# WORDPERFECT® 5.1 MADE EASY

# WORDPERFECT® 5.1

*made Easy*

Mella Mincberg

Osborne **McGraw-Hill**

Berkeley  New York  St. Louis  San Francisco
Auckland  Bogotá  Hamburg  London  Madrid
Mexico City  Milan  Montreal  New Delhi  Panama City
Paris  São Paulo  Singapore  Sydney
Tokyo  Toronto

Osborne **McGraw-Hill**
2600 Tenth Street
Berkeley, California 94710
U.S.A.

For information on translations and book distributors outside of the U.S.A., write to Osborne **McGraw-Hill** at the above address.

A complete list of trademarks appears on page 1047.

**WordPerfect® 5.1 Made Easy**

890 DOC 9987654321

ISBN 0-07-881625-4

# CONTENTS
# AT A GLANCE

# CONTENTS

# ACKNOWLEDGMENTS

Ilene Shapera, associate editor, did a tricky dance to keep this book on schedule, me extremely satisfied with its appearance and design, and our friendship intact. She is the Fred Astaire of the computer book world.

Jan Jue, copy editor, offered an attention to detail that greatly enhanced the book's pages. Cindy Hudson, Dusty Bernard, Kathy Krause (who came in as project editor midway through the book and did so skillfully), and several proofers and typesetters at Osborne/McGraw-Hill did much to put the book together. Scott Maiden, technical reviewer, helped make the material as accurate as possible.

The enthusiastic folks whom I have trained on computers taught me as much about teaching WordPerfect as I taught them about using WordPerfect.

The San Francisco earthquake—the "Big One of '89" that struck as I was revising Chapter 10—mercifully chose to spare most of the Bay Area, including my neighborhood in Oakland and my computer.

Scott Johnson was his usual, supportive, wonderful self. YTAC.

Thank you all!

# INTRODUCTION

Get ready to roll up your sleeves and learn how to use the most popular word-processing package on the market today. WordPerfect will edit your words, rearrange your paragraphs, and print your text with speed and sophistication. And its impressive array of features—such as a 115,000-word dictionary, a thesaurus, outlining and footnoting capabilities, and the ability to combine text with graphics images for desktop publishing, to name only a few—will help you produce professional-looking documents with ease.

## ABOUT THIS BOOK

This book is for the WordPerfect beginner or intermediate user. You will find everything you need to complete your documents, from instructions for installing WordPerfect on your computer to directions for printing your text with fancy fonts and special characters.

The book covers *both* of WordPerfect's recent versions: version 5.0 and version 5.1. Since its introduction more than five years ago, WordPerfect has continued to improve, expand, and develop. WordPerfect version 5.0, released in May, 1988, became a best-seller because of its ability to do the basics such as type, edit, and print documents with ease, along with its more advanced features, such as outstanding printer support and many desktop publishing capabilities. Version 5.1, released in November, 1989, offers additional features to make the program even easier to use: mouse support, pulldown menus, and new features enabling the user to create equations, produce tables, and import spreadsheets. The capabilities of both versions are described in this book; those that refer to only one or the other version are clearly marked as such.

# HOW THIS BOOK IS ORGANIZED

The book is divided into four main sections: "Getting Started," Part I, Part II, and the Appendixes.

**GETTING STARTED**   This section, which is one chapter in length, describes the computer equipment, the various keys on the computer keyboard, and how to start and end a WordPerfect session. Read "Getting Started" if you're unfamiliar with using a computer, you've never started up WordPerfect on your computer before, or you just need a refresher course in computer essentials.

**PART I**   This section, which includes Chapters 1 through 7, explains the WordPerfect fundamentals. You'll learn how to type, edit, save, and print documents. You'll also discover how to perform such essential tasks as altering margins and tab settings; inserting headers and footers; moving a paragraph from one location to another; underlining, boldfacing, and centering text; and checking your document for spelling errors.

At the end of each chapter in Part I is a Review Exercise and Quick Review. The Review Exercise will make you more skillful in using the features described in the chapter. The Quick Review serves as a summary, or can be used before you read a chapter as a way to rapidly learn the basics about the features described.

To create any standard document using WordPerfect, it is essential to know all the information covered in Part I. For the beginning user, the seven chapters are meant to be read in order; the exercises in each build on previous chapters, and you will want to follow along with the procedures step-by-step on your computer. For the intermediate user, you can skim these chapters, reading and performing the exercises in only those chapters that cover topics with which you're unfamiliar.

**PART II** This section covers WordPerfect's special word processing features. Chapter 8 discusses file management capabilities for organizing documents on disk. Chapters 9 through 13 explain how to print with special options, use fonts and graphics for desktop publishing, create text columns and tables, outline and footnote text, and merge form letters and envelopes. Chapter 14 describes macros and styles, which are wonderful time-savers and should not be ignored. And Chapter 15 discusses those extra features that go beyond the bounds of typical word processing, into such areas as WordPerfect's math and sorting capabilities.

At the end of each chapter in Part II is a Review Exercise and Quick Review, just as in Part I. The eight chapters in Part II can be read in any order, depending on your word-processing needs. You may wish to skim the Quick Review in each chapter to decide whether the chapter covers features that would assist with the type of documents that you need to create.

APPENDIXES   This section is important only for certain WordPerfect users. Appendix A is addressed to those of you who have not yet installed WordPerfect to work with your computer or your printer (including any new printer that you may acquire). Appendix B is for users who wish to customize the WordPerfect default settings for particular needs. Appendix C is relevant only if your computer is equipped with a mouse. Appendix D contains lists of the files found on the master WordPerfect disks, which is useful during a customized installation, and contains a complete list of the codes that are inserted into Word-Perfect documents, which is useful during advanced text editing. Appendix E offers sources for additional support, including the address and telephone number of Word-Perfect Corporation.

At the back of this book, you will also find a set of command cards that you can tear out and put beside your computer. They are a condensed guide to WordPerfect's function keys, pulldown menus, and essential features.

# CONVENTIONS USED IN THIS BOOK

A specific notation is used in this book to indicate how to activate each WordPerfect feature. Once you understand the conventions used, you will find the instructions and explanations easy to follow.

A plus sign (+) between keys indicates that you press the keys simultaneously. For example, Ctrl + PgUp means that while holding down the ⌨Ctrl⌨ key you also press ⌨PgUp⌨. Then release both keys. A comma (,) between keys indicates that you should press them sequentially. For example, ⌨Home⌨, ⌨←⌨ means press ⌨Home⌨ and release it; then press ⌨←⌨ and release it.

WordPerfect menu items are sometimes selected by typing a letter, other times by typing a number, and most times by typing either a letter or number. A menu option is followed in parentheses by the corresponding letter and/or number that can be pressed to select it, such as Line (1 or L), Paper Size (7 or S), or File (F).

Function key names, which are assigned in WordPerfect, are shown in FULL CAPITALS. A function key name is followed in parentheses by the corresponding key(s) that can be pressed to select it, such as EXIT (⌨F7⌨) or CENTER (⌨Shift⌨ + ⌨F6⌨) or MERGE CODES (⌨Shift⌨ + ⌨F9⌨). Moreover, since 5.1 users can access features not only by selecting function key names, but by selecting from pulldown menus, pulldown menu keystrokes follow in square brackets. For example, "Press the EXIT (⌨F7⌨) key [*Pulldown menu*: File (F), Exit (X).]"

Most features work the same whether you use WordPerfect version 5.1 or 5.0. But for those features that pertain to only one of the versions, the version to which they apply is clearly marked. For instance, if an entire section discusses a feature available only to 5.1 users, that section's heading is marked: [*5.1 users only*]. Or, if just one paragraph of information pertains only to 5.1 users, that paragraph begins with: *5.1 users only*. And when a feature applies to both versions but the keystrokes required to access it are different, both sets of keystrokes are offered. For example, *5.1 users:* Select New Page Number (1 or N). *5.0 users:* Select New Page Number (6 or N).

# A SPECIAL NOTE TO BEGINNERS

Getting over the hurdle of learning something new can feel intimidating and takes both time and practice, so you must be patient as you learn WordPerfect. Work at your own pace. Tackle a chapter or two every day or every week— whatever is appropriate for you. And since the best way to learn is by doing, make sure that you don't just read the chapters, but that you follow along on your computer, step by step. Pretty soon you'll be using WordPerfect like a pro.

The benefits of learning WordPerfect are innumerable and far outweigh any initial discomfort. Don't worry if at first you feel awkward with the WordPerfect concepts. Give yourself time to gain skill with the basics, the freedom to make mistakes, and the permission to experiment with the more advanced features. Above all, as you use *WordPerfect 5.1 Made Easy*, give yourself the latitude to have some fun!

— Mella Mincberg

# WHY THIS BOOK IS FOR YOU

This book is for the WordPerfect beginner or intermediate user. It is for you if you possess either WordPerfect version 5.1 or version 5.0 and you fall into one of these categories:

- You are just starting to use a personal computer.

- You have worked previously with a personal computer but have never used it as a word processor.

- You know word processing but are new to WordPerfect version 5.1 or 5.0.

- You are familiar with WordPerfect but want to use it more effectively and take advantage of its more sophisticated features.

You will find that, by using this book, you can master WorPerfect easily. You'll learn about the wide range of WordPerfect's capabilities. You'll discover exactly which keys to press so that you can tap those capabilities. And you'll learn it all quickly. To that end, each chapter offers:

- an introductory section which explains the WordPerfect concepts and features to be discussed

- thorough, straightforward explanations of each feature and its business applications

- step-by-step procedures to help you put those WordPerfect features into action right away

- a Review Exercise to help you build confidence as you become proficient using WordPerfect for your own documents

- a Quick Review at the end of the chapter which can be used as both a summary and as a rapid reference guide.

# LEARN MORE ABOUT WORDPERFECT

Here is an excellent selection of other Osborne/McGraw-Hill books on WordPerfect.

*WordPerfect 5.1: The Complete Reference,* by Karen Acerson, is a desktop resource that lists every WordPerfect 5.1 command, feature, and function along with brief yet complete descriptions of how they are used.

For a quick reference of essential commands, see Mella Mincberg's *WordPerfect 5.1: The Pocket Reference, WordPerfect 5: The Pocket Reference,* or *WordPerfect: The Pocket Reference,* which covers release 4.2.

*WordPerfect: Secrets, Solutions, Shortcuts, Series 5 Edition,* by Mella Mincberg, is jam-packed with all the tips, tricks, and hints you could want for extending WordPerfect version 5.0 capabilities. Whether you are only somewhat familiar with WordPerfect or are an experienced user with years of practice, you're bound to learn plenty of new secrets from this book.

# GETTING STARTED

This chapter allows you to become comfortable using your computer with WordPerfect. It begins with a quick overview of computer equipment for those of you who are unfamiliar with the basic parts of a computer, and then provides step-by-step directions for starting up Word-Perfect on your computer.

Once in WordPerfect, you'll discover how it offers a comfortable word processing environment. Its Typing screen is clear of distracting messages so that you can focus not on WordPerfect but on your goal—writing and typing documents. You'll be instructed to type one line of text and see how WordPerfect operates using all the different sections of the keyboard. You'll be introduced to the menus that allow you to access all of WordPerfect's powerful features, and you'll learn how to use WordPerfect's Help facility, so that if you can't remember how to use a feature or accomplish a task, you can get your answer by tapping a few keys on the keyboard.

At the end of the chapter, you'll discover the proper method of exiting the WordPerfect program when you're done for the day. It is critical to exit WordPerfect correctly each time you use the program. The process is swift and easy and will soon become as habitual as closing a door behind you when you leave a building.

For those of you who have just purchased WordPerfect but have yet to prepare your copy to work with your computer, turn now to Appendix A, "Installing WordPerfect for Your Computer and Printer," before you read further.

Those of you who have worked with your computer and WordPerfect before may already be familiar with the information provided in this chapter. Nevertheless, skim over its contents or read through the "Quick Review" section at the end of the chapter just to make sure. That way, you'll be confident that you understand the fundamentals in using WordPerfect.

# YOUR COMPUTER EQUIPMENT

If you're facing a computer for the first time, you're probably unfamiliar with the equipment occupying your desk. Let's briefly examine the basic computer components you need to know about, illustrated in Figure GS-1.

## Keyboard and Mouse

With the computer *keyboard* you type text, enter information, and provide instructions to the computer. There are different keyboard models, with keys located in different places and with varying numbers of keys. Later on in this chapter, after you have started up WordPerfect, you will learn about the functions of each of the keys.

A *mouse* is an optional computer component, which can also provide instructions to the computer. If a computer system is equipped with a mouse, the mouse usually sits near the keyboard, either on a special pad or simply on a desk top. It is controlled by clicking or holding down a mouse button and moving the mouse. You will learn later about the possible uses for a mouse in WordPerfect.

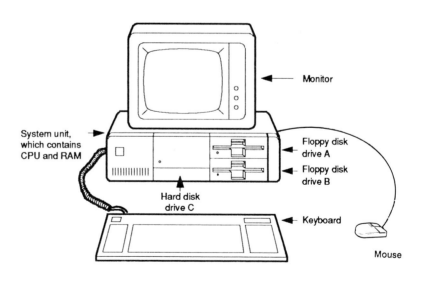

**FIGURE GS-1**   The computer components

# Monitor

The computer *monitor,* which resembles a television screen, displays messages from the computer and also displays any characters that you type on the keyboard. A monochrome monitor displays one-color characters (most often green or amber) on a black background screen. A color monitor can display numerous colors. Most monitors have an 80-column by 25-line display, which means that at any one time you can see 80 characters across the width of the screen and 25 lines of text down the length of the screen. A *cursor,* which resembles a dash that blinks, acts like your pointer on the monitor screen.

# System Unit

The computer *system unit* contains the heart of the computer system. Inside the system unit is the *central processing unit* (CPU), often referred to as the brain of the computer because the CPU interprets all instructions and performs all necessary computations.

Also inside the system unit is the computer's random-access memory (RAM). RAM is circuitry where the computer temporarily stores information to be processed by the CPU. For example, when you type on the keyboard, characters that appear on your monitor are also placed in RAM so that you can then edit those characters. You can think of RAM as the computer's workspace.

Each computer contains a certain amount of RAM as its workspace. RAM is measured in *bytes,* a computer term of measurement equal to one character—such as a letter or a space. For instance, your computer may contain 512 kilobytes of RAM. This means that your computer's workspace can hold more than 512,000 bytes (characters) of information, which is the suggested minimum required to run WordPerfect. With most computers, you can purchase additional RAM to expand the capacity of your computer.

It is important to realize that RAM is only temporary storage. When you turn off your computer, or if the electricity flowing to your computer stops due to a power failure, all the information stored in RAM disappears, along with all the characters displayed on the monitor. For instance, suppose you type a document using WordPerfect. This document is in RAM and is displayed on the computer screen. But, whenever you turn off the computer, the document will vanish (unless you have already saved it, as is discussed next).

## Disk Drives

The computer *disk drives* take information stored in RAM and copy that information more permanently, so that you can use it again in the future. Thus, by means of disk drives, you can save a document and then tomorrow or whenever, you can review, edit, or print out that document again without having to retype it.

One type of disk drive stores information onto *floppy diskettes (disks),* which are like removable file cabinets. If your computer has one floppy disk drive, it is called drive A. If your computer has two, then the one on the left or on top is called drive A, and the other is called drive B.

Disk drives use different types of floppy disks. For instance, some disk drives use floppy disks that are 5 1/4″ in size and can hold up to 360 kilobytes of information. Others use 3 1/2″ floppy disks that can hold up to 720 kilobytes.

Still others use 5 1/4″ floppy disks that can hold 1200 kilobytes (1.2 megabytes) or 3 1/2″ floppy disks that hold 1440 kilobytes (1.44 megabytes).

Another type of disk drive does not use floppy disks at all, but instead stores information onto a *hard disk,* which is like a file cabinet fixed inside the computer. If your computer is equipped with a hard disk, it is usually called drive C.

A hard disk holds many times more information than a floppy disk can. For instance, some hard disks hold as many as 40,000 kilobytes (40 megabytes) of information. As a result, to organize information that is stored on a hard disk, it is important to segregate the hard disk electronically into separate parts, called *directories.* Think of a directory as a separate file drawer in your file cabinet. Related groups of information are then kept together in different directories. (Chapter 8, "Managing Files on Disk," offers information on how to create new directories, delete old ones, and effectively arrange information within directories.)

Figure GS-1 shows an example of a computer system with two floppy disk drives and one hard disk drive. Word-Perfect will operate only if your computer is equipped with, at a minimum, either (1) two floppy disk drives, or (2) one floppy disk drive and one hard disk. *5.1 users only*: If your computer is equipped only with floppy disk drives, then to run WordPerfect those disk drives must be able to use disks that store at least 720 kilobytes.

# START THE WORDPERFECT PROGRAM

When you work with WordPerfect, you are also working with another program called DOS, which stands for Disk Operating System. DOS acts like an interpreter at the

United Nations, taking what you type during a Word-Perfect session and converting it into a language the computer can understand. If your computer has no hard disk, then after you install WordPerfect to work with your computer hardware (Appendix A), both DOS and Word-Perfect are housed on the WordPerfect 1 disk. (However, if your computer requires a special boot disk, then the special boot disk contains DOS, and only WordPerfect is on the WordPerfect 1 disk.) If your computer is equipped with a hard disk, then after you install WordPerfect (Appendix A), both DOS and WorkPerfect are housed on the hard disk.

Whenever you wish to use WordPerfect, you must start up DOS on your computer first and start up WordPerfect second. The computer's RAM will contain both DOS and WordPerfect, and you will be ready to use WordPerfect.

*5.1 users only*: You cannot start up WordPerfect from the master disks. You must use the working disks that you created when you installed WordPerfect, as described in Appendix A.

## Start DOS

When starting up DOS on your computer, you should know about two keys on the keyboard:

- The Enter key, also called the Return key, is used to register instructions into the computer from DOS. It is usually on the right side of the keyboard, marked with the word "Enter" or the word "Return" or with a symbol of a crooked arrow pointing to the left: ⏎ . (Some of you may have two Enter keys on your keyboard. They work identically.)

- The [Backspace] key is used to correct a mistake when you accidentally type the wrong character. It is usually just above the [Enter] key, marked with the word "Backspace" or with a symbol of a long, straight arrow pointing to the left: [←].

With these two keys in mind, let's start up DOS, a procedure known as *booting up* the computer:

1. Floppy disk users should place the WordPerfect 1 disk in drive A—usually the disk drive on the left or on the top—and close the disk drive door. (If your computer requires a special boot disk, then insert this special disk in drive A instead.) Place a data disk where you will store your documents in drive B—usually the disk drive on the right or on the bottom—and close the disk drive door. (For information on formatting a blank disk so that it becomes a data disk to be used to store documents, see Appendix A.) Now turn on the computer. You may have to turn on the monitor separately, especially if you have a color monitor.

   Hard disk users don't need to insert disks in the floppy disk drives because DOS and WordPerfect should be stored on the hard disk, which is fixed inside the computer; simply turn on the computer. If you have a color monitor, you may have to turn it on separately.

   It will take a few moments for the computer to warm up and begin working.

2. For some of you, the computer will respond with a request for the current date; type it in. For example, if today's date is December 9, 1990, type **12-09-90**; if the date is January 15, 1991, type **01-15-91**. Be sure to use real zeros and real ones on the keyboard; a computer

will not accept the letters "o" or "l" as substitutes.

If you make a typing mistake when typing the date, simply press the `Backspace` key to erase the error, and then type the correct character(s).

3. If you typed in the correct date, press the `Enter` key.

4. For some of you, the computer responds with a request for the current time; type it in. The computer works on military time (a 24-hour clock); so if the correct time is, for example, 7:30 A.M., type **7:30**, or if the correct time is 4:30 P.M., type **16:30**.

5. If you typed in the correct time, press the `Enter` key.

You are now ready to start up WordPerfect on the computer, a procedure referred to as *loading* WordPerfect. How you load WordPerfect depends on (1) whether your computer is equipped with a hard disk, and (2) whether you or someone else has written a batch file (a set of computer instructions written in DOS, as described in Appendix A) for your computer so that WordPerfect can be loaded automatically.

## Start WordPerfect from a Floppy Disk System

Floppy disk users who have written a batch file as described in Appendix A to automatically load WordPerfect should proceed as follows:

1. Because of the automatically activated batch file, Word-Perfect automatically begins loading WordPerfect for

you. In a few moments, a WordPerfect screen appears with the following message:

```
Insert diskette labeled "WordPerfect2" and press any key
```

2. Take out your WordPerfect 1 disk from drive A, place it back in its protective envelope, and insert your Word-Perfect 2 disk into drive A.

3. Press Enter to continue loading WordPerfect.

Floppy disk users who have not written a batch file or who require a special boot disk to start up the computer should proceed as follows:

1. After DOS is loaded, you will see the DOS prompt A> appear on the screen, signaling that DOS has been loaded into RAM and that the active drive is drive A. Your cursor should be located just to the right of the A>.

2. Type **b:** (uppercase or lowercase makes no difference), and press Enter. Now the DOS prompt reads B>. This means that the default drive—the drive for storing and retrieving files—has been changed to drive B, where the data disk is stored. (This step is necessary so that Word-Perfect knows to store your documents not on the same disk where the WordPerfect program is housed, but rather on a separate disk. Storing programs and your documents on separate disks is a good idea so that you have an uncluttered space just for your documents and to reduce the chances of inadvertently erasing or damaging the WordPerfect program.)

3. If a special boot disk is in drive A, take this disk out, place it back in its protective envelope, and insert your WordPerfect 1 disk in drive A.

4. Type **a:wp,** and press ⟨Enter⟩. The WordPerfect program begins to load into the computer's RAM. In a few moments, a WordPerfect screen appears with the following message:

```
Insert diskette labeled "WordPerfect 2" and press any key
```

5. Take out your WordPerfect 1 disk from drive A, place it back in its protective envelope, and insert your WordPerfect 2 disk into drive A.

6. Press ⟨Enter⟩ to continue loading WordPerfect.

You will know that WordPerfect has successfully started when you are viewing the WordPerfect Typing screen on your monitor, as shown in Figure GS-2.

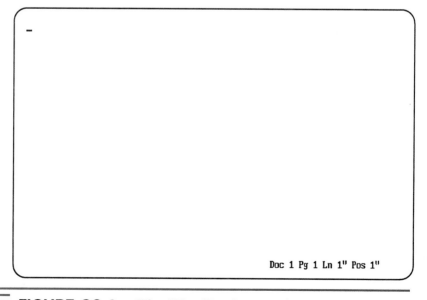

Doc 1 Pg 1 Ln 1" Pos 1"

**FIGURE GS-2**   The WordPerfect Typing screen

# Start WordPerfect from a Hard Disk System

Hard disk users who have written a batch file as described in Appendix A should proceed as follows:

1. You will see a DOS prompt such as C> or C:\> appear on screen, signaling that DOS has been loaded into RAM and that the active drive is drive C, the hard disk. Your cursor should be located just to the right of the C> or C:\>.

2. Type **wp5** (uppercase or lowercase makes no difference), which is the name of the batch file.

3. Press (Enter) to activate the batch file; WordPerfect will be loaded for you.

Hard disk users who have installed WordPerfect without writing a batch file should proceed as follows:

1. You will see a DOS prompt such as C> or C:\> appear on screen, signaling that DOS has been loaded into RAM and that the active drive is drive C, the hard disk. Your cursor should be located just to the right of the C> or C:\>.

2. You must issue a CD (Change Directory) command to switch to the directory on the hard disk where the WordPerfect program instructions are housed. For example, suppose that the WordPerfect program files are housed in a directory named \WP51. Then, type **cd \wp51** and press (Enter). This tells the computer to change directories to \WP51 so that WordPerfect can be started.

3. Type **wp** and press (Enter). Now the WordPerfect program loads into the computer's RAM.

4. Keep in mind that this procedure for loading Word-
Perfect causes the default directory (the directory that
WordPerfect assumes for saving or retrieving your documents) and the directory housing the WordPerfect
program to be one and the same. This is not a good
idea. A better idea is to store your documents in a
different directory from where the WordPerfect program
is housed, thus allowing for better organization of information on the hard disk and reducing the chances
of accidentally erasing or damaging the WordPerfect
program. Once you begin working extensively with
WordPerfect to type documents, you might want to see
Appendix A to learn how to create a separate directory
named \WP51\DATA or \WP50\DATA to store your
documents and how to make this directory the default.
Or you might want to see Chapter 8 to learn how to
create new directories and how to change the default
directory once WordPerfect is loaded.

You will know that WordPerfect has successfully started
when you are viewing the WordPerfect Typing screen on
your monitor, as shown in Figure GS-2.

## Respond to WordPerfect Start Up Messages

Sometimes you may encounter a problem or be faced with
an error message on the screen before WordPerfect will
start. If you are not yet viewing the Typing screen, here's
what may be happening:

- WordPerfect is asking for your registration number because this is your first time loading WordPerfect, and you
are using version 5.1. Look at your original WordPerfect

package to find your registration number, type in that number, and press ⌈Enter⌉. (Or, if you choose, you can simply press ⌈Enter⌉ without typing in your registration number.) Now this number will be easily accessible to you when using the Help facility, as described further on in this chapter. The Typing screen will then appear.

- WordPerfect is requesting your user initials. If you're loading WordPerfect from a network version, then Word-Perfect uses these initials—up to three characters—to keep your special files (overflow files that it needs to run WordPerfect for you) separate from those of other indi-viduals working simultaneously in WordPerfect on the network. If you've been assigned a log-in number, enter that number. Or enter your own initials or three other characters.

- WordPerfect is responding with the following error mes-sage:

`Are other copies of WordPerfect currently running?  Y/N`

This indicates that, when WordPerfect was last loaded on your computer, the computer was shut off before the user had the opportunity to exit WordPerfect properly. (You will learn how to exit WordPerfect properly at the end of this chapter.) As a result, WordPerfect believes that you will run two separate copies of WordPerfect, which is incorrect. Type **N** for "No," so that only one copy of WordPerfect will run. The Typing screen will then appear.

- WordPerfect is refusing to load, or it begins to load, but then the monitor screen freezes. This may indicate that WordPerfect has been installed improperly; refer to the installation procedures as described at the beginning of

Appendix A and consider reinstalling WordPerfect. Another possibility is that your computer does not have enough RAM to run WordPerfect—in which case, you must obtain more memory, available from your computer retailer, to use WordPerfect. Or, this may mean that, to use WordPerfect on your equipment, you must activate special options when starting up WordPerfect, such as /nk or /nc. Turn to the section of Appendix A that discusses "Startup (Slash) Options" for more information.

*Note:* You should know that, even if WordPerfect loads properly for you, you can load WordPerfect slightly differently to activate options that might make your WordPerfect session more productive. For instance, if your computer is equipped with a large amount of RAM, you can load WordPerfect in a way that speeds up its operations. Refer to the section of Appendix A entitled "Startup (Slash) Options" for more details.

# EXAMINE THE TYPING SCREEN

The WordPerfect Typing screen is almost totally blank, so that there is little to distract you from your typing. A blinking line sits at the top left corner of the screen, as shown in Figure GS-2. This is your WordPerfect cursor, which acts like a position marker or pencil point on the screen. A character that you type will appear wherever the cursor is located. The bottom line on the screen, called the *status line,* provides information on the cursor's present location. On a clear Typing screen, the cursor is in the upper left corner and the status line reads

`Doc 1 Pg 1 Ln 1" Pos 1"`

**Doc 1** indicates that the cursor is in document 1; this is important information when you begin working with two documents at once, referred to as Doc 1 and Doc 2, as described in Chapter 3, "Typing and Text Enhancements."

**Pg 1** informs you that the cursor is on page 1 of the document. In WordPerfect, a document can be many pages long, as you'll soon see.

**Ln 1″** signifies that the cursor is positioned 1″ down from the top of the page. In other words, whatever you type on Ln 1″ will appear 1″ from the top edge of a piece of paper when you print out what you've typed, so that your printed document has a 1″ top margin. The 1″ top margin is an assumption, called a *default* or *initial setting,* that Word-Perfect makes about how you wish your document produced. A related default setting is for a 1″ bottom margin. You will learn in Chapter 6 how you can change these top and bottom margin settings for any document.

**Pos** 1″ means that the cursor is located 1″ from the left edge of the page. In other words, whatever you type at Pos 1″ will appear 1″ from the left edge of a piece of paper when you print out what you've typed, so that your printed document has a 1″ left margin. This 1″ left margin is another default setting; a related setting is for a 1″ right margin. You will learn in Chapter 4 how to change these left and right margin settings for any document.

*Note:* If your status line reads something other than **Ln 1″** or **Pos** 1″, then someone has changed either the default settings for your copy of WordPerfect or the units of measure on the status line. Look to the sections "Environment" and "Initial Settings," in Appendix B for further explanation.

# USE THE KEYBOARD IN WORDPERFECT

Let's explore how the computer keyboard works with WordPerfect. Most keyboards consist of three distinct sections: the typewriter keypad, the cursor movement/numeric keypad, and the function keypad. Figures GS-3 and GS-4 illustrate two of the most common keyboard types, with these sections indicated.

## Typewriter Keypad to Insert Text

At the heart of the computer keyboard is the *typewriter keypad,* which contains the standard typing keys as found on a typewriter—a spacebar at the bottom, letters on the

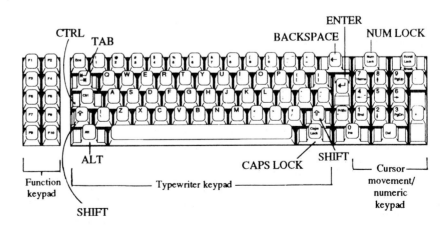

**FIGURE GS-3**   The IBM standard keyboard

middle three rows, numbers on the top row. In general, use these keys as you would on a typewriter. But keep in mind that, unlike on a typewriter, on a computer it is unwise to use the spacebar to indent text—such as the first line in a paragraph. This is because the width and location of spaces can change as you type a document on a computer.

The [Tab] key is used to indent the first line of a paragraph. This key is marked either with the word "Tab" or with one arrow pointing left and one arrow pointing right: [⇆]. Every time you press [Tab], the cursor jumps to the next tab stop to the right, and the characters you type will be fixed at that position. The default setting for tab stop locations is every 0.5".

The typewriter keypad has two [Shift] keys, located on either side of the Spacebar. The [Shift] keys are marked

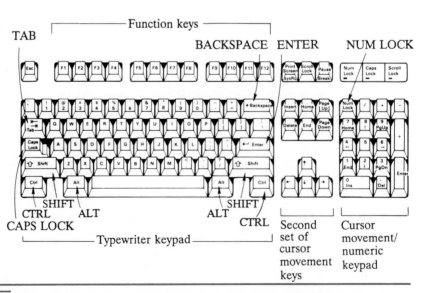

**FIGURE GS-4**    The IBM enhanced keyboard

either with the word "Shift," or with an outline of an arrow pointing upward: [△]. Use the [Shift] key to capitalize an individual letter: Hold down the [Shift] key, and while holding it down, type the letter. And, use the [Shift] key to type symbols such as ! or $ or ?, which are located on the upper portion of the keys: hold down the [Shift] key and type the symbol.

The typewriter keypad also contains some keys not found on a standard typewriter, including

- [Caps Lock] key—acts like a toggle switch to turn capital letters on and off. To type a group of letters in uppercase, press [Caps Lock] to activate the feature. Type the letters and then press [Caps Lock] a second time to turn off capital letters.

  You can tell when [Caps Lock] is active on the Word-Perfect Typing screen: The **Pos** indicator on the status line appears in uppercase—**POS**. On some keyboards, there is also an indicator that lights up when [Caps Lock] is active.

  Be aware that when [Caps Lock] is active, the effect of the [Shift] key is reversed; holding down a [Shift] key and typing a letter will produce that letter in lowercase. Also, the [Caps Lock] key *affects only letters;* even with [Caps Lock] activated, you must use the [Shift] key to type symbols such as ! and &.

- [Ctrl] and [Alt] keys—only work in conjunction with other keys on the keyboard, such as the function keys. You will learn more about these keys as you read on in this chapter.

- [Backspace] key—as previously discussed, erases the character to the left of the cursor.

- (Enter) key—as previously discussed, registers commands into the computer. In addition, in typing documents the (Enter) key is used to end paragraphs, end short lines of text, or insert blank lines. You will learn more about exactly when to press the (Enter) key as this chapter progresses and in Chapter 1.

To get a feel for the typewriter keypad, try the following. If you make a typing mistake, press (Backspace) to erase it, and then type the correct character.

1. Press (Tab) one time. The cursor jumps 0.5″ to the right.

2. Type **Hello!!!** (Remember to use the (Shift) key when typing the uppercase "H" and the three exclamation points.)

3. Press the spacebar twice to insert two empty spaces.

4. Press (Caps Lock). When you do, notice that the position indicator on the status line at the bottom of the computer screen now reads **POS** rather than **Pos**, indicating that uppercase has been activated.

5. Type **welcome**. All the letters appear in uppercase without your using the (Shift) key.

6. Type three more exclamation points. (Remember that, even though (Caps Lock) is active, you must still use the (Shift) key to insert the exclamation points. If you don't use the (Shift) key, you'll type the number 1 rather than the exclamation point.)

7. Press (Caps Lock). Now the status line reads **Pos**, since uppercase has been deactivated. The screen reads

```
Hello!!!  WELCOME!!!_
```

Did you notice how the cursor moved to the right as you typed each new character? The cursor is now just to the right of the characters you typed. The status line always reflects the change in the cursor's position. If you look at the status line, you'll notice that it indicates a new cursor position. For example, when the cursor is at position 3.5" (meaning 3.5" from the left edge of the page), then the status line reads

`Doc 1 Pg 1 Ln 1" Pos 3.5"`

## Cursor Movement/Numeric Keypad to Guide the Cursor and Insert Numbers

The section on the right side of the computer keyboard is the *cursor movement/numeric keypad*. As the name suggests, this keypad serves two purposes.

First, you can use this section as a cursor movement keypad, controlling the whereabouts of your cursor. The bottom half of each key indicates its cursor movement function. For example, the ⬅ key (marked with a left arrow at the bottom and the number 4 at the top) moves the cursor to the left, and the ➡ key (marked with a right arrow and the number 6) moves the cursor to the right. You will learn about the functions of all the cursor movement keys, including those keys with names like Home and PgUp, in the next chapter.

Second, you can use this section as a numeric keypad, typing the numbers shown on those keys. The top half of each key indicates the number to which it corresponds. For example, when you press the ⬅ key (marked with a left arrow at the bottom and the number 4 at the top), you insert the number 4 on screen. Those who frequently type on a ten-key adding machine may prefer to type numbers using this section of the keyboard, rather than using the top row of the typewriter keypad.

The ⟦Num Lock⟧ key acts like a toggle switch, controlling whether this keypad is used for cursor movement or for typing numbers. To switch to a numeric keypad, press ⟦Num Lock⟧ so that the feature is activated. Type the numbers and then press ⟦Num Lock⟧ a second time to return to a cursor movement keypad.

You can tell when ⟦Num Lock⟧ is active on the WordPerfect Typing screen: The **Pos** indicator on the status line blinks. On some keyboards, there is also an indicator that lights up when ⟦Num Lock⟧ is active. Be aware, however, that when ⟦Num Lock⟧ is active, the ⟦Shift⟧ key can temporarily reverse the function of this keypad. For instance, if ⟦Num Lock⟧ is active but you hold down the ⟦Shift⟧ key and then type the key that is marked with the number 4 and the left arrow, the cursor moves to the left.

Those of you with the enhanced keyboard (see Figure GS-4) have a second set of cursor movement keys on your keyboard. Thus, if you wish, you can keep ⟦Num Lock⟧ always activated so that you use the cursor movement/numeric keypad only to type in numbers. This second set of keys can be relied on to move the cursor. Those of you with the standard keyboard (see Figure GS-3) must use the cursor movement/numeric keypad to move the cursor. Of course, regardless of which keyboard you use, you may decide after some practice on the keyboard to type numbers using the top row of the typewriter keypad, and to ignore the ⟦Num Lock⟧ key altogether.

Try the following to explore how the ⟦Num Lock⟧ key affects the function of the cursor movement/numeric keypad:

1. With 〖Num Lock〗 inactive, press the 〖←〗 key (marked with a left arrow and the number 4) five times. The cursor now moves five spaces to the left, and the position indicator on the status line indicates the change in location.

2. Press the 〖→〗 key (marked with a right arrow and the number 6) five times. The cursor now moves five spaces to the right.

3. Press 〖Num Lock〗. Notice that the position indicator on the status line blinks. This indicates that the numeric keypad has been activated.

4. Press the 〖←〗key (marked with a left arrow and the number 4) five times. Notice that you have typed the number 44444.

5. Press the 〖→〗 key (marked with a right arrow and the number 6) five times. Now you have typed the number 66666.

6. Press 〖Num Lock〗. This deactivates the numeric keypad.

7. Press 〖←〗 several times. You'll see that you can again move the cursor; you've switched back to the cursor movement keypad. Now the screen reads

```
Hello!!!  WELCOME!!!4444466666
```

You can move the cursor only within that part of the screen in which you've already typed. So, to move the cursor further to the right, you must continue typing using the typewriter keypad. To end a short amount of text and move the cursor down to a new line, use the 〖Enter〗 key to create a blank line. For example:

1. Press the 〖→〗 key until the cursor stops moving. Notice that the cursor refuses to move any further than one past the last character you typed.

2. Press the ⬇ key. The cursor still won't move past the typed line.

3. Press the spacebar twice. The cursor moves two places to the right.

4. Press Enter. The cursor moves down to the beginning of a new line.

5. Now you can use your arrow keys to maneuver in the slightly larger document: *up* to the first line, *left* to the left margin, *right* to just past the numbers and two spaces, or *down* to the second line.

Notice that when the cursor is situated down on the blank line that you created by pressing the Enter key, the status line reflects the fact that the cursor is on that new line:

`Doc 1 Pg 1 Ln 1.17" Pos 1"`

This indicates that the second line of text will print 1.17″ from the top of the page.

*Note:* You may find that after you press Enter, the status line on your screen indicates that the cursor is at another vertical location, such as at Ln 1.16″ or Ln 1.18″. How WordPerfect spaces each line on a page partially depends on the *printer* and that printer's corresponding *font* (print character) selected to print out your document. Your lines will be spaced based on the printer you or someone else selected when you installed your copy of WordPerfect (as described in Appendix A).

## Function Keypad to Access Features

The third section of the keyboard is the *function keypad*. Depending on your keyboard, the function keypad sits either on the left with keys labeled F1 through F10 (as shown in Figure GS-3) or on top with keys labeled F1 through F12 (as shown in Figure GS-4).

WordPerfect's special features can be accessed via the function keypad, by pressing one of the first ten function keys either by itself or in combination with one of three other keys: Ctrl, Alt, and Shift. Each function key can thus be used in four different ways. For example, you can press F1 on its own; you can press the Alt key and, while holding it down, press F1 (denoted from now on as Alt + F1 ); you can press Shift + F1 ; or you can press Ctrl + F1 . Each key combination invokes a different set of commands; therefore, there are 40 sets of commands at your fingertips on the function keypad.

To remind you which function keys perform which commands, the WordPerfect package comes with two plastic templates. One template is shaped like a rectangular doughnut and is for those keyboards where the function keys are on the left side. The other template is shaped like a ruler and is for those keyboards where the function keys are at the top. The templates indicate function key names, to help you know which function keys access which special features. The templates are color-coded, as follows:

| Function Key Name Color | Corresponding Key Combination |
| --- | --- |
| Black | Function key alone |
| Green | Shift + Function key |
| Blue | Alt + Function key |
| Red | Ctrl + Function key |

*Before you continue, be sure to place the template that is appropriate for your keyboard next to your function keys.*

| Function Key Name | Key Combination |
|---|---|
| BLOCK | Alt + F4 |
| BOLD | F6 |
| CANCEL | F1 |
| CENTER | Shift + F6 |
| COLUMNS/TABLES | Alt + F7 |
| DATE/OUTLINE | Shift + F5 |
| END FIELD | F9 |
| EXIT | F7 |
| FLUSH RIGHT | Alt + F6 |
| FONT | Ctrl + F8 |
| FOOTNOTE | Ctrl + F7 |
| FORMAT | Shift + F8 |
| GRAPHICS | Alt + F9 |
| HELP | F3 |
| →INDENT | F4 |
| →INDENT← | Shift + F4 |
| LIST | F5 |
| MACRO | Alt + F10 |
| MACRO DEFINE | Ctrl + F10 |
| MARK TEXT | Alt + F5 |
| MERGE CODES | Shift + F9 |
| MERGE/SORT | Ctrl + F9 |
| MOVE | Ctrl + F4 |
| PRINT | Shift + F7 |
| REPLACE | Alt + F2 |
| RETRIEVE | Shift + F10 |

**TABLE GS-1**  Alphabetical List: WordPerfect 5.1 Function Key Names

| Function<br>Key Name | Key<br>Combination |
|---|---|
| REVEAL CODES | `Alt` + `F3` |
| SAVE | `F10` |
| SCREEN | `Ctrl` + `F3` |
| ←SEARCH | `F2` |
| ←SEARCH | `Shift` + `F2` |
| SETUP | `Shift` + `F1` |
| SHELL | `Ctrl` + `F1` |
| SPELL | `Ctrl` + `F2` |
| STYLE | `Alt` + `F8` |
| SWITCH | `Shift` + `F3` |
| TAB ALIGN | `Ctrl` + `F6` |
| TEXT IN/OUT | `Ctrl` + `F5` |
| THESAURUS | `Alt` + `F1` |
| UNDERLINE | `F8` |

**Table GS-1**   Alphabetical List: WordPerfect 5.1
Function Key Names (*continued*)

For your convenience, you will also find an alphabetical list of function key names in the two following tables. Table GS-1 is for version 5.1 users, and Table GS-2 is for version 5.0 users. (Three function keys have different names in version 5.1 because of modifications in features.) Another list is provided on the command card at the back of this book.

When you press a function key to select a command, WordPerfect responds in one of several ways:

- WordPerfect may respond with a message on the status line, called a *prompt,* asking for further information before activating a feature. You would enter the appropriate information, and then the command would be carried out.

- WordPerfect may provide you with a list of choices, called a *menu;* this menu may appear at the bottom of the screen, temporarily replacing the status line, or on the full screen, temporarily replacing the Typing screen. You would select a menu item by selecting either the number or the mnemonic letter that corresponds to your selection.

- WordPerfect may simply turn on or off a feature, inserting a symbol called a *code* into the text of your document. (Codes are described in further detail in the next chapter.)

When you press a function key inadvertently and a prompt or a menu appears, you can clear the prompt or menu from the screen by pressing CANCEL, the F1 function key. (The spacebar or Enter key also can usually clear a prompt or menu.) Sometimes you must press CANCEL (F1) more than once to completely back out of a command. When you press a function key and a feature is turned on, you must cancel the feature by erasing the inserted code; you can do so by pressing the Backspace key. (More on codes in the next chapter.)

Here's a chance for you to practice reading the template and viewing different prompts and menus. We'll use the CANCEL (F1) and Backspace keys to back out of the commands.

1. Find the EXIT key on the template (or in Table GS-1 or GS-2). You'll find it located next to the F7 function

| Function Key Name | Key Combination |
|---|---|
| BLOCK | [Alt] + [F4] |
| BOLD | [F6] |
| CANCEL | [F1] |
| CENTER | [Shift] + [F6] |
| DATE/OUTLINE | [Shift] + [F5] |
| EXIT | [F7] |
| FLUSH RIGHT | [Alt] + [F6] |
| FONT | [Ctrl] + [F8] |
| FOOTNOTE | [Ctrl] + [F7] |
| FORMAT | [Shift] + [F8] |
| GRAPHICS | [Alt] + [F9] |
| HELP | [F3] |
| →INDENT | [F4] |
| →INDENT← | [Shift] + [F4] |
| LIST FILES | [F5] |
| MACRO | [Alt] + [F10] |
| MACRO DEFINE | [Ctrl] + [F10] |
| MARK TEXT | [Alt] + [F5] |
| MATH/COLUMNS | [Alt] + [F7] |
| MERGE CODES | [Shift] + [F9] |
| MERGE R | [F9] |
| MERGE/SORT | [Ctrl] + [F9] |
| MOVE | [Ctrl] + [F4] |
| PRINT | [Shift] + [F7] |
| REPLACE | [Alt] + [F2] |
| RETRIEVE | [Shift] + [F10] |
| REVEAL CODES | [Alt] + [F3] |
| SAVE TEXT | [F10] |

**TABLE GS-2**  Alphabetical List: WordPerfect 5.0 Function Key Names

| Function<br>Key Name | Key<br>Combination |
|---|---|
| SCREEN | Ctrl + F3 |
| ✦SEARCH | F2 |
| ✦SEARCH | Shift + F2 |
| SETUP | Shift + F1 |
| SHELL | Ctrl + F1 |
| SPELL | Ctrl + F2 |
| STYLE | Alt + F8 |
| SWITCH | Shift + F3 |
| TAB ALIGN | Ctrl + F6 |
| TEXT IN/OUT | Ctrl + F5 |
| THESAURUS | Alt + F1 |
| UNDERLINE | F8 |

**Table GS-2**  Alphabetical List: WordPerfect 5.0
Function Key Names (*continued*)

key. Since the word "Exit" is written in black on the template, you know that the Exit feature is accessed with the F7 key alone.

2. Press the EXIT ( F7 ) key. On the status line (bottom of screen), you'll see an example of a prompt in the form of a question, which requires a one-character response. The question prompt is slightly different for 5.1 users than for 5.0 users. But, whether you are using version 5.1 or 5.0, the procedure used for answering the question is the same. For 5.1 users, you'll see the following question prompt:

Save document? Yes (No)

For 5.0 users, the prompt reads

`Save document? Y/N Yes`

Whenever WordPerfect prompts with a question, it suggests an answer, placing the cursor under the suggestion. So, in the preceding prompt, WordPerfect is assuming that yes, you do wish to save the document. To *reject* WordPerfect's assumption, type the opposite response; thus, you could reject WordPerfect's suggestion by typing **N** in response to the preceding prompt. To accept WordPerfect's assumption, press any other key on the typewriter keypad—such as the [Enter] key or the letter that the cursor is on, which in the preceding prompt means that you could type **Y**.

3. Let's accept WordPerfect's suggestion. Either Type **Y** or press [Enter]. Now, another prompt appears:

`Document to be saved:`

This is an example of a prompt that requires more than just a "Yes" or "No" response. You could respond to this prompt by typing in a document name and then pressing the [Enter] key to register the name. However, for now, let's abort this command.

4. Press the CANCEL ([F1]) key. The prompt disappears, and the command is canceled.

5. Find the FOOTNOTE key on the template. You'll find the word also located next to the [F7] key, but in red, meaning that the FOOTNOTE key is [Ctrl] + [F7].

6. Press the FOOTNOTE ([Ctrl] + [F7]) key. The following menu appears on the status line:

`1 Footnote; 2 Endnote; 3 Endnote Placement: 0`

This is an example of a one-line menu. WordPerfect is waiting for you to make a Footnote menu selection by typing a number or by typing a mnemonic character. For instance, you could choose option 1, Footnote, by typing either **1** or **F**—which will in the remainder of this book be denoted as follows: Footnote (1 or F).

*Note:* Mnemonic characters on a menu will be indicated on your computer screen in boldface. The section of Appendix B titled "Display" discusses how you can change the appearance of mnemonic characters on menus, if you so desire.

Notice on your screen that the cursor has moved down and is located at the 0, on the far right side of the menu. This means that WordPerfect's current suggestion is for no option to be chosen. Thus, if you press a key on the typewriter keypad that does not correspond to a menu selection—anything other than Footnote by typing **1** or **F**, Endnote by typing **2** or **E**, or Endnote Placement by typing **3** or **P**—WordPerfect will not execute any of the commands listed on the menu. But if you select one of the menu options, the command will be executed.

7. Type **1** or **F** to select the Footnote option on the menu. Notice that, based on your selection, a second menu appears, which can be considered the Footnote submenu.

Footnote: 1 Create; 2 Edit; 3 New Number; 4 Options: <u>0</u>

You could now choose an option from this new submenu. Instead, let's abort the Footnote command.

8. Press the CANCEL (F1) key. The menu disappears.

9. Find the FORMAT key on the template. You'll find it next to the F8 key, in green, meaning that the FORMAT key is Shift + F8.

10. Press the FORMAT (Shift + F8) key. A menu appears, this time on the entire screen, as shown in Figure GS-5. Here you have four items from which to select by either typing a number or a mnemonic character, such as Line (1 or L), or Page (2 or P). The cursor is again at the end of the menu, on the 0 at the bottom.

11. Select a menu option, by typing either its corresponding number or mnemonic character. A submenu appears.

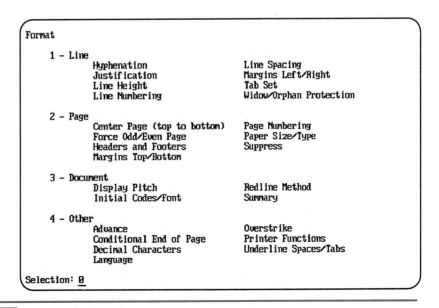

```
Format

      1 - Line
               Hyphenation                    Line Spacing
               Justification                  Margins Left/Right
               Line Height                    Tab Set
               Line Numbering                 Widow/Orphan Protection

      2 - Page
               Center Page (top to bottom)    Page Numbering
               Force Odd/Even Page            Paper Size/Type
               Headers and Footers            Suppress
               Margins Top/Bottom

      3 - Document
               Display Pitch                  Redline Method
               Initial Codes/Font            Summary

      4 - Other
               Advance                        Overstrike
               Conditional End of Page        Printer Functions
               Decimal Characters             Underline Spaces/Tabs
               Language

Selection: 0
```

**FIGURE GS-5**   The Format menu

12. Press the CANCEL (F1) key. This backs you out of the submenu only. You're again viewing the Format menu shown in Figure GS-5.

13. Press the CANCEL (F1) key again. The menu disappears and the Typing screen reappears, with the characters that you previously typed intact.

14. Find the UNDERLINE key on the template. You'll find it next to the F8 key, in black, meaning that the UNDERLINE key is F8.

15. Press the UNDERLINE (F8) key. This is an example of a function key for which no menu appears. Instead, you have turned on the Underline feature; a special, hidden code has been inserted in the text.

16. Press Backspace to cancel the Underline feature. WordPerfect prompts with a question, asking whether you wish to erase the code **[UND]**, which will abort the Underline command:

    `Delete [UND]? No (Yes)`

17. Type **Y.** The prompt clears and the Underline feature has been canceled.

## Pulldown Menus To Access Features [5.1 Users Only]

You've just learned how the function keys select WordPerfect's special features. As a 5.1 user, you have a second alternative for selecting the same features—a *pulldown menu.* A pulldown menu is one where various menus are "pulled down" from a *menu bar.*

 WordPerfect's menu bar is displayed by pressing the ⟨Alt⟩ key and, while holding the ⟨Alt⟩ key down, pressing the key with the symbol of a plus sign (+) on top and an equal sign (=) on the bottom. This will be denoted from now on as ⟨Alt⟩ + ⟨=⟩. The following menu bar displays

File  Edit  Search  Layout  Mark  Tools  Font  Graphics  Help

The first pulldown menu name, File, is always highlighted in reverse video when you first bring up the menu bar.

 From the menu bar, you then "pull down" one of the nine menus available in one of several ways: (1) use the ⟨←⟩ or ⟨→⟩ key to highlight the menu that you wish to select and press the ⟨Enter⟩ key, (2) use the ⟨←⟩ or ⟨→⟩ key to highlight the menu that you wish to select and press the ⟨↓⟩ key, or (3) type the mnemonic letter associated with the menu, such as **F** for File. That pulldown menu is then displayed down the screen.

 You select from that pulldown menu either by using the ⟨↑⟩ or ⟨↓⟩ key to highlight the command and pressing ⟨Enter⟩, or by typing the corresponding mnemonic letter. When a menu item on a pulldown menu is enclosed in brackets, that item cannot be selected. Certain features can only be accessed if you first highlight a portion of text, known as a *block.* Other features can be accessed only if no block is highlighted. Chapter 1 describes how to turn Block on to highlight portions of text, and how to turn Block off.

 Sometimes a pulldown menu leads into a pulldown submenu. Then WordPerfect will respond in one of the same three ways as when you use the function keys; that is, WordPerfect may (1) display a prompt for further information; (2) display a menu of numbered options; or (3) turn on a feature, inserting a code in the text.

Whenever you wish to clear the pulldown menus from the screen, use the CANCEL ([F1]) key. Sometimes you will need to press CANCEL ([F1]) two or three times to back all the way out of the menu structure and back to the Typing screen. (Pressing the spacebar or [Esc] key will also back you out of a menu.) To quickly exit all the way out of the pulldown menus in one operation, press the EXIT ([F7]) key.

Let's use the pulldown menu to access the Exit command, which, as you learned previously, can also be selected with the EXIT ([F7]) function key:

1. Press [Alt] + [=]. (Remember that means to hold down the [Alt] key and, while holding it down, press the [=] key one time. The [=] key is usually found at the top of the typewriter keypad, to the right of the numbers.)

   The menu bar appears, with the first option highlighted.

2. Press [→] nine times for practice in highlighting all the menu items, until you are again highlighting "File."

3. Press [Enter] to select this option. The pulldown file menu displays, as shown in Figure GS-6.

4. Press [↓] until the cursor is highlighting "Exit," and press [Enter] to select the Exit command. (Or you could have selected this command simply by typing **X**, the mnemonic letter for Exit.) The menu structure clears and the following prompt displays at the bottom of the screen:

   Save document? Yes (No)

   Perhaps you remember from the previous section that this is the same prompt that is displayed when you use the function keys rather than the pulldown menu.

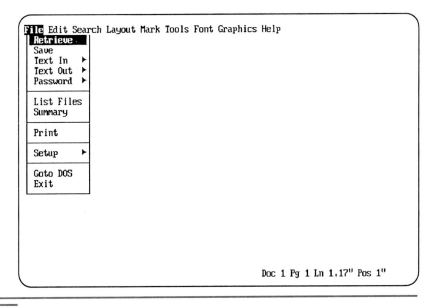

══ **FIGURE GS-6**    The File pulldown menu

5. Press CANCEL [F1] to clear the prompt and cancel the command.

   Now let's use the pulldown menu to access the Footnote feature:

1. Press [Alt] + [=]. The menu bar reappears.

2. Press [→] three times to highlight "Layout."

3. Press [↓] to display the Layout pulldown menu, as shown in Figure GS-7. Many of the items listed are marked with an arrowhead, which means that those items house submenus.

4. Type **F** to select the Footnote option. Now the submenu is revealed, as shown in Figure GS-8. This submenu contains the same four options as when, in the last

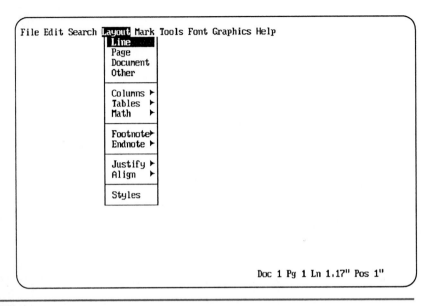

File Edit Search Layout Mark Tools Font Graphics Help

```
Line
Page
Document
Other

Columns  ▶
Tables   ▶
Math     ▶

Footnote▶
Endnote  ▶

Justify ▶
Align    ▶

Styles
```

Doc 1 Pg 1 Ln 1.17" Pos 1"

═══ **FIGURE GS-7**    The Layout pulldown menu

section, you used the function keys to access the footnote feature.

5. Press CANCEL ([F1]) three times, until you back completely out of the pulldown menus. (Or, to back out in one step, you could simply have pressed the EXIT ([F7]) key.)

As you can see, every command that you can select using the function keys can also be selected via the pulldown menus. As you become more familiar with WordPerfect, you will undoubtedly develop your preference for selecting commands. You may decide to stick with the function keys and ignore the pulldown menu. Conversely, you may decide to rely solely on the pulldown menu. Or you may use some combination of both—depending on which allows easiest access to a feature.

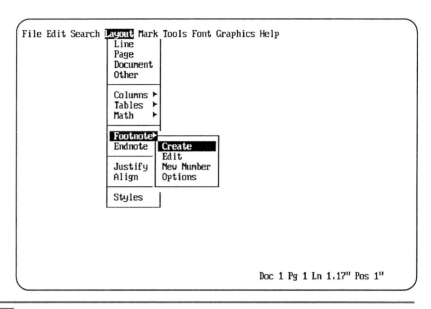

File Edit Search **Layout** Mark Tools Font Graphics Help

Line
Page
Document
Other

Columns ►
Tables ►
Math ►

**Footnote►**
Endnote │ **Create**
            │ Edit
Justify │ New Number
Align   │ Options

Styles

Doc 1 Pg 1 Ln 1.17" Pos 1"

**FIGURE GS-8**   The Footnote pulldown menu, a
submenu of the Layout pulldown menu

Throughout this book, all keystrokes will be provided using both the function keys and the pulldown menu. The function key procedure will be listed first, and the pulldown menu keystrokes will follow in brackets, such as in this example: Press the EXIT ([F7]) key. [*Pulldown menu:* File(F), Exit(X).] Thus, you will be able to experiment with both methods to discover which you fancy.

*Note:* You can change the keystrokes used to call up the menu bar in WordPerfect. Instead of the key combination [Alt] + [=], you can display the menu bar simply by pressing the [Alt] key. You may prefer this simple keystroke if you decide to rely predominantly on the pulldown menus, rather than the function keys, to access WordPerfect's features. The procedure is described in the section titled "Display" in Appendix B.

# USE A MOUSE IN WORDPERFECT [5.1 USERS ONLY]

A mouse is not required in WordPerfect. You can, however, take advantage of a mouse in WordPerfect for three types of operations:

- *Cursor Movement*    Rather than rely on the cursor movement keys, you can use the mouse to point to a specific location.

- *Access Features*    You can use the mouse exclusively to select features: You can display the menu bar, choose a pulldown menu, and then select a menu option, all by moving the mouse and clicking the mouse buttons. Or, you can use the mouse in combination with keystrokes to select features. For instance, you can press a function key to display a menu, and then use the mouse to select from the menu.

- *Block Text*    As you will learn in the next chapter, WordPerfect offers the ability to highlight a portion of text so that you can turn on a feature only for that highlighted area. You can highlight the text using a mouse.

Because not all computer users have mice, this book describes how to move the cursor, select commands, and block text by giving step-by-step keystrokes and not by giving mouse procedures. But if you have a mouse, you will find a full description of how to use it in WordPerfect in Appendix C.

If your computer is equipped with a mouse and you wish to use the mouse with WordPerfect, consider reading the remainder of the current chapter and also Chapters 1 and 2 before turning to Appendix C. In that way you will better understand the concepts of cursor movement, feature selection, and blocking text in a WordPerfect document before you start working with a mouse. And you'll have a point of comparison; you'll be in the position to discover whether it is the mouse or the keyboard that you prefer.

# ACCESS WORDPERFECT'S HELP FACILITY

One of the most useful function keys, especially for beginning users, is the HELP ([F3]) key. With the HELP key, you can discover what features are available to you and which function keys control those features. It's like having an abbreviated version of the WordPerfect manual on screen.

There are two ways to use the Help facility. Once you press the HELP ([F3]) key, either press a letter key to view an alphabetical index of features and commands starting with that letter, or press a function or cursor movement key to view an explanation of that key's purpose. If a letter or number is in boldface on a Help screen, that means that you can display a more detailed Help screen by selecting that letter or number. To exit Help, press either the [Enter] key or the spacebar.

Suppose you wish to know how to center text between your margins (a task you will actually perform in Chapter 3) and also how to exit WordPerfect (a task you will perform at the end of this chapter). Let's use the Help facility to find out how to perform each task.

1. Press the HELP ([F3]) key. [*Pulldown menu:* Help (H).]
   Hard disk users will view the screen shown in Figure
   GS-9, which describes how to use the Help feature. The
   upper right corner of the introductory Help screen lists
   the release date of the copy of WordPerfect that you are
   using on your computer. In addition, version 5.1 users
   will find their license registration number listed on the
   top line (provided you or someone else entered in that
   number when you installed WordPerfect.)

   Floppy disk users will view the following message at
   the bottom of the same screen:

   ```
   WPHELP.FIL not found.  Insert disk and press drive letter:
   ```

   This message means that WordPerfect cannot find the
   Help facility, which is stored on disk in a file named

```
Help            License #:  WP0001234567         WP 5.1   11/06/89

    Press any letter to get an alphabetical list of features.

        The list will include the features that start with that letter,
        along with the name of the key where the feature is found.  You
        can then press that key to get a description of how the feature
        works.

    Press any function key to get information about the use of the key.

        Some keys may let you choose from a menu to get more information
        about various options.  Press HELP again to display the template.




Selection: 0                                    (Press ENTER to exit Help)
```

═══ **FIGURE GS-9**   The Introductory Help screen (5.1 users)

WPHELP.FIL. Floppy disk users should remove the disk currently in drive B, replace it with the Word-Perfect 1 disk that you created when you followed the directions in Appendix A (or the WordPerfect Help disk, if you created such a disk), close the drive door, and type **B**. The screen shown in Figure GS-9 will appear.

2. To learn how to center text, type the letter **C** (for "Center"). The Help index beginning with the letter "C," which is shown in Figure GS-10, appears on the screen (slightly different for 5.0 users). Notice that half-way down the page is listed the feature "Center Text." The middle column indicates that the key name is CENTER. The right column indicates that the CEN-TER key is accessed by pressing [Shift] + [F6] (abbreviated on screen as Shft-F6). (At the bottom of Figure GS-10, WordPerfect is informing you that for more features beginning with the letter "C," type **C** (5.1 users) or type **1** (5.0 users); this means that there are more features and commands starting with the letter "C" than can display on one screen.)

3. Press the CENTER ([Shift] + [F6]) key. Figure GS-11 appears, telling you how to center text between margins or over columns. (5.0 users will see a slightly different screen.)

4. To learn how to exit WordPerfect, type the letter **E**. A new Help index appears, beginning with the letter "E." From this screen you will learn that to exit WordPerfect you must use the EXIT ([F7]) key.

```
╭──────────────────────────────────────────────────────────────────╮
│ Features [C]                    WordPerfect Key   Keystrokes       │
│                                                                    │
│ Cancel                          Cancel            F1               │
│ Cancel Hyphenation Code         Home              Home,/           │
│ Cancel Print Job(s)             Print             Shft-F7,4,1      │
│ Capitalize Block (Block On)     Switch            Shft-F3,1        │
│ Cartridges and Fonts            Print             Shft-F7,s,3,4    │
│ Case Conversion (Block On)      Switch            Shft-F3          │
│ Center Block (Block On)         Center            Shft-F6          │
│ Center Justification            Format            Shft-F8,1,3,2    │
│ Center Page (Top to Bottom)     Format            Shft-F8,2,1      │
│ Center Tab Setting              Format            Shft-F8,1,8,c    │
│ Center Text                     Center            Shft-F6          │
│ Centered Text With Dot Leaders  Center            Shft-F6,Shft-F6  │
│ Centimeters, Units of Measure   Setup             Shft-F1,3,8      │
│ Change Comment to Text          Text In/Out       Ctrl-F5,4,3      │
│ Change Default Directory        List              F5,=,Dir name,Enter │
│ Change Font                     Font              Ctrl-F8          │
│ Change Supplementary Dictionary Spell             Ctrl-F2,4        │
│ Change Text to Comment (Block On) Text In/Out     Shft-F5          │
│ Character Sets                  Compose           Ctrl-v or Ctrl-2 │
│ Character Spacing               Format            Shft-F8,4,6,3    │
│ More... Press c to continue.                                      │
│                                                                    │
│ Selection: 0                           (Press ENTER to exit Help)  │
╰──────────────────────────────────────────────────────────────────╯
```

**FIGURE GS-10**   The Help index starting with "C" (5.1 users)

5. Press the EXIT ( F7 ) key. Now the Help facility offers an explanation for the uses of the EXIT ( F7 ) key.

6. Press the Enter key or spacebar to leave the Help facility. The typing screen reappears.

7. Floppy disk users can now remove the Help disk from drive B and replace it with the disk that was there previously.

Help is useful only for a brief explanation of a feature. Nevertheless, it comes in handy when you are typing a document and want a quick reminder of how to accomplish a specific task. Therefore, whenever you are working with WordPerfect and don't know what to do next, consider the Help feature.

```
Center

        Centers one or several lines between margins or over columns. To place
        dot leaders in front of the centered text, press Center twice. To create
        a Hard Center Tab on the next tab stop, press Home, Center.

        Between margins
          a. To center a line, place the cursor at the left margin and press
             Center. Any text typed will automatically be centered until Tab,
             Flush Right, or Enter is pressed.
          b. With an existing line of text, press Center at the beginning of the
             line. The line will be centered after you press Down Arrow or select
             an action that rewrites the screen.

        Over columns
          a. Over a text column, press Center at the column's left margin.
          b. Over a column created with tabs or indents, tab to where you want
             the text centered, press Center and type the text.

        Several lines
        You can center several lines by blocking the text and pressing Center.
        WordPerfect places a [Just:Center] code at the beginning of the block, and
        a [Just:] code at the end of the block. The second justification code
        returns justification to its setting before the block.
Selection: 0                                              (Press ENTER to exit Help)
```

**FIGURE GS-11**   Help information on the CENTER ( Shift + F6 ) key

You can also turn to Help for an on-screen copy of the function key template. To see the template, press the HELP ( F3 ) key twice in a row. [*Pulldown menu:* Help (H), Template (T).] Press Enter or the spacebar when you're ready to return to the Typing screen.

## Context-Sensitive Help [5.1 Users Only]

Version 5.1 users will find that the Help feature has been enhanced—it is context-sensitive. That means that, in the midst of using a special feature, you can ask for help. For instance, suppose you press the FOOTNOTE ( Ctrl + F7 ) key and now aren't certain which menu item to select. You can press HELP ( F3 ); a Help screen describing the Footnote menu options would be displayed. You can then select a boldfaced number from that Help screen to learn more specifically about one of the menu items. Or press Enter or the spacebar to exit from the Help facility.

# CLEAR THE TYPING SCREEN

As you work at your desk throughout the day, there are times when you clear it of paper. You have two basic alternatives: put the paper in a file folder and slip the folder into your file cabinet, or crumple up the paper and throw it away. Once you've cleared off your desk, you have another set of options: start a new project, or leave your office.

You have the same options in WordPerfect. The EXIT ( F7 ) key is used to exit whatever you're currently working on. [*Pulldown menu:* File (F), Exit (X).] When you select the EXIT ( F7 ) key, WordPerfect first asks whether you wish either to store the document currently on screen onto a disk for use in the future or to just simply "throw it away," clearing the text from RAM. Then WordPerfect asks whether you wish to end your session for the day or to remain in WordPerfect.

To practice with the EXIT key, let's assume that since what appears on your screen right now is just practice material, you wish to throw it away, but you wish to remain in WordPerfect.

1. Press the EXIT ( F7 ) key. [*Pulldown menu:* File (F), Exit (X).] WordPerfect responds with

`Save document? `Y`es (No)`

WordPerfect always makes an assumption when it prompts for a yes/no answer. Since the cursor is on the "Y" in **Yes**, WordPerfect is assuming you wish to save the text. That is incorrect in this case.

2. Type **N**, which overrides the suggestion; WordPerfect understands that you don't wish to save the document. Next WordPerfect responds with

`Exit WP? `N`o (Yes)`

Since the cursor is on the "N" in **No**, WordPerfect is assuming you wish to remain in WordPerfect, which is indeed what you want.

3. Press the ⌨Enter key (or type **N**, or press any letter key other than **Y**) to accept the suggestion. The screen clears, and you remain in WordPerfect. Now you have "fresh paper" for a new project.

# EXIT WORDPERFECT

You may have worked with other word processing packages in which, to end the session, you simply turned off the computer. But whenever you finish using WordPerfect for the day, you should never simply turn off the computer! Rather, you must exit the WordPerfect program first. Only then should you turn off the computer (or load another software program). The EXIT (F7) key accomplishes this task.

Why must you exit WordPerfect before you turn off the computer? If you don't, the program has no opportunity to manage its operations and to delete special temporary files (such as overflow files) that it creates so you can use WordPerfect. You could, over time, harm the WordPerfect program on disk. Let's exit WordPerfect properly.

1. Press the EXIT ([F7]) key. [*Pulldown menu:* File (F), Exit (X).] WordPerfect responds with

   `Save document? Yes (No)`

   WordPerfect is assuming you wish to save the text. However, the screen is blank, so you have nothing to save.

2. Type **N**. WordPerfect responds with

   `Exit WP? No (Yes)`

   WordPerfect is assuming you wish to remain in Word-Perfect. That is not true in this case.

3. Type **Y**. If you are a floppy disk user, the DOS prompt (A> or B>) will appear on screen and you will have successfully exited the program, or WordPerfect will prompt as follows:

   `Insert disk with COMMAND.COM in drive A`
   `and strike any key when ready`

   WordPerfect is requesting that you reinsert the Word-Perfect 1 disk in drive A (the WordPerfect 1 disk contains COMMAND.COM, a part of the DOS program). Take out your WordPerfect 2 disk from drive A, place it back in its protective envelope, and insert your WordPerfect 1 disk into drive A. Then press [Enter] (or any other key). The DOS prompt (such as A> or B>) appears on screen, which means you have successfully exited the program. Now, if you have finished working with the computer for today, you can turn it off.

If you are a hard disk user, DOS is stored on the hard disk, so that the DOS prompt (such as C> or C:\>) appears on screen in moments; you have successfully exited the program. Now, if you have finished working with the computer for today, you can turn it off.

What happens if you or a colleague forgets to exit Word-Perfect before turning off the computer? (This should be a rare occurrence.) Or what if the power in your building flickers and the computer is shut off because of forces beyond your control? The next time you load the Word-Perfect program, a prompt such as the following will appear on the screen:

```
Are other copies of WordPerfect currently running? Y/N
```

Type **N**. The WordPerfect Typing screen will appear, and you will be ready to begin working with WordPerfect again.

## Quick Review

- To start up WordPerfect, you must first start up DOS on your computer. Then, hard disk users should change to the directory where the Word-Perfect program is stored, type **WP**, and press `Enter`. On a floppy disk system, users must first insert a data disk in the B drive and change to the B drive. Next, floppy disk users should insert the Word-Perfect 1 disk into drive A, type **A:WP**, and press `Enter`. When prompted, replace the WordPerfect 1 disk with the WordPerfect 2 disk and press any key.

  When WordPerfect's Typing screen appears, you have successfully loaded WordPerfect into the computer's RAM memory, and you are ready to begin typing.

- The cursor acts like a pointer on the Typing screen, and the status line at the bottom reports the cursor's current location.

- The `Caps Lock` key is a toggle switch that affects letters on the typewriter keypad. If you press `Caps Lock` to turn it on, all the letters you type will appear in UPPER-CASE. Press `Caps Lock` again to turn it off, so that the letters you type appear in lowercase. When `Caps Lock` is off, you can use the `Shift` key to capitalize an individual letter.

- The [Num Lock] key is a toggle switch that affects the cursor movement/numeric keypad. If you press [Num Lock] to turn it on, the right section of the keyboard acts as a numeric keypad for typing numbers. Press [Num Lock] again to turn it off, so that the right section of the keyboard serves as a cursor movement keypad, moving the cursor on the Typing screen.

- The arrow keys on the cursor movement keypad reposition the cursor without affecting your text. You can move the cursor only within the area of the screen where you've already typed.

- WordPerfect features are accessed by the function keys. The function key template fits beside the function keys. The template is a plastic card that lists the names of the features available with each function key, selected by pressing either the function key by itself or in combination with [Ctrl], [Alt], or [Shift]. A list of key names can also be found in Table GS-1 for 5.1 users and GS-2 for 5.0 users.

- 5.1 users can access features not only with the function keys, but with the pulldown menus as well. These menus are accessed from a menu bar, which appears on screen when you press [Alt] + [=].

- Press the HELP (F3) key to get on-screen assistance with WordPerfect features. Or, pulldown menu users can select Help (H).

- You must always exit WordPerfect before you turn off your computer at the end of a working session. Press the EXIT (F7) key. Or pulldown menu users can select File (F), Exit (X). Next, decide whether you wish to save the document on screen, and then, at the prompt "Exit WP?", type **Y** to exit WordPerfect. If you type **N**, the Typing screen will clear, but you will remain in WordPerfect, ready to begin a new document.

# BASIC FEATURES

# TYPING, CURSOR MOVEMENT, AND EDITING

O nce you know how to start up WordPerfect on your computer, you're ready to type a business report, write a short memo, or create "the great American novel."

While Chapter 1 won't start you on the path to novel writing, it will have you typing a short document for a fictitious organization (named the R&R Wine Association). You'll see that typing and editing text with WordPerfect is even simpler than using a typewriter.

You'll also learn what goes on behind the scenes when you type. WordPerfect hides certain symbols, called codes, from you. These codes control how your words appear, and so they are important to be aware of. You will uncover the codes from their hiding places and see how a simple code insertion or deletion can reshuffle paragraphs. Don't let the term "code" make you uncomfortable; in no time you'll be inserting and deleting codes easily.

This chapter also includes a discussion of one of Word-Perfect's most essential features, the Block command. With this command, you can mark a section of text (whether it's one character or 15 paragraphs in size) in order to perform an operation on just that block—such as deleting it. The review exercise that concludes the chapter will prove to you that after one short lesson, you have the skill to type and edit documents on your own.

# TYPE A DOCUMENT USING WORD WRAP

*Word wrap,* which is WordPerfect's automatic carriage return feature, is one of the major timesaving features of a word processor. With a typewriter, it is necessary to slow down and listen for the sound of a bell at the end of every line, so that you know when to press the carriage return. With WordPerfect, there's no need to slow down. As you type and as the cursor reaches the right margin, word wrap moves the cursor and the next word down to begin the next line.

Because of word wrap, the ⟨Enter⟩ key is *not* used in WordPerfect like a carriage return on a typewriter. The ⟨Enter⟩ key should never be pressed at the end of a line that is in the midst of a paragraph. Instead, press ⟨Enter⟩ only when the cursor is positioned where you wish to

- End a paragraph

- End a short line of text

- Insert a blank line

Let's practice typing text so that you can see word wrap in action, and so that you can practice using the ⟨Enter⟩ key properly. You will also use the ⟨Tab⟩ key, which you learned about in "Getting Started," to indent some text.

Make sure you have started WordPerfect (as explained in "Getting Started") so that you are viewing the Typing screen. Follow the steps below to type a document regarding the fictitious R&R Wine Association. If you type a wrong character, remember that you can press ⟨Backspace⟩ to erase it and then retype, just as described in "Getting Started." But don't worry too much about typing mistakes; you will learn various ways to edit your text soon. The final outcome of your typing is shown in Figure 1-1.

1. Type the following paragraph. Remember, do *not* press the ⟨Enter⟩ key at all while typing the paragraph. Just keep typing, and watch word wrap go to work.

   Two of the major wine-producing countries in Europe are France and Italy. France produces a wide variety, and Bordeaux is often considered one of the centers of fine wine. In Italy, wine production takes place in just about every region. Other countries in Europe that produce wine include:

```
 Two of the major wine-producing countries in Europe are France and
 Italy.  France produces a wide variety, and Bordeaux is often
 considered one of the centers of fine wine.  In Italy, wine
 production takes place in just about every region.  Other countries
 in Europe that produce wine include:

 Spain
 Germany
 Portugal
 Switzerland
 Austria
 Hungary
 Greece


 For more information on wine from all over Europe and the rest of
 the world, CONTACT THE R&R WINE ASSOCIATION at (415) 444-1234.  Or,
 write to us at the following address:

             R&R Wine Association
             3345 Whitmore Drive, #505
             San Francisco, CA  94123 _

                                        Doc 1 Pg 1 Ln 4.67" Pos 4.9"
```

**FIGURE 1-1**   Sample text to be typed

2. Press Enter to end the paragraph and to move the cursor to the beginning of the next line.

3. Press Enter to insert a blank line.

4. Type the following countries, making sure to press Enter after each so that you type one country on each line:

```
Spain
Germany
Portugal
Switzerland
Austria
Hungary
Greece
```

Your cursor should now be on a blank line below "Greece."

5. Press ⟨Enter⟩ three times to insert three blank lines.

6. Type the following paragraph. Remember not to press the ⟨Enter⟩ key within the paragraph; instead, let word wrap work for you. Also remember from "Getting Started" that the ⟨Caps Lock⟩ key is available for typing a group of words in uppercase letters. Remember also from "Getting Started" that you should type real ones and zeros, rather than the letters "o" and "l" when typing numbers.

   For more information on wine from all over Europe and the rest of the world, CONTACT THE R&R WINE ASSOCIATION at (415) 444-1234. Or, write to us at the following address:

7. Press ⟨Enter⟩ twice.

8. Press ⟨Tab⟩ three times. (Remember from "Getting Started" that each time you press ⟨Tab⟩, the cursor jumps to the next tab stop, which is 0.5″ to the right.)

9. Type **R&R Wine Association.**

10. Press ⟨Enter⟩.

11. Press ⟨Tab⟩ three times. Type **3345 Whitmore Drive, #505**.

12. Press ⟨Enter⟩.

13. Press ⟨Tab⟩ three times. Type **San Francisco, CA 94123**.

Congratulations to those of you who have just completed your very first WordPerfect document! You've probably noticed that word wrap has helped you type faster, whether you type 5 or 85 words per minute.

If you compare your document to the screen shown in Figure 1-1, you may find that the two screens are identical. On the other hand, you may find that words wrapped differently in paragraphs on your screen. It is important to understand that there are several possible explanations for this.

First, where WordPerfect wraps a word depends on the *settings* as to how text will be organized on the page. As discussed in "Getting Started," WordPerfect starts out with various default settings—its initial assumptions. These include: left margin of 1″; right margin of 1″; and that the document will be printed on standard-size paper, which is 8.5″ wide. (All the default settings are listed in Appendix B.) Given these default settings, WordPerfect will automatically wrap text that would otherwise extend beyond position 7.5″.

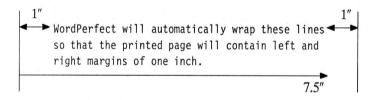

Someone may already have altered these default settings on your copy of WordPerfect, and thus word wrap in your documents may occur at a different location from that shown in Figure 1-1.

Second, where WordPerfect wraps a word partially depends on the *printer* and that printer's corresponding *font* (print character) selected to print out your document. Depending on the printer, there are variations in how many characters can actually fit across a line that extends to position 7.5″. Your document was word wrapped based on the printer you or someone else selected when you installed your copy of WordPerfect (as described in Appendix A)—which may or may not be the same as the one selected for Figure 1-1.

Thus, you may have followed the previous steps perfectly, and yet your document may look different from Figure 1-1. Of course, you will learn how to select different settings—such as change margins—and how to choose different printers and fonts in the following chapters.

# MOVE THE CURSOR BETWEEN WORDS AND LINES

On a standard-size monitor, you can see up to 24 lines of WordPerfect text on the screen at one time. (The 25th is occupied by the status line.) The document you just typed is 24 lines long, so with such a monitor you can see all of it at one time.

There are various methods for moving the cursor between words and lines without altering your text. You learned in "Getting Started" that you can move horizontally with the ⬅ and ➡ keys. You can move only through that portion of the line where you've previously typed characters or pressed the spacebar.

In a similar way, you can move vertically one line at a time with the ⬆ and ⬇ keys, but can move only through that portion of the screen where you've previously typed characters or pressed Enter to insert blank lines.

As you move up and down, WordPerfect will attempt to maintain your current position on the line. For instance, suppose your cursor is in the middle of the screen, on the first line. When you press ⬇, WordPerfect will move your cursor down a line, preserving its position in the middle of the screen. But, suppose that the second line is short, so that text does not extend to the middle of the screen. In that case, when you press ⬇, WordPerfect will move the cursor down, but will place the cursor as close to the middle of the screen as possible.

You can move more quickly on the screen by pressing and holding down any of the arrow keys. The key you press will repeat automatically. For instance, hold down the ➡ key, and the cursor will speed to the right. Also, if you press ➡ or ⬅ when the cursor is where you previously pressed the Tab key, the cursor will jump to the next or previous tab stop, respectively. Try the following:

1. Press and hold down the ⬆ key and watch the cursor zoom up until it stops at the top of the document.

2. Press and hold down the ➡ key for a few moments to watch the cursor speed to the right. When the cursor reaches the end of the first line of text, word wrap moves the cursor down to the beginning of the next line, and the cursor continues speeding along.

3. Use the ⬅ key to position the cursor at the left margin (position 1″).

4. Press and hold down the ⬇ key until the cursor moves to the left margin of the line containing the address "3345 Whitmore Drive."

5. Press ➡ three times. Since you pressed the Tab key before you began typing the address, the cursor jumps from tab stop to tab stop.

6. Press ⬅ three times. The cursor hops between tab stops to the left margin.

There are also quick ways to move the cursor by combining the arrow keys with other keys. One combination uses the Ctrl key. Remember from "Getting Started" that whenever you use the Ctrl key in conjunction with another key, you hold down the Ctrl key and, while holding it down, press the other key. Then release both keys. So, for example, Ctrl + ⬅ signifies that you hold down Ctrl, press ⬅, and then release the keys. (Some keyboards have two keys labeled Ctrl, which are interchangeable.) Use the Ctrl key to move the cursor as follows:

| | | |
|---|---|---|
| Ctrl + ⬅ | Word left—beginning of previous word |
| Ctrl + ➡ | Word right—beginning of next word |
| Ctrl + ⬆ | Paragraph up—beginning of previous paragraph (5.1 users only) |
| Ctrl + ⬇ | Paragraph down—beginning of next paragraph (5.1 users only) |

*Note:* Ctrl + ⬆ or ⬇ works only if you (1) are using WordPerfect version 5.1 and (2) have an enhanced keyboard.

Another combination uses the Home key. The Home key operates differently from the Ctrl key. Whenever a key combination involves the Home key, you press the Home key first, *release it,* and then press the second key. So, for example, Home, ⬅ signifies that you press the Home key once, and then press the ⬅ key once. (Some keyboards have two keys labeled Home. Either key can be used, but if you use the Home key located on the cursor movement/ numeric keypad, remember from "Getting Started" that

[Num Lock] must be inactive for this keypad to be used for cursor movements.) Use the [Home] key to move the cursor as follows:

| | |
|---|---|
| [Home], [←] | Left edge of text on screen |
| [Home], [→] | Right edge of text on screen |
| [Home], [↑] | Top line of text on screen |
| [Home], [↓] | Bottom line of text on screen |

You don't necessarily need to use the [Home] key to move around the screen. WordPerfect offers alternatives. (As you're discovering, WordPerfect frequently offers two or three means by which you can accomplish the same task.) The [−] key, located on the far right side of the cursor movement/numeric keypad, is another option for moving to the top of the screen. Similarly, the [+] key on the cursor movement/numeric keypad is an option for moving to the bottom of the screen. Finally, when a line of text is no wider than the screen (such as in Figure 1-1), the [End] key, also located on the cursor movement/numeric keypad, is another way to move to the right edge of the screen.

1. Press [Home], [↓], or press [+] on the numeric keypad. The cursor moves down to the bottom line on the screen.

2. Press [Home], [↑], or press [−] on the numeric keypad. The cursor moves to the top line.

3. Press [Ctrl] + [→]. The cursor jumps one word to the right.

4. Press the [Ctrl] key, and, while holding it down, press the [→] key five times. The cursor moves five more words to the right.

5. Press ⌨Home, ⌨←. The cursor moves to the left edge of the text on screen.

6. Press ⌨Home, ⌨→, or press ⌨End. The cursor moves to the right edge of the text.

7. Press ⌨Home, ⌨↓, or press ⌨+ on the numeric keypad. The cursor moves to the bottom of the screen.

Pulldown menu users will be interested to know that these cursor movements are also shortcuts for maneuvering horizontally on the pulldown menu bar or vertically within a pulldown menu. For instance, assume that you've just pressed ⌨Alt + ⌨= to display the pulldown menu bar. The cursor is highlighting the first pulldown menu name, File. You can press ⌨Home, ⌨→ to highlight the Help pulldown menu name. Then press ⌨Home, ⌨← to again highlight the File menu.

# DELETE CHARACTERS

Once you know how to control the location of the cursor, you are ready to edit your text. Editing text is easy with WordPerfect because your words appear on the computer screen rather than on a piece of paper. You don't have to reach for an eraser or correction fluid when you want to fix a typing mistake. And you don't have to start typing all over again if you forget to include a paragraph or two at the top of the document. You just press certain keys on the keyboard and the text is changed right on the screen.

The ⌨Backspace and ⌨Del keys will erase text character by character; which one you use depends on where your cursor is. As you've already learned in "Getting Started," to erase a character you've just typed (and that is therefore just to the *left* of the cursor), use the [Backspace] key. To erase a character *at* the cursor, press the DELETE ([Del]) key. If you press and hold down the [Backspace] or [Del] key, it will repeat automatically (just like the arrow keys), so that you can erase many characters in a row.

There are fast ways to delete one word, all or part of a line, and all or part of a page using the [Ctrl] key:

[Ctrl] + [Backspace]   Deletes one word—position the cursor anywhere within the word or on the empty space following the word.

[Ctrl] + [End]   Deletes to end of line (Delete EOL)—position cursor on the first character closest to the left edge of the line that you wish to erase.

[Ctrl] + [PgDn]   Deletes to end of page (Delete EOP)—position the cursor on the first character closest to the top of the page that you wish to erase.

As an example, position the cursor on the middle character in a line and press [Ctrl] + [End] to clear the right half of the line. Or, position the cursor on the first character on a page and press [Ctrl] + [PgDn] to clear an entire page of text.

The [Home] key enables you to quickly erase just a portion of a word as follows:

[Home], [Del]   Characters right of the cursor to the next word

[Home], [Backspace]   Characters left of the cursor through the first letter of that word

When you delete characters, word wrap adjusts the remaining text to fit properly inside the right margin boundary. If you delete several words from the text, you may need to *rewrite* the screen by pressing ⟨↓⟩ once or more to adjust the remaining paragraphs within the margins.

Here's a chance to delete some characters, words, and lines in your text:

1. Position the cursor just to the right of the "3" in the ZIP code "94123" near the bottom of the screen. Press ⟨Backspace⟩ five times. You have erased the ZIP code.

2. Press ⟨↑⟩ to position the cursor on the comma in the string ", #505". Press ⟨Del⟩ six times to erase that string of characters.

3. Press ⟨Home⟩, ⟨←⟩ once and then press ⟨↑⟩ as many times as necessary until the cursor is positioned on the "F" in "For more information." Now press ⟨Ctrl⟩ + ⟨End⟩. The entire line of text is erased.

4. Press ⟨Ctrl⟩ + ⟨Backspace⟩ several times until you erase any additional words that precede the phrase "CONTACT THE R&R WINE ASSOCIATION."

5. Press ⟨↓⟩ once. The revised paragraph readjusts within the margins. The bottom of your document now reads as follows:

```
CONTACT THE R&R WINE ASSOCIATION at (415) 444-1234.  Or write to
us at the following address:

                    R&R Wine Association
                    3345 Whitmore Drive
                    San Francisco, CA
```

# RECOVER DELETED TEXT

Probably, you will one day erase a word, line, paragraph, or page accidentally. Fortunately, rather than retyping the text, you can use WordPerfect's *Undelete* feature to restore a previous deletion. A deletion is considered to be a group of text you erase before typing again or moving the cursor again in the document. For instance, suppose you press [Ctrl] + [End] to delete a line; that's one deletion. Suppose you then resume typing and press [Del] twice in a row; that's another deletion. And assume you move the cursor to the top of the document and press [Ctrl] + [Backspace] four times in a row; that's a third deletion. Any of your three most recent deletions can be restored with Undelete.

You learned in "Getting Started" that if you inadvertently press a function key and then wish to clear the menu or prompt that appears, you can simply press the CANCEL ([F1]) key to clear the menu or prompt. When *no* menu or prompt appears on the screen, the CANCEL key controls the Undelete menu. [*Pulldown menu*: Edit (E) and then Undelete (U).] The most recent deletion reappears in reverse video wherever the cursor is currently located, and a menu appears on the screen enabling you to either restore ("undelete") the text at the current cursor position or view a previous deletion. If, instead, you press CANCEL ([F1]) again, the Undelete menu clears. WordPerfect remembers your last three deletions until you clear the screen or leave WordPerfect using the EXIT ([F7]) key.

Let's delete and then undelete a line of text.

1. Position the cursor in the upper left corner of the screen on the "T" in "Two." (*Hint:* Press [Home], [↑] to move the cursor quickly.)

2. Press (Ctrl) + (End) to erase that first line of text.

3. Press the CANCEL ((F1)) key. [*Pulldown menu:* Edit (E), Undelete (U).] That most recent deletion reappears in reverse video, and the Undelete menu appears at the bottom of the screen, as shown in Figure 1-2. The selections are

```
Undelete: 1 Restore; 2 Previous Deletion: 0
```

4. Select Previous Deletion (2 or P). Your next-to-last deletion now appears in reverse video.

5. Select Previous Deletion (2 or P). Your third-to-last deletion now appears in reverse video.

```
Two of the major wine-producing countries in Europe are France and
Italy.  France produces a wide variety, and Bordeaux is often
considered one of the centers of fine wine.  In Italy, wine
production takes place in just about every region.  Other countries
in Europe that produce wine include:

Spain
Germany
Portugal
Switzerland
Austria
Hungary
Greece


CONTACT THE R&R WINE ASSOCIATION at (415) 444-1234.  Or, write to
us at the following address:

            R&R Wine Association
            3345 Whitmore Drive
            San Francisco, CA

Undelete: 1 Restore; 2 Previous Deletion: 0
```

**FIGURE 1-2**  Undelete menu

6. Select Previous Deletion (2 or P). Since WordPerfect remembers only your last three deletions, the line of text that you erased most recently reappears.

7. Select Restore (1 or R). The line is reinserted into the text at the current cursor position, and the menu clears.

Whenever you inadvertently delete text and wish to use the Undelete feature, make sure to position the cursor wherever you wish to restore the text before you press CANCEL (F1). For instance, suppose you erase a line of text, move the cursor down several lines, and then realize that you wish to restore the line. Move the cursor back to its original position before you press CANCEL to recall your deletion. (Or, if you position the cursor in a different place before recalling the deletion, you can effectively move the text—although the "official" method for moving text is described in Chapter 5.)

Also, remember that WordPerfect retains only your last three deletions. You cannot undelete a line, for instance, if you wait to restore it until after you perform three additional deletions.

# INSERT CHARACTERS

WordPerfect is normally in *Insert mode*. This means that any character you type will be inserted at the current cursor position, and any text following that new character will move to the right to accommodate the insertion. Just as for a deletion, word wrap adjusts the text when you make an insertion so that your paragraph fits properly within the margins. If you insert many words, it may appear that your already-existing text is disappearing off the right edge of the screen, but that is not so. As soon as you press ⬇ to rewrite the text on screen, word wrap will bring the "disappeared" words back into view, adjusting the paragraph within the margins.

An alternative way to insert characters is to switch to *Typeover mode,* where any new character you type will replace whatever character is currently located at the cursor. Use Typeover whenever editing will be more convenient if you can type on top of the existing letters — such as when you mistakenly transpose characters (such as "teh" instead of "the," or "415" instead of "514").

The INSERT (Ins) key activates Typeover mode. Press it once and Typeover mode toggles on; the message "Typeover" appears on the left side on the status line. Press Ins again and Typeover mode is turned off; the message disappears from the screen. (Some keyboards offer two Insert keys, one labeled "Ins" and the other labeled "Insert." Either key can be used.)

Let's add some text to the document to watch how the Insert and Typeover modes operate:

1. Position the cursor at the top left corner of the screen, on the "T" in "Two."

2. Type the following: **Fine wines are produced all over the world.** The text is inserted at the cursor.

3. Press the spacebar twice to insert two spaces. It may appear that text has disappeared to the right.

4. Press ⬇. Word wrap rewrites the paragraph for you.

5. Position the cursor on the "O" of "Other" in the last sentence of the first paragraph.

6. Type the following:

> In fact, Italy has been known to yield more wine per year than any other country in the world. Though white wines are manufactured here, it is Italy's red wines that have achieved a special reputation.

7. Press the spacebar twice to insert two spaces.

8. Press ⬇. Word wrap rewrites the paragraph for you.

9. Position the cursor on the "C" of "CONTACT," near the bottom of the screen.

10. Press (Ins) once and notice that "Typeover" appears in the left corner on the status line. You have just toggled into Typeover mode.

11. Type **Contact**. Notice how, in Typeover mode, text is replaced character for character.

12. On the same line, position the cursor on the "1" of "1234" in the phone number.

13. Type **5678**. The old numbers are replaced.

14. Press (Ins) once to turn off Typeover mode. The message "Typeover" disappears from the status line.

After inserting characters, the screen should now resemble Figure 1-3.

Several keys operate differently when Typeover mode is active. The spacebar will replace the character to the right of the cursor with a space, instead of inserting a space. The (Backspace) key will replace the character to the left of the cursor with a space, instead of erasing that character. (The (Tab) key also works a bit differently in Typeover mode, as will be discussed later in this chapter.)

```
Fine wines are produced all over the world.  Two of the major wine-
producing countries in Europe are France and Italy.  France
produces a wide variety, and Bordeaux is often considered one of
the centers of fine wine.  In Italy, wine production takes place
in just about every region.  In fact, Italy has been known to yield
more wine per year than any other country in the world.  Though
white wines are manufactured here, it is Italy's red wines that
have achieved a special reputation.  Other countries in Europe that
produce wine include:

Spain
Germany
Portugal
Switzerland
Austria
Hungary
Greece


Contact THE R&R WINE ASSOCIATION at (415) 444-5678._ Or, write to
us at the following address:

            R&R Wine Association
                                        Doc 2 Pg 1 Ln 4.33" Pos 6"
```

**FIGURE 1-3**  Sample text after insertions

# MOVE THE CURSOR BETWEEN SCREENS

Notice that after you have inserted additional sentences in your document, the address is no longer visible at the bottom of the screen. This is simply because your document is now longer than 24 lines. The text is still there, but not all of it can be viewed on screen at one time. All you need to do is move the cursor down until the additional text comes into view. This is referred to as *scrolling* down the screen.

If you press and hold down the ⬇ key, you will scroll down the screen. The address will come into view and the top lines of the document will disappear. You must grow accustomed to seeing only 24 lines of text at a time. Approximately two and a half screens of single-spaced text are equal to one printed page.

Now that your text can no longer fit on one screen, let's look at some quick ways to move the cursor vertically. You learned previously that to move to the top of a screen, you press (Home), (↑) or the (−) key on the cursor movement/-numeric keypad. To move to the next screen above, simply press (Home), (↑) or (−) a second time. To move to the very top of the document, no matter how many screens above, press (Home), (Home), (↑) (that is, press (Home) twice and then press (↑)). Similarly, press (Home), (↓) or the (+) key on the cursor movement/numeric keypad to move to the next screen below, and press (Home), (Home), (↓) to move to the bottom of the document.

1. Press (↓) until the cursor is sitting on the last line of text.

2. With the cursor located at the bottom of the document, press (Home), (↑). The cursor moves to the top of the screen.

3. Press (Home), (↑) again. The cursor scrolls up one full screen to the top of the document.

4. Press (Home), (↓). Your cursor is now at the bottom of the screen.

5. Press (Home), (↓) again to scroll down a screen. Since only a few lines of the second screen are occupied, most of that screen is blank.

6. Press (Home), (Home), (↑). The cursor is again at the top of the document.

There are corresponding methods to move the cursor horizontally when lines are so long that they cannot fit on one screen. Press (Home) one extra time to move to the far edges of a line—of significance only when the line is wider than the screen. For instance, you learned that (Home), (→) moves the cursor to the right edge of the screen. Press (Home), (Home), (→) to move the cursor to the far right edge of the line. Similarly, press (Home), (Home), (←) to move the cursor to the far left edge of the line.

You've now learned how to move the cursor quickly between words, lines, and screens. Methods for moving the cursor between pages are discussed when you learn how to work with multiple pages in Chapter 6.

# REVEAL CODES

Hidden from view, codes were inserted as you typed the document now on screen. A code is a command telling the computer how text should be displayed on the screen, how it should be printed, or both. Codes are created whenever you press keys that determine how the text will appear or when you use a WordPerfect feature. For instance, when you press (Tab), a **[Tab]** code is inserted at the cursor. Similarly, when you press (Enter), the code **[HRt]**, which stands for hard carriage return, is inserted. The carriage return is called "hard" because it will not disappear as text readjusts. One code that WordPerfect creates on its own is **[SRt]**, which is inserted at the end of a line whenever word wrap moves a word down to the next line. **[SRt]** stands for soft carriage return—"soft" because it will readjust as you insert or delete text. In WordPerfect, codes are represented as words or phrases enclosed in square brackets []. (A complete list of codes can be found in Appendix D.)

The codes are hidden from you so as not to clutter the Typing screen. As you type, you need not be concerned with where codes are hiding. However, when you wish to edit the appearance of your text on screen, understanding the location of codes becomes vital. You uncover codes with the REVEAL CODES ([Alt] + [F3]) key. [*Pulldown menu:* Edit (E), Reveal Codes (R)]

*Note:* If your computer is equipped with a keyboard containing 12 function keys, then you can reveal codes by pressing either [Alt] + [F3] or, more simply, by pressing [F11]. Both are referred to as the REVEAL CODES key and produce the same effect. Or, 5.1 users can reveal codes using the pulldown menu by selecting Edit (E) and then Reveal Codes (R).

The REVEAL CODES key splits the screen into two separate windows. The top window displays 11 lines of text just as it normally appears on the Typing screen—with codes hidden. The bottom window displays ten lines of text—with codes revealed. Separating the top and bottom windows is the status line as well as a *ruler line* (also called a tab ruler), a solid bar that displays the document's current margin and tab settings. You press the REVEAL CODES ([Alt] + [F3]) key a second time to clear the Reveal Codes screen, returning to the Typing screen.

When viewing the Reveal Codes screen, you can move the cursor by using the arrow keys, just as on the Typing screen, or by using any of the other cursor movement keys. For example, press [Home], [↑] to move the cursor up a screen (only eleven lines at a time in the Reveal Codes screen, since the screen is smaller), or press [Home], [Home], [↑] to move to the top of the document.

You can also insert or delete characters on the Reveal Codes screen just as if you were on the Typing screen. In fact, you can type a whole document with codes revealed (though the main advantage to revealing codes is when you wish to edit, rather than type, your document).

In addition, you can select features on the Reveal Codes screen just as you do on the Typing screen. But if you press a function key and a prompt or menu appears, the prompt or menu is displayed between the top and bottom windows on the Reveal Codes screen, just above the ruler line, instead of at the bottom of the screen.

Figure 1-4 shows how the Reveal Codes screen appears when the screen is clear of all text and codes and you press REVEAL CODES ( Alt + F3 ). The cursor appears twice — once in each window. In the top window, it looks identical to the cursor on the Typing screen; in the bottom, it is represented as a highlighted block as tall as a standard character. The ruler line between the two windows contains triangles that represent tab stop locations, a left brace { that represents the left margin and a right brace } that

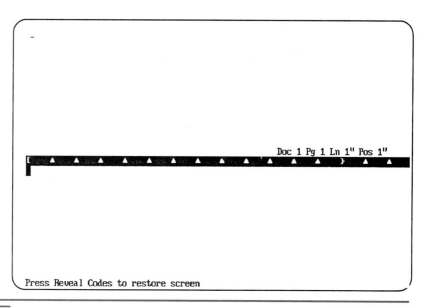

**FIGURE 1-4** A clear Reveal Codes screen

represents the right margin. The ruler line displays the default settings that were discussed previously: left margin of 1″ from the left edge of the page, right margin of 1″ from the right edge, and tab stops every 0.5″. Knowing how a blank Reveal Codes screen displays will help you orient yourself to seeing it when full of text.

Let's reveal codes on the document you just typed. Be warned that while the Typing screen is clutter free, the Reveal Codes screen can confuse the beginning Word-Perfect user. All of a sudden your screen is split into two windows, with some of the same text repeated in both windows. All of a sudden, all sorts of strange codes are surrounding your text in the lower window. And all of a sudden, a thick ruler line is crossing the middle of the screen. But after examining text on the Reveal Codes screen, you will become comfortable with its appearance and quickly see how invaluable it is in controlling exactly how you want the text of a document to appear when printed.

1. Press Home, Home, ↑ to position the cursor at the very top left corner of the document.

2. Press REVEAL CODES (Alt + F3). [*Pulldown menu:* Edit (E), Reveal Codes (R)]. The Reveal Codes screen will appear as shown in Figure 1-5. Notice that your text appears twice, in both the top and bottom windows. In the top window, the cursor is under the "F" in "Fine"; in the bottom window, the cursor highlights the "F." Also notice that in the bottom window where codes are revealed each line of the paragraph ends with an **[SRt]** code, indicating that word wrap took effect at the end of every line in this paragraph. In addition, you can see in the bottom window that the paragraph ends with two **[HRt]** codes, which were inserted where you pressed the Enter key as you typed this document. The

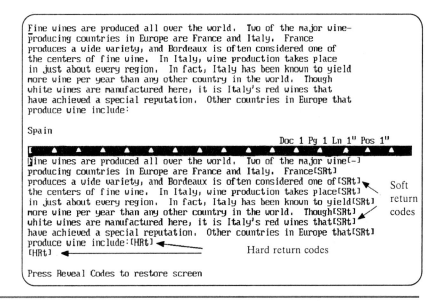

**FIGURE 1-5**   Reveal Codes screen at top of document with cursor highlighting a character

first **[HRt]** ends the last, short line of the paragraph, while the second **[HRt]** creates a blank line between paragraphs.

3. Press ⬇ at least five times and watch how the top and bottom windows start to move independently. This is because the cursor behaves differently in each window: in the top window, the cursor can be located on any line; in the bottom window, WordPerfect always maintains the cursor on the fourth line in version 5.1 and on the third line in version 5.0 (unless the cursor is on the first or second line in the document).

4. Press ⬇ until the cursor is on the line just above the word "Spain," as shown in Figure 1-6. In the top window, it looks as if the cursor is on- a blank line. But check the bottom window. The cursor is actually on an

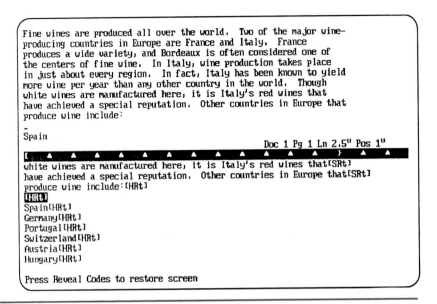

```
Fine wines are produced all over the world.  Two of the major wine-
producing countries in Europe are France and Italy.  France
produces a wide variety, and Bordeaux is often considered one of
the centers of fine wine.  In Italy, wine production takes place
in just about every region.  In fact, Italy has been known to yield
more wine per year than any other country in the world.  Though
white wines are manufactured here, it is Italy's red wines that
have achieved a special reputation.  Other countries in Europe that
produce wine include:
-
Spain
                                                 Doc 1 Pg 1 Ln 2.5" Pos 1"
[  ▲   ▲   ▲   ▲   ▲   ▲   ▲   ▲   ▲   ▲   ▲   ▲   }   ▲   ▲
white wines are manufactured here, it is Italy's red wines that[SRt]
have achieved a special reputation.  Other countries in Europe that[SRt]
produce wine include:[HRt]
[HRt]
Spain[HRt]
Germany[HRt]
Portugal[HRt]
Switzerland[HRt]
Austria[HRt]
Hungary[HRt]

Press Reveal Codes to restore screen
```

**FIGURE 1-6**   Reveal Codes screen with cursor highlighting a hard return code

[HRt] code. When the cursor in the bottom window is on a code, that code becomes highlighted in reverse video. Notice also in the bottom window the short lines ending with **[HRt]** codes, which were inserted where you pressed (Enter) after typing in each country.

5. Press (Home), (Home) (↓) so that the cursor moves to the bottom of the document as shown in Figure 1-7. Notice that in the lower window you can view a string of three **[Tab]** codes on those lines where you pressed the (Tab) key three times before typing in R&R Wine Association's address. Those same lines end with **[HRt]** codes, where you pressed (Enter) to end these short lines.

6. Press REVEAL CODES ((Alt) + (F3)) to again hide the codes. [*Pulldown menu:* Edit (E), Reveal Codes (R).]

You undoubtedly can now appreciate the Typing screen; it hides all distracting codes.

It will now appear as if most of your text has disappeared along with the codes. But remember, all you need to do is scroll up using the cursor movement keypad to again view the full text. Press [Home], [Home], [↑], and the cursor returns to the top of the document. *5.1 users only:* You have the ability to determine the number of lines that will display in the bottom window of the Reveal Codes screen. In fact, if your screen appears different from what is shown in Figures 1-5 through 1-7, someone has previously altered that default setting on your copy of WordPerfect. The section entitled "Display" in Appendix B describes the procedure.

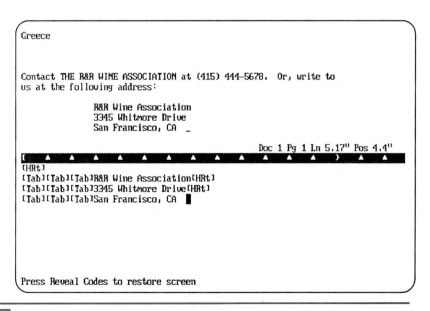

**FIGURE 1-7** Reveal Codes screen at bottom of document

# INSERT CODES

You insert codes just as you insert characters: position the cursor, and then type. Codes can be inserted either on the Typing screen or on the Reveal Codes screen. After codes are inserted, press ⬇ so that the text readjusts to fit within the margin boundaries, just as when you insert text.

For example, suppose you wish to indent the first paragraph of your document. To do so, we will precede the paragraph with a Tab code, so that the paragraph is indented to the next tab stop, which is set by default as 0.5″ from the left margin. (Remember from the discussion in "Getting Started" that it is better to use tabs rather than spaces to indent a paragraph because text may not always line up properly when printed if preceded by spaces.) Let's indent the paragraph on the Typing screen.

1. Position the cursor at the top left corner of the document on the "F" in "Fine."

2. Press Tab once. A hidden **[Tab]** code is inserted.

3. Press ⬇ to readjust the **[SRt]** codes and, thus, rewrite the text on screen.

Suppose you wish to separate the first paragraph into two separate ones. To do so, we will split the paragraph using the Enter key. Let's do so on the Reveal Codes screen.

1. Position the cursor on the "I" at the start of the sentence that begins with "In Italy."

2. Press REVEAL CODES ( Alt + F3 ) to view the Reveal Codes screen. [*Pulldown menu:* Edit (E), Reveal Codes (R).]

3. Press ⌨Enter⌨. A **[HRt]** is inserted at the cursor location, so the text that follows moves down to the next line. You see this code if you glance at the bottom window on screen.

4. Press ⌨Enter⌨ again. Another **[HRt]** has been inserted, creating a blank line.

5. Press ⌨Tab⌨. Now the second paragraph is indented. A **[Tab]** code is displayed in the bottom window.

6. Press ⌨↓⌨ to readjust the text.

7. Press REVEAL CODES ( ⌨Alt⌨ + ⌨F3⌨ ) to return to the Typing screen. [*Pulldown menu:* Edit (E), Reveal Codes (R).]

```
      Fine wines are produced all over the world.  Two of the major
wine-producing countries in Europe are France and Italy.  France
produces a wide variety, and Bordeaux is often considered one of
the centers of fine wine.

      In Italy, wine production takes place in just about every
region.  In fact, Italy has been known to yield more wine per year
than any other country in the world.  Though white wines are
manufactured here, it is Italy's red wines that have achieved a
special reputation.  Other countries in Europe that produce wine
include:

Spain
Germany
Portugal
Switzerland
Austria
Hungary
Greece


Contact THE R&R WINE ASSOCIATION at (415) 444-5678.  Or, write to
us at the following address:
                                      Doc 1 Pg 1 Ln 2" Pos 1.5"
```

**FIGURE 1-8** Sample text after paragraphs re-formed

Figure 1-8 shows the results after splitting a large paragraph into two small paragraphs in the sample text.

You learned previously that text is inserted into your document differently depending on whether you are in Insert mode or Typeover mode. But, when you insert codes, it doesn't matter whether you are in Insert mode or Typeover mode. Codes will never replace text or other codes at the current cursor position, so they will always be inserted as if in Insert mode. However, there is one exception to this: the (Tab) key. While in Insert mode, pressing (Tab) will always insert a **[Tab]** code; in Typeover mode, pressing (Tab) will move the cursor through the text to the next tab stop without inserting a **[Tab]** code.

# DELETE CODES

There are two approaches to deleting codes. First, you can make the codes visible using the REVEAL CODES ((Alt) + (F3)) key. When codes are revealed, look at the bottom half of the screen to see where your cursor is situated in respect to surrounding codes. The (Backspace) key erases the character or code to the cursor's left, while the (Del) key erases the character or code highlighted by the Reveal Codes cursor (the cursor in the bottom window on the Reveal Codes screen). Alternatively, you can delete a code on the Typing screen—if you know where the code is "hiding." Over time, you will be able to detect the location of many codes without needing to reveal them.

Suppose you wish to take the first two paragraphs on screen and combine them back into one. You must delete the **[Tab]** and **[HRt]** codes just inserted. Let's do so on the Reveal Codes screen.

1. Position the cursor at the first letter of the second paragraph, which is the "I" at the start of the sentence "In Italy."

2. Press REVEAL CODES (⟨Alt⟩ + ⟨F3⟩). [*Pulldown menu:* Edit (E), Reveal Codes (R).] Notice in the bottom window that the cursor is just to the right of a **[Tab]** code.

3. Press ⟨Backspace⟩ to erase the **[Tab]** code. Notice that the cursor is just below an **[HRt]** code. Because of the word wrap feature, the ⟨Backspace⟩ key can wrap back up to the previous line and erase that code.

4. Press ⟨Backspace⟩ to erase the **[HRt]** code.

5. Press ⟨Backspace⟩ again to erase another **[HRt]** code. The paragraphs have been combined.

6. Press REVEAL CODES (⟨Alt⟩ + ⟨F3⟩) to return to the Typing screen.

Now you're probably starting to develop an intuitive sense of where **[Tab]** and **[HRt]** codes are positioned in the text. Let's use that intuition to erase some codes on the Typing screen without revealing them first.

1. Position the cursor on the "C" in "Contact," near the bottom of the screen.

2. Realize that since the line above is blank, there must be an **[HRt]** code hidden there.

3. Press ⟨Backspace⟩. The line your cursor is on moves up as an **[HRt]** code is erased.

4. Position the cursor on the "F" in "Fine" at the very top of the document.

5. Realize that the line is indented because you inserted a **[Tab]** there.

6. Press [Backspace]. The **[Tab]** is erased.

7. Press [↓] to see if WordPerfect needs to rewrite the text, adjusting it within the margins.

Because of the position of the text on screen, the location of codes such as **[Tab]** and **[HRt]** can be detected even when you're viewing the Typing screen and the codes are hidden. But, as you will soon learn, other codes are more difficult to detect. Thus, it is a good habit, especially for beginning WordPerfect users, to switch to the Reveal Codes screen before editing text that contains numerous codes.

If you accidentally delete codes, you can restore them using the Undelete feature, as described earlier in this chapter. But, be sure to reveal codes before you use Undelete, so that you can view the codes that you are restoring.

# DELETE BLOCKS OF CHARACTERS AND CODES

WordPerfect provides speedy ways to erase a whole chunk of text at once, no matter what its content—characters, codes, or both—and no matter what its size—six words, six lines, or six paragraphs.

In WordPerfect, a chunk of text is referred to as a *block*. If that block is either a sentence ending with a period and a space, a paragraph ending with an **[HRt]** code, or a page ending with a page break (more on page breaks in Chapter 6), the deletion can be accomplished quickly. Position the cursor anywhere within the sentence, paragraph, or page that you wish to delete. Then, press MOVE ( Ctrl + F4 ). [*Pulldown menu*: Edit (E), Select (E).] Next, you can indicate whether the block is a sentence, paragraph, or page.

Once you indicate whether the block is a sentence, paragraph, or page, WordPerfect highlights the block in reverse video and prompts

1 Move; 2 Copy; 3 Delete; 4 Append: 0

Select Delete (3 or D) to erase the text (Chapter 5 discusses the other options on this menu).

If the block is *not* a sentence, paragraph, or page, you must manually define for WordPerfect the block's contents and dimensions. Position the cursor on the first character or code of the block you want to delete and press BLOCK ( Alt + F4 ). [*Pulldown menu*: Edit (E), Block (B).] The message "Block on" blinks in the left corner on the status line, indicating that the Block feature is active. Also, the **Pos** number in the right corner is displayed in reverse video. You then move the cursor, using the arrow keys, just past the last character or code of the block. WordPerfect highlights the block in reverse video. With the block defined, press either Backspace or Del . [*Pulldown menu*: Edit (E), Delete (D).] WordPerfect prompts you to verify the deletion before completing it. If the block you wish to delete is correctly highlighted, type **Y** for "Yes." If not, type **N** for "No" or type any key except Y, and the Delete command will be canceled.

*Note:* If your computer is equipped with a keyboard containing 12 function keys, you can access the Block command by pressing either Alt + F4 or, more simply, by pressing F12 . Both are referred to as the BLOCK key and produce the same effect.

Suppose you wish to erase the first sentence of the document that is currently on your Typing screen. Here, the MOVE key is appropriate.

1. Position the cursor anywhere within the document's first sentence.

2. Press the MOVE ( Ctrl + F4 ) key. [*Pulldown menu:* Edit (E), Select (E).] WordPerfect responds with the Move menu:

   `Move:  1 Sentence; 2 Paragraph; 3 Page; 4 Retrieve: 0`

3. Select Sentence (1 or S). WordPerfect highlights the sentence in reverse video, as shown in Figure 1-9, and prompts

   `1 Move; 2 Copy; 3 Delete; 4 Append: 0`

4. Select Delete (3 or D). Watch the sentence disappear.

5. Press ↓ to rewrite the text on screen, readjusting the remaining text within the margins.

Now suppose you wish to erase the last three countries from the list in the middle of the document. These three do not comprise a sentence, paragraph, or page; therefore, you

```
Fine wines are produced all over the world. Two of the major wine-
producing countries in Europe are France and Italy. France
produces a wide variety, and Bordeaux is often considered one of
the centers of fine wine. In Italy, wine production takes place
in just about every region. In fact, Italy has been known to yield
more wine per year than any other country in the world. Though
white wines are manufactured here, it is Italy's red wines that
have achieved a special reputation. Other countries in Europe that
produce wine include:

Spain
Germany
Portugal
Switzerland
Austria
Hungary
Greece


Contact THE R&R WINE ASSOCIATION at (415) 444-5678. Or, write to
us at the following address:

                R&R Wine Association
                3345 Whitmore Drive
1 Move; 2 Copy; 3 Delete; 4 Append: 0
```

**FIGURE 1-9**  A highlighted sentence

must use the BLOCK ([Alt] + [F4]) key to erase them all quickly in one command.

1. Position the cursor on the "A" in "Austria," the first character of the block.

2. Press BLOCK ([Alt] + [F4]). [*Pulldown menu:* Edit (E), Block (B).] **Block on** flashes in the left corner on the status line.

3. Press [→] until the cursor is just to the right of the lowercase "a." "Austria" is now highlighted.

4. Press [↓] twice to also highlight the last two countries listed. The screen will appear as shown in Figure 1-10.

```
Two of the major wine-producing countries in Europe are France and
Italy. France produces a wide variety, and Bordeaux is often
considered one of the centers of fine wine. In Italy, wine
production takes place in just about every region. In fact, Italy
has been known to yield more wine per year than any other country
in the world. Though white wines are manufactured here, it is
Italy's red wines that have achieved a special reputation. Other
countries in Europe that produce wine include:

Spain
Germany
Portugal
Switzerland
Austria
Hungary
Greece


Contact THE R&R WINE ASSOCIATION at (415) 444-5678. Or, write to
us at the following address:

            R&R Wine Association
            3345 Whitmore Drive
            San Francisco, CA
Block on                          Doc 1 Pg 1 Ln 3.5" Pos 1.6"
```

═══ **FIGURE 1-10**   A highlighted block

5. Press [Del] or [Backspace] . [*Pulldown menu:* Edit (E), Delete (D).] WordPerfect responds with

   ```
   Delete Block? No (Yes)
   ```

6. Type **Y** to erase the block. The rest of the text moves up because, along with the text, you deleted **[HRt]** codes contained in the block.

# HIGHLIGHT BLOCKS

In later chapters, you will find that it is often necessary to mark off blocks of text for purposes other than deletion. For example, you may wish to boldface a chunk of text, center it, or underline it. You will use the BLOCK key to mark that chunk. There are a variety of shortcuts to use when manually highlighting a block of text. You can use all four directional arrow keys — [↑], [↓], [→], or [←] — as shown in the preceding example, or you can use other cursor movement keys. You can also type the last character of the portion of text to be blocked, and WordPerfect will highlight up through this character. If you've highlighted too much text by accident, simply move the cursor in the opposite direction, or press CANCEL ([F1]) to erase all the highlighting and turn Block off.

Here's some practice in highlighting text and then removing the highlighting.

1. Position the cursor in the upper left corner of the screen, on the "T" in "Two." (*Hint:* Press [Home], [Home], [↑] to move the cursor quickly.)

2. Press BLOCK ([Alt] + [F4]). [*Pulldown menu:* Edit (E), Block (B).] "Block on" flashes on the status line.

3. Type . (period). Notice that the first sentence is now highlighted.

4. Type . again. Now the first two sentences are highlighted.

5. Type **j**. WordPerfect highlights all the way up to and including the "j" in "just."

6. Press [Enter]. WordPerfect highlights up to the end of the first paragraph, where an invisible **[HRt]** code is located.

7. Type **C** (uppercase). WordPerfect highlights to the "C" in "Contact."

8. Press Home, →, or press End. WordPerfect highlights to the end of the line.

9. Press ↑ several times and notice that WordPerfect removes the reverse video from the text as you move up.

10. Press the CANCEL (F1) key. The highlighting disappears, and Block is turned off.

You have not actually done anything to the text that you just highlighted; you just practiced with the Block command. Why become proficient at blocking a section of text? You will see in later chapters that it is often necessary to block a section of text in order to perform a specific operation on only that section. In fact, here is a list of those WordPerfect features that can be performed on a block of text, organized by the chapters where the features are discussed:

| Chapter | Features |
| --- | --- |
| 1 | Delete a block |
| 2 | Save, Print a block |
| 3 | Bold, Underline, Center, Flush Right (situate at the right margin) a block; Switch a block between upper and lowercase; Convert a block from text to a comment |
| 5 | Move/Copy a block; Append a block to the end of a file; Replace characters only within the block |
| 6 | Protect a block from page breaks |
| 7 | Count the words in a block |

| 10 | Change the font appearance or size of a block |
| 11 | Edit or format a block within a table |
| 14 | Change the style of a block |
| 15 | Sort a block; Mark a block for a table of contents/authorities, index, or list |

Obviously, the Block command is one of WordPerfect's most important features, and you'll be using it frequently. Therefore, the practice you just had will soon come in handy.

# SAVE THE TEXT AND CLEAR THE SCREEN

So far, everything that you typed has been stored temporarily in RAM and displayed on the Typing screen. If the computer power shut off suddenly, you would lose the document you have just created; the only way to use the document again would be to retype it.

So that you can use this document later, let's save it on a disk. Remember from the explanation in "Getting Started" that a disk acts like your filing cabinet, storing documents for future use. Documents are saved on disk in separate files, each with a different *filename,* just as paper documents are saved in a filing cabinet in separate file folders. Let's save the document you just created and edited into a file with the name "SAMPLE." (In the chapter that follows, you will learn more about saving files on disk.) After the document is saved, we'll clear the screen. The EXIT ( F7 ) key allows you to perform both tasks.

1. Press the EXIT ( F7 ) key. [*Pulldown menu:* File (F), Exit (X).] WordPerfect responds with

   Save document? Yes (No)

   Since the cursor is on the "Y" in "Yes," WordPerfect is assuming you wish to save the text. That is correct.

2. Press the Enter key (or type **Y** or any key on the type-writer keypad other than **N**). WordPerfect responds with

   Document to be saved:

   (If, instead, WordPerfect responds with the prompt "Long Document Name:," press Enter once until the prompt "Document to be saved:" appears.) WordPerfect is requesting a filename.

3. Type **SAMPLE** (uppercase or lowercase letters make no difference), making sure not to press the spacebar at all when typing in the filename.

4. Press Enter . WordPerfect indicates that the file is now being saved. Then WordPerfect prompts

   Exit WP? No (Yes)

   Since the cursor is on the "N" in "No," WordPerfect is assuming you wish to remain in WordPerfect.

5. Press the Enter key (or type **N** or any letter key other than **Y**) to accept the suggestion.

Now the screen is clear. It seems as if you've just typed a document that no longer exists. But in fact the document does exist—it is residing on disk. You'll see in the next chapter how quickly you can bring it back to the screen anytime you wish.

# REVIEW EXERCISE

So far you've learned quite a bit about typing and editing in WordPerfect. To make sure you're comfortable using the skills you've just learned, follow the instructions below to create and edit a new document, a letter to Mr. Barrett Smith. Refer back to the information in this chapter for guidance. The letter that you complete will be used in Chapter 2 as you learn more about saving documents and printing documents on paper.

1. Once the Typing screen is clear, type the letter shown in Figure 1-11. (*Hint:* Remember to press the (Enter) key only to end a paragraph or short line, or to insert a blank line; otherwise, let word wrap work for you. Also, use the (Tab) key to indent the table. For instance, press (Tab) several times before typing a name, and then press (Tab) several more times before typing an anniversary date. With the (Tab) key, the names and dates will align properly when printed.)

2. Practice moving the cursor to specific locations in the document as quickly as possible using the arrow keys along with the (Home) and (Ctrl) keys.

---

February 3, 1989


Mr. Barrett Smith
FST Accounting
1801 S. Harmon Street
Oakland, CA 94130


Dear Mr. Smith:

As you requested, here are a list of full-time employees who elected to accept the new vacation option, along with their anniversary dates with us. There are only three employees who chose the plan. Please add their names to your record.

|                   |             |
|-------------------|-------------|
| Antonio Abbot     | May 13th    |
| Lois Chang        | April 27th  |
| Paul McClintock   | August 7th  |

The new accrued vacation system should begin for these employees immediately.


Sincerely,


Sandy Peterson
R&R Wine Association


P.S. I've enclosed a copy of our quarterly newsletter for your enjoyment.

---

**FIGURE 1-11**   Review exercise text

February 3, 19~~89~~ 90

Mr. Barrett ^P.^ Smith
FST Accounting
1801 S. Harmon Street
Oakland, CA 94~~130~~ 413

Dear ~~Mr. Smith~~ *Barrett*:

As ~~you requested~~ *we discussed*, here ~~are~~ *is* a list of full-time employees who elected to accept the new vacation option, ^*complete*^ along with their anniversary dates with us. ~~There are only three employees who chose the plan.~~ Please add their names to your record.

|  | Antonio Abbot | May ~~13th~~ **31st** |
| *Tim Fingerman* → | Lois Chang | April 27th |
|  | Paul McClintock | August 7th ← *May 20th* |

The new accrued vacation system should begin for these employees immediately. *Thank you*

Sincerely,

Sandy Peterson *— President*
R&R Wine Association

P.S. I've ~~enclos~~ *includ*ed a copy of our quarterly newsletter for your enjoyment.

**FIGURE 1-12**  Review exercise text to be edited

3. Edit the document as shown in Figure 1-12. (*Hint:* Use both the Insert and Typeover modes for quick editing. For instance, stay in Insert mode to add Barrett Smith's middle initial, but switch to Typeover mode to edit the ZIP code from "94130" to "94413." Also, remember that you can insert a blank line anywhere in a document by positioning the cursor and pressing the [Enter] key; for example, to add a new name to the table, position the cursor just to the right of the "h" in "April 27th" and press [Enter].)

4. Save this document under the filename LETTER. (*Hint:* To do so, press the EXIT ([F7]) key. [*Pulldown menu:* File (F), Exit (X).] Next, type **Y** in response to the prompt **Save document? Yes (No)**. Then, type **LETTER** and press [Enter] to indicate the document name.)

5. If you're done for the day, exit WordPerfect by typing **Y** in response to the prompt **Exit WP? No (Yes)**. If, instead, you're ready to proceed to Chapter 2, just clear the Typing screen, but remain in WordPerfect by pressing [Enter] or typing **N** in response to that prompt.

## Quick Review

- When typing text, use the ⟦Enter⟧ key only to (1) end a paragraph; (2) end a short line of text; or (3) insert a blank line. Otherwise, let word wrap—the automatic carriage return feature—adjust your text within the margins of your document.

- The ⟦←⟧, ⟦→⟧, ⟦↑⟧, and ⟦↓⟧ keys move the cursor one character or line at a time without disturbing the text on screen. There are also quick methods for moving the cursor on screen, as shown in Table 1-1.

- The variety of methods for deleting text are shown in Table 1-2.

- Restore any of your last three deletions using the Undelete feature. To access this feature, press the CANCEL (⟦F1⟧) key. Or, using the pulldown menu select Edit (E) and then Undelete (U). WordPerfect displays your last deletion in reverse video. Select Restore (1 or R) to recall the deletion or Previous Deletion (2 or P) to display another deletion.

- When inserting text, the ⟦Ins⟧ key is a toggle that switches between Insert and Typeover mode. In Insert mode, characters that you type are inserted at the current cursor position, and existing text moves to accommodate the new characters. In Typeover mode, existing text is replaced with new characters that you type.

- Pressing keys such as [Enter] or [Tab] causes codes to be inserted into the text that determine how it will appear on screen and on the printed page. As you view the normal Typing screen, these codes are hidden.

- Make codes visible by switching from the Typing screen to the Reveal Codes screen. To do so, press the REVEAL CODES ([Alt] + [F3]) key. Or, using the pulldown menu, select Edit (E) and then Reveal Codes (R). Now you can position the cursor precisely before inserting or deleting codes. Press REVEAL CODES ([Alt] + [F3]) again, or select Edit (E) and then Reveal Codes (R) from the pulldown menu, to toggle back to the Typing screen.

- Perform tasks on a specific portion of text with the all-important Block command. To use this command, position the cursor on the first character to be included in the block, press the BLOCK ([Alt] + [F4]) key to turn Block on, and then position the cursor one past the last character. Or, pulldown menu users can turn Block on by selecting Edit (E) and then Block (B).

| Cursor Movement | Key Sequence |
|---|---|
| Word left | [Ctrl] + [←] |
| Word right | [Ctrl] + [→] |
| Paragraph up (5.1 only) | [Ctrl] + [↑] |
| Paragraph down (5.1 only) | [Ctrl] + [↓] |
| | |
| Left edge of screen | [Home], [←] |
| Right edge of screen | [Home], [→] |
| Top of screen (or, if cursor is at the top, screen above) | [Home], [↑], or [−] |
| Bottom of screen (or, if cursor is at the bottom, screen below) | [Home], [↓], or [+] |
| | |
| Far left edge of document (for lines wider than the screen) | [Home], [Home], [←] |
| Far right edge of document (for lines wider than the screen) | [Home], [Home], [→], or [End] |
| Top of document | [Home], [Home], [↑] |
| Bottom of document | [Home], [Home], [↓] |

**TABLE 1-1**  Cursor Movement Between Words, Lines, and Screens

| Text Deleted | Key Sequence |
|---|---|
| Character (or code) left of cursor | Backspace |
| Character (or code) at cursor | Del |
| Word at cursor | Ctrl + Backspace |
| Characters left to word boundary | Home , Backspace |
| Characters right to word boundary | Home , Del |
| Characters right to line end | Ctrl + End |
| Characters right and below to page end | Ctrl + PgDn |
| Sentence, paragraph, or page | Block text; Ctrl + F4 , 1 or 2 or 3; 3 |
| Block | Block text; Del or Backspace ; Y |

**TABLE 1-2** Deletion Options

# RETRIEVING, SAVING, AND PRINTING

Y ou have little to show for all your hard work in the last chapter: Neither of the two documents you created is on screen, and neither has been printed. That is now going to change. In this chapter you will learn more about how to store documents on disk and how to get a listing of the stored documents. And you'll retrieve your documents back to the screen for review.

You'll also learn how to transform your words from glowing characters on a computer screen to printed characters on paper. In the pages that follow, you'll print your documents using several different methods. As you settle into using WordPerfect, you will probably start to rely on only one or two of the many possible methods for most of your printing needs.

After completing this chapter, you will understand the basics of saving, retrieving, and printing documents. Word-Perfect version 5.1 users who use the pulldown menus will find that saving, retrieving, and printing commands are all accessed from the File pulldown menu.

# LEARN ABOUT NAMING AND LISTING FILES

In Chapter 1, you typed and then saved two documents for future use: the document with the name SAMPLE and the review exercise document named LETTER. Both documents were placed in a file and stored on disk.

As you work more and more with WordPerfect, you will save literally hundreds of files on disk for future use, each with a different filename. When you name files, you must abide by the following rules:

- A filename can contain from one to eight characters followed by an optional period and a one- to three-character file extension.

- Acceptable characters in a filename and its optional extension include all letters and numbers and any of the following characters:

  ! @ # $ ( ) - { } ` ´ ^ ~

- A filename cannot contain spaces.

The filenames SAMPLE and LETTER are acceptable filenames. Other acceptable filenames include

| | | |
|---|---|---|
| SAMPLE1 | SAMPLE1.SWJ | SAMPLE1.01 |
| BRADY#1 | BRADY#1.LTR | BRADY(1).LTR |
| 007 | OO7.RPT | RPT.OO7 |

Examples of invalid filenames are

| | |
|---|---|
| FIRSTSAMPLE | (Too many characters in filename) |
| SAMPLE.4232 | (Too many characters in extension) |
| BOB SMIT | (Contains a blank space) |
| LETTER*.1 | (Contains *, an unacceptable character in a filename) |

Establishing an orderly naming system for files is essential for identifying documents easily. It is wise to develop a descriptive system based on the type of documents you create. An appropriate naming system if you type different types of documents might specify a document's type in its filename extension. For example, all correspondence could end with the extension .LTR, standing for "letter," all reports could end with the extension .RPT, and so on. An alternative naming system if you share a hard disk with other users might indicate a document's author in its filename extension. For example, if your initials are MRM, you could assign .MRM as the extension for all documents you write; a document discussing the 1989 budget could be called BUD89.MRM. Or a document's author might be included as the first three letters of the filename, with no file extension used. For instance, the budget document could be named MRMBUD89. Whatever naming system you choose, be sure to plan now, before you accumulate too many files.

Unless you specify otherwise, a file is stored in what is called the *default drive* or *directory*. Thus, the documents that you saved in Chapter 1 under the names SAMPLE and LETTER are both stored on your default drive/directory.

The default drive/directory is determined by how you loaded WordPerfect. For those of you with a floppy disk system, if you followed the directions for loading in "Getting Started," the default is drive B. A drive letter is always followed by a colon, so that drive B is denoted as B: or B:\. For those of you with a hard disk system, if you followed the directions for loading with a batch file in "Getting Started," the default is either the directory \WP51\DATA or \WP50\DATA on drive C. This is denoted as C:\WP51\DATA or C:\WP50\DATA. Or, you may have loaded WordPerfect differently, so that your default is something else.

*Note:* 5.1 users can also determine the default drive/directory by specifying a location for your documents, as described in the section entitled "Location of Files" in Appendix B.

The LIST ([F5]) key allows you to determine your default drive/directory. (In version 5.0, the [F5] function key is referred to as the LIST FILES key, rather than as the LIST key.) To determine your default drive/directory:

1. Press the LIST ([F5]) key. [*Pulldown menu:* File (F), List Files (F).] A prompt will appear, such as:

   `Dir B:\*.*`

   This means that the default is drive B.
   Or, you may see

   `Dir C:\WP51\DATA\*.*`

   This means that the default is the directory \WP51 \DATA on drive C, the hard disk.
       The asterisk (*) is a wildcard character; thus, the "*.*" in the prompt signifies that WordPerfect is prepared to list all the files in the default drive or directory, regardless of their filename (the characters that precede the period) or their file extension (the characters following the period).

2. Press CANCEL ([F1]) to clear the prompt.

Through the remainder of this chapter, you will work predominately with files stored in the default drive/directory. However, you should be aware that it is possible to change the default drive/directory at any time during the current working session. This is important for hard disk users because, on a hard disk, keeping an orderly filing system is based not only on naming files with descriptive names, but on grouping similar documents into the same directory. You can, for example, reserve one directory named \WP51\DATA for business documents and reserve another named \WP51\PERS for personal documents. Chapter 8 describes how to create new directories, and then how to alter the default directory in the midst of a working session. (Floppy disk users can group documents together simply by inserting the same disk into drive B before each of the documents is saved.)

# DISPLAY A LIST OF FILES

You can use the LIST key not only to show the default drive directory but also to display a complete list of files stored in the default drive/directory.

1. Press the LIST ( F5 ) key. [*Pulldown menu:* File (F), List Files (F).] A prompt will appear displaying your default drive/directory, such as:

   Dir B:\*.*

   or

   Dir C:\WP51\DATA\*.*

2. Press Enter .

Figure 2-1 shows an example of the List Files screen. At the very top of the List Files screen, in the first line of the List Files header, WordPerfect lists the date and time (which are correct provided that you properly entered the current date and time as described in "Getting Started" or

```
┌─────────────────────────────────────────────────────────────────────┐
│ 01-15-90  02:58p           Directory C:\WP51\DATA\*.*                 │
│ Document size:         0   Free: 1,490,944 Used:    576,247  Files:  41│
│ ┌──────────────────────────────────┐                                  │
│ │ .   Current    <Dir>             │   ..    Parent    <Dir>          │
│ !ACCTS   .       1,329  10-12-89 11:15p  1001     .      46,266 01-15-90 01:29p│
│ 5012     .      35,605  10-04-88 08:41p  5028     .CRG   29,573 10-04-88 08:42p│
│ 88ANN   .RPT    21,212  02-09-88 11:23a  88RENT   .      43,544 06-16-88 03:56p│
│ 89ANN   .RPT    40,656  10-17-89 01:21p  89RENT   .      40,824 10-17-89 01:19p│
│ ACCOUNTS.ADD    36,403  01-15-90 01:30p  BKGROUND.88        778 02-23-88 01:20p│
│ BUDMIN89.        1,961  05-22-88 09:32p  BUDMIN90.       27,764 01-15-90 01:32p│
│ C1      .LTR     1,551  02-09-89 11:05a  C2      .LTR     1,123 10-16-89 07:49p│
│ C3      .LTR     1,340  01-15-90 01:30p  CEO1    .MMO       942 12-21-88 11:15a│
│ DOCLIST1.MS     40,756  10-04-88 08:39p  FINANCE .        2,143 09-09-88 10:30a│
│ FON     .       20,120  10-04-88 08:43p  GAIN    .LTR     1,598 02-09-89 11:05a│
│ J&B     .MMO     2,317  09-16-88 08:36p  JONES1  .MMO     1,356 07-22-88 12:56a│
│ JONES2  .MMO     5,936  02-11-88 01:01a  LE-45   .       40,970 10-04-88 08:40p│
│ LETTER  .        1,123  10-16-89 07:49p  LINKER  .        1,206 09-16-88 08:36p│
│ LINKER2 .       35,651  01-15-90 01:33p  LIST    .        1,799 08-22-88 11:23a│
│ LIST    .NEW     1,939  08-21-88 09:43p  MEYERS-1.MS      1,206 09-16-88 08:36p│
│ P&L     .       35,597  10-04-88 08:40p  R&RBACK .          380 09-20-88 11:51a│
│ SALVA   .LTR     4,537  09-16-88 08:37p  SALVA:  .       29,573 10-04-88 08:43p│
│ SAMPLE  .        1,329  10-12-89 11:15p▼ SEYMORE .LTR       714 02-15-88 03:21a│
│ └──────────────────────────────────┘                                  │
│ 1 Retrieve; 2 Delete; 3 Move/Rename; 4 Print; 5 Short/Long Display;   │
│ 6 Look; 7 Other Directory; 8 Copy; 9 Find; N Name Search: 6           │
└─────────────────────────────────────────────────────────────────────┘
```

═════ **FIGURE 2-1** List Files screen (version 5.1)

that your computer is equipped with an internal clock), and the name of the drive and/or directory for which files are listed. For example, C:\WP51\DATA\*.* in Figure 2-1 indicates that the files listed are from the directory \WP51\DATA in drive C, the hard disk. As another example, B:\*.* would indicate that the files listed are those in drive B, the default for floppy disk users. (Remember that the notation *.* means that WordPerfect is displaying all files in the default drive/directory, no matter what their filenames or extensions.) The second line of the header provides the following information:

- *Document size* This is the size of the document on the Typing screen when you first pressed the LIST key. For instance, if the Typing screen was clear when you pressed LIST, then the document size will read 0 (as shown in

Figure 2-1). If the Typing screen contained text, then WordPerfect reports the size of the text on screen in *bytes,* a computer term of measurement equal to a number, letter, space, or punctuation mark. For comparison purposes, keep in mind that approximately 1500 to 2000 bytes equal one double-spaced page of text.

- *Free*  This is the amount of free space still available to store files on the floppy or hard disk. This is also measured in bytes.

- *Used*  This is the amount of space occupied by files on the floppy disk or on the directory of your hard disk, also measured in bytes.

- *Files*  This is the total number of files on the floppy disk or in the directory of your hard disk.

Below the List Files header, filenames are displayed in two columns and are alphabetized row by row. Filenames that begin with symbols are listed first, followed by filenames that begin with numbers, and then by filenames that begin with letters. Notice in Figure 2-1 that you can see an alphabetized list of files, two of which are SAMPLE and LETTER (shown near the bottom of the first column). At the top of the columns are "Current <Dir>" and "Parent <Dir>." These two entries are used to display files in other directories, as discussed in Chapter 8, and can be ignored for now, except to note that "Current <Dir>" is highlighted in reverse video, meaning that this is where the cursor is located when you first view the List Files screen. Notice that the cursor covers the full width of one column on the List Files screen.

*Note:* For 5.1 users, if your screen displays one column instead of two, then the List Files screen is in "Long" Display, rather than "Short" Display, as is discussed in

Chapter 8. You can switch the display to resemble Figure 2-1 as follows: Select Short/Long Display (5 or S), select Short Display (1 or S), and press [Enter] .

Only 36 filenames can be displayed at one time on the List Files screen. If there are more than 36 files in the drive/directory, then an arrow appears at the bottom of the screen between the two columns (as shown in Figure 2-1). You must then use the arrow keys or the other cursor movement keys to scroll the cursor down to the filenames on the screen below.

Next to each document's filename, the List Files screen provides other useful information. The number just to the right of each filename indicates its size, again in bytes. In Figure 2-1, for example, the size of both SAMPLE (1329 bytes) and LETTER (1123 bytes) indicates that the text of each fills up less than a full page (1500-2000 bytes). Word-Perfect also lists next to each file the date and the time that the file was last saved to disk. By glancing at a file's date and time, you can tell when you or someone else made the most recent typing and editing changes to that document.

At the bottom of the List Files screen is a menu of options for managing files. Three of the options — Retrieve (1 or R), Print (4 or P), and Look (6 or L) — are described later on in this chapter. Additional file-management capabilities are described in Chapter 8.

You can clear the List Files menu and return to the Typing screen at any time using the CANCEL ( [F1] ) key — the same way you back out of any command where WordPerfect displays a menu or prompt; or you can use the spacebar or EXIT ( [F7] ) key.

Here's how to move the cursor on the List Files screen:

1. Press [↓] . The cursor moves down from the phrase

"Current <Dir>" to the first file listed in the first column.

2. Press ➡. The cursor moves to the first file listed in the second column.

3. Press and hold down the ⬇ key until the cursor reaches the last file in column two. (There may be only two files—LETTER and SAMPLE—on your List Files screen, so that the cursor can move down no further.)

4. Press (Home), ⬆. The cursor moves up to the file listed in the upper left corner on screen. If you have already stored many files in this drive or directory, it may be necessary to continue pressing (Home),⬆ until the cursor is back to the very top, on the phrase, "Current <Dir>."

5. Press the CANCEL ((F1)) key. The List Files screen disappears.

You can temporarily list files in a drive or directory other than the default. Press the LIST ((F5)) key, and when WordPerfect suggests the default, type in another drive or directory before pressing (Enter). For instance, if you are a hard disk user and wish to view a list of files on the floppy disk in drive A, press LIST ((F5)), and, when WordPerfect prompts you with

```
Dir C:\WP51\DATA\*.*
```

type the drive letter followed by a colon, writing over the prompt in order to edit it. Type **A:**. (There's no need to type \*.* so that the prompt reads "A:\*.*" because, unless you specify otherwise, WordPerfect assumes you wish to list every file in that drive.) Now the prompt reads

```
Dir A:
```

Press ⌊Enter⌋. The List Files screen now displays a list of files on the floppy disk in drive A.

As another example, suppose you wish to view a list of files in a directory named \WP51\PERS. Press LIST (⌊F5⌋) and, when WordPerfect prompts you with

```
Dir C:\WP51\DATA\*.*
```

use the ⌊Backspace⌋, ⌊Del⌋, and arrow keys to edit the prompt to read

```
Dir C:\WP51\PERS\*.*
```

(or, more simply, to read DIR C:WP51\PERS). Press ⌊Enter⌋. The List Files screen now displays a list of the files in that directory. After examining the screen, press CANCEL (⌊F1⌋) to return to the Typing screen.

# RETRIEVE A DOCUMENT TO THE SCREEN

To review or edit a document stored on disk, you must retrieve that document file to the screen. What you retrieve is actually a copy of the file: the original version remains stored safely on the disk. Therefore, if you retrieve a document for review, but make no editing changes to the document, you can simply clear the screen with the EXIT (⌊F7⌋) key when you are finished reviewing it.

It is critical that before retrieving a document, you make sure that the Typing screen contains no other document. This is trickier than you may think. Many WordPerfect users have accidentally combined documents on screen because the Typing screen wasn't truly blank. While the screen may look clear, a document may be on screen but not in view until you press the ⬆ or ⬇ key to scroll through the text. When a Typing screen is completely void of text and codes, the cursor does not move when you press any of the arrow keys, and the status line reports that the cursor is at Pg 1 Ln 1 ″ Pos 1″ .

What happens if the Typing screen is not clear when you retrieve a document? WordPerfect inserts the contents of a retrieved file wherever the cursor is located. For instance, suppose you typed three paragraphs of text. With your cursor below the third paragraph, if you retrieve a file, the contents of that file will be added onto the end of the three paragraphs. So unless you want to combine text from different sources (further discussed in Chapter 13), make sure that the screen is clear by using the EXIT ( F7 ) key before retrieving text from a new file to the screen.

You can retrieve a file in one of two ways: with the RETRIEVE ( Shift + F10 ) key [*Pulldown menu:* File (F), Retrieve (R)] or with the LIST ( F5 ) key [*Pulldown menu:* File (F), List Files (F)].

Using· the RETRIEVE key is swift and easy, provided that you remember the name of the file you wish to retrieve. On a clear Typing screen, press the RETRIEVE ( Shift + F10 ) key, type in the document's full name (including a period and its extension if it has one), and press Enter . WordPerfect checks the default drive or directory for that file and recalls a copy of its contents onto the Typing screen. Should WordPerfect be unable to locate that file on disk, it responds

ERROR: File not found

If you made a typing mistake, you now have the opportunity to retype or edit the filename you just typed and press [Enter] to retrieve the correct file. If the wrong floppy disk is in the default drive, then you can insert the correct disk and press [Enter]. Or if you wish to back out of the Retrieve command, press CANCEL ([F1]).

When using the RETRIEVE key, there may be times that you wish to retrieve a file from other than the default drive or directory. In that case, you must precede the document's filename with the drive or directory where WordPerfect will find the file. For instance, suppose that your default directory is \WP51\DATA, but that the file named SAMPLE is stored in the directory on the hard disk named \WP51\PERS. After pressing the RETRIEVE key, you would type **C:\WP51\PERS\SAMPLE** and press [Enter]. Or suppose that the file named SAMPLE is stored on drive A. After pressing the RETRIEVE key, you would type **A:\SAMPLE** (or more simply, **A:SAMPLE**) and press [Enter]. (See Chapter 8 for more information on altering the default drive/directory.)

Using the LIST key to retrieve files is handy if you have forgotten the document's filename (a likely occurrence once you've accumulated numerous files on your disk), or if you are a slow typist and prefer to use the cursor rather than typing in a filename. On a clear Typing screen, use the LIST ([F5]) key to list the files in the correct drive or directory. Next, position the cursor on the file to be retrieved. Finally, select Retrieve (1 or R) from the menu of options at the bottom of the List Files screen. A copy of the file's contents appears on the Typing screen.

Suppose you wish to review a document and you know that its filename is SAMPLE. Proceed in these steps:

1. The screen should be completely clear. If not, clear the screen by pressing the EXIT ([F7]) key [*Pulldown menu:* File (F), Exit (X)] and then typing **N** twice.

2. Press the RETRIEVE ([Shift] + [F10]) key. [*Pulldown menu:* File (F), Retrieve (R).] WordPerfect responds with

   `Document to be retrieved:`

3. Type **SAMPLE** (uppercase or lowercase makes no difference) and then press [Enter]. WordPerfect checks the default drive or directory for a file named SAMPLE. In seconds, a copy of that file appears on the screen for you to read or edit.

Suppose after reading through the file named SAMPLE, you wish to retrieve another file, whose filename you forgot. Let's clear the screen and then retrieve that other file.

1. Press the EXIT ([F7]) key. [*Pulldown menu:* File (F), Exit (X).]

2. Since the file named SAMPLE is still safely on disk and you did not revise it on screen, you don't need to save it again. In fact, you'll see the message "(Text was not modified)" in the lower right corner of the status line, verifying that the version on screen is identical to the version on disk. Simply type **N** twice to clear the screen.

3. Press the LIST ([F5]) key. [*Pulldown menu:* File (F), List Files (F).]

4. Press [Enter]. The List Files menu appears, showing the names of files in your default drive or directory.

5. Use the cursor movement keys to position the cursor on the filename LETTER.

6. Select Retrieve (1 or R). In seconds, a copy of the file is retrieved to the screen.

You'll find that whenever you retrieve to the screen a document previously saved to disk, the drive or directory location where it is stored, followed by its filename, is listed in the lower left corner of the status line. For instance, if you use a floppy disk system and LETTER has been stored on the disk in drive B, when you retrieve that file, the lower left corner of the status line reads

`B:\LETTER`

A hard disk user whose default directory is \WP51\DATA will see

`C:\WP51\DATA\LETTER`

This information helps remind you of the name of the file you are working on, as well as its location on disk. A document's location on disk is referred to as its *path*. Thus, C:\WP51\DATA\LETTER signifies that the path for the document file named LETTER is C:\WP51\DATA. Should you find the display of a document's path and filename distracting when shown on the status line, you can ask WordPerfect to suppress this information. See the information under the heading "Display" in Appendix B.

# LOOK AT THE CONTENTS OF A FILE

You've learned that the Retrieve feature is used when you wish to recall a file to the screen for review or editing. WordPerfect offers a related feature, the Look feature, whereby you can review (but not edit) the contents of a file *without actually recalling the text to the screen.* Look is handy when you don't wish to disrupt the text currently on the Typing screen but want to take a quick glance at the contents of another document.

You initiate the Look feature from the List Files screen by positioning the cursor on the file you wish to take a peek at and then either selecting Look (6 or L) or pressing the Enter key. (Pressing the Enter key is the alternative because, as shown in Figure 2-1, the assumed menu option—at the end of the List Files menu at the bottom of the screen—is number 6, Look.) You can then use the cursor keys to scroll through the document on the Look screen. Press CANCEL (F1) or EXIT (F7) when you wish to return to the List Files screen.

Let's take a glance at the file named SAMPLE, even though the file named LETTER is currently on screen.

1. Press the LIST (F5) key. [*Pulldown menu:* File (F), List Files (F).]

2. Press Enter. The List Files menu appears, showing the names of files in your default drive or directory.

3. Position the cursor on the filename SAMPLE.

4. Press Enter. Or select Look (6 or L). A Look screen appears, displaying the contents of the file named SAMPLE. The Look screen for 5.1 users is shown in Figure 2-2. At the top of the Look screen is a header that displays the file's path and name, such as C:\WP51\DATA\SAMPLE, meaning that the file into which you are looking is named SAMPLE and stored in the directory \WP51\DATA on the hard disk. Also, the header displays the date and time that the document was last revised—the last time that it was stored on disk.

At the bottom of the screen is the following menu:

**Look 1** Next Doc; **2** Prev Doc: **0**

This allows you to select Next Doc (1 or N) or Prev Doc (2 or P) to view the Look screen for the next or previous document listed on the List Files screen, respectively.

The Look screen for 5.0 users is different from Figure 2-2 in two ways: first, there is no menu at the bottom of the screen, so that, to look at the contents of another file, you must press CANCEL ( $\boxed{\text{F1}}$ ) to return to the List Files screen, reposition the cursor, and then reselect the Look feature. Second, the header displays the file's size rather than the date it was last revised.

```
File: C:\WP51\DATA\SAMPLE                WP5.1      Revised: 10-12-89 11:15p

Two of the major wine-producing countries in Europe are France and
Italy.  France produces a wide variety, and Bordeaux is often
considered one of the centers of fine wine.  In Italy, wine
production takes place in just about every region.  In fact, Italy
has been known to yield more wine per year than any other country
in the world.  Though white wines are manufactured here, it is
Italy's red wines that have achieved a special reputation.  Other
countries in Europe that produce wine include:

Spain
Germany
Portugal
Switzerland


Contact THE R&R WINE ASSOCIATION at (415) 444-5678.  Or, write to
us at the following address:

          R&R Wine Association

Look: 1 Next Doc; 2 Prev Doc: 0
```

══ **FIGURE 2-2**    Look screen showing the contents of SAMPLE (version 5.1)

5. Use the cursor movement keys (such as ⊞, ⊟, ⊟, and ⊞ on the cursor movement keypad) and watch as you move to different lines in the file.

6. Press CANCEL (F1) twice—once to exit the Look screen and a second time to exit the List Files screen. You are returned to the Typing screen. Notice that the text on screen has been unaffected by your having looked quickly at the contents of another file.

# SAVE A DOCUMENT AT REGULAR INTERVALS

After you've retrieved a document to screen and revised it, you must remember to save it again if you want to keep a copy of the revised document. As in retrieving, there are two methods for saving a document to disk, one using the EXIT (F7) key [*Pulldown menu:* File (F), Exit (X)] and the other using the SAVE (F10) key [*Pulldown menu*: File (F), Save (S)].

Use the EXIT (F7) key if you wish to save the document and you've finished working with it for the moment; using this key allows you either to clear the screen and start something new or to end your WordPerfect session. (In Chapter 1, you were introduced to this method for saving files.) When you press the EXIT (F7) key, WordPerfect responds with

**Save document? Yes (No)**

Press (Enter) or type **Y** or any key other than **N** to save the document and WordPerfect prompts

```
Document to be saved:
```

After you type in a filename and press `Enter`, the document is saved on disk, and WordPerfect prompts

```
Exit WP? No (Yes)          (Cancel to return to document)
```

Type **Y** to exit WordPerfect, or press `Enter` or type **N** or any key other than **Y** to clear the screen and remain in Word-Perfect. Either way, you will exit the document. If you decide instead to return to the document after saving it, you should press the CANCEL (`F1`) key when you see the "Exit WP?" prompt, as suggested on the right side of the prompt.

Use the SAVE (`F10`) key if you wish to save the document in its present form and continue working on it. Why save a document to disk before you're done? Remember that every word you type is temporarily stored in RAM: Unless you save your text to a disk, it will disappear as soon as you clear the screen or should you experience a power failure. Just imagine having typed and edited a ten-page document for four hours, only to have the electricity go off with just one more paragraph to go. If you haven't saved any part of that document to disk, you'll have lost a full four hours of work! On the other hand, if you saved your work 15 minutes before the blackout, you'll have lost only your last 15 minutes of work.

Thus, as you begin to spend long hours typing and editing documents, you should acquire the habit of saving documents to disk at regular intervals of 10 to 30 minutes — not just when you have finished typing or editing them. Because the SAVE key automatically returns you to your document after storing it on disk, using the SAVE key is a quick and easy way to periodically safeguard against losing your new text.

When you press the SAVE ( F10 ) key, there are fewer prompts to contend with than when using the EXIT ( F7 ) key. WordPerfect will simply respond with

`Document to be saved:`

You should type in a filename and press Enter . The document is saved on disk; at the same time, it remains on screen.

After the first time you store a document on disk, WordPerfect knows the document by its filename; every time thereafter that you begin to save the same document— whether using the SAVE ( F10 ) key or the EXIT ( F7 ) key—WordPerfect suggests the known name. If you press Enter to accept the known name, WordPerfect requests verification to replace the file stored on disk with the current version shown on screen, in which case you'll store on disk just one copy of a document, the most current version. If you instead type in a new filename, the current version will be stored as a separate file with that new filename, and the earlier version will remain unchanged.

*Note:* For 5.1 users, whether you press the EXIT or the SAVE key, you may find that instead of the prompt "Document to be saved:," you see the following:

`Long Document Name:`

This signifies that someone has altered a default setting for your copy of WordPerfect to activate the Long Document Name feature, whereby you can name a file with up to 40 characters. Press Enter and the "Document to be saved:" prompt appears. To learn about the Long Document Name feature, turn to Chapter 8, which covers advanced features for managing files on disk.

Pretend that you've just spent 20 minutes revising the letter now on screen. Let's again save the document under the filename LETTER to safeguard against a power failure, and then leave the document on screen for further editing.

1. Press the SAVE ([F10]) key. [*Pulldown menu:* File (F), Save (S).] WordPerfect assumes you wish to save the file under the known name, so it responds with that name. For floppy disk users, the prompt reads

   Document to be saved: B:\LETTER

   For hard disk users, the prompt reads

   Document to be saved: C:\WP51\DATA\LETTER

2. Press [Enter] to accept the suggestion. WordPerfect prompts for verification that you wish to replace the original screen file with the current screen version. For floppy disk users, the prompt reads

   Replace B:\LETTER? No (Yes)

   WordPerfect suggests the response "No." WordPerfect assumes that you wish *not* to replace the old version to be as conservative as possible so that you don't inadvertently overwrite a file.

3. Type **Y**. WordPerfect saves the file on disk, replacing the old file with the current version of the letter, while displaying a message that, for floppy disk users, reads

   Saving B:\LETTER

Now you can continue editing, knowing that if the power goes out, you'll be able to retrieve this file to the screen when the power comes back on and have lost none of your revisions.

Religiously save files to disk every 15 to 30 minutes and you will avoid disaster. If you think you won't remember to save to disk that often, give WordPerfect the responsibility. WordPerfect has an automatic backup option that saves the file on screen into a temporary file at regular intervals. You activate this option with WordPerfect's Setup menu. To learn how to set up timed backup, refer to the sections entitled "Environment" in Appendix B.

# SAVE A PORTION OF A DOCUMENT

Sometimes you may wish to save to disk just a portion of what's on the screen. With WordPerfect, you can save a block of text into a separate file, referred to as a Block Save.

A Block Save is useful when you've typed text on screen as part of a document and realize that you wish to save that text separately. For instance, you may wish to store a paragraph into its own file so that it can later be used independently from the rest of the letter. First use the BLOCK (Alt + F4) key to highlight the portion of text you wish to save. [*Pulldown menu:* Edit (E), Block (B)] The message "Block on" is displayed, flashing at the bottom of the screen. (See Chapter 1 for a review of how to highlight blocks of text.) When you press the SAVE (F10) key [*Pulldown menu:* File (F), Save (S)], a special prompt appears:

Block name:

WordPerfect is requesting a filename to save this text under. Type in a filename and press (Enter). If a file by that name already exists, WordPerfect will ask whether you wish to replace the existing file. Type **Y** to replace the old version on disk, or type **N** and enter in a different filename.

Currently on your monitor screen is a letter addressed to Mr. Barrett P. Smith. Suppose that you frequently use Mr. Smith's name and address when typing letters or documents. You may wish to save his name and address in a separate file so that in the future you won't have to retype them. Use the Block Save feature as follows:

1. Position the cursor on the "M" in "Mr. Barrett P. Smith," near the top left corner of the document on the screen.

2. Press the BLOCK ((Alt) + (F4)) key. [*Pulldown menu:* Edit (E), Block (B).] The message "Block on" appears on the status line.

3. Press (↓) four times. The inside address is highlighted, as shown in Figure 2-3.

4. Press the SAVE ((F10)) key. [*Pulldown menu:* File (F), Save (S).] WordPerfect responds with

Block name:

5. Type **SMITH.ADD** (a name that reminds you that this file will contain Mr. Smith's address) and press (Enter). WordPerfect saves the block independently under that filename.

```
February 3, 1990

Mr. Barrett P. Smith
FST Accounting
1001 S. Harmon Street
Oakland, CA  94413

Dear Barrett:

     As we discussed, here is a complete list of full-time
employees who elected to accept the new vacation option, along with
their anniversary dates with us.  Please add their names to your
record.

          Antonio Abbot        May 31st
          Lois Chang           April 27th
          Tim Fingerman        May 20th
          Paul McClintock      August 7th

The new accrued vacation system should begin for these employees
immediately.  Thank you.

Block on                              Doc 1 Pg 1 Ln 2.17" Pos ⬛
```

**FIGURE 2-3**    A highlighted block to be saved into its own file

Nothing on the screen has changed. And yet, you've also created a new, separate file on disk that contains only Smith's name and address.

# CHECK FOR A SELECTED PRINTER

Once you've typed and edited a document so that it says exactly what you want it to, you will want not only to save that document but also to print it on paper.

When you print a document, WordPerfect must know what type of printer you are using. Is it an IBM Proprinter? An Epson LQ-1000? A Diablo 630? In addition, the program must know what type of paper you are using. Will you feed single sheets manually? Do you have a sheet feeder that feeds single sheets for you? Are you using continuous-feed paper (a long stack of paper separated by perforations)?

The following discussions on printing assume that you have already installed and selected a printer in Word-Perfect. You can tell whether a printer has been selected by pressing the PRINT ( Shift + F7 ) key and then checking the column to the right of the Select Printer option.

If a printer is listed in the second column—for example, the HP LaserJet Series II is shown in Figure 2-4—then one has previously been installed and selected and you can read on. But if no printer is listed, then choose Select Printer (S). Should a list of one or more printers appear, position the cursor on the name of your printer, choose Select (1 or

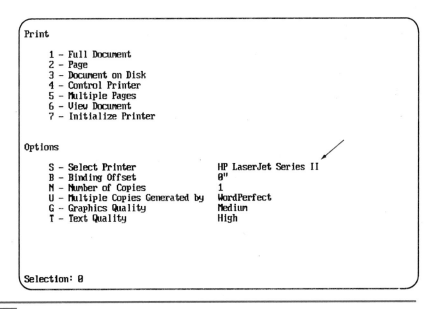

```
Print

     1 - Full Document
     2 - Page
     3 - Document on Disk
     4 - Control Printer
     5 - Multiple Pages
     6 - View Document
     7 - Initialize Printer


Options

     S - Select Printer                    HP LaserJet Series II
     B - Binding Offset                    0"
     N - Number of Copies                  1
     U - Multiple Copies Generated by      WordPerfect
     G - Graphics Quality                  Medium
     T - Text Quality                      High



Selection: 0
```

═══ **FIGURE 2-4**   Print screen

S), and then press EXIT ( F7 ) to return to the typing screen. (Chapter 9 discusses the Select Printer option in more detail.) Or, should no list of printers appear, then turn to the section of Appendix A that discusses installation of your printer to work with WordPerfect before you read further.

# PRINT FROM THE SCREEN

When a document is already on screen, printing it is quick and easy. To print the entire document or just one page, press the PRINT ( Shift + F7 ) key. [*Pulldown menu:* File (F), Print (P).] A full screen menu appears, as shown in Figure 2-4 for 5.1 users, with the HP LaserJet Series II as the selected printer. Select Full Document (1 or F) to print the entire document, or select Page (2 or P) to print only the page on which the cursor is located. If the document is only one page long, as is the case for the document currently on your screen, then these two selections are identical.

    *5.1 users only:* You can also print any specified number of pages directly from screen. Select Multiple Pages (5 or M). WordPerfect prompts

Page(s):

Type in the number of pages and press Enter . If you separate pages with a hyphen, WordPerfect will print the range. If you separate pages with a comma, WordPerfect will print the individual pages. For instance, to print pages 2 and 3, type **2,3**. To print pages 1 through 4 and page 6, type **1-4,6**. (5.0 users can only print a specified number of pages by printing from disk, as described in the next section.)

You can also print a block of text—perhaps just one paragraph from a screenful of text. First, use the Block feature to highlight the block (as described in Chapter 1). With Block on, press the PRINT (⟦Shift⟧ + ⟦F7⟧) key. [*Pulldown menu:* File (F), Print (P).] Now instead of displaying the Print screen, WordPerfect prompts

`Print block? No (Yes)`

Type **Y** to print the block; type **N** or press ⟦Enter⟧ to abort the print.

For sheet-feeder and continuous-paper users, when the paper is present in the printer, the printing will begin immediately. If the paper is not initially in the printer or your printer has been defined for manually fed paper, the computer may pause and sound a beep, indicating that it is waiting for a signal that you have placed a fresh piece of paper in the printer. To give it that signal, press the PRINT (⟦Shift⟧ + ⟦F7⟧) key again, select Control Printer (4 or C), and then select Go (Start Printer) (4 or G). (More information on the Control Printer screen is provided further on in this chapter.) Continue to insert a new sheet of paper and select Go for each page to be printed. Then press CANCEL (⟦F1⟧) to return to the Typing screen.

Here's some practice printing the document that is currently on the screen.

1. Turn your printer on and insert paper. Sheet-feeder users should place a stack of sheets into the feeder. Continuous-feed users should insert the paper and line up the top of one sheet (at the perforation) with the printhead (the mechanism that creates the characters on paper). Manual-feed users should insert a sheet of paper and roll it up just above the printhead.

2. Press the PRINT ( Shift + F7 ) key. [*Pulldown menu:* File (F), Print (P).] The Print screen appears, as shown in Figure 2-4.

3. Select Full Document (1 or F). Alternatively, you can instead select Page (2 or P).

4. The printing should begin. If, however, WordPerfect sounds a beep, your printer has been defined for hand-fed paper or with the paper not initially present.

Manual-feed-paper users should then proceed as follows:

1. Press the PRINT ( Shift + F7 ) key.

2. Select Control Printer (4 or C).

3. Select Go (4 or G), and the printing begins.

4. Press the CANCEL ( F1 ) key twice to clear the Control Printer screen and return to your document.

*Note:* Your printer may fail to print for reasons having nothing to do with the insertion of paper. If your printer refuses to print, refer to the "Control Print Jobs" section further on in this chapter to learn how to uncover problems and correct them.

Now let's print only the list of names and dates found in the middle of the letter (that is, print a block of text from the screen):

1. Make sure that the printer is turned on and paper is inserted.

2. Position the cursor at the left margin of the line that reads "Antonio Abbot . . ."

3. Press the BLOCK (Alt + F4) key. [*Pulldown menu:* Edit (E), Block (B).]

4. Press the ⬇ four times. All four names are highlighted.

5. Press the PRINT (Shift + F7) key. [*Pulldown menu:* File (F), Print (P).] WordPerfect prompts

   `Print block? No (Yes)`

6. Type **Y** to print the block.

7. The printing should begin. If, instead, WordPerfect sounds a beep, your printer has been defined for manual-feed paper or as not initially present. In that case, follow the procedure for manual-feed paper as described previously.

Printing all or part of a document directly from the screen is handy, especially because you will most often want to print a document when you've finished editing it and the document is still on screen. In fact, you'll probably find yourself printing in this way more times than not.

Printing from the screen is also versatile. You can print text without ever saving it to disk. For instance, perhaps you want to type and distribute a short memo. If you will have no future use for this memo, don't bother storing it on disk where it will occupy space. Just type the letter, print it from the screen, and then clear the screen. You've produced the memo, and you haven't taken up valuable storage space.

# PRINT A FILE FROM DISK

In addition to printing the document on screen, you can print a document directly from disk, which is convenient when you wish to print a long document, one that isn't on screen, or when you have many documents to print. Rather than retrieving and printing each one in turn, print directly from the disk. It makes no difference whether the Typing screen is clear or contains a document. There are two methods for printing from disk: using the Print screen, which is convenient when you remember a document's filename, or using the List Files screen, which is effective if you can't remember a document's filename or are a slow typist.

To print from disk using the Print screen, press the PRINT ( Shift + F7 ) key [*Pulldown menu:* File (F), Print (P)] and, from the menu illustrated in Figure 2-4, select Document on Disk (3 or D). WordPerfect prompts

```
Document name:
```

Type in the file's name, including a period and the extension if that file has one, and press Enter . (If the file you wish to print is in other than the default drive/directory, precede the filename with its path. For instance, suppose the default directory is C:\WP51\DATA. If the file SAMPLE is in that directory, simply type **SAMPLE**, but if the file is on drive A, then type **A:SAMPLE**.)

Next, WordPerfect wants to know how many pages of the document you wish to print, prompting with

```
Page(s): (All)
```

WordPerfect assumes that you wish to print the entire document. You have four alternatives:

- Press (Enter) to print the entire document (all pages).

- Type in any page number and press (Enter) to print that specific page.

- Type in page numbers joined by a hyphen (no spaces) and press (Enter) to print a range of consecutive pages.

- Type in numbers separated by commas and press (Enter) to print nonconsecutive pages.

For instance, to print pages 5 through 10, type **5-10**. To print pages 1 through 5, type **1-5** or **-5** (page 1 is assumed). To print pages 14 through the end of the document, type **14-** (the last page is assumed). To print pages 5 and 9, type **5,9**. And you can even combine hyphens and commas in the same command: to print pages 5 through 10 and page 20, type **5-10,20**.

The printing begins immediately, except when paper is manually fed or defined as not initially present, in which case you must follow the previously outlined procedure for printing with manually fed paper.

To print from disk using the List Files screen, press the LIST FILES ((F5)) key [*Pulldown menu:* File (F), List Files (F)] and press (Enter) to display a list of files. Next, position the cursor on the file to be printed. (Chapter 8 describes how you can also mark a group of files so that they will all be printed in one command.) Select Print (4 or P) from the menu of options at the bottom of the screen. WordPerfect prompts

```
Page(s): (All)
```

With the List Files screen, you have the same four options for indicating which pages you wish to print as you do when using the Print menu's Document on Disk option. Indicate

the pages you wish to print and press ⟨Enter⟩. Press CAN-
CEL (⟨F1⟩) to return to the Typing screen.

Let's print the file named SAMPLE. It doesn't matter
that another file is currently on the Typing screen since
you'll be printing directly from disk.

1. Make sure that the printer is turned on and paper has
   been inserted.

2. Press the PRINT (⟨Shift⟩ + ⟨F7⟩) key. [*Pulldown menu:*
   File (F), Print (P).] WordPerfect responds with the Print
   screen.

3. Select Document on Disk (3 or D). WordPerfect responds with

   `Document name:`

4. Type **SAMPLE** and press ⟨Enter⟩. (If SAMPLE is stored
   on other than the default drive or directory, indicate
   where the file is stored. For example, type **B:SAMPLE**
   and press ⟨Enter⟩.) WordPerfect responds with

   `Page(s): (All)`

5. Press ⟨Enter⟩ to print all the pages (here, just one page).

6. The document will begin printing. (Again, if Word-
   Perfect sounds a beep, you must signal that paper has
   been inserted into the printer as described previously in
   this chapter.)

7. Press the CANCEL (⟨F1⟩) key until you return to the
   Typing screen.

*Note:* For 5.0 users, if you attempt to print from disk
and WordPerfect refuses to print your document, display-

ing the error message "Document was Fast Saved—Must be retrieved to print," then a default setting has been changed as to how WordPerfect stores documents on disk. WordPerfect offers the Fast Save option, whereby you can speed up the time it takes WordPerfect to store your text. The trade-off, however, is that the Fast Save option restricts how you can print your documents. Refer to Appendix B for more on the Fast Save feature.

Pretend you wish to print a file whose name you can't remember. In that case:

1. Turn your printer on and insert paper.

2. Press the LIST ([F5]) key. [*Pulldown menu:* File (F), List Files (F).] WordPerfect prompts you with your default drive or directory.

3. Press [Enter]. A list of files in the default drive or directory is displayed on the screen. Now you can find the name of the file you forgot.

4. Position the cursor on the filename SAMPLE.

5. Select Print (4 or P). WordPerfect responds with

   Page(s): (All)

6. Press [Enter] to print all the pages (here, just one page).

7. The document will begin printing. (Again, if Word-Perfect sounds a beep, you must signal that paper has been inserted into the printer as described previously in this chapter.)

8. Press the CANCEL ([F1]) key to clear the List Files screen and return to the Typing screen.

Keep in mind that printing from screen and printing from disk are distinct commands. Whatever is currently on screen will be ignored should you decide to print from disk. For example, let's suppose that you retrieve to the screen and edit the document named SAMPLE and now wish to print out the edited version. You can either resave the edited document and print it from disk or print directly from the screen. But if you print from disk *before resaving,* you'll be printing the old, unedited version of SAMPLE, instead of the document on screen containing the revisions.

# CONTROL PRINT JOBS

Every time you ask WordPerfect to print a document, no matter whether you're printing from screen or from disk, a *print job* is created, assigned a job number, and added to the list of jobs waiting their turn to be printed. As a result, you don't have to wait until one document has finished printing before continuing to work with WordPerfect. After you've sent one job to the printer, you can either continue to request additional print jobs, or you can return to the Typing screen and perform a nonprinting task like editing another document. Or you can do both. For instance, request three print jobs so that the printer will print three documents one after another in the order that they were created in the job list; then, while the printer is working in the background, retrieve and start editing a fourth document. Keep in mind, however, that if you do perform an editing task while documents are printing, WordPerfect will proceed a bit more slowly because it is performing two tasks at once.

At any time you can check the status of your print jobs. To do so, press the PRINT ( Shift + F7 ) key [*Pulldown menu:* File (F), Print (P)], and then select Control Printer (4 or C). Using the Control Printer menu, you can also cancel a job so that it won't print, or you can change the order in which jobs will be printed.

The Control Printer screen is separated into three sections. Figure 2-5 illustrates the Control Printer screen when no jobs have been sent to the printer; Figure 2-6 shows the same screen with three jobs listed. The top section of the screen provides information on the current job (the one being sent to the printer). Notice in Figure 2-5 that Word-Perfect reports "No print jobs" next to the heading "Status." In Figure 2-6, on the other hand, WordPerfect indicates that (1) job 1 is printing, (2) WordPerfect assumes 8.5- by 11-inch paper for the print job, (3) the paper

```
Print: Control Printer

Current Job

Job Number:  None                      Page Number:  None
Status:      No print jobs             Current Copy: None
Message:     None
Paper:       None
Location:    None
Action:      None


Job List

Job  Document              Destination        Print Options




Additional Jobs Not Shown: 0



1 Cancel Job(s); 2 Rush Job; 3 Display Jobs; 4 Go (start printer); 5 Stop: 0
```

**FIGURE 2-5**   Control Printer screen with no print jobs

is fed continuously into the printer, (4) no action is required since the job is printing, (5) page 1 is printing, and (6) only one copy of the job has been requested (see Chapter 9 for directions on how to direct WordPerfect to print multiple copies of a document, one of the options on the Print screen).

The middle section offers information about the job list of all jobs that have been sent to the printer. For instance, Figure 2-6 indicates that (1) job 1 is being printed from screen, while jobs 2 and 3 are specific files on disk named SAMPLE and J&B.MMO, both stored in C:\WP51\DATA, (2) all three jobs are being sent to the printer attached to LPT 1 (the specific plug at the back of the computer to which that printer is attached), and (3) no print options have been activated (refer to Chapter 9 for more on print options). Only three jobs are shown on the list at one time,

```
Print: Control Printer

Current Job

Job Number: 1                          Page Number:  1
Status:     Printing                   Current Copy: 1 of 1
Message:    None
Paper:      Standard 8.5" x 11"
Location:   Continuous feed
Action:     None


Job List

Job  Document            Destination     Print Options
 1   (Screen)            LPT 1
 2   C:\WP51\DATA\SAMPLE LPT 1
 3   C:\WP51\DATA\J&B.MMO LPT 1

Additional Jobs Not Shown: 0


1 Cancel Job(s); 2 Rush Job; 3 Display Jobs; 4 Go (start printer); 5 Stop: 0
```

**FIGURE 2-6**   Control Printer screen showing three print jobs in the job list

so WordPerfect also indicates how many additional jobs are not shown; the "0" in Figure 2-6 means that, in this particular case, there are only three jobs in the job list.

The third section is a menu at the bottom of the screen which provides five options for controlling the print jobs in the job list. Perhaps you accidentally sent the wrong document to the printer, the paper has jammed in the printer, or the printer isn't working at all. The Control Printer menu provides the following options:

- *Cancel Job(s) (1 or C)*  This option erases from the job list a print job. If you're currently printing job 1, then when you type **1** or **C**, WordPerfect responds with

Cancel which job? (*=all jobs) 1

To cancel the current job, press [Enter]. Or, type in a different job number and press [Enter]. If more than one print job is in the job list and you wish to cancel every one, type an asterisk (*). WordPerfect asks for verification, prompting

**Cancel all print jobs?** No (Yes)

Type **Y** to verify that you wish to cancel all jobs.

- *Rush Job (2 or R)*  This option rearranges the order of print jobs listed. For instance, suppose you had jobs 1,2,3, and 4 in the job list to be printed. As job 1 is printing, type **2** or **R**, and WordPerfect prompts

Rush which job? 4

WordPerfect assumes you wish to rush the last print job. Press [Enter] and job 4 is printed next, or type in another job number and press [Enter] to move that job ahead of the others. WordPerfect will also ask whether you wish to interrupt the current job; type **Y** to do so, or type **N** to print the rush job after the current job is completed.

- *Display Jobs (3 or D)* This option shows a complete list of jobs waiting to be printed, temporarily replacing the Control Printer screen. Use this option if there are more than three print jobs. As many as 24 jobs in the list are displayed at one time. Press any key to return to the Control Printer screen.

- *Go (start printer) (4 or G)* This option resumes printing after a pause to insert paper or a new print wheel or cartridge, or restarts the printer after you've selected the Stop option (see the next item in this list).

- *Stop (5 or S)* This option stops the printer temporarily, without actually canceling the print job, which is useful in case of a paper jam or if the ribbon runs out. When you're ready to begin printing again, select the Go option. The printing begins at the beginning of the document unless page 1 has already been printing, in which case WordPerfect prompts you for the page number to begin with.

Depending on your printer, you may find that even when you attempt to stop or cancel a print job, the printing continues for a while. Because the computer has already sent part or all of the text to the printer, the printing continues for the text that has been sent. To cancel the current print job immediately, first turn off the printer, and then cancel the print job as described previously. Turn the printer back on when you are ready to print again. However, be aware that when you turn off the printer, you will lose all the text already sent from the computer unless you previously stored a copy of that text on disk. Also, when you turn the printer back on, you may need to advance the printer paper to the top of the next page and to initialize your printer (if you need to load soft fonts before you print, as described in Chapter 9) in order to print properly again.

If you ever issue a print command and the printer doesn't print, don't issue another print command. Instead, always check the top section on the Control Printer screen. Indication of a printing problem or error is listed next to the heading "Message." For instance, Figure 2-7 shows the following information next to "Message": "Printer not accepting characters." This usually means that the connection between the computer and the printer is inoperative. Perhaps the printer is turned off or is not on line, or the cable connecting the two pieces of equipment is worn, cracked, or plugged in incorrectly. The information next to the

```
Print: Control Printer

Current Job

Job Number: 1                                    Page Number:  None
Status:      Starting print job                  Current Copy: None
Message:     Printer not accepting characters
Paper:       None
Location:    None
Action:      Check cable, make sure printer is turned ON


Job List

Job  Document            Destination      Print Options
 1   (Screen)            LPT 1
 2   C:\WP51\DATA\SAMPLE LPT 1
 3   C:\WP51\DATA\J&B.MMO LPT 1

Additional Jobs Not Shown: 0




1 Cancel Job(s); 2 Rush Job; 3 Display Jobs; 4 Go (start printer); 5 Stop: 0
```

**FIGURE 2-7**  Error message: Printer not accepting characters

heading "Action" indicates possible solutions: "Check cable, make sure printer is turned ON." Once you've read the information under "Current Job," you can correct the problem, or select an item from the Control Printer menu, such as to cancel a print job.

As you can see, WordPerfect allows enormous control over print jobs. Feel free to send jobs to the printer one after another. There's no need to print only one document at a time if there's a whole group to print. You can follow and manage the progress of each job by using the Control Printer menu.

You should know that WordPerfect offers a variety of special options for printing out your document. For instance, you can request that WordPerfect print a specific number of copies of your document. Or you can request that WordPerfect initialize the printer, downloading special fonts into the printer. Or you can even use an option called View Document, whereby you can preview how your document will appear on the printed page, a valuable feature especially when working with WordPerfect in desktop publishing. Look to Chapter 9 for more details on special print options and enhancements.

# REVIEW EXERCISE

In the following exercise you will practice saving and printing a document. Find a short memo or report around your office that you want to practice on. The document should be a simple one, without any fancy features or enhancements like underlining or centered text—you will learn how to enhance text in the next chapter.

1. Clear the screen by pressing EXIT (F7) [*Pulldown menu:* File (F), Exit (X)] and typing **N** twice. Then type the first several paragraphs of one of your own documents.

2. Assume that 15 minutes have elapsed. Use the SAVE (F10) key [*Pulldown menu:* File (F), Save (S)] to save the document on disk, safeguarding against a power failure. Select a filename that abides by the rules for naming files discussed at the beginning of this chapter.

3. Print your short document. (*Hint:* As long as the document is on screen, you can print directly from the screen by pressing the PRINT (Shift + F7) key [*Pulldown menu:* File (F), Print (P)] and selecting Full Document (1 or F) or Page (2 or P).) If you encounter problems printing, don't forget to display the Control Printer screen, so that you can uncover the problem and manage the print job.

4. Add another paragraph or so to your document.

5. After another 15 minutes have elapsed, you must again save the current version of your text to disk. But suppose this time you wish to save the document and clear the screen. Use the EXIT (F7) key [*Pulldown menu:* File (F), Exit (X)] to do so. (*Hint:* After pressing the EXIT (F7) key, type **Y** to save the document, press Enter to use the same filename, and type **Y** to replace the file on disk. Then type **N** to clear the screen without leaving WordPerfect.)

6. Print the document. (*Hint:* Since the document is no longer on screen, print it from disk using either the Document on Disk option from the Print screen, or the Print option from the List Files screen.)

## Quick Review

- Save an entire document on disk and then exit from that document using the EXIT ([F7]) key. Press EXIT ([F7]), type **Y** to save, and enter a document filename. If WordPerfect prompts "Replace?," type **Y** to overwrite the document with the same name on disk, or type **N** and enter a different filename. Next, at the prompt "Exit WP?," type **Y** to exit Word-Perfect or type N if you wish to clear the screen but remain in WordPerfect. Pulldown menu users can select File (F) and then Exit (X) instead of pressing EXIT.

- Save an entire document on disk and then remain in that document by pressing SAVE ([F10]). Or pull-down menu users can select File (F) and then Save (S). Next, enter a document filename. If Word-Perfect prompts "Replace?," type **Y** to overwrite the document with the same name on disk, or type **N** and enter a different filename.

- Remember to save a file on disk frequently as you're typing and editing it, and not just when you've completed the final product. This protects against your losing hours of work because of power failure or human error. The SAVE ([F10]) key is most convenient for doing so.

- Save a portion of a document on disk by highlighting that text using the Block feature ( Alt + F4 ). Next, press the SAVE ( F10 ) key and, at WordPerfect's prompt, enter the block's filename.

- The List Files screen presents information about the documents stored on your floppy disks or in directories on your hard disk—including each document's filename, size (measured in bytes), and the date and time each was last saved to disk. Display the List Files screen using the LIST ( F5 ) key. Or pulldown menu users can select File (F), and then List Files (F).

- Retrieve a file to screen when you don't remember its name by displaying the List Files screen for the drive/directory where the file is stored. Then, position the cursor on the file you wish to bring to the screen and select Retrieve (1 or R).

- Retrieve a file to screen when you remember its name by pressing the RETRIEVE ( Shift + F10 ) key. Or pulldown menu users can select File (F) and then Retrieve (R). Then enter the name of the file you wish to retrieve, preceded by that file's drive/directory if different from the default drive/directory.

- When you wish to glance at the contents of a file but don't wish to retrieve that file to screen, employ the Look feature. From the List Files screen, position the cursor on the file you wish to look at and select Look (6 or L).

- The variety of methods for printing—either directly from the screen or from a file on disk—are provided in Table 2-1.

- If you have a printing problem, check the Control Printer screen for information on the status of print jobs or for print errors: Press PRINT (Shift + F7), to display the print screen. Or, pulldown menu users can select File (F) and then Print (P). Next, choose Control Printer (4 or C). Make changes to print jobs by selecting from the menu of options at the bottom of the Control Printer screen.

| Print | Key Sequence |
|---|---|
| Entire document from screen | (Shift) + (F7), **1** |
| One page from screen | Position cursor, (Shift) + (F7), **2** |
| Multiple pages from screen (*5.1 users only*) | (Shift) + (F7), **5**, enter pages |
| Block of text from screen | Block text, (Shift) + (F7), **Y** |
| Entire document or range of pages from disk (by typing in a filename) | (Shift) + (F7), **3**, enter filename, enter pages |
| Entire document or range of pages from disk (by positioning the cursor on a filename) | (F5), enter drive/directory, position cursor, **4**, enter pages |

**Table 2-1**  Printing Options from Screen or Disk

# TYPING ENHANCEMENTS

This chapter covers the basics that make your readers notice words you want to stand out from the rest. You'll learn how to position words centered or flush at the right margin, how to boldface and underline words, how to switch between uppercase and lowercase in seconds, and how to indent whole paragraphs on a tab stop.

You'll also learn WordPerfect features that make the job of typing easier. One example, the Date feature, inserts the current date or time in a document for you. Another provides the ability to work simultaneously with two separate documents, jumping from one to the other as often as you like. You'll also discover how to split the screen in half to view two independent documents at the same time. You'll type several documents and use all these special typing features along the way.

# CENTER AND FLUSH RIGHT TEXT

WordPerfect text is typically aligned flush left, meaning that each line starts flush against the left margin. As an alternative, you can have any short line of text centered between the left and right margins, such as this line:

Journey to the Center

You can also align text flush right, meaning that the last character of the line sits at the right margin, such as the following date:

June 16, 1990

You can reposition text either as you type or after you've typed. To center text that you are about to type, make sure the cursor is at the left margin and press the

CENTER (⬚Shift⬚ + ⬚F6⬚) key. [*Pulldown menu:* Layout (L), Align (A), Center (C).] The cursor jumps to the center of the line. Now type the text and press ⬚Enter⬚ to end the line. The text is centered between the margins. Similarly, if you wish to align text flush right, you press the FLUSH RIGHT (⬚Alt⬚ + ⬚F6⬚) key. [*Pulldown menu:* Layout (L), Align (A), Flush Right (F).] The cursor jumps to the right edge of the line. Type the text and then press ⬚Enter⬚ to end the line.

You can type flush left, centered, and flush right text all on the same line. For example, with the cursor at the left margin of a blank line, you could type **Anita Robbins**, press the CENTER (⬚Shift⬚ + ⬚F6⬚) key, type **President**, press the FLUSH RIGHT (⬚Alt⬚ + ⬚F6⬚) key, and type **ABC Company** to get the following results:

```
Anita Robbins                  President                  ABC Company
```

If you align text in different ways on one line, make sure that each segment of text is short; otherwise text will overlap, and it will seem as if some of the text has disappeared.

To center or align flush right a line of text you've already typed, place the cursor at the left margin of a short line of text that you wish to reposition. Press CENTER or FLUSH RIGHT. Then press ⬚↓⬚ to rewrite the screen so that the text is centered or aligned flush right.

What keeps text centered or aligned flush right are hidden codes inserted around the text. But remember from Chapter 1 that codes are always hidden; you must use the REVEAL CODES (⬚Alt⬚ + ⬚F3⬚) key to view the codes. [*Pulldown menu:* Edit (E), Reveal Codes (R)]

The codes are different for 5.1 or 5.0, depending on which version you use. *5.1 users:* centered text is preceded by the code **[Center]**. Text aligned flush right is preceded by **[Flsh Rt]**. And, when you press the [Enter] key after typing the text, a hard return code **[HRt]** ends the centering or flush right. *5.0 users:* a pair of codes surrounds the centered or right aligned text like a pair of bookends, the first code turns the feature on and the second code turns it off. The following pair of hidden codes surrounds centered text: **[Cntr]** and **[C/A / Flrt]**. The following pair surrounds text aligned flush right: **[Flsh Rt]** and **[C/A/Flrt]**. Notice that the code to turn the feature off is identical for both centering and aligning text flush right; it stands for "Center/Align/Flush Right."

If you change your mind and decide to cancel the centering or flush right aligning of text on a line, you must locate and delete the codes that surround the text. You need only erase one code if they are in pairs—WordPerfect automatically erases the other. You can erase a code on the Reveal Codes screen or on the Typing screen. Erasing on the Reveal Codes screen allows you to view the code you are deleting. Erasing on the Typing screen means that you must deduce where one of the pair of codes is hiding (which is quite straightforward since the code pair surrounds the text). For instance, on the Typing screen you can position the cursor on the first character of centered text and press [Backspace]. The code is deleted and the text returns to the left margin, no longer centered.

You can also center or align flush right many lines of text at once. From lines typed like this:

Wine Tasting
Through the Ages
by
Jan Miller

You can produce this:

Wine Tasting
Through the Ages
by
Jan Miller

You must first highlight the lines using the Block feature. Then, with Block on, center the block by pressing the CENTER ([Shift] + [F6]) key. Or, align the text flush right by pressing the FLUSH RIGHT ([Alt] + [F6]) key. Word-Perfect prompts you for verification that you wish to center the block; type **Y** for "Yes" if you wish to do so. For 5.1 users, this procedure causes WordPerfect to activate the Justification feature; the codes inserted are different, as described in the section called "Modify a Document's Justi-fication" in Chapter 4. For 5.0 users, this procedure causes WordPerfect to place a pair of codes around each line of the text in the block when it is centered or aligned flush right just as if you centered or aligned each line individu-ally.

Let's practice centering and aligning text flush right.

1. Make sure the typing screen is clear. If not, clear the typing screen by pressing the EXIT ([F7]) key and typ-ing **N, N**. The cursor should now be at the top left corner of an empty screen.

2. Press the CENTER ([Shift] + [F6]) key. [*Pulldown menu:* Layout (L), Align (A), Center (C).]

3. Type **Urgent Notice**. This title is automatically centered as you type.

4. Press (Enter) twice to end the line and insert a blank line.

5. Type **To: All Employees**.

6. Press the FLUSH RIGHT ((Alt) + (F6)) key. [*Pulldown menu:* Layout (L), Align (A), Flush Right (F).]

7. Type **From: Sandy Peterson**. This text is aligned flush right for you.

8. Press (Enter) to move down one line.

9. Press (Home), (Home) (↑) to position the cursor at the top of the document, and then press the REVEAL CODES ((Alt) + (F3)) key to view the codes inserted to center and align the text flush right.

Figure 3-1 illustrates how the Reveal Codes screen will appear if you're a version 5.1 user. The top window shows

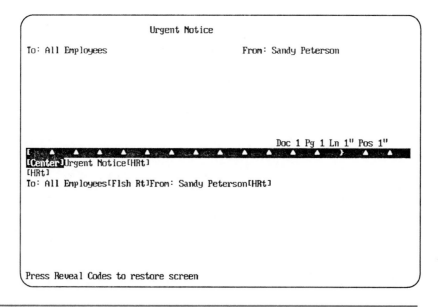

Urgent Notice

To: All Employees                          From: Sandy Peterson

Doc 1 Pg 1 Ln 1" Pos 1"

[Center]Urgent Notice[HRt]
[HRt]
To: All Employees[Flsh Rt]From: Sandy Peterson[HRt]

Press Reveal Codes to restore screen

**FIGURE 3-1**   Reveal Codes screen showing Center and Flush Right codes (version 5.1)

centered and flush right text. The bottom window shows the codes instead of the actual positioning of the text. For example, the title for 5.1 users is preceded by a center code and followed by a hard return code:

`[Center]Urgent Notice[HRt]`

For version 5.0 users, the title is surrounded by a pair of center codes and then a hard return code:

`[Cntr]Urgent Notice[C/A/Flrt][HRt]`

Suppose you wish to cancel the centering of the phrase "Urgent Notice." Remain in the Reveal Codes screen so that you can watch as the code (or code pair) is deleted:

1. Check the bottom window in the Reveal Codes screen to make sure the cursor is positioned on the **[Center]** or **[Cntr]** code.

2. Press ⌷Del⌷. Notice that the center code (or pair of codes for 5.0 users) disappears and that the text is no longer centered.

Now suppose you change your mind and decide to center the title after all. Remain in the Reveal Codes screen so that you can watch as the code pair is reinserted:

1. The cursor should already be positioned under the "U" in "Urgent." Press the CENTER (⌷Shift⌷ + ⌷F6⌷) key.

2. Press ⌷↓⌷ to rewrite the screen. The title is again centered.

3. Press REVEAL CODES (⌷Alt⌷ + ⌷F3⌷) to exit the Reveal Codes screen.

# INSERT THE DATE OR TIME

Your computer knows the current date and time if either of the following two conditions is met: (1) you entered the date and time before loading WordPerfect (as described in "Getting Started"), in which case the computer keeps track of the correct date and time until you turn it off again; or (2) your computer has an internal, battery-operated clock, so it automatically keeps track of the correct date and time whether it is on or off.

If your computer knows the correct date and time, you can let WordPerfect insert the date or the time into the text of a document for you. The DATE/OUTLINE (Shift + F5) key controls this feature. When you press the DATE/OUTLINE (Shift + F5) key, the following menu is displayed:

1 Date Text; 2 Date Code; 3 Date Format; 4 Outline; 5 Para Num;
6 Define: 0

Menu options 1, 2, and 3 relate to the Date feature. [*Pull-down menu:* Select Tools (T) and then either Date Text (T), Date Code (C), or Date Format (F).]

The first option, Date Text, simply inserts the date at the current cursor position. WordPerfect's default for the appearance of the date in your text is as follows:

Month #, 19##

For example, if the date is the 9th of May, 1990, then, unless you alter the default for the format of the date (as described further on), WordPerfect will insert the date as

May 9, 1990

To insert the date, position the cursor where you want the date to appear, press the DATE/OUTLINE (Shift + F5)

key, and select Date Text (1 or T). [*Pulldown menu:* Tools (T), then Date Text (T).] The date appears as if you had typed it out yourself, only faster. This is especially useful for inserting the date at the top of a letter.

The second option, Date Code, appears at first glance to be identical to the first option. If you position the cursor, press the DATE/OUTLINE (Shift + F5 ) key, and select Date Code (2 or C), the current date appears at the cursor. But while it looks as if all you have done is insert text, you actually have inserted a hidden code. If the Date format is the default (Month #, 19##), then the code you have inserted is **[Date: 3 1, 4]**, with the characters **3 1, 4** standing for month, day, and year. (The numbers 3 1, 4 are derived from the Date Format menu, shown in Figure 3-2 which will be described next.) Of course, the code is hidden, and what you see is the text instead.

```
Date Format

     Character   Meaning
        1        Day of the Month
        2        Month (number)
        3        Month (word)
        4        Year (all four digits)
        5        Year (last two digits)
        6        Day of the Week (word)
        7        Hour (24-hour clock)
        8        Hour (12-hour clock)
        9        Minute
        0        am / pm
       %,$       Used before a number, will:
                   Pad numbers less than 10 with a leading zero or space
                   Abbreviate the month or day of the week

     Examples:  3 1, 4        = December 25, 1984
                %6 %3 1, 4    = Tue Dec 25, 1984
                %2/%1/5 (6)   = 01/01/85 (Tuesday)
                $2/$1/5 ($6) =  1/ 1/85 (Tue)
                8:90          = 10:55am

Date format: 3 1, 4
```

**FIGURE 3-2** Date Format menu

Because you inserted the code with the Date Code option, the date will automatically be updated when you next retrieve the document to the screen or print it from disk. For example, suppose that tomorrow you retrieve to the screen a letter that contains a date code. The letter will appear with tomorrow's date. Or suppose that the week after next, you print the same letter from disk. The printed result will show the current date. This feature is especially handy when included in a header or footer—the current date can be printed on every page, whenever you print (headers and footers are discussed in Chapter 6).

The third option, Date Format, enables you to select a different default style for the display of the date, tailoring it to meet your needs. When you select Date Format (3 or F), the screen shown in Figure 3-2 appears. Here you can select exactly how the date will appear when inserted automatically. Notice that the bottom left corner of the screen indicates that the current date format is **3 1, 4**—the default pattern. The two columns in the center of the Date Format menu indicate your other format choices; you can pick and choose as you like. You can insert not only the month, the day of the month, and the year, but also the current hour, the current minute, and the day of the week. You can also include symbols or words in the format pattern, so long as the date format does not exceed 29 characters. A percentage symbol (%) can be used to insert a leading zero for numbers less than ten or to shorten the month or day of the week to three letters. *5.1 users only:* A dollar sign ($) can also be used to insert a leading space. Table 3-1 shows some date format examples, assuming that today is Wednesday, May 9, 1990, and that the time is 1:30 P.M.

When you change the date format, no codes are inserted into the text. Instead, you are directing how information will appear every time you use the DATE/OUTLINE

| Date Format Pattern | Display of Date on Screen |
|---|---|
| 2/1/5 | 5/9/90 |
| 2-1-4 | 5-9-1990 |
| %2-%1-4 | 05-09-1990 |
| $2-$1-4 | 5- 9-1990 |
| Time — 8:9 0 | Time — 1:30 pm |
| Time — 7:9 | Time — 13:30 |
| 6, 3 1, 4 | Wednesday, May 9, 1990 |
| %6, 3 1, 4 | Wed, May 9, 1990 |
| Signed on 3 1, 4 | Signed on May 9, 1990 |
| Signed on 3 1 at 8:9 0 | Signed on May 9 at 1:30 pm |

**TABLE 3-1**  Formatting the Date

( [Shift] + [F5] ) key to insert the date — either as text or as code — until you change the date format again or exit WordPerfect. (Next time you load WordPerfect, the default date format returns.) Suppose, for example, that you change the date format to **2-1 at 8:9 0**. When you select Date Text (1 or T) the following appears at the current cursor position:

```
5-9 at 1:30 pm
```

Or, if you select Date Code (2 or C), the same information appears, but tucked behind this text would be the hidden code **[Date:2-1 at 8:9 0]**, and the date and time would update automatically the next time you retrieved or printed the document.

Remember that in order for the Date feature to work properly, the computer must know the correct date and time; otherwise, the wrong date will be inserted. If your computer is not equipped with a battery-operated clock and you forgot to enter the current date and time before starting WordPerfect, you can exit WordPerfect, reboot your computer, and then reload WordPerfect all over again—this time making sure to enter the proper date and time when prompted. An easier alternative is to exit to DOS temporarily in order to enter the date and time (a procedure described in the "Go to DOS" section in Chapter 8).

Let's change the date format to include the date and the day of the week and then insert that information into the memo on the Typing screen.

1. Press [Home], [Home], [↓] to position the cursor at the bottom of the document, where you left off typing the document on screen.

2. Press [Enter] to insert a blank line.

3. Press the DATE/OUTLINE ([Shift] + [F5]) key. [*Pull-down menu:* Tools (T).] WordPerfect responds with

   `1 Date Text; 2 Date Code; 3 Date Format; 4 Outline; 5 Para Num; 6 Define: 0`

4. Select Date Format (3 or F). The Date Format menu appears, as shown in Figure 3-2.

5. Type **(6) 3 1, 4** and press [Enter]. The Date menu returns to the bottom of the screen.

6. Select Date Text (1 or T). Watch as WordPerfect inserts the date for you, in a fraction of a second, in the following format:

   `(Day) Month #, 19##`

Remember that the date format will remain as you specified it until you alter it again or exit WordPerfect.

# UNDERLINE AND BOLDFACE

If you wish to stress important words, you can <u>underline</u> them, or you can make them **boldface** (darker than the rest of the text). You can underline text or make it boldfaced either as you type or after you type.

To underline as you type, press the UNDERLINE (F8) key and type all the text you want underlined. Then press the UNDERLINE (F8) key again to turn off the feature. Similarly, you make text boldface by pressing the BOLD (F6) key, typing the text, and then pressing the BOLD (F6) key a second time to turn the feature off. You can also create an underscore without text: Press the UNDERLINE (F6) key; press the spacebar until the line is as long as you desire, and press the UNDERLINE (F8) key again to turn underline off.

You can tell if underline or boldface is active by checking the Pos number on the status line. Normally, the Pos number is the only number not boldfaced on the status line, as follows:

`Doc 1 Pg 1 Ln 2" Pos 3.2"`

On a monochrome monitor, when you press the UNDER-LINE (F8) key to turn on the feature, the Pos number on the status line is underscored as follows:

`Doc 1 Pg 1 Ln 2" Pos `<u>`3.2"`</u>

When you press the BOLD ( F6 ) key to turn on bold-facing, the Pos number becomes boldfaced, like the rest of the status line.

Doc 1 Pg 1 Ln 2" Pos 3.2"

On a color monitor, the Pos number changes color when either feature is activated. When you turn off these features, the status line returns to normal.

To underline or boldface text you've already typed, use the Block feature to highlight the portion of text you wish to underline or change to boldface. Then, with "Block on" flashing, press either the UNDERLINE ( F8 ) or the BOLD ( F6 ) key. WordPerfect activates the feature for just the highlighted text and turns Block off automatically.

Whether you underline or boldface text, a code pair surrounds that portion of text, just like when you center or align text flush right. The code pair **[UND]** and **[und]** is inserted to mark the boundaries of the underlined text. For boldfaced text, the codes are **[BOLD]** and **[bold]**. Of course, the codes are shown only on the Reveal Codes screen. To remove the underlining or boldface, you must delete the codes. Although they come in pairs, you need only delete one of the codes; the other will be erased automatically by WordPerfect.

How underlined and boldfaced text is displayed on the Typing screen depends on your monitor. If you have a monochrome monitor, the underline appears as a line below your text, and boldfaced words appear brighter than regular text. (If boldface does not appear on your monochrome monitor, adjust the contrast and brightness knobs.) If you have a color monitor, the underlined and boldfaced text appears in different colors than the rest of the text; color monitor users usually see the underlining and bold-facing only on the printed page. (You can change how

```
                        Urgent Notice

To: All Employees                    From: Sandy Peterson

(Wednesday) October 10, 1990

As you know, we announced on September 15th a new vacation option
for employees who are full-time or who work more than twenty hours
per week. Here is the list of those employees who have already
signed up for the new option:

Name                      Department

Antonio Abbott            Distribution, East Coast
Lois Chang                Personnel
Tim Fingerman             Public Relations
Paul McClintock           Distribution, West Coast

If you wish to sign up, but your name is not on the list, then you
must telephone our Personnel Director, John Samsone, by October
15th at (415) 333-9215. Thank you._


                                    Doc 1 Pg 1 Ln 4.33" Pos 4.5"
```

**FIGURE 3-3**   Sample document with underlined and boldfaced text

text with enhancements—such as underlining and bold-facing—is displayed on the Typing screen. In fact, some color monitor users can even view underlining on screen. Refer to "Display" in Appendix B for more details.)

Let's continue with the "Urgent Notice" memo, underlining and creating boldfaced text along the way. Figure 3-3 shows the result.

1. Your cursor should be just to the right of today's date. Press [Enter] twice to insert a blank line.

2. Type the following:

```
As you know, we announced on September 15th a new vacation option
for employees who are
```

3. Press the spacebar once, and then press the UNDER-LINE ( F8 ) key to turn on the Underline feature.

4. Type **full-time**.

5. Press the UNDERLINE ( F8 ) key to turn off the Underline feature, and press the spacebar once.

6. Type **or who work**

7. Press the spacebar once, and then press the UNDER-LINE ( F8 ) key to turn on underlining.

8. Type **more than twenty hours per week**.

9. Press the UNDERLINE ( F8 ) key to turn off under-lining. Then type a period, press the spacebar twice, and type the following:

   Here is the list of those employees who have

10. Press the BOLD ( F6 ) key to turn on the boldface feature.

11. Type **already signed up**.

12. Press the BOLD ( F6 ) key to turn off the boldface feature, and type **for the new option:**

13. Press Enter twice to insert a blank line.

14. Press the UNDERLINE ( F8 ) key to turn on underlin-ing and type **Name**.

15. Press ( Tab ) five times and type **Department**.

16. Press the UNDERLINE ( F8 ) key to turn underlining off.

17. Type the remainder of the document as shown in Figure 3-3. (When typing the two columns of information under the headings "Name" and "Department," remember to use the [Tab] key. That is, type the information under the heading "Name," then press [Tab] until the cursor moves to the heading "Department," type in the information under the heading, and press [Enter]. As discussed previously, using the [Tab] key is more effective than pressing the spacebar when moving the cursor by a certain increment to the right so that text under a heading such as "Department" lines up evenly in columns when printed.)

Now that the document has been typed, suppose you decide in the last paragraph to underline the name John Samsone and change the date, October 15th, to boldface. Since the information has already been typed, you must use the Block feature to highlight the text, as follows:

1. Position the cursor on the "J" in "John Samsone."

2. Press the BLOCK ([Alt] + [F4]) key, and type **e** to highlight the first and last names. (Remember from Chapter 1 that you can quickly move the cursor to the end of a block simply by typing the last character in the block.)

3. Press the UNDERLINE ([F8]) key. The name becomes underlined.

4. Position the cursor on the capital "O" in "October 15th."

5. Press the BLOCK ([Alt] + [F4]) key, and then type **h** to highlight the date.

6. Press the BOLD ([F6]) key. The date becomes boldfaced.

In addition to underlining and boldfacing, there are many other alternatives for changing the appearance of characters to make text stand out. For instance, you can increase or decrease the size of characters or use italics. Or you can direct WordPerfect to underline with a double underscore rather than a single underscore. Also, while the UNDERLINE (F8) and BOLD (F6) function keys are the quickest methods for underlining and boldfacing text, you can also access these features with the FONT key or with the Font pulldown menu. Refer to Chapter 10 for more on using the FONT key or pulldown menu to change the appearance of characters.

# CHANGE THE UNDERLINE STYLE

Depending on the capability of your printer, you can change the style with which WordPerfect underlines text when printed. The default setting is for WordPerfect to underline all spaces located between the On Underline and Off Underline codes, but not to underline any tabs. Examples of this and of other available underline style options are shown in Figure 3-4.

To change the underline style, position the cursor at the left margin of the line where you want to change the style. Press the FORMAT (Shift + F8) key and select Other (4 or O). [*Pulldown menu:* Layout (L), Other (O).] The Other Format menu, as shown in Figure 3-5, appears. Notice that the default settings—underlining spaces but not tabs—are indicated on this menu. Next, select Underline (7 or U) and then type **Y** or **N** to determine whether spaces and/or tabs are to be underlined. As a last step, press EXIT (F7) to return to the Typing screen.

**Spaces Underlined: Yes**
**Tabs Underlined: No**

| Last Name | First Name | Employee Number |

**Spaces: No**
**Tabs: Yes**

| Last Name | First Name | Employee Number |

**Spaces: No**
**Tabs: No**

| Last Name | First Name | Employee Number |

**Spaces: Yes**
**Tabs: Yes**

| Last Name | First Name | Employee Number |

**FIGURE 3-4**  Underline styles

```
Format: Other

    1 - Advance

    2 - Conditional End of Page

    3 - Decimal/Align Character      ,
        Thousands' Separator         ,

    4 - Language                    US

    5 - Overstrike

    6 - Printer Functions

    7 - Underline - Spaces         Yes
                     Tabs          No




Selection: 0
```

**FIGURE 3-5**  Other Format menu

When you alter the underline style, a code is inserted at the cursor location. For instance, if you decide to change the style so that both spaces and tabs are underlined, the code inserted is **[Undrln:Spaces,Tabs]**. Or, if you decide to underline only tabs, the code inserted is **[Undrln:Tabs]**.

An underline style code affects all underlined text from the location where it is inserted all the way to the end of the document, or until another underline style code is encountered farther forward in the document. For instance, suppose you decide to underline both spaces and tabs starting at the top of the document. Position the cursor at the top of the document and use the FORMAT ( Shift + F8 ) key to insert the code **[Undrln:Spaces, Tabs]**. Farther forward in the text, suppose you choose to underline tabs only. Then reposition the cursor where you want to change the style and insert the code **[Undrln: Tabs]**.

Suppose you want WordPerfect to underline the tabs between the headings "Name" and "Department." Remember that WordPerfect assumes you wish to underline only spaces and not tabs. Thus, you must insert an Underline style code just above these two headings to change the underline style in effect.

1. Position the cursor on the blank line above the "N" in "Name."

2. Press the FORMAT ( Shift + F8 ) key. [*Pulldown menu: Layout (L).*]

3. Select Other Format (4 or O). [*Pulldown menu: Other (O).*] The menu shown in Figure 3-5 appears.

4. Select Underline (7 or U).

5. Type **Y** twice to indicate that you desire both spaces and tabs underlined.

6. Press EXIT ( F7 ) to leave the Other Format menu and return to the Typing screen.

Monochrome monitor users will see that the tabs are now underlined, continuing from the heading "Name" to the heading "Department," as shown in Figure 3-6.

Color monitor users who view underlined text in a different color rather than with an underscore will see the change only on the printed page; print out the page if you wish to verify the change in the underline style. You can also verify the alteration by revealing codes so that you can view the Underline style code that you inserted. If you erase the Underline style code, then the underline style for

```
                        Urgent Notice

To: All Employees                    From: Sandy Peterson

(Wednesday) October 10, 1990

As you know, we announced on September 15th a new vacation option
for employees who are full-time or who work more than twenty hours
per week. Here is the list of those employees who have already
signed up for the new option:

Name                     Department

Antonio Abbott           Distribution, East Coast
Lois Chang               Personnel
Tim Fingerman            Public Relations
Paul McClintock          Distribution, West Coast

If you wish to sign up, but your name is not on the list, then you
must telephone our Personnel Director, John Samsone, by October
15th at (415) 333-9215. Thank you.


                                  Doc 1 Pg 1 Ln 2.67" Pos 1"
```

**FIGURE 3-6**  Sample document where underline style is changed to underscore tabs as well as spaces

the lower portion of the document returns to the default underline style: spaces underlined but tabs not underlined.

# A REMINDER: SAVE THE DOCUMENT PERIODICALLY

As you've been reading this chapter and typing the practice document, 15 minutes or so have probably gone by. Remember from the discussion in Chapter 2 that you must save to disk regularly; otherwise, you risk losing your text to a power failure or an operator error. Let's take a moment to save the typing done so far.

1. Press the SAVE ( F10 ) key. [*Pulldown menu:* File (F), Save (S).] WordPerfect requests a document filename.

2. Type **URGNOTE** (standing for urgent notice) and press Enter . (Remember to type the correct drive/directory designation in front of URGNOTE if you want that file stored somewhere other than the default—for example, B:URGNOTE.)

You can now continue, knowing that a copy of the text you've typed is safely stored on disk. If you experience a power failure, you can reload WordPerfect, retrieve the document named URGNOTE, and continue from this point.

# REPEAT A KEYSTROKE WITH THE ESCAPE KEY

The ESCAPE ( Esc ) key, usually located on the top row of the keyboard, can be used in WordPerfect to repeat a character a specified number of times—a quick typing aid. The default repeat value is 8. Therefore, to repeat a character eight times, position the cursor where you want that character to appear and press (Esc). WordPerfect responds with

```
Repeat Value = 8
```

Press any character to insert it eight times. For instance, if you type the plus sign, the following appears:

```
++++++++
```

When you want a character repeated more or fewer than eight times, press (Esc), type in the desired repeat value, and type the character.

   Suppose that you wish to insert eight exclamation points after the words "Thank you" at the end of the "Urgent Notice" document.

1. Position the cursor at the period just to the right of the words "Thank you," and press (Del) to erase the period.

2. Press (Esc). WordPerfect prompts

```
Repeat Value = 8
```

3. Type !. WordPerfect inserts eight exclamation points

   Now let's draw a blank line 20 spaces long at the bottom of the document as a place for a signature. What that means is that you will want to turn on the Underline feature, insert 20 spaces, and turn underlining off. The (Esc) key makes this easy.

1. Press ⌊Enter⌋ twice to move to a blank line.

2. Press the UNDERLINE (⌊F8⌋) key to turn on the feature.

3. Press ⌊Esc⌋. WordPerfect prompts

   ```
   Repeat Value = 8
   ```

4. Type **20**. Now the prompt reads

   ```
   Repeat Value = 20
   ```

5. Press the spacebar. Twenty spaces are now inserted, all underlined.

6. Press the UNDERLINE (⌊F8⌋) key to turn off the Underline feature.

You can also alter the repetition number for an entire working session. Suppose you were typing a document where, every page or so, you inserted a row of 35 asterisks. You could change the repetition number to 35 for the working session and insert those asterisks quickly. To change the default repeat value, press ⌊Esc⌋, type in a new repetition number, and press ⌊Enter⌋. From then on until the end of the working session, every time you pressed ⌊Esc⌋, the prompt would reflect the new number:

```
Repeat Value = 35
```

The ⌊Esc⌋ key can be used not only to repeat a specific character, but to repeat a cursor movement or deletion operation as well. For instance, press ⌊Esc⌋ and then press the ⌊→⌋ key to move 8 places to the right. Or, press ⌊Esc⌋, type **12**, and press ⌦ to delete 12 characters in a row, just as if you had pressed the ⌦ key 12 times. Besides the arrow keys and ⌦, other keys that work with the ⎋ key include

- ⌃ + ← and ⌃ + →, to move the cursor by a specific number of words

- ⌃ + ↑ and ⌃ + ↓, to move the cursor by a specific number of paragraphs (*5.1 users with enhanced keyboards only*)

- ⇞ and ⇟, to move the cursor by a specific number of pages

- − and + (on the cursor movement/numeric keypad), to move the cursor by a specific number of screens

- ⌃ + ⌫, to delete a specific number of words

- ⌃ + ⇥, to delete a specific number of lines

# CONTROL WORD WRAP WITH SPACES AND HYPHENS

Sometimes word wrap will break a line at an awkward or inappropriate spot. For instance, word wrap may split a name, a date, or a phone number between two lines. Following are several examples of an awkward split at the end of a line:

```
According to my calendar, Mr. Patterson is due back on September
14th. He will call you then.
```

```
Ms. Cindy Ballenger can be reached in New York City at (212)
455-1299.
```

You can control how word wrap operates so that you can keep dates, telephone numbers, or names together on one line. Your lines can look like the following instead:

```
According to my calendar, Mr. Patterson is due back on
September 14th. He will call you then.
```

```
Ms. Cindy Ballenger can be reached in New York City at
(212) 455-1299.
```

To keep together words that are separated by a space, you must create a "hard" space—one that glues words together. Type the first word, press (Home), press the spacebar, and type the second word. You have thus created a Hard Space code, which, on the Reveal Codes screen, looks like [ ]. The two words on either side of the hard space will be kept on the same line. If you had already typed the words that you wanted kept together, you would delete the space between them before pressing (Home), and then spacebar.

To keep together words joined by a hyphen (-), the process is similar. Type the first word, press (Home), type in a hyphen, and type the second word. You have created a Hard Hyphen code, which on the Reveal Codes screen resembles an ordinary, non-boldfaced hyphen: -. (If you press the hyphen without first pressing (Home), you insert a hyphen character, and the code inserted is [-]. This hyphen character *won't* protect two words from being split by word wrap.)

Notice that the date "October 15th" in the last paragraph is separated onto two separate lines in Figure 3-6. (This may also be the case on your computer screen, though not necessarily. Remember from Chapter 1 that the printer you defined to work with WordPerfect determines where word wrap will break a line; thus, your words may wrap differently than what is shown in Figure 3-6.) Suppose you wish to make sure that WordPerfect keeps "October 15th" on the same line, and you wish to ensure that the phone number "(415) 333-9215," stays together on one line as well.

1. Position the cursor on the blank space after "October."

2. Press [Del] to delete the space. The text readjusts.

3. Press [Home], then spacebar. A hard space code is inserted in the text.

4. Press [↓] to readjust the text. "October 15th" is treated like one word for purposes of word wrap; the two words remain together on one line, even though, for some of you, the word "October" could, by itself, fit at the end of the line above.

5. Position the cursor on the blank space after "(415)."

6. Press [Del] to delete the space.

7. Press [Home], spacebar. A hard space code is inserted in the text.

8. Position the cursor on the hyphen after "333."

9. Press [Del] to delete the hyphen.

10. Press [Home], and a hyphen. A hard hyphen is inserted, keeping the complete phone number on one line.

Now no matter how you edit your text, neither the date nor the phone number will be split by word wrap. You may wish to experiment by inserting or deleting random words to verify that word wrap will no longer split the date or phone number on separate lines. WordPerfect will leave extra space at the end of a line instead.

# CONVERT LOWERCASE AND UPPERCASE LETTERS

WordPerfect provides a slick feature that lets you change uppercase text that you've already typed to lowercase or vice versa. You first use the BLOCK ( (Alt) + (F4) ) key to highlight the text you wish to convert between lowercase and uppercase. Next, with "Block on" flashing, press the SWITCH ( (Shift) + (F3) ) key and select to switch all letters to either uppercase or lowercase [*Pulldown menu:* Select Edit (E), Convert Case (V).] If you select lowercase and the block of text you highlighted contains any sentences, then the first letter of each sentence remains in uppercase automatically.

Let's change the words "Urgent Notice" to all uppercase letters:

1. Press (Home), (Home), (↑), and then press (→) to position the cursor on the "U" in "Urgent Notice."

2. Press the BLOCK ( (Alt) + (F4) ) key. [*Pulldown menu:* Edit (E), Block (B).]

3. Press (End) to highlight the text to the end of the line.

4. Press the SWITCH ( (Shift) + (F3) ) key. [*Pulldown menu:* Edit (E), Convert Case (V).] WordPerfect prompts

`1 Uppercase; 2 Lowercase: 0`

5. Select Uppercase (1 or U). The title is switched to uppercase letters—URGENT NOTICE. The Block feature is turned off automatically.

# CREATE DOCUMENT COMMENTS

WordPerfect offers the Comment feature, whereby you can type information that will appear in a double-line box in the document on screen, but will not appear on the printed page. This is convenient if you wish to leave within a document a mental reminder for yourself or someone else who will be viewing this document on screen. For instance, in a draft document you might sprinkle comments containing ideas for adding to the text. Or, you might insert a comment that informs the next person who will edit the document how you have altered it. A comment is also handy for indicating what information should be typed at a specific location in a document, such as in a form that you designed on the computer and that other people will be filling out in WordPerfect.

To insert a document comment, position the cursor where you wish the comment to appear, press the TEXT IN/OUT ( Ctrl + F5 ) key, and select the Comment option. [*Pulldown menu:* Select Edit (E), Comment (O).] WordPerfect then displays the following Comment menu:

`Comment: 1 Create; 2 Edit; 3 Convert to Text: 0`

Next, select Create (1 or C).

Once you select to create a comment, a comment box appears on screen, in which you can type up to 1157 characters. When you are done typing, you must press the EXIT (F7) key. The comment appears in your document in a double-line box. If you reveal codes, you'll see that the hidden code **[Comment]** is inserted in the text; this code creates the double-line box and contains the comment text.

A document comment can be deceiving. While the comment may occupy various lines on screen, it occupies no space at all in the actual printed document. As a result, the status line ignores the position of the comment. When the cursor is located just before or after the comment box, simply use the ← and → keys to pass over the code (and the box) in one keystroke.

Suppose you wish to insert a reminder to yourself that employees must receive the "URGENT NOTICE" memo by Friday. Proceed as follows:

1. Press Home, Home, ↑ to position the cursor at the top left corner of the document.

2. Press the TEXT IN/OUT (Ctrl + F5) key. [*Pulldown menu:* Edit (E).] The Text In/out menu appears on screen.

3. *5.1 users:* Select Comment (4 or C). [*Pulldown menu:* Comment (O).] *5.0 users:* Select Comment (5 or C). A new menu appears:

   `Comment: 1 Create; 2 Edit; 3 Convert to Text: 0`

4. Select Create (1 or C). An empty document comment box appears on screen, as shown in Figure 3-7.

5. Type the following:

   `Make sure employees receive memo by Friday. Special courier`
   `to distribution centers on the East Coast.`

6. Press the EXIT ( F7 ) key. You are returned to the Typing screen, with the comment at the top of the screen, as Figure 3-8 shows.

7. Press ← . The cursor moves before the **[Comment]** code, so that on the Typing screen the cursor is above the comment.

8. Press → . The cursor moves below the comment.

Remember that the comment will not appear when you print this document; it is solely an on-screen feature. You may wish to print this document to verify that, in fact, the comment doesn't appear as part of the printed document.

You can edit the contents of the comment box at any time by positioning the cursor below the comment, following steps 2 and 3 above, and then selecting the Edit Option

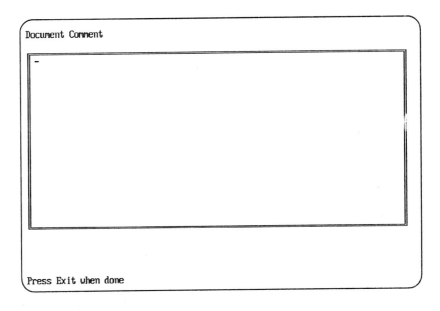

Document Comment

Press Exit when done

**FIGURE 3-7** Document Comment screen

```
┌─────────────────────────────────────────────────────────────┐
│  ╔═══════════════════════════════════════════════════════╗  │
│  ║ Make sure employees receive memo by Friday.  Special courier to ║  │
│  ║ distribution centers on the East Coast.               ║  │
│  ╚═══════════════════════════════════════════════════════╝  │
│                          URGENT NOTICE                      │
│  ▬                                                          │
│  To: All Employees                      From: Sandy Peterson │
│                                                             │
│  (Wednesday) October 10, 1990                               │
│                                                             │
│  As you know, we announced on September 15th a new vacation option │
│  for employees who are full-time or who work more than twenty hours │
│  per week.  Here is the list of those employees who have already │
│  signed up for the new option:                              │
│                                                             │
│  Name                    Department                         │
│                                                             │
│  Antonio Abbott          Distribution, East Coast           │
│  Lois Chang              Personnel                          │
│  Tim Fingerman           Public Relations                   │
│  Paul McClintock         Distribution, West Coast           │
│                                                             │
│  If you wish to sign up, but your name is not on the list, then you │
│  C:\WP51\DATA\URGNOTE                         Doc 1 Pg 1 Ln 1" Pos 1" │
└─────────────────────────────────────────────────────────────┘
```

**FIGURE 3-8**   Sample document with an on-screen comment

(2 or E). The comment appears on the screen for editing. Press the EXIT ( F7 ) key when you have completed editing the comment.

You can also convert the contents of the comment box into standard text. For instance, suppose you typed text into a comment box and now decide you want that text incorporated into the document. Or, suppose you wish to print the comment. Position the cursor just below the comment, follow steps 2 and 3 above, and then select Convert to Text (3 or T). The double-line box disappears, but the comment text remains in the document.

Conversely, you can convert a portion of text into a comment. As an example, suppose you type a sentence in a document and then realize that the sentence is more appropriate as a comment; that is, text that appears only when the document is on screen. Use the Block feature to highlight the sentence, and with "Block on" flashing, press the TEXT IN/OUT ([Ctrl] + [F5]) key. [*Pulldown menu:* Edit (E), Comment (O), Create (C).] WordPerfect prompts

**Create a comment?** No (Yes)

Type **Y** to convert that text into a comment, or type **N** or press [Enter] to abort the command but leave Block on.

If you wish to erase a comment, including the comment text, you must delete the **[Comment]** code. For instance, with your document on the screen, you can press the RE-VEAL CODES ([Alt] + [F3]) key, position the cursor to the right of the code, and press [Backspace]. If you inadvertently erase a comment, remember from Chapter 1 that you can use the Undelete feature to restore the comment just as you would recover other deleted text.

One final option allows you to hide the display of all document comments. The default setting is to display comments; to change the default, refer to the "Display" section in Appendix B.

# SWITCH BETWEEN TWO DOCUMENT SCREENS

With WordPerfect, you can work on two Typing screens at one time, each containing a separate document. Both documents remain in the computer's RAM; you simply switch between them at will by pressing the SWITCH ([Shift] + [F3]) key. [*Pulldown menu:* Edit (E), Switch Document (S).] The first Typing screen is referred to as the Doc 1 window, while the second is the Doc 2 window. Both windows are always available to you; so far, we haven't accessed the Doc 2 window.

Why work with two documents at one time? Doc 1 might contain an outline you wish to refer to periodically when creating a report in Doc 2. Or Doc 1 might contain a memo you wish to refer to when typing a letter in the other Doc window. Or Doc 2 could be reserved for your random thoughts as you type a report in Doc 1. Also, dual document typing is especially handy when you want to copy a paragraph from one document to another. You can retrieve one document in the Doc 1 window and copy text from it to the Doc 2 window. (The Move/Copy command is described in Chapter 5.)

All of WordPerfect's features operate the same in the Doc 2 window as in the Doc 1 window. For instance, you could retrieve a document into the Doc 2 window in the usual manner—using the RETRIEVE ([Shift] + [F10]) or the LIST ([F5]) key. You must make sure the cursor is in the Doc 2 window before retrieving.

Suppose that while working on the "URGENT NOTICE" memo, you have a brainstorm regarding another memo you wish to write. Let's switch between the Doc 1 and Doc 2 windows.

1. Press the SWITCH ([Shift] + [F3]) key. [*Pulldown menu:* Edit (E), Switch Document (S).] Now the screen becomes blank. Notice at the bottom of the screen that the status line reads **Doc 2**. You have switched to the second Typing screen.

2. Press the SWITCH ([Shift] + [F3]) key. You are returned to Doc 1 and the memo it contains. When you switch between documents in separate Typing screens, you don't lose any text from either one.

3. As this chapter continues, you will create a memo in the Doc 2 window. The "URGENT NOTICE" memo in Doc 1 will remain in RAM. But because you have substantially edited the memo in Doc 1 since you last saved it, it is a good idea to again save the contents of what's in the Doc 1 window, just in case there's a power failure. Press the SAVE (F10) key, press Enter, and type **Y** to save the document in the Doc 1 window.

4. Press the SWITCH (Shift + F3) key. You are returned to Doc 2, ready to work on a new document.

# LEARN ABOUT INDENTING AND ALIGNING TEXT ON TAB STOPS

You learned previously that as a default setting tab stops are set every 0.5″. When you wish to jump to a tab stop, you press the Tab key; a **[Tab]** code is inserted and the text that you type following that code will be aligned at the tab stop. Thus, as you saw when typing documents in Chapter 1, the Tab key is used to indent the first line of a paragraph, or to align the left side of text in a table.

In addition to the Tab key, there are other alternatives for aligning text on tab stops. These features include: →Indent, →Indent←, ←Margin Release, Center, and Tab Align. All of these features are accessed directly from the function keys, as is discussed shortly. [*Pulldown menu:* You can also access each of these features by selecting Layout (L) and then Align (A).] As illustrated in Figure 3-9, each key has a slightly different effect on the text.

**Tab stop**
↓

When you use the TAB key, only one line is indented. As
a result, the TAB key is commonly used to indent the first line
of a paragraph.

When you press the ->INDENT (F4) key and type a paragraph, the entire paragraph is indented to the next tab
stop, no matter how many lines that one paragraph
contains.

When you press the -> INDENT <- (SHIFT + F4)
key, the whole paragraph is indented not only
from the left side, but from the right side as
well -- quite a convenient feature if you wish
to type a long, indented quote.

You can create a hanging paragraph by first pressing the
->INDENT (F4) key, pressing the <- MARGIN RELEASE (SHIFT
+ TAB) key, and then typing your text. The first line of
the paragraph hangs out farther than the remaining lines
of the paragraph.

↑

**Tab stop**

| Centered on the Tab ↓ | Tab aligned on a Decimal ↓ | Tab aligned on a Dollar Sign ↓ |
|:---:|:---:|:---:|
| This | 44.55 | $44.55 |
| is | 3.40 | $3.40 |
| centered | 112.0 | $112.00 |
| on | 1500.05 | $1500.89 |
| a tab stop. | 33.44 | $2.33 |

≡≡≡ **FIGURE 3-9**  Different features that operate on tab
stops

# Indent

While the ⌊Tab⌋ key indents a single line, the ➔INDENT (⌊F4⌋) key indents an entire paragraph. Each time you press the ➔INDENT (⌊F4⌋) key, an [➔Indent] code is inserted, indenting all lines to the next tab stop until an [HRt] code is encountered. This key widens the left margin for a single paragraph. If you edit the text of the paragraph, the margins are readjusted so that the paragraph remains indented.

A related key is the ➔INDENT◄ (⌊Shift⌋ + ⌊F4⌋) key, which indents both the left and right edges of all lines in a paragraph by an equal amount. This key widens both the left and right margins for a single paragraph, such as a long quotation. An [➔Indent◄] code is inserted.

# Margin Release

The ◄MARGIN RELEASE (⌊Shift⌋ + ⌊Tab⌋) key is used to move a single line of text back one tab stop to the left. It has the reverse effect of the ⌊Tab⌋ key, and will even move text to the left of the left margin. An [◄Mar Rel] code is inserted.

When you press the ◄MARGIN RELEASE (⌊Shift⌋ + ⌊Tab⌋) key immediately after pressing the ➔INDENT (⌊F4⌋) key, you create a hanging paragraph, whereby the first line of a paragraph begins one tab stop to the left of the remaining paragraph lines. The hanging paragraph style is useful in bibliographies or in documents where a list of topics is presented in paragraph form.

# Center

The CENTER ([Shift] + [F6]) key can center a short entry on a tab stop. To center text you *must first press* [Tab] to position the cursor on the correct tab stop. (This is different from how the other features operate.) Then press the CENTER ([Shift] + [F6]) key and type the entry. Now press [Tab] to move to the next tab stop or [Enter] to move down to a new line. *5.1 users:* [Center] is inserted in front of the centered text. *5.0 users:* The following pair of Center codes is inserted around the text like bookends: [Cntr] and [C/A/Flrt].

*5.1 users only:* You have another method for centering on the next tab stop. Instead of pressing [Tab] to position the cursor before pressing CENTER ([Shift] + [F6]), press [Home], CENTER ([Shift] + [F6]). The code [CNTR TAB] is inserted in front of the centered text.

# Tab Align

The TAB ALIGN ([Ctrl] + [F6]) key lines up all the text at a tab stop on a specific character. The default character is the decimal point (period) so that you can easily align numbers in a column on a decimal, as shown in the second column at the bottom of Figure 3-9.

When you press the TAB ALIGN ([Ctrl] + [F6]) key, the cursor jumps to the next tab setting, and WordPerfect prompts

```
Align char =.
```

reminding you that the align character is the decimal point (period). You can type in text or a number, including a period. Then press Ⓣab or the TAB ALIGN ( Ⓒtrl + Ⓕ6 ) key if you wish to move to the next tab stop, or you can press Ⓔnter to move down to the next line. If you type text that didn't contain a period before moving to the next tab stop or line, that text will be right justified, meaning that the right edge of the text will be aligned on the tab stop.

The codes inserted around text aligned on the decimal point are different depending on whether you are using version 5.1 or 5.0. *5.1 users:* A decimal tab code **[DEC TAB]** is inserted in front of the text to align it on the decimal point. Here's an example:

```
[DEC TAB]33.66
```

*5.0 users:* A pair of codes is inserted, and it is only inserted around the text that precedes the decimal point: **[Align]** and **[C/A/Flrt]**. Here's an example:

```
[Align]33[C/A/Flrt].66
```

The Tab Align feature is quite flexible because you can alter the character that aligns on the tab for a particular document. For example, perhaps you want the tab stop to align with the colon (:). Or perhaps you wish to align numbers on the dollar sign ($), as shown in the third column at the bottom of Figure 3-9. If so, you must change the alignment character *before* using the TAB ALIGN ( Ⓒtrl + Ⓕ6 ) key. Position the cursor where you want the new alignment character to take effect. Then press the FOR-MAT ( Ⓢhift + Ⓕ8 ) key and select Other (4 or O). [*Pulldown menu:* Layout (L), Other (O).] The Other Format menu, as shown in Figure 3-5, appears. Notice that the period (.) is indicated as the default decimal/align character. Select Decimal/Align Character (3 or D), and type the new character on which you want the text to align. Then press [Enter] to bypass changing the thousands' separator (which is related to the Math feature). As a last step, press EXIT ([F7]) to return to the Typing screen. A code is inserted in the text at the current cursor position. For instance, if the align character is changed to the dollar sign ($), the code inserted is **[Decml/Algn Char:$,,]**. The code determines what character will be aligned on the tab when you use the Tab Align feature at any point following the location of the code.

# WORK WITH TAB STOP KEYS

Here's a chance to practice with various keys that operate on a tab stop. You'll first create a bulleted list with the →Indent feature, using the lowercase "o" as your bullet character. (Your printer may have the ability to produce an actual bullet character. Refer to the section of Chapter 15 entitled "Insert Special Characters" for details.) Then, you'll type two columns, the first aligned on the decimal point and the second with the text centered on the tab. The result of your typing is shown in Figure 3-10.

1. Your cursor should be in Doc 2, a blank screen. If you are still in Doc 1, press the SWITCH ([Shift] + [F3]) key.

2. Type the following:

   I spoke to John Samsone on January 3rd about our financial situation. He reported the following highlights:

3. Press [Enter] twice.

```
I spoke to John Samsone on January 3rd about our financial
situation. He reported the following highlights:

o     He is meeting with a venture capitalist next week who is
      interested in investing with us.

o     Our debt stands at $159,000 as of December 31st, 10% lower
      than we anticipated. Financial forecasts project that we'll
      be out of debt in two years time. Here are the debt figures
      (in thousands):

      Amount Owed              Name of Bank

        $40.5                  Floyd Interstate
          9.8                    Center Bank
        100.7                  Bank of Stevenson

 _



                                             Doc 2 Pg 1 Ln 3.67" Pos 1"
```

**FIGURE 3-10**  Sample document for working with tab stop keys

4. Type **o**, to represent a bullet, and press the ➔INDENT ( F4 ) key.

5. Type the following:

   ```
   He is meeting with a venture capitalist next week who is
   interested in investing with us.
   ```

6. Press Enter twice.

7. Type **o** and press the ➔INDENT ( F4 ) key.

8. Type the following:

   ```
   Our debt stands at $159,000 as of December 31st, 10% lower
   than we anticipated. Financial forecasts project that we'll be
   out of debt in two years time. Here are the debt figures (in
   thousands):
   ```

9. Press [Enter] twice.

10. Press [Tab] twice, and then press the CENTER ([Shift] + [F6]) key.

11. Type **Amount Owed,** and watch as the heading is centered on the tab stop.

12. Press [Tab] four times, and then press the CENTER ([Shift] + [F6]) key.

13. Type **Name of Bank**, and watch as the heading is centered on the tab stop.

14. Press [Enter] twice.

15. Press the TAB ALIGN ([Ctrl] + [F6]) key twice. Word-Perfect responds with

    ```
    Align char =.
    ```

16. Type **$48.5**. When you press the decimal point (period), the prompt at the bottom of the screen disappears. The number is aligned on the decimal.

17. Press [Tab] five times, and then press the CENTER ([Shift] + [F6]) key.

18. Type **Floyd Interstate** and then press [Enter]. The bank name is centered on the tab stop.

19. Press TAB ALIGN ([Ctrl] + [F6]) twice and type **9.8**.

20. Press [Tab] five times, press CENTER ([Shift] + [F6]), type **Center Bank,** and press [Enter].

21. Press TAB ALIGN ([Ctrl] + [F6]) twice and type **100.7**.

22. Press ⌨Tab five times, press CENTER (⌨Shift + ⌨F6 ),
    type **Bank of Stevenson**, and press ⌨Enter.

Notice that for the document you just created, it was
necessary to press the ⌨Tab key numerous times before
typing the entries in the second column, so that the text
would align properly. Since tab stops are initially set every
0.5″, the interval between each tab stop was too small. With
WordPerfect, you can change the location of tab stops (as
well as the tab stop style) so that you can more easily type a
table, such as the one you just completed, by pressing ⌨Tab
just once to move to each column in a table. This is especially important if you need to type tables with numerous
entries (more than the three lines of entries in the current
document). The procedure to alter tab settings for typing
tables is discussed in Chapter 4. Also, 5.1 users have available the Tables feature, which makes the process of setting
tab stops and typing text into tables even easier. Look to
Chapter 11 for more on the Tables feature.

If you decide to cancel an indent, margin release, center,
or tab align command for a text entry, you must delete the
code or code pair that you inserted around that text. For
instance, suppose you indented a paragraph using the
→INDENT (⌨F4 ) key, and now wish to cancel the indent
and instead, align the text against the left margin. On the
Typing screen, either position the cursor at the left margin
of that paragraph and press ⌨Del or position the cursor on
the first character of the indented paragraph and press
⌨Backspace. The hidden [→**Indent**] code is erased, and the
paragraph realigns against the left margin. Or, you can
switch to the Reveal Codes screen to view the code before
deleting it: Position the cursor on the code and press ⌨Del,
or position the cursor just to the right of the code and press
⌨Backspace

# SPLIT THE SCREEN IN HALF

While practicing with tab stops, did you forget about the document still occupying the Doc 1 screen? The document is still there. In fact, with WordPerfect, not only can you work with two documents on separate screens, but you can view and edit two documents on the *same* screen! To do this, you must reduce the size of either the Doc 1 or Doc 2 Typing screen's window by pressing the SCREEN (Ctrl + F3) key and selecting Window (1 or W). [*Pulldown menu:* Edit (E), Window (W).] Then, as prompted by Word-Perfect, type the desired size (in number of lines) for the Typing screen you are now viewing, and press Enter.

You can size both windows evenly or make one window larger than the other. You learned previously that Word-Perfect displays 24 lines of text on a standard-sized monitor, with the 25th serving as the status line. If you shrink a Typing screen to an 11-line window, the screen splits in half: Doc 1 and its status line appear in the top 12 lines, and Doc 2 and its status line appear on the bottom. A ruler line splits the two windows (the same ruler line that appears to split the windows on the Reveal Codes screen). Or you can make one window larger than the other by sizing it at a number larger than 11 but smaller than 23. Once the screen is split, you can type, edit, and move the cursor in one window while referring to text in the other window.

Suppose that in Doc 2 you wish to insert a phone number that you haven't memorized but that you know can be found in the document located in the Doc 1 window. Let's split the screen in half to work with both documents at the same time. You'll first position the cursor at the top of each document.

1. With Doc 2 on the Typing screen, press [Home], [Home], [↑].

2. Press the SWITCH ([Shift] + [F3]) key to go to Doc 1. [*Pulldown menu:* Edit (E), Switch Document (S).]

3. Press [Home], [Home], [↑].

4. Press the SCREEN ([Ctrl] + [F3]) key. [*Pulldown menu:* Edit (E).] WordPerfect responds with the following menu:

   `0 Rewrite; 1 Window; 2 Line Draw: 0`

5. Select Window (1 or W). WordPerfect prompts

   `Number of lines in this window: 24`

6. Type **11** and press [Enter]. The screen splits in half, and a ruler line appears in the middle of the screen, as shown in Figure 3-11. Notice that the tab stop markers (triangles) on the ruler line are pointing upward. This indicates that the cursor is currently in Doc 1.

7. Press [↓] until John Samsone's phone number comes into view in the top window. Now that you can view the phone number, you're ready to type it into Doc 2.

8. Press the SWITCH ([Shift] + [F3]) key. Now the tab stop markers are pointing downward; the cursor is in Doc 2.

9. Press [Home], [Home], [↓] to position the cursor at the bottom of the second document.

10. Press [Enter] once to insert a blank line. Your screen will now look like the one in Figure 3-12.

11. Type the following:

    `For more detail, call John at (415) 333-9215.`

```
┌──────────────────────────────────────────────────────────┐
│  ┌────────────────────────────────────────────────────┐  │
│  │ Make sure employees receive memo by Friday.  Special courier to │  │
│  │ distribution centers on the East Coast.            │  │
│  └────────────────────────────────────────────────────┘  │
│                       URGENT NOTICE                       │
│  ─                                                        │
│  To: All Employees                    From: Sandy Peterson│
│                                                           │
│  (Wednesday) October 10, 1990                             │
│                                                           │
│  C:\WP51\DATA\URGNOTE                    Doc 1 Pg 1 Ln 1" Pos 1" │
│  ▆▆▆▆▆▆▆▆▆▆▆▆▆▆▆▆▆▆▆▆▆▆▆▆▆▆▆▆▆▆▆▆▆▆▆▆▆▆▆▆▆▆▆▆▆▆▆▆▆▆▆▆▆▆  │
│  I spoke to John Samsone on January 3rd about our financial │
│  situation.  He reported the following highlights:         │
│                                                           │
│  o    He is meeting with a venture capitalist next week who is │
│       interested in investing with us.                    │
│                                                           │
│  o    Our debt stands at $159,000 as of December 31st, 10% lower │
│       than we anticipated.  Financial forecasts project that we'll │
│       be out of debt in two years time.  Here are the debt figures │
│       (in thousands):                                     │
│                                         Doc 2 Pg 1 Ln 1" Pos 1" │
└──────────────────────────────────────────────────────────┘
```

═══════  **FIGURE 3-11**   A split screen, displaying the Doc 1 and
Doc 2 windows

You were able to quickly reference John's phone number by viewing the Doc 1 screen. You should know that it is
also possible to copy John's phone number from the Doc 1
to the Doc 2 screen, rather than retype it. Copying text
from one screen to another is quite handy; refer to Chapter
5 for more on the Copy feature.

You can return a window to its standard, full-screen size
by pressing the same keys as when you split it in half, but
sizing one of the windows at 24 lines (or at 0 lines). Let's
return to the full-size screen.

1. Press the SCREEN (Ctrl + F3) key to view the
Screen menu. [*Pulldown menu:* Edit (E).]

2. Select Window (1 or W). WordPerfect prompts you with

   `Number of lines in this window: 11`

3. Type **24** and press [Enter]. Now only Doc 2 is displayed because that's the window the cursor was located in when you returned the screen to full size. Doc 1 is still in RAM, but it cannot be displayed on the screen unless you use the SWITCH ([Shift] + [F3]) key to switch to it.

# EXIT FROM TWO SCREENS

WordPerfect keeps track of whether or not you've been working with two Typing screens. If both Typing screens

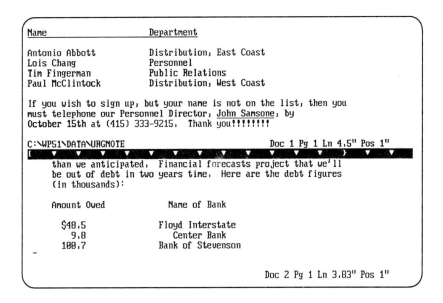

```
Name                    Department

Antonio Abbott          Distribution, East Coast
Lois Chang              Personnel
Tim Fingerman           Public Relations
Paul McClintock         Distribution, West Coast

If you wish to sign up, but your name is not on the list, then you
must telephone our Personnel Director, John Samsone, by
October 15th at (415) 333-9215.  Thank you!!!!!!!!

C:\WP51\DATA\URGNOTE                          Doc 1 Pg 1 Ln 4.5" Pos 1"
[    ▼     ▼     ▼     ▼     ▼     ▼     ▼     ▼     ▼   }  ▼     ▼
      than we anticipated.  Financial forecasts project that we'll
      be out of debt in two years time.  Here are the debt figures
      (in thousands):

      Amount Owed            Name of Bank

          $48.5             Floyd Interstate
            9.8             Center Bank
          108.7            Bank of Stevenson
  -
                                              Doc 2 Pg 1 Ln 3.83" Pos 1"
```

**FIGURE 3-12** A split screen, with the cursor in the bottom window

contain text, when you use the EXIT ([F7]) key to clear a screen or exit WordPerfect the prompts are a bit different. WordPerfect won't allow you to exit the program until you decide on the fate of both documents. Rather than asking whether you wish to exit WordPerfect, the prompt asks whether you wish to leave the document you're currently in. Once you have exited one of the screens, you can then exit the other in the usual manner.

Suppose you've completed both memos. You wish to save the memo in Doc 2 under the name FINANCE and save the memo in Doc 1 under the name URGNOTE again.

1. If you're not viewing Doc 2, press the SWITCH ([Shift] + [F3]) key to do so.

2. Press the EXIT ([F7]) key [*Pulldown menu:* File (F), Exit (X).] to save the document in the Doc 2 screen. Type **Y** to save the document, and then type the name **FINANCE**.

3. Notice that after WordPerfect saves the document on disk, the following prompt displays:

    `Exit doc 2? No (Yes)`

4. Type **Y** to leave Doc 2. The screen switches to Doc 1—Doc 2 has been cleared. (Alternatively, you could type **N**, in which case WordPerfect would remain in Doc 2, but the screen would clear.)

5. Press the EXIT ([F7]) key, type **4** to resave the document, and then resave the document in the Doc 1 window under the name URGNOTE by pressing [Enter] to accept the suggested name and typing **Y** to replace

the earlier file on disk. Now WordPerfect prompts you with

`Exit WP? No (Yes)`

WordPerfect enables you to exit now because the second document is clear.

6. Type **N** so that you may remain in WordPerfect and proceed with the review exercise that follows.

# REVIEW EXERCISE

The following steps will help you to gain skill in using enhancements as you type a document. Find a document containing several paragraphs of text that you can practice with. You will perform tasks such as underlining and bold-facing. Then you will work with two documents at once — each in a different Typing screen window.

1. On a clear Typing screen, begin to type your own practice document. As you do so, practice underlining and boldfacing words and sentences. Also practice centering and aligning flush right as you type, and use the →INDENT and other features that work on tab stops as you type paragraphs or type text in columns aligned on tabs.

2. Change the date format to display the current date and time as follows: Month ##, 19## at #.## am. (*Hint:* This translates to the following date format: 3 1, 4 at 8:9 0.) Then position the cursor where you would like the date and time to appear and insert the date and time as text.

3. Switch to the Doc 2 Typing screen. Make sure that the screen is clear, and retrieve the file named SAMPLE.

4. Practice underlining and boldfacing individual words and sentences in SAMPLE. (*Hint:* Since the text has already been typed, you must highlight the text with the Block feature before you can underline or boldface it.)

5. Center all of the countries that are listed on individual lines in the document. (*Hint:* Use the Block feature to highlight the list of countries, and then press the CEN-TER (Shift + F6) key and type **Y** to center them all at once.)

6. Use the EXIT (F7) key to exit WordPerfect *without* saving either of the documents on screen. *Hint:* Since you have text on both the Doc 1 screen and the Doc 2 screen, WordPerfect won't allow you to exit the program until you decide on the fate of both documents. So after pressing the EXIT (F7) key, type **N**, indicating that you do not wish to resave the file named SAMPLE. Next, type **Y** to exit the Doc 2 screen. Now you must repeat this procedure—press EXIT (F7), type **N**, and type **Y**—to exit the Doc 1 screen and WordPerfect.)

# Quick Review

- Center text between the left and right margins with the CENTER (Shift + F6) key. With the cursor at the left margin, press the CENTER (Shift + F6) key and then type the text to be centered. Or, to center text that's already been typed, use the Block feature to highlight the text, and then press the CENTER (Shift + F6) key. Or, pulldown menu users can select Layout (L), Align (A), Center (C).

- Align text against the right margin with the FLUSH RIGHT (Alt + F6) key. Press the FLUSH RIGHT (Alt + F6) key and then type the text to be aligned. Or, to align text that's already been typed, use the Block feature to highlight the text, and then press the FLUSH RIGHT (Alt + F6) key. Or, pulldown menu users can select Layout (L), Align (A), Flush Right (F).

- The UNDERLINE (F8) key underscores text. Press the UNDERLINE (F8) key once, type the text, and then make sure to press UNDERLINE a second time to turn off the feature. You can also type the text first, then use the Block feature to highlight the text you want underlined, and finally press the UNDERLINE (F8) key. Using the Other Format menu, you can decide whether you wish spaces and tabs underlined.

- The BOLD (F6) key boldfaces text. Press the BOLD (F6) key once, type the text, and then make sure to press BOLD again to turn off the feature. You can also type the text first, then use the Block feature to highlight the text you want boldfaced, and finally press the BOLD (F6) key.

- To insert the date at the current cursor position, press the DATE/OUTLINE (Shift + F5) key and select Date Text (1 or T) or Date Code (2 or C). If you insert the date as a code, the date will automatically be updated when you retrieve or print the document containing that date code. You can also specify the format in which the date will appear by selecting the Date Format (3 or F) option. Pulldown menu users can access these features from the Tools menu.

- The Esc key can be used to repeat a character a specific number of times or to repeat a cursor movement or a deletion a certain number of times. Press Esc, type a number to specify the repetitions, and then press the character or cursor movement key. The default repeat value is 8.

- Use the Home key to control where word wrap breaks a line of text. Press Home, then spacebar to ensure that two words separated by a space remain together on a line. Press [Home], then a hyphen to ensure that two words separated by a hyphen remain together on a line.

- Convert text between lowercase and uppercase by first using the Block feature to highlight the text. Next, press the SWITCH ([Shift] + [F3]) key and choose an option from the Switch menu. Or, pulldown menu users can select Edit (E), Convert Case (O).

- On-screen comments that will never be printed can be incorporated into a document. You can create or edit a comment, or convert that comment to text via the TEXT IN/OUT ([Ctrl] + [F5]) key, or pulldown menu users can select Edit (E), Comment (C).

- A number of keys in addition to [Tab] can affect how text is positioned on a tab stop: the ➔INDENT ([F4]) key indents an entire paragraph to the next tab stop; the ➔INDENT◄([Shift] + [F4]) key indents from both the left and the right; the ◄MARGIN RELEASE ([Shift] + [Tab]) key moves one line of text back to the previous tab stop; the TAB ALIGN ([Ctrl] + [F6]) key aligns text on a specific character at the tab stop; and the CENTER ([Shift] + [F6]) key centers text on a tab stop if you press the [Tab] key first. Pulldown menu users can access the same features by selecting Layout (L), Align (A).

- Work with two documents at once by typing or retrieving the first on the Doc 1 screen and the second on the Doc 2 screen. Switch between the document screens by pressing the SWITCH (Shift + F3) key. Or, pulldown menu users can select Edit (E), Switch Document (S).

- Split the Typing screen by pressing the SCREEN (Ctrl + F3) key or by selecting Edit (E), Window (W) from the pulldown menu and then entering the number of lines for the current window. The Doc 1 and Doc 2 text can then be viewed simultaneously. A window size of 11 splits the screen in half.

*chapter* **4**

# CHANGING MARGINS, TABS, LINE FORMAT FEATURES

**W**hen you make decisions about how text will appear on the printed page, you are said to be setting the document's *format*. You made no format decisions when you worked with documents in the preceding chapters, and as a result WordPerfect assumed the initial or default format settings—settings that the designers of the Word-Perfect program established for you. (A complete list of these settings can be found in Appendix B.)

You don't have to abide by the default settings: You can alter the appearance of each document you create, and you can do so at any time—before you start typing a document, while you're typing it, or when you're done.

You'll learn in this chapter about the default settings for left and right margins, tabs, and other basic settings that affect each line of text. Using one of the documents you created in a previous chapter, you'll establish new margins. You'll also work with the justification and hyphenation settings and make the whole document double rather than single spaced. To help you become skillful with tabs, step-by-step instructions will show you how to change tab stop locations. By the chapter's end, you will have become skilled at working with the hidden codes inserted into your document whenever you make margin, tab, and other line format changes.

# INITIAL LINE FORMAT SETTINGS

The initial settings for formatting each line of text in a document are as follows:

Left and right margins    1″ borders on either side of
                          the printed page

| | |
|---|---|
| Full justification | WordPerfect will adjust the spacing between characters when printing the text to establish left and right margins that are even |
| Hyphenation | Off, meaning that WordPerfect will wrap a long word that extends beyond the right margin down to the next line rather than split the word with a hyphen |
| Spacing | Single |
| Tab stops | One every 0.5″(up to 14″) across the width of the page |

If you do not specify otherwise, the above defaults will take effect in each line you type, providing a printed result as illustrated in Figure 4-1.

*Note:* The preceding are the defaults as initially set up at WordPerfect Corporation. If some of your default settings appear different, then a coworker may have altered these default settings for your copy of WordPerfect. The procedure to alter the standard defaults is described in the "Initial Settings" section of Appendix B.

You can change any or all of the format defaults for a particular document by inserting format codes within the document. These codes serve to override the default settings.

Placement of format codes is critical. Any code that you insert in a document controls all text from that location *forward,* all the way either to the end of the document or up

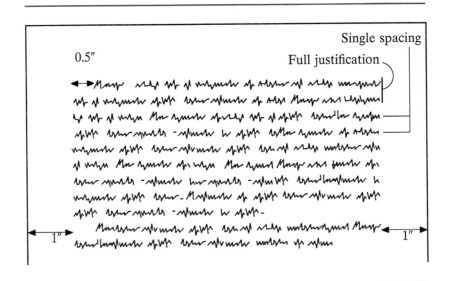

**FIGURE 4-1**   Printed lines based on default line format settings

to the next code of its type farther down in the document. For instance, position the cursor at the top of a document to change margins for the entire document. Or position the cursor just before the third paragraph to change margins for paragraph three and all succeeding paragraphs; paragraphs one and two will abide by the original margin settings.

You insert a format code in a document by pressing the FORMAT ([Shift] + [F8]) key. When you do so, the menu in Figure 4-2 appears. Notice in Figure 4-2 that there are four types of format changes that can be made: line format changes, which will be discussed in this chapter; page format changes, which affect the layout of text on a page and will be discussed in Chapter 6; document format changes, which are special and affect an entire document (one of

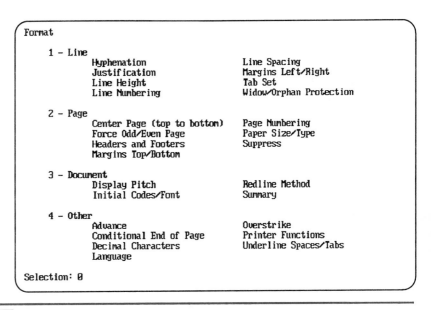

```
Format
    1 - Line
            Hyphenation                    Line Spacing
            Justification                  Margins Left/Right
            Line Height                    Tab Set
            Line Numbering                 Widow/Orphan Protection

    2 - Page
            Center Page (top to bottom)    Page Numbering
            Force Odd/Even Page            Paper Size/Type
            Headers and Footers            Suppress
            Margins Top/Bottom

    3 - Document
            Display Pitch                  Redline Method
            Initial Codes/Font             Summary

    4 - Other
            Advance                        Overstrike
            Conditional End of Page        Printer Functions
            Decimal Characters             Underline Spaces/Tabs
            Language

Selection: 0
```

**FIGURE 4-2**   Format menu

which will also be discussed in this chapter); and other format changes, which cover special formatting, such as a document's underline style (as described in Chapter 3). You select the appropriate menu option to change a format; a format code is inserted at the current cursor position, which is displayed in the document when you reveal codes. [*Pulldown menu:* Initiate format changes by selecting Layout (L). Then, depending on the type of format change you desire, select Line (L), Page (P), Document (D), or Other (O). In using the pulldown menu, you bypass Figure 4-2.]

You will insert various format codes as this chapter continues. Remember that if you lose your bearings as you press function keys and select menu items, press CANCEL ( F1 ) until you back out of the menus and then start again.

(In a few circumstances, CANCEL won't back you out of a menu, and you must press EXIT (F7) instead, as is usually indicated at the bottom of the menu screen.)

# CHANGE LEFT AND RIGHT MARGINS

WordPerfect's initial left and right margin settings are 1″. This means that WordPerfect will insert 1″ of blank space on both the left and right edges of the printed page. Since WordPerfect assumes that you will be printing on paper that is 8.5″ wide (paper size of 8.5″ by 11″ is another assumption that can be changed, as discussed in Chapter 9), this means that WordPerfect assumes you want each line of text to be 6.5″ long—8.5″ minus 1″ left margin minus 1″ right margin. You saw the 1″ left and right margins when you printed two documents in Chapter 2.

*Note:* If you followed the directions in Chapter 2 to print your documents, but your printed result had left/right margins other than 1″, then the paper may have been improperly aligned in your printer. For example, if the paper has been placed in the printer too far to the right, the right margin would be wider than the left. Try printing again by shifting where paper is inserted into the printer.

You can set new margins, thus increasing or decreasing the width of each line of text. To set new margins, position the cursor at the beginning of the line where you want the new margins to take effect. For example, you would position the cursor at the top of the document to alter margins throughout, or at the very top left corner of page 2 to change margins starting on that page. Positioning the cursor is critical: remember that a margin change will take effect from the cursor position on down.

Once the cursor is properly positioned, press the FORMAT ([Shift] + [F8]) key. The Format menu shown in Figure 4-2 appears. Select Line (1 or L), and the Line Format menu as shown in Figure 4-3 appears. (5.0 users will see a slightly different menu.) [*Pulldown menu:* Layout (L), and then Line (L).] Select Margins Left and Right (7 or M), and then enter both your left and right margin settings, measured from the edges of the page. Finally, press EXIT ([F7]) to return to the Typing screen.

When you alter margins within a document, a Left and Right Margin code is inserted at the current cursor position. For instance, if you changed left and right margins to 2″, then the code inserted is **[L/R Mar:2″,2″]**. As with any

```
Format: Line

      1 - Hyphenation                        No

      2 - Hyphenation Zone - Left            10%
                            Right            4%

      3 - Justification                      Full

      4 - Line Height                        Auto

      5 - Line Numbering                     No

      6 - Line Spacing                       1

      7 - Margins - Left                     1"
                    Right                    1"

      8 - Tab Set                            Rel: -1", every 0.5"

      9 - Widow/Orphan Protection            No


  Selection: 0
```

────────── **FIGURE 4-3**  Line Format menu (version 5.1)

other code placed in a document, a Left/Right Margin code is visible only when you reveal codes. This code affects margins from that point and forward, or to another **[L/R Mar:]** code located farther down in the document.

Let's alter margins for an entire document. We'll set the left margin to 1.5″ and the right margin to 1″.

1. On a clear Typing screen, retrieve the file named SAMPLE by using either the LIST (F5) or the RETRIEVE (Shift + F10) key. (Both methods for retrieving a document are described in Chapter 2.)

2. Make sure the cursor is at the top left corner of the document.

3. Press the FORMAT (Shift + F8) key. [*Pulldown menu:* Layout (L).] The Format menu appears.

4. Select Line (1 or L). The Line Format menu appears, as shown in Figure 4-3. Notice that option 7, Margins, indicates that the current default settings are 1″ for both the left and right margins.

5. Select Margins Left and Right (7 or M).

6. Type **1.5″** and press Enter to set a left margin. (Word-Perfect automatically assumes inches and inserts the ″ symbol if you don't type it.)

7. Type **1″** and press Enter to set a right margin.

8. Press EXIT (F7) to return to the Typing screen.

9. Press ↓ to readjust the text on screen.

Word wrap has readjusted the text to fit properly within the new margin settings. Notice that with the cursor at the left margin the position indicator on the status line now reads **Pos** 1.5″ indicating a new left margin setting. This is because the Margin code **[L/R Mar:1.5″,1″]** has been inserted at the top of the document. This code overrides the default settings. Since it is the only margin code in the document and is at the top, it affects the entire document.

What if you wish the bottom portion of the text to have different margins? In that case, you would insert a second Margin code farther down in the text. Let's set the bottom portion of the text to wider margins of 2.5″ on both the left and the right.

1. Position the cursor on the "C" at the left margin on the line that reads "Contact THE R&R WINE. . . ."

2. Press the FORMAT ( Shift + F8 ) key. [*Pulldown menu:* Layout (L).] The Format menu appears.

3. Select Line (1 or L). The Line Format menu appears. Notice on your screen that option 7, Margins, indicates that the current settings are 1.5″ for the left margin and 1″ for the right margin. This is a result of the Margin code we previously inserted at the top of the document.

4. Select Margins Left and Right (7 or M).

5. Type **2.5″** and press Enter to set a left margin. (Word-Perfect automatically assumes inches and inserts the ″ symbol if you don't type it.)

6. Type **2.5″** and press Enter to set a right margin.

7. Press EXIT ( F7 ) to return to the Typing screen.

8. Press ⬇ to rewrite the text on screen.

You have just inserted a second Margin code **[L/R Mar:2.5″,2.5″]** into the text so that the first and second halves of the document have different margin settings. The first Margin code stays in control of the text up to the point where the second code appears. Though the codes are invisible, they can be viewed if you reveal codes.

# REVISE MARGIN CODES

It is common to change your mind once you've reset your margins (or changed any other format). If you wish to cancel a margin change, you must find and erase the **[L/R Mar:]** code that controls it. And, if you wish to revise a margin change, you must erase the existing code and insert a new one. Remember from Chapter 1 that to uncover the location of a code, you can use the Reveal Codes screen. If you don't know where the Margin code is hiding, the Reveal Codes screen enables you to find it quickly. Let's reveal codes to view those codes you just set and erase the second Margin code:

1. Position the cursor on the "C" in "Contact THE R&R. . . ."

2. Press the REVEAL CODES ((Alt) + (F3)) key. [*Pull-down menu:* Edit (E), Reveal Codes (R).] In the bottom window, you should be able to spot the **[L/R Mar:2.5″,2.5″]** code.

3. If the cursor is just to the right of the Margin code, press (Backspace) to delete the code. If the cursor is on the Margin code, press (Del) to delete the code.

4. Press REVEAL CODES ( [Alt] + [F3] ) to return to the Typing screen.

5. Press [Home], [Home], [↑] to move to the top of the document. As you can see, the bottom portion of the document has been adjusted to abide by the only Margin code in the text, which is located at the top of the document, dictating left and right margins of 1.5″ and 1″, respectively.

Now suppose that you wish to return the document to the default left and right margin settings of 1″. To do so, we must erase the **[L/R Mar:1.5″,1″]** code located at the top of the document; when WordPerfect finds no Margin codes in the text, the default margins will again take effect. Remember from Chapter 1 that you don't necessarily have to erase a code using the Reveal Codes screen. If you know where a code is hiding, you can erase it on the Typing screen.

When you attempt to erase a format code on the Typing screen, you'll find that WordPerfect always prompts to verify the deletion—just in case you don't realize that there's a format code that you're about to erase. If you wish to erase the code, type **Y**. If you bumped up against the code accidentally and don't wish to erase it, press [Enter] or type **N** or any key other than **Y**.

Let's erase the remaining Margin code on the Typing screen.

1. Press [Home], [Home], [↑] to position the cursor at the top of the document.

2. Press [Backspace] . WordPerfect prompts

`Delete [L/R Mar:1.5",1"]? No (Yes)`

WordPerfect is informing you that you have bumped up against a hidden code. Notice from the prompt that WordPerfect is assuming that you do not wish to delete this code, with the cursor under the "N" in "No."

3. Type **Y**. The margin code is deleted.

There are now no Margin codes in the text; if you press ⏎ to rewrite the screen, the text returns to the default settings.

But suppose you change your mind one more time; that is, you decide that you *did* want a left margin of 1.5″. In other words, you wish to reinstate the Margin code you just deleted. To do so, there are two alternatives. You could use the FORMAT ( Shift + F8 ) key over again to insert a new Margin code. An easier way, however, is to simply recover the deleted code using the Undelete feature, which you learned about in Chapter 1. (See the "Recover Deleted Text" section of Chapter 1 for a refresher.) The Undelete feature will work because you just deleted the Margin code:

1. Move the cursor to the top of the document, where you wish to reinsert the margin code.

2. Press CANCEL ( F1 ). [*Pulldown menu:* Edit (E), Undelete (U).] The Undelete menu appears:

Undelete: 1 Restore; 2 Previous Deletion: 0

No text appears in reverse video on screen because you just deleted a code — not text.

3. Select Restore (1 or R). The **[L/R Mar:1.5″,1″]** code is recovered, and the text readjusts for the new margins.

If you find the Undelete feature mysterious when work-ing with codes, just remember that on the Typing screen a code is hidden. You may wish to erase the Margin code again and this time switch to the REVEAL CODES screen key before you use the Undelete feature. In that way, you can view the Margin code as it reappears in the text.

# MODIFY A DOCUMENT'S JUSTIFICATION

Justification determines how text in a document is aligned in relation to the left and right margins. The default setting is for the text in paragraphs to be justified at both the left and right margins when printed; space between words is expanded or compressed to justify the text. This is referred to in version 5.1 as *Full Justification,* and in version 5.0 as *Justification On.* Since the justification feature is distinct in the two versions, it is next discussed separately for each version.

## Justification [5.1 Users]

WordPerfect 5.1 offers four alternatives for justifying text. Each is illustrated in Figure 4-4, as follows:

- *Full*   Text is aligned at both the left and right margins.

- *Left*   Text is aligned at the left margin, but ragged at the right margin.

- *Right*   Text is aligned at the right margin, but ragged at the left margin.

- *Center*   Text is centered between the margins, similar to the Center feature discussed in the previous chapter, but all lines of text are centered as a group, rather than as individual lines.

Full justification, the default setting, is common for newsletters and when working in text columns. It is also commonly used in reports and other standard documents, although you may prefer left justification in standard documents. Center and right justification are used for special effects or in tables.

As with margins, justification is altered for a document on the Line Format menu. Notice in Figure 4-3 that the menu indicates that justification is "Full," which is the default setting. When you select Justification (3 or J), the following menu displays:

`Justification: 1 Left; 2 Center; 3 Right; 4 Full: 0`

Select an item and then press EXIT (F7) to return to the Typing screen. WordPerfect inserts a Justification code at the current cursor position indicating the justification type you selected, such as **[Just:Left]** or **[Just:Right]**. All text from the code is affected to the end of the document or until the next Justification code you insert further forward in the text. If you change your mind and decide to return to the default setting for justification, erase the Justification code that you inserted.

You can alter the justification for an entire document, or for a portion of the text, depending on where you position the cursor before you display the Line Format menu. For instance, position the cursor at the top of the document to

**Full Justification**

Two of the major wine-producing countries in Europe are France and Italy. France produces a wide variety, and Bordeaux is often considered one of the centers of fine wine. In Italy, wine production takes place in just about every region. Italy has been known to yield more wine per year than any other country in the world.

**Left Justification**

Two of the major wine-producing countries in Europe are France and Italy. France produces a wide variety, and Bordeaux is often considered one of the centers of fine wine. In Italy, wine production takes place in just about every region. Italy has been known to yield more wine per year than any other country in the world.

**Right Justification**

Two of the major wine-producing countries in Europe are France and Italy. France produces a wide variety, and Bordeaux is often considered one of the centers of fine wine. In Italy, wine production takes place in just about every region. Italy has been known to yield more wine per year than any other country in the world.

**Center Justification**

Two of the major wine-producing countries in Europe are France and Italy. France produces a wide variety, and Bordeaux is often considered one of the centers of fine wine. In Italy, wine production takes place in just about every region. Italy has been known to yield more wine per year than any other country in the world.

**FIGURE 4-4**  Printed results with different justification types (version 5.1)

alter justification for the entire document. Or, position the cursor at the top of page two and insert a **[Just:Left]** code to turn on left justification for page 2 and all pages that follow. Or, select center justification for only the fourth through sixth paragraphs by inserting a **[Just:Center]** just before the fourth paragraph and then inserting a **[Just: Full]** code just after the sixth paragraph to return the rest of the document to full justification.

In fact, if you wish to modify the justification for one section in the middle of the text (such as the fourth through sixth paragraphs) to either right or center justification and then return the rest of the text to the original justification setting, it is even simpler to do so using the Block feature. Highlight the block and then, with Block on, select right justification by pressing the FLUSH RIGHT ( [Alt] + [F6] ) key. Or, choose center justification by pressing the CENTER ( [Shift] + [F6] ) key. WordPerfect prompts you for verification that you wish to right justify or center the block; type **Y** for Yes if you wish to do so. WordPerfect inserts a **[Just:Right]** or **[Just:Center]** at the start of the block, and then inserts another Justification code at the end of the block that returns the justification to its original setting, such as **[Just:Full]** if full justification was in effect above the block.

It is important to note that all but full justification are displayed on screen. With full justification, text on screen appears with a ragged right margin, as if left justification were in effect. This is because your computer screen cannot expand or compress spaces the way that your printer can. Full justification occurs only when you print out your document (or if you use the View Document feature to preview the printed result, as described in Chapter 9). So, remember that full justification is not displayed on the Typing screen; it looks instead like left justification.

## Justification [5.0 Users]

Version 5.0 offers two alternatives for justifying text. These are illustrated in Figure 4-5, as follows:

- *Justification On*  Text is aligned at both the left and right margin.
- *Justification Off*  Text is aligned at the left margin, but ragged at the right margin.

The default setting is for justification on. As with margins, justification is altered for a document on the Line Format menu. When you select Justification (3 or J), you

**Justification On**

Two of the major wine-producing countries in Europe are France and Italy. France produces a wide variety, and Bordeaux is often considered one of the centers of fine wine. In Italy, wine production takes place in just about every region. Italy has been known to yield more wine per year than any other country in the world.

**Justification Off**

Two of the major wine-producing countries in Europe are France and Italy. France produces a wide variety, and Bordeaux is often considered one of the centers of fine wine. In Italy, wine production takes place in just about every region. Italy has been known to yield more wine per year than any other country in the world.

**FIGURE 4-5**  Printed results with justification on and off (version 5.0)

can then type **N** for No, to turn justification off, or, if you previously turned it off, type **Y** for Yes, to turn justification on. Then press EXIT (F7) to return to the Typing screen. WordPerfect inserts a justification code at the current cursor position indicating the justification type you selected, either **[Just Off]** or **[Just On]**. All text after the code is affected to the end of the document or until the next Justification code you insert further forward in the text. If you change your mind and decide to return to the default setting for justification, erase the Justification code that you inserted.

You can alter the justification for an entire document, or for a portion of the text, depending on where you position the cursor before you display the Line Format menu. For instance, position the cursor at the top of the document to alter justification for the entire document. Or, position the cursor at the top of page two and insert a **[Just Off]** code to turn off justification for page 2 and all pages that follow.

It is important to note that when justification is on, it is not shown on the Typing screen. Text on screen appears with a ragged right margin. This is because your computer screen cannot expand or compress spaces the way that your printer can. Justification occurs only when you print out your document (or if you use the View Document feature to preview the printed result, as described in Chapter 9).

(In version 5.0, center or flush right justification is not available from the Line Format menu, as it is for version 5.1 users. However, you can get the same effect by specifying that a certain block of text be centered or aligned flush right. Highlight the block and then, with Block on, select right justification by pressing the FLUSH RIGHT (Alt + F6) key. Or, choose center justification by pressing the CENTER (Shift + F6) key. See Chapter 3 for more details.)

# Change the Justification Setting
# [5.1 and 5.0 Users]

Let's alter justification in the document on screen so that the text in paragraphs is justified only at the left margin, and is ragged at the right margin. In WordPerfect terms, 5.1 users will want to change justification to "left," while 5.0 users will want to turn justification to "off."

Before you begin, notice that on screen, the right margin of text currently looks ragged, even though the default setting, which calls for an even right margin, is in effect. Thus, even though you are about to change to a ragged right margin, text on screen will appear no different once you alter this setting (although word wrap may readjust the ends of lines slightly).

1. Press [Home], [Home], [↑] to position the cursor at the top of the document.

2. Press the FORMAT ([Shift] + [F8]) key. [*Pulldown menu:* Layout (L).]

3. Select Line (1 or L). The Line Format menu appears.

4. Select Justification (3 or J).

5. *5.1 users:* Select Left (1 or L). *5.0 users:* Type **N** to turn off justification.

6. Press EXIT ([F7]) to return to the text of your document.

Remember that it is at the printer, and not on screen, that a change from an even right to a ragged right margin is shown. But, if you reveal codes, you can verify that you

inserted a Justification code, and thus that the text produced by the printer will no longer have an even right
margin. By printing the document, you can also see the
change; you will be directed to print out your results further on in this chapter.

# WORK WITH HYPHENATION

Hyphens at the ends of lines can improve the look of the
printed page. Figure 4-6 illustrates the line-by-line differences for identical text with and without hyphenation,

---

**Hyphenation Off**

Here is a standard paragraph to show the
noticeable effects of hyphenation in your
documents. Hyphenation is off as the default
but can be turned on easily enough.
Hyphenation is preferred by some people but
disliked by others.

**Hyphenation On**

Here is a standard paragraph to show the noticeable effects of hyphenation in your documents. Hyphenation is off as the default but
can be turned on easily enough. Hyphenation
is preferred by some people but disliked by
others.

---

**FIGURE 4-6**   Hyphenation effects with a ragged right
margin

assuming a ragged right margin (which, as just discussed, is referred to as "Left Justification" in version 5.1 and "Justification Off" in version 5.0). Notice how the right margin is *less* ragged with hyphenation in effect; that is, there are smaller gaps at the right side of the text. If justification is set for an even right margin, then hyphenation has another effect; it reduces the number of extra spaces necessary to make the right margin straight.

The default is for hyphenation off, so that WordPerfect automatically wraps down to the next line any word that extends too far beyond the right margin. When you turn hyphenation on, words at the ends of lines become candidates for hyphenation. First let's explore how WordPerfect decides what words to hyphenate. Then you'll learn how to turn on and use the Hyphenation feature—which is different for version 5.1 users than for 5.0 users.

## The Hyphenation Zone

Which words are candidates for hyphenation depends on what in WordPerfect is called the *hyphenation zone*. This zone has a left boundary and a right boundary, both measured as a percentage of the line's length and based on the right margin location. The default is for a left hyphenation zone of 10% and a right hyphenation zone of 4%. So, for instance, let's take a line that is 6.5″ long (as is the case when all the default settings are intact—your paper width is 8.5″ and left/right margins are 1″). The left hyphenation zone equals 10% of 6.5″, or 0.65″. The right hyphenation zone equals 4% of 6.5″, or 0.26″. (You may be surprised that the right hyphenation zone is not set at 0%. The default setting is greater than 0% so that text can extend a bit beyond the right margin, which allows for a more reliable average right margin setting.) So, here's the hyphenation zone in relation to the right margin:

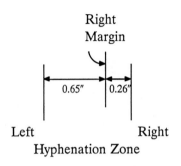

Only if a word starts on or before the left hyphenation zone boundary and extends past the right hyphenation zone boundary is it a candidate for hyphenation. Figure 4-7 illustrates words at the end of four separate lines in a document. The first two words, "Approximately" and "Volleyball," are candidates for hyphenation. The word "Dictionary" does not extend far enough to be hyphenated, and so would remain at the end of the current line. The word "Personal" begins after the start of the hyphenation zone, so the entire word would be wrapped down to the next line.

You can widen the hyphenation zone by inserting larger percentages; as a result, fewer words will be candidates for hyphenation. Or, you can narrow the hyphenation zone by inserting smaller percentages; as a result, more words will be candidates for hyphenation. For instance, suppose you change the left hyphenation zone to 5% and the right hyphenation zone to 0%. The percentages are now less, so

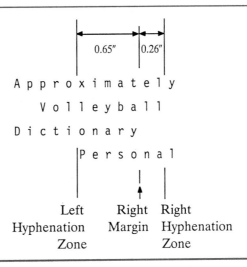

**FIGURE 4-7** The hyphenation zone dictates that only the first two words are hyphenation candidates

you have narrowed the hyphenation zone: the left hyphenation zone equals 5% of 6.5″, or 0.325″, and the right hyphenation zone equals 0% of 6.5″, or 0″. As a result, all of the words in Figure 4-7 would now become hyphenation candidates.

It is unnecessary to change a document's hyphenation zone before turning on hyphenation. You can simply use the default setting. But, if you wish to change the default, position the cursor where in the document you wish the new hyphenation zone to take effect. Then, from the Line Format menu (which you previously used to alter margins and justification), select Hyphenation Zone (2 or Z). Type a new left hyphenation zone setting and press ⌊Enter⌋. You can simply type in a number, such as 5, without the percent sign because WordPerfect assumes percentages and inserts the percent sign once you press (Enter). Next, type the right hyphenation zone setting and press (Enter). Now, press EXIT ((F7)) to return to the Typing screen.

WordPerfect inserts a Hyphenation Zone code at the current cursor position indicating the settings, such as **[HZone:5%,0%]**. All text from the code to the end of the document will be examined for possible hyphenation based on that new hyphenation zone setting—provided that hyphenation has also been turned on for that portion of the text, as described shortly.

Let's alter the hyphenation zone. You'll narrow the zone, so that more words have the potential to be hyphenation candidates when, in the next section, you turn on hyphenation.

1. Press (Home), (Home), (↑) if the cursor is not already at the top of the document.

2. Press the FORMAT ((Shift) + (F8)) key. [*Pulldown menu:* Layout.]

3. Select Line (1 or L). Notice that, as shown in Figure 4-3, the current hyphenation zone settings are 10% and 4%.

4. Select Hyphenation Zone (2 or Z).

5. Type **5**, press (Enter), type **0**, and press (Enter). Notice that WordPerfect assumes that you are entering the hyphenation zone in percentage numbers, so the % symbol is inserted automatically.

6. Finally, press EXIT ((F7)). You have now inserted a **[HZone:5%,0%]** code at the top of the document.

## Turn Hyphenation On/Off

If you plan to use hyphenation in a document, you can turn it on at any time, such as before you begin typing or after editing. To turn hyphenation on, move the cursor to the line where you want hyphenation to begin—for instance, at the top of the document if you want to initiate hyphenation for the entire document. If you've previously inserted a Hyphenation Zone code (as described earlier) in the location where you want hyphenation to begin, position the cursor next to that code. Then, from the Line Format menu, select Hyphenation (1 or Y). The last steps depend on whether you use WordPerfect version 5.1 or 5.0.

*5.1 users:* Type **Y** for Yes to turn hyphenation on, or, if you previously turned it on, you can type **N** for No, to turn it off. Then press EXIT (F7) to return to the Typing screen.

*5.0 users:* A menu appears at the bottom of the screen for you to select from, as follows:

`1 Off; 2 Manual; 3 Auto: 0`

Off (1 or F) turns off hyphenation if it had been turned on previously. Manual (2 or M) turns on hyphenation whereby WordPerfect will always prompt, asking for you to indicate where to position the hyphen in each word to be hyphenated. Auto (3 or A) turns on hyphenation whereby WordPerfect will determine the positioning of the hyphen and will prompt for a hyphenation decision only when WordPerfect cannot determine it. Once you make a selection, press EXIT (F7) to return to the Typing screen.

Whether you are a 5.1 or 5.0 user, a **[Hyph Off]** code is inserted when you turn off hyphenation, while a **[Hyph On]** code is inserted when you turn on hyphenation. For text already typed that exists forward from the **[Hyph On]** code, WordPerfect checks for hyphenation candidates when you move the cursor or begin to edit. Or, if no text exists below the **[Hyph On]** code, WordPerfect checks for hyphenation candidates as you type. As previously discussed, Word-Perfect determines which words require hyphenation based on the current settings for the hyphenation zone.

Should a word require hyphenation, WordPerfect will try to determine where to hyphenate the word. In version 5.1, WordPerfect uses a special hyphenation dictionary named WP{WP}US.HYC and the Speller dictionary named WP{WP}.LEX to determine where to hyphenate. For hard disk users these are housed along with the Speller files on the hard disk and for floppy disk users on the Speller disk. (If you attempt to hyphenate and WordPerfect responds indicating that this file is not found, then hard disk users must install this file properly wherever the Speller files are found; see the section "Install WordPerfect" in Appendix A for details. Floppy disk users must insert the Speller disk into drive B to access the hyphenation dictionary.) In version 5.0, WordPerfect uses an internal formula to determine where to hyphenate.

Once WordPerfect analyzes where to insert a hyphen, it responds in one of two ways. Sometimes, WordPerfect will hyphenate the word automatically, inserting a *soft hyphen* for you. The hyphen is "soft" because it will disappear if, later on, you edit your text in such a way that the word containing the hyphen no longer requires hyphenation. A soft hyphen looks on the Typing screen like a regular hyphen. Reveal codes, however, and you can see the difference. Whereas a hyphen character that you type appears on the Reveal Codes screen bolded and in brackets [-], a soft hyphen appears bolded but without brackets -. A regular hyphen remains in the text; a soft hyphen vanishes if it is no longer required, and thus is the appropriate style of hyphen to insert for hyphenation.

Other times, WordPerfect will display a prompt at the bottom of the screen, asking you to determine the location of the hyphen, but suggesting a hyphen location. For instance, suppose the word "approximately" needs hyphenation. WordPerfect may prompt with that word at the bottom of the screen as follows (you may be unable to see where that word is located in the actual text):

```
Position hyphen; Press ESC   approxi-mately
```

In this example, WordPerfect is suggesting that you hyphenate between the "i" and "m" in "approximately." You have three choices for the WordPerfect prompt:

- To accept the hyphen location suggestion, simply press the (Esc) key; a soft hyphen is inserted wherever suggested by WordPerfect.

- To reject the suggestion and reposition the hyphen, use the (→) or (←) key to relocate the hyphen. (Sometimes, the area in which you can move the cursor within the word is limited, due to the size of the hyphenation zone.) Then, press (Esc); a soft hyphen is inserted wherever you indicated.

- To cancel hyphenation for that one word, press the CANCEL ((F1)) key; a cancel hyphenation code [/] is inserted before that word (only displayed on the Reveal Codes screen), and the entire word is wrapped down to the beginning of the next line. (Also, if WordPerfect prompts and you wish to temporarily cancel hyphenation, press the EXIT ((F7)) key.)

*5.1 users:* WordPerfect almost always inserts a hyphen automatically; WordPerfect prompts for a cursor position only when the program cannot determine a proper hyphenation location. This is because WordPerfect is set up, by default, to use the special hyphenation dictionary, WP{WP}US.HYC.

*5.0 users:* If you select Auto from the Hyphenation menu, WordPerfect inserts hyphens on its own, prompting only in rare instances when it cannot determine a proper location for the hyphen. If you select Manual, however, then a prompt will appear in every instance where Word-Perfect encounters a hyphenation candidate.

*Note:* 5.1 users have the ability to alter the procedure by which WordPerfect hyphenates, changing the default so that WordPerfect *always* prompts you, or, conversely, *never* prompts you. In addition, you can dictate that instead of using WP{WP}US.HYC to determine hyphenation, Word-Perfect use an internal dictionary; see the section entitled "Environment" in Appendix B for details.

5.0 users have the ability to change the source Word-Perfect uses to determine where to hyphenate each word. Normally, WordPerfect hyphenates based on its own internal rules; however, if you plan to use auto hyphenation in your documents, you should know that WordPerfect Corporation offers a hyphenation module for version 5.0, where words are hyphenated according to a dictionary and, therefore, where the hyphenation is more reliable. The hyphenation module is sold separately. Contact Word-Perfect Corporation for details.

You may prefer to turn hyphenation on before you type your document, in which case WordPerfect will hyphenate as you type. Or, you may prefer to turn on hyphenation after completing a document, in which case you would position the cursor at the top of the completed document, turn on hyphenation, and then move the cursor down to the bottom of the document, which triggers WordPerfect to check for hyphenation candidates. The choice is up to you. However, you may wish to wait until you've finished typing, so you won't continually be bothered with hyphenation prompts. And, if you are a 5.1 user and are working on a floppy disk system, consider hyphenating a document after you type it, so that you can keep the Speller disk in drive B while the Hyphenation feature is operating.

For the document on screen, let's turn on hyphenation. Then you'll edit the text by inserting a new word, and watch as hyphenation readjusts.

1. Press [Home], [Home], [↑] if the cursor is not already at the top of the document.

2. Press the FORMAT ([Shift] + [F8]) key. [*Pulldown menu:* Layout.]

3. Select Line (1 or L).

4. Select Hyphenation (1 or Y).

5. *5.1 Users:* Type **Y**. *5.0 Users:* Select either Auto (1 or A) or Manual (2 or M).

6. Press EXIT ([F7]). You have now inserted a **[Hyph On]** code at the top of the document.

7. Press [↓] to readjust the text. For some of you, hyphens may appear in your text. For others, WordPerfect may request hyphenation, with a prompt such as:

```
Position hyphen; Press ESC    Bor-deaux
```

In that case, either press CANCEL ([F1]) so as not to hyphenate, or press [Esc] to hyphenate.

8. Position the cursor at the end of the second line of text on screen, just after the phrase "France produces a wide variety, and"

9. Insert a space, type **delightful,** and press ⬇ to reformat the text. WordPerfect may hyphenate "delightful," or prompt for you to position the cursor. Respond to all remaining hyphenation prompts.

Your document will now contain one or more hyphenated words. Here's an example of part of what you may be viewing now on screen:

```
Two of the major wine-producing countries in Europe are
France and Italy. France produces a wide variety, and de-
lightful Bordeaux is often considered one of the centers of
fine wine.
```

Remember that hyphens inserted during hyphenation are "soft" hyphens, so that they will vanish later if you edit so that the words containing the soft hyphens no longer fall at the end of a line. For instance, if you were to edit the first two sentences above and then press ⬇ to adjust the text, the hyphen in "delightful" will vanish:

```
Two of the wine-producing countries in Europe are France and
Italy. France produces a variety, and delightful Bordeaux
is often considered one of the centers of fine wine.
```

The soft hyphen remains as a hidden code even if it disappears from the Typing screen; it stays around in case you edit further and the hyphen is again required.

Once WordPerfect inserts hyphens at the end of lines in your document, you may change your mind and decide to reposition hyphens in various locations, or even cancel hyphenation of certain words. You can do so manually. To reposition the hyphen in a word, insert a soft hyphen on your own by pressing Ctrl + hyphen, and then delete the soft hyphen that previously existed there; WordPerfect will reposition the hyphen if it is allowed in the hyphenation zone. (Remember that pressing the hyphen without first pressing the Ctrl key inserts a hyphen character that remains in the word regardless of where that word falls on a line, which is appropriate for words such as "wine-producing" or "mother-in-law," but not when you want the hyphen to disappear if a word moves away from the margin during editing.) In addition, to cancel hyphenation of a word, position the cursor in front of the word containing a soft hyphen, press Home, / to insert the code [/]. Then, delete the soft hyphen.

Table 4-1 provides a summary of the methods for inserting hyphens or canceling hyphenation for a word. (One style, the hard hyphen, was discussed in Chapter 3, but is included here so that you have a table of the full spectrum of hyphen styles.)

# MODIFY LINE SPACING

Line spacing increases or decreases the amount of space between lines. WordPerfect assumes you want all your text single spaced. To alter spacing, you must position the cursor at the left margin of the line where you want to make

| Hyphen Style | Key Sequence | Hidden Code | Purpose |
|---|---|---|---|
| Hyphen Character | hyphen | [-] | Inserts a hyphen that always remains in a word. |
| Soft Hyphen | Ctrl + hyphen | - | Inserts a hyphen that remains only when a word falls at the end of a line. |
| Hard Hyphen | Home, hyphen | - | Inserts a hyphen and also ensures that a word remains together on one line. |
| Cancel Hyphenation | Home, / | [/] | Negates hyphenation for a word, so it remains together on one line without hyphenation. |

**TABLE 4-1** Methods for Inserting Hyphens

the change, and, as with margins, justification, and hyphenation, use the Line Format menu to make the change. Select Line Spacing (6 or S), and then enter the spacing you desire—providing that your printer supports the spacing increment you entered. For instance, you can type **2** to request double spacing, or **1.5** to change to one-and-one-half-line spacing. Some printers will even support fractional spacing such as **1.25** or **1.1**, allowing you the flexibility to refine the spacing between lines.

The screen can show spacing only to the nearest whole number. If you selected one-and-one-half-line spacing, for example, the screen will show double spacing, but when printed, the text will have one-and-one-half spacing. A **[Ln Spacing:]** code is inserted when you change line spacing, affecting all text down to the next spacing code or the end of the document.

Here's the step-by-step procedure to double space the document that is currently on screen.

1. Press [Home], [Home], [↑]. The cursor moves to the top of the document.

2. Press the FORMAT ([Shift] + [F8]) key. [*Pulldown menu:* Layout (L).]

3. Select Line (1 or L). Notice that, as shown in Figure 4-3, the number 1 appears next to the Line Spacing option. The **1** indicates that the document is currently single spaced.

4. Select Line Spacing (6 or S).

5. Type **2** and press [Enter].

6. Press EXIT ([F7]) to return to the document. The entire document is now double spaced.

*Note:* Technically, WordPerfect determines the spacing between lines of text on the printed page by multiplying line spacing by a feature called line height, which is the amount of space assigned to a single line. For instance, a common line height is 0.16″. As a result, 0.16″ times single spacing means that lines will be printed 0.16″ apart, so that there will be six lines per one vertical inch. Or, 0.16″ times double spacing means that lines will be printed 0.32″ apart. See Chapter 10 for more on the Line Height feature and your ability to control the amount of space assigned to each line of text.

# LEARN MORE ABOUT FORMAT CODES

The format codes that you inserted thus far in this chapter are referred to as *open* codes. A format code is "open" because it takes effect from its position forward—all the way to the end of the document or until it is overshadowed by another code of the same type. (These codes for formatting a document are distinct from the *paired* codes for features such as underlining or boldfacing, which, as you learned about in Chapter 3, are inserted to mark the boundaries of text.) Thus, it is critical to position the cursor properly before you insert any format codes in your text. And it is important to keep those codes in mind when you edit your text.

But when your documents become intricate, with numerous format codes throughout, it becomes difficult to remember what changes you have made and where they take effect. You can find out by switching to the Reveal Codes screen. You can reveal codes and scroll down through the document to survey the location of format codes. And, of course, you can erase any codes you no longer desire or that you inserted by accident.

In fact, inserting extra or unwanted codes is quite common, especially for beginners. For example, you may set margins and then, realizing you made a typing mistake in entering the margins, insert another Margin code to reset them. You would then have two codes side by side in the text.

```
[L/R Mar:2.5",2.5"][L/R Mar:1.5",1.5"]
```

Remember that a format code's effect on a document is canceled as soon as another code of the same type is encountered farther on in the text. As a result, the first Margin code's effect on the text is overshadowed by the second code; in the example, the 1.5″ margins will control the text. Nonetheless, you will still want to delete that first, unnecessary code.

Why delete extra codes? They have a tendency to create problems. For instance, if you happened to position the cursor between two **[L/R Mar:]** codes and then began typing, the first code would affect the new text, and the results might be awkward. Therefore, always tidy up your documents by erasing unwanted codes.

Let's reveal codes to check the format settings. Once you have verified that the format settings are correct, you'll print the document to see the changes.

1. Press Home, Home, ↑ to position the cursor at the top of the document.

2. Press the REVEAL CODES (Alt + F3) key. [*Pull-down menu:* Edit (E), Reveal Codes (R).] You should see a long string of codes in the bottom window, as shown in Figure 4-8. (Your codes may appear in a different order.)

3. Check your screen against Figure 4-8. If there are extra codes shown in the bottom window, delete them. Posi-

tion the cursor just to the right of an unwanted code and press [Backspace] , or position it on the code and press [Del] .

4. If any codes are missing, insert them as described earlier in this chapter. (*5.0 users:* If the Justification code refuses to appear, it may be that the default for your copy of WordPerfect has been set for right justification off. If so, it would be unnecessary to insert a **[Just Off]** code.)

5. Press REVEAL CODES ([Alt] + [F3]) to return to the typing screen.

6. Turn on your printer, insert paper, and print the page. One quick way to do so is to press the PRINT ([Shift] + [F7]) key and select Page (2 or P).

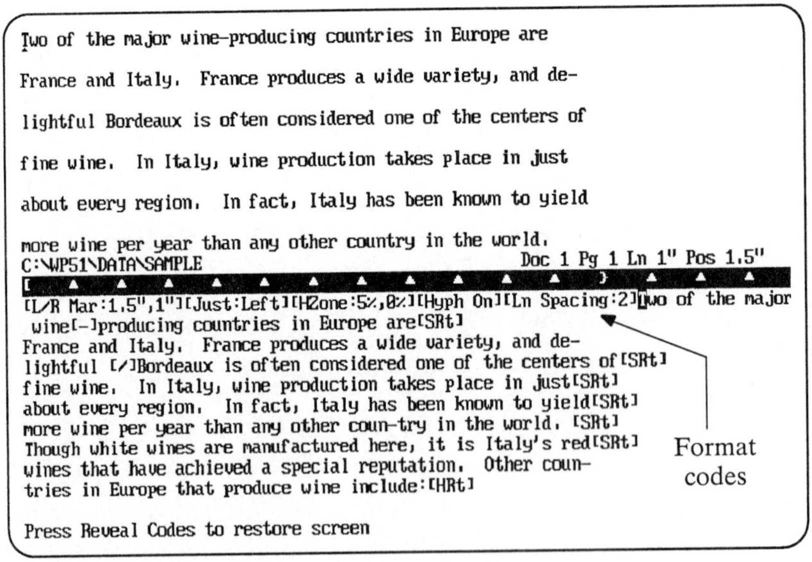

---

```
Two of the major wine-producing countries in Europe are

France and Italy.  France produces a wide variety, and de-

lightful Bordeaux is often considered one of the centers of

fine wine.  In Italy, wine production takes place in just

about every region.  In fact, Italy has been known to yield

more wine per year than any other country in the world.
C:\WP51\DATA\SAMPLE                                Doc 1 Pg 1 Ln 1" Pos 1.5"
[   ▲    ▲    ▲    ▲    ▲    ▲    ▲    ▲    ▲    ▲  }  ▲    ▲    ▲
[L/R Mar:1.5",1"][Just:Left][HZone:5%,8%][Hyph On][Ln Spacing:2]Two of the major
wine[-]producing countries in Europe are[SRt]
France and Italy.  France produces a wide variety, and de-
lightful [/]Bordeaux is often considered one of the centers of[SRt]
fine wine.  In Italy, wine production takes place in just[SRt]
about every region.  In fact, Italy has been known to yield[SRt]    Format
more wine per year than any other coun-try in the world. [SRt]      codes
Though white wines are manufactured here, it is Italy's red[SRt]
wines that have achieved a special reputation.  Other coun-
tries in Europe that produce wine include:[HRt]

Press Reveal Codes to restore screen
```

---

**FIGURE 4-8** Numerous format codes on the Reveal Codes screen (version 5.1)

You should see the following results:

| | |
|---|---|
| Left and right margins | 1.5″ and 1″, respectively |
| Justification | Left (5.1 users) or Off (5.0 users) |
| Hyphenation | On, with various words hyphenated according to the new hyphenation zone setting |
| Spacing | Double |

These format changes affect only the document currently on screen. If you clear the screen to begin typing a new document, the new document starts out with all the default settings.

Now let's save this document on disk with the changes made to it and then clear the screen:

1. Press the EXIT ([F7]) key, type **Y**, and press [Enter] to save the document on screen under the filename SAMPLE.

2. Type **Y** when WordPerfect asks whether you wish to replace SAMPLE.

3. Type **N** when WordPerfect asks whether you wish to exit the program.

The screen is clear, and the revised document is safely stored on disk, format codes and all. You are returned to the default settings on the Typing screen, ready to begin a new document. Notice, for example, that with the cursor at the left margin of the blank screen, the status line indicates **Pos 1″**: 1″ is the default left margin setting.

# CHANGE TAB STOP LOCATIONS

As you've previously learned, the default for tab stop locations is every 0.5″ across the full width of a page. But you can alter your tab stop locations. For instance, you may wish to type a report where you indent all paragraphs 0.75″. Or, you may wish to type a table comprised of three columns, one starting at 1.4″, another at 3.5″, and a third at 6.0″.

Moreover, you can change not only the location of tab stops, but the style of tab stops as well. The default tab style is left justified, which means that when you press the ⟨Tab⟩ key and then type text, that text is aligned with its left edge (first character) at the tab stop. The left-justified style is the most commonly used tab style—to indent the first line of a paragraph or to align text in tables. But there are actually four tab stop styles:

- *Left*  Text is aligned with its left edge at the tab stop.

- *Right*  Text is aligned with its right edge at the tab stop (like the FLUSH RIGHT key).

- *Decimal*  Text is aligned with a specific character (usually the decimal point) at the tab stop (like the TAB ALIGN key).

- *Center*  Text is centered at the tab stop (like the CENTER key).

In addition, the left, right, and decimal styles can all be preceded by a dot leader, meaning that when you press ⟨Tab⟩, a row of dots is inserted as the cursor jumps to the next tab stop. Figure 4-9 shows the effects of the various tab styles.

You change tab settings and styles on the Line Format menu, the same menu used to alter other features discussed in this chapter, such as left/right margins. On the

**Without Dot Leaders:**

| Center | Left | Right | Decimal |
|--------|------|-------|---------|
| ^ | ^ | ^ | ^ |
| 1 | June | Smith | $ 33.66 |
| 222 | Peter | Wild | 5.00 |
| 33333 | Marilyn | Gold | 1,236.17 |
| 4444444 | Kim | Wallens | 14.50 |

**With Dot Leaders:**

| | Left | Right | Decimal |
|--|------|-------|---------|
| | ^ | ^ | ^ |
| 1. . . . . . . . | June . . . . . | Smith . . . . . | $33.66 |
| 222. . . . . . . | Peter . . . . . | Wild . . . . . . | 5.00 |
| 33333. . . . . . | Marilyn . . . . | Gold . . . . | 1,236.17 |
| 4444444. . . . . | Kim. . . . . | Wallens . . . . . | .14.50 |

^ represents tab stop location

===== **FIGURE 4-9** Tab stop styles

Line Format menu, select Tab Set (8 or S). WordPerfect displays at the bottom of the Typing screen a Tab menu. On the Tab menu a tab ruler displays the current tab settings, where the letter L represents the location of a left-justified tab, R represents a right-justified tab, D represents a decimal-aligned tab, and C represents a center tab. If any of the letters L, R, or D is highlighted, this represents a tab stop that has been defined for a dot leader.

*5.1 users:* Here's the Tab menu, assuming the default settings:

```
L....L....L....L....L....L....L....L....L....L....L....L....L....L....L....L...
   !    ^    !    ^    !    ^    !    ^    !    ^    !    ^    !    ^    !    ^
  0"       +1"       +2"       +3"       +4"       +5"       +6"       +7"
Delete EOL (clear tabs); Enter Number (set tab); Del (clear tab);
Type; Left; Center; Right; Decimal; .= Dot Leader; Press Exit when done.
```

In version 5.1, position 0″ corresponds to the left margin. The tabs that you set are *relative* to the left margin. For that reason, the tab ruler shows a plus sign "+" in front of the inch measurements on the Tab menu; this indicates a relative measurement from the margin and to the right. (A minus sign "−" would indicate a relative measurement from the margin and to the left.) When you change your left margin setting, the tab stops will shift by a corresponding amount. For instance, suppose that the left margin is currently at 1″ and you want a tab stop 0.6″ from the margin. In that case, set a tab stop at location 0.6″. If you later increase the left margin to 1.5″, that tab stop will shift so that it remains 0.6″ from the left margin.

*5.0 users:* Here's the Tab menu, assuming the default settings:

```
L....L....L....L....L....L....L....L....L....L....L....L....L....L....L....L...
   !    ^    !    ^    !    ^    !    ^    !    ^    !    ^    !    ^    !    ^
  1"       2"        3"        4"        5"        6"        7"        8"
Delete EOL (clear tabs); Enter Number (set tab); Del (clear tab);
Left; Center; Right; Decimal; .= Dot Leader; Press Exit when done.
```

In version 5.0, position 0″ corresponds to the left edge of the page. The tabs that you set are *absolute,* which means that they are set based on the left edge of the page and have no relevance to the left margin. For instance, suppose that the left margin is currently at 1″ and you want a tab stop 0.6″ from the margin. In that case, set a tab stop at location 1.6″. If you later increase the left margin to 1.5″, that tab stop will remain at location 1.6″, which is now only

0.1″ from the left margin. As a result, you may wish to decide on and, if necessary, change your margins before setting new tab stops. And keep these margins in mind when setting new tab stop locations.

*5.1 users only:* You can instead switch to the absolute type of tab as discussed above for 5.0 users; from the Tab menu, type **T**. The following menu appears on the Tab menu:

`Tab Type: 1 Absolute; 2 Relative to Margins: 0`

Select Absolute (1 or A) and the plus signs disappear from the Tab menu. If you select Relative to Margins (2 or R), the pluses reappear.

On the Tab menu for both 5.1 and 5.0 users, there are two ways to delete tab stops. To delete a single tab stop, use the ➡ or the ⬅ key to position the cursor on the tab stop and press Del. To delete *all* tab stops from the current cursor position to the right end of the row, position the cursor on the first tab stop you wish to delete and press DELETE EOL ( Ctrl + End ). To delete every tab, including those left of the left margin, be sure to position the cursor at the very left end of the tab ruler before pressing Ctrl + End .

There are several ways to insert tab stops, depending on the number and style of tabs you wish to set:

- To insert a single, left-justified tab stop, you have two choices. You can either (1) move the cursor to the location where you want a tab stop and then type **L** or press Tab to insert a left-justified tab, or (2) type a location where you want a tab to appear and press Enter ; for instance, type **1.4″** and press Enter to place a tab at position 1.4″. When entering fractional numbers, precede them with a 0. For instance, type **0.5″** and not .5″.

- To insert a row of evenly spaced, left-justified tab stops, type the starting tab stop location, type a comma, type the incremental spacing, and press (Enter). For instance, to set tabs starting at the 1.5″ position and every inch after that, you would type **1.5″,1″** and press (Enter). (Or, more simply, you would type **1.5,1** and press (Enter); WordPerfect assumes inches.)

- To insert a single tab stop using a style other than left justified or using a dot leader, move the cursor to the location where you want a tab stop and type **R** to insert a right-justified tab, type **D** to insert a decimal tab, type **L** to insert a left-justified tab, or type **C** to insert a center tab. Then if you wish to create a dot leader, type a period; the "L," "R," or "D" on screen becomes highlighted in reverse video, signifying a tab with a dot leader.

- To insert a row of evenly spaced tab stops using a style other than left justified, first set a single tab at the starting tab stop location. Then enter the starting tab stop location and the incremental spacing, separated by a comma. For example, to set decimal tabs every inch starting at position 2.4″, first set a single decimal tab at position 2.4″. Then type **2.4,1** and press (Enter).

Once tab stops are set to your specifications, press the EXIT ((F7)) key to leave the Tab menu.

A **[Tab Set:]** code is inserted into the text, listing each tab stop that you set. The code does not indicate the style of each tab stop, only the location. And, for 5.1 users, the code also indicates whether the tab stops are set as absolute or as relative to the margin. As an example, if you inserted two tab stops only, at positions 2″ and 3.4″, then the code for 5.1 users would be [**Tab Set:Rel: + 2″, + 3.4″**] or [**Tab Set:Abs:2″,3.4″**], depending on whether the tabs were set as absolute or relative. The code for 5.0 users would be [**Tab Set:2″,3.4″**]. Or, if you inserted tab stops starting at 1.5″ and every inch thereafter, the code inserted would be [**Tab Set:Rel: + 1.5″, every 1″**] or [**Tab Set:Abs:1.5″, every 1″**] for 5.1 users, and [**Tab Set:1.5″,every 1″**] for 5.0 users. If you set many individual tab stops, then the code can be quite long.

Like other format codes, the Tab Set code affects all text forward in the text, to the end of the document or until another code is encountered. Thus, you can insert a Tab Set code, type a table, and then insert another Tab Set code below the table to again change the tab settings. For instance, you can change the tab stops back to the default setting by positioning the cursor below a typed table, and then setting tabs as follows:

*5.1 users:* Relative tabs, starting at −1″, in increments of 0.5″ (−1″,0.5″)

*5.0 users:* Tabs starting at 0″, in increments of 0.5″ (0″,0.5″)

What happens if you insert a Tab Set code and then realize that you need to readjust the tab stop locations? You can erase the existing Tab Set code and insert a new one. However, a simpler method if you wish to readjust the tab stops only slightly is to reveal codes, position the cursor just to the right of the existing Tab Set code, and use the Line Format menu to again display the Tab menu. Because the cursor is located forward from the Tab Set codes, the recently set tab locations are shown on the tab ruler. Now, reset tabs and press EXIT (F7) to insert the new Tab Set code. Then you will have two codes side by side, the first code on the left and the newly revised code on the right, such as:

`[Tab Set:Rel:+2",+3.4",+5.5"] [Tab Set:Rel:+2",+3.4",+6.1"]`

Be sure to erase the *first* Tab Set code, which is the old code that you no longer desire, so that you clear the document of unnecessary codes. Existing text found below the code will adjust according to the new Tab Set code. (However, if you alter a tab stop style in addition to its location, version 5.1 users will find that existing text will be readjusted according to the new style, while version 5.0 users will find that the existing text will not be readjusted. Thus, 5.0 users may need to re-enter the text positioned on the tab stop with the new style.)

You learned previously that you use the Tab key to move the cursor from tab stop to tab stop when typing, such as when moving from place to place when typing a table. You also learned in Chapter 3 about other keys that can work on tab stops as well, such as →INDENT (F4) or CENTER (Shift + F6) or TAB ALIGN (Ctrl + F6), which cause different effects on tab stops. How do each of these keys work in relation to different tab stop styles? Pressing Tab to position the cursor preserves whatever tab style you set—whether left, right, center, or decimal—for one line of text. However, pressing another key overrides the tab style. For instance, suppose you set a tab stop with a right tab style. When you press Tab to move to that tab stop, a line of text will be right aligned. But when you press →INDENT to move to that tab stop, many lines of text will be left aligned. And when you press TAB ALIGN to move to that tab stop, the decimal point will be aligned on the tab stop (just as if you set a decimal tab).

Suppose you want to type the document shown in Figure 4-10. Follow the steps below to practice setting individual tabs and typing a table on the newly defined tab stops.

1. Starting with a clear Typing screen, press ⌷Tab⌷. So far, the default settings are in effect: the cursor moves 0.5" to the right.

2. Type the following paragraph:

   ```
   Here are the names that were left off the list of deliveries
   to the Northwestern territory.  Please make sure to add these
   names immediately:
   ```

3. Press ⌷Enter⌷ twice to insert empty lines. The cursor is now positioned where you will modify tab stops.

---

```
   Here are the names that were left off the list of deliveries
to the Northwestern territory. Please make sure to add these
names immediately:
```

| Customer | City | Order # | Cases |
|----------|------|---------|-------|
| Chou | Seattle | AB-1 | 128 cases of Chardonnay from container 744; 25 cases from 333 |
| Goldberg | Seattle | AB-12 | 2 cases of Sauvignon Blanc from container 55; 8 cases from 334 |
| Johnson | Portland | AL-12 | 88 cases of Chardonnay from container 100; 142 from container 15 |

**FIGURE 4-10**  Sample table to be typed

4. Press the FORMAT ([Shift] + [F8]) key. [*Pulldown menu:* Layout (L).] WordPerfect responds with the Format menu.

5. Select Line (1 or L) to display the Line Format menu, indicating the default tab stop settings in the right column.

6. Select Tab Set (8 or T). The Tab menu appears.

7. Press [←] until the cursor moves all the way to the left edge of the page, which is position −1″ or 0″, depending on your version of WordPerfect. (You can also press [Home], [Home], [←] to move to the left edge of the Tab menu more quickly.)

8. Press [Ctrl] + [End] to delete all tabs starting from the current cursor position.

9. *5.1 users only:* Select **T** for Type, and then select **A** for Absolute, so that you will set tabs according to the left edge of the page, rather than the left margin.

10. Set three tab stops as follows: type **2.5″** and press [Enter]; type **4″** and press [Enter]; type **5.4″** and press [Enter]. Now you have established three left-aligned tab stops, which will be positioned 2.5″, 4″, and 5.4″ from the left edge of the paper on which the document will be typed.

11. Press the EXIT ([F7]) key twice to return to the document. A [**Tab Set: Abs: 2.5″,4″,5.4″**] code is inserted in the document. This determines tab stop locations from the current cursor location down. (The Tab Set code is invisible on the Typing screen, of course.)

12. To type the first line of the table, which contains the headings, type **Customer,** press [Tab], type **City,** press [Tab], type **Order #,** press [Tab], type **Cases,** and press [Enter] twice to insert a blank line.

13. To type the first entry, notice in Figure 4-10 that the "Cases" column contains multiple lines. Thus, to line up the text properly for the "Cases" column, you will want to press →INDENT (F4), rather than Tab, before typing the "Cases" entry. (See Chapter 3 for a review of the →INDENT feature, which allows you to align an entire paragraph of text, rather than just one line.)

Thus, to type the first entry, type **Chou**, press Tab, type **Seattle**, press Tab, type **AB-1**, press →INDENT (F4), and then type **128 cases of Chardonnay from container 744; 25 cases from 333**. Then press Enter twice to move to the next line and insert a blank line.

14. Complete the table shown in Figure 4-10.

After typing the table, suppose you wish to return tab stops to their default settings, one every 0.5″. To do so, you must insert another Tab Set code below the table. Here's the quick procedure for doing so.

1. After typing the last entry of the table, press Enter twice to position the cursor below the table, and to insert a blank line.

2. Press the FORMAT (Shift + F8) key. [*Pulldown menu:* Layout (L).] WordPerfect responds with the Format menu.

3. Select Line (1 or L) to display the Line Format menu, indicating the tab stop settings for the table.

4. Select Tab Set (8 or T). The Tab menu appears.

5. Press Home , Home , ← and then press Ctrl + End to delete all tabs.

6. *5.1 users only:* Select T for Type, and then select R for Relative so that you will again set tabs according to the left margin, rather than the left edge of the paper.

7. *5.1 users:* Type −1",0.5". *5.0 users:* Type 0",0.5". Notice that what you just typed now appears in the lower right corner of the tab ruler.

8. Press Enter . Tab stops now appear every 0.5".

9. Press the EXIT ( F7 ) key twice. A new Tab Set code is inserted in the document. This determines tab stop locations from the current cursor location down. (The Tab Set code is invisible on the Typing screen, of course.)

10. Press Tab . Notice that the default settings are in effect; the cursor jumped 0.5" to the next tab stop.

11. Type the following sentence:

    ```
    I should have a list for the Northeastern territory by
    tomorrow morning.
    ```

By changing the location and style of tab stops, you can more easily type a chart, a table, or an invoice. In addition, you should be aware of the Columns feature, which is useful when most of your table's columns contain entries that are more than one line in length. Also, 5.1 users should also be aware of the Tables feature, which can calculate tab settings for you, and makes the process of typing text into tables still easier. Look to Chapter 11 for more on the Columns and Tables features.

# KEEP TRACK OF TABS AND MARGINS

When your document contains many different Tab Set codes, it becomes difficult to remember which portion of text is affected by which tab settings. Some word processing packages maintain a ruler line on screen so that you can quickly check your current tab and margin settings. This feature is available in WordPerfect, but at a price: it reduces the number of text lines you can see on the screen. The ruler line that appears is the same one displayed between windows on the Reveal Codes screen, with symbols to represent tab stops as well as margins. Triangles represent tab stop locations, a square bracket [ or ] represents a margin setting, and a curly brace { or } represents a margin where a tab stop is also located.

The standard monitor, which displays 24 lines of text, must be reduced to 23 lines for the ruler line to appear. You would press the SCREEN (Ctrl + F3) key and select Window (1 or W). [*Pulldown menu:* Edit (E), Window (W).] When WordPerfect prompts you for the window size, either press ⬆ or type **23** and press Enter. (This is similar to how you split screens, a feature discussed in Chapter 3; the difference is that to insert a ruler line you reduce the screen by only one line.)

Let's display the ruler line right now. The cursor can be located anywhere in the document:

1. Press the SCREEN (Ctrl + F3) key. [*Pulldown menu:* Edit (E).]

2. Select Window (1 or W). WordPerfect prompts you with

```
Number of lines in this window: 24
```

3. Type **23** and press ⌨Enter⌨. (Or you can press ⬆ and then press ⌨Enter⌨.)

A ruler line is now fixed at the bottom of the screen. If you move the cursor through the text, you'll find that the tab markers on the ruler line change to reflect the different tab settings in the document. Within the table, there are only three triangles on the ruler line, representing the three tab stops you set, as shown in Figure 4-11. But when you move the cursor either above or below the table, there are many more tab stops where the tab setting is the default.

The ruler line remains on the screen—regardless of what document is on screen, even if the screen is clear. If you're used to another word processing package that continually displays margin and tab settings, you may welcome the ruler line. To type and edit your text with the ruler line always on screen, shrink your window by one line at the

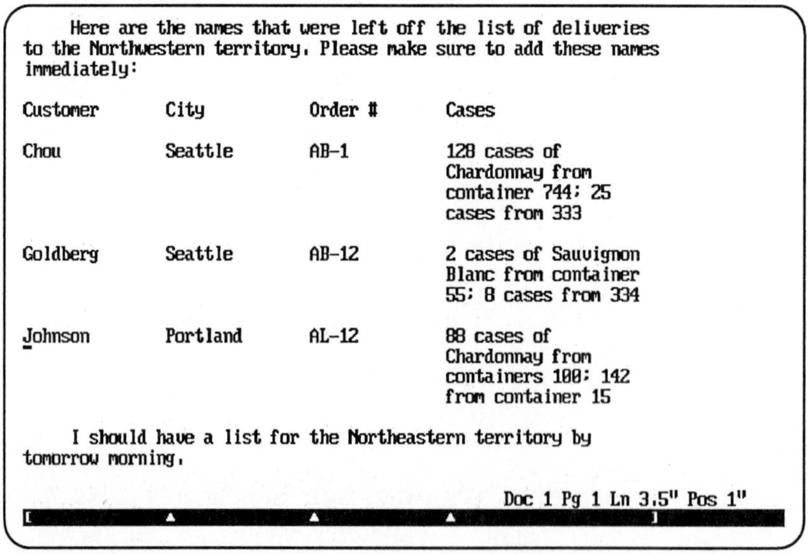

```
┌─────────────────────────────────────────────────────────┐
│      Here are the names that were left off the list of deliveries │
│  to the Northwestern territory. Please make sure to add these names │
│  immediately:                                            │
│                                                          │
│  Customer      City        Order #      Cases            │
│                                                          │
│  Chou          Seattle     AB-1         128 cases of     │
│                                         Chardonnay from   │
│                                         container 744; 25 │
│                                         cases from 333    │
│                                                          │
│  Goldberg      Seattle     AB-12        2 cases of Sauvignon │
│                                         Blanc from container │
│                                         55; 8 cases from 334 │
│                                                          │
│  Johnson       Portland    AL-12        88 cases of      │
│                                         Chardonnay from   │
│                                         containers 100; 142 │
│                                         from container 15 │
│                                                          │
│      I should have a list for the Northeastern territory by │
│  tomorrow morning.                                       │
│                                                          │
│                              Doc 1 Pg 1 Ln 3.5" Pos 1"   │
│  [         ▲          ▲          ▲              ]        │
└─────────────────────────────────────────────────────────┘
```

**FIGURE 4-11**    A Ruler line on screen

beginning of each WordPerfect session. The ruler line will remain on screen until you return the window to full size or until you exit WordPerfect.

On the other hand, you may find the ruler line distracting. To return the window to full size, you would follow the steps just outlined, specifying a window size of 24. Let's save the document you just typed under the filename LIST, clear the screen, and then get rid of the ruler line.

1. Press the EXIT (F7) key, type **Y**, and save the document under the filename LIST.

2. Type **N** when WordPerfect asks whether you wish to exit the program. Notice that while the screen is clear, the ruler line remains, but now the tab stops are returned to their default settings.

3. Press the SCREEN (Ctrl + F3) key. [*Pulldown menu:* Edit (E).]

4. Select Window (1 or W). WordPerfect prompts you with

   `Number of lines in this window: 23`

5. Type **24** and press (Enter). (Or, you can press ⏷ and then press (Enter).)

If you dislike keeping the ruler line on screen as you type, you have, of course, other alternatives for keeping track of tab stops. First, you can position the cursor on the line where you wish to check tabs, then return to the Line Format menu, and select Tab Set to view the tab ruler line. Then press the CANCEL (F1) key to back out of the Tab command. (Be sure to press CANCEL and not EXIT. If you press EXIT (F7), you will insert an extra, unneeded

Tab Set code.) Another way to keep track of tab stops is to reveal the Tab Set code. Press the REVEAL CODES (⌨Alt + ⌨F3) key to display the Reveal Codes screen, and move the cursor until the **[Tab Set:]** code appears on the screen. The code reports the location of each tab stop.

# REVIEW EXERCISE

You have now explored a number of ways to control the overall format of lines in a document. The following exercise has you working with the letter that you typed to Mr. Barrett Smith in Chapter 1. You will make format changes in the letter and print it out.

1. On a clear screen, retrieve the file named LETTER in order to make format changes.

2. For the whole document, change the left margin to 1.5″ and the right margin to 1.5″. (*Hint:* Since you are changing margins for the whole document, position the cursor at the very top.)

3. Switch to left justification (version 5.1) or turn justification off (version 5.0) for the whole document. (*Hint:* Again, since you are changing the justification default for the whole document, place the Justification code at the top of the document.)

4. Double space only the list of names. (*Hint:* Position the cursor at the left margin of the line that reads "Antonio Abbot," and set double spacing. Then position the cursor on the blank line below the table and set line spacing back to single spacing.)

5. *5.1 users:* Reset tabs for the list of names so that the first tab is 1.2″ from the left margin and other tabs follow in 0.5″ increments. (*Hint:* Position the cursor at the left margin of the line that reads "Antonio Abbot" before you begin to set tabs. Then, display the Tab menu. Since the default is for tabs relative to the left margin, there's no need to select Type. Simply delete the old tabs, and set new ones by typing **1.2″,0.5″** and pressing [Enter].)

   *5.0 users:* Reset tabs for the list of names so that the first tab stop is 2.7″ from the left edge of the page and other tabs follow in 0.5″ increments. (*Hint:* Position the cursor at the left margin of the line that reads "Antonio Abbot" before you begin to set tabs. Then, display the Tab menu, delete the old tabs, and set new ones by typing **2.7″,0.5″** and pressing [Enter].)

6. Reveal codes to make sure that the Margin, Justification, Tab Set, and Line Spacing codes are correct.

7. Print the document to see the final product, as shown in Figure 4-12.

8. Resave the document under the same filename (LETTER) and clear the screen.

---

February 3, 1990


Mr. Barrett P. Smith
FST Accounting
1801 S. Harmon Street
Oakland, CA 94413

Dear Barrett:

As we discussed, here is a complete list of full-
time employees who elected to accept the new vacation
option, along with their anniversary dates with us.
Please add their names to your record.

Antonio Abbot          May 31st

Lois Chang             April 27th

Tim Fingerman          May 20th

Paul McClintock        August 7th

The new accrued vacation system should begin for these
employees immediately. Thank you.

Sincerely,


Sandy Peterson
President
R&R Wine Association

P.S. I've included a copy of our quarterly newsletter
for your enjoyment.

---

**FIGURE 4-12**   Review exercise text with format changes

# Quick Review

• While default settings control the format of your documents, the Line Format menu allows you to insert format codes in your text to change the default settings for left/right margin, tab, justification, and hyphenation settings in each document. Display the Line Format menu by pressing the FORMAT (⌈Shift⌋ + ⌈F8⌋) key and selecting Line (1 or L). Or, pulldown menu users can select Layout (L), then Line (L).

• Change the left/right margins from the Line Format menu by selecting Margins (7 or M) and entering the new margin settings.

• Determine how text will be justified when printed from the Line Format menu by selecting Justification (3 or J). 5.1 users can then select Full Justification, where text will be aligned evenly at both the left and right margins. Or, select Left, Right, or Center Justification. 5.0 users can select to turn Justification On, where text will be aligned evenly at both the left and right margins, or turn Justification Off, where the text will print with a ragged right margin.

• Hyphenation assistance is available from the Line Format menu by selecting Hyphenation (1 or Y) and then turning it on (5.1 users), or selecting either

Manual or Automatic assistance (5.0 users). When hyphenation is on, WordPerfect determines which words to hyphenate based on the size of the hyphenation zone, which can be adjusted from the Line Format menu. Words are hyphenated with a soft hyphen—"soft" because it will be concealed if subsequent editing relocates the word away from the margin. To enter a soft hyphen on your own, press Ctrl + hyphen.

* Change tab stop locations from the Line Format menu by selecting Tab Set (8 or T) and then inserting and deleting tab stops which are marked on a tab ruler. Left, right, center, or decimal tabs can be set. In addition, 5.1 users can decide whether the tabs should be set in relation to the left margin (relative) or based on the left edge of the printed page (absolute). For 5.0 users, tabs are always set as absolute from the left edge of the page.

* Format codes—such as those inserted to alter margin, justification, hyphenation, or tab settings—affect all the text forward to the end of the document or until the next code of the same format type. Thus, make sure to position the cursor where you want a format change to occur before displaying the Line Format menu to insert a format code. To cancel a format change, delete the corresponding format code.

- To keep track of margin and tab settings wherever the cursor is located, establish a ruler line at the bottom of the screen. Press SCREEN ( Ctrl + F3 ) and select Window (1 or W). Or, using the pulldown menus, select Edit (E) and then Window (W). Next, press ⬆ and Enter so that the Typing screen is reduced in size by one line. Cancel the ruler line by following the same procedure, but this time press ⬇ and Enter .

*chapter* **5**

# EDITING ENHANCEMENTS, SEARCH & REPLACE, MOVE & COPY

Search for Characters in Text
Search for Codes in Text
Replace Text and/or Codes
Move/Copy/Append Text
Compare Documents After Editing
Review Exercise
Quick Review

**R**eworking words, rearranging sentences, reordering paragraphs—these are some of the constants in document editing. WordPerfect makes the rewriting process less arduous with some special editing enhancements. One editing timesaver is the Search feature. WordPerfect can look through a long document and position the cursor on the specific word or phrase you can't seem to locate, or it can find a hidden code that is eluding you. A related feature is Replace, whereby WordPerfect locates a certain word or phrase everywhere it occurs and swaps it for another phrase of your choice.

Another handy feature enables you to perform a cut-and-paste procedure—moving text from one part of the document to another—without having to use scissors or tape. You can also copy text from one place to another, and even from one separate file to another.

Should you decide to edit your document and keep track of editing changes, you can ask that WordPerfect compare the edited version of a document on screen with the old version on disk. This is useful if you want to contrast an original contract with a revision, or the draft of a report with the final version. In this chapter, the various editing features will be explained, and you will practice using them with documents that you created in previous chapters.

# SEARCH FOR CHARACTERS IN TEXT

Searching through the text for a specific character, word, or phrase can be a time-consuming process. Imagine, for instance, needing to reread a 30-page report just to find one reference to wine sales in San Francisco. Rather than scroll through the document screen by screen, you can start with the cursor at the top of the document and request that WordPerfect find the phrase "San Francisco." WordPerfect moves the cursor to that phrase in moments. A character, phrase, or word that you are searching for is referred to as a *string*.

## The GOTO Key

If the string you wish to find is just one character, then you can use the GOTO ( Ctrl + Home ) key to move there. [*Pulldown menu:* Search (S), Goto (G).] When you press Ctrl + Home , WordPerfect prompts

Go to

Type a letter or symbol (such as !, *, or %) and the cursor moves just to the right of the first occurrence of that letter or symbol—as long as it appears within the next 2000 characters. The GOTO ( Ctrl + Home ) key only moves the cursor forward in the text, so you must position the cursor before the character you seek. (You cannot use GOTO to find a *number* in the text; as you'll learn in the next chapter, if you press Ctrl + Home and enter a number, WordPerfect assumes the number refers to a page and moves the cursor to the top of that page.)

As practice, let's first move the cursor using the GOTO key. You are going to search in the short document you created in Chapter 4. (Be aware that the time savings in using the Search feature are even more dramatic on a long document.)

1. On a clear Typing screen, retrieve the file named LIST.

2. With the cursor at the top of the document, suppose you want to move the cursor to the end of the first full sentence. Press Ctrl + Home . [*Pulldown menu:* Search (S), Goto (G).] WordPerfect prompts you with

Go to

3. Type a period (.). The cursor moves past the end of the sentence in an instant.

4. Press [Ctrl] + [Home] again.

5. Type a colon (:). The cursor moves to the end of the first paragraph, where the colon is located.

# The Search Feature

If the string you want to locate is at least 1 character long but less than 59 characters long, you will rely on the Search feature. With the Search feature, you're not limited to looking within the next 2000 characters; rather, an entire document can be scanned. You can search either forward from the current cursor position with the →SEARCH ([F2]) key or backwards with the ←SEARCH ([Shift] + [F2]) key. To search an entire document, for example, move the cursor to the top of the document and press the →SEARCH ([F2]) key, or move the cursor to the bottom of the document and press the ←SEARCH ([Shift] + [F2]) key. [*Pulldown menu:* Search (S), and then either Forward (F) or Backward (B).] WordPerfect prompts asking for the string of characters for which you wish to search. The prompt contains an arrow pointing to the right for a forward search:

```
->Srch:
```

And it contains an arrow pointing to the left for a backward search:

```
<-Srch:
```

At the search prompt, type in the string and then press either the ➔SEARCH (F2) key or the ◄SEARCH (Shift) + F2) key or the Esc key to execute the command. Or press the CANCEL (F1) key to abort the search. When you initiate a search and the search string is found, the cursor will move just to the right of the first occurrence of the string. Otherwise, WordPerfect will prompt with

```
* Not found *
```

In a search string, WordPerfect is sensitive to uppercase letters. An uppercase string will match only uppercase in the text, while a lowercase string will match either. For instance, suppose your string is "CHAMPAGNE". Word-Perfect will stop after "CHAMPAGNE" in the text but not after "champagne" or "Champagne". However, if the string is "champagne", then it will stop after any of the three variations. Be careful of typos, however. If the string you typed is "hcampagne", the word would not be found in the text, and WordPerfect would respond with a "* Not found *" message.

You have several options when performing a search. One is to execute an Extended Search, whereby Word-Perfect searches through headers, footers, footnotes, endnotes, text boxes, and graphic box captions, as well as the main body of text. To do so, press (Home) before pressing the ➔SEARCH (F2) or the ◄SEARCH (Shift) + F2) key. [*Pulldown menu:* Search (S), Extended (E), and then either Forward (F) or Backward (B).] Then type in the search string and press ➔SEARCH (F2) or Esc) to initiate the search. Press (Home) again before pressing ➔SEARCH to continue the Extended Search.

Furthermore, you can include a "wild card" in the search string to represent any single character, as long as the wild card isn't the first character in the string. To include a wild card when typing the search string, you would press Ctrl + V and then press Ctrl + X. The wild card character ^X is inserted. So, for example, the string "wa^Xt" would match "wait", "walt", "want", "wart", and "watt".

Here's some practice using the →SEARCH (F2) key. Suppose you're searching through the entire document on screen for a reference to Chardonnay, a type of white wine. You know that the reference to it appears further forward in the document, so you will search in the forward direction.

1. Press the →SEARCH (F2) key. [*Pulldown menu:* Search (S), Forward (F).] WordPerfect responds with

   ->Srch

2. Type **Chardonnay**. (You can also type **chardonnay**.)

3. Press the →SEARCH (F2) key to initiate the search.

In seconds, the cursor flies down the document, just to the right of "Chardonnay." If you typed the string with a typo, WordPerfect would be unable to locate the string and would prompt you with

   * Not Found *

If that prompt appeared on screen, try again, being sure to type the word correctly in step 2.

Once you indicate a search string, WordPerfect remembers that string for subsequent searches. The next time you press →SEARCH or ←SEARCH, the search prompt appears displaying the most recent string. As a result, you can quickly move to all locations containing the same search string in your text. For instance, suppose the cursor is at the top of a report in which you quickly wish to move forward to each instance where a client named "Murphy" is mentioned. Using the function keys, you would:

- Press the →SEARCH ( F2 ) key, type **Murphy**, and press →SEARCH ( F2 ) again to move to the first instance.

- Press →SEARCH ( F2 ) twice quickly to move to the second instance.

- Press →SEARCH ( F2 ) twice again to move to the third instance, and so on.

(Or, to move backward, use the ←SEARCH ( Shift + F2 ) key in the same way.)
 Using the pulldown menus in version 5.1, you would

- Select Search (S), Forward (F), type **Murphy**, and press →SEARCH ( F2 ) to move to the first instance.

- Select Search (S), Next (N) to move to the second instance.

- Select Search (S), Next (N) again to move to the third instance, and so on.

(Or, to move backward, select Search (S), Backward (B) for the first instance, and then Search (S), Previous (P) thereafter.)

When you wish to search for a new search string, simply press →SEARCH [*Pulldown menu:* Search (S), Forward (F)] and type over or edit the search string that is displayed before continuing. For instance:

1. Press the →SEARCH ([F2]) key. WordPerfect responds with

   ->Srch: Chardonnay

   Notice that WordPerfect remembers the last search string, and so suggests it again.

2. Press the →SEARCH ([F2]) key to initiate the search. The cursor moves just past the next occurrence of "Chardonnay."

3. Repeat steps 1 and 2 again. WordPerfect prompts "* Not found *," meaning that the search string does not appear farther forward in the document.

4. Press the ←SEARCH ([Shift] + [F2]) key. WordPerfect responds with a backwards search prompt, still remembering the most recent search string:

   <-Srch: Chardonnay

5. Suppose you wish to search for the reference to Seattle. Type **Seattle**. As soon as you begin typing the new search string, the old one is erased—you don't even need to use the [Backspace] or [Del] key. Now the prompt reads

   <-Srch: Seattle

6. Press the [Esc] key to initiate the search. Now the cursor moves backwards in the text and stops just past the closest occurrence of "Seattle."

The Search feature can be used as a convenient way to leapfrog from one section of a document to the next. For instance, suppose you are writing a report but must talk to several experts before you include some statistics. At each place in the document where you are missing a statistic, you can type a string of characters that you would not otherwise find in the document, such as **??**. After you have talked to the experts, you can use the Search feature to move quickly to the places where you must fill in the statistics.

The Search feature can also help you to quickly define the end of a block. Position the cursor on the first character in the text that you wish to highlight, press BLOCK ([Alt] + [F4]) to turn block on, and then initiate a search. The text will be highlighted up to and including the search string that you specify.

In addition, the Search feature is impressive when used along with the Look feature. Remember from Chapter 2 that, when viewing a list of files, you can use the Look feature to peek at the contents of files without actually retrieving them to the screen. Once viewing the Look screen for a certain document, you can use the →SEARCH ([F2]) or ←SEARCH ([Shift] + [F2]) key, rather than the cursor movement keys, to scroll through the text of that file. The cursor will move to the beginning of the line where the search string that you specify is located. In that way, you can quickly find files that refer to a specific topic.

As you begin to use the Search feature in your documents, keep in mind that a search is *not* executed with the

[Enter] key. Rather, it is the →SEARCH ([F2]), ←SEARCH ([Shift] + [F2]) or [Esc] key that executes a search.

What happens if, as is common with beginning users, you mistakenly press the [Enter] key after typing a search string? You'll insert an **[HRt]** code in the search string rather than execute the search. For instance, suppose you press the →SEARCH ([F2]) key and type **Europe**. The prompt reads

```
->Srch: Europe
```

Now if you press [Enter] the search doesn't begin! Instead, you have added an **[HRt]** code to the search string. Word-Perfect considers this code part of the string and will only find the phrase "Europe" when it is followed by a hard return. The prompt appears as

```
->Srch: Europe[HRt]
```

To correct the mistake, press [Backspace] to erase the **[HRt]** code from the search string and then press the →SEARCH ([F2]) key, →SEARCH ([Shift] + [F2]), or [Esc] key to execute the search. The next section describes more about how you can locate codes such as **[HRt]** using the Search feature.

# SEARCH FOR CODES IN TEXT

One of the Search command's most compelling features is the ability to quickly locate hidden codes, either by themselves or along with text. This frees you from having to reveal codes and then move slowly through the text to find a code you're looking for. For instance, what if you printed out a document only to find that the margins shifted unexpectedly on page 3. By now you know that the culprit is most likely a **[L/R Mar:]** code or perhaps an **[→Indent]** code that you accidentally placed on that page. With the Search command, you could find that troublesome code instantly and use the Backspace key to erase it, since Word-Perfect positions the cursor just to the right of the code you're seeking.

To include a code in a search string, you use the same function key combination as when you inserted that code in the text in the first place. For instance, you would press the Enter key to search for a Hard Return code **[HRt]**, or press the BOLD (F6) key to search for a beginning Bold code **[BOLD]**, or press BOLD (F6) twice and then erase the beginning Bold code to search for an ending Bold code **[bold]**. Or use the FORMAT (Shift + F8) key and then follow the procedure as if changing left/right margins to search for a Left/Right Margin code **[L/R Mar:]**. Although any WordPerfect code can be part of a search string, there's no way to specify a particular parameter within a code. For example, you can search for a Left/Right Margin code, but not for only those Left/Right Margin codes with margins of 1.5″.

*Note:* When inserting a code in a search string, you must use the function keys to do so, and not the pulldown menu. Whenever the "Srch:" prompt is displayed at the bottom of the screen, the pulldown menus cannot be accessed.

As an example, let's search for **[Tab]** codes.

1. Press Home, Home, ↑ to position the cursor at the top of the document.

2. Press the ➔SEARCH ( F2 ) key. [*Pulldown menu:* Search (S), Forward (F).] WordPerfect responds with

   ->Srch: Seattle

   Notice that WordPerfect remembers the last string you searched for. You can type right over that string.

3. Press the Tab key. Now the search string reads

   ->Srch: [Tab]

4. Press the ➔SEARCH ( F2 ) key to begin the search. The cursor moves just to the right of a **[Tab]** code. You can verify this by revealing codes.

5. Press ➔SEARCH ( F2 ) twice and watch how the cursor jumps just past the next **[Tab]** code located forward in the document.

6. Repeat step 5 above several more times and watch how the cursor jumps to each **[Tab]** code. You may wish to switch to the Reveal Codes screen as you use the Search feature, so that you can watch as the cursor repositions just to the right of each successive Tab code. (If Word-Perfect doesn't pause at a spot where you believe a Tab code is located, reveal codes; you may find that an **[➔Indent]** code is located there instead.) Once Word-Perfect responds with "* Not found *," then you have verified the absence of any more Tab codes located forward from the cursor.

Suppose that you now wish to position the cursor next to any **[Tab Set]** code that may exist in the document and erase one of those codes.

1. Press `Home`, `Home`, `↑` to move the cursor to the top of the document.

2. Press the →SEARCH (`F2`) key. [*Pulldown menu:* Search (S), Forward (F).] WordPerfect responds with

   `->Srch: [Tab]`

   WordPerfect remembers the last code you searched for.

3. Press the LINE FORMAT (`Shift` + `F8`) key (the key sequence that enables you to insert Tab Set codes into a document). Because you are in the midst of a search, a slightly different menu appears than when you actually changed margins. This menu is

   `1 Line; 2 Page; 3 Other: 0`

   WordPerfect is asking whether the code you wish to search for is inserted into the document using the Line Format, Page Format, or Other Format menu.

4. Select Line (1 or L). The following menu appears:

   `1 Hyphen; 2 HZone; 3 /; 4 Justification; 5 Line; 6 Margins; 7 Tab Set; 8 W/O: 0`

   Each of these options represents a different type of Line Format code.

5. Select Tab Set (7 or T). The search prompt reappears and reads

   `->Srch: [Tab Set]`

6. Press the →SEARCH (`F2`) key again. The cursor moves forward in the text. If you reveal codes, you'll see that the cursor is now just to the right of a **[Tab Set]** code.

7. Press the ➔SEARCH (F2) key twice; the cursor moves to the next **[Tab Set]** code in the text.

8. Press Backspace to erase this second Tab Set code. If you're viewing the Typing screen, WordPerfect asks for verification. For instance, 5.1 users see the following:

`Delete [Tab Set:Rel:-1", every 0.5"]? No (Yes)`

9. Type **Y** and the code will disappear; once you move the cursor to rewrite the screen, notice that the last sentence is now indented a full 1.5″. This is because a **[Tab]** code precedes the sentence, which abides by the Tab Set code located near the top of the text.

10. Press Del to erase the **[Tab]** code. The sentence moves back to the left margin.

Appendix D provides a complete list of codes—even some codes that have yet to be discussed but that will be covered in future chapters. Using this appendix, you can more easily identify codes as you edit your text and as you include codes in a search string. Refer to it when you find a code on the Reveal Codes screen that you can't identify so that you can look up the associated feature, learn how the code will affect the text when printed, and decide whether or not to delete or move it.

# REPLACE TEXT AND/OR CODES

The Replace feature goes one step further than Search. Not only will WordPerfect locate an occurrence of a specific string, but it can also automatically substitute a new phrase for that string, continuing along until all such occurrences in the document are found and replaced. For example, you could search for all the places where you referred to "ABC Company" in a proposal and change them to "XYZ Company"—tailoring the proposal to a different organization in moments.

In a Replace, there are the following two strings:

| | |
|---|---|
| Search string | The phrase that you are looking for |
| Replace string | The phrase that will be substituted for the search string |

Both the search and replace strings can include text, codes, or both, up to 59 characters in length.

There are two ways that the Replace feature can operate. First, you can request the Replace with confirmation, meaning that when the search string is found, WordPerfect pauses and asks if you wish to substitute the replace string. Alternatively, you can request Replace without confirmation, whereby WordPerfect performs the substitution of all search strings found in the document without stopping.

Depending on what the replace string is, it can serve as a straight substitution, an insertion, or a deletion. For example, if you searched for "Joe Smith" and replaced with "Hanna Jones", that would be a straight substitution. If you searched for "Joe" and replaced it with "Joe W. Smith, Sr.", that would be more like an insertion. If you searched for an Underline code and left the replace string blank, you effectively would be deleting all underlining from the text.

You can execute the Replace in either the forward or the backward direction from the current cursor position.

First position the cursor. Next press the REPLACE ([Alt] + [F2]) key. [*Pulldown menu:* Search (S), Replace (R).] WordPerfect prompts you with

`w/Confirm? No (Yes)`

WordPerfect assumes that you want the Replace command to work on the document without confirmation. Type **N** or press [Enter] to accept this assumption, or type **Y** to perform the Replace with confirmation. After you type **Y** or **N**, WordPerfect assumes you wish to proceed in the forward direction and prompts for a search string with an arrow pointing to the right:

`->Srch:`

Only if you wish to perform a backward replace, press the [↑] key. Now the prompt reads

`<-Srch:`

Next type the search string and press any of the following keys to register the search string: REPLACE ([Alt] + [F2]) key, →SEARCH ([F2]), ←SEARCH ([Shift] + [F2]), or [Esc]. Now a prompt appears for the replace string:

`Replace with:`

Type in the replace string and then press REPLACE ([Alt] + [F2]), →SEARCH ([F2]), ←SEARCH ([Shift] + [F2]), or [Esc] to execute the replacement (or press the CANCEL ([F1]) key to abort it).

    For a replacement without confirmation, the substitutions occur in moments.

For a replacement with confirmation, WordPerfect pauses with the cursor at the first occurrence of the search string and prompts

`Confirm? No (Yes)`

Type **Y** to make the substitution or type **N** or press ⌈Enter⌉ to skip over that string and to look for the next occurrence. This would continue to the end of the text unless you pressed the CANCEL (⌈F1⌉) key during the Replace to stop the procedure.

Some of the same options apply to the Replace command as to the Search command. For instance, both the search string and the replace string are sensitive to uppercase letters. You can also perform an Extended Replace, including headers, footers, footnotes, endnotes, text boxes, and graphics box captions in the search by pressing the ⌈Home⌉ key before pressing the REPLACE (⌈Alt⌉ + ⌈F2⌉) key.

You can also specify that the Replace feature operate on only a portion of your document. First, highlight that portion using the Block feature. Then, with Block on, press REPLACE (⌈Alt⌉ + ⌈F2⌉) to initiate a replace. The search string you specify will be located and substituted only within the highlighted text.

As you practice with Replace, notice that the document currently on your Typing screen contains the word "territory" several times, once near the top of the document and once near the bottom. Suppose that you decide to refer to a section of the country as a "region," rather than as a "territory."

1. Position the cursor at the top of the document.

2. Press the REPLACE ( Alt + F2 ) key. [*Pulldown menu:* Search (S), Replace (R).] WordPerfect prompts

   `w/Confirm? No (Yes)`

3. Type **N**. Now WordPerfect prompts

   `->Srch: [Tab Set]`

   Notice that even though you are performing a replace, WordPerfect remembers your last search string.

4. Type **territory**. The prompt reads

   `->Srch: territory`

5. Press the Esc key. Now WordPerfect asks for the replace string.

   `Replace with:`

6. Type **region**.

7. Press the Esc key.

8. Move to the top of the document to see the results.

In moments, WordPerfect makes the substitution everywhere that the word "territory" appears on screen and then rewrites the screen so that when "region" is inserted, the document adjusts within the margins. It doesn't matter whether a replace string is shorter or longer than the search string; WordPerfect adjusts the text accordingly once the substitutions are made.

You can even use the Replace feature to quickly add codes to the text. For instance, you can search for a specific phrase that you wish to enhance with boldface through a document, and boldface that phrase. The search string is the phrase. The replace string is the same phrase, only with boldface codes surrounding it. For instance, let's boldface the word "region" in the document on screen:

1. Position the cursor at the top of the document.

2. Press the REPLACE (⌑Alt⌑ + ⌑F2⌑) key. WordPerfect prompts

   `w/Confirm? No (Yes)`

3. Type **N**. Now WordPerfect prompts

   `->Srch: territory`

   Notice that even though you are performing a replace, WordPerfect remembers your last search string.

4. Type **region**. The prompt reads

   `->Srch: region`

5. Press the ⌑Esc⌑ key. Now WordPerfect asks for the replace string.

   `Replace with:`

6. Press BOLD (⌑F6⌑), type **region**, and press BOLD (⌑F6⌑) again. The prompt reads

   `Replace with: [BOLD]region[bold]`

7. Press the (Esc) key. In moments the substitution is complete. Position the cursor back at the top of the document to see the results.

Some of the best uses for the Replace command occur when you want to eliminate codes. For instance, you can use Replace to delete unnecessary hard returns or to delete any underlining or boldfacing from a document. Indicate in the search string the code or codes you are searching for. For instance, the search string could read →**Srch: [BOLD]**. Then leave the replace string blank to erase all boldfacing from the text.

As discussed previously, although any WordPerfect code can be part of the search string, there's no way to specify a particular parameter within a code. For example, you can search for a Left/Right Margin code, but not for only those Left/Right Margin codes with margins of 1.5″. Because you cannot specify a particular parameter within a code, format codes cannot be included in a *replace* string. The codes that can be included in a replace string include

| | | |
|---|---|---|
| Center | Hard Space | Math On/Off |
| Center Page | Hyphen | Math Operators |
| Columns On/Off | Hyphenation Cancel | Merge Codes |
| Flush Right | →Indent | Soft Hyphen |
| Font Appearance | →Indent← | Tab |
| Font Size | Justification | Tab Align |
| Hard Page | →Margin Release | Widow/Orphan On/Off |

Be careful when you execute a Replace without confirmation. WordPerfect replaces *every* occurrence of a string—even if it's a part of another word—and you may be surprised at the results. For instance, if you replace all occurrences of "pen" with "ballpoint", you'd also change "*pen*cil" to "*ballpoint*cil", and you'd swap "indis*pen*sable" with "indis*ballpoint*sable". An alternative would be to search for "pen" both preceded and followed by a blank space. But then WordPerfect wouldn't find the word if it were followed by a period at the end of a sentence—or by any other punctuation—or if it were the first word in a paragraph (where it is usually preceded by a Tab code and not a space). The safest method for replacing a fairly common character string is to execute with confirmation.

# MOVE/COPY/APPEND TEXT

WordPerfect offers three features for reorganizing your text once it has been typed:

- *Move*  Erase the text from its current location and reinsert it at another location on screen.

- *Copy*  Preserve the text at its current location and, in addition, place it at another location on screen.

- *Append*  Preserve the text at its current location and, in addition, place it at the end of a document already stored on disk.

How you move, copy, or append text depends on the size and shape of that text. Use a shortcut if the text is one sentence, one paragraph, or one page. Otherwise, use another method. Both methods are described below, first to move or copy text and then to append text.

# Move or Copy a Complete Sentence, Paragraph, or Page

WordPerfect recognizes several discrete units of text. A sentence is considered to be text that ends with a period, exclamation point, or question mark, followed by one to three spaces. A paragraph is text that ends with a hard return **[HRt]** code. A page is text that is bounded by a soft or hard page code (as is described in Chapter 6).

If you wish to move or copy a discrete unit—a complete sentence, paragraph, or page—then the procedure is accomplished in two stages.

In stage one, you indicate which text you wish to relocate. To do so, position the cursor anywhere within the text. For example, to move a sentence, position the cursor within the text of the sentence or on the ending punctuation mark. Or, to move a paragraph, position the cursor anywhere within the paragraph or on the ending Hard Return code. Or, to copy a page, position the cursor on that page.

Next, press the MOVE ( Ctrl + F4 ) key and select either Sentence (1 or S), Paragraph (2 or P), or Page (3 or A). [*Pulldown menu:* Edit (E), Select (E), and then either Sentence (S), Paragraph (P), or Page (A).] WordPerfect highlights the text in reverse video and prompts you with

1 Move; 2 Copy; 3 Delete; 4 Append: 0

If you select Move (1 or M), the text disappears from the screen and is placed in WordPerfect's move/copy *buffer,* which is like a temporary holding tank; the text is preserved in the buffer so that it can be relocated. If you select Copy (2 or C), the block remains, but a copy is placed in the buffer. A prompt at the bottom of the screen now reads:

`Move cursor; press `**`Enter`**` to retrieve.`

In stage two, you "paste" the text back into the docu-ment; that is, you indicate where you want the text that is currently in the buffer to be moved or copied. You have two choices. If you're ready to recall the text from the buffer onto the screen immediately, position the cursor where you want the text inserted and press ⌈Enter⌉ .

On the other hand, you can wait before placing the text into a new location. Instead of pressing ⌈Enter⌉, press the CANCEL (⌈F1⌉) key. The prompt "Move cursor; press **Enter** to retrieve" disappears. Now, you can continue edit-ing the text. When you're ready to reinsert the text on screen, position the cursor where you want it to appear. Next, press the MOVE (⌈Ctrl⌉ + ⌈F4⌉) key and select Re-trieve (4 or R). [*Pulldown menu:* Edit (E), Paste (P).] WordPerfect prompts with

`Retrieve: 1 Block; 2 Tabular Column; 3 Rectangle: 0`

Choose Block (1 or B). Now the block — the sentence, para-graph, or page stored in the buffer — is reinserted into the document. (In fact, a block of text remains in the buffer until you wish to move/copy another block, so you can retrieve the same block of text many times; reposition the cursor, and then again press MOVE (⌈Ctrl⌉ + ⌈F4⌉), select Retrieve, and select Block.)

There are a fair number of keys you must press to move or copy text, so becoming comfortable with the process takes a few tries. Let's practice on a document you've already typed and stored under the filename FINANCE, which contains two bulleted, indented paragraphs. Pretend that you want to reverse the order of the two paragraphs. Since you're moving a paragraph, you can use the MOVE (Ctrl + F4) key to do so.

1. Press the SWITCH (Shift + F3) key to shift to the Doc 2 Typing screen. [*Pulldown menu:* Edit (E), Switch (S).] This screen should be clear. (For a review of Dual Document typing, whereby you can use both the Doc 1 and Doc 2 screens, refer to Chapter 3.)

2. Retrieve the file named FINANCE into the Doc 2 screen.

3. Position the cursor anywhere on the first bulleted item. For example, position the cursor on the "v" in "venture capitalist."

4. Press the MOVE (Ctrl + F4) key. [*Pulldown menu:* Edit (E), Select (E).] WordPerfect responds with the Move menu:

Move: 1 Sentence; 2 Paragraph; 3 Page; 4 Retrieve: 0

5. Select Paragraph (2 or P). WordPerfect highlights the paragraph in reverse video, as shown in Figure 5-1, and prompts

1 Move; 2 Copy; 3 Delete; 4 Append: 0

6. Select Move (1 or M). Now the sentence has disappeared — but not for long. A prompt at the bottom of the screen reads

Move cursor; press **Enter** to retrieve.

7. Position the cursor on the last line of text, on the "F" in "For more detail."

8. Press the [Enter] key. The result of the move is shown in Figure 5-2.

Imagine what a timesaver the MOVE ([Ctrl] + [F4]) key is for restructuring whole pages of text. Also imagine how powerful the MOVE ([Ctrl] + [F4]) key is in working between two different documents on the Doc 1 and Doc 2 screens. For instance, suppose that you want to write a

```
I spoke to John Samsone on January 3rd about our financial
situation.  He reported the following highlights:

o    He is meeting with a venture capitalist next week who is
     interested in investing with us.

o    Our debt stands at $159,000 as of December 31st, 10% lower
     than we anticipated.  Financial forecasts project that we'll
     be out of debt in two years time.  Here are the debt figures
     (in thousands):

     Amount Owed            Name of Bank

       $48.5                Floyd Interstate
         9.8                Center Bank
       100.7                Bank of Stevenson

For more detail, call John at (415) 333-9215.




1 Move: 2 Copy: 3 Delete: 4 Append: 0
```

**FIGURE 5-1** A paragraph highlighted during a move

```
 I spoke to John Samsone on January 3rd about our financial
 situation. He reported the following highlights:

 o    Our debt stands at $159,000 as of December 31st, 10% lower
      than we anticipated. Financial forecasts project that we'll
      be out of debt in two years time. Here are the debt figures
      (in thousands):

      Amount Owed              Name of Bank

       $48.5               Floyd Interstate
        9.8                    Center Bank
       100.7                Bank of Stevenson

 o    He is meeting with a venture capitalist next week who is
      interested in investing with us.

 For more detail, call John at (415) 333-9215.




 C:\WP51\DATA\FINANCE                    Doc 2 Pg 1 Ln 3.33" Pos 1"
```

**FIGURE 5-2**   Sample text after a paragraph is moved

report based on a letter you had already created. You could retrieve the letter into the Doc 1 window and begin writing the report in the Doc 2 window, copying selected paragraphs from the letter as needed. For instance, in the Doc 1 window, you would use the MOVE (Ctrl + F4 ) key to copy a paragraph from the letter. Then you would press the SWITCH (Shift + F3 ) key to jump to the Doc 2 window, position the cursor where you wanted the paragraph to appear in the report, and press Enter to retrieve the text. Thus, you can assemble one document quickly by copying text from another.

# Move or Copy Blocks of Other Sizes, Including Columns and Rectangles

What if the block you wish to move, copy, or append is not a sentence, paragraph, or page? This requires an extra step. *Before* you press the MOVE ([Ctrl] + [F4]) key, define for WordPerfect the block's contents and dimensions.

When the block is standard text—perhaps just three words, three paragraphs, or half a page—then highlight it just as you've learned in Chapter 1; position the cursor on the first character in the block, press BLOCK ([Alt] + [F4]), and then position the cursor one past the last character in the block. After the text is highlighted, press the MOVE ([Ctrl] + [F4]) key. With "Block on" flashing, a different menu appears:

Move:   1 Block; 2 Tabular Column; 3 Rectangle: 0

Choose Block (1 or B) and then WordPerfect prompts:

1 Move; 2 Copy; 3 Delete 4 Append: 0

Select Move (1 or M) so that the block disappears from the screen and is placed in WordPerfect's buffer. Or, select Copy (2 or C) so that the block remains, but a copy is placed in the buffer. [*Pulldown menu:* Once you've highlighted the text, select Edit (E), and then either Move (M) or Copy (C).] The following prompt appears:

Move cursor; press **Enter** to retrieve.

*Note:* WordPerfect offers 5.1 users with enhanced keyboards a shortcut for moving or copying a standard block of text. Once you have used the Block feature to highlight the text, simply press Ctrl + Del to specify a move or press Ctrl + Ins to signal a copy. The "Move cursor; press **Enter** to retrieve" prompt appears.

Now, in stage two, you have the same choices for pasting the block back into the text as when moving/copying a sentence, paragraph, or page—either position the cursor where you want the block to reappear and press Enter, or press the CANCEL (F1) key, in which case the prompt "Move cursor; press **Enter** to retrieve" disappears, so that when you're ready to retrieve that block, you must press the MOVE (Ctrl + F4) key, and select Retrieve (4 or R). [*Pulldown menu:* Edit (E), Paste (P).] Now, when WordPerfect prompts:

`Retrieve: 1 Block; 2 Tabular Column; 3 Rectangle: 0`

Choose Block (1 or B).

This procedure enables you to move or copy not only a standard block of text, but a tabular column or rectangle as well. A tabular column is a column of text where each entry is aligned on the left margin or on a tab stop with a tab or decimal tab code. A rectangle is a rectangular portion of text, where opposing corners are composed of the first and last characters in that block. Figure 5-3 illustrates the differences between highlighted blocks, tabular columns, and rectangles.

To move or copy a tabular column, position the cursor anywhere on the *first line* in the column you wish to move copy, press BLOCK (Alt + F4), and then position the cursor anywhere on the last line in that same column. WordPerfect highlights the entire block, as if it were a standard block. Now select MOVE (Ctrl + F4) and select Tabular Column (2 or C). [*Pulldown menu:* Edit (E), Select

**Standard Block**

> Here are the names that were left off the list of deliveries to the Northwestern region. Please make sure to add these names immediately:

**Tabular Column**

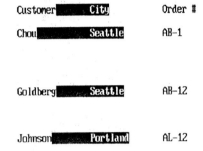

**Two Separate Rectangles**

> Here are the names that were left off the list of deliveries to the Northwestern region. Please make sure to add these names immediately:

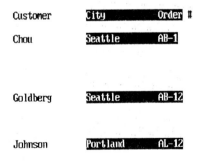

**FIGURE 5-3** Examples of a highlighted block, column, rectangle

(E), Tabular Column (C).] Once you indicate the block as a column, WordPerfect highlights only that column. Now, you can select to move or copy that tabular column just like for a standard block.

To move or copy a rectangle, position the cursor on the first character that sits at the upper lefthand corner of the rectangle, press BLOCK (Alt + F4), and then position the cursor one past the character that sits at the lower right corner of the rectangle. Now select MOVE (Ctrl + F4) and select Rectangle (3 or R). [*Pulldown menu:* Edit (E), Select (E), Rectangle (R).] Once you indicate the block as a rectangle, WordPerfect highlights only that rectangular portion of text. Now, you can select to move or copy that rectangle just like a standard block.

Suppose you wish to change the order of words in the sentence on the Doc 2 screen that reads, "Our debt stands at $159,000 as of December 31st, 10% lower than we anticipated." You will reverse the order of words and change the sentence to read, "Our debt as of December 31st stands at $159,000, 10% lower than we anticipated." The three words you will be moving do not comprise a complete sentence; therefore, you must use the BLOCK (Alt + F4) key and select to move a standard block.

1. Position the cursor on the blank space between "debt" and "stands." The space will be the first character of the block.

2. Press the BLOCK (Alt + F4) key. [*Pulldown menu:* Edit (E), Block (B).] "Block on" flashes on the status line.

3. Press → until the cursor is highlighting "stands at $159,000" as shown in Figure 5-4.

4. Now press the MOVE (Ctrl + F4) key. WordPerfect prompts

Move:  1 Block; 2 Tabular Column; 3 Rectangle: 0

[*Pulldown menu:* Edit (E) and then skip to step 6.]

5. Select Block (1 or B). Another prompt appears:

1 Move; 2 Copy; 3 Delete; 4 Append: 0

6. Select Move (1 or M). The highlighted text disappears from the screen and WordPerfect reminds you

Move cursor; press **Enter** to retrieve.

7. Position the cursor on the comma (,) in the middle of the sentence.

8. Press (Enter). You have now reordered words in a sentence without needing to retype.

```
I spoke to John Samsone on January 3rd about our financial
situation. He reported the following highlights:

o    Our debt stands at $159,000 as of December 31st, 10% lower
     than we anticipated. Financial forecasts project that we'll
     be out of debt in two years time. Here are the debt figures
     (in thousands):

     Amount Owed              Name of Bank

        $48.5                 Floyd Interstate
          9.8                    Center Bank
        100.7                 Bank of Stevenson

o    He is meeting with a venture capitalist next week who is
     interested in investing with us.

For more detail, call John at (415) 333-9215.




Block on                                    Doc 2 Pg 1 Ln 1.5" Pos 4.2"
```

**FIGURE 5-4**  A portion of a sentence highlighted for a move

Now suppose that you wish to edit the table on the Doc 1 screen. The four columns are currently in the following order:

```
Customer    City      Order #    Cases
Chou        Seattle   AB-1       128 cases of
  .           .         .           .

  .           .         .           .

  .           .         .           .
```

Assume that you want to move the third column, "Order #," over one column to the left. You can't use the Block option on the Move menu as you did for the previous example because, in addition to moving the third column, WordPerfect would also move parts of other columns. But you can use the Tabular Column option because each column is aligned on a tab.

1. Press SWITCH (Shift + F3) to return to the document named LIST that appears on the Doc 1 screen. [*Pull-down menu:* Edit (E), Switch Document (S).]

2. To define the first line of the tabular column, position the cursor anywhere on the heading "Order #" in the third column, such as on the "O".

3. Press the BLOCK (Alt + F4) key. [*Pulldown menu:* Edit (E), Block (B).]

4. To define the last line of the tabular column, first press ↓ until your cursor sits anywhere on the last line in the table. WordPerfect highlights as follows:

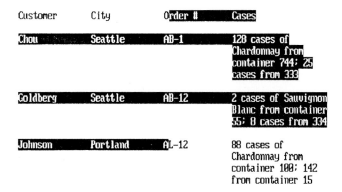

```
Customer        City        Order #       Cases

Chou            Seattle     AB-1          128 cases of
                                          Chardonnay from
                                          container 744; 25
                                          cases from 333

Goldberg        Seattle     AB-12         2 cases of Sauvignon
                                          Blanc from container
                                          55; 8 cases from 334

Johnson         Portland    AL-12         88 cases of
                                          Chardonnay from
                                          container 100; 142
                                          from container 15
```

5. Press the MOVE ( Ctrl + F4 ) key. You will see Word-Perfect prompt

**Move:  1 B**lock; **2** Tabular Column; **3** Rectangle: **0**

[*Pulldown menu:* Edit (E), Select (E).]

6. Select Tabular Column (2 or C). Now WordPerfect highlights only the portion of text that forms a column, including the **[Tab]** code that precedes each entry.

```
Customer        City         Order #      Cases

Chou            Seattle      AB-1         128 cases of
                                          Chardonnay from
                                          container 744; 25
                                          cases from 333

Goldberg        Seattle      AB-12        2 cases of Sauvignon
                                          Blanc from container
                                          55; 8 cases from 334

Johnson         Portland     AL-12        88 cases of
                                          Chardonnay from
                                          container 100; 142
                                          from container 15
```

Another prompt appears:

`1 Move; 2 Copy; 3 Delete; 4 Append: 0`

7. Select Move (1 or M). The highlighted text disappears from the screen and you are left with only three columns:

```
Customer      City          Cases

Chou          Seattle       128 cases of Chardonnay from
                            container 744; 25 cases from 333

Goldberg      Seattle       2 cases of Sauvignon Blanc from
                            container 55; 8 cases from 334

Johnson       Portland      88 cases of Chardonnay from
                            container 100; 142 from container 15
```

The following prompt appears at the bottom of the screen:

`Move cursor; press Enter to retrieve.`

8. Now you're ready to reinsert the deleted tabular column. Position the cursor on the "C" in "City" since you want the column you cut to come just before the "City" column.

9. Press Enter. Now the columns appear in the following order:

```
Customer      Order #    City        Cases
Chou          AB-1       Seattle     128 cases of
   .             .          .            .
   .             .          .            .
   .             .          .            .
```

"Order #" is now the second—rather than the third—column.

When you move or copy a block that you define using the Block feature—whether a standard block, a tabular column, or a rectangle—make sure to include in the block any hidden codes you want to take along in the process. For instance, it was important to include the **[Tab]** codes in the last example so that, when moved, the tabular column would align properly. As another example, if you were copying a table to another place, you would want to include in the block the **[Tab Set:]** code that may precede the table to reset tab stops. Thus, it is often a good idea to perform the move or copy procedure when viewing the Reveal Codes screen, rather than the Typing screen, so that you can position the cursor precisely, including or excluding codes depending on what you are moving/copying.

Also, keep in mind that working with tabular columns and rectangles can be tricky. In standard editing, Word-Perfect operates from horizontal line to line. Any insertions are made on one particular line, and all text already on the screen that follows the insertion is pushed out of the way. Working with columns and rectangles, however, Word-Perfect operates with text in a vertical orientation; if you insert a column, you are actually inserting text on many lines at once, and many individual lines of text need to be pushed out of the way. This can cause word wrap to re-adjust text in unexpected ways. Therefore, make sure that you have stored a file on disk before you start moving and copying columns and rectangles. If the text is reshuffled so extremely that a document is ruined, you can always re-trieve the file from disk and try again.

# Append a Sentence, Paragraph, Page or Block

The Append feature works similarly to the Move and Copy features. To Append a sentence, paragraph, or page to a file on disk, position the cursor anywhere within the text. So, for example, to append a paragraph, position the cursor anywhere within the paragraph or on the ending Hard Return code.

Next, press the MOVE (Ctrl + F4) key and select either Sentence (1 or S), Paragraph (2 or P), or Page (3 or A). [*Pulldown menu:* Edit (E), Select (E), and then either Sentence (S), Paragraph (P), or Page (A).] WordPerfect highlights the text in reverse video and prompts you with

`1 Move; 2 Copy; 3 Delete; 4 Append: 0`

Select Append (4 or A), and a prompt at the bottom of the screen now reads:

`Append to:`

Type in the name of the file on disk where a copy of this sentence, paragraph, or page should be placed, and press Enter. A copy of the text will be placed at the end of the file (or, if WordPerfect cannot locate that file, a new file by that name will be created). Make sure to precede the filename by the drive/directory where the file is located, if different from the default. For instance, suppose you wish to append text to a file named BUDMIN90. If BUDMIN90 is stored in the default drive/directory, simply enter **BUDMIN90.** But, if the file is stored on a disk in C:\WP51\PERS, which is not the default, then enter **C:\WP51\PERS\BUDMIN90.**

The Append feature for a standard block, tabular column, or rectangle works similarly to the Move and Copy features. To Append to a file on disk, use the Block feature to highlight the text you want to move or copy, as previously described. Next, press the MOVE (Ctrl + F4) key and select either Block (1 or B), Tabular Column (2 or C), or Rectangle (3 or R). WordPerfect highlights the text in reverse video and prompts you with

`1 Move; 2 Copy; 3 Delete; 4 Append: 0`

Select Append (4 or A), and a prompt at the bottom of the screen now reads:

`Append to:`

[*Pulldown menu:* Choose Edit (E) and then either Append (A), To File (F) for a standard block; Select (E), Tabular Column (C), Append (4 or A) for a tabular column; or Select (E), Rectangle (R), Append (4 or A) for a rectangle.]

Type in the name of the file on disk where a copy of this text should be placed, and press (Enter). A copy of the text will be placed at the end of the file (or, if WordPerfect cannot locate that file, a new file by that name will be created). You must make sure to precede the filename by the drive/directory where the file is located, if different from the default.

# COMPARE DOCUMENTS AFTER EDITING

WordPerfect offers a feature whereby any editing changes made to a document on screen can be compared to the original version on disk. The documents are compared phrase by phrase, where a phrase is defined as text between punctuation marks like a period, colon, question mark, exclamation point, or comma. The Document Compare feature is useful when you wish to compare an edited article or contract with the original.

On-screen text that has been added so that it does not exist in the file on disk is redlined; the codes **[REDLN]** and **[redln]** are inserted around that text. Once you print the on-screen text, redline on your printer may result in shading that appears over characters, such as in this example:

The last three words of this sentence are redlined.

Redline may also appear as a vertical bar in the left margin or in a different color than the rest of your text. How redline appears on the printed page depends on your printer.

On-screen text that has been deleted is recalled onto the screen and marked with strikeout; the codes **[STKOUT]** and **[stkout]** are inserted around that text. Strikeout on your printer may result in a solid line through the characters, such as in this example:

The last three words here contain strikeout marks.

Strikeout may also appear as a broken line through the characters. As with redline, how strikeout appears depends on your printer.

Moreover, any on-screen text that has been moved from one location to another compared to the text on disk is bordered by two messages on screen—"THE FOLLOWING TEXT WAS MOVED" and "THE PRECEDING TEXT WAS MOVED."

*Note*: Neither the redline nor the strikeout marks are visible on the Typing screen; they appear only on the printed page. But you can decide exactly how the text should appear on screen. To determine how redline and strikeout will appear on screen, refer to the "Display" section of Appendix B. (You can also mark sections of text for redline and strikeout by yourself, inserting the redline and strikeout codes manually. In addition, you can change the redline method used when your printer prints out your document; see Chapter 10 for details.)

To compare an edited document to the original on disk, make sure that the edited version is on screen. Then press the MARK TEXT ( Alt + F5 ) key. The following menu appears:

```
1 Cross Ref; 2 Subdoc; 3 Index; 4 ToA Short Form; 5 Define;
6 Generate: 0
```

[*Pulldown menu:* Mark (M).] Select Generate (6 or G) and the Generate menu, as shown in Figure 5-5, appears. Select Compare Screen and Disk Documents and Add Redline and Strikeout (2 or C). WordPerfect prompts for a file-name (and usually suggests as a response the name of the file you retrieved to the screen before initiating the Document Compare), such as:

```
Other document: C:\WP51\DATA\FINANCE
```

Press Enter to accept the suggested filename or type a filename and then press Enter .

In moments, WordPerfect marks the on-screen document. On-screen text that does not exist in the file on disk is redlined. Text in the file on disk that does not exist in the document on screen is copied to the on-screen document with Strikeout codes inserted.

After WordPerfect has compared the two documents, you have a variety of options. First, you can simply print out the result. That way you can see the changes quite clearly and can even solicit suggestions for the final version of your document by distributing the printed text.

Second, you can move the cursor phrase by phrase to each Redline or Strikeout code in the text and decide which version of that phrase you prefer. (The Search feature is convenient for moving the cursor to each **[REDLN]** or **[STKOUT]** code; see Chapter 10 for the procedure to insert one of these codes individually, so that you'll know how to include one in the search string.) Delete the rejected text along with the accompanying Redline or Strikeout codes.

Third, you can decide to remove all the Redline codes and strikeout text from the document. In that way, you are

```
Mark Text: Generate

    1 - Remove Redline Markings and Strikeout Text from Document

    2 - Compare Screen and Disk Documents and Add Redline and Strikeout

    3 - Expand Master Document

    4 - Condense Master Document

    5 - Generate Tables, Indexes, Cross References, etc.




Selection: 0
```

═══ **FIGURE 5-5** Generate menu

returning the on-screen text to the way it appeared before WordPerfect performed a Document Compare for you — meaning that you prefer the on-screen version as compared to the disk version of the document. To remove all the Redline codes and strikeout text, return to the Generate menu (as shown in Figure 5-5). Then select Remove Redline Markings and Strikeout Text from Document (1 or R). To verify, WordPerfect prompts with the following:

`Delete redline markings and strikeout text? No (Yes)`

Type **Y** and in moments all redline marks will be gone, and all strikeout text will be deleted. Or type **N** or press `Enter` and the command is aborted.

Here's an example. Your Doc 2 screen contains an edited version of the file named FINANCE. Following instructions found in earlier sections of this chapter, you edited the document by moving a paragraph and several words. Let's take a look at the changes:

1. Press SWITCH (`Shift` + `F3`) to return to the document named FINANCE that appears on the Doc 2 screen. [*Pulldown menu:* Edit (E), Switch Document (S).]

2. To view the redline and strikeout more clearly, edit a few more words in the document. For example, in the first sentence, change "spoke" to "talked." In the last sentence, change "John" to "him."

3. Press the MARK TEXT (`Alt` + `F5`) key to display the following menu:

`1 Cross Ref; 2 Subdoc; 3 Index; 4 ToA Short Form; 5 Define;`
`6 Generate:  0`

[*Pulldown menu:* Mark (M).]

4. Select Generate (6 or G). The Generate Mark Text menu appears, as shown in Figure 5-5.

5. Select Compare Screen and Disk Documents for Redline and Strikeout (2 or C). WordPerfect prompts for the name of the document on disk, assuming it is the same document as you retrieved before editing. For instance, floppy disk users will see

```
Other document: B:\FINANCE
```

6. Press Enter to accept the suggested filename.

7. Print out the document. You'll get a result similar to Figure 5-6 (depending on how you edited the document and also depending on how your printer handles redline and strikeout).

Notice in Figure 5-6, for example, that WordPerfect indicates that several phrases were moved. Also notice that WordPerfect redlined "call him at (415) 333-9215." and marked for strikeout "call John at (415) 333-9215." because the phrase is different on screen—"John" has been changed to "him."

Now suppose that after reviewing the editing changes you wish to return the text on screen to the edited version. You wish to remove all the Redline codes and all the text marked for strikeout. Proceed as follows:

1. Press the MARK TEXT (Alt + F5) key to display the following menu:

```
1 Auto Ref; 2 Subdoc; 3 Index; 4 ToA short form; 5 Define;
6 Generate: 0
```

[*Pulldown menu:* Mark (M).]

2. Select Generate (6 or G). The Generate Mark Text menu appears, as shown in Figure 5-5.

3. Select Remove Redline Markings and Strikeout Text from Document (1 or R). To verify, WordPerfect prompts with the following:

`Delete redline markings and strikeout text? No (Yes)`

4. Type **Y**. The document returns to its edited version, with Redline and Strikeout codes no longer in the text.

---

I talked to John Samsone on January 3rd about our financial situation.I spoke to John Samsone on January 3rd about our financial situation.  He reported the following highlights:

```
o   Our debt as of December 31st stands at $159,000, 10% lower
    than we anticipated.  Financial forecasts project that we'll
    be out of debt in two years time.  Here are the debt figures
    (in thousands):

    Amount Owed                 Name of Bank

        $48.5                   Floyd Interstate
          9.8                     Center Bank
        100.7                 Bank of Stevenson
```

THE FOLLOWING TEXT WAS MOVED
```
o   He is meeting with a venture capitalist next week who is
    interested in investing with us.
```

o   Our debt stands at $159,000 as of December 31st,
THE PRECEDING TEXT WAS MOVED
For more detail, call him at (415) 333-9215. call John at (415) 333-9215.

---

**Figure 5-6**   Redline and strikeout on the printed page after WordPerfect compared documents

# REVIEW EXERCISE

Practice some editing tasks as suggested below. You will then be quite ready to revise any document that comes your way.

1. Save the documents that are currently on the Doc 1 and Doc 2 screen, and then clear the screens. But remain in WordPerfect.

2. On a clear Doc 1 Typing screen, retrieve the file named URGNOTE, which you created in Chapter 3.

3. The "Urgent Notice" memo's date is near the top of the document. Insert two hard returns at the bottom of your document, and then move the date down to the bottom. (*Hint:* Since the date is a short line of text ending with an **[HRt]** code, you can move it as if it were a paragraph.)

4. Delete the column entitled "Department" from the memo. (*Hint:* If this column is aligned on tabs, it can be deleted by using the Tabular Column option on the Move menu; otherwise, use the Rectangle option.)

5. Substitute the word "plan" for the word "option" every time it occurs in the document. (*Hint:* Use the Replace feature to perform this task quickly. Search for "option" and replace with "plan".)

6. Use the Document Compare feature to view the changes that you've made to this document, and print out the results so that you can compare the edited to the original version of the document.

7. Return the document on screen to its edited version with no Redline or Strikeout codes. (*Hint:* Use the Generate menu to perform this task quickly.)

8. Suppose you plan to write another memo. Copy the top portion of the memo — up to and including the first sentence — to the Doc 2 screen. (*Hint:* Press Home, Home, ↑ and use the Block feature to highlight the text all the way up to the period that ends the first sentence. Next, use the MOVE (Ctrl + F4) key to specify a copy of a standard block. When the prompt "Move cursor; Press **Enter** to retrieve" appears, switch to the Doc 2 screen and press Enter.)

9. Go ahead and complete the new memo that you started on the Doc 2 screen with sentences of your own.

10. Save these documents to disk and clear the screen. You can resave the text in the Doc 1 screen again under the name URGNOTE. Select your own filename for the practice document in the Doc 2 screen.

# Quick Review

- Reposition the cursor at the next occurrence of a letter or symbol by pressing the GOTO key combination ( Ctrl + Home ) and typing the character. In the pulldown menus, access GOTO by selecting Search (S), Goto (G).

- Reposition the cursor at the next occurrence of a string of characters and/or codes with the Search feature. Press →SEARCH ( F2 ), type the string, and press Esc to initiate the search. Or, for a backwards search, use the ←SEARCH ( Shift + F2 ) key instead. In the pulldown menus, select Search (S) and then choose either the forward or backward direction for the search.

- Substitute a string of characters and/or codes for a new string everywhere it occurs in your text with the Replace feature. Press REPLACE ( Alt + F2 ), indicate whether you want the substitutions to occur with or without confirmation, type the search string, press Esc, type the replace string, and press Esc again. In the pulldown menus, select Search (S), Replace (R) to initiate the Replace feature.

- The Search and Replace features are effective for finding or eliminating not only phrases in the text, but codes as well. Include codes in a search or replace string by pressing the same keys as when you insert those codes directly into the text.

- The variety of methods for moving or copying text is shown in Table 5-1 for function key users and in Table 5-2 for pulldown menu users.

- Use the Append feature to attach a block of text currently on screen to the end of a document on disk. For text that is a complete sentence, paragraph, or page, position the cursor in the text, press MOVE (Ctrl + F4), select Sentence (1 or S), Paragraph (2 or P), or Page (3 or A), choose Append (4 or A), and enter in the name of the file to which the text should be copied. Otherwise, first use the Block feature to define the boundaries of the block. Next, press MOVE (Ctrl + F4), select Block (1 or B), Tabular Column (2 or C), or Rectangle (3 or R), and choose Append (4 or A). Then, enter in the name of the file. Append can also be accessed from the pulldown menus by choosing Edit (E) and then either Append (A) for a standard block or Select (E) for a sentence, paragraph, page, tabular column, or rectangle.

- Track your editing changes in a document with the Document Compare feature. Place the edited text on screen, press MARK TEXT (Alt + F5), select Generate (6 or G), and then choose Compare (2 or C). When prompted, enter the name of the file where the original text is stored on disk. WordPerfect inserts redline codes where text appears on screen only and inserts Strikeout codes where text-appears on disk only. This feature is also accessed via the pulldown menus by selecting Mark (M).

| Move (or Copy) | Key Sequence |
|---|---|
| Sentence | Position cursor, Ctrl + F4 , **1, 1** (or **2**), reposition cursor, Enter |
| Paragraph | Position cursor, Ctrl + F4 , **2, 1** (or **2**), reposition cursor, Enter |
| Page | Position cursor, Ctrl + F4 , **3, 1** (or **2**), reposition cursor, Enter |
| Standard Block | Block text, Ctrl + F4 , **1, 1** (or **2**), reposition cursor, Enter |
| Standard Block (5.1 shortcut) | Block text, Ctrl + Del (or Ctrl + Ins ), reposition cursor, Enter |
| Tabular Column | Block from first line to last line in the column, Ctrl + F4 , **2, 1** (or **2**), reposition cursor, Enter |
| Rectangle | Block from upper left to lower right corner of rectangle, Ctrl + F4 , **3, 1** (or **2**), reposition cursor, Enter |

**Table 5-1** Moving/Copying with Function Keys

| Move (or Copy) | Pulldown Menus Sequence |
|---|---|
| Sentence | Position cursor, [Alt] + [≡], E, E, S, 1 (or 2), reposition cursor, [Enter] |
| Paragraph | Position cursor, [Alt] + [≡], E, E, P, 1 (or 2), reposition cursor, [Enter] |
| Page | Position cursor, [Alt] + [≡], E, E, A, 1 (or 2), reposition cursor, [Enter] |
| Standard Block | Block text, [Alt] + [≡], E, M (or C), reposition cursor, [Enter] |
| Tabular Column | Block from first line to last line in the column, [Alt] + [≡], E, E, C, 1 (or 2), reposition cursor, [Enter] |
| Rectangle | Block from upper left to lower right corner of rectangle, [Alt] + [≡], E, E, R, 1 (or 2), reposition cursor, [Enter] |

**Table 5-2**  Moving/Copying with Pulldown Menus (5.1 Users Only)

*chapter* **6**

# WORKING WITH MULTIPLE-PAGE AND PAGE FORMAT FEATURES

The documents you created in the previous chapters were all less than one page in length. Few documents, however, are limited to one page. In this chapter, you'll add text to a document you've already created and watch as WordPerfect breaks that document into distinct pages automatically. You'll also see how you can control exactly where one page ends and another begins. You'll find that most of WordPerfect's page features are on the Page Format menu, accessed via the FORMAT ( Shift + F8 ) key or the Layout pulldown menu.

Farther on in the chapter, you'll establish headers and footers, which are standard lines of text at the top and bottom of each page in a document. You'll also activate the Page Numbering feature—and never have to number pages manually again!

# INITIAL PAGE FORMAT SETTINGS

The default settings for the basics of how each page of text is formatted in a document are as follows:

| | |
|---|---|
| Top and bottom margins | 1″ borders on the top and bottom of the printed page |
| Widow/orphan protection | Off, meaning that a page break may result in a widow (first line of a paragraph appearing on the last line of a page) or an orphan (last line of a paragraph appearing on the first line of a page) |

| | |
|---|---|
| Headers and footers | None |
| Page numbering | None |

If you do not specify otherwise, the preceding defaults will take effect in each page of a document you type, providing a printed result as illustrated in Figure 6-1. (For a complete list of default settings, refer to Appendix B.)

As you learned in Chapter 4, you can change any or all of the format defaults for a particular document by inserting format codes within the document. These codes serve to override the default settings. Also remember that the placement of format codes is critical. Any code that you insert in a document controls all text from that location *forward,* all the way to either the end of the document or to the next code of its type further down in the document. With that in mind, let's create a document with several pages, and then insert codes to change the defaults.

# CREATE A MULTIPLE-PAGE DOCUMENT

WordPerfect automatically breaks your text into pages as you type. This Page Break feature is as much a timesaver as is word wrap: There's no need to keep track of whether you're typing more lines than can fit on one page.

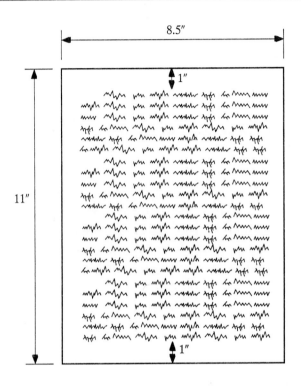

**FIGURE 6-1** Printed page based on default page format settings

When does WordPerfect break pages? Since WordPerfect's default is for a top margin of 1″ and a bottom margin of 1″, and since WordPerfect assumes you will be printing on 11″ long paper (paper size is discussed in Chapter 9), the program will break to a new page after 9″ of text have been typed—11″ minus 1″ top margin minus 1″ bottom margin. Thus, your last line of text on a page will be typed on approximately line 9.8″ (the exact position depends on your printer). When your cursor moves down to the next line, the status line does *not* indicate **Doc 1 Pg 1 Ln 10″ Pos**

1″ because this would violate the bottom margin settings. Instead, it indicates the top of a new page — **Doc 1 Pg 2 Ln 1″ Pos 1″**.

Where a page break occurs, WordPerfect inserts an **[SPg]** code, which stands for soft page — "soft" because it will adjust as you insert or delete text. (This is comparable to the soft return **[SRt]** code created by word wrap at the end of a line.) Like all codes, **[SPg]** is hidden from view on the Typing screen. To indicate that a new page has begun on the Typing screen, WordPerfect draws a page bar (a single dashed line) just below the last line of the page. A new page begins below the page bar.

Let's retrieve a document you've already created and add some text so that it becomes long enough to break into pages.

1. Retrieve the document saved under the filename SAM-PLE. This document is double spaced, with a left margin of 1.5″ and a right margin of 1″. Justification is set to left (5.1 users) or off (5.0 users) and manual hyphenation is on. This is all because of the line format codes you inserted into that document as you followed the directions in Chapter 4.

2. Press (Home), (Home), (↓) to move to the bottom of the document.

3. Press (Enter) twice to insert a blank line.

4. Type the following paragraph to add length to the text:

   R&R WINE ASSOCIATION, established in 1982, boasts a
   membership of over 100 outstanding wineries from California,
   New York, Europe, South America, and Australia. We
   disseminate information about wine tasting, production, and
   enjoyment. In addition, we distribute wine produced by our
   member wineries.

   Then press (Enter) to end the paragraph.

(As you'll recall from Chapter 4, you turned on hyphenation for this document. As a result, WordPerfect will hyphenate as you type the preceding paragraph. You may find that WordPerfect prompts asking for you to position the hyphen; see Chapter 4 if you need a refresher on the possible responses.)

Notice that as you typed, a page bar appeared across the screen. Figure 6-2 shows the page bar. (Your page break may occur at a different spot, depending on how many blank lines you inserted in your document and on how WordPerfect wraps words in your document based on your printer selection.) This page bar is inserted just below a

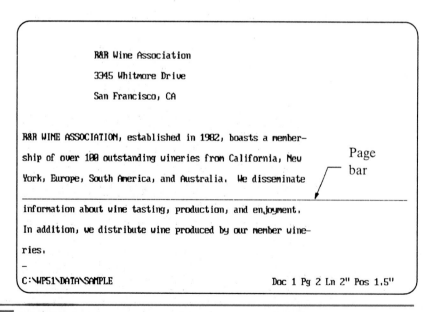

**FIGURE 6-2** Single dashed line, indicating a soft page break

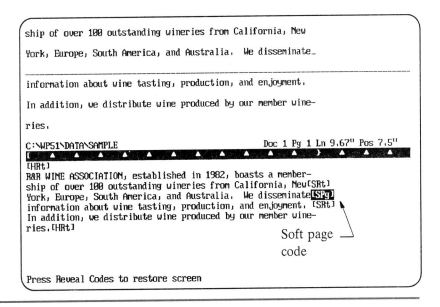

ship of over 100 outstanding wineries from California, New

York, Europe, South America, and Australia. We disseminate_

information about wine tasting, production, and enjoyment.

In addition, we distribute wine produced by our member wine-

ries.

C:\WP51\DATA\SAMPLE        Doc 1 Pg 1 Ln 9.67" Pos 7.5"

[HRt]
R&R WINE ASSOCIATION, established in 1982, boasts a membership of over 100 outstanding wineries from California, New[SRt]
York, Europe, South America, and Australia. We disseminate[SPg]
information about wine tasting, production, and enjoyment. [SRt]
In addition, we distribute wine produced by our member wineries.[HRt]

Soft page — 
code

Press Reveal Codes to restore screen

**FIGURE 6-3**    Soft Page code on the Reveal Codes
screen

hidden **[SPg]** code. If you reveal codes and position the
cursor at the bottom of page 1 or at the top of page 2, you
will see the **[SPg]** code, as illustrated in Figure 6-3.

If you add lines of text to a page, the page bar will
automatically adjust to retain only nine vertical inches of
text on that page. You are free from concern about adjusting page breaks yourself. To illustrate WordPerfect's page
break readjustment, here you'll add five short lines of text
to the middle of page 1.

1. Position the cursor on page 1 at the end of the line that
   reads "Switzerland," just to the right of the "d."

2. Press Enter and type **Austria**.

3. Press Enter and type **Hungary**.

4. Press ⟨Enter⟩ and type **Greece**.

5. Press ⟨Enter⟩ and type **Romania**.

6. Press ⟨Enter⟩ and type **Yugoslavia**.

7. Press ⟨↓⟩ until the page bar comes into view. Notice that the page bar has relocated.

As you can see, when you create a lengthy document, you can just keep typing along without worry; WordPerfect readjusts the page breaks to maintain the default top/bottom margins.

*5.1 users only*: If a soft page break occurs just before a hard return **[HRt]** code in the text, WordPerfect turns that code into a dormant hard return **[Dorm HRt]**. The hard return is suppressed—meaning that the blank line that would otherwise appear at the top of the new page is suppressed—until the text is edited so that the hard return is no longer at the top of the page. This Dormant Hard Return feature is helpful in preventing a blank line from appearing at the top of a page where a soft page break falls between the two hard returns that typically end a paragraph.

# CHANGE TOP AND BOTTOM MARGINS

Because of WordPerfect's initial top margin setting of 1″, WordPerfect will roll the paper up in the printer so that the first line of text begins 1″ below the top edge of the page. And, because of WordPerfect's automatic page breaks, a page will stop printing 1″ from the bottom edge of the page.

*Note:* If you followed the directions in Chapter 2 to print your document, but your printed result had top/ bottom margins other than 1″, then the paper may have been improperly aligned. For example, if the paper had been rolled up too far from the printhead, the top margin would be larger than 1″. Try printing again by shifting the location where paper is inserted into the printer.

You can set new margins, increasing or decreasing the number of lines of text on a page, and thus altering the white space at the top and bottom when printed. To set new margins, position the cursor at the beginning of the page where you want the new margins to take effect. For instance, place the cursor at the top of the document to change top/bottom margins starting at page 1. Or position the cursor at the very top left corner of page 3 to change margins starting on that page. Positioning the cursor is critical: Remember that a margin change will take effect from the cursor position on down. If you position the cursor in the middle of page 2 and change the top/bottom margins, the change will not take effect until page 3!

After positioning the cursor, press the FORMAT (⟦Shift⟧ + ⟦F8⟧) key to display the Format menu, and then select Page (2 or P). [*Pulldown menu:* Layout (L), Page (P).] The Page Format menu as shown in Figure 6-4 appears. (5.0 users will see a slightly different menu.) To change margins, select Margins Top and Bottom (5 or M), and then enter both your top and bottom margin settings. Finally, press EXIT (⟦F7⟧) to return to the Typing screen or press CANCEL (⟦F1⟧) to return to the Format menu.

When you alter top and bottom margins within a document, a Top/Bottom Margin code is inserted at the current cursor position. For instance, if you changed top and bottom margins to 2″, then the code inserted is

```
Format: Page

     1 - Center Page (top to bottom)    No

     2 - Force Odd/Even Page

     3 - Headers

     4 - Footers

     5 - Margins - Top              1"
                   Bottom           1"

     6 - Page Numbering

     7 - Paper Size                 8.5" x 11"
                   Type             Standard

     8 - Suppress (this page only)




Selection: 0
```

═══ **FIGURE 6-4**   Page Format menu

**[T/B Mar:2″,2″]**. This code affects margins from that point forward or up to another **[T/B Mar:]** code located further down in the document.

Let's change the top margin of the document on the screen to 2″ and leave the bottom margin at 1″:

1. Press Home, Home, ↑ to move to the top of the document.

2. Press the FORMAT (Shift + F8) key. [*Pulldown menu:* Layout (L).]

3. Select Page (2 or P). The Page Format menu appears as shown in Figure 6-4.

4. Select Margins Top and Bottom (5 or M). Notice that top and bottom margins of 1″ are currently indicated.

5. Type **2″** and press [Enter] and then type **1″** and press [Enter] to set margins.

6. Press EXIT ( [F7] ) to return to the text of your document.

Notice that with the cursor at the top of the document the status line indicates **Ln 2″**. This is because the new top margin setting of 2″ is now in effect. Because of this top margin change, WordPerfect also readjusted the soft page break to retain a bottom margin of 1″. If you now switch to the Reveal Codes screen, you can view the code which causes the change in the top margin: **[T/B Mar:2″,1″]**. (You will also see various other codes at the top of the document, including a code to change the left/right margins, to alter the justification, to change the hyphenation zone, to turn on hyphenation, and to change the line spacing. These are all line format codes that you learned about and inserted into this document when you read Chapter 4.)

# CONTROL PAGE BREAKS

Unfortunately, sometimes WordPerfect's Automatic Page Break feature ends a page at an awkward spot. Fortunately, you do have some control over the location of page breaks. You can adjust the location of a soft page break, and thus override the bottom margin setting, with the following features: Widow/Orphan Protection, Conditional End of Page, Block Protect, or Hard Page Break. These are described below.

## Widow and Orphan Protection

When a paragraph's first line appears at the bottom of the preceding page, it is called a *widow*. When a paragraph's last line appears at the top of the following page, it is called an *orphan.* You can request protection against one line of a paragraph being left stranded. By asking for widow/orphan protection, you are giving WordPerfect the license to break the page one line earlier or later than it might otherwise.

To protect against "family" separations, position the cursor at the top of the page where you want to activate the feature. Then press the FORMAT ( Shift + F8 ) key and select Line (1 or L). [*Pulldown menu:* Layout (L), Line (L).] The Line Format menu shown in Figure 6-5 appears. Notice in Figure 6-5 that Widow/Orphan Protection is off, as indicated by "No." This is the default setting. Select Widow/Orphan Protection (9 or W), and then type **Y** to turn on the feature (or type **N** to turn it off if it had been turned on for previous pages in the document). Finally,

```
Format: Line

    1 - Hyphenation                     No

    2 - Hyphenation Zone - Left         10%
                          Right         4%

    3 - Justification                   Full

    4 - Line Height                     Auto

    5 - Line Numbering                  No

    6 - Line Spacing                    1

    7 - Margins - Left                  1"
                  Right                 1"

    8 - Tab Set                         Rel: -1", every 0.5"

    9 - Widow/Orphan Protection         No


Selection: 0
```

─────── **FIGURE 6-5**  Line Format menu

press EXIT (F7) to return to the Typing screen or press CANCEL (F1) to return to the Format menu. A **[W/O On]** code is inserted at the current cursor position if you turned the feature on, and **[W/O Off]** is inserted if you turned it off.

## Keep Lines Together

You can also protect against a particular group of lines being split by a page break. For instance, suppose you commonly type a heading followed by two hard returns and then a paragraph. You can request that WordPerfect keep the heading, the blank lines, and the first few lines of the paragraph on the same page, without the threat of their being split by a page break. Or suppose you included a table in a document, and you want to make sure that WordPerfect inserts a page break either above or below the table, but not through the table. You have your pick of two features to keep specific lines together: Conditional EOP (end of page) and Block Protect.

The Conditional EOP feature is most useful for keeping a specified number of lines together where the contents of those lines may change—such as a heading and the first two lines of the paragraph that follows. To use Conditional EOP, you must count the number of lines you wish to keep together—for example, a one-line heading, two blank lines, and two lines of text equal five lines. Then move the cursor to the line *just above* where you want the feature to take effect; for example, the line above the heading. Press the FORMAT (Shift + F8) key, and select Other Format (4 or O). [*Pulldown menu:* Layout (L), Other (O).] Then, choose Conditional End Of Page (2 or C). WordPerfect prompts at the bottom of the Other Format menu:

```
Number of Lines to Keep Together:
```

Type in the number of lines you wish to keep together, press [Enter], and then press EXIT ([F7]) to return to your text. A code is inserted in the text. For example, if you wish to keep five lines together, the **[Cndl EOP:5]** code is inserted at the cursor.

With the Block Protect feature you don't have to count the number of lines to be kept together. An advantage of Block Protect is that you can add lines within the block, and the entire block will remain protected from a page break. Thus, Block Protect is most useful for keeping together tables, charts, or other portions of a document where you may later add more lines. To use Block Protect, highlight the text you want kept together with the Block feature. Then press the FORMAT ([Shift] + [F8]) key. Because Block is on, instead of displaying the Format menu, WordPerfect will ask you whether you wish to protect the highlighted block with the following prompt:

```
Protect block? No (Yes)
```

Type **Y** to protect the block and WordPerfect inserts a **[Block Pro:On]** code in front of the block and a **[Block Pro:Off]** code at the end of the block, marking off the lines that must not be separated by a page break. [*Pulldown menu:* Edit (E), Protect Block (T).] Or type **N** or [Enter] to cancel the Block Protect command.

When using the Block Protect feature, it is a good idea to highlight blocks from character to character, rather than from code to code—especially if you are protecting numerous blocks in the same document. This is because two consecutive protected blocks must be separated by at least

```
┌─────────────────────────────────────────────────────────────┐
│  Greece                                                     │
│                                                             │
│  Romania                                                    │
│                                                             │
│  Yugoslavia                                                 │
│                                                             │
│                                                             │
│                                                             │
│                                                             │
│  Contact THE R&R WINE ASSOCIATION at (415) 444-5678.  Or,   │
│                                                             │
│  write to us at the following address:                      │
│  ─────────────────────────────────────────────────────────  │
│            R&R Wine Association                              │
│                                                             │
│            3345 Whitmore Drive                              │
│                                                             │
│            San Francisco, CA                                │
│                                                             │
│  Block on                            Doc 1 Pg 2 Ln 2.67" Pos 4.8" │
└─────────────────────────────────────────────────────────────┘
```

═══ **FIGURE 6-6**  Highlighting text for a block protect

a **[SRt]** or **[HRt]** code, or they will be treated like one block. So, for instance, if you wish to protect a paragraph, define the block as the first character to the last character in the paragraph.

As practice, suppose that you plan to edit the document on screen. You want to make sure, however, that R&R Wine Association's phone number and address are always kept together on the same page. To protect them from being split between different pages, proceed as follows, using the Block Protect feature:

1. Move the cursor to the left margin (at the bottom of page 1) of the line that reads "Contact THE R&R..."

2. Use the Block feature to highlight the text up to and including "San Francisco, CA" as shown in Figure 6-6. (If you'll remember from Chapter 1, one quick method

to highlight the text would be to type **A**—in uppercase—until the entire block is highlighted up to and including the "A" in "San Francisco, CA".)

3. Press the FORMAT ( Shift + F8 ) key. [*Pulldown menu*: Edit (E).] WordPerfect prompts you with

    `Protect block? No (Yes)`

4. Type **Y**. [*Pulldown menu:* Protect Block (T).] Word-Perfect inserts the **[Block Pro:On]** and **[Block Pro:Off]** codes around the block like bookends.

If you switch to the Reveal Codes screen, you can locate the two codes that now surround the block, as shown in Figure 6-7. If the association's phone number and address

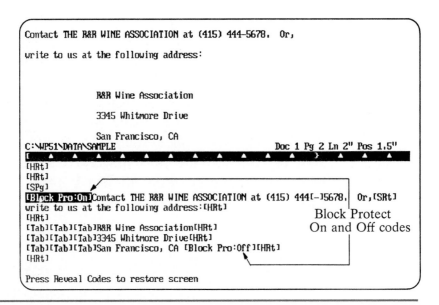

```
Contact THE R&R WINE ASSOCIATION at (415) 444-5678.  Or,

write to us at the following address:


              R&R Wine Association

              3345 Whitmore Drive

              San Francisco, CA
C:\WP51\DATA\SAMPLE                              Doc 1 Pg 2 Ln 2" Pos 1.5"
[HRt]
[HRt]
[SPg]
[Block Pro:On]Contact THE R&R WINE ASSOCIATION at (415) 444[-]5678,  Or,[SRt]
write to us at the following address:[HRt]            Block Protect
[HRt]                                                 On and Off codes
[Tab][Tab][Tab]R&R Wine Association[HRt]
[Tab][Tab][Tab]3345 Whitmore Drive[HRt]
[Tab][Tab][Tab]San Francisco, CA [Block Pro:Off][HRt]
[HRt]

Press Reveal Codes to restore screen
```

**FIGURE 6-7**   Block Protect codes on the Reveal Codes screen

had previously been split by a page break, the text is now readjusted to fall below the page break. Whether you add text above the address or below, those lines of text will not be split by a page break as long as the **[Block Pro:]** codes border those lines.

## Insert Hard Page Breaks

There are instances when you will want even more control over page breaks—for example, when you wish to end a short page of text and begin typing a new page. You might want a title page, a table of contents, and a list of illustrations each on a distinct page of a report. That control is available to you.

To end a short page of text, position the cursor where you want a page bar to appear and simply press Ctrl + Enter. [*Pulldown menu:* Layout (L), Align (A), Hard Page (P).] A Hard Page code **[HPg]** is inserted. The code is "hard" because the page end will not adjust, no matter how you edit the text; a page boundary will always be located at that spot. Of course, the code is hidden on the Typing screen. You will see a page bar of *equal signs*—a double dashed line rather than a single dashed line—so that you can distinguish a hard page from a soft page on the Typing screen.

Suppose that you want to place the last paragraph of the document that you've been working with on a separate page. Proceed as follows:

1. Move the cursor to the left margin of the line that begins "R&R WINE ASSOCIATION, established in 1982. . ."

2. Press [Ctrl] + [Enter]. A page bar appears, and the status line now indicates that the cursor is on page 3.

`Doc 1 Pg 3 Ln 2" Pos 1.5"`

You have ended page 2 early so that the description of the wine association appears on a separate page. If you reveal codes and position the cursor at the bottom of page 2, you will see the **[HPg]** code, as illustrated in Figure 6-8.

In general, it is wise to allow WordPerfect's Automatic Page Break feature to work for you, inserting soft page breaks that will readjust as you edit your text. Reserve hard page breaks for those times when you want to end a short page of text or have a page break at a specific point no

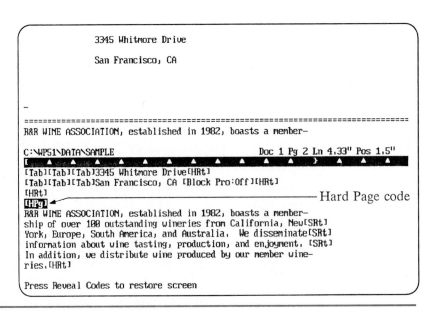

**FIGURE 6-8**   Hard Page code on the Reveal Codes screen

matter how the document changes. Otherwise, you may find that if you use hard pages and then substantially edit a document, pages end at awkward places.

Should you decide to cancel a hard page, you must erase the **[HPg]** code just as you would any other code — either on the Reveal Codes screen or on the Typing screen. Since the page bar gives its location away, an **[HPg]** code can be erased easily on the Typing screen; position the cursor at the left margin just below the page bar and use the Backspace key to delete the code.

# CENTER PAGE TOP TO BOTTOM

WordPerfect offers a feature that will center a short page of text vertically. Maybe you've typed a short letter that you wish to center. Or, perhaps you've created a title page by typing the title, pressing Enter several times to insert blank lines, typing the author's name, and pressing Ctrl + Enter to end the page. To center that short page, position the cursor at the top of the page you wish to center — before any other format codes that may be located there. Then, press the FORMAT (Shift + F8) key and select Page (2 or P). [*Pulldown menu:* Layout (L), Page (P).] The first option, Center Page Top to Bottom, is defaulted at "No," but you can select Center Page Top to Bottom (1 or C) and alter this setting to "Yes." Press EXIT (F7) to return to the document. A **[Center Pg]** code is inserted in the text. For just that one page (*and only that one page* — unlike how most codes operate), the top and bottom margin settings are overridden. The centering occurs only at the printer, not on screen. Figure 6-9 shows a printed page centered in this way.

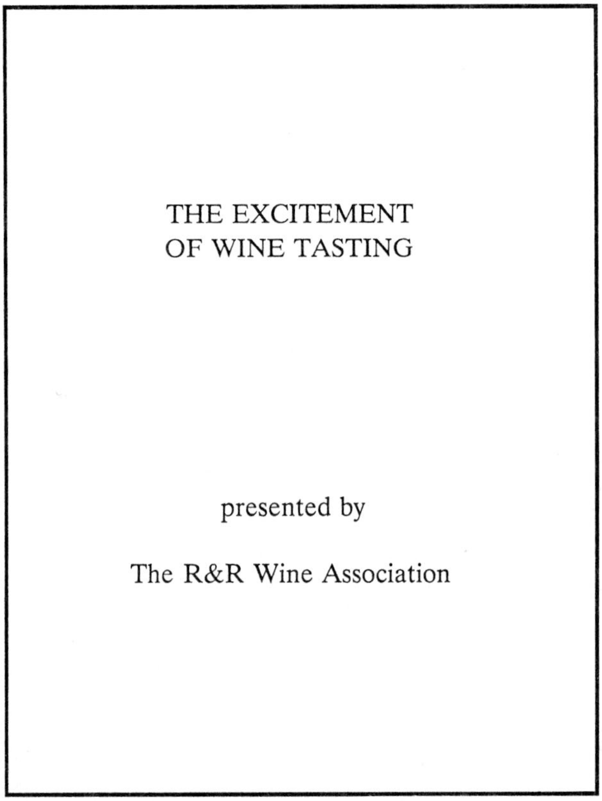

THE EXCITEMENT
OF WINE TASTING


presented by

The R&R Wine Association

**FIGURE 6-9**   A page centered vertically

As an example, let's vertically center the last page of the document on screen:

1. Position the cursor at the very top of page 3.

2. Press the FORMAT ((Shift) + (F8)) key to display the Format menu. [*Pulldown menu:* Layout (L).]

3. Select Page (2 or P) to display the Page Format menu.

4. Select Center Page (1 or C).

5. *5.1 users:* Type **Y**. *5.0 users:* The "No" is automatically changed to "Yes."

6. Press EXIT ( F7 ) to return to the Typing screen.

Remember that the vertical centering is not displayed on screen but takes effect at the printer. To prove that the page will, in fact, center when printed, you can reveal codes to view the **[Center Pg]** code you just inserted. Or you can print the page. Remember that a quick way to do so is to turn on your printer, to press PRINT ( Shift + F7 ), and select (2 or P).

Keep in mind that WordPerfect includes all blank lines occupied by hard return **[HRt]** codes when centering a page. Thus, suppose that at the top of a page, you press Enter twice, type six lines of text, press the Enter key six times to insert six blank lines, and then press Ctrl + Enter to insert a hard page code. WordPerfect will center all 14 lines on the page—two blank lines at the top, six lines of text, six blank lines at the bottom. If you want to center only from the first to the last line of actual text on the page, be sure to delete any hard return **[HRt]** codes located at the top of the page or located at the bottom of the page just before the hard page **[HPg]** code that ends the page.

# INSERT HEADERS/FOOTERS

A *header* prints the same line or lines of text at the top of every page, while a *footer* prints text at the bottom of every page. WordPerfect offers a feature whereby you can create a header or footer. In fact, you can create different headers or footers for alternating pages. For example, in a report, you can insert your company's name at the top of even-numbered pages and the report's topic at the top of odd-numbered pages. An example is shown in Figure 6-10. A header or footer can be one, two, or many lines long.

To create a header or footer, you must position the cursor at the very top of the first page on which you want

R&R Wine Association

Wine Tasting

**FIGURE 6-10**  Alternating headers

the header or footer to appear, before any text. Otherwise, the header or footer won't take effect until the next page. For instance, if you want a header or footer to start at page 1, position the cursor at the top of the document. Also, sometimes a header code must precede other codes at the top of the page—except for a Top/Bottom Margin code or a Paper Size/Type code (described in Chapter 9)—to have an effect on that page.

Once the cursor is positioned, press the FORMAT ( Shift + F8 ) key and select Page (2 or P). [*Pulldown menu:* Layout (L), Page (P).] Then select either Headers (3 or H) or Footers (4 or F). WordPerfect provides a menu with two choices, asking whether you wish to choose a header/footer A or B. For instance, if you select Headers (3 or H), then the following menu appears at the bottom of the Page Format menu:

```
1 Header A; 2 Header B: 0
```

Select the type you want—Header A or B, or Footer A or B. Generally select Header or Footer A first. Select Header or Footer B only if you are creating a second header or footer—for example, you've already created one header in the document on even-numbered pages and you wish to create a second one on odd-numbered pages. Next, Word-Perfect offers options on the frequency with which the header or footer should occur: should WordPerfect print it on every page? On even-numbered pages? The following menu appears:

```
1 Discontinue; 2 Every Page; 3 Odd Pages; 4 Even Pages;
5 Edit: 0
```

Select an option (2, 3, or 4) to choose the pages on which you want the header or footer to appear.

WordPerfect then provides a blank screen on which you would type the header or footer just as you want it to appear. You can use enhancements when typing a header or footer. For instance, use the CENTER (Shift + F6) key if you wish to center the header/footer on each page. Or use the UNDERLINE (F8) key to underscore all or part of the header/footer text. After typing the header or footer, press EXIT (F7) to leave the Header/Footer screen. You are returned to the Page Format menu. The Page Format menu will now indicate the frequency of occurrence of any headers or footers that you created. For instance, next to option 3, Headers, WordPerfect might insert on the Page Format menu "HA Every Page," standing for Header A, Every Page.

When you press EXIT (F7) to return to your document, a Header or Footer code will be inserted in the text, indicating the type and frequency of the header or footer, as well as up to the first 50 characters contained in the header or footer. For instance, suppose you insert a Header A on every page that reads "R&R Wine Association Annual Report." In that case, the code inserted for 5.1 users is **[Header A:Every Page;[UND]**R&R Wine Association Annual Report**[und]]**. For 5.0 users, the code indicates the frequency with which the header will occur with a number corresponding to the item in the Header menu. For instance, since "Every Page" is option 2 on the Header menu, the code inserted for 5.0 users is **[Header A:2;[UND]**R&R Wine Association Annual Report**[und]]**.

Headers and footers appear on the printed page but not on the Typing screen. When printed, a header will start on the first text line of a page and be followed by one blank line to separate it from the first line of the text. A footer will appear on the last text line on each page, preceded by a blank line. For more than one line separating a header from the rest of the page, insert hard returns below the text when you create the header. Similarly, you can insert hard returns above the text of the footer. Top and bottom margins are preserved even when you insert headers or footers in your text; WordPerfect adjusts its soft page breaks to accommodate any headers or footers.

You can also edit the text of a header or footer once you've created it. Suppose, for example, that you inserted a header and now realize that you'd like to change it. Position the cursor after the **[Header:]** code and follow the procedure described above to return to the following menu:

```
1 Discontinue; 2 Every Page; 3 Odd Pages; 4 Even Pages;
5 Edit: 0
```

Then select Edit (5 or E). The Header/Footer screen appears, with the text of your header displayed. When you have corrected the header, press the EXIT (F7) key to save the editing changes.

And you can discontinue a header or footer. Position the cursor at the top of the page where the header/footer will be terminated, return to the Header/Footer menu, and select Discontinue (1 or D). A code such as **[Header A:Discontinue]** for 5.1 users or **[Header A:1]** for 5.0 users is inserted; this code signifies that header A, as defined by the header code further back in the text, is discontinued for the rest of the document.

Here's an opportunity to practice creating a header in the top left corner on every page of the document on screen.

1. Press Home, Home, ↑.

2. Press the FORMAT ([Shift] + [F8]) key. [*Pulldown menu:* Layout (L).]

3. Select Page (2 or P) to display the Page Format menu.

4. Select Headers (3 or H). The following menu appears:

   1 Header **A**; 2 Header **B**: **0**

5. Select Header A (1 or A). Another menu appears:

   1 Discontinue; 2 Every Page; 3 Odd Pages; 4 Even Pages;
   5 Edit: 0

6. Select Every Page (2 or P). A blank Header/Footer screen now displays in order for you to type the header just as it should appear on every page.

7. Type **R&R Wine Association**.

8. Press [Enter] to create an *extra* line of separation between the header and the body of the text.

9. Press the EXIT ([F7]) key to return to the Page Format menu. Notice that this menu now indicates "HA Every Page" next to the item "Headers."

10. Press EXIT ([F7]) to return to the Typing screen.

If you now switch to the Reveal Codes screen, you'll see that the following code has been inserted at the top of the document: **[Header A:Every Page;** R&R Wine Association**[HRt]]**. Remember that a header or footer is never displayed on the Typing screen. If you desire, you can print any one or all three of the pages to find that the header appears on each page, with two blank lines separating it from the body of the text.

# INSERT PAGE NUMBERS

WordPerfect is capable of numbering pages consecutively when you print your document, but only when you direct the program to do so. The page numbers that are printed correspond to the **Pg** number as indicated on the status line. There are two different page numbering methods — within headers and footers, or using the Page Numbering feature.

## Numbering in Headers/Footers

You can insert page numbering within a document by inserting the code ^B within the text of a header or footer. You insert the code ^B on the Header/Footer screen where you want the page number to be printed. For instance, if you want the bottom of each page to read "Page 1," "Page 2," and so on, type **Page ^B** as the footer text. Or, to be more complicated, type the footer to read **R&R Wine Association (Page ^B).** The ^B code is automatically replaced by the appropriate page number when the document is printed.

You create a ^B code by pressing Ctrl + B. Do not create the ^B by typing a caret (^) and then typing **B**; it looks the same on screen, but Ctrl + B is the correct special symbol that WordPerfect recognizes for page numbering in a header or footer.

*Note:* The ^B code can also be used to insert the current page number anywhere within the body of your text, into footnotes, or into endnotes. For instance, press Ctrl + B while typing a paragraph, and, on the printed page, the current page number will appear wherever you inserted the ^B.

## Choosing a Page Number Position

A second method for having WordPerfect number pages for you is with the Page Numbering feature. With this feature, you can swiftly indicate exactly where a page number will appear—whether at the top left, top center, top right, bottom left, bottom center, or bottom right of each page. To do so, position the cursor at the top of the page on which you want numbering to start. Display the Page Format menu by pressing FORMAT ([Shift] + [F8]) and selecting Page (2 or P). [*Pulldown menu:* Layout (L), Page (P).] Then, the procedure is different depending on whether you use WordPerfect version 5.1 or 5.0. *5.1 users:* Select Page Numbering (6 or N) to display the menu shown in Figure 6-11, and then choose Page Number Position (4 or P). *5.0 users:* Select Page Numbering (7 or P).

For both 5.1 and 5.0 users, the menu shown in Figure 6-12 then appears, providing options for where you want page numbers to appear on each printed page. Six of the options are for page numbering in the same position on every page; for instance, type **2** to insert page numbers in the top center of every page. Two other options are for alternating page number locations; for example, type **4** to insert page numbers in the top left corner on even-numbered pages and in the top right corner on odd-numbered pages. Then press EXIT ([F7]) to return to your text. A code is inserted at the current cursor position. For example, if you selected page numbering at the bottom center of every page, the code inserted is **[Pg Numbering: Bottom Center]**.

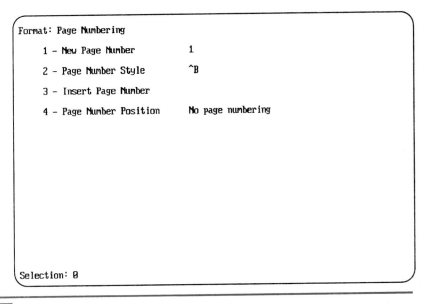

**FIGURE 6-11**  Page Numbering menu (5.1 users only)

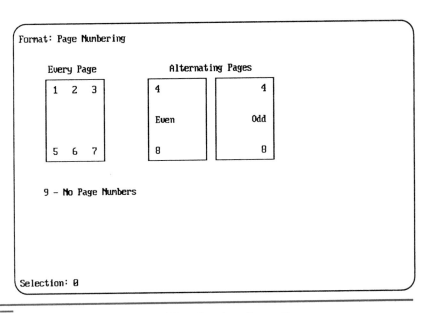

**FIGURE 6-12**  Page Numbering Location menu

Like headers and footers, page numbers added to a document with the Page Numbering feature appear on the printed page but not on the Typing screen. Also like headers and footers, a page number at the top of the page is followed by one blank line, and a page number at the bottom is preceded by one blank line. Soft page breaks adjust to accommodate the page numbering.

Be cautious that you don't create conflicts when choosing both a header or footer and a page number position option. For instance, since you've already created a header that will print in the top left corner of every page for the document on screen, you shouldn't also select page numbers at the top left of every page. Instead, let's insert page numbers at the bottom center of every page:

1. Press [Home], [Home], [↑] to move to the top of the document.

2. Press the FORMAT ([Shift] + [F8]) key. [*Pulldown menu:* Layout (L).]

3. Select Page (2 or P) to display the Page Format menu.

4. *5.1 users:* Select Page Numbering (6 or N) and then Page Number Position (4 or P). *5.0 users:* Select Page Numbering (7 or P). The menu shown in Figure 6-12 appears.

5. Type **6** to center page numbers at the bottom of every page. You are returned to the previous menu. Notice that this menu now indicates "Bottom Center" as the Page Number Position.

6. Press EXIT ([F7]) to return to the document.

The code [**Pg Numbering: Bottom Center**] is inserted at the top of the document. You've now activated WordPerfect's Automatic Page Numbering feature for each page of this document when printed.

*5.1 users only:* You have the added option of including words or phrases with the page number. From the Page Numbering menu shown in Figure 6-11, select Page Number Style (2 or S). WordPerfect displays only the ^B code, which represents the page number. Instead, you can add text to the page number style entry, so that the entry has a maximum of 30 characters. For instance, edit the style to read "Page ^B", or "Introduction—^B". (As discussed previously, remember that it is the keystroke sequence [Ctrl] + [B] that inserts the ^B code.) Then press [Enter]. Now you can choose the Page Number Position item, if you haven't already done so. When you press EXIT ([F7]) to return to the Typing screen, WordPerfect inserts a [**Pg Num Style:**] code in the text that specifies the new page number style. (5.0 users who wish to combine text with page numbers cannot use this method, but must instead include the ^B code within a header or footer. 5.1 users can combine text with page numbers either using the Page Numbering feature or in headers/footers.)

Also on the Page Numbering menu for 5.1 users is Insert Page Number (3 or I), which will insert the current page number on screen wherever the cursor was located before you displayed the Page Numbering menu. The page number will be inserted in whatever page numbering style was previously specified. You are automatically returned to the Typing screen, and WordPerfect inserts an [**Insert Pg Num:**] code in the text.

The remaining item on the Page Numbering menu, New Page Number (1 or N), is described next.

# RENUMBER PAGES AND FORCE ODD/EVEN PAGES

The New Page Number feature allows you to reset page numbers so that you can print out whatever page numbers you choose. For instance, you may have written a book with each chapter saved into its own file. When you print, you will want to number the pages sequentially. Perhaps Chapter 1 ends with page 50; you'll want Chapter 2 to begin at page 51.

When you renumber pages, WordPerfect offers you a choice between Arabic numerals (1, 2, 3...) and lowercase Roman numerals (i, ii, iii...). In that way, a table of contents, abstract, appendix, or bibliography can be numbered with Roman numerals, while the body of your book can be numbered with Arabic numerals. 5.1 users can also specify uppercase Roman numerals (I, II, III...).

To renumber pages, position the cursor at the top of the page where you want to start the renumbering (before any Page Numbering or Header/Footer codes already inserted on that page). *5.1 users:* Select New Page Number (1 or N) from the Page Numbering menu as shown in Figure 6-11. *5.0 users:* Select New Page Number (6 or N) from the Page Format menu. Then type in the new page number in either Arabic style or as a Roman numeral and press ⌐Enter⌐. Press EXIT (⌐F7⌐) to return to the document.

WordPerfect inserts a Page Numbering code in the text. For instance, **[Pg Num:51]** indicates page 51 in Arabic style, while **[Pg Num:i]** indicates page 1 in lowercase Roman numeral style. When the cursor is to the right of or below that Page Numbering code, the **Pg** indicator on the status line reflects the new page number—*but not the numbering style.* The status line shows Arabic numerals on screen even when you choose Roman—the Roman numerals appear only at the printer. All subsequent pages are renumbered consecutively to the end of the document or up to the next **[Pg Num:]** code found farther forward in the document.

Besides renumbering pages, WordPerfect allows you to dictate that a certain page be assigned an odd or even number. This is useful, for instance, to ensure that the first page of a report or book chapter is an odd-numbered page. To use the Force Odd/Even Page feature, make sure that the cursor is at the top of the page, before any Page Numbering or Header/Footer codes that may be located on that page. Select Force Odd/Even (2 or O) on the Page Format menu. WordPerfect responds by displaying the following menu at the bottom of the screen:

`1 Odd; 2 Even: 0`

Select from these two options and then press EXIT ( F7 ) to return to your document. A **[Force:Odd]** or **[Force: Even]** code is inserted on that page. You may find that WordPerfect inserts a blank page as a result of this feature. If, for example, you insert a **[Force:Odd]** code at the top of page 2, then the page is renumbered to page 3 and a blank page is inserted as page 2. If, however, you insert a **[Force: Even]** code at the top of page 2, the page retains its number since it is, in fact, an even-numbered page.

# SUPPRESS HEADERS, FOOTERS, AND PAGE NUMBERING

What if you wish to print a header, a footer, or page numbers on all but a select page? You can suppress those features on specific pages. For instance, you can insert a

Header code on page 1 and then also suppress that code on page 1; a header will appear on all but the first page of the document.

To suppress headers, footers, and/or page numbers, position the cursor at the top of the page on which you wish to suppress a feature, and from the Page Format menu select Suppress (8 or U for 5.1 users; 9 or U for 5.0 users). The menu in Figure 6-13 appears. Next indicate what feature or combination of features you want to suppress. For instance, select Suppress Page Numbering (4 or P) and type **Y** so that page numbers inserted using the Page Numbering feature do not appear on that page—although headers and footers will appear (as well as page numbers if inserted in a header or footer using ^B). Or select Suppress Header A (5 or H) and type **Y** to suppress only header A on that page. Or select Suppress Headers and Footers (2 or

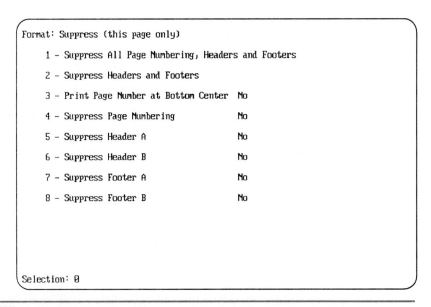

```
Format: Suppress (this page only)

      1 - Suppress All Page Numbering, Headers and Footers

      2 - Suppress Headers and Footers

      3 - Print Page Number at Bottom Center   No

      4 - Suppress Page Numbering              No

      5 - Suppress Header A                     No

      6 - Suppress Header B                     No

      7 - Suppress Footer A                     No

      8 - Suppress Footer B                     No



Selection: 8
```

**FIGURE 6-13**   Suppress (this page only) menu

S) to suppress all headers and footers on that page —
although page numbers will appear. (When you select
option 1 or 2 on the Suppress menu, it is unnecessary to
type **Y** or **N**; WordPerfect changes "No" to "Yes" where
appropriate.) Now press EXIT ( [F7] ) to return to the Typing screen.

When you suppress headers, footers, and/or page numbering on a specific page, a **[Suppress:]** code is inserted.
For instance, if you elect to suppress headers and footers,
then the code inserted is **[Suppress:HA,HB,FA,FB]**. Unlike
most other codes, this one takes effect *only for the current
page.*

Suppose you wish to suppress the page numbering,
headers, and footers for the last page of your document on
screen:

1. Press [PgDn] until you're at the top of page 3.

2. Press the FORMAT ( [Shift] + [F8] ) key. [*Pulldown
   menu:* Layout (L).]

3. Select Page (2 or P) to display the Page Format menu.

4. Select Suppress (8 or U for 5.1 users; 9 or U for 5.0
   users). The menu shown in Figure 6-13 appears.

5. Select Suppress All Page Numbering, Headers and Foot
   ers (1 or A). Notice that WordPerfect changes "No" to
   "Yes" for options 4 through 8.

6. Press EXIT ( [F7] ) to return to the Typing screen.

If you now reveal codes, you'll view the following new
code that you inserted: **[Suppress:PgNum,HA,HB,FA,FB]**.
Print page 3 and you'll see that, in fact, there is no page
number or header on the page. In fact, print all three

pages. Since the start of this chapter, you've inserted various page format codes into the text. You'll find when you print that there are page numbers and headers on pages 1 and 2 and that page 3 is centered vertically.

*Note*: You should know that there is a method for previewing the format of your document before it is actually printed. The View Document feature displays a replica of each page of your document, showing the current settings for margins, headers, footers, and page numbers. For instance, if you use the View Document feature with the document currently on your computer screen, you can see pages with top and bottom margins as you set them earlier in this chapter and with page numbers and headers on pages 1 and 2. This feature enables you to save paper, printing a document only after checking to make sure that the format of your document meets your approval. Refer to Chapter 9 for more on the View Document feature.

# MOVE THE CURSOR BETWEEN PAGES AND AROUND CODES

As you've followed the step-by-step instructions in this chapter, you've created and worked with a three-page document. You will undoubtedly find yourself typing documents with even more pages. WordPerfect offers a number of keystrokes to quickly move between pages.

The (PgUp) and (PgDn) keys, located on the cursor movement keypad, move the cursor between pages, as follows:

| | |
|---|---|
| [PgUp] | Top line of previous page |
| [PgDn] | Top line of next page |

In addition, there are a variety of ways to move page by page with the GOTO ([Ctrl] + [Home]). [*Pulldown menu: Search (S), Goto (G).*] When you press [Ctrl] + [Home], WordPerfect prompts

Go to

Now you can type an arrow key or enter a number to move the cursor as follows:

| | |
|---|---|
| [Ctrl] + [Home], [↑] | Top line of page (the page where the cursor is currently located) |
| [Ctrl] + [Home], [↓] | Bottom line of page |
| [Ctrl] + [Home], *page number,* [Enter] | Top of a specified page |

There are quick ways to move to the first or last page of a document as well. You learned previously that [Home], [Home], [↓] takes the cursor to the bottom of a document and [Home], [Home], [↑] takes the cursor to the top of the document. This applies no matter what page the cursor is on. For instance, if you are on page 1 and you press [Home], [Home], [↓], the cursor moves to the bottom of the document even if the document is 35 pages long (although it might take WordPerfect a few moments to do so when the document is long).

Now that you know about format codes, there are subtleties that you should also be aware of when you move the cursor with the [Home] key on lines containing codes. As you now know, numerous codes may reside at the top of a document—codes to change the document's default format settings. [Home], [Home], [↑] places the cursor at the top of the document, but *after* all format codes that reside there. Press [Home] one more time—that is, press [Home], [Home], [Home], [↑]—and the cursor moves to the top of the document, but *before* all codes that reside there. Similarly, [Home], [Home], [←] positions the cursor at the beginning of a line and after codes, while [Home], [Home], [Home], [←] positions the cursor at the beginning of the line and before codes. As an example, suppose you've inserted five format codes at the top of your document. If you press [Home], [Home], [↑], then the cursor moves to the top of the document, but not before the codes residing there:

```
[L/R Mar:1,5",1"][Just:Left][HZone:5%,8%][Hyph On][Ln Spacing:2]Two of the major
wine[-]producing countries in Europe are[SRt]
```

Notice that the cursor is highlighting the "T" in "Two". But, here's what results if you press [Home], [Home], [Home], [↑]:

```
[L/R Mar:1,5",1"][Just:Left][HZone:5%,8%][Hyph On][Ln Spacing:2]Two of the major
wine[-]producing countries in Europe are[SRt]
```

The cursor moves to the absolute top of the document, before the codes, so that it resides on the **[L/R Mar:]** code. These differences are only apparent on the Reveal Codes screen. But, as you work more and more with WordPerfect, and as you insert more and more codes into documents, precise cursor control will become important.

For the document on screen, try the following to become comfortable moving from page to page in a document:

1. Press [Home], [Home], [↓] to move to the bottom of the document.

2. Press [Ctrl] + [Home], [↑]. The cursor moves to the top of page 3.

3. Press [PgUp]. The cursor moves to the top of page 2.

4. Press [PgDn]. The cursor moves back to the top of page 3.

5. Press [Home], [Home], [↑] to move to the top of the document. Now the cursor is located after the codes, on the "T" in "Two." If you Reveal Codes, you'll see the screen shown in Figure 6-14, with the cursor situated after the three lines of codes.

6. Press [Ctrl] + [Home] and, when you see the "Goto" prompt, type **3** and press [Enter]. The cursor moves to the top of page 3.

7. Press [Home], [Home], [Home], [↑] to move to the top of the document before any codes. The cursor is at the far left side of the screen because it is now located before the Left/Right Margin code that establishes a left margin of 1.5″.

# PLACE CODES ON THE DOCUMENT INITIAL CODES SCREEN

As shown in Figure 6-14, you can amass many format codes together on a certain line in a document. In Figure 6-14, they are all located at the top of the document.

```
     Two of the major wine-producing countries in Europe are

     France and Italy.  France produces a wide variety, and de-

     lightful Bordeaux is often considered one of the centers of

     fine wine.  In Italy, wine production takes place in just

     about every region.  In fact, Italy has been known to yield

     more wine per year than any other country in the world.
C:\WP51\DATA\SAMPLE                          Doc 1 Pg 1 Ln 2.5" Pos 1.5"
     ▲   ▲    ▲    ▲    ▲    ▲    ▲    ▲    ▲    ▲    ▲    }    ▲    ▲
[L/R Mar:1.5",1"][Just:Left][HZone:5%,0%][Hyph On][Ln Spacing:2][T/B Mar:2",1"][
Header A:Every page;R&R Wine Association[HRt]
][Pg Numbering:Bottom Center]Two of the major wine[-]producing countries in Euro
pe are[SRt]
France and Italy.  France produces a wide variety, and de-
lightful [/]Bordeaux is often considered one of the centers of[SRt]
fine wine.  In Italy, wine production takes place in just[SRt]
about every region.  In fact, Italy has been known to yield[SRt]
more wine per year than any other coun-try in the world. [SRt]
Though white wines are manufactured here, it is Italy's red[SRt]

Press Reveal Codes to restore screen
```

**FIGURE 6-14**   Cursor at top of document but after
format codes

WordPerfect offers the ability to place many format codes that would otherwise appear at the top of the document on a special screen, the Document Initial Codes screen. By inserting format codes on this screen rather than in the document itself, you (1) reduce the clutter at the top of the document, and (2) safeguard against accidentally moving or erasing a code, something that is all too easy to do when a code is in the document itself.

Place a format code on the Document Initial Codes screen only if you wish to change a document's format starting *at the top* of the document. Any format codes of the same type that are found in the document itself override any codes on the Document Initial Codes screen. Thus, the hierarchy of how a document is formatted is as follows: (1) when a document is first created, WordPerfect assumes default settings; (2) if a format code is located on the

Document Initial Codes screen, then the default setting is overridden by that format code; (3) if a format code is located in the text of the document itself, then the format code on the Document Initial Codes screen is overridden by the code in the text, from the point where that code is located until the end of the document or until the next code of its type farther forward in the text.

You can access the Document Initial Codes screen with your cursor positioned anywhere on screen. Press the FORMAT ( Shift + F8 ) key. Then select Document (3 or D), in which case the Document Format menu shown in Figure 6-15 appears. [*Pulldown menu:* Layout (L), Document (D).] Select Initial Codes (2 or C). A screen that resembles a Reveal Codes screen appears. Then proceed as if you were placing a format code within the document itself. When

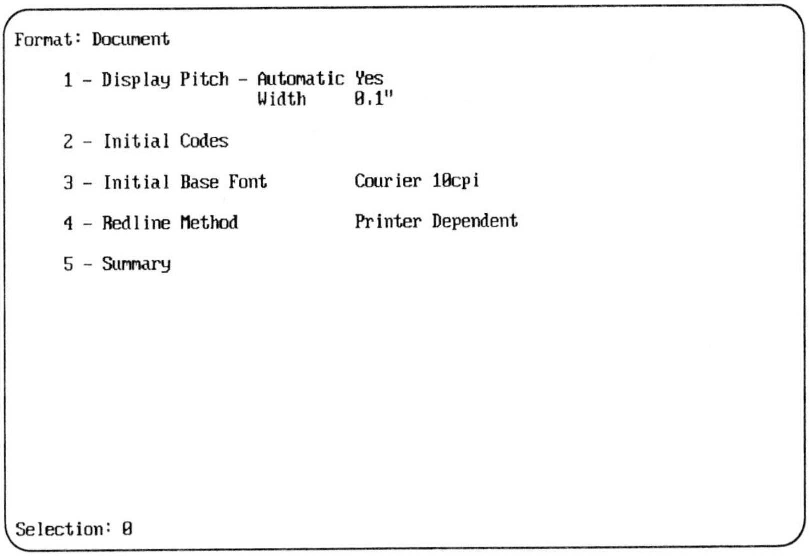

```
Format: Document

      1 - Display Pitch - Automatic  Yes
                          Width      0.1"

      2 - Initial Codes

      3 - Initial Base Font          Courier 10cpi

      4 - Redline Method             Printer Dependent

      5 - Summary




Selection: 0
```

**FIGURE 6-15**  Document Format menu

you exit the Document Initial Codes screen using the EXIT ( F7 ) key, your cursor repositions at the top of the document on screen.

Codes inserted on the Document Initial Codes screen are never displayed when you reveal codes in a document. You can see the erase, or edit codes only when you return to the Document Initial Codes screen.

Let's view the current Document Initial Codes screen for the file named SAMPLE:

1. With the cursor positioned anywhere in the document, press the FORMAT ( Shift + F8 ) key. [*Pulldown menu:* Layout (L).]

2. Select Document (3 or D). You will then see the Document Format menu, as shown in Figure 6-15.

3. Select Initial Codes (2 or C). The Document Initial Codes screen appears, as shown in Figure 6-16. This screen is split into two windows and separated by a tab ruler line (which shows the default margin and tab settings), just like the Reveal Codes screen. The Document Initial Codes screen is blank. If there were codes on this screen, however, the codes would be hidden in the top window and displayed in the bottom window. (*5.0 Users:* On your Document Initial Codes screen, the words "Initial Codes:" are omitted.)

4. Press the EXIT ( F7 ) key to exit the Document Initial Codes screen.

5. Press EXIT ( F7 ) to return to your document.

Because the Document Initial Codes screen is blank, you can tell that no changes have yet been made to the default settings. However, format codes in the text serve to override the defaults.

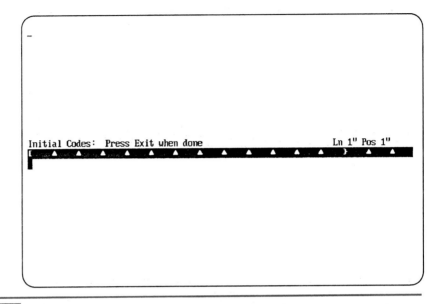

Initial Codes: Press Exit when done                    Ln 1" Pos 1"

**FIGURE 6-16**   A clear Document Initial Codes screen

*Note*: If on your screen you find that one or more codes appear in the bottom window of the Document Initial Codes screen, then someone else has altered certain default settings for the copy of WordPerfect you are using. Besides changing default formats for particular documents, you also have the ability to change the default format settings permanently—for all documents that you create from that point on.

Now that you know about the Document Initial Codes screen and the advantage to keeping the amount of codes within a document to a minimum, let's place the first six codes found at the top of the document on the Document Initial Codes screen. Then these codes can be erased from the top of the document, reducing the clutter at the top and safeguarding against tampering with them if the text is later edited. One way would be to erase these codes, display the Document Initial Codes screen, and then reinsert each code one-by-one using the Line and Page format menus. However, the codes are already in the document. You learned in the last chapter that WordPerfect allows you to move blocks of text and/or codes. Thus, as a short-cut, let's use the Move feature to relocate the codes.

1. Press Home, Home, Home, ⬆ to position the cursor at the top of the document before any codes.

2. Press REVEAL CODES (Alt + F3) to display the codes at the top of the document. [*Pulldown menu:* Edit (E), Reveal Codes (R).]

3. Press BLOCK (Alt + F4) to turn on the Block feature. [*Pulldown menu:* Edit (E), Block (B).]

4. Press the ➡ key six times to define the block as including the first six codes. The cursor should be positioned past the sixth code, which is a Top/Bottom Margin code that you inserted at the start of this chapter.

5. Press MOVE (Ctrl + F4), Block (1 or B), Move (1 or M). [*Pulldown menu:* Edit (E), Move (M).] Above the tab ruler line WordPerfect prompts "Move cursor; press **Enter** to retrieve."

6. Press FORMAT (Shift + F8) and select Document (3 or D), Initial Codes (2 or C) to display the Document Initial Codes screen.

7. Press Enter. The codes are inserted, as shown in Figure 6-17.

8. Press EXIT (F7) twice to return to the Typing screen.

The document is still formatted with special left/right margin, top/bottom margin, hyphenation, and justification

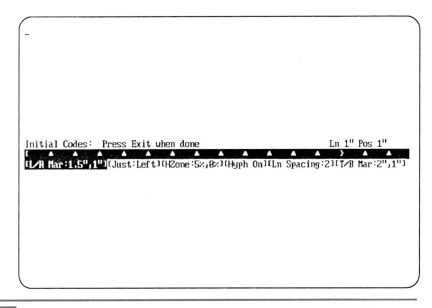

Initial Codes: Press Exit when done                          Ln 1" Pos 1"
[L/R Mar:1.5",1"][Just:Left][HZone:5%,8%][Hyph On][Ln Spacing:2][T/B Mar:2",1"]

**FIGURE 6-17**   Document Initial Codes screen with codes inserted

settings—even though those codes are not in the text of the document itself. These codes are instead on the Document Initial Codes screen. If you wish to view or edit the codes, you must return to that screen.

Most format codes are allowed on the Document Initial Codes screen. Exceptions include header or footer codes; these must be inserted within the text of the document itself.

Format changes made on the Document Initial Codes screen affect only the one document to which the changes were made, just like format changes made within the text of the document itself. If you clear the screen to begin typing a new document, the new document starts out with all the default settings. For instance:

1. Press EXIT ( F7 ) to resave this document.

2. Resave this document under the name SAMPLE, and then clear the screen (but remain in WordPerfect).

3. Use the Document Format menu to again display the Document Initial Codes screen, this time for the clear screen. The Document Initial Codes screen is again free of codes.

4. Press EXIT ( F7 ) twice to return to the Typing screen.

# REVIEW EXERCISE

You are now ready to tackle a document of any length! For practice, find a two- to three-page document that's on your desk and follow the suggestions below. You'll reassure yourself that you can easily format pages any way you desire.

1. Clear the screen.

2. For the document that you're about to type, change the top and bottom margins to 2″. (*Hint:* Since you are changing top/bottom margins starting at the top of the document, insert the Top/Bottom Margin code on the Document Initial Codes screen.)

3. Turn on Widow/Orphan Protection so that WordPerfect is given flexibility in inserting page breaks. (*Hint:* This code can also be inserted on the Document Initial Codes screen.)

4. Type and edit your multiple-page document. Now Word-Perfect inserts automatic page breaks after 7″ of text are typed (11″ minus 2″ minus 2″, or after Line 8.8″ approximately).

5. Create the following header, which will insert a page number on every page:

   Review Exercise -- ^B

   (*Hint:* Before pressing the FORMAT ( Shift + F8 ) key to insert the header, be sure to move to the very top of the document. **[Header:]** and **[Footer:]** codes cannot be inserted on the Document Initial Codes screen. Remember to use Ctrl + B to create the "^B" character.)

6. Scroll through the document. Notice that since you created the header, page breaks have adjusted to accommodate the one-line header and its accompanying blank line.

7. Print the document to examine the final results of your work, and then clear the screen (making sure to save your document if you plan to edit, print, or reuse the document later on).

## Quick Review

• WordPerfect automatically inserts page breaks in your text after the maximum number of lines that can fit on a page are typed. These page breaks are "soft" because they will readjust when add or delete lines during text editing.

• Change the top/bottom margins of your text by pressing FORMAT ([Shift] + [F8]) and selecting Page (2 or P). Or, pulldown menu users can select Layout (L), Page (P). From the Page Format menu that displays, select Margins (5 or M) and enter the new margin settings. Soft page breaks adjust based on the new margin settings.

• Widow/Orphan Protection guards against the first or last line of a paragraph being separated from the rest of the paragraph because of a soft page break. Turn on this feature by pressing FORMAT ([Shift] + [F8]) and selecting Line (1 or L). Or, pulldown menu users can select Layout (L), Line (L). Then, from the Line Format menu select Widow/Orphan Protection (9 or W). WordPerfect will then readjust any soft page breaks that would otherwise cause an awkward separation of a line or a paragraph.

• To protect a block against being split onto separate pages because of an untimely soft page break, use the Block feature to highlight the block of text. Then, press FORMAT ([Shift] + [F8]) and type **Y** to protect the block. Or, pulldown menu users can select Edit (E), Protect Block (T). Block Protection is especially useful for keeping the text of charts or tables together on the same page.

- To protect a specific number of lines from being split onto separate pages, position the cursor just above those lines, press FORMAT ([Shift] + [F8]), and select Other (4 or O). Or pulldown menu users can select Layout (L), Other (O). Then select Conditional End of Page (2 or C), and enter a number representing the lines to be kept together. Conditional EOP is especially useful for keeping headings together with a few lines of text on the same page.

- Press [Ctrl] + [Enter] to insert a page break only if a new page must start at a specific location in your text. Or pulldown menu users can select Layout (L), Align (A), Hard Page (P). Otherwise, let WordPerfect's Automatic Page Break feature adjust your page ends.

- Center a short page of text by positioning the cursor at the top of that page, pressing FORMAT ([Shift] + [F8]), and selecting Page (2 or P). Or, pulldown menu users can select Layout (L), Page (P). From the Page Format menu that displays, select Center Page (1 or C). Top/bottom margins are' overridden for the current page only.

- Insert headers or footers in your document from the Page Format menu by selecting Header (3 or H) or

Footer (4 or F). Then, choose either a first (A) or second (B) header/footer, indicate the frequency with which you want the header/footer to appear, and type the text of the header/footer. Headers and footers appear on the printed page, but not on the Typing screen.

- Number pages in your printed document from the Page Format menu. *5.1 users*: select Page Numbering (6 or N), and then select Page Number Position (4 or P). *5.0 users*: select Page Numbering (7 or P). Then enter a page numbering location to activate automatic page numbering.

  Or, you can have WordPerfect number your pages within a header or footer. Insert the ^B code into the text of the header/footer by pressing [Ctrl] + [B]. ^B will be replaced by the current page number when the text is printed. Page numbers appear on the printed page, but not on the Typing screen.

- Suppress headers/footers and/or page numbering for a specific page on the Page Format menu by selecting Suppress (8 or U for 5.1 users, 9 or U for 5.0 users) and then choosing the specific headers, footers, and/or page numbering that you wish to suppress. Headers, footers, and/or page numbering are ignored for the current page only.

- The methods for moving the cursor quickly between pages and around format codes in a document are summarized in Table 6-1.

- Most format codes can be inserted on the Document Initial Codes screen to affect the format starting at the beginning of the document. Press FORMAT ( Shift + F8 ) and select Document (3 or D). Or, pulldown menu users can select Layout (L), Document (D). From the Document Format menu that appears, choose Initial Codes (2 or C) to display the Document Initial Codes screen. Insert codes on this screen to avoid the possible clutter of codes at the top of the document and to guard against accidentally erasing a code when you edit the document text.

  Format codes inserted into the text of a document itself override any code of the same type on the Document Initial Codes screen and affect all text forward to the end of the document or until the next code of the same type. It is thus critical to position the cursor carefully before inserting a format code.

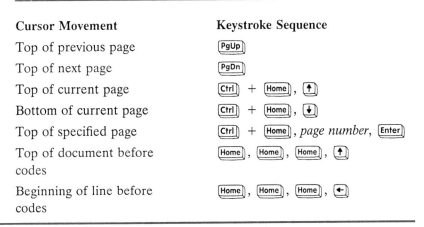

| Cursor Movement | Keystroke Sequence |
| --- | --- |
| Top of previous page | PgUp |
| Top of next page | PgDn |
| Top of current page | Ctrl + Home , ↑ |
| Bottom of current page | Ctrl + Home , ↓ |
| Top of specified page | Ctrl + Home , *page number*, Enter |
| Top of document before codes | Home , Home , Home , ↑ |
| Beginning of line before codes | Home , Home , Home , ← |

**TABLE 6-1**  Cursor Movement Between Pages and Around Codes

# THE SPELLER AND
# THE THESAURUS

When proofreading a document, you can easily miss spelling errors—especially if you're the author and all too familiar with the material. WordPerfect offers a comprehensive spelling checker packed with more than 100,000 words in its dictionary. The Spell feature makes sure that all the words in a document are spelled correctly by comparing each word with those in its dictionary. You can thus ensure that there are no misspellings before you print.

Another bonus is WordPerfect's Thesaurus feature, which helps you find just the right phrase as you're writing a document. It is also useful when you're not sure of the exact meaning of a word: it provides synonyms and antonyms for some 10,000 common words. In this chapter, you'll learn how to access a dictionary and thesaurus as you write your documents by tapping keys rather than by lifting heavy books.

# SPELL CHECK A WORD

WordPerfect's Spell feature lets you verify the spelling of a word before you type it or check spelling in a document that you've finished typing. WordPerfect's dictionary is split into two separate lists: a common word list of 2500 words and a main word list of 115,000 words. The latter is quite comprehensive—it even includes some technical terms, such as "endocrinology," and some proper nouns, such as "John" and "Smith." When you use the spell checker, the common word list is always checked first; this makes for a speedy spelling check.

The dictionary is stored on the Speller disk, in a file called WP{WP}US.LEX. (The letters "US" in the filename indicate the U.S. English dictionary. If you purchased one of the first releases of version 5, then your dictionary may be in a file named WP{WP}*EN*.LEX, rather than in the file WP{WP}*US*.LEX. When WordPerfect Corporation first released version 5, the United States English dictionary was identified with the letters "EN," which stood for "English," and was later changed to "US.") To have access to the dictionary, floppy disk users must insert into drive B the Speller disk that you created when installing WordPerfect.

Hard disk users should already have the dictionary stored on the hard disk. (If not, hard disk users should turn to Appendix A to learn how to install the dictionary onto your hard disk.) You are now ready to use the Spell feature.

*Note:* You can purchase additional dictionaries (at an additional charge) in several languages. The two initials that follow the "WP{WP}" in the dictionary's filename indicate the language. For instance, WP{WP}US.LEX is the United States English version, while WP{WP}PO.LEX is the Portuguese dictionary. WordPerfect offers dictionaries for version 5.0 and 5.1 in a variety of languages, including: Catalonian (CA); Danish (DK); Dutch (NL in version 5.1, NE in version 5.0); Finnish (SU); French (FR); French, Canadian (CF in version 5.1, CA in version 5.0); English, United States (US or EN); German (DE); German, Swiss (SD); Icelandic (IS in version 5.1, IC in version 5.0); Italian (IT); Norwegian (NO); Portuguese (PO); Spanish (ES); Swedish (SV). New dictionaries are developed all the time, so check WordPerfect Corporation for the most current list and if you wish to purchase foreign language dictionaries.

When you have acquired a foreign language dictionary and wish to use it in a document, you must inform Word-Perfect by using the Language feature, which inserts a Language code in the text. Position the cursor where another dictionary should be used during the spell check, press FORMAT ( Shift + F8 ) and select Other (4 or O). [*Pulldown menu:* Layout (L), Other (O).] Then select Language (4 or L), and then enter the two letters representing that language (such as FR for French). WordPerfect inserts a Language code into the text, such as **[Lang:FR]**, which informs WordPerfect which language to use from that point forward in the document. (The Language code also affects which hyphenation file and thesaurus file are used.)

## Check a Word Before You Type

Suppose you're typing a document and you aren't sure how to spell a word. You're probably used to reaching over to a shelf of books and grabbing *Webster's.* Instead, you can rely on WordPerfect. When you are about to type a word, press the SPELL (Ctrl + F2 ) key. [*Pulldown menu:* Tools (T), Spell (E).] WordPerfect prompts you to wait as it accesses the dictionary. The following menu then appears on the screen:

```
Check: 1 Word; 2 Page; 3 Document; 4 New Sup. Dictionary;
5 Look Up; 6 Count: 0
```

Select Look Up (5 or L), and WordPerfect responds with

```
Word or word pattern:
```

You must provide WordPerfect with some indication of the word you want to look up, so that it can respond with some correctly spelled words from the dictionary. You have two alternatives. First, you can type in the word *as you think it should be spelled.* Where there are letters you aren't sure of, you can use the wild cards ? and *. The question mark (?) substitutes for one letter, while the asterisk (*) substitutes for any number of letters. For example, if you can't remember how to spell "hippopotamus," you can type **hippo\*** and then press Enter . The screen splits in half, and the lower portion displays a list of possibilities, as shown in Figure 7-1. As another example, if you don't remember which vowels are where in the word "repetition," you can type **r?p?t?tion** and press (Enter). WordPerfect responds with "repetition" and "reputation." Alternatively, if you have no idea how a word is spelled, you can type in the word *as it sounds*—that is, spell it out phonetically. For instance, suppose you didn't remember how to spell the word "cinnamon." You can sound it out and type what you hear—for example, "sinomon." Or, if you try the word pattern "fobea," you'd find out how to spell "phobia" and "phoebe."

When you are done verifying the spelling of a word, press the CANCEL ((F1)) key, EXIT ((F7)) key, (Enter), or

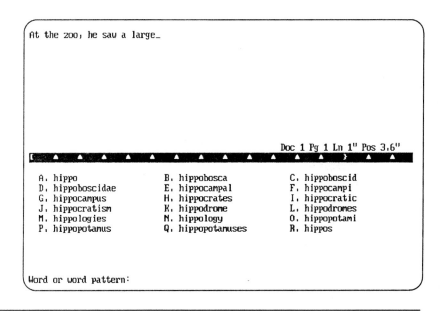

**FIGURE 7-1**  Speller screen when looking up "hippo*"

spacebar twice—once to return to the Spell menu and a second time to exit the Spell feature. Now you can type the word you just looked up and continue writing your document.

For practice, suppose you can't remember how to spell the word "peculiar." Let's use the Spell feature and sound out the word phonetically.

1. *Floppy disk users:* Replace the disk currently in drive B with the disk you labelled as the Speller disk. *Hard disk users:* Proceed directly to step 2. (If you have not installed the Speller on a floppy or hard disk, refer to the installation instructions in Appendix A.)

2. Press the SPELL (Ctrl + F2) key. [*Pulldown menu:* Tools (T), Spell (E).] After a few moments, Word-Perfect responds with

   ```
   Check: 1 Word; 2 Page; 3 Document; 4 New Sup. Dictionary;
   5 Look Up; 6 Count: 0
   ```

3. Select Look Up (5 or L). WordPerfect responds with

   ```
   Word or word pattern:
   ```

4. Type **pakular** (one possible guess as to how the word sounds) and press (Enter). After a few moments, Word-Perfect lists the word "peculiar," the only word in its dictionary that sounds like the word pattern you typed. After a few more moments of checking its dictionary, WordPerfect asks for a new word pattern.

5. Press the CANCEL (F1) key twice to exit the Spell feature.

6. *Floppy disk users:* Remove the Speller disk from drive
B and reinsert the disk used to store your documents.
(When done using the Spell feature, floppy disk users
should always remember to remove the Speller disk
from drive B and reinsert the disk previously stored
there; otherwise, when you later save a document to
disk, you could accidentally store a file on the Speller
disk, which you don't want to do. You will want to leave
any available room on the Speller disk to store some of
your own dictionary words in a supplementary dictionary, described later in this chapter.)

*Note:* If you attempt to use the Spell feature and Word-
Perfect cannot find where the dictionary is stored, the
following menu will appear:

```
WP{WP}US.LEX not found: 1 Enter Path; 2 Skip Language;
3 Exit Spell: 3
```

In that case, Select Enter Path (1 or P), type in the drive
and/or directory where the dictionary can be found (such as
**B:** if the Speller disk is in the B drive or **C:WP51\SPELL** if
the dictionary has been stored in a directory on the hard
disk named \WP51\SPELL), and press Enter. Then proceed
with the Spell feature. Skip Language (2 or S) would allow
you to proceed with other features of the Speller, as described further, but not to check the spelling of words. Exit
Spell (3 or S) would cancel the Spell feature. If this
"WP{WP}US.LEX not found" menu appears in every
working session when you try to access the Spell feature,
then permanently indicate to WordPerfect where the dictionary is located. Refer to the section entitled "Location
of Files" in Appendix B for details.

## Check a Word Already Typed

If you wish to check the spelling of a word that has already been typed on screen, position the cursor anywhere within that word and press the SPELL (Ctrl + F2) key. [*Pull-down menu:* Tools (T), Spell (E).] The Spell Check menu appears; select Word (1 or W).

When that word is found in the dictionary (meaning that it is properly spelled), the word is passed over; the cursor simply jumps to the next word on screen, and the Spell Check menu remains at the bottom of the screen. You can then either select another option from the menu or press the CANCEL (F1) key to exit the Spell feature.

When that word is not in the dictionary, it will be highlighted in reverse video at the top of the screen. Just as when you were finding out how to spell "peculiar," the screen splits in half. In the lower portion, WordPerfect suggests replacements for the highlighted word, guessing at what you had intended to type; a Not Found menu appears at the very bottom of the screen.

Not Found: **1** Skip Once; **2** Skip; **3** Add; **4** Edit; **5** Look Up; **6** Ignore Numbers: **0**

An example is shown in Figure 7-2 where WordPerfect cannot find the word "takked" in the dictionary. From here, you have several choices.

*If the word is misspelled and WordPerfect has suggested a proper replacement,* you can press the corresponding letter to select that word. For instance, Figure 7-2 shows that WordPerfect suggests 21 possible replacements for the misspelled "takked." Type **B** and WordPerfect will replace "takked" with "talked." The cursor will then jump to the next word on the screen, preparing for a spell check of the next word.

*If the word is misspelled but WordPerfect has not suggested the correct replacement,* then you have two possible options available on the Not Found menu displayed at the bottom of the screen:

- *Edit (4)*   Select this option to correct the word yourself. (Or you can select the Edit option by pressing the ⬅ or ➡.) The cursor moves up to the word in the text so that you can correct the misspelling using all the standard editing keys, such as Del or Backspace. You then press the EXIT (F7) key, as indicated at the bottom of the screen, to continue with the spell check.

- *Look Up (5)*   Select this option to request a new list of

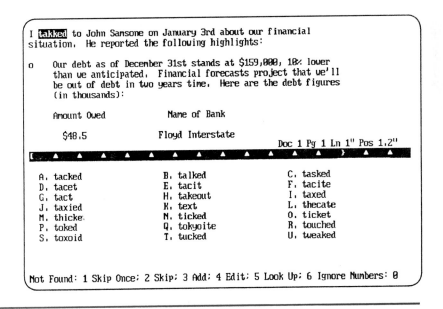

I **takked** to John Sansone on January 3rd about our financial situation. He reported the following highlights:

o    Our debt as of December 31st stands at $159,000, 18% lower than we anticipated. Financial forecasts project that we'll be out of debt in two years time. Here are the debt figures (in thousands):

      Amount Owed              Name of Bank

      $48.5                    Floyd Interstate

                                              Doc 1 Pg 1 Ln 1" Pos 1.2"

| A. tacked | B. talked | C. tasked |
| D. tacet | E. tacit | F. tacite |
| G. tact | H. takeout | I. taxed |
| J. taxied | K. text | L. thecate |
| M. thicke. | N. ticked | O. ticket |
| P. toked | Q. tokyoite | R. touched |
| S. toxoid | T. tucked | U. tweaked |

Not Found: 1 Skip Once; 2 Skip; 3 Add; 4 Edit; 5 Look Up; 6 Ignore Numbers: 0

**FIGURE 7-2**   Speller screen with replacements for "takked"

replacement words. WordPerfect prompts you for a word pattern; you can then spell out the word as best you can, using the asterisk (*) to substitute for any number of characters and the question mark (?) to substitute for one character, as described previously. WordPerfect will provide a new list of possible replacements. Choose a word from the new list, type in a new word pattern, or press the CANCEL ((F1)) key or (Enter) to return to the Spell menu.

*If the highlighted word is spelled correctly,* then it is most likely a technical word or a proper noun that the dictionary doesn't contain. It might also be a word containing numbers; WordPerfect doesn't spell check words containing only numbers (such as 200 or 9555), but does check words containing a mix of letters and numbers (such as 555A or AB14). You'd want to select from among the remaining options on the Not Found menu:

- *Skip Once (1)* Select this option to skip the word once— the spell check continues without tampering with the word, even though it is not listed in the dictionary. This option is an appropriate selection if the highlighted word is spelled correctly and is used just once in the document.

- *Select Skip (2)* Select this option to skip the word for the remainder of the spell check. Spell check will treat the word as correctly spelled for the rest of the spell check. The cursor jumps to the next word, and the Spell menu remains on screen. This option is an appropriate selection if the word is spelled correctly and is repeated throughout the document.

- *Add (3)* Select this option to add the word to a supplementary dictionary. This option is appropriate if you wish WordPerfect to recognize a certain technical word, proper name, or other word as correctly spelled permanently—every time that you use the spell check feature from this day forward. The word is stored on disk, added to a supplemental dictionary file named WP{WP}US.SUP, which is distinct from the main dictionary file. (Technically, the first time you add a word to the supplemental dictionary, the file is actually created; from then on, words are added to that file.)

- *Ignore Numbers (6)* Select this option to have Word-Perfect ignore occurrences of words containing numbers. From this point on and until you press CANCEL ([F1]) to exit the spell check, WordPerfect will skip over any words that are a combination of letters and numbers, such as 334AB or AMT334.

Whichever of the Not Found menu options you choose, the cursor jumps to the next word, and the Spell menu returns to the screen, so that you can select to spell check another word, select another option, or press CANCEL ([F1]) or EXIT ([F7]) to exit the Spell feature.

# SPELL CHECK MORE THAN ONE WORD

In addition to spell checking a single word, you can wait until you've finished typing a document and then check all or part of that document for spelling mistakes.

Checking a page or a document is similar to checking one word. You must make sure that the page or the document you wish to check is on the screen. To spell check the whole document, you can place the cursor anywhere; to check a page, you must place the cursor on that page. Then press the SPELL ([Ctrl] + [F2]) key [*Pulldown menu:* Tools (T), Spell (E)] so that the Spell Check menu appears:

```
Check: 1 Word; 2 Page; 3 Document; 4 New Sup. Dictionary;
5 Look Up; 6 Count: 0
```

Select Page (2 or P) or Document (3 or D). Each word on the page or in the document will be checked. If a certain word is not found in the dictionary, then the Not Found menu appears, just as in a word check (Figure 7-2). You have the same six options to choose from on the Not Found menu as described previously.

Once you decide what to do about the first highlighted word, the spell check continues with the next unrecognized word until WordPerfect has highlighted and you have dealt with all the occurrences of words not found in the Speller's dictionaries. After a page check, WordPerfect lists the total number of words on that page. Press any key to return to the Spell menu. Then you can either select a new option from the Spell menu or press the CANCEL ([F1]) or EXIT ([F7]) key to exit the Spell feature. After a document check, WordPerfect also provides a word count, but it does not return you to the Spell menu. When you press any key, you are exited automatically from the Spell feature.

You can also spell check just a portion of a document or a page by using the Block feature in combination with the Speller. First, use the BLOCK ([Alt] + [F4]) key to high-light the text you wish to spell check. Next, press the SPELL ([Ctrl] + [F2]) key. WordPerfect immediately begins to check that block for spelling mistakes in the same way that it checks through a page or a document. After a block check, WordPerfect provides a word count of that block. Press any key to exit automatically from the Spell feature.

If a word appears twice in a row when you spell check a page, a document, or a block, the Speller stops to highlight both occurrences of that word and provides a Double Word menu, from which you can choose to skip over both words, delete the second of the two words, edit the word yourself, or disable double-word checking for the rest of the spell check. Figure 7-3 shows an example of the screen when a double word is encountered.

*5.1 users only:* If a word appears in an irregular case, the Speller stops to highlight that word. An irregular case is where upper and lowercase letters are found in the same word, such as where the first letter of a word is lowercase and the second letter is uppercase (for example, mAny), or where the first two letters of a word are both uppercase (for example, MAny). An Irregular Case menu appears, an example of which is shown in Figure 7-4. From this menu,

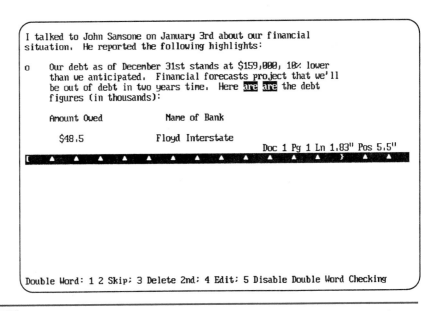

**FIGURE 7-3** Speller screen paused at a double word

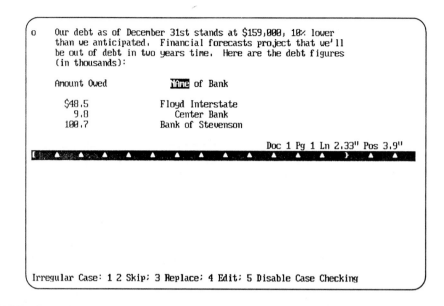

```
o    Our debt as of December 31st stands at $159,000, 10% lower
     than we anticipated.  Financial forecasts project that we'll
     be out of debt in two years time.  Here are the debt figures
     (in thousands):

     Amount Owed              Name of Bank

        $48.5                 Floyd Interstate
          9.8                 Center Bank
        100.7                 Bank of Stevenson

                                      Doc 1 Pg 1 Ln 2.33" Pos 3.9"
```

Irregular Case: 1 2 Skip; 3 Replace; 4 Edit; 5 Disable Case Checking

**FIGURE 7-4**   Speller screen paused for an irregular case (5.1 users only)

you can choose to skip over the word, replace the word with a different capitalization pattern, edit the word yourself, or disable the checking of the case in words for the rest of the spell check.

If you select the Replace option, WordPerfect determines how to capitalize the highlighted word by checking the case of the first three letters of that word. Here are examples of irregular cases and the resulting capitalization pattern:

| Irregular Case | Resulting Capitalization Pattern |
|---|---|
| MAny | Proper Case — Many |
| mAny | Proper Case — Many |

mANY                     Uppercase — MANY

maNy                     Lowercase — many


If a word contains only two letters with an irregular case such as "nO," WordPerfect capitalizes the first letter only: "No."

For both 5.0 and 5.1 users, the Speller will automatically check any headers, footers, captions, footnotes, endnotes, or graphics boxes that are located in the page, document, or block to be checked. If a word in a note is misspelled, the footnote or endnote screen will appear, with the misspelled word highlighted for your correction. Once you select an option from the Spell menu, WordPerfect will then return to the main text to continue the spell check.

You can stop a spell check at any time by pressing CANCEL ([F1]). You may need to press CANCEL ([F1]) two or three times to completely back out of the Spell feature.

Keep in mind that a spell check is no substitute for a final proofreading. The program will not catch grammatical errors. For instance, it cannot check for homonyms such as "no" and "know" or "see" and "sea." For example, suppose one sentence in your document reads as follows:

```
I hope to sea you soon.
```

WordPerfect won't pause during the spell check, even though the sentence should read *"see* you soon."

Nor can WordPerfect figure out whether a sentence makes sense. For instance, suppose your document contained the following sentence:

```
We hope to distribute bonus cheeks by December 15th.
```

You undoubtedly realize that the sentence was meant to read "bonus *checks*" and not "bonus cheeks." But since "cheeks" is in the dictionary, WordPerfect won't pause during the spell check to alert you to a problem in the sentence. Thus, while the spell check will catch all your misspellings, remember that it is no substitute for a final proofreading.

Let's spell check the document named LETTER, which you created back in Chapter 1 and have revised in other chapters. The file is only one page long, so the result will be the same whether you select spell check for a page or for the whole document.

1. On a clear screen, retrieve the file named LETTER. To make the spell check more interesting, purposely misspell some words. In the first paragraph, remove the last "s" in "discussed" and the "p" in "complete" so that the sentence begins "As we *discused,* here is a *comlete* list. . ."

2. *Floppy disk users:* Replace the disk currently in drive B with the Speller disk. *Hard disk users:* Proceed directly to step 3.

3. Press the SPELL ( Ctrl + F2 ) key. [*Pulldown menu:* Tools (T), Spell (E).] After a few moments, Word-Perfect responds with

   ```
   Check: 1 Word; 2 Page; 3 Document; 4 New Sup. Dictionary;
   5 Look Up; 6 Count: 0
   ```

4. Select Page (2 or P). WordPerfect highlights "Barrett" and, in moments, suggests numerous replacement words, as shown in Figure 7-5. (In fact, notice that the screen is full of replacement words—so full that not all of them

can fit on one screen; thus, the bottom of the screen indicates to press [Enter] if you wish to view more replacement words.) "Barrett" is correctly spelled and appears *more than once* in this document.

5. Select Skip (2). WordPerfect highlights "FST." Suppose that the correct name of the accounting firm is FSST Accounting.

6. Select Edit (4).

7. Edit "FST" to read "FSST," and then press EXIT ([F7]), as indicated at the bottom of the screen, to return to the spell check. WordPerfect again highlights "FSST," because this newly edited word is *still* not in its dictionary.

8. Select Skip Once (1). WordPerfect highlights the word "Harmon." Suppose that this is correctly spelled.

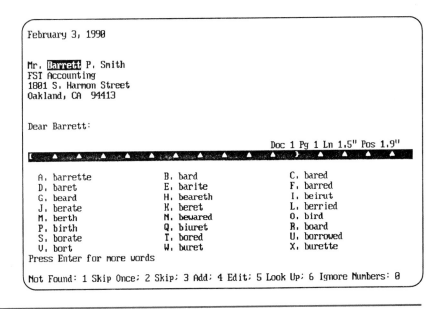

```
February 3, 1990

Mr. Barrett P. Smith
FST Accounting
1801 S. Harmon Street
Oakland, CA  94413


Dear Barrett:
                                            Doc 1 Pg 1 Ln 1.5" Pos 1.9"

 A. barrette          B. bard             C. bared
 D. baret             E. barite           F. barred
 G. beard             H. beareth          I. beirut
 J. berate            K. beret            L. berried
 M. berth             N. bewared          O. bird
 P. birth             Q. biuret           R. board
 S. borate            T. bored            U. borrowed
 V. bort              W. buret            X. burette
Press Enter for more words

Not Found: 1 Skip Once; 2 Skip; 3 Add; 4 Edit; 5 Look Up; 6 Ignore Numbers: 0
```

**FIGURE 7-5**   Speller screen with replacements for "Barrett"

9. Select Skip Once (1). WordPerfect highlights the word "discused" and suggests replacements at the bottom of the screen. (Notice that WordPerfect skips over the second occurrence of the word "Barrett" because you previously selected the option informing WordPerfect to consider that word correctly spelled for the rest of this spell check.)

10. Type **B** to insert the correctly spelled word, which is "discussed." WordPerfect highlights "comlete" and suggests alternatives.

11. Type **B** to insert the correct word, which is "complete." WordPerfect may highlight the word "31st."

12. Select Ignore Numbers (6). WordPerfect will no longer pause at words such as "27th" that are found further down in the document. WordPerfect highlights the word "Lois." Suppose that you frequently type letters containing the name "Lois"—perhaps that's your boss's first name.

13. Select Add (3). The word will be added to your supplementary dictionary (if a supplementary dictionary does not yet exist, it will be created).

14. Continue until the spell check ends. WordPerfect will provide a word count at the bottom of the screen with a message indicating to press any key.

15. Press any key to return to the Spell menu.

16. Press CANCEL (F1) to exit the Spell feature. (If you decided to spell check the document, rather than just a page, then the Spell feature is exited automatically.)

17. *Floppy disk users:* Remove the Speller disk from drive B and reinsert the disk used to store your documents.

You can also count the number of words in a document in a way that bypasses the spell check process. Simply press the SPELL ( Ctrl + F2 ) key and select Count (6 or C). In moments, a word count for the whole document appears on screen. You can then press any key to return to the Spell menu. Select a new option or press CANCEL ( F1 ) to exit the Spell feature.

# WORK WITH SUPPLEMENTARY DICTIONARIES

As previously discussed, WordPerfect lets you customize the Spell feature to your needs by adding words to a supplementary dictionary named WP{WP}US.SUP. To add a word to WP{WP}US.SUP, select Add (3) from the Not Found menu when WordPerfect highlights the word during a spell check. Words in the supplementary dictionary are recognized as correct for all succeeding spell checks.

Actually, when you use the Add option to append a word to WP{WP}US.SUP, WordPerfect places that word temporarily in RAM memory until the spell check is complete. When spell check is complete, all the words in RAM are then copied to WP{WP}US.SUP. Thus, there may be instances when you add so many words during a spell check that RAM memory becomes full, so that when you try to add one more word to the supplementary dictionary, Word-Perfect prompts with a "Dictionary Full" message. In this case use the CANCEL ( F1 ) key to exit the Speller. The words in RAM are copied to the supplementary dictionary. Then you can use the Block feature to highlight the portion of text not yet spell checked and initiate the Spell feature again. (If the "Dictionary Full" message appears frequently during spell checks, refer to the next section for a method to add the words in the supplementary dictionary to the main WordPerfect dictionary.)

WordPerfect offers the ability to add words to WP{WP}US.SUP independent of the Spell feature. In addition, you can delete words, which is an important ability. For instance, suppose that during a spell check, you accidentally select the Add option when WordPerfect is highlighting a word that is spelled incorrectly. In that case, you will want to delete that word from WP{WP}US.SUP. To add or delete words, make sure to clear the screen, and then retrieve WP{WP}US.SUP in the same way you'd retrieve any WordPerfect document. If this file is in other than the default drive/directory, be sure to specify its full pathname when retrieving. For instance, the supplementary dictionary may for hard disk users be stored in the same location as the main dictionary, which is in C:\WP51. In that case, retrieve C:\WP51\WP{WP}US.SUP.

Once you retrieve the supplementary dictionary, you'll notice that all the words are alphabetized from A to Z. Each word is on its own line, in lowercase, and followed by a hard return **[HRt]** code. (Of course, the code can only be seen on screen if you switch to the Reveal Codes screen.) Here's an example of how words appear in the supplementary dictionary:

```
acc
alyce
brendon
osborne
ocr
samsone
```

To remove a word from the dictionary, delete the word and the Hard Return code that follows it. To add a word, position the cursor at the beginning of the line where the word should appear alphabetically, type the word, and then press [Enter] to insert a Hard Return code. Once you've edited the supplementary dictionary, resave this file just as you would a document file.

Do not try this method with the main dictionary. Also, do not try this with the supplementary dictionary if it has been compressed (as described in the next section). See the next section regarding ways to add or delete words from the main dictionary or from supplementary dictionaries that have been compressed.

WordPerfect also offers the ability to create and use supplementary dictionaries other than WP{WP}US.SUP. Separate supplementary dictionaries are convenient if you work with different types of documents.

Perhaps you wish to create one to check legal documents and another to check personal documents. To create a supplementary dictionary, start with a clear Typing screen. Type each word on a separate line. Then save this file using a name which reminds you it's a supplementary dictionary, such as LEGAL.SUP. (The next section describes how you can also create a new supplementary dictionary using the Speller Utility.)

When you're ready to use a supplementary dictionary other than WP{WP}US.SUP, press the SPELL ([Ctrl] + [F2]) key and select New Sup. Dictionary (4 or N). Type in the filename of the new supplementary dictionary (preceded by the appropriate drive/directory) and press [Enter]. Now as you initiate a word, page, or document check, WordPerfect will use the file you specified as the supplementary dictionary. And, if you select the Add option on the Not Found menu during the succeeding spell check, words will be added to the supplementary dictionary you specified.

*Note:* In WordPerfect you can indicate where the supplementary dictionary can be found whenever you initiate the Spell feature. This feature is convenient for hard disk users to indicate one location where all supplemental dictionaries are found; otherwise, WordPerfect creates the supplementary dictionary in the default directory and will be unable to locate the original supplementary dictionary when you change the default and perform a new spell check. Refer to the "Location of Files" section of Appendix B for more on this feature.

# SPELLER UTILITY

WordPerfect provides a separate program that can help manage WordPerfect's dictionary and supplementary dictionaries in a variety of ways. For instance, you can add or delete words, display words in the common word list, or check to see if a word is in the main dictionary. You can also create your own dictionary.

A specific use of the Speller Utility is to transfer the words you created during a spell check from the supplementary dictionary to the main dictionary. In general, this will be necessary only if you compile so many words in the supplement that when you attempt to add another word, the message "Dictionary Full" appears on screen during a spell check. You could add these supplementary words to the main dictionary and then begin a new supplementary dictionary. (On the other hand, if you wanted simply to erase the supplementary dictionary, you would not use the Speller Utility; you would just erase the file named WP{WP}US.SUP from your floppy or hard disk.)

Do not use the Speller Utility casually! Adding or deleting just a few words from the dictionary is impractical, because the process could take up to 20 minutes. Moreover, you could accidentally erase part of the dictionary when shuffling words. In general, you will rarely (if ever) need to use the utility. Nevertheless, this feature is briefly discussed below.

The Speller Utility can be accessed only when you are working in DOS. At the DOS prompt, floppy disk users should (1) place the Speller disk created when you installed WordPerfect in drive A and a data disk in drive B (which may be blank or contain a supplementary dictionary that you wish to combine into the main dictionary); (2) type **A:** and press [Enter] so that the DOS prompt reads **A>**; and (3) type **SPELL** and press [Enter]. Hard disk users should first switch to the directory where the file SPELL.EXE is stored (which is generally where the WordPerfect program is stored); and then type **SPELL** and press [Enter].

In a few moments, you'll see the Speller Utility main menu, as shown in Figure 7-6. (WordPerfect 5.0 users will not find items A, B, or C on screen.) Notice that the upper right corner says "WP{WP}US.LEX," meaning that you're working with the main dictionary. The options on this menu are as follows:

- *Exit (0)* This option returns you to the DOS prompt after you've finished using the Speller Utility. From DOS, you could then return to WordPerfect.

- *Change/Create Dictionary (1)* This option switches you from WP{WP}US.LEX to another dictionary. If the filename of that dictionary is not found on disk, WordPerfect prompts whether you wish to create a new dictionary by the name indicated. Whatever dictionary

```
Spell -- WordPerfect Speller Utility                    WP{WP}US.LEX

0 - Exit
1 - Change/Create Dictionary
2 - Add Words to Dictionary
3 - Delete Words from Dictionary
4 - Optimize Dictionary
5 - Display Common Word List
6 - Check Location of a Word
7 - Look Up
8 - Phonetic Look Up
9 - Convert 4.2 Dictionary to 5.1
A - Combine Other 5.0 or 5.1 Dictionary
B - Compress/Expand Supplemental Dictionary
C - Extract Added Words from Wordlist-based Dictionary

Selection:
```

**FIGURE 7-6**  Speller Utility menu

you specify is the one on which the other items in the Speller Utility menu are performed.

- *Add Words to Dictionary (2)*   This option allows you to add words to the main dictionary, to the common word list, or to a dictionary you created. You would add words either by typing the words from the keyboard (pressing (Enter) or the spacebar after entering each word) or by transferring them from a file where you'd already typed the words. This option allows you to transfer words from the file WP{WP}US.SUP, the supplement, into the main dictionary. Afterwards, you would erase the file named WP{WP}US.SUP.

- *Delete Words from Dictionary (3)*   This option is similar to option 2, but is used for deleting words.

- *Optimize Dictionary (4)* This option is used after you've created a dictionary to reshuffle it into alphabetical order and compress the dictionary. This reduces the amount of disk space required to store the file. Also, if you compress a dictionary, words in that dictionary will never be ignored if the computer's RAM memory is insufficient and will appear as possible replacements on the Not Found menu during a spell check.

- *Display Common Word List (5)* This option shows you the common word list screen by screen.

- *Check Location of a Word (6)* This option allows you to determine whether a word is in the main dictionary, and, if so, whether it is in the common word list or the main word list.

- *Look Up (7)* This option enables you to look up a word based on its spelling, using a question mark (?) or asterisk (*) in those places where you're unsure of a word's spelling (same as the Look Up option on the Not Found menu).

- *Phonetic Look Up (8)* This option enables you to look up a word based on how that word sounds.

- *Convert 4.2 Dictionary to 5.1 (or 5.0) (9)* This option provides the ability to convert a dictionary you created using WordPerfect version 4.2 into version 5.1 (or 5.0) format.

- *Combine Other 5.0 or 5.1 Dictionary (A)* This option allows you to combine several dictionaries into one. It is especially useful if you often use more than one language in your documents and therefore want a dictionary that contains words in two languages. For instance, you can combine WordPerfect's Italian dictionary into WP{WP}US.LEX.

- *Compress/Expand Supplementary Dictionary (B)* This option allows you to compress a supplementary dictionary, so that it reduces the amount of disk space required to store the file. Also, if you compress a supplementary dictionary, words in that dictionary will never be ignored if the computer's RAM memory is insufficient and will appear as possible replacements from the Not Found menu. Or, you can expand a supplementary dictionary and thereby edit the dictionary by retrieving it to screen like a standard WordPerfect document.

- *Extract Added Words from Wordlist-based Dictionary (C)* This option lets you change from a word list to an algorithmic dictionary that uses specific rules rather than word lists to check spelling. WordPerfect prompts for the name of the Wordlist Dictionary, the algorithmic dictionary, and a supplementary dictionary. The Spell utility then spell checks the words in the Wordlist Dictionary based on the algorithmic dictionary and adds to the supplementary dictionary any words that are not recognized by the algorithmic dictionary.

Floppy disk users should be sure to remove the Speller disk from drive A after using the Speller Utility and selecting Exit (0) to leave the utility.

# USE THE THESAURUS

The Thesaurus feature can help you to learn the meaning of a word or find an alternative that fits better in your text.

You can look up synonyms and antonyms for over 10,000 words. A synonym is a word with the same meaning as the word you're looking up, while an antonym has an opposite meaning. For instance, a synonym for the word "dark" is "unlit"; an antonym for the word "dark" is "light."

Each of the 10,000 words that can be looked up is called a *headword*. The headwords, along with their synonyms and antonyms, are stored on the Thesaurus disk in a file called WP{WP}US.THS. If a word is not a headword, Word-Perfect cannot provide synonyms or antonyms for that word; you must try looking up another word instead. (If you purchased one of the first releases of version 5, then your United States version of the thesaurus may be named WP{WP}*EN*.THS, rather than WP{WP}*US*.THS. As with the Spell feature, you can purchase additional thesauri in several foreign languages. You would use the Language feature to insert a Language code in the text; see the note at the beginning of this chapter for details.)

To have access to the Thesaurus, floppy disk users should place the Thesaurus disk created when you installed WordPerfect in drive B. Hard disk users should have copied the Thesaurus file onto the hard disk during installation. (If not, see Appendix A for installation instructions.) You then position the cursor on the word you wish to look up and press the THESAURUS ( Alt + F1 ) key. [*Pulldown menu:* Tools (T), Thesaurus (H).] If the word is a headword, the screen divides. The top displays several lines of your text and highlights the word you are looking up. The bottom of the screen lists alternative words in up to three columns, grouping them into parts of speech — verbs (v), nouns (n), adjectives (a), and antonyms (ant). The following menu appears at the bottom of the screen:

1 Replace Word; **2** View Doc; **3** Look Up Word; **4** Clear Column: **0**

For instance, Figure 7-7 illustrates the Thesaurus screen for the word "accept." There are two columns of references for this word.

You might find an appropriate word in one of the columns. If you find the right word in the first column, you can select Replace Word (1) from the menu. WordPerfect then prompts you with

```
Press letter for word
```

You simply type the letter that corresponds to the word you wish to substitute. That word replaces the original word and the Thesaurus screen clears.

If you find the right word in another column, you must press ⮕ before selecting to replace the word, so that the highlighted letters move over to that column. Then you can

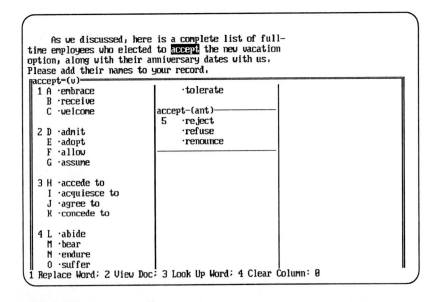

**FIGURE 7-7** Thesaurus screen for the word "accept"

press Replace Word (1) and make a letter selection. There may be more alternatives offered by WordPerfect for a certain word than can fit in the three columns; you can press ⊡ to see the rest of the words.

You have other choices as well. Perhaps you haven't found exactly the word you were looking for. All the words preceded by dots are also headwords. In Figure 7-7, every alternative offered is a headword, and thus can also be looked up in the Thesaurus. Any synonyms or antonyms not preceded by a dot are not headwords and cannot be looked up.

To continue looking up headwords, simply type the letter corresponding to that word (without first selecting an item from the menu at the bottom of the screen). Alternatives for the first word are restricted to the first column, while replacements for the new headword are displayed in the second (and perhaps third) column. Alternatives for up to three different words could be placed side by side in columns in this way. For instance, Figure 7-8 shows the Thesaurus suggesting alternatives not only for "accept" but also for "adopt." You can move between columns with the ⟵ and ⟶ keys and up and down a column with the ⬆ and ⬇ keys or with ⟦PgUp⟧ and ⟦PgDn⟧. (When you have alternatives for two or three words on screen, WordPerfect can only display a partial list of alternatives for each word, and so moving the cursor up and down a column becomes important.) When you want to clear the last column and again view alternatives for the previous word, you can press ⟦Backspace⟧ or select Clear Column (4).

You can also look up a word not found in one of the columns. Select Look Up Word (3). WordPerfect prompts you with

Word:

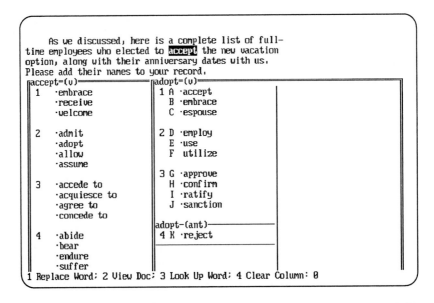

As we discussed, here is a complete list of full-
time employees who elected to `accept` the new vacation
option, along with their anniversary dates with us.
Please add their names to your record.
```
accept=(v)            adopt=(v)
 1    ·embrace        1 A ·accept
      ·receive          B ·embrace
      ·welcome          C ·espouse

 2    ·admit          2 D ·employ
      ·adopt            E ·use
      ·allow            F utilize
      ·assume
                      3 G ·approve
 3    ·accede to        H ·confirm
      ·acquiesce to     I ·ratify
      ·agree to         J ·sanction
      ·concede to
                      adopt-(ant)
 4    ·abide          4 K ·reject
      ·bear
      ·endure
      ·suffer
 1 Replace Word; 2 View Doc; 3 Look Up Word; 4 Clear Column: 0
```

**FIGURE 7-8**   Thesaurus screen for the words "accept" and "adopt"

and you can type the word and press Enter.

A last alternative is to exit the Thesaurus temporarily. You can select View Doc (2); the Thesaurus screen remains, but the cursor moves to the text at the top of the screen. You can then use the cursor movement keys to reposition the cursor as you read through the text before deciding on a replacement word or move to another word that you wish to look up. But you cannot edit your text when you leave the Thesaurus temporarily. Press the EXIT (F7) key to return to the Thesaurus and to make a selection from the menu at the bottom of the screen.

If you wish to leave the Thesaurus at any time, press the CANCEL (F1) key.

*Note:* If you attempt to use the Thesaurus feature and WordPerfect cannot find where on disk the Thesaurus is stored, the following prompt appears:

```
ERROR: File not found--WP{WP}US.THS
```

Floppy disk users should check to make sure that the Thesaurus disk is in the default drive. Hard disk users should make sure that the Thesaurus file has been installed onto the hard disk. For hard disk users where the Thesaurus file is located somewhere other than where the WordPerfect program files are stored, you must indicate to WordPerfect where the Thesaurus can be found; see the "Location of Files" section of Appendix B.

The document LETTER should be on screen. Let's use it to find an alternative for the word "begin."

1. Position the cursor anywhere within the word "begin" in the sentence near the bottom of the letter that reads "The new accrued vacation system should begin for. . ."

2. *Floppy disk users:* Place the Thesaurus disk in drive B. *Hard disk users:* Proceed directly to step 3.

3. Press the THESAURUS ([Alt] + [F1]) key. [*Pulldown menu:* Tools (T), Thesaurus (H).] In moments, the Thesaurus screen appears with suggestions for alternatives as shown in Figure 7-9. Suppose that you wish to find more alternatives, this time for "start."

4. Type **O**. Now the first column is restricted to alternatives for "begin," and the second and third columns contain alternatives for "start." Suppose that you wish to find more alternatives, this time for "initiate."

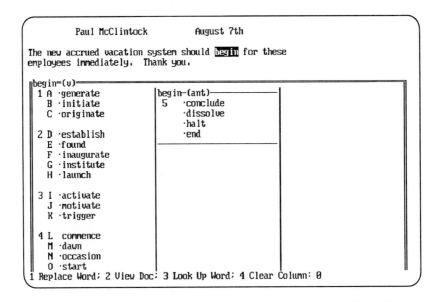

```
        Paul McClintock            August 7th

The new accrued vacation system should begin for these
employees immediately.  Thank you.

begin=(v)
  1 A ·generate            begin-(ant)
    B ·initiate              5     ·conclude
    C ·originate                   ·dissolve
                                   ·halt
  2 D ·establish                   ·end
    E ·found
    F ·inaugurate
    G ·institute
    H ·launch

  3 I ·activate
    J ·motivate
    K ·trigger

  4 L  commence
    M ·dawn
    N ·occasion
    O ·start
1 Replace Word; 2 View Doc; 3 Look Up Word; 4 Clear Column: 0
```

**FIGURE 7-9**  Thesaurus screen for the word "begin"

5. Press 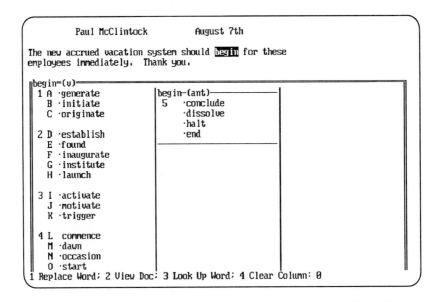. The letters move to the next column.

6. Type **B**. Now all three columns contain alternatives for different headwords, as shown in Figure 7-10. The third column contains alternatives for "initiate." Suppose you wish to clear the last column.

7. Select Clear Column (4). Now you wish to review all the alternatives for "start" in column 2.

8. Press (PgUp) to see the complete list of alternatives for "start." Since column 3 has been cleared, alternatives for "start" can spill over into that column.

9. Select Replace Word (1). WordPerfect prompts for the letter corresponding to the replacement word.

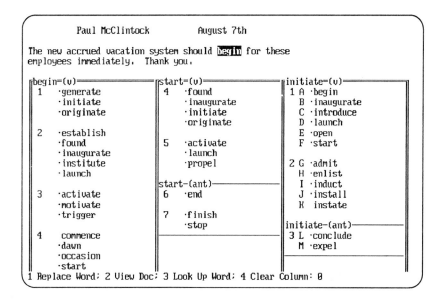

**FIGURE 7-10** Thesaurus screen for three words

10. Type **K**. The word "commence" is inserted in place of "begin," and the Thesaurus is exited automatically.

11. *Floppy disk users:* Remove the Thesaurus disk from drive B and reinsert the disk used to store your documents.

Get accustomed to using the Thesaurus, and you may find that your writing improves dramatically.

# REVIEW EXERCISE

You may wish to use the Speller and Thesaurus on your own documents, or you can practice on the file named FINANCE, which you created in Chapter 3. Here's an exercise using FINANCE.

1. Clear the screen and retrieve the file named FINANCE.

2. On purpose, misspell some words. Then perform a spell check on the whole document. Notice that WordPerfect highlights names such as "Samsone" and "Floyd." You can either skip over these words, or, if any of them are common in your documents, you can add them to your supplementary dictionary.

3. Look up synonyms for the word "debt," which is a word in a bulleted paragraph. One of the alternatives listed is "deficit"; go ahead and look up alternatives for that word as well. Then clear the column of alternatives for "deficit" and select "deficit" as the replacement word.

## Quick Review

- Spell check one word, one page, or one document. With the text on screen, position the cursor and then select SPELL (Ctrl + F2). Or, pulldown menu users can select Tools (T), Spell (E). The Spell menu displays, from which you can then choose the option Word, Page, or Document.

- Spell check a section of text of any size by using the Block feature to highlight that section. Then, press the SPELL (Ctrl + F2) key. WordPerfect begins to check the spelling of the block immediately.

- WordPerfect highlights a word during a spell check when that word is not listed in either the Word-Perfect dictionary or in a supplementary dictionary that you create for specialized terms or proper nouns found often in your documents. From the Not Found menu that displays, you can choose to edit the word, choose from a list of suggested replacements, or skip over the word. Another option lets you customize the spell checker by adding the word to your own supplementary dictionary so that, from that point on, WordPerfect will recognize that word as correctly spelled.

- Have WordPerfect look up the spelling of a word for you. Press SPELL (Ctrl + F2), and, from the Spell menu, select the Look Up (5) option. Next, type out the word as it sounds phonetically, or type the word using the wild cards ? (to represent one letter) and * (to represent one or more letters) in places where you're not sure of the spelling. Word-Perfect will display correctly spelled words as suggestions.

- The Speller cannot check for grammatical errors and is thus no substitute for a final proofreading.

- Count the number of words in a document on screen without checking its spelling by pressing SPELL (Ctrl + F2) and selecting Count (6).

- The Speller Utility is an independent program that can add your supplementary dictionary words to the main dictionary, verify whether a word is in the dictionary, and display the common word list. It can also be used to combine or compress dictionaries. Access the Speller Utility from DOS. Floppy disk users must place the Speller disk that was created when WordPerfect was installed into drive A, and a data disk into drive B. Hard disk users must switch to the drive/directory where the Speller Utility is located. Type **SPELL** and press Enter to display the Speller Utility menu.

- Find a synonym or antonym to a word by positioning the cursor on that word. Next, press THESAURUS (Alt + F1). Or, pulldown menu users can select

Tools (T), Thesaurus (H). From the Thesaurus menu that displays, you can choose to replace the word with one of the others suggested on screen, or continue to seek out additional synonyms or antonyms. WordPerfect's Thesaurus contains synonyms and antonyms for over 10,000 words. It is useful not only when looking for substitutes, but for acquiring a better understanding of a word's meaning.

# SPECIAL FEATURES

Managing Files on Disk
Printing Options and Enhancements
Changing Fonts and Inserting Graphics for Desktop Publishing
Creating Text Columns and Tables
Outlining, Paragraph and Line Numbering, Footnoting
Producing Repetitive Documents and Merging
Using Macros and Styles
Taking Advantage of WordPerfect Extras

*chapter* **8**

# MANAGING FILES ON DISK

**B**y now, after following the instructions in Part I of this book, you've created as many files on disk as chapters that you've read. You've seen how easy it is to accumulate files. In fact, you will find that within weeks of working with WordPerfect, you'll have more files on disk than you can remember. WordPerfect offers many sophisticated features for working with files, helping you to manage the documents that stack up in no time. This chapter explores those vital features.

The first half of the chapter explains how to effectively maintain your disks and directories, including how to keep track of available disk storage space and to reorganize files already on disk, whether by deleting, renaming, or copying. The Copy feature deserves some extra attention; this command can be used to make backup copies of your files—thus averting disaster should your original file disappear because of a mechanical problem or human error. And, you'll learn how to create new directories and to alter the default drive/directory.

The second half of the chapter looks at other file-management tools. You'll lock up a file with a secret password and create a document summary that lets you keep a record of a document's development. You will also learn about the search capabilities of WordPerfect, so that you can find a certain file even if you forget its filename. WordPerfect's ability to temporarily exit to DOS, an option that you'll appreciate if you're comfortable using DOS commands to manage files on disk, is also described.

# MONITOR DISK AND FILE CAPACITY

You learned in Chapter 2 about the List Files screen, which displays a list of the files stored on a floppy disk or in a specific directory on your hard disk. Figure 8-1 displays a List Files screen. To display this screen, press LIST ([F5]). [*Pulldown menu:* File (F), List Files (F).] WordPerfect displays a prompt listing the default drive or directory—the one that WordPerfect assumes is where you wish to store files to or retrieve files from—such as the following:

```
Dir C:\WP51\DATA\*.*
```

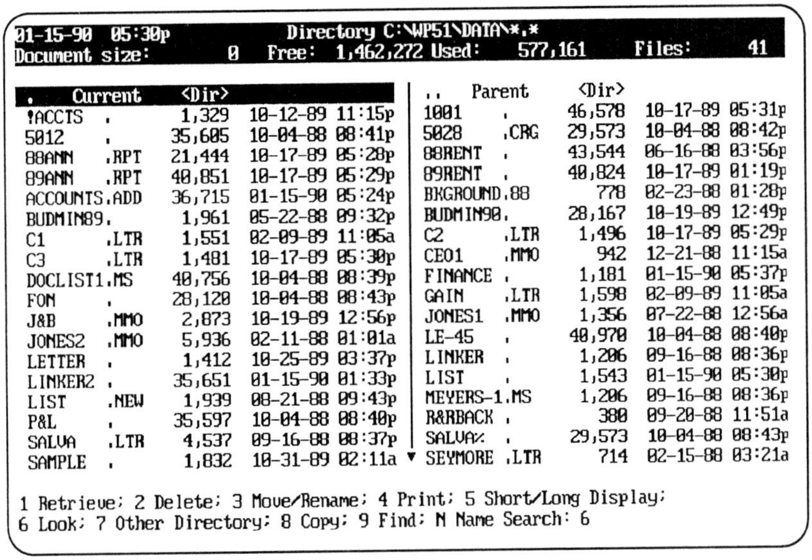

```
┌─────────────────────────────────────────────────────────────────────────┐
│ 01-15-90  05:30p              Directory C:\WP51\DATA\*.*                   │
│ Document size:        0   Free: 1,462,272 Used:     577,161   Files:    41 │
│                                                                           │
│ .     Current    <Dir>              .. Parent     <Dir>                    │
│ !ACCTS  .          1,329 10-12-89 11:15p  1001  .        46,578 10-17-89 05:31p │
│ 5012    .         35,605 10-04-88 08:41p  5028  .CRG     29,573 10-04-88 08:42p │
│ 88ANN   .RPT      21,444 10-17-89 05:28p  88RENT .       43,544 06-16-88 03:56p │
│ 89ANN   .RPT      40,851 10-17-89 05:29p  89RENT .       40,824 10-17-89 01:19p │
│ ACCOUNTS.ADD      36,715 01-15-90 05:24p  BKGROUND.88       778 02-23-88 01:28p │
│ BUDMIN89.          1,961 05-22-88 09:32p  BUDMIN90.      28,167 10-19-89 12:49p │
│ C1      .LTR       1,551 02-09-89 11:05a  C2     .LTR      1,496 10-17-89 05:29p │
│ C3      .LTR       1,481 10-17-89 05:30p  CEO1   .MMO       942 12-21-88 11:15a │
│ DOCLIST1.MS       40,756 10-04-88 08:39p  FINANCE .       1,181 01-15-90 05:37p │
│ FON     .         28,128 10-04-88 08:43p  GAIN   .LTR      1,598 02-09-89 11:05a │
│ J&B     .MMO       2,873 10-19-89 12:56p  JONES1 .MMO      1,356 07-22-88 12:56a │
│ JONES2  .MMO       5,936 02-11-88 01:01a  LE-45  .       40,970 10-04-88 08:40p │
│ LETTER  .          1,412 10-25-89 03:37p  LINKER .        1,206 09-16-88 08:36p │
│ LINKER2 .         35,651 01-15-90 01:33p  LIST   .        1,543 01-15-90 05:30p │
│ LIST    .NEW       1,939 08-21-88 09:43p  MEYERS-1.MS     1,206 09-16-88 08:36p │
│ P&L     .         35,597 10-04-88 08:40p  R&RBACK .         380 09-28-88 11:51a │
│ SALVA   .LTR       4,537 09-16-88 08:37p  SALVAX .       29,573 10-04-88 08:43p │
│ SAMPLE  .          1,832 10-31-89 02:11a ▼ SEYMORE .LTR     714 02-15-88 03:21a │
│                                                                           │
│ 1 Retrieve; 2 Delete; 3 Move/Rename; 4 Print; 5 Short/Long Display;       │
│ 6 Look; 7 Other Directory; 8 Copy; 9 Find; N Name Search: 6               │
└─────────────────────────────────────────────────────────────────────────┘
```

**FIGURE 8-1**  List Files screen for C:\WP51\DATA

You then either press (Enter) to display files in the default drive/directory or type in another drive/directory and press (Enter) to display files in that other drive/directory.

As you know, the header at the top of the List Files screen indicates the drive or directory for which files are displayed. So, in Figure 8-1, "C:\WP51\DATA\*.*" means that WordPerfect is displaying files in the path \WP51 \DATA\ on the hard disk (drive C). The "*.*" means that WordPerfect is displaying every file stored there, regardless of its filename or file extension. As another example, if a List Files screen reads "B:\*.*", that means that Word-Perfect is displaying all files on the floppy disk in drive B (assuming that the floppy disk has no directories).

This header also displays the amount of disk space available on the floppy or hard disk for storing files, next to the heading "Free:". Because disk capacity is limited, it is important (especially for floppy disk users) to check this heading periodically, to know when you're approaching your storage capacity. How much information can one disk hold? It depends on the type of disk that your computer disk drives can use. Some floppy disks hold approximately 360 kilobytes (K) of information in a maximum of 112 files. (Remember from the "Getting Started" chapter that a byte is equal to one character—such as a letter or number—and that slightly more than 1000 bytes equals 1K). A 360K disk can hold about 150 to 200 pages of double-spaced text. Other floppy disks (720K) hold twice as much information. Still others (1200K or 1.2 megabytes) hold almost four times as much information. And, hard disks hold many times more information than floppy disks. For instance, the smallest hard disks hold 29 times as much information as the 360K disks can store.

Floppy disks fill to capacity quickly, so you should watch to see when a disk is becoming full. As a general rule, you should switch to another floppy disk or delete some obsolete files from the floppy before the amount of free disk space becomes smaller than the largest file on disk. (The deletion procedure is described next.) For instance, if you want room to revise files and the largest file on your disk is 20,000 bytes, you need *at least* 20,000 bytes of free disk space because WordPerfect temporarily saves the original and the revision on disk when saving a revised file.

Hard disks take longer to fill up, but they too will reach capacity eventually. It is good practice, therefore, to check the available storage on your hard disk periodically. When near capacity, consider deleting files or moving rarely used files to a floppy disk. (The procedures for deleting and moving files are described next.)

Besides monitoring storage capacity, it's also a good idea to watch the size of a document you're typing. WordPerfect indicates the size of the file currently on screen next to the heading "Document size:" at the top of the List Files screen. When does a document become so large that it should be split into two separate files? That depends on your computer's RAM and storage capacity. For instance, a file may become cumbersome to edit on some computers if it becomes larger than 64,000 bytes.

Finally, hard disk users should be aware of the number of files that are stored in a directory. This is displayed next to the heading "Files:" on the List Files screen. Storing a maximum of about 200 files in each directory creates an organized, efficient filing system; if, instead, you store hundreds of files in one directory, the List Files screen will be bogged down, and you'll have a difficult time searching for and finding files. Read on in this chapter to learn how to create new directories, and how, if you've already stored hundreds of files in one directory, to move files between directories.

# ORGANIZE FILES ON DISK

You learned in Chapter 2 about three menu options at the bottom of the List Files screen: Retrieve (1 or R) to recall a document to the screen; Print (4 or P), to print out a document on paper; and Look (6 or L), to display the contents of a document without actually retrieving it to the screen. Other items on the List Files menu aid in keeping the files on your floppy disks or in your hard disk directories neat and orderly and free of unnecessary files. These are described below.

## Look at List Files Screens for Other Drives/Directories

Suppose that you display the List Files screen for a drive/ directory and, not finding the file that you are looking for, decide to display the List Files screen for another drive/directory. You could press CANCEL ([F1]) to return to the Typing screen, and then again use the LIST ([F5]) key to display the List Files screen, this time for another drive/directory.

But it would be quicker to remain on the List Files screen and position the cursor on the item ".Current < Dir>." This signifies the current drive/directory, the one that WordPerfect is now displaying the List Files screen for. Select Look (6 or L). Or, you can select Look by pressing [Enter], because WordPerfect assumes that you want to choose the Look option. (Notice in Figure 8-1 that the List Files menu at the bottom of the screen is defaulted at "6," which is the Look option.) Now WordPerfect displays a prompt, listing that current drive/directory, such as

```
Dir C:\WP51\DATA\*.*
```

Press [Enter], and WordPerfect will rewrite the List Files screen for the current drive/directory. (Sometimes, WordPerfect will not automatically update the List Files screen to reflect changes when you copy or move files, and so this becomes useful.) Or, edit this prompt to list another drive or directory and press [Enter] to display a different List Files screen.

An additional option is to position the cursor on the item ".. Parent < Dir>." This signifies the parent directory. (Remember from the "Getting Started" chapter that each subdirectory is said to have a parent. As an example, if the current directory is C:\WP51\DATA, then the parent directory is C:\WP51. And, the parent of \WP51 is C:\, the main hard disk directory from which all others diverge.) Select Look (6 or L or [Enter]). Now WordPerfect displays a prompt showing the parent directory, such as

```
Dir C:\WP51\*.*
```

(If the current directory has no parent, such as is typical on a floppy disk, the current directory is again listed.) Press [Enter] and WordPerfect will rewrite the List Files screen showing the files in the parent directory.

Or, suppose you wish to view the List Files screen for a subdirectory of the current directory. The subdirectories of the current directory are listed just below ". Current <Dir>" and ".. Parent <Dir>" on the List Files screen. These subdirectories are identified because the phrase "<Dir>" appears in place of a file size. For instance, Figure 8-1 shows that there are no subdirectories of C:\WP51\DATA. Figure 8-2 shows that there are four subdirectories of C:\WP51, and the cursor is on one of them, "LEARN <Dir>." Select Look (6 or L or [Enter]).

```
01-15-90  07:20p              Directory C:\WP51\*.*
Document size:    5,020  Free: 1,458,176 Used:  3,965,305      Files:      128

  .   Current   <Dir>                ..   Parent    <Dir>
DATA       .     <Dir> 10-17-89 01:16p  LEARN      .      <Dir> 10-04-89 02:00p
MACROS     .     <Dir> 01-15-90 07:20p  PRINT      .      <Dir> 10-10-89 11:16p
8514A    .VRS    4,797 09-22-89 10:48a  ALTB     .WPM        83 10-14-89 01:42p
ALTC     .WPM      115 01-15-90 03:46p  ALTD     .WPM       123 10-12-89 03:02p
ALTG     .WPM       93 10-04-89 05:39p  ALTO     .WPM        84 10-05-89 01:27p
ALTRNAT  .WPK      919 09-22-89 10:35a  ALTU     .WPM        88 10-14-89 01:42p
ALTW     .WPM      101 10-05-89 01:26p  ARROW-22 .WPG       116 09-22-89 10:48a
ATI      .VRS    4,937 09-22-89 10:48a  BALLOONS .WPG     2,806 09-22-89 10:48a
BANNER-3 .WPG      648 09-22-89 10:48a  BICYCLE  .WPG       607 09-22-89 10:48a
BKGRND-1 .WPG   11,391 09-22-89 10:48a  BORDER-8 .WPG       144 09-22-89 10:48a
BULB     .WPG    2,030 09-22-89 10:48a  BURST-1  .WPG       748 09-22-89 10:48a
BUTTRFLY .WPG    5,278 09-22-89 10:48a  CALENDAR .WPG       300 09-22-89 10:48a
CERTIF   .WPG      608 09-22-89 10:48a  CHARACTR .DOC    41,968 09-22-89 10:35a
CHARMAP  .TST   40,440 09-22-89 10:48a  CHKBOX-1 .WPG       582 09-22-89 10:48a
CLOCK    .WPG    1,811 09-22-89 10:48a  CNTRCT-2 .WPG     2,678 09-22-89 10:48a
CODES    .WPM    5,117 09-22-89 10:35a  CONVERT  .EXE   104,689 09-22-89 10:35a
CURSOR   .COM    1,452 09-22-89 10:35a  DEVICE-2 .WPG       657 09-22-89 10:48a
DIPLOMA  .WPG    2,342 09-22-89 10:48a ▼ EGA512   .FRS     3,584 09-22-89 10:48a

1 Retrieve; 2 Delete; 3 Move/Rename; 4 Print; 5 Short/Long Display;
6 Look; 7 Other Directory; 8 Copy; 9 Find; N Name Search: 6
```

**FIGURE 8-2**  List Files screen for C:\WP51

Now WordPerfect displays a prompt showing the indicated subdirectory, such as

`Dir C:\WP51\LEARN\*.*`

Press ⟦Enter⟧ and WordPerfect will rewrite the List Files screen showing the files in that subdirectory.

Once you press CANCEL (⟦F1⟧) to leave the List Files screen and return to the Typing screen, WordPerfect also offers a quick method to return to the last List Files screen that you displayed. If the last List Files screen was on the same drive as the default, then press LIST (⟦F5⟧) twice in a row to again see that List Files screen. For instance, suppose that the default is C:\WP51\DATA, and you just viewed the List Files screen for C:\WP51\LEARN and then pressed CANCEL to return to the Typing screen. If you press the LIST key twice, you'll return to the List Files screen you just viewed, that of C:\WP51\LEARN. Your cursor will even be positioned in the same place as before. But, if instead you press LIST and ⟦Enter⟧, you'll return to the List Files screen for the default.

As another example, suppose that you just viewed the List Files screen for the disk in drive A. In that case, since drive A is not the same as the default drive (drive C), when you press LIST twice, you'll view the List Files screen for the default, C:\WP51\DATA—the same result as when you press the LIST (⟦F5⟧)key and then press ⟦Enter⟧.

## Delete a File

A disk can become cluttered quickly with obsolete files. Not only does a cluttered disk make the work of finding a particular file more cumbersome, but it also takes space away from other files that could be stored there.

You can delete files directly from the List Files screen by positioning the cursor on the file you wish to delete and selecting Delete (2 or D). WordPerfect prompts for confirmation that you wish to delete that file. Type **Y** to delete it or type any other character to abort the deletion. You should think carefully before typing **Y** to confirm a deletion. Once a file is deleted, it is removed from that disk for good.

Here you'll see how quickly a file can be deleted from a disk. Let's delete the file named LETTER, which you used frequently to practice various features in the first part of this book.

1. Press the LIST (F5) key, and then press Enter to view those files in the default drive or directory.

2. Position the cursor on the file named LETTER.

3. Select Delete (2 or D). WordPerfect prompts you for verification. For instance, floppy disk users will see

   `Delete B:\LETTER? No (Yes)`

4. Type **Y**, and the file will be deleted from disk permanently.

Once a file is deleted, it is no longer listed as a file on the disk. The only way you could work with the LETTER file would be to type it all over again.

Don't use the Delete feature casually. When you delete files, be very careful not to accidentally erase files you wish to refer to in the future. And don't erase WordPerfect files—files that on a hard disk are stored in the directory

\WP51 and on a floppy disk system are stored on drive A. Most WordPerfect program files begin with the letters "WP". For instance, the file WP.EXE is the WordPerfect program file; make sure that you don't tamper with that file, or you could erase the program.

## Rename/Move a File

After saving various files on disk, you may change your mind about your naming system. Perhaps the filenames aren't descriptive enough, or maybe you want to add file extensions such as .LTR or .MMO to some of them. You can rename files quickly. Position the cursor on the file you wish to rename and select Move/Rename (3 or M) on the List Files screen. WordPerfect prompts you for a new name, listing the current drive/directory and filename, such as

New name: C:\WP51\DATA\SAMPLE

Change the WordPerfect prompt by either typing over the old filename or by using the arrow keys and deletion keys to edit the filename. Then, press (Enter). For instance, edit the prompt to read

New name: C:\WP51\DATA\SAMPLE.MMO

When you press (Enter), the name change (to SAM-PLE.MMO) is reflected in moments on the List Files screen. Don't forget that there are rules for naming files (as discussed in Chapter 2), such as a limit of eight characters in a filename and three characters in a filename extension.

You may also use this same option to move a file to a

different drive or directory. For instance, suppose you wish to move a file named SMITH.ADD stored on the hard disk to the disk in drive A. Position the cursor on the filename SMITH.ADD and select Move/Rename (3 or M) from the List Files screen. WordPerfect prompts

```
New name: C:\WP51\DATA\SMITH.ADD
```

Edit the prompt (using the ⬅ and ➡ keys and the Del and Backspace keys), leaving the filename the same but changing the drive onto which it is stored so that it reads

```
New name: A:\SMITH.ADD
```

When you press Enter, the file is moved to the disk in the A drive, and the file named SMITH.ADD is erased from the List Files screen.

You must make sure that if you're moving a file to the floppy disk in a different drive, a formatted disk is inserted in that drive before you give the Move/Rename command. (Appendix A describes how to format a disk.) If you're moving a file from one directory to another, both directories must already have been created on the hard disk (you'll learn about creating a new directory further on in this chapter.)

## Copy a File

Unfortunately, disks are not indestructible. On occasion, a hard disk will crash, meaning that it will lose all the information stored on it, whether 5 documents or 500. Or someone in your office (not you, of course!) will accidentally pour coffee on a floppy disk, ruining it and all its files—a tragedy of large proportions. What if you had completed seven chapters of a book, only to have your disk lose them!

The key to avoiding this disaster is to regularly make backup copies of all your important files. Hard disk users usually store backups on floppy disks (though some hard disk users employ tape backup systems), while floppy disk users should maintain a second set of floppies. With backups, if your hard disk crashed with all seven chapters aboard, you would have another copy on floppy to bail you out.

To copy a file, display the List Files screen, position the cursor on the file you wish to copy, and select Copy (8 or C). WordPerfect responds with

```
Copy this file to:
```

Now you must type in the drive or directory to which you wish to save a copy of this file. Make sure to type a colon (:) after the drive letter and to type backslashes (\) to separate the different directories on the hard disk. For instance, if you want a copy stored on the disk in drive A, you would type

```
A:
```

Or if you wanted a copy stored on the directory named \WP51\KIM on the hard disk, you would type

```
C:\WP51\KIM
```

Then press [Enter]. The copy is stored under the same filename as the original.

You must make sure that if you're copying to a drive that uses floppy disks, a formatted disk is inserted in that drive before you activate the Copy command (again, Appendix A describes how to format a disk). If you're copying a file from one directory to another, both directories must already have been created on the hard disk.

It is also possible to copy a file to the same drive or directory so that you have two copies of that file in the same location. For instance, perhaps you have a file on disk named JONES.LTR containing a letter. You wish to write a similar letter to a different person. You can copy the letter using a different filename. For instance, when Word-Perfect prompts

`Copy this file to:`

you can enter

`JONES2.LTR`

Now you have two identical files (until you edit one of them) on the same drive or directory—one under the original filename and one under the filename JONES2.LTR.

## Mark Files

You can mark a group of files on the List Files screen so that the group can be deleted, printed, moved, or copied in one command. By marking files, you can, for example, delete three files at once or copy ten files to another disk as a backup.

To mark files one by one, move the cursor to a file you wish to mark and type an asterisk (*). *5.1 users:* An asterisk appears to the left of the filename. *5.0 users:* An asterisk appears to the right of the file's size indicator. Continue to mark as many files as you desire. You can also remove the marking from a file. The asterisk (*) key acts like a toggle switch: Press it once to mark a file, press it a second time to unmark the file.

You can also use the MARK TEXT ([Alt] + [F5]) key to mark and unmark files. If no files are marked when you press the MARK TEXT ([Alt] + [F5]) key, all the files become marked. You can then unmark individual files. If some files are already marked when you press the MARK TEXT ([Alt] + [F5]) key, all the files become unmarked.

Once files are marked, you can choose to delete, print, move, or copy them by selecting the appropriate option from the menu at the bottom of the List Files screen. WordPerfect prompts you to verify that you wish to perform the operation on the marked files. For instance, suppose that you mark certain files and then select Copy (8 or C). Figure 8-3 shows the marked files. Notice that the upper right corner of the screen indicates how many files

```
01-15-90  05:32p            Directory C:\WP51\DATA\*.*
Document size:        0  Free:  1,464,320 Used:      304,100    Marked:        12

     Current    <Dir>                    .. Parent      <Dir>
*!ACCTS  .          1,329  10-12-89 11:15p  *1001    .         46,578  10-17-89 05:31p
*5012    .         35,605  10-04-88 08:41p  *5028    .CRG      29,573  10-04-88 08:42p
*88ANN   .RPT      21,444  10-17-89 05:28p  *88RENT  .         43,544  06-16-88 03:56p
*89ANN   .RPT      40,851  10-17-89 05:29p  *89RENT  .         40,824  10-17-89 01:19p
 ACCOUNTS.ADD      36,715  01-15-90 05:24p   BKGROUND.88          778  02-23-88 01:28p
 BUDMIN89.          1,961  05-22-88 09:32p   BUDMIN90.         28,167  10-19-89 12:49p
 C1      .LTR       1,551  02-09-89 11:05a   C2      .LTR       1,496  10-17-89 05:29p
*C3      .LTR       1,401  10-17-89 05:30p  *CEO1    .MMO         942  12-21-88 11:15a
*DOCLIST1.MS       40,756  10-04-88 08:39p  *FINANCE .          1,181  01-15-90 05:37p
 FON     .         28,120  10-04-88 08:43p   GAIN    .LTR       1,598  02-09-89 11:05a
 J&B     .MMO       2,873  10-19-89 12:56p   JONES1  .MMO       1,356  07-22-88 12:56a
 JONES2  .MMO       5,936  02-11-88 01:01a   LE-45   .         40,970  10-04-88 08:40p
 LETTER  .          1,412  10-25-89 03:37p   LINKER  .          1,206  09-16-88 08:36p
 LINKER2 .         35,651  01-15-90 01:33p   LIST    .NEW       1,939  08-21-88 09:43p
 MEYERS-1.MS        1,206  09-16-88 08:36p   P&L     .         35,597  10-04-88 08:40p
 R&RBACK .            380  09-20-88 11:51a   SALVA   .LTR       4,537  09-16-88 08:37p
 SALVAX  .         29,573  10-04-88 08:43p   SAMPLE  .          1,832  10-31-89 02:11a
 SEYMORE .LTR         714  02-15-88 03:21a   SMITH   .ADD         153  08-10-88 12:59p

Copy marked files? No (Yes)
```

**FIGURE 8-3**  Twelve marked files about to be copied

are marked (12 files are marked in Figure 8-3). Also, a prompt appears at the bottom of the screen:

`Copy marked files? No (Yes)`

If you type **Y**, WordPerfect responds with

`Copy all marked files to:`

Type in the drive/directory path and press `Enter`. Word-Perfect will copy the marked files in the order listed. On the other hand, if you type **N** or another key, WordPerfect ignores the file markers and assumes that you want to copy only the file that the cursor is currently highlighting.

## Print the List Files Screen

You can print a copy of the List Files screen as a way of keeping track of files on disk. To do so, display the List Files screen that you wish to print, turn on your printer, and then simply press the PRINT (`Shift` + `F7`) key. A sample is shown in Figure 8-4. This printout lists the current date and time, the amount of free disk space, and lists each file stored in the specified drive/directory.

## Change Between Long and Short File Displays [5.1 Users Only]

As you've learned in Chapter 2, a filename must be one to eight characters long, with an optional dot and an extension of one to three characters. Moreover, neither the

```
01-15-90   05:35p      Directory C:\WP51\DATA\*.*
Free:  1,464,320

. Current  <Dir>            |  .. Parent   <Dir>
!ACCTS  .       1,329  10-12-89  11:15P  |  1001    .       46,578  10-17-89  05:31p
5012    .      35,605  10-04-88  08:41p  |  5028    .CRG   29,573  10-04-88  08:42p
88ANN   .RPT   21,444  10-17-89  05:28p  |  88RENT  .      43,544  06-16-88  03:56p
89ANN   .RPT   40,851  10-17-89  05:29p  |  89RENT  .      40,824  10-17-89  01:19p
ACCOUNTS.ADD   36,715  01-15-90  05:24p  |  BKGROUND.88       778  02-23-88  01:28p
BUDMIN89.        1,961  05-22-88  09:32p  |  BUDMIN90.      28,167  10-19-89  05:29p
C1      .LTR    1,551  02-09-89  11:05a  |  C2      .LTR    1,496  10-17-89  05:29p
C3      .LTR    1,481  10-17-89  05:30p  |  CEO1    .MMO      942  12-21-88  11:15a
DOCLIST1.MS    40,756  10-04-88  08:39p  |  FINANCE .MMO    1,181  01-15-90  05:37p
FON     .      28,120  10-04-88  08:43p  |  GAIN    .LTR    1,598  02-09-89  11:05a
J&B     .MMO    2,873  10-19-89  12:56p  |  JONES1  .MMO    1,356  07-22-88  12:56a
JONES2  .MMO    5,936  02-11-88  01:01a  |  LE-45   .      40,970  10-04-88  08:40p
LETTER  .       1,412  10-25-89  03:37p  |  LINKER  .       1,206  09-16-88  08:36p
LINKER2 .      35,651  01-15-90  01:33p  |  LIST    .NEW    1,939  08-21-88  09:43p
MEYERS-1.MS     1,206  09-16-88  08:36p  |  P&L     .      35,597  10-04-88  08:40p
R&RBACK .         380  09-20-88  11:51a  |  SALVA   .LTR    4,537  09-16-88  08:37p
SALVA%  .      29,573  10-04-88  08:43p  |  SAMPLE  .       1,832  10-31-89  02:11a
SEYMORE .LTR      714  02-15-88  03:21a  |  SMITH   .ADD      153  08-10-88  12:59p
T18     .MMO      921  04-04-88  07:58p  |  T6      .MMO    1,463  02-22-88  11:31a
URGNOTE .       1,735  10-26-89  11:36p  |  URGNOTE .ORG    1,670  08-12-88  12:13a
```

**FIGURE 8-4**   Printout of the List Files screen

filename nor the extension can contain spaces. This naming convention is limiting and is imposed by your computer's Disk Operating System (DOS).

However, to get around this naming limitation, WordPerfect version 5.1 offers the Long Document Name feature. If you activate the Long Document Name feature, you can indicate a filename of up to 68 characters long, an extension of up to 20 characters, and even include spaces in your filenames. The filename can be more descriptive, the extension can specify the type of document (such as a letter or memorandum), and thus, you can more easily identify the file's contents by its filename.

The Long Document Name feature is activated via the

Setup menu, a menu described extensively in Appendix B. The following basic keystrokes will activate the feature: Press SETUP ( Shift + F1 ) and select Environment (3 or E). [*Pulldown menu:* File (F), Setup (T), Environment (E).] Then, select Document Management/Summary (4 or D), Long Document Names (3 or N), type **Y** to turn on the feature, and then press EXIT ( F7 ) to return to the Typing screen. (See the section "Environment" in Appendix B for more detail on the keystrokes involved in turning on this feature, and also for a discussion on how to establish a default long document name type.)

Once this feature is activated, whenever you save or exit a document, WordPerfect will first prompt for a long document name; you can type up to 68 characters, such as "1989 Annual Report" or "R&R Wine Association Objectives." Then, WordPerfect will prompt for a document type; you can type up to 20 characters, such as "CEO Memorandum" or "Report." WordPerfect will then prompt for the usual DOS filename—the name that can contain at most eight characters, with an optional three-character extension, and will suggest a truncated version of the long document name and type, such as 1989ANNU.CEO or RRWINEAS.REP. Press Enter to accept this suggestion, or enter your own DOS filename. When WordPerfect prompts for the long document name, if you press Enter without typing any characters, you can save a document without a long document name or long document type. You can also specify a long document name when creating a document summary, as described later in this chapter.

On the List Files screen, you can display a file's long document name. Select Short/Long Display (5 or S). WordPerfect prompts with the following menu:

`1 Short Display; 2 Long Display: 2`

(WordPerfect assumes the opposite of the current display.) Select Long Display (2 or L) to display the long document names. Or, select Short Display (1 or S) for the more familiar, short display. WordPerfect then prompts for the drive/directory, such as

```
Dir C:\WP51\DATA\*.*
```

Press [Enter] or type in a new drive/directory and press [Enter].

If you selected the Long Display, then instead of two files listed in each row, as shown in Figures 8-1, 8-2, or 8-3, the screen displays just one file in each row. An example is shown in Figure 8-5. In each row, the Long Display first lists up to 30 characters in the Long Document Descriptive Name and up to nine characters in the Long Document

```
11-01-89  09:47p            Directory C:\WP51\DATA\*.*
Document size:       0   Free: 1,458,176 Used:     575,618    Files:      39
Descriptive Name            Type    Filename      Size   Revision Date

Current Directory                     .           <Dir>
Parent Directory                      ..          <Dir>
                                    !ACCTS   .     1,329   10-12-89 11:15p
1988 Annual Report          Rpt     88ANN    .RPT  21,444  10-17-89 05:28p
1989 Annual Report          Rpt     89ANN    .RPT  40,851  10-17-89 05:29p
                                    5012     .     35,605  10-04-88 08:41p
                                    5028     .CRG  29,573  10-04-88 08:42p
                                    88RENT   .     43,544  06-16-88 03:56p
                                    89RENT   .     40,824  10-17-89 01:19p
Accounts Added in 1990      Add     ACCOUNTS.ADD  36,715  11-01-89 09:47p
                                    BKGROUND.88      778   02-23-88 01:28p
                                    BUDMIN89.       1,961  05-22-88 09:32p
                                    BUDMIN90.      28,167  10-19-89 12:49p
                                    C1       .LTR   1,551  02-09-89 11:05a
                                    CEO1     .MMO     942   12-21-88 11:15a
Client 1001 Description and Co      1001     .     46,578  10-17-89 05:31p
Clover Co. 2nd Letter       Ltr     C2       .LTR   1,496  10-17-89 05:29p
Clover Co. 3rd Letter       Ltr     C3       .LTR   1,481  10-17-89 05:30p

1 Retrieve; 2 Delete; 3 Move/Rename; 4 Print; 5 Short/Long Display;
6 Look; 7 Other Directory; 8 Copy; 9 Find; N Name Search: 6
```

**FIGURE 8-5**  Long display of the List Files screen (version 5.1 only)

Type. This is followed by the shorter DOS filename, the size, and the revision date. All the features that operate on the Short Display—such as copying files or marking files or printing the List Files screen—work equally when viewing the Long Display.

Once you switch to either the Long or Short Display, WordPerfect will show that display for the List Files screen during the remainder of the working session or until you again select the Short/Long Display option and change the display. The next time you load WordPerfect, WordPerfect will assume the Long Display if the Long Document Name feature has been activated using the Setup menu. If this feature has not been activated, WordPerfect shows the Short Display. Of course, you can always switch to the other display at any time.

When deciding whether you wish to use the Long Document Name feature, be aware that it takes longer for WordPerfect to show the Long Display than the Short Display. This is because WordPerfect must read a portion of each file in order to show each file's Long Document Name.

# CREATE/DELETE DIRECTORIES

As you now know, it is critical to divide a hard disk electronically into various directories, often organized by general topic or person or software program (such as WordPerfect). These directories can contain files and can also be further divided into subdirectories.

Here's one example of how a hard disk could be divided, assuming that WordPerfect and Lotus 1-2-3 are the programs stored on the hard disk:

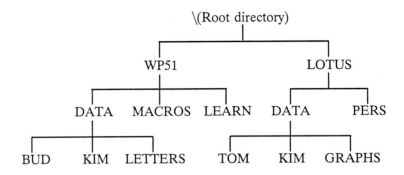

In this example, the WordPerfect program could be stored in the \WP51 directory, and Lotus 1-2-3 in the \LOTUS directory. The subdirectories could store related files. For instance, \WP51\DATA could store the document files, which in turn is divided into \WP51\DATA\BUD, \WP51\DATA\KIM, and \WP51\DATA\LETTERS. You could then segregate different groups of related files into each subdirectory based on whether it was related to budget matters, Kim, or correspondence.

Here's another example assuming that WordPerfect is the only program stored on the hard disk.

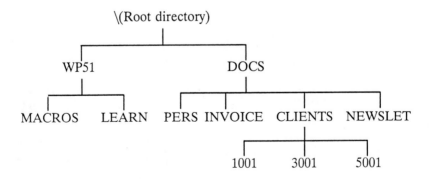

Notice how the WordPerfect program files and the document files are separated into \WP51 and \DOCS, and these are in turn subdivided.

How you organize your hard disk depends on the number of people who share the computer, the type of software packages that you use, and the structure of your business. However, do keep the directory names short, so that switching between directories does not become cumbersome. (There is an 80-character limit to a pathname. For instance, C:\WP51\DATA\BUD is 16 characters long.)

You can use WordPerfect to split a directory into subdirectories by working from the List Files screen. To do so, display the List Files screen for the directory that you wish to divide, position the cursor on the item ". Current <Dir>", and select Other Directory (7 or O). WordPerfect prompts with the name of the current directory. Edit the prompt to indicate the name of the directory you wish to create and press (Enter). Then, type **Y** to confirm the creation of a new directory. The List Files screen will be revised, with the name of the new directory displayed.

Suppose, for instance, that you wish to create a subdirectory within \WP51\DATA that is related only to budget matters. Thus, you wish to create \WP51\DATA\BUD. In that case, hard disk users should proceed as follows: (*5.0 users:* Substitute "WP50" where you read "WP51"):

1. Display the List Files screen for C:\WP51\DATA, which, if you installed WordPerfect according to Appendix A, is the default directory.

2. With the cursor positioned on ". Current <Dir>", select Other Directory (7 or O). WordPerfect prompts

```
New Directory = C:\WP51\DATA
```

3. Press (Home), (→), or press (End) to move to the end of the prompt.

4. Type **\BUD**. Now the prompt reads

New Directory = C:\WP51\DATA\BUD

5. Press (Enter). Now WordPerfect will prompt asking you to verify whether you wish to create this new directory.

Create C:\WP51\DATA\BUD?  No (Yes)

6. Type **Y**. In a few moments, WordPerfect rewrites the screen, and now the item "BUD . <Dir>" is displayed.

You can also have WordPerfect delete a directory for you, but only if that directory contains no files. If the directory contains even one file, WordPerfect will not remove the directory until you delete the file.

To delete a directory, display the List Files screen for the parent directory, and then position the cursor on the name of the directory that you wish to delete, such as "BUD . <Dir>". Next, select Delete (2 or D). WordPerfect will prompt asking for verification before deleting, such as

Delete C:\WP51\DATA\BUD? No (Yes)

Type **Y** to confirm the deletion. If the directory is empty, it will be deleted; otherwise, WordPerfect will return an "ERROR" message and ignore the command.

# CHANGE THE DEFAULT DRIVE/DIRECTORY

You previously learned about the default drive/directory, which is the path WordPerfect assumes you wish to save files to and retrieve files from. There can be only one default at one time. You also learned that you can override the default by preceding a filename with the intended drive and directory path. For instance, you can save a file by pressing the SAVE ( F10 ) key and typing the filename as **A:LETTER**. In that case, the file LETTER is stored on drive A, regardless of the default. Or, you can retrieve a file by pressing the RETRIEVE ( Shift + F10 ) key and typing the filename as C:\WP51\DATA\BUD\J&B1. In that case, WordPerfect looks to the directory C:\WP51\DATA\BUD in order to retrieve the file named J&B1.

There may be instances when, for convenience, you wish to change the default. You can change the default either for a particular working session, or more permanently.

## Change the Default for a Particular Working Session

You can change the default until you turn off the computer at the end of the day or until you change it later on in the current working session. For instance, perhaps you share a computer with two other colleagues. Each of you stores your WordPerfect files in a directory designated by your first name. You can use the LIST ( F5 ) key to change the default to the directory named after you for the whole time that you are working on the computer.

There are two ways to change the default for a working session. One option is available while you're on the Typing screen. You begin by pressing the LIST ( F5 ) key. Word-Perfect responds with the current default listed on the left side of the status line and with a prompt instructing you to change the default on the right side. For instance, for a hard disk user, the prompt after pressing the LIST ( F5 ) key might be

```
Dir C:\WP51\DATA\*.*              (Type = to change default Dir)
```

To change the default, press the equal ( = ) key. Word-Perfect responds by asking for a new default, suggesting the current one:

```
New directory = C:\WP51\DATA
```

Type over or edit this prompt to reflect the new default drive or directory and then press Enter . For instance, you might simply type over the current directory, changing it to read

```
New directory = A:
```

Or you might edit the current directory (using the cursor movement and editing keys) to read

```
New directory = C:\WP51\KIM
```

Then press [Enter] again. WordPerfect will confirm the new default with a prompt such as

```
Dir A:\*.*
```

or

```
Dir C:\WP51\KIM\*.*
```

You have now changed the default. To see a list of files in the new default, press [Enter]. To clear the prompt and continue on the Typing screen instead, press the CANCEL ([F1]) key. The next time you save a new document, it will be saved to the default (such as drive A or the subdirectory \WP51\KIM on the hard disk); the next time you retrieve a document, WordPerfect will search that same default for the file.

The second option for changing the default for a working session is available when you are actually viewing the List Files screen. Select Other Directory (7 or O) and WordPerfect prompts with the current default, such as

```
New directory = C:\WP51\DATA
```

Type in the name of an existing drive or directory you wish for the default and press [Enter]. The default is altered; press [Enter] again and a list of files in the new default is displayed.

## Change the Default at the Start of Every Working Session

WordPerfect also offers a method for establishing a certain default whenever you first load WordPerfect. Rather than change the default manually as just described, you can alter the default by changing the way in which WordPerfect is set up to load; see Appendix A for information about creating a batch file for loading WordPerfect that can set the default for you.

*5.1 users only:* In addition, you can specify a default drive/directory in the Setup menu; see the section "Location of Files" in Appendix B for details. That way, every time you start up WordPerfect, the default that is correct for you will automatically be set.

# LOCK FILES WITH A PASSWORD

Some documents typed in an office are confidential, to be read only by yourself or by a specific group of individuals. When you find yourself typing a top-secret document, WordPerfect offers the ability to save a file with a password. Only the individuals who know the file's password can retrieve it or print it from disk. This is especially handy for those of you who store files on a hard disk and do not have the option of locking the hard disk in a desk drawer as you can with a floppy disk.

To lock a file with a password, make sure the file is on screen, press the TEXT IN/OUT (Ctrl + F5) key, and then select Password (2 or P). WordPerfect displays the following Password menu:

Password: 1 Add/Change; 2 Remove: 0

Select Add/Change (1 or A). [*Pulldown menu:* File (F), Password (W), Add/Change (A).] WordPerfect prompts for you to enter a password, which can contain up to 23 characters and can include numbers, letters, symbols, or spaces. As you type the password, your typing is invisible on screen—a precaution against someone looking over your shoulder to read the password.

Once you type a password and press (Enter), WordPerfect prompts you to reenter the password. You are always asked to enter a password twice to verify that you typed the password exactly as you intended. Type in the password a second time and press (Enter). If the two passwords are different, WordPerfect sounds a beep and prompts you to start again, entering and then reentering the password. If the two attempts at typing a password match, the password is registered. As a last step, you must remember to *resave* your document. When you do, the password is attached to that file.

After a file is locked with a password, WordPerfect will ask for that password whenever you try to view the contents of that file—whether by using the Look option on the List Files menu, by retrieving that file (using the RETRIEVE key or the Retrieve option on the List Files menu), or by printing a document from disk (using the PRINT key or the Print option on the List Files menu). Enter the correct password in order to view, retrieve, or print the file. Enter an incorrect password, however, and WordPerfect aborts the command, with a prompt such as

```
ERROR: File is Locked
```

Don't forget your password! If you do, you'll be locked out of your own file. Keep a written copy of each password somewhere convenient (perhaps in your appointment calendar or wallet), or use a password that you won't easily forget (like your social security number or your mother's birthdate) but that an office mate won't figure out.

You can change a file's password at any time. Make sure you retrieve the file to the Typing screen. Then follow the same steps as outlined above, again selecting Add/Change (1 or A) from the Password menu. Type in the new password twice and make sure to resave your file after changing the password so that the new password takes effect.

You can also remove the password at any time. Again, make sure that the document is on screen. Display the Password menu as outlined above and then select Remove (2 or R). The password is erased. Once you resave the file, the password will become unattached and the file will be unlocked.

Here's an opportunity for you to lock a file. Suppose that a document previously stored on disk is one that you want accessed by you alone. Pretend that your ZIP code at home is 90046. Let's use that ZIP code as the password. Then we'll resave the file so that the password is attached.

1. On a clear screen, retrieve the file named FINANCE.

2. Press the TEXT IN/OUT (⌨Ctrl⌨ + ⌨F5⌨) key. [*Pulldown menu:* File (F).] A menu appears on screen (slightly different for 5.0 users):

   1 DOS Text; 2 Password; 3 Save As; 4 Comment;
   5 Spreadsheet: 0

3. Select Password (2 or P). [*Pulldown menu:* Password (W).] A new menu appears:

   Password: 1 Add/Change; 2 Remove: 0

4. Select Add/Change (1 or A). WordPerfect prompts

```
Enter Password:
```

5. Type **90046** (the numbers will not appear as you type) and press [Enter]. WordPerfect prompts

```
Re-enter Password:
```

6. Type **90046** and press [Enter]. The password has been registered.

7. Use the EXIT ([F7]) key to resave this file under the name FINANCE and to clear the screen (but remain in WordPerfect).

As proof that the file has been locked, let's attempt to retrieve the document.

1. Press the RETRIEVE ([Shift] + [F10]) key. [*Pulldown menu:* File (F), Retrieve (R).] WordPerfect prompts

```
Document to be retrieved:
```

2. Type **FINANCE** and press [Enter]. WordPerfect responds with

```
Enter Password (FINANCE):
```

3. Type **99999** (an incorrect password) and press [Enter]. Since the password is incorrect, WordPerfect responds with an error message indicating that the file is locked and then offers the opportunity to try again, assuming that you still wish to retrieve the same file, with the prompt

```
Document to be retrieved: FINANCE
```

4. Press [Enter] to accept WordPerfect's suggestion that you wish to retrieve the file named FINANCE. WordPerfect prompts

```
Enter Password (FINANCE):
```

5. Type **90046** and press [Enter]. Now the file is retrieved.

Keep in mind that whenever you add, change, or remove a password, you must again save your document for the modification in the password to take effect. Also, remember your password!

# CREATE DOCUMENT SUMMARIES

The Document Summary feature attaches a summary form to a file. The form helps you keep track of the contents of or progress on a document and is often useful for billing purposes. It is also handy for searching for a file based on its content, subject, author, or typist. In version 5.1, a document summary can be both displayed on screen and printed. In version 5.0, however, a document summary is used on screen only; WordPerfect will not print out the summary when you print out the document.

You can create the summary before or after you complete the document or while you're working on it. (However, if you are a version 5.0 user and want the date that WordPerfect automatically inserts on the document summary form to reflect the day you actually started the document, remember to create a summary on the same day.) Your cursor can be anywhere in the document when you create a document summary. To begin, press the FOR-MAT ([Shift] + [F8]) key, select Document (3 or D), and then, on the Document Format menu, select Summary (5 or S). [*Pulldown menu:* File (F), Summary (M).] A Document Summary screen appears. Since the Document Summary feature is different in versions 5.1 and 5.0, it is discussed separately below for each version.

## Document Summary [5.1 Users]

When you first display the Document Summary screen as shown in Figure 8-6, WordPerfect fills out certain items automatically.

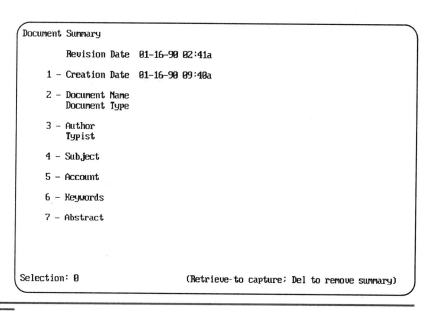

```
Document Summary

         Revision Date  01-16-90 02:41a

 1 - Creation Date  01-16-90 09:40a

 2 - Document Name
     Document Type

 3 - Author
     Typist

 4 - Subject

 5 - Account

 6 - Keywords

 7 - Abstract



Selection: 0                    (Retrieve-to capture; Del to remove summary)
```

**FIGURE 8-6**   Document Summary screen (version 5.1)

- *Revision Date*   The date/time when the *document* was last revised and saved to disk is inserted. This item is left blank if you are creating a Document Summary for a brand new document and have yet to save that document on disk. This date is updated continually according to your computer's current date and time whenever you edit and then resave a document. This date can only be changed by WordPerfect, not by you.

- *Creation Date*   Today's date/time—when the *document summary* is being established—is inserted. (As discussed in "Getting Started," the computer knows today's date only if your computer is equipped with an internal clock or you indicate the current date when you turn on your computer to load WordPerfect.)

- *Document Name/Type*   WordPerfect checks to see if you indicated a Long Document Name and Type for this document (as described previously under the section "Organize Files on Disk "). If so, these are inserted into the document summary.

You can enter or edit seven items on the summary form. These include the following:

- *Creation Date (1 or D)*   This items allows you to enter something other than the current date/time. Enter the date with the month, day, and year always separated by two slashes, such as 1/8/90 or 01/08/1990. Enter the time with the hour and minute separated by a colon and followed by "a" for A.M. or "p" for P.M., such as 10:15a.

- *Document Name/Type (2 or N)*   This item allows you to edit the Long Document Name or Type. Or, if no Long Document Name or Type exist, you can enter them— even if the Long Document Name feature is not activated. The Document Name can contain 68 characters, while the Document Type can contain 20, and both can contain spaces. See the section "Organize Files on Disk" earlier in this chapter for more on this feature.

- *Author/Typist (3 or T)*    This item allows you 60 characters for indicating the author and 60 characters for indicating the typist. Or, if you press the RETRIEVE ([Shift] + [F10]) key, WordPerfect will retrieve the most recent Author and Typist entries saved in a Document Summary during the current working session.

- *Subject (4 or S)*    This item allows you 160 characters for helping to identify the document by subject. Or, if you press the RETRIEVE ([Shift] + [F10]) key, WordPerfect searches the document for the characters "RE:" (or another Subject Search entry, as described in the note at the end of this section). If the characters are found, WordPerfect inserts the text that follows the "RE:", either up to the next hard return or until 39 characters have been inserted.

- *Account (5 or C)*    This item allows you 160 characters for helping to identify the document by account.

- *Keywords (6 or K)*    This item allows you 160 characters for helping find the document based on key words that describe the document. (The Find feature is described later on in this chapter.)

- *Abstract (7 or A)*    This item allows you up to 780 characters. Or, if you press the RETRIEVE ([Shift] + [F10]) key, WordPerfect will retrieve the first 400 characters of the document.

Select an item, type the appropriate information, and then press EXIT ([F7]) or [Enter] before selecting another option.

For instance, if the document relates to an account, select Account (5 or C), type in information of up to 160 characters in length, and press the EXIT key. (When you select the Abstract option, you must press EXIT ([F7]) when done editing the comment; pressing [Enter] will insert a hard return in the abstract, moving the cursor down to the next line.) Once you fill in information for some or all of these items, press EXIT ([F7]) to return to the Typing screen.

After you create a document summary, save that document on disk. The document summary becomes attached to that file. Or, if you ever wish to delete the summary from the document, display the document summary on screen, press the [Del] key and type **Y** to erase it; then resave the file.

The document summary does not automatically display on the Typing screen. To review or edit the contents of the document summary, proceed as if you intend to create a summary for the first time by selecting Summary (5 or S) from the Document Format menu. The form that you previously filled out appears on screen. Now you can select an item for editing or simply press EXIT ([F7]) to return to the Typing screen.

The document summary is quite flexible and can be saved as text to another file. This allows you to keep a copy of all document summaries. One application, for instance, is to save a document summary to a file named 1001.SUM every time that you work on a given file named 1001. That way, you can have a record of revisions on the file for billing purposes. To save a document summary, display the document summary on screen, press the SAVE ([F10]) key, and enter a filename. A filename is created to store the summary as text. Or, if a filename by that name exists, WordPerfect prompts with a menu; select Replace (1 or R) to overwrite the existing text in that file, or select Append

(2 or A) to attach this document summary as a new page at the end of the existing file — the right choice if you want to continue compiling document summaries into one file. (You can also save the document summary using the Look feature, as described momentarily.)

You can print the document summary in one of four ways. First, you can display the document summary on screen, and then press PRINT ([Shift] + [F7]). Second, when the document is not on screen, print the summary by printing from disk (either using the Document on Disk option from the Print menu or directly from the List Files menu). When WordPerfect prompts for the pages you wish to print of a given file that you indicate, type **s** and press [Enter] to print the summary. Or, you can print the summary and additional pages. For instance, type **s,2-5** and press [Enter] to print the summary and pages 2 through 5. The third method for printing a document summary applies if you saved the summary as text into another file. If so, then print that other file as you would any WordPerfect document file. Fourth, you can print the summary from the menu that appears when you use the Look feature to view the contents of a file, as described next.

You can review (but not edit) a document summary when you use the Look feature to peek at the contents of documents. You'll remember from Chapter 2 that the Look feature is accessed from the List Files screen by positioning the cursor on the file whose contents you wish to peruse and either selecting Look (6 or L) or pressing the [Enter] key. The Look screen first displays the document summary for a file (if that file has one); to display the actual file contents, press [↓]. Or, select an item from the menu that appears at the bottom screen, which includes the following options: Next (1 or N) — look at the document summary/contents of the next document; Prev (2 or P) — look at

```
Document Summary

        System Filename          C:\WP51\DATA\FINANCE

        Date of Creation         January 16, 1990

   1 - Descriptive Filename

   2 - Subject/Account

   3 - Author

   4 - Typist

   5 - Comments
  ┌──────────────────────────────────────────────────────────────┐
  │ I talked to John Samsone on January 3rd about our financial situation.  He │
  │ reported the following highlights:  o Our debt as of December 31st stands │
  │ at $159,000, 10% lower than we anticipated.  Financial forecasts project │
  │ that we'll be out of debt in two years time.  Here are the debt figures │
  │ (in thousands):     Amount Owed      Name of Bank :    $40 .5      Floyd │
  └──────────────────────────────────────────────────────────────┘

Selection: 0
```

════════ **FIGURE 8-7**  Document Summary screen (version 5.0)

the previous document; Look at Text (3 or L)—look at the text for the current document, which is the same as when you press ⏎; Print (4 or R)—print the summary; or Save to File (5 or S)—save a copy of the document summary as text in a file.

## Document Summary [5.0 Users]

When you first display the Document Summary screen as shown in Figure 8-7 (where the document named FI-NANCE was on screen before the document summary form was displayed), WordPerfect fills out four items for you automatically:

- *System Filename*   The name with which you stored this document on disk, along with the drive/directory where it is stored, is inserted. (If you haven't yet stored this document on disk, the phrase, "Not named yet" appears on the document summary form until you store the document on disk.)

- *Date of Creation*   Today's date (When the document summary is being established) is inserted. (As discussed in "Getting Started," the computer knows today's date only if your computer is equipped with an internal clock or you indicate the current date when you turn on your computer.)

- *Subject/Account*   WordPerfect searches the first 400 bytes (approximately 400 characters) of the document for the characters "RE:" (or another Subject Search entry, as described in the note at the end of this section). If the characters are found, WordPerfect inserts the text that follows "RE:", either up to the next hard return or until 39 characters have been inserted, whichever comes first. If the characters are not found, the item Subject/Account remains blank.

- *Comment*   If the text has been entered into the document, the first 400 characters are inserted in a double-line box at the bottom of the form. If no text has yet been entered for the document, the comments box remains clear of text.

You can enter or edit five items on the summary form. These include

- *Descriptive Filename (1 or D)*   This item allows you up to 39 characters with which to describe what the system filename stands for. As an example, if the system file-name is 89ANN.RPT, you can fill out the descriptive filename as "1989 Annual Report."

If you enter a descriptive filename before the file has been stored on disk, WordPerfect suggests a system file-name. For instance, suppose you enter the descriptive filename "Status Report on 1989 Budget." WordPerfect will suggest the system filename STATREPO.ON on screen and when you store the file on disk. You can accept the suggestion or type in a system filename of your own.

- *Subject/Account (2 or S)* This item allows you 39 charac-ters to help identify the document by indicating the document's subject or account number.

- *Author (3 or A)* This item allows you 39 characters for typing the author of the document.

- *Typist (4 or T)* This item allows you 39 characters for indicating who is typing the document.

- *Comments (5 or C)* This item allows up to 780 charac-ters in the comments box at the bottom of the screen. You can edit text that WordPerfect automatically in-serted or erase that text and insert your own comments. Only five lines of text can be displayed in the box at one time; use the cursor movement keys (such as ⬇ and ⬆) to view additional text.

Select an item, type in the appropriate information, and then press EXIT ( F7 ) or Enter before selecting another option. For instance, select Author (3 or A), type in a name up to 39 characters in length, and press the EXIT key. (When you select the Comments option, you mustpress EXIT ( F7 ) when done editing the comment; pressing (Enter) will insert a hard return in the comments box, moving the cursor down to the next line.) Once you fill in information for some or all of these five items, press EXIT ( (F7) ) to return to the Typing screen.

After you create a document summary, save that document on disk. The document summary becomes attached to that file.

The document summary does not automatically display on the Typing screen. To review or edit the contents of a document summary, simply proceed as if you intend to create a summary for the first time by selecting Summary (5 or S) from the Document Format menu. The form that you previously filled out appears on screen. Now you can select an item for editing or simply press EXIT ( (F7) ) to return to the Typing screen.

In addition, you can review (but not edit) a document summary when you use the Look feature to peek into the contents of documents. You'll remember from Chapter 2 that the Look feature is accessed from the List Files screen by positioning the cursor on the file whose contents you wish to peruse and either selecting Look (6 or L) or pressing the (Enter) key. The Look screen first displays the document summary for a file (if that file has one); to display the actual file contents, press (↓).

## Add a Document Summary [5.1 and 5.0 Users]

Suppose you've decided that you want to create a document summary for each of your important documents. That way you'll know a document's contents and status from a quick glance at the summary. Let's create a summary for the file named FINANCE, which is now on your Typing screen, and fill out several pieces of information.

1. With the cursor positioned anywhere in the document, press the FORMAT (⟦Shift⟧ + ⟦F8⟧) key [*Pulldown menu:* File (F).] and select Document (3 or D). The Document Format menu appears.

2. Select Summary (5 or S). [*Pulldown menu:* Summary (M).] The Document Summary screen appears, as shown in Figure 8-6 for 5.1 users, or Figure 8-7 for 5.0 users.

3. *5.1 users:* Select Subject (4 or S). *5.0 users:* Select Subject/Account (2 or S). *5.1 and 5.0 users:* Type **Financial Status**, and press ⟦Enter⟧.

4. *5.1 users:* Select Author/Typist (3 or T) and press ⟦Enter⟧ to move to the "Typist" heading. *5.0 users:* Select Typist (4 or T). *5.1 and 5.0 users:* Type your name as the typist, and press ⟦Enter⟧.

5. *5.1 users:* Select Abstract (7 or A). *5.0 users:* Select Comments (5 or C). The cursor moves into the comment box for 5.0 users.

6. Type **Confidential memo to the CEO**. 5.0 users can then press ⟦Enter⟧ twice and use the arrow keys to scroll up and down the comment box.

7. Press EXIT (⟦F7⟧) to exit the comment box. Your screen will now resemble Figure 8-8 for 5.1 users or Figure 8-9 for 5.0 users.

8. Press the EXIT (⟦F7⟧) key to return to your document.

9. Use the EXIT (⟦F7⟧) key to resave this file under the name FINANCE and to clear the screen (but remain in WordPerfect).

```
Document Summary

        Revision Date  01-16-90 03:01a

  1 - Creation Date  01-16-90 09:40a

  2 - Document Name
      Document Type

  3 - Author
      Typist          Scott White

  4 - Subject         Financial Status

  5 - Account

  6 - Keywords

  7 - Abstract        Confidential memo to the CEO.




Selection: 1                    (Retrieve to capture; Del to remove summary)
```

**FIGURE 8-8**   Document Summary screen after entering information (version 5.1)

With the screen clear, suppose that you wish to use the Look feature to peruse the contents of the file named FINANCE without actually retrieving that file to the screen. Proceed as follows:

1. Press the LIST ( F5 ) key. [*Pulldown menu:* File (F), List Files (F).] WordPerfect prompts with the default drive/directory, for instance, Dir B:\*.* or Dir C\:WP51\DATA\*.*.

2. Since FINANCE is stored in the default drive/directory, press Enter . The List Files menu appears, showing the names of files in your default drive or directory. (If FINANCE is not stored in the default, type in the correct drive/directory before pressing Enter .)

```
Document Summary

        System Filename              C:\WP51\DATA\FINANCE

        Date of Creation             January 16, 1990

    1 - Descriptive Filename

    2 - Subject/Account              Financial Status

    3 - Author

    4 - Typist                       Scott White

    5 - Comments
  ┌────────────────────────────────────────────────────────────┐
  │ Confidential memo to the CEO.                                │
  │                                                              │
  │ I talked to John Samsone on January 3rd about our financial situation.  He │
  │ reported the following highlights:  o Our debt as of December 31st stands │
  │ at $159,000, 10% lower than we anticipated.  Financial forecasts project │
  └────────────────────────────────────────────────────────────┘

Selection: 0
```

**FIGURE 8-9**   Document Summary screen after entering
information (version 5.0)

3. Position the cursor on the filename FINANCE.

4. Press (Enter) or select Look (6 or L). Because this file is
   locked from our previous exercise, WordPerfect asks for
   the password, with a prompt such as

   `Enter Password: C:\WP51\DATA\FINANCE`

5. Type **90046** and press (Enter). A Look screen appears as
   shown in Figure 8-10 for 5.1 users and 8-11 for 5.0 users.
   Notice the header at the top of the screen. Below the
   header, WordPerfect displays not the contents of the
   file, but the document summary, since a summary had
   previously been created for the file named FINANCE.

6. Press ⬇. Or, 5.1 users can also select Look at text (3 or L). Now the Look screen shows the actual contents of the file.

7. Press EXIT (F7) or CANCEL (F1) twice — once to exit the Look screen and a second time to exit the List Files screen. You are returned to the Typing screen.

As you will learn in the next section, document summaries can be used when you are seeking a certain file or group of files. Therefore, it is worth your while to devise a systematic method for filling out information in a summary. For instance, 5.1 users can decide that all documents related to your company's finances be assigned the key words

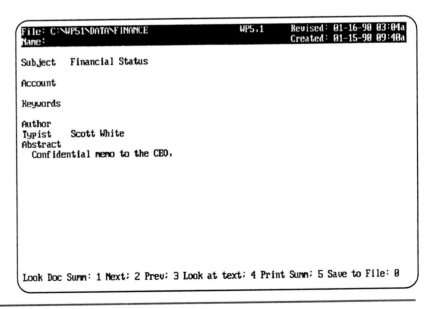

```
File: C:\WP51\DATA\FINANCE              WP5.1    Revised: 01-16-90 03:04a
Name:                                            Created: 01-15-90 09:40a

Subject    Financial Status

Account

Keywords

Author
Typist     Scott White
Abstract
     Confidential memo to the CEO.




Look Doc Summ: 1 Next; 2 Prev; 3 Look at text; 4 Print Summ; 5 Save to File: 0
```

**FIGURE 8-10**   Look screen showing the FINANCE document summary (version 5.1)

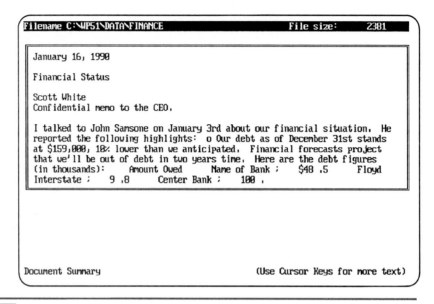

```
Filename C:\WP51\DATA\FINANCE                     File size:    2381

    January 16, 1990

    Financial Status

    Scott White
    Confidential memo to the CEO.

    I talked to John Sansone on January 3rd about our financial situation. He
    reported the following highlights:  o Our debt as of December 31st stands
    at $159,000, 18% lower than we anticipated. Financial forecasts project
    that we'll be out of debt in two years time. Here are the debt figures
    (in thousands):    Amount Owed      Name of Bank ;   $48 .5     Floyd
    Interstate ;   9 .8     Center Bank ;    100 .



    Document Summary                          (Use Cursor Keys for more text)
```

**FIGURE 8-11** Look screen showing the FINANCE document summary (version 5.0)

"financial status". And, while 5.0 users don't have a Keywords item, you can enter "financial status" in the Subject/Account item.

*Note:* WordPerfect offers two features that change how the Document Summary feature operates. First, you can direct WordPerfect to display a document summary form whenever a document is saved without a document summary already created. In this way, you can rely on WordPerfect to remind you to fill out a summary for each new document, rather than attempting to remember yourself. Second, you can change the text for which WordPerfect searches when attempting to fill in the "Subject" heading (version 5.1) or "Subject/Account" heading (version 5.0). As described previously, the default search text is "RE:". But if you type memorandums using the term "MEMO TOPIC:" instead, you can alter the subject search text accordingly. Refer to the "Environment" section in Appendix B for further details on both of these options.

# SEARCH FOR SPECIFIC FILES

No matter how diligent you are about assigning each file a unique filename, once numerous files are accumulated on disk, it becomes difficult to remember which file contains which document. You could stare at the List Files screen for hours and still not remember the name of the file you're looking for. But you don't have to retrieve each file one by one until you find the one you want; WordPerfect offers several features to help you keep track of those files and quickly narrow down the search on the List Files screen.

## Specify Filename or File Extension Patterns

As you know, when you first press the LIST ( [F5] ) key, you see a prompt such as

`Dir B:\*.*`

or

`Dir C:\WP51\DATA\*.*`

The \*.\* means that WordPerfect will display all files in that drive or directory. When you press [Enter], a List Files screen appears containing all the files in that drive/directory.

But you can temporarily narrow down the display of files in a drive/directory to those with similar names by using the wild card characters * and ?. Those of you familiar with DOS will recognize these wild cards. The asterisk (*) represents any number of characters, while the question mark (?) represents just one character—that's why *.* means that all files will be displayed, no matter what their filenames or extensions.

You can edit the *.* and thereby limit what files are displayed. For example, perhaps you know that the file you are looking for ends with the file extension .LTR. You can display all files, with any filename, that have the file extension .LTR. You must edit the prompt when you first press the LIST FILES (F5) key so that instead of *.*, the prompt reads

```
Dir C:\WP51\DATA\*.LTR
```

When you press Enter, the List Files screen shows only those files with the extension .LTR.

Or suppose you are looking for a document named JONES, but can't remember its extension (or even whether it had one). To list all files with the filename JONES and with any extension, change the prompt to read

```
Dir C:\WP51\DATA\JONES.*
```

When you press Enter, WordPerfect will list files such as JONES, JONES.IHM, or JONES.44.

Or suppose you are looking for documents with any filename whose extension starts with any character and ends with "MM." Then change the prompt to read

```
Dir C:\WP51\DATA\*.?MM
```

before pressing `Enter`.

Here's an example whereby you can narrow the List Files screen to only files with the extension ADD.

1. Press the LIST (`F5`) key. [*Pulldown menu:* File (F), List Files (F).] WordPerfect prompts with the default drive /directory, for instance, "Dir B:\*.*" or "Dir C:\WP51\DATA\*.*".

2. Press the `→` key until the cursor won't move any farther (or you can press `End` or `Home`, `→` to move the cursor more quickly); the cursor will be located just to the right of the very last character, which is the second asterisk (*).

3. Press `Backspace` to erase that asterisk.

4. Type **ADD** (uppercase or lowercase makes no difference). Now the prompt will read "Dir B:\*.ADD" or "Dir C:\WP51\DATA\*.ADD".

5. Press `Enter`. A List Files screen like that shown in Figure 8-12 appears. Notice that the top of the screen indicates that the files listed are from C:\WP51\DATA\*.ADD, which means files stored on the hard disk in the directory \WP51\DATA, with any filename with the extension ADD. Figure 8-12 displays two files with an extension of .ADD. Your screen may display only one file named SMITH.ADD, which you created in Chapter 2.

6. Press EXIT (`F7`) or CANCEL (`F1`) to return to the Typing screen.

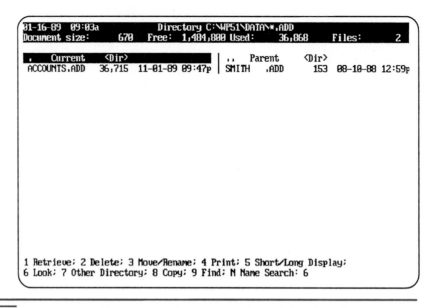

─────────────── **FIGURE 8-12**  List Files screen for files with the
filename extension .ADD

## Name Search

Once you're viewing the List Files screen, you can use the
Name Search feature to move the cursor to a file quickly
based on its first few characters. Instead of using the cursor
movement keys to scroll through the files, type the letter **N**
or press the ➔SEARCH ( F2 ) key. This activates the
Name Search. The List Files menu at the bottom of the
screen is temporarily replaced by the message "(Name
Search; Enter or arrows to Exit)". Instead of using the
cursor movement keys, type the first few characters of the
document's filename. The cursor will move to the filename
that begins with those characters (or most closely matches
them). For instance, if you type **b**, the cursor moves to the
first filename starting with the letter "b." If you then type

**u,** the cursor moves to the first filename starting with "bu"—which might be the file named BUDMIN. Press [Enter] or an arrow key to end the search. The menu of options returns to the bottom of the List Files screen. Here's an example:

1. Press the LIST ([F5]) key. WordPerfect prompts with the default drive/directory, for instance, "Dir B:\*.*" or "Dir C:\WP51\DATA\*.*".

2. Press [Enter] to display the list of files.

3. Type **N** to activate Name Search.

4. Type **U.** The cursor moves down to the first file beginning with the letter "U"; on your screen, this may be the file named URGNOTE that you created in a previous chapter.

5. Press [Enter] to exit Name Search.

6. Press CANCEL ([F1]) to exit the List Files screen.

## Find (Word Search)

The Find feature (referred to as Word Search in version 5.0) can hunt down files by looking not only at each document's filename, but also at its contents. To use this feature, you must first display the List Files screen for the files that you wish involved in the search. For instance, if you wish to search through all the files in the default drive/directory, press LIST ([F5]) and press [Enter]. Or type in another drive/directory and press [Enter]. When viewing a list of files, you can also narrow down the search even further by marking those files you wish to search with an asterisk.

The next step depends on whether you use version 5.1 or 5.0. *5.1 users:* Select Find (9 or F). The following menu appears:

```
Find: 1 Name; 2 Doc Summary; 3 First Pg; 4 Entire Doc; 5 Conditions;
6 Undo: 0
```

*5.0 users:* Select Word Search (9 or W) to view the following menu:

```
Search: 1 Doc Summary; 2 First Page; 3 Entire Doc; 4 Conditions: 0
```

There are two categories for the find operation. You can either indicate a *word pattern,* or you can specify *conditions.*

## Find Files Based on a Word Pattern

When you indicate a word pattern, you specify a certain word, several words, or a phrase of up to 39 characters (20 characters in version 5.0). For instance, you could find all those documents in which the word "computer" is mentioned. WordPerfect can search multiple files for that word pattern in every document summary, the first page of each document, or all pages of each document, whichever you specify. Select either Doc Summary, First Page, or Entire Doc from the Find (or Search) menu and WordPerfect prompts

```
Word pattern:
```

In the word pattern, you can use the wild card character * to represent any number of characters or ? to represent a single character. For instance, the word pattern

```
*computer*
```

will find documents that contain the words *microcomputer, microcomputers, minicomputer, minicomputers, computer,* and *computers,* just to name a few. The word pattern

```
m?re
```

will find documents that contain the words *mare, mere, mire, more,* or *mure.*

If the word pattern contains two or more words, you can separate the words by a space or a semicolon (;) to represent the logical operator AND and separate the words by a comma (,) to represent the logical operator OR. If you type the words in quotation marks, the words are treated as a distinct phrase that must be located. For instance, the word pattern

```
wine price
```

will locate files that contain *both* the word *wine* and the word *price.* The pattern

```
wine, price
```

will locate files that contain *either* word. The pattern

```
"wine price"
```

will locate files that contain the phrase *wine price.*

After you type in a word pattern, press [Enter]. A prompt at the bottom of the screen indicates that the search is progressing. When the search is complete, WordPerfect will rewrite the List Files screen, listing only those files that contain the specified word pattern (version 5.1), or displaying an asterisk next to those files that contain the specified word pattern (version 5.0). Or, if no files are found that contain the specified word pattern, WordPerfect prompts with a "∗ Not found ∗" message.

*5.1 users only:* You can specify a word pattern not only within the file's contents, but also in its name. Unlike the Name Search feature, where WordPerfect searches only the beginning of a filename, in Find, WordPerfect searches anywhere within a filename. Select Name (1 or N) from the Find menu and then type in a word pattern as previously specified. For instance, enter the pattern LTR and WordPerfect will display the files named 1LTR.89, AA6LTR, C1.LTR, C2.LTR, GENLTR, LTRJONES, and SEYMORE.LTR.

Here's an example for either 5.1 or 5.0 users that requires you to use the Find (Word Search) feature. Pretend you want to find those files that mention a person named "samsone" in the document.

1. Display the List Files screen for the default drive or directory.

2. *5.1 users:* Select Find (9 or F). *5.0 users:* Select Word Search (9 or W). WordPerfect responds with the Find menu.

3. *5.1 users:* Select Entire Document (4 or E). *5.0 users:* Select Entire Document (3 or E). WordPerfect prompts for a word pattern.

4. Type **samsone** and press ⌷Enter⌷.

5. As it is checking each file, WordPerfect will prompt for the password for FINANCE; otherwise, WordPerfect won't perform a search on that file. Type **90046** and press ⌷Enter⌷. The search continues in other files.

6. After several moments, WordPerfect displays or marks the two files that contain that name — FINANCE and URGNOTE.

## Find Files Based on Conditions

The second Find (Word Search) method searches for certain conditions. Using the conditions method, you can specify that WordPerfect search based on a word pattern as described previously, and also based on the creation date or the revision date — the date when you last saved a file to disk. Moreover, you can search on more than just one condition at a time. For instance, you can search for files where (1) the word pattern *Scott White* is found under the Author category in the Document Summary, (2) the word pattern *wine opener* is found on the first page of the document, and (3) the document was last edited in February 1990. In this way, you can be quite precise in the document for which you are looking.

To use the conditions method, select Conditions from the Find (Word Search) menu. The screen is different in version 5.1 than in version 5.0.

*5.1 users:* Figure 8-13 illustrates the Find Conditions screen. Items 3 through 5 allow you to specify conditions. Revision Date (3 or D) allows you to search for files which have been edited between certain dates. Text (4 or T) allows you to specify word patterns in a document summary, first page, and/or entire document. Document Summary (5 or S) allows you to specify word patterns for specific items within document summaries.

*5.0 users:* Figure 8-14 shows the Word Search Conditions screen. Items 4 through 7 allow you to specify conditions.

```
┌────────────────────────────────────────────────────────────────┐
│ Find: Conditions                              Files Selected:  42 │
│                                                                   │
│      1 - Perform Search                                           │
│      2 - Reset Conditions                                         │
│                                                                   │
│      3 - Revision Date - From                                     │
│                           To                                      │
│                                                                   │
│      4 - Text - Document Summary                                  │
│               First Page                                          │
│               Entire Document                                     │
│                                                                   │
│      5 - Document Summary                                         │
│          Creation Date - From                                     │
│                           To                                      │
│          Document Name                                            │
│          Document Type                                            │
│          Author                                                   │
│          Typist                                                   │
│          Subject                                                  │
│          Account                                                  │
│          Keywords                                                 │
│          Abstract                                                 │
│                                                                   │
│ Selection: 1                                                      │
└────────────────────────────────────────────────────────────────┘
```

**FIGURE 8-13**  Find screen (version 5.1)

File Date (4 or D) allows you to search for files that have been edited between certain dates. First Page (5 or F) allows you to specify a word pattern for the first page of each file. Entire Doc (6 or E) allows you to specify a word pattern for the entire document. Document Summary (7 or S) allows you to specify a word pattern for anywhere in document summaries if you type the pattern on the first line, or for specific items within document summaries if you type the word pattern next to a specified heading.

For both 5.1 users and 5.0 users, keep in mind when typing in a date to separate the month, day, and year with slashes. For instance, type **12/9/90** or **12/09/1990**. *5.0 users only:* You can leave the month, day, or year unspecified, but be sure to include the slashes. For instance, in order to search for files last revised in February 1990, enter the

```
Word Search

   1 - Perform Search on           All 42 File(s)

   2 - Undo Last Search

   3 - Reset Search Conditions

   4 - File Date                   No
         From (MM/DD/YY):          (All)
         To   (MM/DD/YY):          (All)

                  Word Pattern(s)

   5 - First Page
   6 - Entire Doc
   7 - Document Summary
         Creation Date (e.g, Nov)
         Descriptive Name
         Subject/Account
         Author
         Typist
         Comments

Selection: 1
```

**FIGURE 8-14**   Word Search screen (version 5.0)

"From" and "To" categories as 2//90. Or, to search for all files revised since the start of 1990, enter //90 in the "From" category, and leave the "To" category unspecified.

After you set all conditions, select Perform Search (1 or P) to initiate the search. (You can also press Enter to initiate the search, since WordPerfect always assumes that your selection is option 1, as shown on the status line at the bottom of Figure 8-13 (5.1 users) or 8-14 (5.0 users). A prompt appears indicating that the search is progressing. When the search is complete, WordPerfect will rewrite the List Files screen, displaying only those files that contain the specified conditions (version 5.1) or displaying an asterisk next to those files that meet the conditions (version 5.0). Or, if WordPerfect cannot find files that meet all the conditions, WordPerfect will prompt "* Not found *".

Once you've found the file you were looking for, you are ready to perform whatever task is at hand—whether you peruse the contents of each of the marked documents using the Look feature, retrieve one of the marked documents, or print one of them. Or you can perform another word search. From the List Files screen, with certain files selected because of the previous word search, again select Find (Word Search) and Conditions. The menu reappears, but instead of performing the search on all the files, Word-Perfect will assume you wish to perform the next search on just the selected files. The number of files assumed for the next search is always indicated at the top of the Find (Word Search) Conditions screen. Or, you can undo the most recent search, which will return the List Files screen to the way it was before you performed the search.

As an example, suppose that you search based on certain conditions on a List Files screen containing 100 files. Afterwards, the Find (Word Search) menu narrows down the list to 50 files. Now you can perform a search on just those 50, or use the Undo feature to return to a search on all 100 files. WordPerfect version 5.1 users can select Undo (6 or U) from the Find menu. Version 5.0 users must return to the Word Search Conditions menu and then select Undo Last Search (2 or U).

Keep in mind that WordPerfect remembers the search conditions you set until you change them or exit WordPerfect. Therefore, when you wish to perform a completely different search, select Reset Search Conditions on the menu shown in Figure 8-13 (5.1 users) or 8-14 (5.0 users). The conditions are reset to their original status. Then proceed to set new search conditions and perform another word search.

# TEMPORARILY EXIT TO DOS

Most of the basic file-management and disk-management operations described previously—such as creating a subdirectory, deleting a file, and copying a file—can be performed directly from DOS (Disk Operating System). Other operations, such as formatting a floppy disk, can *only* be accomplished when you exit WordPerfect to DOS.

You can exit WordPerfect to DOS temporarily if you prefer using DOS to copy files, create subdirectories, and the like (though you will probably discover that using the List Files screen is easier), or if you wish to perform an operation not available through WordPerfect. To do so, press the SHELL ( Ctrl + F1 ) key. [*Pulldown menu:* File (F), Go to DOS (G).] Then, select Go to DOS (1 or G). (If you use WordPerfect Library in addition to WordPerfect, you must first select Go to Shell; from here, you can exit to DOS.)

WordPerfect temporarily disappears. A DOS prompt (such as B> or C> or C:WP51\DATA>) appears indicating that you are in DOS, working from the default drive. Now you can type in DOS commands. (See your DOS manual for a full discussion of DOS commands.)

For instance, suppose that you neglected to enter the correct date at the beginning of the day's session, and the computer had no internal clock to automatically tell it the correct date when you turned it on. To inform the computer of the date, you could type **DATE** at the DOS prompt and press Enter . The computer responds with what it believed to be the correct date and prompts you with

ENTER new date

Type in the current date and press (Enter). The DOS prompt returns to the screen, ready for your next command.

Certain DOS commands require access to files that reside on the DOS disk. One such command is FORMAT. To format a disk, floppy disk users must insert the DOS disk in the default drive and a blank disk to be formatted in the second drive. Hard disk users may need to switch the default to the directory containing the DOS files.

You should always be very careful when you format a disk—the Format command is dangerous! When you format a disk, you prepare it to store files. In the process, everything previously stored on that disk is erased. So if you're not cautious, you can accidentally erase important files!

As a general rule, don't simply type **Format** without specifying a drive. If you wish to format a brand new disk in drive A, the correct command is

```
format a:
```

meaning specifically that the disk in drive A should be formatted. If you put that brand new disk in drive B, the correct command is

```
format b:
```

Without specifying a drive, floppy disk users could destroy all the files on the DOS disk, and hard disk users could delete all the hundreds of files that might be stored on the hard disk!

When you are ready to return to WordPerfect, simply type **exit** at the DOS prompt and then press (Enter). (Actually type the word "exit." Do not press the EXIT ((F7)) key instead; the EXIT ((F7)) key operates only when in WordPerfect, not in DOS.)

It is easy to forget about WordPerfect and, after exiting to DOS temporarily, simply turn off the computer. But then you are not exiting WordPerfect properly. Therefore, remember that if you go to DOS in the middle of a Word-Perfect session, you need to return to WordPerfect and exit properly (using the EXIT key or the File pulldown menu) before turning off the computer.

Your computer must be equipped with sufficient RAM memory to exit to DOS temporarily. You might find that WordPerfect won't allow you to exit because you have insufficient memory to do so.

*5.1 users only:* You have the added ability to initiate a DOS command without temporarily exiting WordPerfect. Press the SHELL ([Ctrl] + [F1]) key and, instead of selecting Go to DOS, select DOS Command (2 or C). Word-Perfect prompts for you to type one DOS command. Enter the DOS command and it will be carried out. Then, as prompted, press any key to continue in WordPerfect.

# REVIEW EXERCISE

If you are systematic in how you manage files on disk, you'll have little difficulty finding a file when you need it. Practice by performing the following tasks, and you'll be ready to maintain order for the hundreds of files that will soon find their way onto your hard disk or floppy disks.

1. Remove the password from the file named FINANCE. (*Hint:* To retrieve that file to the screen, remember that the password is 90046. Also, don't forget to resave the file after you remove the password from it.)

2. Pretend that the files named URGNOTE and FI-NANCE are important files that you must maintain a record of. To safeguard against a disk malfunctioning, place copies of these two files on a floppy disk. (*Hint:* Make sure that you have a formatted disk and that you insert that disk in drive A. Also, mark these two files with asterisks on the List Files screen and copy them at one time to A:.)

3. Print out a list of files in your default drive/directory.

4. If you followed the instructions in this chapter to create a subdirectory named C:\WP51\DATA\BUD, delete that subdirectory. (*Hint:* Remember that a subdirectory must be empty to be deleted.)

5. If you haven't yet made backups of your important files, copy those files onto separate floppy disks. You will protect yourself against accidentally erasing an important file or against a disk failure. (*Hint:* Remember that you can mark a group of files with an asterisk and, in that way, copy more than one in a single Copy command.)

6. If you have already stored numerous files on disk, and those files are in disarray, take a bit of time to rearrange your files. The reorganization will save you time and headaches in the long run. Hard disk users may wish to create new subdirectories, and then move files from one directory to another. Floppy disk users may wish to move certain files from one disk to another; you can do so by displaying the List Files screen for drive B, inserting another data disk into drive A, and using the Move feature on the List Files menu.

## Quick Review

- Keep track of the status of files and directories using statistics provided at the top of the List Files screen. Display the List Files screen using the LIST ([F5]) key. Or, pulldown menu users can select File (F), List Files (F).

- Delete a file by positioning the cursor on a specific file when viewing the List Files screen, selecting Delete (2 or D), and typing **Y** to confirm the deletion. Take caution to delete only files you no longer wish to store for future use.

- Move or rename a file by positioning the cursor on a specific file when viewing the List Files screen and selecting Move/Rename (3 or M). Then enter either a new drive/directory for moving the file and/or a new filename for renaming it.

- Copy a file by positioning the cursor on a specific file when viewing the List Files screen, selecting Copy (8 or C), and entering a different drive/directory.

- Mark files on the List Files screen so that you can move, print, copy, or delete all those files in one command. Mark a file by positioning the cursor and typing an asterisk. Or, when no files are marked, mark every file by pressing MARK TEXT ([Alt] + [F5]), and then unmark individual files with the asterisk.

- Print the information on the List Files screen to maintain a paper record of files. From the List Files screen, press PRINT ( Shift + F7 ) and type **Y** to confirm the printing.

- Create a subdirectory on the List Files screen by selecting Other Directory (7 or O), editing the prompt to reflect the new directory name, pressing Enter , and typing **Y** to confirm the creation. Conversely, delete a subdirectory by displaying the List Files screen for the parent directory, positioning the cursor on the subdirectory name, and selecting Delete (2 or D). A subdirectory can be erased only if it is empty of files.

- Change the default drive/directory by displaying the List Files screen, selecting Other Directory (7 or O), and entering the name for the new default. Or, press the LIST ( F5 ) key, type the equal sign =, and enter the name for the new default. The default, which is the location where WordPerfect assumes you wish to store files to and retrieve files from, remains for the remainder of the working session or until you change it again.

- Protect files by assigning a password to them. With the file on screen, press TEXT IN/OUT ( Ctrl + F5 ) and select Password (2 or P). Or, pulldown menu users can select File (F), Password (W). Choose Add/Change (1 or A) and enter a password twice. Remember to resave the file, so that the password is stored along with the file. And remember the password, or you too will be locked out from the file.

- The Document Summary feature allows an organized method for tracking the history and progress of a document. Press the FORMAT (Shift + F8) key, and select Document (3 or D) to display the Document Format screen. Or, pulldown menu users can select Layout (L), Document (D). Choose Summary (5 or S) and a Document Summary screen appears. Press EXIT (F7) when you've filled out the pertinent information. Remember to resave the file so that the Document Summary is stored along with the file.

- Find files quickly on a floppy disk or in a hard disk directory based on (1) a word pattern in the filenames (5.1 users only), the document summaries, the first pages, or the entire documents; (2) the date that the files were last revised; or (3) a combination of word pattern and date conditions. From the List Files screen, 5.1 users select Find (9 or F), while 5.0 users select Word Search (9 or W).

- Exit to DOS temporarily by pressing SHELL (Ctrl + F1). Or, pulldown menu users select File (F), Goto DOS (G). Then select Go to DOS (1 or G). After entering DOS commands, type **exit**—the four letters, and not the F7 key—to return to Word-Perfect.

# PRINTING OPTIONS AND ENHANCEMENTS

You learned in Chapter 2 the basics of printing a document. This chapter covers some of the features offered by WordPerfect for when you wish to direct the printer to do something special. You'll first learn about the options on the Print menu not covered in Chapter 2. These include the View feature, which lets you preview a document before printing, and print options such as how to switch between printers (if you have more than one), how to print a specific number of copies of the print job, or how to change the quality of the text and graphics that print.

Later on in the chapter, you will learn about other features related to controlling your printer. You'll discover how the Advance feature can direct the printer to a precise location on the page before it prints. You'll alter your paper size/type so that you can print out text sideways on a page or on paper of various sizes, such as on envelopes. And, you will learn how to edit printer definitions so that you can control how your printer works with your copy of WordPerfect.

# VIEW A DOCUMENT BEFORE PRINTING

The View Document feature can show you on screen as close in appearance as possible how your document will appear on the printed page. It displays the document's format and many features not shown on the Typing screen, including margins, headers, footers, page numbers, footnotes, endnotes, and full justification of your text. With monitors that have graphics capabilities, it can also display graphics images as well as various font attributes such as small caps or large print and proportional spacing (see Chapter 10 for more on font changes). It is also a convenient way to check the layout and format of your document before you actually print. Use View Document wisely and you can save paper—discovering format mistakes before a document is actually printed.

To preview a document before printing, the document must be on screen. Position the cursor on the first page you wish to view, and press the PRINT ( Shift + F7 ) key to display the Print menu, as shown in Figure 9-1. [*Pulldown menu:* File (F), Print (P).] Then select View Document (6 or V). In moments, WordPerfect rewrites the screen, showing the full page on which your cursor is located, an example of which is shown in Figure 9-2. WordPerfect offers four options at the bottom of the View Document screen:

1 100% **2** 200% **3** Full Page **4** Facing Pages: **3**

For a look at a portion of the page at its actual size, enabling you to read the text, select 100% (1). For a look at a portion of the text at twice its actual size, select 200% (2). This magnified look is useful for detailed work, such as in desktop publishing. To view the full page, select Full

```
Print

        1 - Full Document
        2 - Page
        3 - Document on Disk
        4 - Control Printer
        5 - Multiple Pages
        6 - View Document
        7 - Initialize Printer


Options

        S - Select Printer              HP LaserJet Series II
        B - Binding Offset              0"
        N - Number of Copies            1
        U - Multiple Copies Generated by WordPerfect
        G - Graphics Quality            Medium
        T - Text Quality                High




Selection: 0
```

**FIGURE 9-1**   Print screen

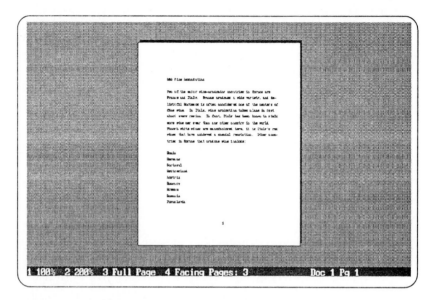

—————— **FIGURE 9-2** View Document screen

Page (3). Or, for a look at an even-numbered page and an odd-numbered page at the same time, select Facing Pages (4).

You can use the cursor movement keys to view a different portion of the document. For instance, if you're looking at the top portion of a page using the 100% option and wish to view the bottom portion, press [Home], [↓] or press [+] (on the cursor movement/numeric keypad). Press [↓] to move down one line at a time. If you're looking at a full page and wish to view the next page, press [PgDn]. Another way to move to a specific page is to press [Ctrl] + [Home] and when WordPerfect prompts "Go to," enter a page number. Or, press [Home], [Home], [↓] to move to the last page. The lower right corner of the screen always indicates the current page you're viewing and whether it's on the Doc 1 or Doc 2 screen.

After examining the text on the View Document screen, press the CANCEL (F1) key to return to the Print screen or press the EXIT (F7) key to return to the Typing screen.

Let's retrieve a file to the screen and then use the View Document feature.

1. Retrieve the file named SAMPLE. You worked with this document in Chapter 6 to practice features such as headers, footers, and page numbering.

2. Press the PRINT (Shift + F7) key. [*Pulldown menu:* File (F), Print (P).]

3. Select View Document (6 or V). In moments, the View Document screen appears, as shown in Figure 9-2. The bottom right corner of the screen indicates that you are looking at page 1 in the Doc 1 window. Notice that you can view the margins on that page.

4. Press PgDn. Now you're viewing page 2. Notice that you can see the header at the top and the page number at the bottom of the page.

5. Select 100% (1). Now you can clearly read the header and the top portion of text.

6. Press the + key on the cursor movement/numeric keypad. Now you can view the bottom portion of the page, which contains only a page number.

7. Select Facing Pages (4). Page 2 is now shown on the left and page 3 on the right side of the View Document screen.

8. Select Full Page (3). Page 2 is now the only text displayed.

9. Press EXIT (F7) to return to the Typing screen.

Because the View Document feature allows you to pre-view how text and graphics will be integrated on the page, it is a critical tool when creating elaborate publications using WordPerfect. The file named SAMPLE that you just viewed contains no graphics. If you haven't yet followed the instructions in Chapter 10 to insert graphics in your docu-ment, you can quickly see how graphics are shown on screen by viewing the file named PRINTER.TST in the WordPerfect package. This file is a WordPerfect document that can test how various WordPerfect features—such as font changes and graphics—operate with your printer.

You may wish to retrieve PRINTER.TST to screen and then use the View Document feature to see how the inte-gration of text and graphics will appear on the page. *5.1 users:* PRINTER.TST can be found in the same directory where the WordPerfect program is housed (hard disk us-ers) or on the WordPerfect 1 disk (floppy disk users). *5.0 users:* PRINTER.TST can be found in the directory into which you copied the files from the Conversion disk (hard disk users) or on the Conversion disk (floppy disk users).

*Note:* If you have a color monitor, you can determine whether WordPerfect displays graphics and text in black/white or in color on the View Document screen. See "Display" in Appendix B for more details.

# CHANGE PRINT OPTIONS

Print options deal with some of the more mechanical as-pects of printing. As described previously, you can print a document directly from screen using the Full Document or

Page options on the Print menu, or you can print a document from disk using the Document on Disk option on the Print menu or the Print option on the List Files menu. Whatever method you use to print, WordPerfect always makes assumptions for each print job about how the printer will operate with respect to the selected printer, binding, number of copies, and graphics and text quality. You can check these defaults by reading the bottom portion of the Print screen, below the heading "Options," as shown in Figure 9-1. Any number of these defaults can be changed before you send a print job to your printer. Each of these options is described below.

*Note:* You have the ability to change the print option defaults permanently, rather than just during each working session. This is useful if you find yourself changing a certain option every time that you start up WordPerfect. See "Initial Settings" in Appendix B for more details.

## Select Printer

The Select Printer option has two main functions. First, it allows you to define or edit the printer(s) attached to your computer so that they will work properly with WordPerfect. As part of the installation procedures, the printer attached to your computer must be defined to work with Word-Perfect. Every time you attach a new brand of printer to your computer, you must define it for WordPerfect. The method for defining new printers, which is part of the installation procedures, is described in Appendix A. The method to edit an existing printer definition is discussed later on in this chapter.

Second, the Select Printer option enables you to select the printer that you wish to use for a document from among the available, already defined printers. WordPerfect uses the printer that you choose for a given document to format that document. The printer name is recorded when the document is stored on disk. The next time you retrieve that document, WordPerfect also recalls the selected printer for that document.

The current printer is whatever printer you last selected. For example, suppose that the selected printer is the HP LaserJet Series II. When you begin to type a new document, WordPerfect will assume that you wish to use the LaserJet to print your document, and will format the text accordingly. The currently selected printer is always shown on the Print screen. In Figure 9-1, for example, the HP LaserJet Series II is indicated as the selected printer.

If you have defined only one printer, then that one printer would have been selected during the installation procedures; it will be unnecessary for you to change that selection.

But if you have more than one printer attached to your computer and have defined all your printers to work with WordPerfect, then you will want to consciously select a specific printer for each new document you type. Make sure that the document for which you wish to select a new printer is on screen. (Or, the screen may be clear because you intend to type a new document as soon as you select a printer.) Then press the PRINT ((Shift) + (F7)) key to view the Print screen as shown in Figure 9-1. [*Pulldown menu:* File (F), Print (P).] The printer listed next to the heading "Select Printer" indicates the currently selected printer, which will be used for this document if you make no change. If you wish to change the printer selection, then choose Select Printer (S). The Select Printer screen appears, listing all the printers that you defined to work with your computer. A sample is shown in Figure 9-3. An aster-isk appears next to the currently selected printer. Position the cursor on the name of the new printer you wish to use for your document and choose Select (1 or S) from the menu at the bottom of the screen. You are automatically returned to the Print screen, and the printer listed next to the heading "Select Printer" reflects the change. The text will now be formatted for the newly selected printer.

Once you select a different printer, that printer stays in effect for the current document as long as you save the document with the new printer selected. In addition, this new printer is now in effect for *all future documents* that you create until you select a new printer. Documents already created and stored on disk are unaffected by the new printer selection, since a printer selection is stored on disk along with the document.

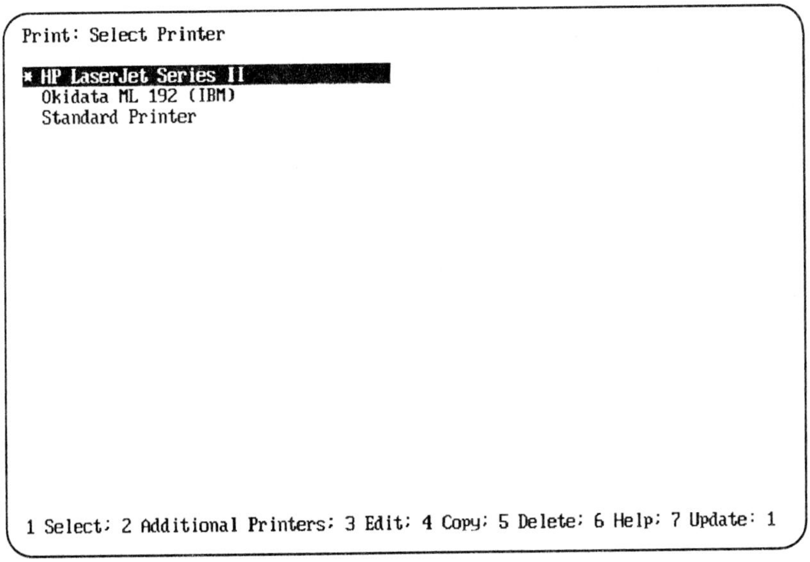

```
Print: Select Printer

* HP LaserJet Series II
  Okidata ML 192 (IBM)
  Standard Printer

 1 Select; 2 Additional Printers; 3 Edit; 4 Copy; 5 Delete; 6 Help; 7 Update: 1
```

**FIGURE 9-3**  Select Printer screen

You can, however, change your mind as to the printer you wish to use for a given document. Suppose that you retrieve a document to screen, press the PRINT ( [Shift] + [F7] ) key, and notice on the Print screen that the document had been last saved with a printer you no longer wish to use. Simply select a different printer using the procedure described above. WordPerfect will reformat the document, which you can now print on the new printer. If you resave your document, the newly selected printer will be saved along with the document. If you don't resave the document, then the next time you retrieve it, the old printer selection will be in effect.

*Note:* A default setting specifies that the printer selected when a document was saved be maintained when the document is retrieved. You can alter this setting so that, whenever you retrieve a document, WordPerfect formats it automatically for the currently selected printer. See "Initial Settings" in Appendix B for more details.

## Binding

A second printing option default shown in Figure 9-1 is that the binding offset is 0″—meaning that there is no provision for documents that you plan to have bound in book format. But what if you wish to print two-sided pages so that they can be bound? In that case, you'll want to reset the binding width, shifting the text of even-numbered pages to the left and the text of odd-numbered pages to the right, leaving extra space for where the book will be bound. (If you plan to bind one-sided pages, you can retain the binding setting as 0″ and simply increase the left margin for the entire document to accommodate the binding.)

Binding offset is measured in inches. If you want the text of each page shifted 0.5″ to accommodate the binding, for example, you would change the binding width to 0.5″. To do so, select Binding Offset (B) from the Print screen. Then type in the desired binding width, such as 0.5, and press (Enter). Once changed, binding takes effect for every print job until you change it again or until you turn off the computer. Therefore, if you wish to print out several print jobs and you want a binding width only for the first one, remember to reset the binding back to 0″ before printing the second job. The next time you load WordPerfect, a binding of 0″ is again assumed.

## Number of Copies

WordPerfect assumes that you wish to print only one copy of each print job. This is often correct, but you may occasionally wish to print multiple copies of one document. Rather than create multiple print jobs, you can create one print job requesting that WordPerfect print a specific number of copies.

Print many copies at once by selecting Number of Copies (N) from the Print screen, typing in a number, and then pressing (Enter). Like the Binding Offset option, the Number of Copies option takes effect for every print job until you change it again or turn off the computer. The next time you load WordPerfect, the Number of Copies value returns to 1.

## Multiple Copies [5.1 Users Only]

WordPerfect assumes that when you wish to print out multiple copies of a print job, you will change the Number of

Copies item on the Print screen. However, certain laser printers have their own command for printing multiple copies. If your printer has such a feature, then the pages will be printed faster by using the *printer* to specify multiple copies, rather than the Number of Copies option— especially if those pages contain graphics or a variety of fonts.

Specify that your printer will control multiple copies by selecting Multiple Copies Generated by (U) and, from the menu that appears, selecting Printer (2 or P). Then make sure to specify the number of copies via your printer. The Multiple Copies option takes effect for every print job during the rest of the working session until you change it again or turn off the computer. When you reload Word-Perfect, Multiple Copies is again reset to be controlled by WordPerfect.

## Graphics and Text Quality

WordPerfect's last two options on the Print screen dictate the quality with which your text and graphics are printed. If your document contains graphics images (see Chapter 10 for a discussion of inserting graphics images into your document), special characters, or equations printed as graphics, WordPerfect assumes you wish to print out the graphics in medium quality. For text, WordPerfect assumes high quality. With most printers, better quality means a better resolution on the printed page; the better the quality, the longer it takes for the printer to print out graphics or text. (Be aware, however, that on some printers, changing the quality has no effect on the printed result.)

To alter the quality, or to request that the graphics or text not be printed during a print job, select Graphics Quality (G) or Text Quality (T) from the Print screen.

WordPerfect displays a menu with four options. For instance, the Graphics Quality menu reads

`Graphics Quality:  1 Do Not Print; 2 Draft; 3 Medium; 4 High: 3`

The same four options are available for text quality. Select one of the options; the change is reflected on the Print screen. Like the Binding and Number of Copies options, the Graphics and Text Quality options remain in effect until you change them again or exit WordPerfect.

# ADVANCE THE PRINTER ON THE PAGE

The Advance feature allows you to indicate exactly where a certain section of a document should begin printing. This feature is useful as a substitute for pressing the spacebar or the [Tab] key repeatedly to position text horizontally and as a substitute for pressing the [Enter] key to position text vertically. It is useful for printing on a preprinted form, for printing two sections of a document (such as a paragraph of text and a shaded graphics box) in the same location, or for spreading out characters in a title or heading.

You can use the Advance Up or Down options to position the printer vertically a certain number of inches from the *current cursor position.* Or use the Advance To Line option to position the printer up or down a certain number of inches from the *top of the page.* (Not all printers have the ability to advance back up the page.) Similarly, use the Advance Left or Right options to position the printer horizontally a certain number of inches from the *current cursor position.* Or use the Advance To Position option to position the printer left or right a certain number of inches from the *left edge of the page.*

Move the cursor just before the character or section of a document where you want the Advance feature to take effect. Press the FORMAT ( Shift + F8 ) key, and select Other (4 or O). [*Pulldown menu:* Layout (L), Other (O).] Then select Advance (1 or A). WordPerfect prompts with the Advance menu at the bottom of the screen:

```
Advance:  1 Up; 2 Down; 3 Line; 4 Left; 5 Right; 6 Position: 0
```

Choose an Advance option and then enter a distance. For instance, to position the printer 3″ down from the current cursor position, select Down (2 or D), type **3″**, and press Enter . Or, to position the printer 0.5 ″ down from the top of the page, select Line (3 or I), type **.5″**, and press Enter . Then press EXIT ( F7 ) to return to the Typing screen.

WordPerfect inserts an Advance code at the current cursor position. The code indicates the Advance option you selected, as well as the measurement that you specified. Here are examples for all six Advance options: **[AdvUp:3″]** **[AdvDn:1.5″]** **[AdvToLn:4.16″]** **[AdvLft:2″]** **[AdvRgt:2″]** **[AdvToPos:.5″]**. Text that follows such a code will be printed at the location specified in the code.

Be aware, however, that the cursor will not change its position on the screen following an Advance code. Only the status line will reflect the change. For instance, suppose that in the middle of the line that is 5″ from the top of the page, you insert a code to advance down 1.5″. The code inserted would be **[AdvDn:1.5″]**. With the cursor just after the code, the status line will read

```
Doc 1 Pg 1 Ln 6.5" Pos 1"
```

If you press ← to move just before the Advance Down code, the status line will read

`Doc 1 Pg 1 Ln 5" Pos 1"`

There would be no extra space between the two parts of the line on the Typing screen, but the status line would inform you that once the document is printed, there will be 1.5" between the two halves of the line. If you preview your document using the View Document feature, you will be able to see where on the page your text will print due to the Advance code.

The Advance feature is often used to position text that will be inserted on a preprinted form. You must first use a ruler to measure exactly where on the form the blanks you wish to fill in are located. As you type the information, use the Advance feature to position the information on the blank lines.

For instance, suppose you wish to print a person's name in the blank line provided on a preprinted form. You measure the form to discover that in order to sit on the blank line, the name must be printed 4" in from the left edge and 3.5" down from the top of the page. (When you measure from the top of the page, keep in mind that you should measure down to where the *top of the line* will be printed rather than to its baseline — unless you set the Baseline Placement feature to Yes. The Baseline Placement feature is discussed in Chapter 10.) Position the cursor where you are about to type the person's name. Use the Advance to Position option and enter a measurement of 4". Then, use the Advance to Line option and enter a measurement of **3.5"**. Now type in the person's name. When you insert the preprinted form and print, the person's name should fill in the appropriate blank.

A similar application involves letterhead. When you type a letter, the first page is often printed on letterhead, while the following pages are printed on blank sheets of the same paper stock. You can use the Advance feature to position the first page of the letter below the letterhead logo. That way, you won't have to tamper with changing the top margin setting twice—once on the first page and then again for all succeeding pages.

For instance, suppose that your letterhead logo occupies the first 2″ of a page. You want an additional 0.5″ of white space between the logo and the first line of a communiqué that you are about to print. Thus, you want to start text 2.5″ from the top of the page.

Let's practice on a document named LIST that you created previously. In this example, you can use the Advance to Line feature and specify a 2.5″ advance from the top of the page. (Since the top margin of LIST is at the default setting of 1″, an alternative is to use the Advance Down feature and specify a 1.5″ advance.)

1. Clear the Typing screen and retrieve the file named LIST.

2. Position the cursor at the top of the document.

3. Press the FORMAT ( Shift + F8 ) key to display the Format menu. [*Pulldown menu:* Layout (L).]

4. Select Other (4 or O). The Other Format menu appears.

5. Select Advance (1 or A). The following appears at the bottom of the screen:

    Advance:  1 Up; 2 Down; 3 Line; 4 Left; 5 Right; 6 Position: 0

6. Select Line (3 or I). WordPefect prompts

    Adv. to line 1"

This means that the cursor is currently at line 1″, which is the current top margin.

7. Type **2.5″** and press Enter.

8. Press EXIT ( F7 ) to return to the document. Notice that the status line now indicates that this line of text will print on Ln 2.5″. This is because of the **[AdvToLn:2.5″]** code you inserted.

You can print out this document to see that, in fact, it will begin 2.5″ from the top of the page, and thus would not overwrite a letterhead logo. If the printer does not advance, it could be that this feature is unsupported on your printer.

# USE TYPE-THROUGH [5.0 USERS ONLY]

WordPerfect 5.0 users will find that option 5 on the Print screen reads "Type Through," rather than "Multiple Pages." In the past, WordPerfect offered the Type Through feature, which allowed you to turn your keyboard and printer into a typewriter. Whatever you typed on the keyboard could be sent directly to the printer—either line by line, or character by character. It was handy for completing preprinted forms, but was limited in that it worked only on a narrow range of printers. For instance, Type Through did not operate on laser printers. To help you in filling out preprinted forms, WordPerfect has enhanced existing features (such as the Advance feature) and added new ones (such as the Tables feature). As a result, Type Through has been removed from most copies of version 5.0, and all copies of version 5.1. You can, however, order it; call WordPerfect Corporation at (801) 225-5000 for details on whether this feature works on your printer, and how to place an order.

# CHANGE THE SIZE AND TYPE OF PAPER FOR PRINTING

WordPerfect's paper form definition setting provides WordPerfect with the information required to print your text on paper. It is comprised of two parts: a paper size, and a paper type. The default paper size is 8.5″ wide by 11″ long. (This is the default for WordPerfect versions sold in the United States. In other countries, the default paper size differs.) The default paper type, which carries with it information about the position and location of the paper in your printer, is referred to as the "Standard" type. What "Standard" means depends on your currently selected printer. For instance, the paper type for the HP LaserJet II specifies that the paper is fed continuously and in portrait orientation, which means that the characters are printed parallel to how the paper is inserted into the printer. For another printer, the paper type might specify that the paper be fed manually and in portrait orientation.

Using the Paper Type/Size feature, you can specify that pages print differently. You can specify a different size—such as 8.5″ wide by 14″ long—to print a legal document on legal-size paper. Or, you can specify the same paper size but a different type—such as landscape orientation, which means to rotate the page so that the characters are printed perpendicularly to how the paper is inserted into the printer. This effectively results in paper dimensions of 11″

wide by 8.5″ long, useful for printing a wide chart. Or, you can specify a different size and a different type—such as 9.5″ wide by 4″ long and feeding the paper manually—to print out an envelope. With the Paper Size/Type feature, you choose from other common paper sizes/types, or create your own.

When you specify a different paper definition, you will see an effect on screen only if the result is a paper size change. This is because WordPerfect adjusts your text to maintain your margin settings. For instance, suppose your left/right and top/bottom margins are set at 1″, which are the default settings. This means that on a piece of paper 8.5″ wide, 6.5″ of text will fit horizontally across the page (8.5″ minus 1″ minus 1″). Similarly, on a piece of paper that is 11″ long, 9″ of text will fit vertically down the page (11″ minus 1″ minus 1″). Now, if you change your paper size for a business envelope, which is 9.5″ wide by 4″ long, the text readjusts so that 7.5″ of text can fit across the page (9.5″ minus 1″ minus 1″) and 2″ of text can fit down the page (4″ minus 1″ minus 1″). (Because of the dynamic link between paper size and margins, it is often necessary to alter margins after you alter the paper size.) However, if you modify the paper definition such that only the paper type—and not the paper size—changes, then the effect of this paper definition modification is revealed only when you print out your document.

The steps to change your text's paper size/type differ based on whether you are a 5.1 or 5.0 user, and are therefore discussed separately below.

## Paper Size/Type [5.1 Users]

To specify a different paper definition, position the cursor at the very top of the page where you want the new paper size or type instructions to begin. For instance, if you want to change the paper definition for an entire document, position the cursor either at the very top of the document or on the Document Initial Codes screen, which, as you learned in Chapter 6, initiates a format change starting at the first page of a document. Or, if you wish to alter the paper definition only for the last page of your document, position the cursor at the top of the last page.

When the cursor is positioned properly, press the FOR-MAT ( Shift + F8 ) key and select Page (2 or P) to display the Page Format menu. [*Pulldown menu:* Layout (L), Page (P).] The Document Format menu that displays indicates that, for item 7, the current paper size is 8.5″ by 11″, and that the current type is Standard. Select Paper Size/Type (7 or S). The Paper Size/Type screen displays, which contains all the predefined paper size/type combinations. For instance, Figure 9-4 shows the Paper Size/Type screen for the HP LaserJet Series II printer. Position the cursor on the Paper definition that you desire for your text, and press Select (1 or S). You can also press Enter since, as shown at the bottom of Figure 9-4, WordPerfect assumes item 1 on the menu. You are returned to the Page Format menu, where your selections will be indicated next to the Paper Size/Type heading. Press EXIT ( F7 ) to return to your document. WordPerfect inserts a Paper Size/Type code at that location. For instance, suppose you selected the paper definition that the cursor is currently highlighting in Figure 9-4. Then the code inserted when you press Enter is [**Paper Sz/Type:9.5″x 4″,Envelope**].

If there is no paper definition for the size/type combination that you desire, then you can create a new one. When you are viewing the Paper Size/Type screen as shown in Figure 9-4, select Add (2 or A). Now, WordPerfect displays a Paper Type screen, as shown in Figure 9-5. Select a name for the type of paper to be used in this paper definition. (If

```
Format: Paper Size/Type
                                                        Font Double
Paper type and Orientation     Paper Size    Prompt Loc  Type Sided  Labels

Envelope - Wide                9.5" x 4"      No  Manual  Land  No
Standard                       8.5" x 11"     No  Contin  Port  No
Standard                       8.5" x 14"     No  Contin  Port  No
Standard - Wide                11" x 8.5"     No  Contin  Land  No
Standard - Wide                14" x 8.5"     No  Contin  Land  No
[ALL OTHERS]                   Width ≤ 8.5"   Yes Manual        No














1 Select; 2 Add; 3 Copy; 4 Delete; 5 Edit; N Name Search: 1
```

════ **FIGURE 9-4** Paper Size/Type screen for the HP
LaserJet Series II (version 5.1 only)

you wish to indicate a paper type not on this list, then select the Other (9) option, and enter a different name.) Next, the Edit Paper Definition screen appears, as shown in Figure 9-6. Here, you define the various components of the paper definition as follows:

- *Paper Size* Indicates the dimension of the paper that will be used.

- *Paper Type* Indicates the paper type, which you chose from Figure 9-5. If the paper size's width is greater than its length, WordPerfect automatically inserts the text "-Wide", next to the paper type, indicating a landscape orientation.

```
Format: Paper Type
     1 - Standard
     2 - Bond
     3 - Letterhead
     4 - Labels
     5 - Envelope
     6 - Transparency
     7 - Cardstock
     8 - [ALL OTHERS]
     9 - Other




Selection: 1
```

═══ **FIGURE 9-5**   Paper Type screen (version 5.1 only)

- *Font Type*   Indicates the orientation of fonts used to print out the form. The two types are Portrait, meaning parallel to how the paper is inserted into the printer, and Landscape, meaning sideways—perpendicular to the paper. Set this to Landscape only if you wish to print text sideways and you use a printer where the paper cannot be turned sideways, but where the font must be rotated to print text sideways. In that case, you will only be able to select from fonts that print in landscape mode (more on fonts in Chapter 10). Landscape mode is common, for example, on laser printers when you wish to print out an address on an envelope.

- *Prompt to Load*   Indicates whether you want Word-Perfect to prompt you to insert paper before the printing begins. If you plan to have the correct paper in the printer before you print, then this item can be set to

"No". But, if this item is set to "Yes", then when you send a page to the printer, WordPerfect will sound a beep. You must insert the paper, and then, from the Control Printer screen, select "Go" to start the printing (see Chapter 2 for more on the Control Printer screen).

- *Location*   Indicates where to find the paper that will be used. The options are as follows: manual—used for hand-feeding forms into the printer; continuous—used when paper is fed automatically into the printer (such as using the standard paper tray on an HP LaserJet Series II or using continuous-feed paper on dot matrix or daisy wheel printers); and bin number—used if you have a sheet-feeder with various bins, where you specify a particular bin number.

```
Format: Edit Paper Definition

        Filename                HPLASEII.PRS

    1 - Paper Size              8.5" x 11"

    2 - Paper Type              Standard

    3 - Font Type               Portrait

    4 - Prompt to Load          No

    5 - Location                Continuous

    6 - Double Sided Binding    No

    7 - Labels                  No

    8 - Text Adjustment - Top   0"
                         Side   0"


Selection: 0
```

**FIGURE 9-6**   Edit Paper Definition screen (version 5.1 only)

- *Double Sided Binding*  Indicates whether the text will print on both sides of the page. If your printer can print on both sides of the page, then, for double-sided binding, either set this item to "Top", where the back will print upside down from the front of the page so that the document is top-bound, or to "Side", where the back and the front are printed the same for side-bound text.

- *Labels*  Indicates whether the page will be broken up into discrete units for special printing purposes. For text that flows according to how it is displayed on screen, this item can be set to "No". But if you wish to print labels, or set up a document where you insert hard pages to break text into pages on screen and then have those pages printed in adjoining columns and/or rows at the printer, you will want to change this item to "Yes". (Make sure that the dimensions of the paper are correct before selecting this item; for instance, if you use labels that come on sheets, then make sure the paper size is set to the size of each individual sheet, such as 8.5″ by 11″ if those are the dimensions of the sheet. Or, if you use labels that are on a long roll of continuous paper, then set the paper width to be the width of the labels across the page, and the height to be the length of one row of labels — measured from the top of one label to the top of the next.)

    When you select "Yes", the menu shown in Figure 9-7 appears. On the Format Labels screen, you specify for WordPerfect the size and type of labels that you use, and how text should be positioned on those labels during printing, including (1) the actual dimensions of each individual label; (2) the number of columns of labels across each page, and the number of rows of labels down each page (the number of rows should equal 1 if you use a continuous-feed roll of labels and should equal the

```
Format: Labels

    1 - Label Size
                    Width           2.63"
                    Height          1"

    2 - Number of Labels
                    Columns         3
                    Rows            10

    3 - Top Left Corner
                    Top             0.5"
                    Left            0.188"

    4 - Distance Between Labels
                    Column          0.125"
                    Row             0"

    5 - Label Margins
                    Left            0.013"
                    Right           0.123"
                    Top             0"
                    Bottom          0"

Selection: 0
```

**FIGURE 9-7**  Format Labels screen (version 5.1 only)

actual number if you use sheets); (3) the location where WordPerfect should begin printing on the first label, in which case WordPerfect will then print the following labels in the same relative location; (4) the distance between labels that are positioned side by side in a column, and the distance between each row of labels (the distance between rows should equal 0 if you use a continuous-feed roll of labels and should equal the actual distance if you use sheets); and (5) any margins you wish to specify for each individual label. Then, press EXIT ([F7]) to return to the Paper Type screen.

- *Text Adjustment*  Compensates for paper loaded into the printer at vertical or horizontal positions different than what WordPerfect otherwise assumes. Indicate a text adjustment only if your text never prints with the margins you specified. The following menu appears:

`Adjust Text: 1 Up; 2 Down; 3 Left; 4 Right: 0`

Select a direction and then enter the distance of the adjustment you want to make.

After specifying a new paper definition, press EXIT (F7) to return to the Paper Size/Type screen (Figure 9-4). You can then select this new paper definition for your document. Other options on the menu at the bottom of this screen enable you to copy, delete, or edit an existing paper definition. Just position the cursor on the paper definition before selecting an item—either by using the cursor movement keys, or by selecting Name Search (N), typing the name of the paper type, and then pressing Enter. If you wish to create a new paper definition that is similar to an existing one, it is often more convenient to copy a definition and then edit it, rather than to select Add and start from scratch to define a new paper size/type.

One special paper definition that can be edited is the [ALL OTHERS] definition. This specifies the maximum width the paper can have in order to be inserted in the printer, as well as the location and position of text that has no paper definition.

## Paper Size/Type [5.0 Users]

To specify a different paper definition, position the cursor at the very top of the page where you want the new paper size or type instructions to begin. For instance, if you want to change the paper definition for an entire document, position the cursor either at the very top of the document or on the Document Initial Codes screen, which, as you learned in Chapter 6, initiates a format change starting at the first page of a document. Or, if you wish to alter the paper definition only for the last page of your document, position the cursor at the top of the last page.

When the cursor is positioned properly, press the FOR-MAT ( Shift + F8 ) key and select Page (2 or P) to display the Page Format menu. The Document Format menu that displays indicates that, for item 8, the current paper size is 8.5″ by 11″, and that the current type is Standard. Select Paper Size/ Type (8 or S). The Paper Size menu in Figure 9-8 appears, from which you select the appropriate paper size. (If the paper size on which you wish to print is not listed as a menu item, then select the last option, which is Other (0 or O), and then type in the appropriate paper dimensions.) Next, WordPerfect displays the Paper Type menu, as illustrated in Figure 9-9, from which you select the appropriate paper type. (If the form type you wish to select is not listed, then select the last

```
Format: Paper Size                 Width  Height

      1 - Standard                 (8.5" x 11")

      2 - Standard Landscape       (11" x 8.5")

      3 - Legal                    (8.5" x 14")

      4 - Legal Landscape          (14" x 8.5")

      5 - Envelope                 (9.5" x 4")

      6 - Half Sheet               (5.5" x 8.5")

      7 - US Government            (8" x 11")

      8 - A4                       (210mm x 297mm)

      9 - A4 Landscape             (297mm x 210mm)

      o - Other

Selection: 1
```

**FIGURE 9-8** Paper Size screen (version 5.0 only)

```
Format: Paper Type

    1 - Standard

    2 - Bond

    3 - Letterhead

    4 - Labels

    5 - Envelope

    6 - Transparency

    7 - Cardstock

    8 - Other




Selection: 1
```

**FIGURE 9-9**   Paper Type screen (version 5.0 only)

option, which is Other (8 or O), and then choose from the list of special form types previously defined to operate with your printer.) You are returned to the Page Format menu, where your selections will be indicated next to the Paper Size/Type heading. Press EXIT (F7) to return to your document. WordPerfect inserts a Paper Size/Type code at that location. For instance, suppose you select envelope size (9.5″ by 4″) and envelope type. Then the code inserted is **[Paper Sz/Type:9.5″ × 4″,Envelope]**.

If you select a paper size/type combination that has not been previously defined, WordPerfect indicates this on the Page Format menu. Next to the Paper Size/Type heading, WordPerfect will display the message "requested form is unavailable." In that case, WordPerfect uses the [ALL OTHERS] paper definition, or finds the closest match, for the instructions on how to print out the document.

If there is no paper definition for the size/type combination that you desire, then you can create a new one (or edit an existing one). You cannot, however, do so on the Page Format menu, but must create and edit paper definitions by editing your printer definition. See "Edit Printer Definitions" later on in this chapter for more information on doing this.

## Change the Paper Size/Type Setting [5.1 and 5.0 Users]

Let's use LIST, the document currently on screen, to change the paper size to 11″ by 8.5″, as if planning to print sideways on the page.

1. Press [Home], [Home], [Home], [↑] to position the cursor at the top of the page. (It is important to press [Home] three times before pressing [↑] so that the cursor is positioned at the very top of the page and before all codes—which in this case is the Advance code we inserted earlier in this chapter. Look to Chapter 6 if you need a review of methods for moving the cursor around codes.)

2. Press the FORMAT ([Shift] + [F8]) key. [*Pulldown menu:* Layout (L).]

3. Select Page (2 or P) to display the Page Format menu.

4. Select Paper Size/Type (7 or S for 5.1 users, 8 or S for 5.0 users).

5. *5.1 users:* Position the cursor on the paper definition that shows the combination of a Standard-wide paper type and 11″ by 8.5″ paper size. If such a paper defini-

tion does not exist, then select the Add option, and proceed to create this new paper definition.) *5.0 users:* Select Standard Landscape (2 or T).

6. *5.1 users:* With the cursor positioned on the Standard-wide/11″ by 8.5″ definition, choose Select (1 or S). Now, the Page Format menu reappears, with the newly se-lected paper definition indicated next to item 7.

   *5.0 users:* Select Standard (1 or S). The Page For-mat menu reappears. (Selecting Standard allows you to see the effects of changing the paper size on your screen, no matter what printer you are using. However, choosing Standard paper type is technically correct at the printer only for those of you with printers that allow you to place your paper sideways into the printer and where the Standard paper type is defined for manually fed paper to allow you to insert the paper sideways before printing. If you can feed paper sideways but the paper is defined for continuous-feed, then to print this document sideways on the page, you need to (1) define a form type where you hand-feed the paper, so that the printer will pause for you to insert the paper; and (2) select the corresponding paper type rather than Stan-dard. If you are a laser printer user, where the printer doesn't allow you to feed the paper sideways, then to actually print this document sideways, you need to (1) define a form where the printer prints in a landscape orientation, and (2) select the corresponding paper type rather than Standard. (See the next section, which dis-cusses how to edit printer definitions, for more details on defining paper (form) types.)

7. Press EXIT ( F7 ) to return to the document.

8. Press ⟨↓⟩ to readjust the text; WordPerfect rewrites the screen based on the same margins, but for a new paper size.

On the Typing screen, you will notice that it appears as if some of the text in LIST disappears off the right edge of the screen, as shown in Figure 9-10. This is because the margins are now such that a line is wider than what can display on screen; only a portion of each line is displayed at one time on a standard, 80-column monitor. Whenever the width of your lines is longer than what can be displayed on screen, you will need to use the cursor movement keys to read a full line of text. You can move in a wide document quickly by using the ⟨Home⟩ key. Remember that ⟨Home⟩, ⟨→⟩, positions the cursor at the right edge of the text on

```
    Here are the names that were left off the list of deliveries to the Northwe
Please make sure to add these names immediately:

Customer      Order #        City           Cases

Chou          AB-1           Seattle        128 cases of Chardonnay from contain
                                            cases from 333

Goldberg      AB-12          Seattle        2 cases of Sauvignon Blanc from cont
                                            8 cases from 334

Johnson       AL-12          Portland       88 cases of Chardonnay from containe
                                            from container 15

I should have a list for the Northeastern region by tomorrow morning.




C:\WP51\DATA\LIST                                     Doc 1 Pg 1 Ln 2.67" Pos 1"
```

**FIGURE 9-10**   LIST with lines wider than are displayed on screen

screen. But, since the line of text is wider than the screen, you should press `Home`, `Home`, `→` or press `End` if you wish to move to the far right end of the line. Similarly, while `Home`, `←` moves the cursor to the left edge of the text on screen, press `Home`, `Home`, `←` to move to the far left end of the line.

If you reveal codes, you can see that you have inserted a code into the text: **[Paper Sz/Typ:11″ x 8.5″;Standard]**. It is this code that caused the screen to adjust for the new paper size. To see the dimensions of the page that WordPerfect now assumes, you can use the View Document feature to preview the page. On the View Document screen, Word-Perfect will draw the page based on its new size, with the paper's width wider than its length, and illustrate how the text will fit on the page. You can also print out the page to see the results. (Remember, however, that if you are a 5.0 user and haven't yet created a paper definition for printing sideways on a page, you must do so before this page will print out correctly.)

One important aspect to remember about altering the paper size/type is that when you change the paper size, the text is adjusted to maintain current margins. As a result, it is often necessary to first alter your margin settings so that the text prints at the proper spot on the page. For instance, most offices use business-size envelopes, with the compa-ny's return address already printed, so that all you need to do is type the name and address of the person to receive the envelope. If you change your paper size to 9.5″ by 4″, type the address, but retain a top margin of 1″, then when you print the address onto an envelope, the name and address will print too high on the envelope.

The paper size/type, top/bottom margin, and left/right margin settings that work best on your printer for a given paper type, such as an envelope, depend on how your printer works. Often, trial and error is required to determine the proper settings for your printer.

Here's an example of settings you can try to print an address on an envelope assuming 9.5″ by 4″ size and assuming that the return address is already printed on it. (Be aware that, on your particular printer, different margin settings may be more appropriate. Also, if your printer cannot fit an envelope sideways or cannot print fonts in landscape mode, you won't be able to print envelopes.)

1. At the top of a blank page, insert a Top/Bottom Margin code for a top margin of 2.5″ and a small bottom margin, such as 0″ or .3″ (to allow room for a multiline address). Or, if you will insert the envelope into the printer manually, you can simply advance the envelope in the printer about 2″ yourself; in that case, you can set the top margin to 0″.

2. Insert a Left/Right Margin code for a left margin of 4.5″ and a small right margin, such as 0″ or .3″ (to allow room for a lengthy line in an address).

3. Insert a Paper Size/Type code for envelopes. If the envelopes you use are standard business size, which is 9.5″ by 4″, use the predefined Envelope size/type. If the envelopes you use are of a size other than 9.5″ by 4″, then you must have previously created another paper definition for envelopes of another size (by selecting a paper size of Other and typing in the true dimensions of your envelope, and then defining a type that corresponded to how you can print envelopes on your printer), and would now select the paper size/type that matched that other paper definition.

4. Type in the name and address.

5. Feed an envelope into your printer in the way you specified in the paper definition for envelopes, and then print the envelope.

You should get a result such as that shown in Figure 9-11. If not, or if you prefer different margins, change the margin settings and try again. Once you determine the best settings for your printer, you will quickly be able to address envelopes on it. Then, you can create a whole document full of addresses for printing on envelopes: repeat steps 1 through 4 above, press [Ctrl] + [Enter] to insert a hard page so that the cursor is now on a new page, type a second address, and so on, pressing [Ctrl] + [Enter] between each address.

*Note:* Suppose in addition to printing out the occasional envelope, you need to print numerous letters and envelopes

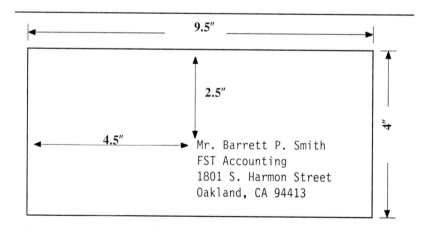

**FIGURE 9-11** Envelope printed after paper size/type and margin changes

for a mass mailing. Or, you may wish to print out mailing labels, rather than envelopes, for that mailing. In printing out labels, you must also change the margins in addition to the paper size/type. Refer to Chapter 13 for information on WordPerfect's Merge feature, which allows you to take a list of names and addresses, and quickly produce personalized letters and corresponding envelopes or mailing labels.

# EDIT PRINTER DEFINITIONS

Appendix A describes how, when you install WordPerfect to work with your computer, you also install it to work with your printer. During installation, WordPerfect creates an individual file with a .PRS extension (which stands for Printer ReSource file) for your printer, which is thereafter used whenever you wish to print a document. For example, HPLASEII.PRS stores the printer definition for the HP LaserJet Series II.

You must establish a printer definition file for each printer you plan to use on your computer system with WordPerfect; see Appendix A for more on creating a printer definition for a new printer on which you plan to print your documents. Then, from within WordPerfect, you can edit that printer definition.

Editing a printer definition is important if any of the specifications related to the printer change. For instance, you may purchase a sheet feeder for the printer. Or, you decide that you want a different font to be assumed as the initial font (more on fonts in Chapter 10). Or, you purchase a new font cartridge or additional downloadable fonts for your printer; whenever you purchase additional fonts for your computer, you must edit your printer definition so that WordPerfect is aware that these new fonts are available. Also, editing a printer definition is important for version 5.0 users in order to establish new paper definitions, such as for odd-shaped envelopes or for labels so you can insert the corresponding Paper Size/Type code—as described previously.

To edit an existing printer definition file, you return to the Select Printer screen, as shown in Figure 9-3, and position the cursor on the name of the printer you wish to edit. Then, select Edit (3 or E). A menu appears, such as that shown in Figure 9-12. (5.0 users have one more item, which is called "Forms", on this menu.) The options on the Select Printer Edit screen that you can alter are as follows.

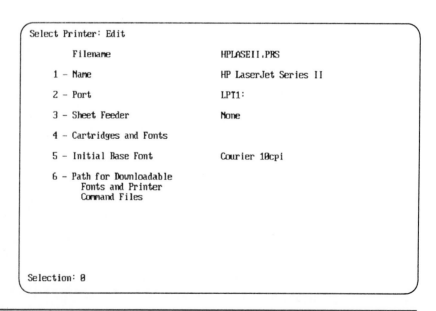

FIGURE 9-12   Printer Edit screen (version 5.1)

**NAME**  This printer setting specifies the name that will be listed for that printer definition whenever you display the Select Printer screen in the future. You can change this name, making it more descriptive, by choosing Name (1 or N) and typing up to 36 characters. Then, press (Enter).

**PORT**  This setting indicates the type and number of the port (plug) on the back of the computer to which the printer is attached. When you select Port (2 or P), a menu appears as follows:

```
Port: 1 LPT 1; 2 LPT 2; 3 LPT 3; 4 COM 1; 5 COM 2; 6 COM 3;
7 COM 4; 8 Other: 0
```

LPT 1 through LPT 3 imply a parallel printer, where the number indicates the parallel plug to which your printer is attached. If your printer is a parallel printer, generally it is plugged into LPT1, which is the default setting. COM 1 through COM 4 indicate a serial printer, where the number indicates the serial plug to which your printer is attached. When you specify a port for a serial printer, WordPerfect prompts for the printer's baud, parity, stop bits, character length, and whether the XON/XOFF protocol is on or off. See your printer manual for the appropriate settings.

**SHEET FEEDER**  If you use a sheet feeder that automatically feeds paper into the printer, use this option to define it. Select Sheet Feeder (3 or S). A Sheet Feeder screen appears, listing possible sheet feeder brands for that printer. (*5.0 users:* If this screen does not appear, then it is because WordPerfect does not have access to the Printer disk containing the original driver for your printer. Word-Perfect prompts, "Directory for printer files:". Insert the correct Printer disk in drive A or B, and then type **A:** or **B:** and press (Enter), or, if the printer file is on the hard disk, then type the correct directory and press (Enter).)

Move the cursor to highlight the sheet feeder that you have and press (Enter) to select that brand. A Helps and Hints screen appears for that sheet feeder brand. Read the information provided, and then press EXIT ((F7)) to return to the Select Printer Edit screen. (You should then make sure to create paper (form) definitions to indicate the location of the available forms in the sheet feeder.)

**FORMS [5.0 USERS ONLY]**   This setting allows you to establish new paper (form) definitions for use with your printer. WordPerfect uses this information when it encounters a Paper Size/Type code in your document (as described previously) and assumes an 8.5″ by 11″ paper size and the Standard type if no code is inserted in your document.

When you select Forms (4 or F), the Select Printer Forms screen appears, an example of which is shown in Figure 9-13, listing the paper definitions (forms) that have already been established. For instance, Figure 9-13 shows the definitions for an envelope with dimensions of 4″ by 9.5″, standard paper with dimensions of 8.5″ by 11″, and an [ALL OTHERS] form type for the HP LaserJet Series II printer. (The [ALL OTHERS] option is used if you insert a Paper Size/Type code in your document for a paper type that is unavailable, meaning that the type you indicated in the code hasn't been defined.) You can delete a form by positioning the cursor and pressing Delete (2 or D). Or, you can add a form to that list by pressing Add (1 or A). You can edit a form by positioning the cursor and pressing Edit (3 or E).

If you select to add a paper (form) definition, then WordPerfect displays a menu listing seven basic paper definition (form) types, an [ALL OTHERS] form type, and an Other option. Select an item to choose the type of form you are defining; or choose Other and then indicate a type with

```
Select Printer: Forms                    Font
                                         Orient  Init            Offset
 Form type                 Size           P L    Pres Location  Top    Side

 Envelope                  4" x 9.5"      N Y     N   Manual     0"     0"
 Standard                  8.5" x 11"     Y Y     Y   Contin     0"     0"
 [ALL OTHERS]              Width ≤ 8.5"           N   Manual     0"     0"










 If the requested form is not available, then printing stops and WordPerfect
 waits for a form to be inserted in the ALL OTHERS location.  If the requested
 form is larger than the ALL OTHERS form, the width is set to the maximum width.

 1 Add; 2 Delete; 3 Edit: 3
```

**FIGURE 9-13**  Select Printer Forms screen for the HP LaserJet Series II (version 5.0 only)

a name of your choosing. It is this type that will carry along with it a number of characteristics of the form on which you will be printing.

Then, whether you selected to add a form and indicated a form type, or you selected to edit an existing form type, the Select Printer Forms menu appears for that specific form type, an example of which is shown in Figure 9-14 for the Envelope form type on the HP LaserJet Series II. You now can specify the following characteristics for that paper definition (form) type:

• *Form Size*  Indicates the dimensions of the paper that will be used. If you select this option, several commonly used dimensions are offered. Or, select Other, and enter a specific height and width of your choosing to match the size of the form you are defining.

- *Orientation*    Indicates the direction in which the font will print, of importance in printers where you are unable to insert the paper sideways into the printer and thus must tell the printer to print sideways on the form. Portrait orientation prints lines parallel to how the form is inserted into the printer. Landscape orientation prints lines perpendicular to how the form is inserted into the printer (sideways) — for printing envelopes or printing documents across the width of a page.

  Notice, for example, that the orientation for the envelope in Figure 9-14 is Landscape. This is because, with an HP LaserJet Series II printer, an envelope can only be inserted with its narrow end first, which is perpendicular to how you want it to actually print.

- *Initially Present*    Indicates whether you want Word-Perfect to prompt you to insert paper before the printing begins. If you plan to have the correct paper in the printer before you print, and do not need prompting, then this item can be set to "No." But if you indicate that the paper is not initially present, then when WordPerfect encounters the Paper Size/Type code for the paper type you are defining, WordPerfect will sound a beep. You must then select the Control Printer option on the Print screen and select "Go" to start the printing, which is discussed in Chapter 2.

- *Location*    Indicates where and how the paper will be fed into the printer: continuously, manually, or from a specific bin in a sheet feeder. For instance, select Continuous if you use continuous-feed paper on a dot matrix or daisy wheel printer, or if paper is fed through a single tray on a laser printer. Select manual if you plan to feed each sheet of paper manually. Select sheet feeder if you defined a sheet feeder for use with your printer.

- *Page Offsets* Indicates whether an adjustment is necessary to compensate for how paper is loaded into the printer. You can specify a top edge offset and/or a side offset, either with a positive number for forms that must be adjusted downward or to the right, or with a negative number for forms that must be adjusted upward or to the left.

Next, press [Enter] or EXIT ([F7]) to return to the Select Printer Forms screen, which lists all paper definitions (forms) defined for your printer, including the form you just defined. You can define a number of forms for the same printer. For instance, if you use a sheet feeder, you will want to define a form type for each sheet feeder bin.

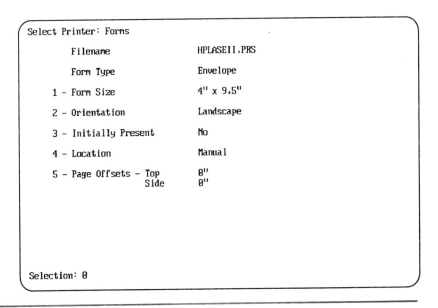

```
Select Printer: Forms

        Filename                HPLASEII.PRS

        Form Type               Envelope

    1 - Form Size               4" x 9.5"

    2 - Orientation             Landscape

    3 - Initially Present       No

    4 - Location                Manual

    5 - Page Offsets - Top      0"
                        Side    0"




Selection: 0
```

**FIGURE 9-14**  Forms screen for 4″ by 9.5″ size/envelope type with the HP LaserJet Series II (version 5.0 only)

Or, if you plan to feed both envelopes and labels into your printer, then create an Envelope form type and set the appropriate characteristics, and then a Label form type and its appropriate characteristics.

When you have defined all the forms you will use for your printer, press EXIT ([F7]) to return to the Select Printer Edit screen.

**CARTRIDGES AND FONTS**   Some printers allow you to insert different print cartridges or to download font files so that you have a variety of extra fonts available for printing. In that case, use this printer setting to list all possible cartridges or fonts you plan to use with your printer. Word-Perfect uses this information when it encounters a Font Change code in your document (see Chapter 10).

When you select Cartridges and Fonts (4 or C for 5.1 users, 5 or C for 5.0 users), the Select Printer Cartridges and Fonts screen appears; an example is shown in Figure 9-15. (*5.0 users:* If this screen does not appear, then it is because WordPerfect does not have access to the Printer disk containing the original driver for your printer, which is contained in the file with an extension of .ALL. Word-Perfect prompts, "Directory for printer files:". Insert the correct Printer disk in drive A or B, and then type **A:** or **B:** and press [Enter], or, if the printer file is on the hard disk, then type the correct directory and press [Enter].) This screen indicates under the heading "Font Category" (or under the category "Resource" for 5.0 users) whether your printer has built-in fonts, or uses cartridge fonts, print wheels, and/or downloadable font files, each as a separate option. *5.1 users:* The heading "Quantity" indicates the number of slots available in your printer for cartridges, the print wheels that can be used, or the amount of memory available for downloadable font files. The heading "Avail-

```
┌─────────────────────────────────────────────────────────────────────┐
│ Select Printer: Cartridges and Fonts                                │
│                                                                     │
│ Font Category                          Quantity         Available   │
│ ▓▓▓▓▓▓▓▓▓▓▓▓▓▓▓▓▓▓▓▓▓▓▓▓▓▓▓▓▓▓▓▓▓▓▓▓▓▓▓▓▓▓▓▓▓▓▓▓▓▓▓▓▓▓▓▓▓▓▓▓▓▓▓▓▓▓▓▓│
│ Built-In                                                            │
│ Cartridges                                2                2        │
│ Soft Fonts                              350 K            350 K      │
│                                                                     │
│                                                                     │
│                                                                     │
│                                                                     │
│                                                                     │
│                                                                     │
│                                                                     │
│                                                                     │
│ NOTE: Most items listed under the Font Category (with the exception │
│ of Built-In) are optional and must be purchased separately from     │
│ your dealer or manufacturer.                                        │
│                                                                     │
│ 1 Select; 2 Change Quantity; N Name search: 1                       │
└─────────────────────────────────────────────────────────────────────┘
```

**FIGURE 9-15**   Cartridges and Fonts screen

able" indicates how many of the total number have yet to be used. *5.0 users:* There is only the heading "Quantity," which indicates how many of the total number of cartridges or print wheels, or how much memory has yet to be used.

You can select Change Quantity (2 or Q) to indicate that you have added more slots or memory to your printer than is preset for your printer, and then enter the appropriate number.

You can also move the cursor to the font category of your choice and choose Select (1 or S) or simply press Enter . A list of the available cartridges or fonts for that font category appears. Move the cursor to a cartridge or font you want to use with your printer, and then, depending on the instructions at the bottom of the screen, you may do one of the following:

- Type an asterisk (∗) to mark it as Present When Print Job Begins, which means that the cartridge or font is in a slot or in the printer memory when you start a print job. Fonts marked with this option are downloaded when you select the Initialize Printer option on the Print menu (as described in the next section). Also, for printers where fonts cannot be swapped, memory is automatically decreased when you mark a font with ∗.

- Type a plus sign (+) to mark it as Can be Loaded (Unloaded) During Print Job, which means that Word-Perfect will load (or unload) the font or ask you to insert (or remove) the cartridge during a print job. For printers where fonts cannot be swapped, fonts can only be loaded during a print job or unloaded afterwards. If fonts can be swapped, fonts can be loaded or unloaded during a print job.

- Type both ∗ and +, in which case WordPerfect down-loads the font and if necessary, unloads it to load another font. That font is then reloaded at the end of the print job.

Continue to mark all fonts that you wish to use (or until memory is almost used up), and then press EXIT (F7) to return to the Select Printer Cartridges and Fonts screen. Press EXIT (F7) again to return to the Select Printer Edit screen.

**INITIAL FONT**　　This setting specifies the default font for the printer you are defining. WordPerfect uses the specified font when it prints out all documents with this printer, unless a Font Change code is inserted in the document to override the initial font (see Chapter 10).

When you select Initial Font (5 or I for 5.1 users, 6 or I for 5.0 users), the Select Printer Initial Font screen appears, which lists the possible fonts available for your printer (including built-in fonts and those you marked with the Cartridges and Fonts option, described above). Move the cursor to the font of your choice and choose Select (1 or S) or simply press Enter. An asterisk is inserted next to that font, indicating that it has been chosen as the initial font, and you are immediately returned to the Select Printer Edit screen.

**PATH FOR DOWNLOADABLE FONTS AND PRINTER COMMANDS** This setting indicates the drive/directory where WordPerfect should look for downloadable font files and printer command files. When you select Path for Downloadable Fonts and Printer Commands (6 or D for 5.1 users; 7 or D for 5.0 users), you should then enter a drive/directory. For instance, if all downloadable fonts are stored on the hard disk in a directory named \WP51\FONTS, then enter **C:\WP51\FONTS**.

Once you edit a printer definition, press EXIT (F7) to store the printer definition you just created on disk in a file with the extension .PRS, and to return to the Select Printer screen, as shown in Figure 9-3.

On the Select Printer screen, you can perform other tasks in addition to editing a printer definition. Position the cursor on the name of the printer and then select Copy (4 or C) to create a duplicate of an existing .PRS file — a useful feature if you wish to define a new printer that is similar to an existing one. You can copy and then edit the copied printer definition. Select Delete (5 or D) to delete a printer definition. Select Help (6 or H) to view a screen of information about that printer. Or, select Update (7 or U), if you received a new version of WordPerfect that contains new Printer disks and you wish to replace a printer definition with a new, updated copy.

A final option allows you to display a different list of printers. Should you wish to edit a printer definition for a printer that is not currently listed on the Select Printer screen, select Additional Printers (2 or A). WordPerfect will display a new list of printer files. Or, if WordPerfect cannot find a different list of printers, you then have the option of indicating an alternative location for the additional printer files by selecting the Other Disk item. (*5.1 users*: you cannot use any of the original Printer disks that come in the WordPerfect package to create or edit a printer definition. Because the original disks contain files that are compressed, you must install the Printer disks first, as described in Appendix A.)

# INITIALIZE YOUR PRINTER FOR SOFT FONTS

A variety of laser and PostScript printers allow for soft fonts, which you can purchase so that your printer can print out using fancy type styles and sizes. (See Chapter 10 for a detailed explanation of the set of characteristics that define a given font.) Soft fonts are stored on disk and must be downloaded to the printer before they can be used, which means that the instructions for how to print using those fonts are sent from disk to the printer's memory.

If you have purchased soft fonts for your printer, then you must inform WordPerfect which ones you have available and where those soft fonts are stored on disk. You can designate certain fonts as "always present" when a print job begins and other soft fonts as "available to be loaded" for a particular print job. These procedures are performed when you edit your printer definition, as previously described in this chapter.

The soft fonts that you designate as "always present" in your printer must always be downloaded the *first time* that you wish to use them after turning on the printer. On the Print screen, check to see that the currently selected printer is the one that accepts soft fonts; if not, select the correct printer. Then, select Initialize Printer (I or 7). WordPerfect sends a print job to the printer, which downloads the fonts; other fonts that were previously loaded into the printer's memory are erased. Once the print job is complete, you are ready to print out documents using the fonts marked for "always present" throughout your Word-Perfect working session—provided that you keep your printer turned on. If you turn your printer off and then turn it on again, you must again initialize for those fonts to be ready for printing.

# INSERT PRINTER COMMANDS

There may be features that your printer supports but that you cannot access by any of the methods discussed so far. WordPerfect allows you to send special commands to your printer to tap such features. You must find these commands in your printer manual. They will be numbers, letters, or a combination of numbers and letters, where the numbers are surrounded by angle brackets < >. Most printer commands start with the Escape control code; in that case, the first part of the command will be <27>. Thus, a printer command for your printer may be <27>A or <27> <15>.

To insert a printer command into the text, position the cursor where you want the command to take effect. Then press the FORMAT (Shift + F8 ) key, select Other (4 or O), select Printer Functions (6 or P), and select Printer Command (2 or P). WordPerfect prompts

`1 Command; 2 Filename: 0`

Select Command (1 or C) and enter the command. Or you can create a file on disk that contains printer commands, in which case you would then select Filename (2 or F) and enter in the correct filename. WordPerfect inserts a hidden code in the text, such as **[PtrCmnd: < 27 > A]**. During printing this code will be sent to the printer.

Needless to say, you must rely on your printer manual to tell you the right command. In general, unless your printer has a capability that you're not able to access using Word-Perfect codes, there's no need to employ this feature.

# REVIEW EXERCISE

Many of the features explained in this chapter depend on your printer's capabilities. Certain other features, such as Number of Copies, should work no matter what type of printer you use and no matter how many printers are attached to your computer. Here are some features that will work no matter what your printer:

1. Clear the screen and then retrieve the file named URGNOTE.

2. Use the Advance feature to insert a code that will advance this document down an extra 2″ on the page when printed.

3. Use the View Document feature to preview on screen how the document will appear when printed; if your printer supports the Advance feature, then the document should appear lower on the page in the View Document screen.

4. Print three copies of the document in one print job. (*Hint:* To do so, set the Number of Copies option on the Print screen to "3" before sending the print job to the printer.)

5. Reset the Number of Copies option on the Print screen back to "1"; otherwise you'll get three copies of everything you print until the next time you reload WordPerfect.

6. Clear the screen and then retrieve the file named SMITH.ADD. This is a file that contains the address for Mr. Barrett Smith, which you saved using the Block Save feature in Chapter 2.

7. Make the proper format changes to print out the name and address onto a 9.5″ by 4″ envelope. (*Hint:* If you haven't already done so, establish a paper definition (form) for envelopes—based on the method your printer uses to print envelopes, and providing that your printer can print envelopes. Then, position the cursor at the top of the document and insert a Top/Bottom Margin code, a Left/Right Margin code, and a Paper Size/Type code for envelopes.)

8. Use the View Document feature to preview the printed result. The View Document screen should show the page in the shape of an envelope. If you desire, you can also print the envelope to examine the final results of your work.

# Quick Review

- To preview a document that is currently on screen before printing, select PRINT ([Shift] + [F7]) to display the Print screen. Or, pulldown menu users can select File (F), Print (P). Then, select View Document (6 or V). The View Document screen displays features that don't otherwise appear on the Typing screen, such as margins, headers, footers, and page numbers. By using the View Document screen regularly, you can save on the cost of printing supplies by printing out a document only after you verify it will print in the desired format.

- Choose a different printer for a document from the Print screen by choosing Select Printer (S). Next, position the cursor on one of the printers listed and choose Select (1 or S). The text is reformatted for the newly selected printer. All future documents that you create will also be formatted for the new printer, unless you select a new printer. All existing files will retain the printer that had been selected when the documents were most recently stored on disk.

- Control the mechanics of print jobs by choosing an item under the heading "Print Options" on the Print screen. These items include the following: Binding Offset, which establishes a width for binding a document like a book; Number of Copies, which enables you to print out multiple copies of a document in one print job; or Graphics/Text Quality, which determines the quality used to print out text and/or graphics. 5.1 users also have the ability to specify whether the generation of multiple copies is controlled by WordPerfect or the printer.

If you alter a print option for a particular print job, remember to return it to the previous setting once the print job is complete, unless you want to maintain that new print option setting for future print jobs during the current working session.

- Advance the printer to an exact horizontal or vertical position on the page by pressing FORMAT (Shift + F8) and selecting Other (4 or O) to display the Other Format menu. Or, pulldown menu users can select Layout (L), Other (O). Next, select Advance (1 or A). A menu appears, from which you can select Up, Down, Left, or Right to advance a certain measurement from the cursor position. Or, select Line or Position to advance a certain measurement from the top or left edge of the page. The Advance feature is especially useful for positioning text on letterhead or preprinted forms or for overlapping text in desktop publishing applications.

- Indicate to WordPerfect that you will print on paper of a different size or type by positioning the cursor at the top of the page, pressing FORMAT (Shift + F8), selecting Page (2 or P) to display the Page Format menu, and then choosing Paper Size/Type (7 or S for 5.1 users, 8 or S for 5.0 users). Choose the paper definition (form) for the size and type of paper you wish to print on. The text will reformat if the paper modification specifies a change in size.

If a paper size/type combination that you wish to select does not currently exist, you should establish a new paper definition (form) before selecting the corresponding paper size/type.

- Edit a printer definition from the Print screen by choosing Select Printer (S). Next, position the cursor on one of the printers listed and select Edit (3 or E). Now you can change the settings that WordPerfect uses when communicating with the printer. 5.0 users will also want to edit a printer definition to create a new paper definition (form), which can then be chosen for a specific document using the Paper Size/Type feature.

- When your printer uses downloadable (soft) fonts, you must initialize your printer to use those fonts previously defined as initially present in your printer. Initialize your printer by selecting Initialize (7 or I) on the Print screen. A print job is sent to the printer, which loads the fonts into the printer's memory.

- Should WordPerfect not directly support a feature available on your printer, you can insert a printer command into a document to activate that feature. Press FORMAT ( Shift + F8 ), select Other (4 or O), select Printer Functions (6 or P), and then choose Printer Command (2 or P). You can enter a command or the name of the file where printer commands have been stored.

*chapter* **10**

# CHANGING FONTS
# AND INSERTING
# GRAPHICS FOR
# DESKTOP
# PUBLISHING

**W**ith the advent of desktop publishing, computers have created a publishing revolution. Desktop publishing is the ability to control the writing and publishing process using the computer equipment that sits on your desk. You will be interested in WordPerfect's desktop publishing abilities if, instead of sending your text to a designer, typesetter, and printer, you want to produce newsletters, business reports, company publications, or manuals by yourself.

This chapter describes the features that WordPerfect offers in order to undertake desktop publishing. You'll learn how to print characters using fancy fonts. For instance, you can print all headings in a large type size and in italics, while printing the main body of the text in a smaller type size, with a Courier typeface and proportional spacing. Font changes offer true sophistication in enhancing different sections of your text and giving your documents a slick, professional look.

You'll also insert graphics into your documents. With WordPerfect, you can effectively merge pictures with text— such as inserting a map of the United States near a discussion of the R&R Wine Association's national growth. And you can insert graphics lines or shaded boxes in your text to emphasize certain sections of text.

Be aware that the desktop features available to you depend on the capabilities of your printer. Laser printers usually offer the most features for desktop publishing; they can produce printed documents of nearly typeset quality using a variety of fancy fonts and can print graphics of good quality.

# MODIFY THE INITIAL OR BASE FONT

In WordPerfect, a font is a set of characteristics that defines how text will print, as shown in Figure 10-1. These include the following:

- *Typeface*  This is the style of the characters, such as Courier, Times Roman, Presentation, or Helvetica.

- *Pitch*  This is the density of characters per inch (CPI) on a line. The larger the pitch size, the smaller or more tightly packed the character; for instance, a pitch of 10 CPI means that 10 characters fit in 1″ of horizontal space on a page, while a pitch of 12 CPI means that 12 characters are squeezed into that same inch. The smaller the pitch, the wider or farther apart the characters. Pitch applies when the text is monospaced; standard monospaced text usually prints in 10, 11, or 12 pitch.

- *Horizontal spacing*  This is how characters are spaced on a line. *Monospacing* means that each character occupies the same amount of space. *Proportional spacing* means that each character occupies a different amount of space in proportion to its width, so that a narrow letter like "i" is allotted less space on the page than a wide letter like "w." Proportional spacing gives documents a more typeset look.

- *Type style or appearance*  This is the specific style of characters to add emphasis or contrast, such as italics, boldface, shadow, or small caps. The style applies for a particular typeface.

- *Character set*  This is the collection of symbols and characters that can be printed in the selected font, such as Roman Eight, Legal, or Math.

- *Type size*  This is the size or height of characters, typically measured in points, where approximately 72 points equal 1 vertical inch. Standard text usually prints in type sizes of 8, 10, or 12 points.

Courier typeface, monospaced, pitch of 10 CPI, type size
of 12-point. Courier is the most common typeface.

Times Roman typeface, proportionally spaced, type size of 10-point.
Proportional spacing provides a more professional look to the text.

*Times Roman typeface, proportionally spaced, type size of 10-point, with italics
appearance. Italics means that letters are slanted to provide a light and
cursive effect.*

**Century Schoolbook typeface, proportionally spaced, type
size of 14-point, boldface. An increase in type size
results in a larger character, so WordPerfect adjusts
the line height automatically to accommodate the
increase.**

**PRESENTATION TYPEFACE, MONOSPACED,
6.5 CPI, 18-POINT, BOLDFACE. A
DECREASE IN PITCH MEANS FEWER
CHARACTERS FIT ON A LINE, SO
WORDPERFECT ADJUSTS THE LENGTH OF
LINES BOTH ON SCREEN AND AT THE
PRINTER.**

# Century Schoolbook, proportionally spaced, 30-point, boldface. Perfect for headlines!!

**FIGURE 10-1** Examples of different fonts

At installation an *initial font* is assigned to each printer. (The process for editing printer definitions, whereby you can alter the initial font for a particular printer, is described in Chapter 9.)

## Alter the Initial Font

You are not limited to using the initial font, however. Most printers offer a variety of font options. Some printers have many different fonts built in. With other printers, you can have access to more fonts by purchasing printer extras. For instance, most laser printers allow you to insert cartridges containing additional fonts. Laser printers also allow for soft fonts, which are fonts stored on disk that must be read by the printer (downloaded) before they can be used.

*Note:* If you acquire additional cartridges or soft fonts for your printer, you must inform WordPerfect before you attempt to use them by editing your printer definition. Moreover, before printing a document that uses soft fonts, you may need to initialize your printer, which means that WordPerfect will download the fonts to your printer so that they will be available for use. Refer to Chapter 9 for details.

For laser printer users, your alternative font options also depend on the paper size and type you are using. If Word-Perfect assumes that you will print the characters parallel to how the paper is inserted into the printer (portrait mode), then only the fonts that print in portrait mode are available. If you insert a Paper Size/Type code so that the characters print perpendicular to how the paper is inserted into the printer (landscape mode), then only the fonts that print in landscape mode are available.

For each document, you can ascertain a document's initial font, display a list of other fonts available, and/or change the initial font. With the document on screen, press the FORMAT (⟨Shift⟩ + ⟨F8⟩) key and select Document Format (3 or D). [*Pulldown menu:* Layout (L), Document (D).] The Document Format menu, as shown in Figure 10-2, appears. Next to the heading Initial Base Font (called "initial font," and not "initial base font" in version 5.0), WordPerfect indicates the initial font for your document. If you wish to retain that initial font, simply press CANCEL (⟨F1⟩) until you return to the Typing screen. If you wish to change the initial font, select Initial Base Font (3 or F) from the Document Format menu. A screen appears listing the available fonts for your printer; an example for the HP LaserJet Series II (with several cartridges defined) is shown in Figure 10-3. WordPerfect displays an asterisk next to the currently selected initial font. Position the cursor on the font you wish to select either by using the cursor movement keys (such as ⟨↓⟩ and ⟨PgDn⟩) or by typing **N** to select the Name Search option, typing the first few letters of the font

```
Format: Document

       1 - Display Pitch - Automatic  Yes
                           Width      0.1"

       2 - Initial Codes

       3 - Initial Base Font          Courier 10cpi

       4 - Redline Method             Printer Dependent

       5 - Summary




Selection: 0
```

**FIGURE 10-2**   Document Format menu

```
Document: Initial Font

* Courier 10cpi
  Courier 10cpi Bold
  Helv 14.4pt Bold (B)
  Letter Gothic 10cpi (Legal) (R)
  Letter Gothic 10cpi (R)
  Line Draw 10cpi (Full)
  Line Draw 10cpi 14pt (R)
  Line Printer 16.67cpi
  PC Line Draw 10cpi 14pt (Land) (R)
  PC Line Draw 10cpi 14pt (R)
  Presentation  6.5cpi Bold (Legal) (R)
  Presentation  6.5cpi Bold (R)
  Presentation  8.1cpi Bold (Legal) (R)
  Presentation  8.1cpi Bold (R)
  Presentation 10cpi Bold (Legal) (R)
  Presentation 10cpi Bold (R)
  TmsRmn  8pt (B)
  TmsRmn 10pt (B)
  TmsRmn 10pt Bold (B)
  TmsRmn 10pt Italic (B)

1 Select; N Name search: 1
```

**FIGURE 10-3**  A Document Initial Font screen: HP Laser-Jet Series II with several cartridges

name until the cursor moves to that font, and pressing [Enter]. Now choose Select (1 or S). You are returned to the Document Format screen, where your new font selection is now indicated next to the Initial Base Font heading.

When you alter the initial base font, WordPerfect assumes the change begins at the top of the document and will affect not only the main body of text, but also headers, footers, endnotes, footnotes, and graphics box captions. No code is inserted in the text. If you change your mind and wish to select a different initial font, you can again return to the Initial Font screen.

## Alter the Base Font

In addition to changing the font starting at the top of a document, you can also change a font for a specific section of your document. When you do so, you are altering the *base font* of your document. The procedure is quite different from the method for altering the initial font. First, you must position the cursor wherever you want the font change to take effect. For instance, if you want the change to start on page 2, position the cursor at the top of page 2. Press the FONT ( Ctrl + F8 ) key. WordPerfect displays the Font menu:

```
1 Size; 2 Appearance; 3 Normal; 4 Base Font; 5 Print Color: 0
```

Select the Base Font (4 or F). [*Pulldown menu:* Font (O), Base Font (O).] WordPerfect displays the Base Font screen, listing the available fonts for your printer. This screen is identical to the Document Initial Font screen (Figure 10-3) for a given printer, except that the top of the screen reads "Base Font" rather than "Document: Initial Font." An asterisk appears next to the currently selected font. To change that font, position the cursor on the font you wish to select either by using the cursor movement keys (such as ↓ and PgDn ) or by typing **N** to select the Name Search option, typing the first few letters of the font name until the cursor moves to that font, and pressing Enter . Now choose Select (1 or S). You are returned to the Typing screen.

You can alter the base font as many times as you desire in the same document. Each time, WordPerfect inserts a Font code at the current cursor position. For instance, suppose that your printer has available the Times Roman, 10-point font, which you select. The following font code is inserted: **[Font:Tms Rmn 10pt]**. The font change takes effect from the hidden code until the end of the document or until another Font code is inserted farther forward in the text.

A base font change will affect the main body of the text and Header and Footer codes that follow the Base Font code. Or, you can insert a Base Font code into a header or footer. If you change your mind and decide to cancel a base font change, then erase the hidden font code — in the same way you would erase a format code, such as a Margin or Tab Set code.

When you change your initial or base font, the characters on screen will appear the same, but line and page breaks may readjust if the font's pitch, horizontal spacing, and/or type size changes.

For instance, suppose you change from a font with a pitch of 10 CPI to a font with a pitch of 12 CPI. Now more characters can fit on a line when printed, so the Soft Return codes at the end of lines readjust. In fact, you may no longer be able to see a full line of text at one time across the width of your screen, but will need to press [Home], [Home], [→] to view text at the far right end of the line. (Remember from previous chapters that, when moving horizontally, pressing [Home] an extra time moves the cursor to the end of the line, rather than to the end of the screen. For instance, [Home], [Home], [←] positions the cursor at the left end of the line, while [Home], [←] positions the cursor at the left edge of the screen. When the line is wider than the screen, this difference is noticeable.) Conversely, if you change to a pitch of 6.5 CPI, then fewer characters can fit on a line and on each page; the length of each line may extend only halfway across the width of the screen.

As another example, suppose that you change from a font with a type size of 12 points to a font of 18 points. Since the characters will now be taller when printed, Word-Perfect automatically adjusts the height of each line of text. Fewer lines can fit on a page, so page breaks readjust. (Line height is discussed in more detail farther on in this chapter.)

Let's retrieve a document and then change the base font for the middle portion only. Since we will make a font change starting somewhere other than at the top of the document, we'll use the FONT key to make the change.

1. On a clear screen, retrieve the file named FINANCE. (If you saved this file with a password during an exercise in Chapter 9, you will need to enter the password, **90046**, for WordPerfect to retrieve FINANCE.)

2. Position the cursor on the blank line above the first bulleted paragraph.

3. Press the FONT (Ctrl + F8) key. WordPerfect displays the Font menu:

   1 Size; 2 Appearance; 3 Normal; 4 Base Font; 5 Print Color: 0

   [*Pulldown menu:* Font (O).]

4. Select Base Font (4 or F). [*Pulldown menu:* Base Font (O).] WordPerfect displays a Base Font screen, which lists the available fonts for your printer. An asterisk appears next to the font assumed for your printer. Notice the name of the initial font that WordPerfect assumes for your printer.

5. Use the ↓ key and position the cursor on any other font selection of your choosing.

6. Choose Select (1 or S) to select that font. You are now returned to the Typing screen. If your font change resulted in a different pitch or type size, then when you move the cursor, WordPerfect rewrites the screen, readjusting the line and page breaks for text below that code on screen. If you reveal codes, you can view the Font code you just inserted.

7. To return the bottom portion of the document to the initial font, position the cursor on the blank line below the second bulleted paragraph, and repeat steps 3 through 6, but this time selecting the initial (original) font.

If you reveal codes, you can view the Font codes that you just inserted.

WordPerfect will again readjust the text if your font change resulted in a different pitch or type size. In fact, you may find that your margins on screen appear quite different in the middle of the document, where the font change has an effect. Remember that this is because WordPerfect is showing you how many characters will actually fit across each line when the document is printed using the font selected. You may wish to manually readjust text based on the new font changes. When you print out this document, you can see the font change take effect for the middle portion of the text.

You learned in Chapter 9 that you can select a new printer for a document at any time. When you select a different printer for a document that contains a Font Change code, WordPerfect selects a font available for the newly selected printer that most closely matches the font for the previous printer.

# MODIFY A FONT ATTRIBUTE

To add emphasis to a section of text, you can alter one or more attributes of a font for that section without actually asking WordPerfect to change the font itself. In Word-Perfect, there are two categories of font attributes that you can control for each font.

The first attribute relates to a font's type size. Each font is assigned a specific normal size. You can instead select different sizes in the following percentages of normal: Fine (60%), Small (80%), Large (120%), Very Large (150%), and Extra Large (200%). *5.1 users only:* The percentages of normal for the different sizes can be altered, as described in the section "Initial Settings" in Appendix B.

Here's an example of different size changes using the same font.

This is fine size,

while this is small size,

and this is normal for the current font.

**Meanwhile, this is a sample of large,**

while this is very large,

and here's extra large.

(Changing the type size may, depending on your printer, sometimes result in a typeface change as well.)

Also within the size category are superscript and subscript, which position characters slightly above or below the normal line of text, and, depending on a printer's capabilities, may reduce their size to 60% of normal at the same time.

Superscript moves $^{\text{characters up}}$ in a line.

Subscript moves $_{\text{characters down}}$ in a line.

Superscript and subscript come in handy when typing scientific or mathematical information, such as $X^{14}$ or $H_20$. (Superscript is automatically used to denote footnotes, as described in Chapter 12.)

The second attribute you can control relates to a font's appearance or typestyle. Each font is assigned a normal appearance. You can instead select from the following: italics, where characters are slanted to provide a cursive effect; outline, where characters appear as white and outlined in black; shadow, where edges of characters are darkened or characters are printed twice, one slightly to the right of the other, to produce a shadow effect; small caps, where characters are printed as if in uppercase, but smaller in size; redline, where characters are marked either with a shaded background, a dotted line under the characters, a vertical bar in the left margin, or in a different color; strikeout, where a solid or dashed line is printed through the characters; bold; underline; and double underline. Here's an example of different styles using the same font:

This is normal for the current font.

This is Redline, ~~while this is Strikeout.~~

Here is Underline, while <u>here is Double Underline.</u>

*Here's Italic appearance.* **This is Shadow.** **Here's Bold!!!!!!**

The way you control font attributes depends on whether you've already typed the text. One method is used to add an attribute to a portion of text *as you type.* Another is used to add an attribute to a portion of text that *you've already typed* into your document.

# Alter Attributes as You Type

To alter an attribute as you type, position the cursor where you want a change in size or appearance to occur and press the FONT ( Ctrl + F8 ) key. The Font menu appears:

1 Size; 2 Appearance; 3 Normal; 4 Base Font; 5 Print Color: 0

If you select Size (1 or S), the following menu appears:

1 Suprscpt; 2 Subscpt; 3 Fine; 4 Small; 5 Large; 6 Vry Large; 7 Ext Large: 0

If you select Appearance (2 or A) from the Font menu, this menu appears:

1 Bold; 2 Undrln; 3 Dbl Und; 4 Italc; 5 Outln; 6 Shadw; 7 Sm Cap; 8 Redln; 9 Stkout: 0

Choose a size or appearance attribute. [*Pulldown menu:* Select Font (O) to display a font menu; then choose a size attribute, or select Appearance (A) and choose an appearance attribute.] Once you choose a size or appearance attribute, you have activated that attribute.

Your next step is to type the text that you want enhanced with that attribute. (However, if you wish to activate more than one attribute for the same portion of text, select a second attribute—repeating the process as described above—before you type the text.) Type the complete portion of text to be affected.

As a final step, you must turn off the special attribute. You can do so in several ways:

- Repeat the same procedure as when you turned on the feature. That is, press FONT ( Ctrl + F8 ), select Size

(1 or S) or Appearance (2 or A), and choose the attribute again to turn it off.

- Press the ⮕ key to position the cursor outside the Attribute codes. This is the quickest method if you have activated only one attribute.

- Press FONT ( Ctrl + F8 ) and select Normal (3 or N). [*Pulldown menu:* Font (O), Normal (N).] This is the quickest method if you have activated more than one attribute. For instance, perhaps you turned on large size, italics, and underline. Using the Normal option turns off all three at the same time, returning the font to normal.

## Alter Attributes for Existing Text

To change a font attribute for text you've already typed, use the Block feature to highlight the portion of text you wish to affect. Then, with "Block on" flashing, press the FONT ( Ctrl + F8 ) key. With Block on, WordPerfect displays a special attribute menu:

Attribute: 1 Size; 2 Appearance: 0

Select Size (1 or S) or Appearance (2 or A), and then select the attribute you desire. [*Pulldown menu:* With Block on, select Font (O). Next, either select from the size attribute options, or select Appearance (A) and select from the appearance attribute options.] WordPerfect activates the feature for just the highlighted text and turns Block off automatically.

Regardless of which of the two methods you use to alter attributes, WordPerfect surrounds the text designated for a different size or appearance attribute with a pair of codes. An On code for the attribute precedes the text and an Off code follows the text. The codes are

| Size Attribute Codes | Appearance Attribute Codes |
|---|---|
| [SUPRSCPT] [suprscpt] | [BOLD] [bold] |
| [SUBSCPT] [subscpt] | [UND] [und] |
| [FINE] [fine] | [DBL UND] [dbl und] |
| [SMALL] [small] | [ITALC] [italc] |
| [LARGE] [large] | [OUTLN] [outln] |
| [VRY LARGE] [vry large] | [SHADW] [shadw] |
| [EXT LARGE] [ext large] | [SM CAP] [sm cap] |
| | [REDLN] [redln] |
| | [STKOUT] [stkout] |

Delete one of the pair of codes and the attribute is removed from your text.

(Bold and underline can be inserted in your text not only with the FONT key, but also using the BOLD (F6) and UNDERLINE (F8) keys; refer to Chapter 3 for a review of the quick methods for enhancing text with bold or underline. Redline and strikeout can also be inserted with the Compare Document feature, where the screen and disk versions of a document are compared; refer to Chapter 5 for a review of this feature.)

## How Attributes Display and Print

How text with a given attribute appears on your Typing screen depends on your monitor. On a monochrome monitor, each of the attribute changes may appear brighter than the rest of the text, underlined, highlighted, or blinking. On a color monitor, the attribute changes may appear in a different color. Also, if your computer is equipped with a Ramfont graphics card, then you'll actually be able to view attributes such as italics and different-sized characters right on screen.

*Note:* With WordPerfect you can change the way that text with font attribute enhancements is displayed on the Typing screen. Refer to the "Display" section of Appendix B for more details.

How each of these attributes appears on the printed page depends on two factors. First, it depends on the printer you're using. Some printers do not support certain attributes. For instance, on PostScript printers, you can print all the size attributes with the percentages of normal as set up by WordPerfect. Other printers can't support italics, and so show underlining instead. Some printers can only change a size attribute if this is accompanied by a typeface change. And, some printers are capable only of standard Courier at 10-pitch; they will not support any size attribute and may be quite limited in appearance attributes as well.

The second factor that determines how attributes appear is the currently active font. Font size and appearance attributes are variations of the current font only. Thus, even if a certain attribute is available with your printer, it may not be available for the current font.

You must therefore remember that a change in an attribute will not change text at the printer unless the printer supports different type sizes and appearances, and supports them in the font that you are currently using. You need to discover your own printer's capabilities. You can do so with a test document. Create your own test document by typing text on screen using all the different size and appearance attributes. Or, use a document provided by WordPerfect with the filename PRINTER.TST, a file that can be used to test the attribute, graphics, and other advanced Word-Perfect features on your printer. *5.1 users:* This file is housed on your hard disk in the same directory on which the WordPerfect program is found, or on the WordPerfect 1 disk if you installed the WordPerfect program onto floppy disks. *5.0 users:* This file is housed on the Conversion disk. Retrieve this document to screen.

Once a test document—either your own document or PRINTER.TST—is on screen, print it. Then, position the cursor at the top of the document, select a new base font, and print. Repeat this process by deleting the Base Font code, selecting a different base font, and printing again. Print the test file as many times as fonts you have available. You may discover that your printer doesn't support certain attributes.

With the redline attribute, you have a choice as to how the redline marks appear on the printed page. Redline is set up as printer dependent. Once you print either PRINTER.TST or a test document that includes Redline codes,you'll uncover what "printer dependent" means for your printer. You can instead select that redline print as a certain character in the left margin. Or you can select that redline print as a certain character in alternating margins— in the left margin of odd pages and in the right margin of even pages. To change the current method of redline print-ing for a specific document, make sure that the document is on screen. The cursor can be positioned anywhere. Press the FORMAT ( Shift + F8 ) key and select Document (3 or D). [*Pulldown menu:* Layout (L), Document (D).] The

Document Format menu appears as shown in Figure 10-2. Notice that the redline method is "Printer Dependent." Select Redline Method (4 or R), and WordPerfect displays a redline menu:

**Redline Method: 1** Printer Dependent; **2** Left; **3** Alternating: **1**

If you select Left (2 or L) or Alternating (3 or A), Word-Perfect prompts for the character to be used as the redline character, suggesting the ¦ symbol. Press [Enter] to accept that symbol or enter one of your own. Press EXIT ([F7]) to return to the Typing screen.

If you have a printer that prints in color, you can enhance text not only by changing a font attribute, but by altering the color of text as well. To print in a specified color, position the cursor where you want the color change to take effect in your document. Press the FONT ([Ctrl] + [F8]) key and then select Print Color (5 or C). [*Pulldown menu:* Font (O), Print Color (C).] The menu shown in Figure 10-4 appears. Select a color option from the 11 predefined colors or create a color of your own by selecting Other (O) and entering the new intensity percentage for red, green, and blue in the three columns on screen. (Check your color printer manual to see which colors are supported.) When you press EXIT ([F7]) to return to the text, a code such as **[Color:Red]** is inserted.

## Practice with Attributes

Here's some practice changing font attributes for the document named FINANCE, which is currently on screen. We'll

```
┌─────────────────────────────────────────────────────────────┐
│ Print Color                                                   │
│                                                               │
│                        Primary Color Mixture                  │
│                      Red      Green     Blue                  │
│         1 - Black        0%        0%        0%               │
│         2 - White      100%      100%      100%               │
│         3 - Red         67%        0%        0%               │
│         4 - Green        0%       67%        0%               │
│         5 - Blue         0%        0%       67%               │
│         6 - Yellow      67%       67%        0%               │
│         7 - Magenta     67%        0%       67%               │
│         8 - Cyan         0%       67%       67%               │
│         9 - Orange      67%       25%        0%               │
│         A - Gray        50%       50%       50%               │
│         N - Brown       67%       33%        0%               │
│         0 - Other                                             │
│                                                               │
│         Current Color    0%        0%        0%               │
│                                                               │
│                                                               │
│                                                               │
│ Selection: 0                                                  │
└─────────────────────────────────────────────────────────────┘
```

**FIGURE 10-4**   Print Color menu

change the font attributes both for text already typed and for text as we type.

1. Use the Block feature to highlight the words "venture capitalist", located in one of the bulleted paragraphs.

2. With Block on, press the FONT (Ctrl + F8) key. [*Pull-down menu:* Font (O).] WordPerfect prompts

   **Attribute: 1 S**ize; **2 A**ppearance: **0**

3. Select Appearance (2 or A). The following menu appears:

   **1 B**old; **2 U**ndrln; **3 D**bl Und; **4 I**talc; **5 O**utln; **6 S**hadw; **7 S**m Cap;
   **8 R**edln; **9 S**tkout: **0**

4. Select Italics (4 or I). A hidden **[ITALC]** code is placed to the left of the block, and an **[italc]** code is placed to the right of the block. How italics displays on your screen depends on your monitor.

5. Use the Block feature to highlight the words "10% lower than we anticipated," located in the other bulleted paragraph.

6. With Block on, press FONT (Ctrl + F8 ). [*Pulldown menu:* Font (O).]

7. Select Size (1 or S). [*Pulldown menu:* remain on the font menu.] The following menu appears:

   1 Suprscpt; 2 Subscpt; 3 Fine; 4 Small; 5 Large; 6 Vry Large; 7 Ext Large: 0

8. Select Very Large (6 or V). A hidden **[VRY LARGE]** code is placed to the left of the block, and a **[vry large]** code is placed to the right of the block. How a very large type size displays on your screen depends on your monitor.

9. Position the cursor at the very end of the document, just to the right of the last line. Press the spacebar twice.

10. Press the FONT (Ctrl + F8 ) key. With Block off, WordPerfect displays the Font menu:

    1 Size; 2 Appearance; 3 Normal; 4 Base Font; 5 Print Color: 0

11. Select Appearance (2 or A). The following menu appears:

    1 Bold 2 Undln 3 Dbl Und 4 Italic 5 Outln 6 Shadw 7 Sm Cap 8 Redln 9 Stkout: 0

12. Select Dbl Und (3 or D).

13. Type the following text:

```
He will be sending you a memo regarding his meeting with the
venture capitalist by next Friday.
```

14. Press ⏎ to end the double underlining. How double underlining appears on screen depends upon your monitor.

You have now inserted three types of attribute codes in your document – for italics, very large type size, and double underlining. In addition, remember that you also inserted a Base Font code in the text so that the top and bottom portions of the text are governed by different fonts. You can print the document to see how the font and attribute changes will take effect at the printer. Or, use the View Document feature (discussed in Chapter 9) to preview how the text will appear on the printed page before you actually print; if your monitor has graphics capabilities, you can see the font attribute changes on screen.

Keep in mind that a font attribute is based on both the printer and the currently selected font. Therefore, an attribute for one font may appear different for another font, even for the same printer. For example, Figure 10-5 shows a printout of FINANCE with an HP LaserJet Series II printer using Courier font throughout. The words "venture capitalist" in the first bulleted item were set for italics, a phrase in the second bulleted item was set to very large type size, and the last sentence was set to double underlining. Figure 10-6 shows the same document, using the same printer, but using a Century Schoolbook font. Notice that "venture capitalist" is underlined rather than changed to

I talked to John Samsone on January 3rd about our financial situation. He reported the following highlights:

o  He is meeting with a <u>venture capitalist</u> next week who is interested in investing with us.

o  Our debt stands at $159,000 as of December 31st, **10% lower than we anticipated.** Financial forecasts project that we'll be out of debt in two years time. Here are the debt figures (in thousands):

Amount Owed                    Name of Bank

  $48.5                      Floyd Interstate
    9.8                         Center Bank
  100.7                      Bank of Stevenson

For more detail, call him at (415) 333-9215. <u>He will be sending you a memo regarding his meeting with the venture capitalist by next Friday.</u>

**FIGURE 10-5**  Printed page using Courier as the base font

italics in Figure 10-5. On the other hand, the same words are changed to italics in Figure 10-6. For this specific printer, italics is unavailable in Courier but available in Century Schoolbook.

I talked to John Samsone on January 3rd about our financial situation. He reported the following highlights:

o  He is meeting with a *venture capitalist* next week who is interested in investing with us.

o  Our debt stands at $159,000 as of December 31st, **10% lower than we anticipated**. Financial forecasts project that we'll be out of debt in two years time. Here are the debt figures (in thousands):

Amount Owed                    Name of Bank

  $48.5                      Floyd Interstate
    9.8                         Center Bank
  100.7                      Bank of Stevenson

For more detail, call him at (415) 333-9215. <u>He will be sending you a memo regarding his meeting with the venture capitalist by next Friday.</u>

**FIGURE 10-6**  Printed page using Century Schoolbook as the base font

# ADJUST THE CHARACTER SPACING

In addition to allowing different fonts and font attributes for your text, WordPerfect also offers the ability to refine the spacing between characters and between lines of text. The features available include Line Height, Kerning, Word and Letter Spacing, and Word Spacing Justification Limits. Keep in mind that these features are available to you only if supported by your printer.

## Line Height

Line height is the amount of vertical space allotted to each line, measured from the bottom (baseline) of one line to the bottom of the next. WordPerfect assigns a line-height measurement to each font and each font attribute available for your printer. As an example, when you are using a font with the standard type size of 12 points, most printers are assigned a line height equal to approximately 0.167″, so that there are six lines of text to one vertical inch of space on a page.

By default, line height is set automatically, meaning it adjusts automatically for each font or font attribute in your text. For instance, if you change from a 12-point to a 30-point font, the line height is increased. Look to Figure 10-1 for examples. Instead, you can request that your line height be evenly spaced regardless of the fonts or attributes you are using. Move the cursor to where you want to change the line-height setting. Press the FORMAT ( Shift + F8 ) key and select Line (1 or L) to display the Line Format menu. [*Pulldown menu:* Layout (L), Line (L).] Next to the heading "Line Height," WordPerfect indicates the default setting, which is Auto (automatic). Select Line Height (4 or H) and WordPerfect offers two choices:

1 Auto; 2 Fixed: 0

Select Fixed (2 or F) and WordPerfect displays the current line height, such as 0.167″. Press Enter to accept that suggestion or type in a line-height setting of your own and press Enter. WordPerfect inserts a Line Height code that indicates the new measurement, such as **[Ln Height:0.2″]**. This code affects text from the current cursor position forward. Or, select Auto (1 or A) and WordPerfect inserts a Line Height code **[Ln Height:Auto]** that returns line height to the default setting from the cursor position. Press EXIT ( F7 ) to return to the Typing screen.

Be aware that some printers do not support varying line heights. Thus, on some printers, changing the line height will have no effect on your printed results.

A feature related to line height is Baseline Placement for Typesetters. WordPerfect normally places the *top* of the first line of text even with the top margin so that no text prints within the top margin. As a result, the baseline of the first line of text is below the top margin. Consequently, the baseline will vary when the font is altered in the text, resulting in problems when you wish to place characters precisely on the page relative to the first baseline.

You can make sure that the baseline remains constant. To do so, specify that you want a fixed height, as previously described. Then, set the *bottom* of the first line of text even with the top margin; to do so, press the FORMAT ( Shift + F8 ) key, and select Other (4 or O) to display the Other Format menu. [*Pulldown menu:* Layout (L), Other (O)]. Now select Printer Functions (6 or P) to display the menu shown in Figure 10-7. From the Printer Functions menu, select Baseline Placement for Typesetters (5 or B), and type **Y** for Yes. Now, the first baseline on the page will remain constant, regardless of font.

*5.1 users only:* Leading is another feature related to line height. Leading is the extra white space added between lines of text. In WordPerfect version 5.1, the default setting is for 2 points of leading to be automatically added for proportionally spaced fonts, and no leading to be added for monospaced (since the leading is already built in). In version 5.0, leading varies from font to font, and cannot be altered from within WordPerfect.

In version 5.1, you can alter the default leading, both for lines that end with Soft Return **[SRt]** codes, which are those within paragraphs, or for lines that end with Hard Return **[HRt]** codes, useful for lines that separate paragraphs. To do so, return to the Printer Functions menu, as shown in Figure 10-7.

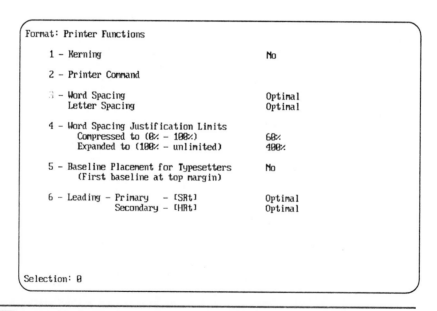

FIGURE 10-7  Printer Functions menu (version 5.1)

From the Printer Functions menu in version 5.1, select Leading Adjustment (6 or L). Now enter a leading adjustment of your own. You can enter this measurement in inches, although you may wish to enter the leading measurement in points. To do so, type in a number and then type **p**. For instance, enter **4p** to set a 4-point leading. (You can enter all measurements in WordPerfect in points; see "Units of Measurement" in Appendix B for a complete discussion.)

# Kerning

Kerning allows for reduction in the space between specific pairs of letters. It is commonly used in large-sized fonts to eliminate excessive white space between letters, such as the space between the "A" and "V" in "BRAVE." (When kerned, the word looks like this: "BRAVE") Kerning often makes it easier to read a heading. Be aware, however, that kerning may or may not be available for fonts used with your printer. Moreover, kerning in WordPerfect relates only to proportionally spaced fonts. You can switch to a proportionally spaced font, turn on kerning, and then print your document to see whether or not it is supported.

If the printer and font you are using support kerning, position the cursor where you want the kerning to begin, press the FORMAT ([Shift] + [F8]) key, and select Other (4 or O). [*Pulldown menu:* Layout (L), Other (O).] Then select Printer Functions (6 or P). The Printer Functions menu appears as shown in Figure 10-7. (5.0 users will not see all of the items on this menu.) Select Kerning (1 or K) and then type either **Y** to turn it on or **N** to turn it off. A **[Kern:On]** or **[Kern:Off]** code is inserted at the current cursor position, affecting text from that point forward.

# Word and Letter Spacing

The Word and Letter Spacing feature adjusts the spacing between neighboring words and letters. WordPerfect Corporation has set what it considers to be the optimal spacing between words and letters for each font available with your printer. However, if your printer supports this feature, you can adjust the spacing yourself.

Position the cursor where you want the change in word and/or letter spacing to begin, press the FORMAT ( Shift + F8 ) key, select Other (4 or O), and then select Printer Functions (6 or P). As shown in Figure 10-7, the default setting is for "Optimal" word and letter spacing. Select Word and Letter Spacing (3 or W) and WordPerfect displays the following menu:

```
Word Spacing: 1 Normal; 2 Optimal; 3 Percent of Optimal;
4 Set Pitch; 2
```

In addition to Optimal, your options are Normal, the spacing that looks best according to the printer manufacturer (which, for some printers, is the same as the Optimal setting); Percent of Optimal, which allows you to set your own spacing—100% is comparable to using the Optimal setting, so that numbers less than 100% reduce the space, and numbers greater than 100% increase the space; and Set Pitch, which allows you to set spacing at an exact pitch, such as 10 or 12 characters per inch. The pitch setting is then converted by WordPerfect to a percentage of the Optimal setting.

Select an option and, if you selected options 3 or 4, enter in a word spacing measurement. WordPerfect then displays an identical menu for letter spacing. Again select an option and enter a letter spacing measurement if prompted to do so. Now press EXIT (F7) to return to your document.

WordPerfect inserts a code at the current cursor position, such as **[Wrd/Ltr Spacing:Normal,Normal]**, which affects all text from that code forward. You can now print your document to view the result.

## Word Spacing Justification Limits

If your document is set for full justification, then WordPerfect assumes that the space between words can be compressed by 60% or expanded by 400% to produce an even right margin. (Refer to Chapter 4 for a review of the Justification feature and how to turn it on or off.) Once these compression and expansion limits are reached, then and only then will WordPerfect adjust spacing between characters. However, assuming that your printer supports it, you can change these compression and expansion limits for a document, fine-tuning justification for your printer.

Position the cursor where you want to change the justification limits, press the FORMAT (Shift + F8) key, select Other (4 or O), and then select Printer Functions (6 or P). As shown in Figure 10-7, the default setting is for 60% compression and 400% expansion. Select Word Spacing Justification Limits (4 or J) and then enter numbers representing a compression and expansion percentage. Press EXIT (F7) to return to the document.

WordPerfect inserts a Justification Limit code into the text listing both percentages, such as **[Just lim:75,700]**. The larger the percentage, the more flexibility WordPerfect has in adjusting spacing between words. WordPerfect considers an expansion percentage of anything over 999% as an unlimited expansion ability.

# INSERT GRAPHICS LINES

WordPerfect has the ability to insert horizontal or vertical graphics lines—of any thickness or shading—anywhere on a page. You can use graphics lines, for example, to separate headings from text, to separate columns, or to border a page. Your printer must support graphics in order to print these lines.

To insert a graphics line, position the cursor where you wish to create a line and press the GRAPHICS ( Alt + F9 ) key. [*Pulldown menu:* Graphics (G).] The Graphics menu is displayed (5.0 users will see only the first five items):

1 Figure; 2 Table Box; 3 Text Box; 4 User-defined Box; 5 Line;
6 Equation: 0

Select Line (5 or L) and the following menu displays:

Create Line: 1 Horizontal; 2 Vertical; Edit Line: 3 Horizontal;
4 Vertical: 0

When you select Horizontal Line (1 or H), the menu shown in Figure 10-8 appears. (Version 5.0 users won't see the "Vertical Position" option.) You can now define the loca-

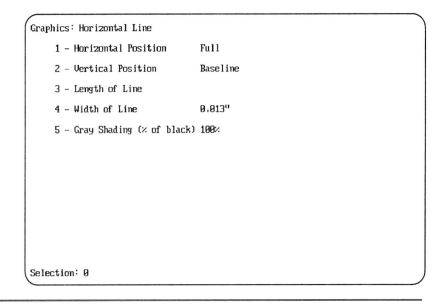

**FIGURE 10-8** Horizontal Line Graphics menu

tion and dimensions of the horizontal line you desire as follows:

- *Horizontal Position* WordPerfect assumes that you want to position the line horizontally beginning at the left margin and ending at the right margin, referred to as "Full" in version 5.1 and "Left & Right" in version 5.0. Instead, you can position the line beginning at the left margin, ending at the right margin, centered between margins, or, by selecting the Set Position option, at a specific position from the left edge of the page. If you select the Set Position option, WordPerfect displays the cursor's current horizontal position. For example, if the status line indicates that the cursor is located at Pos 1″ just before you display the Graphics menu, then when you select Set Position, WordPerfect responds

```
Offset from left edge of page: 1"
```

Press (Enter) to accept this suggestion, or type in another horizontal position.

- *Vertical Position*   WordPerfect assumes that you want the graphics line to be aligned with the baseline (bottom) of the line where the cursor is located when you display the Graphics menu. *5.1 users:* You can instead select Set Position to specify a specific position from the top edge of the page; WordPerfect will display the cursor's current vertical position. Type in another horizontal position and press (Enter). *5.0 users:* You cannot alter the vertical position option, and therefore, it is important for 5.0 users to position the cursor on the line where the line is to appear before displaying the Graphics menu.

- *Length of Line*   If the horizontal position is set as Full (version 5.1) or Left & Right (version 5.0), then the length of line is automatically calculated as the distance between the left and right margins and cannot be altered. If the horizontal position is set to another option, then the line length is set as the current cursor position up to the margin specified with the horizontal position option. You can accept the suggestion or enter a length measurement of your own.

- *Width of Line*   WordPerfect assumes that you want a line 0.013" (version 5.1) or 0.01" (version 5.0) wide (thick). You can specify a different line thickness. In fact, if you enter a very large measurement, then you can define a shaded rectangle rather than a line. The bottom of the line stays in the same position, and the line expands upward.

(However, 5.1 users who change the Vertical Position option from "Baseline" to a specific position will find that it is the top of the line that stays in the same position, and the line expands down.)

- *Gray Shading* WordPerfect assumes that the shading should be 100% to produce a black line. The lower the percentage entered, the lighter the gray shading.

If you make no changes on the menu shown in Figure 10-8, then WordPerfect will assume you wish to insert a black line, 0.013″ (5.1 users) or 0.01″ (5.0 users) thick, from the left margin to the right at the baseline of the line where the cursor is located, as follows:

———————————————————————————————

Once you press EXIT (F7) to return to the Typing screen, a hidden code is inserted. *5.1 users:* The hidden code **[HLine:Full,Baseline,6.5″,0.013″ 100%]** is inserted (assuming that the distance between the margins is 6.5″, as is the case for the default margin settings). *5.0 users:* The code is **[HLine:Left&Right,6.5″,0.01″,100%]**. If you change any of the options on the Horizontal Line Graphics menu, then the changes are reflected in the hidden code.

When you select Vertical Line (2 or V), the menu shown in Figure 10-9 appears. You can now define the location and dimensions of the vertical line as follows:

- *Horizontal Position* WordPerfect assumes you want to position the line horizontally slightly to the left of the left margin, referred to as "Left Margin." Instead, you can position the line slightly to the right of the right margin, between any two text columns by specifying the number of the first column (refer to Chapter 11 for a discussion of the text column feature), or, with the Set Position option, at a specific position from the left edge of the page. If you select the Set Position option, WordPerfect suggests the cursor's current horizontal position.

- *Vertical Position*  WordPerfect assumes that you want to position the line vertically beginning at the top margin and ending at the bottom margin, referred to as "Full Page." Instead, you can position the line beginning at the top margin, ending against the bottom margin, centered between the top and bottom margins, or at a specific position from the top edge of the page.

- *Length of Line*  If the vertical position is set as "Full Page," then the length of line is automatically calculated as the distance between the top and bottom margins and cannot be altered. If the vertical position is set to another option, then the line length is set as the current cursor position up to the margin specified as the Vertical Position option. You can accept the suggestion or enter a length measurement of your own.

- *Width of Line*  WordPerfect assumes that you want a line 0.013″ (version 5.1) or 0.01″ (version 5.0) wide (thick). You can specify a different line thickness. In fact, if you enter a large measurement, then you will be defining a shaded rectangle rather than a line. The left edge of the line stays in the same position, and the line expands to the right.

- *Gray Shading*  WordPerfect assumes that the shading should be 100% to produce a black line. The lower the percentage entered, the lighter the gray shading.

If you make no changes on the menu shown in Figure 10-9, then WordPerfect will assume you wish to insert a black line, 0.013" (version 5.1) or 0.01" (version 5.0) thick, all the way from the top margin to the bottom margin on the page, just to the left of the left margin.

When you press EXIT ([F7]) to return to the Typing screen, the hidden code **[VLine:Left Margin,Full Page, 9",0.013",100%]** is inserted (assuming that the distance between the top/bottom margins is 9", as is the case for the default margin settings). If you change any of the options on the Vertical Line Graphics menu, then the changes are reflected in the hidden code.

Be aware that a graphics line—whether horizontal or vertical—is never displayed on the Typing screen. It is displayed on the printed page, or it is displayed using the

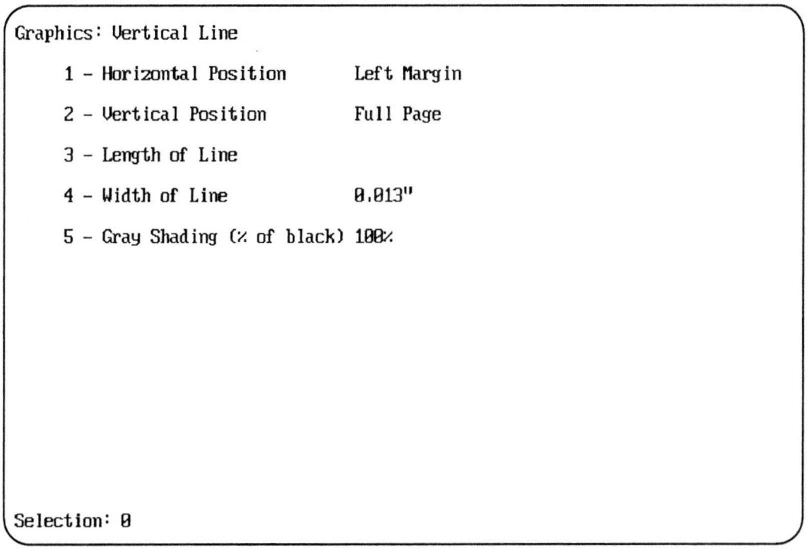

```
Graphics: Vertical Line

     1 - Horizontal Position       Left Margin

     2 - Vertical Position         Full Page

     3 - Length of Line

     4 - Width of Line             0.013"

     5 - Gray Shading (% of black) 100%




Selection: 0
```

**FIGURE 10-9** Vertical Line Graphics menu

View Document feature (as described in Chapter 9) providing that you use a monitor that can display graphics. If you insert a graphics line, be careful not to also type text in the same location, or you'll overwrite text with the graphics line when the document is printed.

Also keep in mind that a graphics line will print only if your printer supports graphics. Moreover, even if your printer can print graphics lines, it may not be able to support shading other than 100% (black). If your printer does not support graphics, then an alternative for inserting lines on a page is the Line Draw feature. Line Draw (discussed in Chapter 15, "WordPerfect Extras") allows you to draw lines and outlines of boxes using special characters.

As an example of inserting graphics lines in text, suppose you wish to create letterhead in WordPerfect where you insert a black line 0.03″ thick just below your name and address. Proceed as follows:

1. Clear the screen and make sure that the cursor is positioned at the top of the document.

2. Center your (or your company's) name and address. You may wish to select a fancy font or font attribute for the name and address. (You may also wish to move to the top of the document and alter margins.)

3. Position the cursor two blank lines below the address.

4. Press the GRAPHICS (⌐Alt⌐ + ⌐F9⌐) key. [*Pulldown menu:* Graphics (G).] WordPerfect responds with the Graphics menu:

   1 Figure; 2 Table Box; 3 Text Box; 4 User-defined Box; 5 Line;
   6 Equation: 0

5. Select Line (5 or L) and another menu displays:

   Create Line: 1 Horizontal; 2 Vertical; Edit Line: 3 Horizontal;
   4 Vertical: 0

6. Select Horizontal Line (1 or H). The full screen menu shown in Figure 10-8 appears.

7. Select Width of Line (4 or W for 5.1 users, 3 or W for 5.0 users).

8. Type **.03″** and press (Enter).

9. Press EXIT ((F7)) to return to your document.

The hidden code **[HLine:Full,Baseline,6.5″,0.03″,100%]** for 5.1 users or **[HLine:Left & Right,6.5″,0.03″,100%]** for 5.0 users is inserted in the text. The horizontal line is not displayed on the Typing screen. You can see the result of your efforts, however, by printing the page or by using the View Document feature (as described in Chapter 9). If you have a printer that supports graphics, you can get results as shown in Figure 10-10.

Once a graphics line is in your text, you can delete the line by deleting the corresponding code—just like you delete any WordPerfect code. Or you can edit the line. To edit a graphics line, position the cursor to the right or below the graphics line code for that line, return to the Graphics Line menu, and select Edit Horizontal Line (3 or O) or Edit Vertical Line (4 or E). WordPerfect searches backward in the text for the first graphics line of the type you specified, either horizontal or vertical. Then the Graphics Line menu for that particular line is displayed. Edit any of the options and then press EXIT (F7) to return to the Typing screen.

# INSERT GRAPHICS BOXES

In addition to inserting graphics lines, WordPerfect also supports the inclusion of graphics boxes in your text. These boxes can remain empty or can contain either text or

R&R Wine Association
3345 Whitemore Drive, #505
San Francisco, CA 94123

**FIGURE 10-10**  Letterhead: graphics line below the address

graphics images. *5.1 users:* These boxes can also contain equations.

## Create a Graphics Box

To create a graphics box, you must position the cursor where you wish to insert a box. This will depend on how you want the box situated on a page. If you want a box associated with a particular paragraph, position the cursor within that paragraph; if your document is edited later on, the graphics box will move with the paragraph. If you want a box treated like any character, position the cursor precisely in the line of text where you want the box to appear. If you want a box placed at a fixed position on the page, position the cursor at the top of that page—above any text that you may have already typed on that page. (You can also insert boxes into headers, footers, footnotes, and endnotes.)

Once you have positioned the cursor, press the GRAPHICS ( Alt + F9 ) key. [*Pulldown menu:* Graphics (G).] The Graphics menu is displayed:

1 Figure; 2 Table Box; 3 Text Box; 4 User-defined Box; 5 Line; 6 Equation: 0

Now you can select from five different styles for inserting a graphics box into your text: figure, table, text, user-defined, or equation. (The Line option on the Graphics menu is for creating graphics lines rather than graphics boxes, as discussed previously in this chapter. Also, 5.0 users will see only the first five items on the Graphics menu. You have all but the equation style available and should thus ignore the mention of equation box styles in the following discussion.)

The style of a box does *not* determine the contents of that box. For instance, you can create a figure box that contains text, or a text box that contains an equation. What the box style does determine is

- How WordPerfect will number that box. All boxes are numbered separately. So, in your text, you may have four figure boxes and three user-defined boxes. WordPerfect keeps track of two sets of boxes. As a result, you can generate a list of captions for each box style; more on generating lists in Chapter 15.

- The default settings for that box. For instance, figures will be printed with a single-line border around the text or image, while user-defined boxes will be printed with no borders. As another example, figures are numbered with Arabic numerals (Figure 1, and so on), while table boxes are numbered with Roman numerals (Table I, and so on). You can, of course, change the default options for any of the graphics box styles; the method for doing so is described farther on in this chapter.

Thus, you can select any box style, regardless of what you plan to insert into that box. But it is a good idea to be consistent when choosing a box style. For instance, if you wish to number boxes consecutively in a document, select the same box style for each box you create. Or, you may wish to abide by the style of box that each name suggests — using the figure box style only for graphics images and diagrams, the table box style for tables of text or statistical data, the text box style for quotes or sidebars, the equation style for scientific equations, and the user-defined box style for images or text that you want set apart from the rest of the document but that don't fall into any of the other box style categories.

From the Graphics menu, select an option to create a box of a certain style. A menu for that box style then appears on screen. For instance, if you selected the Figure option, WordPerfect displays

Figure: 1 Create; 2 Edit; 3 New Number; 4 Options: 0

Select Create (1 or C). WordPerfect displays a full-screen Definition menu for that box style. If the box style is "Figure," for example then the menu shown in Figure 10-11 displays (Version 5.0 users will see all but the Contents option.) You can now define the image, location, and dimensions of the graphics box.

- *Filename*  This option allows you to specify a file—containing either a graphics image, an equation, or text (which must be less than one page in length)—that you wish to place into the graphics box.

  WordPerfect will prompt for a filename. Specify a filename by typing in the name of the file you wish to retrieve, preceded by the proper drive/directory if that file is not stored in the default graphics drive/directory. *5.1 users:* The default is the drive/directory specified for graphics files in the Setup menu; see "Location of Files" in Appendix B. *5.0 users:* The default graphics drive/directory is the same as the default drive/directory for all of your documents.

  Or, specify a filename by using the LIST ([F5]) key to display a list of files, and then, from the List Files screen, positioning the cursor on the file you wish to retrieve and pressing Retrieve (1 or R).

  Once you specify a filename, WordPerfect determines the format of the file, whether text or graphics, and, providing that the format is acceptable, retrieves the file into the box. Acceptable formats include: text in Word-

```
Definition: Figure

        1 - Filename

        2 - Contents           Empty

        3 - Caption

        4 - Anchor Type         Paragraph

        5 - Vertical Position   0"

        6 - Horizontal Position Right

        7 - Size                3.25" wide x 3.25" (high)

        8 - Wrap Text Around Box Yes

        9 - Edit




Selection: 0
```

**FIGURE 10-11**   Figure Definition menu

Perfect format, text in DOS format, or graphics in any of the WordPerfect-supported graphics formats, which are listed in Table 10-1. Should the format of the file be inconsistent with what WordPerfect can accept, an error message displays

In addition to placing text into a graphics box by retrieving a file, you can also insert text by typing directly into the graphics box. To do so, bypass the Filename option and, instead, select the Edit option, as described below.

Or, you can leave the graphics box empty, and paste a photo or logo into that location on the printed page.

- *Contents (5.1 users only)*   This option determines the format of the information in the box. You have the following choices:

  *Graphics*   This is the default setting whenever you retrieve a file containing a graphics image into a box.

| WordPerfect-Supported Graphics Format | Graphics Programs That Can Create This Format* |
|---|---|
| Computer Graphics MetaFile (CGM) | Arts & Letters, Freelance Plus, Framework II, Graphwriter, Harvard Graphics, Pictur-ePaks, PlanPerfect (for versions of PlanPerfect before version 4.0, obtain the graphics driver named META.SYS from WordPerfect Corporation), Pixie, Lotus 1-2-3 |
| Dr. Halo PIC Format (DHP) | Dr. Halo II, III |
| AutoCAD Format (DXF) | AutoCAD, AutoSketch |
| Encapsulated PostScript (EPS) | Adobe Illustrator, Harvard Graphics, Quattro, Chemtext, GRAFPLUS |
| Hewlett-Packard Graphics Language Plotter File (HPGL) | Anvil-5000, Harvard Graphics, AutoCAD, AutoSketch, IBM CBDS, IBM CATIA, IBM GPG, SlideWrite Plus, Microsoft Chart, VersaCAD, IBM CADAM, IBM CDDM, Graph-in-the-Box, Diagram-Master, Chart-Master, CCS Designer, SignMaster, Diagraph, Generic CADD, Chemfile, Easyflow, Windows Draw, VP Graphics, Schema, Mirage, GRAFPLUS |
| GEM Paint Format (IMG) | GEM Scan, DFI Handy Scanner, Boeing Graph, GEM Paint, EnerGraphics |
| Tagged Image File Format (TIFF) | GEM Scan, DFI Handy Scanner, GEM Paint, EnerGraphics, SlideWrite Plus, CIES (Compuscan), HP Graphics Gallery, HP Scanning Gallery, VGA Paint, Scan Man, GeniScan |

*Some programs can be saved in more than one graphics format.

**TABLE 10-1**  WordPerfect-Supported Graphics Formats

| WordPerfect-Supported Graphics Format | Graphics Programs That Can Create This Format |
|---|---|
| Microsoft Windows Paint Format (MSP) | Windows Paint |
| PC Paintbrush Format (PCX) | PC Paintbrush, SlideWrite Plus, HP Graphics Gallery, HP Scanning Gallery, PicturePaks, PFS: First Publishing Pizazz, Lotus 1-2-3 |
| Lotus 1-2-3 Format (PIC) | Symphony, VP Planner, SuperCalc 4, Words & Figures, Lotus 1-2-3, Quattro, Reflex, Paradox |
| MacPaint Format (PNTG) | MacPaint |
| PC Paint Plus Format (PPIC) | PC Paint Plus |
| WordPerfect Graphics Format (WPG) | PicturePaks, VGA Paint, Hotshot, HIJAAK |

**TABLE 10-1**   WordPerfect-Supported Graphics Formats (*continued*)

*Graphics on Disk*   The graphics image will be kept in a separate file on disk rather than being saved with the document—useful for conserving space in a document if you will be inserting the same graphics image many times into the same document and necessary if you intend to insert the graphics box in a style (Chapter 14 describes the Styles feature). You can choose Contents (2 or O) and specify the Graphics on Disk item before or after you retrieve the graphics image.

*Text*   This is the default setting whenever you retrieve a file containing text into a box or whenever you type text directly into a box.

*Equation*   Should you wish to retrieve an equation into a box or type an equation directly into a box, it is critical to choose Contents (2 or O) and specify the Equation option first; if you do not, WordPerfect will assume that the file contains text and not an equation. (5.1 users who wish to learn more about the Equation feature for inserting equations into a graphics box should turn to Chapter 15.)

- *Caption*   WordPerfect assumes you want no caption accompanying a graphics box. You can add a caption easily by selecting the Caption option. WordPerfect automatically inserts the default caption for that box style and shows it on a Box Caption screen.

  Assume that you are creating your first graphics box. For a figure, the default caption style is "Figure 1"; for a table, "Table I"; for a text or user-defined box, simply "1"; and for an equation box, "(1)". WordPerfect assumes that all captions will number the boxes consecutively and be boldfaced. If you reveal codes while looking at the caption WordPerfect inserted, you'll discover that the default caption is actually a code. The code inserted is **[Box Num]**.

  You can accept WordPerfect's suggested caption by not editing it on the Caption screen. (You can change the default caption or its location using the Options item; for details, see "Change Graphics Box Default Options" later in this chapter.)

Or, you can edit the caption, perhaps adding a phrase after the code, so that, for example, the caption can read "Figure 1 -- Diagram of Distribution Centers". Or, you can delete the code and insert your own caption, which is useful if you don't want captions to number each box. For instance, you can delete the code and then type a phrase so that the caption reads simply "Diagram of Distribution Centers". If you delete the default caption and then decide to reinstate it, press GRAPHICS ( Alt + F9 ).

Once you are satisfied with the box caption, press EXIT to exit the Caption screen.

- *Anchor Type*   This option allows you to indicate how a graphics box will be anchored to the surrounding text. The type of anchor you select determines how Word-Perfect will situate that graphics box on the page and how the box will move if you later edit your text.

   *Paragraph Type*   This is the anchor type that Word-Perfect assumes, and means that the box will remain with the paragraph with which it is associated. If the paragraph is so close to the bottom of the page that the graphics box cannot fit, the box will be moved to the top of the next page.

   *Page Type*   This type treats the box as part of the page, and you can specify a fixed position on the page where the box will remain using the Vertical and Horizontal Position options, as described below. Make sure to position the cursor at the top of a page, before any text, prior to creating a graphics box with a page anchor; otherwise, WordPerfect will bump the graphics box to the next page. When selecting the page type, version 5.1 users also have the option of selecting how many pages to skip before inserting the graphics box. For instance, enter **0** as the number of pages to be skipped if you want the box to be inserted on the current page; or enter **1** if you want the box to appear on the next page.

*Character Type* This type treats the box like any other character, so that the box appears exactly where the cursor was positioned when you created the box. Any text that follows the box will be wrapped below the box. Character type anchors are useful when placing equations in a line and are the only type allowed in footnotes and endnotes.

- *Vertical Position* This option establishes the graphics box's position vertically on the page and this is dependent on the graphics box anchor type.

  If you have selected a paragraph-type box, WordPerfect assumes that the box is to be inserted on the line where the cursor was located when you began to create the box. You can instead enter a value measured from the top line of the paragraph. For instance, to start the box even with the first line of the paragraph, enter a value of 0″.

  If you have selected a Page-type box, WordPerfect assumes that the box should be aligned with the top margin of the page. You can instead choose that the box occupy the full page, be centered on the page, be aligned with the bottom margin of the page, or be situated at a specific position from the top of the page with the Set Position option. If you select Set Position, WordPerfect suggests the cursor's current vertical position.

If you selected a character-type box, WordPerfect assumes that the text on the same line as the box should be aligned with the bottom of the box. You can instead choose to align the text with the top or center of the box.

*5.1 users only:* You can also specify that the baseline of an equation be aligned with the text on the same line as the box or, for text, that the baseline of the last line of text in the box be aligned with the text outside the box on the same line. To do so, select the Baseline option.

- *Horizontal Position*  This option establishes the graphics box's position horizontally on the page, which, like the vertical position, is dependent on the graphics box anchor type.

  If you have selected a paragraph-type box, WordPerfect assumes that the box should be aligned at the right margin. You can instead align the box at the left margin, in the center between the left and right margins, or stretch the box to fill the area from the left to the right margin by selecting the Full option.

  If you have selected a page-type box, WordPerfect assumes you wish to align the box with the right margin. You can instead align the box with the left margin, with the center, or stretch the box to fill the area from the left to the right margin. You can also align the box between text columns. First indicate a column or a range of columns (such as 1-3) and then align the box with the left margin, with the right margin, with the center, or stretch the box to fill the area from the left to the right margin of the column or range of columns. (See Chapter 11 for a discussion on creating text columns. When you choose to center a graphics box between two columns, text will flow around *both* sides of the box.) You can also set the box at a specific position from the left edge of the page.

If you have selected a character-type box, then the horizontal position is already set by the location of the cursor when you began to create the graphics box. You cannot specify another position.

- *Size* This option sets the height and/or width of the graphics box. The default setting is determined automatically by WordPerfect based on the shape of the graphics image or text to be inserted in the box and the options you selected for the horizontal and vertical position of the box. You can change the default setting by specifying a particular width, in which case WordPerfect calculates the height to preserve the graphic image's original shape; specifying a particular height, in which case WordPerfect calculates the width; or by specifying both a width and height.

- *Wrap Text Around Box* WordPerfect assumes that text should always wrap around graphics boxes. You can instead choose that text not wrap around graphics boxes.

    Setting this option to N is useful when you wish to print text on top of a graphics box (such as when the graphics box contains a border) or to superimpose a graphics box on top of another. For instance, suppose that you wish to superimpose a graphics box containing an image of an arrow on top of another graphics box containing an image of a map. Create the graphics box for the map, and then either use the View Document feature or print out the document in order to figure out where you want the arrow to appear. Then, use the Advance feature (as described in Chapter 9) to reposition the cursor where you want the arrow to appear and create the second box, which will contain the arrow. You will set the "Wrap Text Around Box" for the first box to N and for the second box to Y.

- *Edit* This option has three functions. If the graphics box is empty or it contains text, then when you select the Edit option WordPerfect displays a Typing screen for you to enter or edit text. Left and right margins are adjusted to conform with the width of the graphics box. You can enhance text using the Center, Flush Right, Bold, Underline, Base Font, and Font Attribute features, among others. Press EXIT ( F7 ) to return to the Definition screen.

  If the graphics box contains a graphics image, then when you select the Edit option, you can rotate, scale, or move the image, as discussed in the next section.

  If the graphics box contains an equation, then the equation editor is displayed, as discussed in Chapter 15.

Once you have decided on the definition for the figure, table, text box, or user-defined box, press EXIT ( F7 ) to return to the Typing screen. A code is inserted in the text at the current cursor position or at the beginning of the current paragraph if the box is defined as a paragraph type. For instance, suppose you just defined your first figure in a document, which contains a graphics image that is stored in a file named BOOK.WPG. Then the code inserted is **[Figure: 1;BOOK.WPG]**. Or, if you inserted the same figure but also selected to insert the default caption, then **[Box Num]** is inserted in the code as follows: **[Figure: 1; BOOK.WPG [Box Num]]**. Or suppose you defined your first text box, inserting text directly into the box. The code inserted is **[Text Box:1;;]**.

Once a graphics box is created, what you see on screen depends on the box type you chose. If you created a paragraph or page box, an outline of the box begins to form as you type text on the same line where the graphics box was inserted. This outline takes full form as soon as you type all the text that will appear around the box. The top of the box outline indicates the box style and number. For instance, Figure 10-12 shows a box outline after the text has been typed around the box. "FIG 1" indicates that this box outline represents Figure 1. However, if you set the Wrap Text Around Box option to No, the box outline won't appear. If you created a character-type box, then a highlighted rectangle the size of one character appears. With a character-type box, you can't see how much space the graphics box will occupy while viewing the Typing screen.

Whatever type of graphics box you create, the text or image inside the box does not appear on the Typing screen. To view the document showing the text and contents of all graphics boxes, use the View Document feature; however,

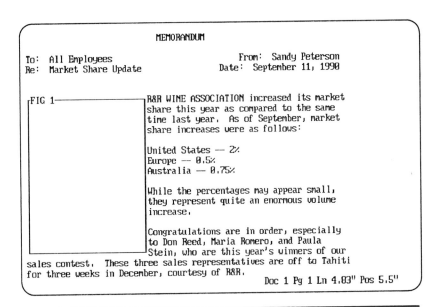

**FIGURE 10-12**  Figure box outline in the text

it takes a monitor that supports graphics to clearly view a box containing a graphics image. You could also print the document; but again, your printer must support graphics to print out a graphics image.

## Insert a Graphics Image

Where do you find a graphics image to insert into a graphics box? One possibility is to use another software package that produces graphics. Table 10-1 lists the graphics formats supported by WordPerfect. (More graphics programs are added to this list all the time.) You can create a graphics image using any of the graphics software packages indicated and save it into a WordPerfect-supported format. For instance, you can use Lotus 1-2-3 to create a pie chart and store it on disk in Lotus's PIC format. Or use Harvard Graphics to create a bar graph and store it on disk in CGM format. Or use AutoCAD to draw a diagram and store it on disk in HPGL format. Then load WordPerfect and retrieve that pie chart, bar graph, or diagram into a WordPerfect graphics box. (If your graphics software package is not listed in Table 10-1, then you may still be able to bring a graphics image into WordPerfect using GRAB.COM; see Chapter 15.)

If you don't currently own a graphics package, you can still incorporate graphics images into your document. WordPerfect Corporation has included 30 graphics images on the WordPerfect disks so that you can get started using graphics right away. These 30 images all have the filename extension .WPG. In 5.1, they were created by WordPerfect's DrawPerfect program. In 5.0 they are part of the

Publisher's PicturePaks series created by Marketing Graphics Inc. (MGI). Figure 10-13 illustrates all 30 images packaged in version 5.1. Figure 10-14 illustrates the version 5.0 images. (If you upgraded from version 5.0 to 5.1, you thus have 60 images available.) All are ready to be incorporated into a WordPerfect document at any time. *5.1 users:* you must have installed the Fonts/Graphics files in order to have access to the .WPG graphics images.

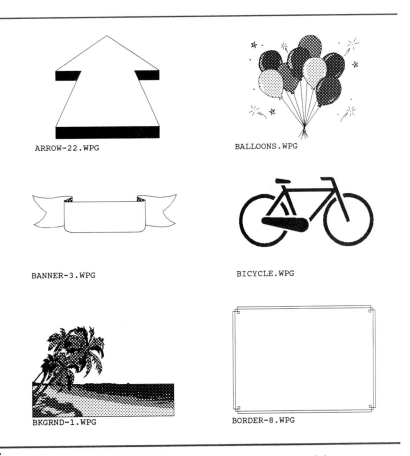

ARROW-22.WPG

BALLOONS.WPG

BANNER-3.WPG

BICYCLE.WPG

BKGRND-1.WPG

BORDER-8.WPG

**FIGURE 10-13** Graphics images included with version 5.1

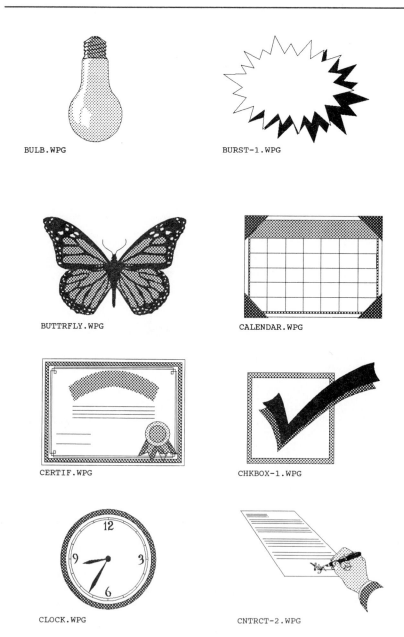

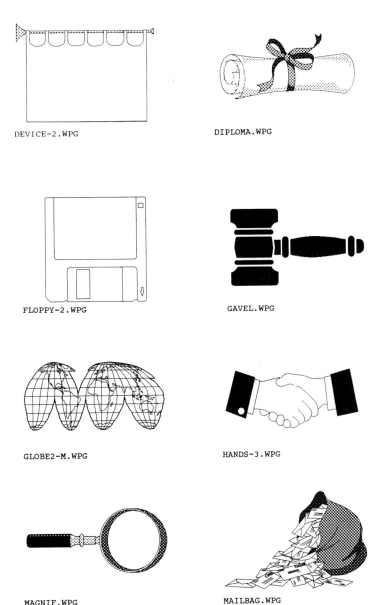

DEVICE-2.WPG

DIPLOMA.WPG

FLOPPY-2.WPG

GAVEL.WPG

GLOBE2-M.WPG

HANDS-3.WPG

MAGNIF.WPG

MAILBAG.WPG

**FIGURE 10-13**   Graphics images included with version 5.1 *(continued)*

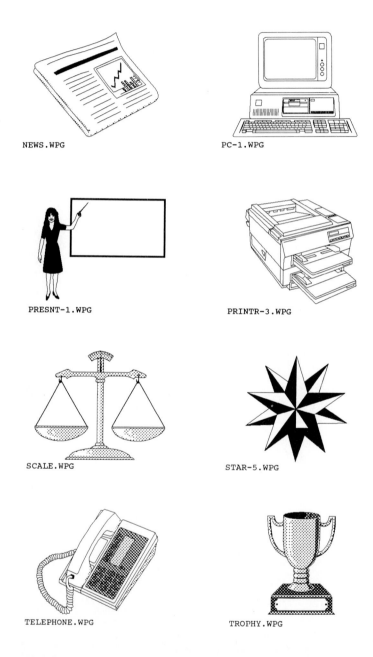

NEWS.WPG

PC-1.WPG

PRESNT-1.WPG

PRINTR-3.WPG

SCALE.WPG

STAR-5.WPG

TELEPHONE.WPG

TROPHY.WPG

**FIGURE 10-13** Graphics images included with version 5.1 *(continued)*

AIRPLANE.WPG

AND.WPG

ANNOUNCE.WPG

APPLAUSE.WPG

ARROW1.WPG

ARROW2.WPG

BADNEWS.WPG

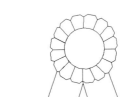

AWARD.WPG

**FIGURE 10-14** Graphics images included with version 5.0

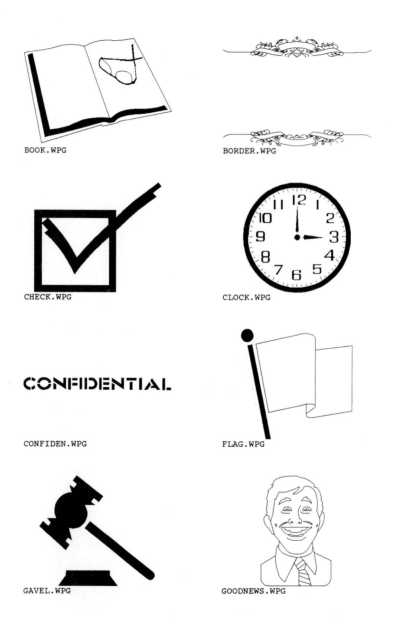

BOOK.WPG

BORDER.WPG

CHECK.WPG

CLOCK.WPG

CONFIDENTIAL

CONFIDEN.WPG

FLAG.WPG

GAVEL.WPG

GOODNEWS.WPG

**FIGURE 10-14**   Graphics images included with version 5.0 (*continued*)

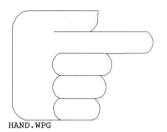

HAND.WPG

HOURGLAS.WPG

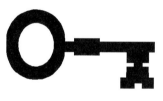

KEY.WPG

MAPSYMBL.WPG

NEWSPAPR.WPG

NO1.WPG

**FIGURE 10-14** Graphics images included with version 5.0 *(continued)*

PC.WPG

PENCIL.WPG

PHONE.WPG

PRESENT.WPG

QUILL.WPG

RPTCARD.WPG

**FIGURE 10-14**   Graphics images included with version 5.0 (*continued*)

THINKER.WPG

USAMAP.WPG

**FIGURE 10-14** Graphics images included with version 5.0 *(continued)*

## Practice with Graphics Boxes

As an example in incorporating graphics boxes into a document, let's create a document that contains a graphics image. *5.1 users:* You will create the document shown in Figure 10-15, which contains one of the DrawPerfect images stored on disk in the file named BALLOONS.WPG. *5.0 users:* You will create the document shown in Figure 10-16, which contains one of the PicturePaks images stored on disk in the file named APPLAUSE.WPG. Since the graph needs to stay with the first paragraph, we'll create a paragraph-type box. We'll also place the graphics box at the left margin and reduce the size of the graphics image.

1. On a clear screen, center **MEMORANDUM** and type the information following "To:", "From:", "Re:", and "Date:," as shown in Figure 10-15 or 10-16. (If you need

a refresher on how to center the title or position the "From:" and "Date:" headings flush against the right margin, refer to Chapter 3.)

2. Press `Enter` twice to position the cursor where the text of the memorandum is to begin.

3. Type the following paragraph:

R&R WINE ASSOCIATION increased its market share this year as compared to the same time last year. As of September, market share increases were as follows:

4. Use the `↑` and `←` keys to position the cursor anywhere within the paragraph you just typed.

5. Press the GRAPHICS (`Alt` + `F9`) key. [*Pulldown menu:* Graphics (G).] WordPerfect responds with

1 Figure; **2** Table Box; **3** Text Box; **4** User-defined Box; **5** Line; **6** Equation: **0**

---

MEMORANDUM

To: All Employees                     From:  Sandy Peterson
Re: Market Share Update               Date:  September 11, 1990

R&R WINE ASSOCIATION increased its market share this year as compared to the same time last year. As of September, market share increases were as follows:

United States -- 2%
Europe -- 0.5%
Australia -- 0.75%

While the percentages may appear small, they represent quite an enormous volume increase.

Congratulations are in order, especially to Don Reed, Maria Romero, and Paula Stein, who are this year's winners of our sales contest.  These three sales representatives are off to Tahiti for three weeks in December, courtesy of R&R.

---

**FIGURE 10-15**  Printed page: practice document merging text with graphics (version 5.1)

6. Select Figure (1 or F). The following menu appears:

   Figure: 1 Create; 2 Edit; 3 New Number; 4 Options: 0

7. Select Create (1 or C). Now the Figure Definition menu appears, as shown in Figure 10-11.

8. Select Filename (1 or F). WordPerfect prompts

   Enter Filename:

9. Enter the filename BALLOONS.WPG (5.1 users) or APPLAUSE.WPG (5.0 users), preceded by the drive or directory where this image can be found if not in the default. (Floppy disk users must place the Graphics disk that you installed in drive B before retrieving the image.) WordPerfect retrieves the image.

---

MEMORANDUM

To:  All Employees                    From:  Sandy Peterson
Re:  Market Share Update              Date:  September 11, 1990

R&R WINE ASSOCIATION increased its
market share this year as compared to
the same time last year.  As of
September, market share increases were
as follows:

United States -- 2%
Europe -- 0.5%
Australia -- 0.75%

While the percentages may appear small,
they represent quite an enormous volume
increase.

Congratulations are in order,
especially to Don Reed, Maria Romero,
and Paula Stein, who are this year's winners of our sales
contest.  These three sales representatives are off to Tahiti for
three weeks in December, courtesy of R&R.

---

**FIGURE 10-16**  Printed page: practice document merging text with graphics (version 5.0)

10. Notice that the default setting for the type of graphics box is Paragraph. Thus, this setting requires no modification.

11. Select Vertical Position (5 or V for 5.1 users, 4 or V for 5.0 users). Because the box is paragraph type, WordPerfect prompts

    ```
    Offset from top of paragraph:
    ```

    and suggests an offset based on the current location of the cursor in relation to the paragraph.

12. Type **0″** and press [Enter] so that the graphics box lines up evenly with the first sentence of this paragraph.

```
Definition: Figure

     1 - Filename           BALLOONS.WPG

     2 - Contents           Graphic

     3 - Caption

     4 - Anchor Type        Paragraph

     5 - Vertical Position  0"

     6 - Horizontal Position Left

     7 - Size               3.45" (wide) x 2.5" high

     8 - Wrap Text Around Box Yes

     9 - Edit



Selection: 0
```

**FIGURE 10-17**   Figure Definition menu with BALLOONS.WPG sized and positioned

13. Select Horizontal Position (6 or H for 5.1 users, 5 or H for 5.0 users). Because the box is paragraph type, WordPerfect prompts

    `Horizontal Position: 1 Left; 2 Right; 3 Center; 4 Full: 0`

14. Select Left (1 or L) to position the box at the left margin.

15. Select Size (7 or S for 5.1 users, 6 or S for 5.0 users).

16. Select Height/Auto Width (2 or H). WordPerfect prompts

    `Height =`

    and suggests the default height for that graphics image.

17. Type **2.5″** and press ⟨Enter⟩. WordPerfect automatically adjusts the width to keep the proper proportions for the graphics image. Your screen will now resemble Figure 10-17. (WordPerfect 5.0 users will see a slightly different screen: the filename will be APPLAUSE .WPG, there will be no Contents item, and the size will be specified as "2.38″ wide × 2.5″ high").

18. Press EXIT (⟨F7⟩) to register the graphics box and return to your document. The box outline begins to form on screen.

19. Press ⟨Home⟩, ⟨Home⟩, ⟨↓⟩ to position the cursor at the bottom of the document. The text will readjust, and more of the box outline will form.

20. Type the remainder of the document as shown in Figure 10-15 or 10-16. As you type, the box outline will completely form. (Remember that the graphics image will appear only when printed; your final result on screen will appear as shown in Figure 10-12.)

21. To preview the graphics image within the document, use the View Document feature by pressing PRINT ( Shift + F7 ). [*Pulldown menu:* File (F), Print (P).] Then, select View Document (6 or V). The graphics image will display as part of the document.

22. Press EXIT ( F7 ) to return to the Typing screen.

23. Use the SAVE ( F10 ) key to save this document using the filename MARKETSH.MMO (which stands for market share, memorandum).

If your printer supports graphics, go ahead and print this document. The result is shown in Figure 10-15 or 10-16. On some printers it takes a few moments for the graphics image to be read by the printer before printing begins.

When a document contains both text and graphics, you have the option of printing only the text, only the graphics, or printing the text in one type quality and the graphics in another. (See the "Print Options" section in Chapter 9 for more details.) Also, depending on your printer, you may need to increase the memory in your printer to print a page that contains more than one or two graphics images. (If you have insufficient memory, you may need to first print the text, then print the graphics, and merge the two with scissors and tape or at the copy machine.)

# EDIT GRAPHICS BOXES

After you create a graphics box, you can edit its contents at any time. Position the cursor in the text before the graphics box. Press the GRAPHICS ( Alt + F9 ) key. [*Pulldown menu:* Graphics (G).] Then select the menu option corresponding to the style of graphics box you wish to edit—figure, table, text box, or user-defined box. For a figure, for example, the following menu appears:

Figure: 1 Create; 2 Edit; 3 New Number; 4 Options: 0

Select Edit (2 or E). WordPerfect asks which graphics box you wish to edit, suggesting a number. For instance, if you selected to edit a figure, the prompt that appears may be

Figure number? 2

Type in the number of the figure you wish to edit and press Enter . The Definition menu for that graphics box appears on screen, as shown in Figure 10-17.

Select any option and edit as you desire. For instance, you can select Filename and enter a new filename, effectively changing the graphics image to be inserted in the graphics box. Or, select Caption and alter the wording of the caption that will appear near the box. Or, select Vertical Position to alter the graphics box's vertical position on the page.

By selecting the Edit option, you can refine the appearance of the text or graphics image in the box. If your graphics box contains text, the text appears on screen, formatted properly for the margins within that graphics box. Edit the text and press EXIT ( F7 ) to return to the Definition screen for that graphics box. Now you can alter any of the other settings on that screen. Press EXIT ( F7 ) to return to the Typing screen.

If your graphics box contains a graphics image, then when you select Edit, the graphics image appears on the Graphics Edit screen, as shown in Figure 10-18. Now you have a variety of options for rotating, scaling, or moving the image *within the graphics box:*

- *Indicate a % Change* This option determines the extent to which the cursor movement keys affect an image for moving, scaling, and rotating (as described below). The default setting is 10%, as indicated in the lower right corner of Figure 10-18. This percentage can be changed to 1%, 5%, or 25% by pressing the INSERT (Ins) key repeatedly until the desired percentage appears.

- *Move* This option moves the image horizontally or vertically in the box. Use the arrow keys to move the image by a certain percentage as displayed in the lower right corner of the screen.

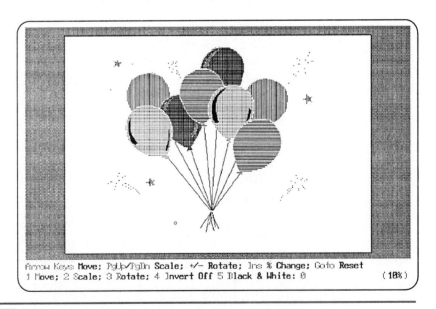

≣≣≣ **FIGURE 10-18** Graphics Edit screen showing BALLOONS.WPG

You can also select Move (1 or M) from the menu at the bottom of the screen and enter horizontal and vertical measurements. A positive number (such as 0.3″) moves the image up when specifying the vertical movement and to the right;-1q when specifying the horizontal movement. A negative number (such as −2″) moves the image down when specifying the vertical movement and to the left when specifying the horizontal movement.

- *Scale* This option expands or contracts the image. Press [PgUp] to expand the image and [PgDn] to contract the image horizontally and vertically by a certain percentage as displayed in the lower right corner of the screen.

  You can also select Scale (2 or S) from the menu at the bottom of the screen and enter vertical (Y) and horizontal (X) scale factors. A scale factor represents a percentage of the original size. For instance, to keep the vertical scale as is and to reduce the horizontal scale by half, enter scale X as 50 and scale Y as 100.

- *Rotate* This option turns the image in a circle. *5.1 users:* Press the [−] on the numeric keypad to rotate the image in a counterclockwise direction or the [+] key on the numeric keypad to rotate the image in a clockwise direction. *5.0 users:* Press [−] on the numeric keypad to rotate the image in a clockwise direction or [+] on the numeric keypad to rotate the image in a counterclockwise direction. The image is rotated based on a certain percentage, as displayed in the lower right corner of the screen.

  You can also select Rotate (3 or R) and enter the number of degrees you wish to rotate the image. For instance, to rotate an image so that it becomes upside down, enter 180 degrees. After you indicate a measurement for the rotation, WordPerfect asks whether you wish to mirror the image. Type **Y** to mirror the image or **N** to maintain the image in its usual state. For instance, suppose the image is of an arrow pointing to the right. If you mirror the image, it will point to the left.

- *Invert*  This option switches a bitmap image so that the complementary color of each dot is displayed; black becomes white and white becomes black. This item has an effect only on bitmap images, where images are depicted as a matrix of black dots, and has no effect on line (vector) drawings. The graphics images that come with WordPerfect are line drawings and cannot be inverted.

- *Black & White*  This option allows you to display and print a color image with black and white instead of a shading or fill pattern. Type **Y** to activate the Black & White option.

You can also reset an image back to its initial appearance on the Graphics Edit screen by pressing GOTO ([Ctrl] + [Home]).

Once you have altered the image on the Graphics Edit screen, press EXIT ([F7]) to return to the Definition screen for that graphics box. Finally, press EXIT ([F7]) to return to the Typing screen.

Besides editing the contents or location of a graphics box, you can also alter the box number. Position the cursor in the text where you want the new number to take effect, such as before a certain graphics box. Press the GRAPH-ICS ([Alt] + [F9]) key and then select the menu option corresponding to the style of graphics box you wish to edit—figure, table, text box, or user-defined box. For a figure, for example, the following menu appears:

Figure: 1 Create; 2 Edit; 3 New Number; 4 Options: 0

Select New Number (3 or N). WordPerfect prompts for which number you wish to use. With the figure style, for example, WordPerfect prompts

Figure number?

Type in a new number and press [Enter]. A code is inserted in the text, renumbering all graphics boxes of the indicated style from the cursor location forward, starting with the new number. For instance, suppose you indicate that you wish to renumber all figures in a document starting with number 5. The code inserted is **[New Fig Num:5]**, and the first figure-style graphics box created below that code will be renumbered as "Figure 5." All subsequent figure-style graphics boxes will be renumbered accordingly. As another example, the code after renumbering a text-style box to number 10 is **[New Txt Num:10]**.

# CHANGE GRAPHICS BOX DEFAULT OPTIONS

In addition to adjusting the settings for a particular graphics box, you can alter the default settings assumed for each of the five graphics box styles: figure, table, text box, user-defined box, or equation. The default options are shown in Table 10-2. To change one or more options for a particular box style in a document, position the cursor where you want the changes to take effect.

For instance, position the cursor on the Document Initial Codes screen to alter the options for a particular box style starting at the top of the document. Or position the

| | Figure Box | Table Box | Text Box | User-defined Box | Equation Box |
|---|---|---|---|---|---|
| **Border Style** | | | | | |
| Left | Single | None | None | None | None |
| Right | Single | None | None | None | None |
| Top | Single | Thick | Thick | Thick | None |
| Bottom | Single | Thick | Thick | Thick | None |
| | | | | | |
| **Outside Border Space** | | | | | |
| Left | 0.167″ | 0.167″ | 0.167″ | 0.167″ | 0.083″ |
| Right | 0.167″ | 0.167″ | 0.167″ | 0.167″ | 0.083″ |
| Top | 0.167″ | 0.167″ | 0.167″ | 0.167″ | 0.083″ |
| Bottom | 0.167″ | 0.167″ | 0.167″ | 0.167″ | 0.083″ |
| | | | | | |
| **Inside Border Space** | | | | | |
| Left | 0″ | 0.167″ | 0.167″ | 0″ | 0.083″ |
| Right | 0″ | 0.167″ | 0.167″ | 0″ | 0.083″ |
| Top | 0″ | 0.167″ | 0.167″ | 0″ | 0.083″ |
| Bottom | 0″ | 0.167″ | 0.167″ | 0″ | 0.083″ |
| | | | | | |
| **Numbering Method** | | | | | |
| First Level | Numbers | Roman | Numbers | Numbers | Numbers |
| Second Level | Off | Off | Off | Off | Off |

Note: 5.0 users should substitute 0.16″ for 0.167″.

**TABLE 10-2**   Default Settings for the Five Graphics Box Styles

|  | Figure Box | Table Box | Text Box | User-defined Box | Equation Box |
|---|---|---|---|---|---|
| **Caption Number Style & Position from Box** | | | | | |
| Style | [BOLD] Figure 1 [bold] | [BOLD] Table 1 [bold] | [BOLD] 1 [bold] | [BOLD] 1 [bold] | [BOLD] (1) [bold] |
| Position | Below, Outside | Above, Outside | Below, Outside | Below, Outside | Right, Inside |
| **Minimum Offset from Paragraph** | | | | | |
|  | 0″ | 0″ | 0″ | 0″ | 0″ |
| **Gray Shading (% of black)** | | | | | |
|  | 0% | 0% | 10% | 0% | 0% |

**TABLE 10-2**    Default Settings for the Five Graphics Box Styles (*continued*)

cursor above Table 5 to change the options for that table and all graphics boxes of the table style that follow. Press the GRAPHICS ( Alt + F9 ) key and then select the menu option corresponding to the style of graphics box you wish to alter—whether a figure, table, text box, or user-defined box. For a figure, the following menu appears:

Figure: 1 Create; 2 Edit; 3 New Number; 4 Options: 0

Select Options (4 or O). A menu, such as that shown in Figure 10-19, appears. Notice in Figure 10-19 that the default settings for the figure-style box options are indicated on the right side of the screen. When you select a different graphics box style, the corresponding default settings are indicated on screen.

The options that you can alter are as follows:

- *Border Style*  This option sets the style for all four borders of the graphics box. The choices are None, Single Line, Double Line, Dashed Line, Dotted Line, Thick Line, or Extra Thick Line.

```
Options: Figure

      1 - Border Style
            Left                            Single
            Right                           Single
            Top                             Single
            Bottom                          Single
      2 - Outside Border Space
            Left                            0.167"
            Right                           0.167"
            Top                             0.167"
            Bottom                          0.167"
      3 - Inside Border Space
            Left                            0"
            Right                           0"
            Top                             0"
            Bottom                          0"
      4 - First Level Numbering Method     Numbers
      5 - Second Level Numbering Method     Off
      6 - Caption Number Style             [BOLD]Figure 1[bold]
      7 - Position of Caption              Below box, Outside borders
      8 - Minimum Offset from Paragraph    0"
      9 - Gray Shading (% of black)        0%

Selection: 0
```

**FIGURE 10-19** . Figure Graphics Box Options menu

- *Outside Border Space*  This option sets the amount of space between the borders of the box and the text *outside* the box.

- *Inside Border Space*  This option sets the amount of space between the borders of the box and the image or text *inside* the box.

- *First Level and Second Level Numbering Method*  This option sets the format for the graphics box number to appear in the caption for each box. The choices are Off, Numbers (Arabic), Letters, or Roman Numerals. Letters and Roman numerals are displayed in uppercase for first-level numbers and in lowercase for second-level numbers. For instance, if you selected Numbers as the first level and Letters as the second level, then the first three figures would be labeled "Figure 1a," "Figure 1b," and "Figure 1c."

- *Caption Number Style*  This option sets the style for a graphics box caption. Type **1** where you want the first level number to appear, and type **2** where you want the second level number to appear. For instance, suppose that you selected Numbers as the first-level numbering method and Letters as the second-level numbering method (as discussed in the bulleted paragraph above). Now you want the figures labeled in boldface as **"Chapter 1, Figure a," "Chapter 1, Figure b,"** and so on. Enter the caption number style as **[BOLD]Chapter 1, Figure 2[bold]**.

- *Position of Caption*  This option sets the position of the caption. You have two sets of choices for all but equation boxes: below or above the graphics box, and outside or inside the graphics box. For equation boxes, you can also place the caption to the left or the right of the box.

- *Minimum Offset from Paragraph*   For a paragraph-style graphics box, this option determines the amount of space the graphics box can be offset from the top of the paragraph.

    As you've learned, you can specify a certain vertical distance from the top of the paragraph to the top of the graphics box. If necessary, WordPerfect will move the image higher in the paragraph than the vertical distance you specified so that the image can fit on the same page as the text; but it can move the image up only as far as allowed by the Minimum Offset from Paragraph option. When there isn't enough room for the graphics box to fit on the page, even when WordPerfect moves the image up as much as allowed by the Minimum Offset from Paragraph option, the box is moved to the next page.

- *Gray Shading*   This option sets the shading within graphics boxes of a particular style. A value of 0% represents no shading. If your printer supports various levels of shading, then a value of 100% represents a black box and you can specify different levels of shading (such as 10%, which is very light gray shading; 20%, which is slightly darker; and so on).

Once you alter any of the default settings, press EXIT (F7) to return to your document. A Graphics Option code is placed at the current cursor position, affecting all graphics boxes of the style you specified from that position forward or until the next Graphics Option code. For instance, the code after altering the options for figure-style graphics boxes is **[Fig Opt]**; the code after altering text-style boxes is **[Txt Opt]**.

Figure 10-20 shows some examples of the effects after graphics options are altered. To produce the text box for the newsletter banner shown at the top of Figure 10-20, the text box options were altered as follows:

- *Border Style*   Extra Thick on all sides

- *Shading*   20%

---

**REST & RELAXATION WINE NEWS**

*Published by the R&R Wine Association*                                    *Vol. 1, No.1*

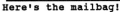

**Here's the mailbag!**

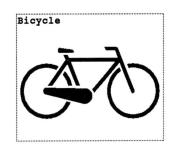

**FIGURE 10-20**   Graphics examples with Box Options altered

To produce the figure box for the image of a mailbag, the figure box options were altered as follows:

- *Border Style*  Thick on the right and bottom, single on the left and top (which provides a three-dimensional look to the box, available only in version 5.1)

- *Position of Caption*  Below box, Outside Borders

To produce a user-defined box for the image of a bicycle, the user-defined box options were altered as follows:

- *Border Style*  Dotted

- *Position of Caption*  Above box, Inside borders

Remember that Graphics options do not determine the size, contents, or position of a graphics box or the text of that box's caption; these are determined when you create the graphics box itself.

# REVIEW EXERCISE

Here's some practice using the special font and graphics features in WordPerfect. Remember, however, that the fonts available and the ability to print graphics both depend on your printer.

1. If it is not currently on screen, retrieve the file MAR-KETSH.MMO, which contains a graphics image.

2. Alter the font attribute for the word "MEMORAN-DUM" at the top of the document so that it prints in very large letters. Then, alter the base font for the rest of the document.

3. On the blank line just below the word "MEMORAN-DUM," draw a horizontal line that extends from the left margin to the right and is 0.05″ thick. After creating the graphics line (remember that the line will not display on the Typing screen), press `Enter` to insert extra white space below the graphics line.

4. Alter the font attribute for the phrase "Congratulations are in order" in the last paragraph so that it prints in italics. (If italics is not available with your printer, the text may print with an underline.)

5. Position the figure at the right margin, rather than at the left margin. (*Hint:* Press the GRAPHICS (`Alt` + `F9`) key and then select to edit Figure 1. On the Figure Definition screen, change the Horizontal Position to "Right" instead of "Left." When you press the EXIT (`F7`) key to return to your document, it may appear jumbled. Simply move the cursor down so that Word-Perfect will rewrite the screen.)

6. You may wish to print your document. (Results are shown in Figure 10-21, assuming you're a 5.1 user. For 5.0 users, only the graphics image will be different.)

## MEMORANDUM

To: All Employees                              From: Sandy Peterson
Re: Market Share Update                        Date: September 11, 1990

R&R WINE ASSOCIATION increased its market share this year as compared to the same time last year. As of September, market share increases were as follows:

United States -- 2%
Europe -- 0.5%
Australia -- 0.75%

While the percentages may appear small, they represent quite an enormous volume increase.

*Congratulations are in order*, especially to Don Reed, Maria Romero, and Paula Stein, who are this year's winners of our sales contest. These three sales representatives are off to Tahiti for three weeks in December, courtesy of R&R.

**FIGURE 10-21**   Printed page after completing Review Exercise

## Quick Review

- Change the initial font starting at the top of a document — and for headers, footers, footnotes, and endnotes — by pressing FORMAT ([Shift] + [F8]) and selecting Document (3 or D) to display the Document Format menu. Or, pulldown menu users can select Layout (L), Document (D). Then select Initial Base Font (3 or F), position the cursor on the font you desire, and choose Select (1 or S).

- Change the base font for a portion of text, starting at the current cursor position, by pressing FONT ([Ctrl] + [F8]) and selecting Base Font (4 or F). Or, pulldown menu users can select Font (O), Base Font (O). Then position the cursor on the font you desire, and choose Select (1 or S).

- Change a font's size or appearance attribute for a portion of text *before* you type the text: Press FONT ([Ctrl] + [F8]) to display the Font menu, select Size (1 or S) or Appearance (2 or A), and choose an attribute. Or, from the pulldown menus, select Font (O), and then choose a size attribute, or select Appearance (A), and then choose an appearance attribute. Now type the text. Then, to turn off the size or appearance attribute, repeat the keystrokes used to turn on the attribute, or select the Normal option from the font menu, or press the [→] key to move the cursor outside the pair of attribute codes.

You can also change an attribute *after* you type the text: Use the Block feature to highlight the text, and then display the Font menu to select an attribute.

• Alter the Line Height from the Line Format menu by pressing the FORMAT (Shift + F8) key and selecting Line (1 or L). Or, pulldown menu users can select Layout (L), Line (L). Then select Line Height (4 or H) and choose either a fixed line height or auto line height, the default setting, where WordPerfect automatically adjusts for each font change in your text.

• Refine the spacing between characters and lines from the Printer Functions menu. Press FORMAT (Shift + F8), select Other (4 or O), and select Printer Functions (6 or P). Or, pulldown menu users can select Layout (L), Other (O), and then Printer Functions (6 or P). Now you can specify Kerning, Word and Letter Spacing, Word Spacing Justification Limits, or Baseline Placement. 5.1 users can also adjust the Leading. Whether these features affect a document depends on the capabilities of your printer.

• Place a graphics line in a document by positioning the cursor, pressing GRAPHICS (Alt + F9), and selecting Line (5 or V). Or, choose Graphics (G), Line (L) from the pulldown menus. Now, choose either to create a vertical or horizontal line, and then define the position of the line, the line's width and length, and the line's shading. Graphics lines are displayed on the printed page, but not on the Typing screen.

- Place a graphics box in a document by positioning the cursor based on how that box will be anchored in the text—either in a paragraph to anchor the box to that paragraph, at the top of a page to anchor the box to a position on a page, or in a specific location to treat the box like a character. Then, press GRAPHICS ( Alt + F9 ), select the style of box you desire, and choose Create (1 or C). Or, from the pulldown menus, choose Graphics (G), select a box style, and select Create (C). Once a graphics box is created, define its contents, position, and size on that box's Definition menu.

- WordPerfect provides 30 graphics images that you can use right away to insert into your graphics boxes. You can also create an original image using a graphics package: save your graphics image in a WordPerfect-supported format, and then retrieve that image into a WordPerfect graphics box.

- Edit a graphics box by pressing GRAPHICS ( Alt + F9 ), selecting the style of box you wish to edit, choosing Edit (2 or E), and entering the number of the box. Or, from the pulldown menus, choose

Graphics (G), select a box style, and select Edit (E) and enter the box number. You can revise the box's contents, position, or size. Or, select Edit (9 or E): If the box contains text, you can edit the text, or, if the box contains a graphics image, you can move, scale, rotate, or invert the image.

- Change the default options for a certain graphics box style: Press GRAPHICS (⟨Alt⟩ + ⟨F9⟩), select the style of box you wish to alter, and choose Options (4 or O). Now you can specify the default for that box style's caption, shading, border style, and border space.

# CREATING TEXT COLUMNS AND TABLES

A common need in typing documents is the ability to align text in columns. You learned in Chapter 4 how to reset tab stop locations and then use the [Tab] key or other keys such as → INDENT or CENTER to align text at tab stop locations. However, for complicated tables, using tabular columns can be tedious. It is difficult to calculate the correct tab stop locations for the columns. It is hard to type multiple-line entries into these columns. And, it is cumbersome to edit the multiline entries within these columns.

WordPerfect offers several features to help you type columns into a document. First is WordPerfect's Text Column feature. WordPerfect calculates the column margins and the spacing between columns for you. Once you start typing text into these columns, word wrap operates independently for each column; you can type and let WordPerfect do the job of confining the text to each column. In addition, if you edit the text in one column, the other columns will not become misaligned.

You can create up to 24 columns on a page with the Text Column feature. Discussed in this chapter are the two basic styles of columns that you can select from:

- *Newspaper style*   The text flows down the page in each column, as in a magazine or newspaper—each column is independent of the others.

- *Parallel*   The text reads across the page as in an address or inventory list—a related group of information is kept together in adjacent columns, side by side.

You'll learn the four basic steps in creating text columns, and you'll practice editing text and moving the cursor within the columns that you create.

Also discussed in this chapter is WordPerfect 5.1's Tables feature. Like the Text Column feature, Tables allows you to align information in columns. But this feature is often easier to use than parallel columns for keeping text side by side in columns. It also offers special options for moving/copying text within tables, and for formatting each entry, referred to as a cell. With Tables, you can quickly create an inventory list, a chart, an invoice, or even a fill-in-the-blanks form. 5.1 users will be able to compare the Text Column and Tables features side by side.

# CREATE NEWSPAPER-STYLE COLUMNS

Newspaper-style columns are those in which the text begins at the top of the first column on a page, continues down to the bottom of that column, and then starts at the top of the next column, as shown in Figure 11-1. You find this type of column in your daily newspapers and in magazines, where you read all of the first column before your eyes move up to the top of the second. A common use for the newspaper-style column is in producing a company newsletter.

There are four basic steps for working with columns (whether newspaper style or parallel): defining the columns, turning on the Column feature, typing text into the columns, and turning off the Column feature.

## Define Columns

The first step in working with newspaper columns is to define your column layout. You must specify the number of columns you desire and the left and right margins of each

R&R WINE ASSOCIATION
EMPLOYEE NEWS

### NEW SERVICE OFFERED

All R&R Wine Association employees are now eligible for two valuable company services.

First is the new <u>R&R Money Market Fund.</u> Any percentage of your monthly salary can be automatically invested in the Money Market Fund, an established mutual fund with assets so far of over $1 million. The R&R Money Market Fund is just a part of a larger fund, which is over $45 million strong.

You will earn high yields and enjoy a variety of extras. These include free check writing on your account. The service is unlimited; write as many checks as you need. In addition, there's free reinvestment of your dividends so that your earnings grow faster.

The R&R Money Market Fund is professionally managed by The Thomas Corporation, one of the nation's leading mutual fund companies.

Second, and as a complimentary feature, we now offer a <u>financial planning service</u>, free to all employees. You'll learn how to minimize taxes, what to do about life insurance, and how to handle emergency needs. You'll also be advised on pension plan options.

Why do we offer the Money Market Fund? So that your investments are wise ones, so that you get long-term profit from your earnings at R&R.

Why do we offer the FREE financial planning service? For the same reasons.

To find out more about the benefits of joining our company's Money Market Fund, call Karl Nottingsworth at (415) 666-9444. He's also the person you'll want to speak with about setting up an appointment for financial planning!

### WORLD OF WINES

In our last newsletter, we completed a five-part series on wines produced in the United States. Next month, we begin a new series on the wines of Europe. Our first nation in Europe? By popular request, it will be France.

France is most often considered the greatest wine-producing country in the world. The variety of wines grown here is absolutely amazing: the sparkling wines of Champagne, the red wines of Bordeaux, the red and white wines of Burgundy, the sweet wines of Barsac--just to name a few!

You'll learn about all the French wines we ship around the country in our next edition of R&R Wine News.

**FIGURE 11-1** Sample of newspaper columns

column. If you desire columns of equal size, WordPerfect can calculate the margins for each column automatically.

To define columns, position the cursor where you want the columns to take effect. For instance, to initiate columns starting at the top of the document, you can position the cursor at the top of the document or, to reduce the number of codes at the top, on the Document Initial Codes screen. If you want to type columns starting in the middle of page 2, position the cursor there.

Next you need to display the Text Column Definition menu. The process is different depending on whether you are a 5.1 or 5.0 user.

*5.1 users:* Press the COLUMNS/TABLES ( Alt + F7 ) key and select Columns (1 or C). [*Pulldown menu:* Layout (L), Columns (C).] The following Columns menu appears:

`Columns: 1 On; 2 Off; 3 Define: 0`

Select Define (3 or D) to display the menu shown in Figure 11-2.

*5.0 users:* Press the MATH/COLUMNS ( Alt + F7 ) key to display the following menu for columns:

`1 Math On; 2 Math Def; 3 Column On/Off; 4 Column Def: 0`

(Though accessed with the same function key, the Math and Column features are distinct; see Chapter 15 for a discussion of the Math feature.) Select Column Def (4 or D) to display the menu shown in Figure 11-2.

Whether a 5.1 or 5.0 user, you are then ready to define your columns by making the following choices:

- *Type (1 or T)* The default setting for this option is newspaper style. Therefore, there is no need to alter this setting for newspaper columns. (To indicate a parallel style, choose an option from the Type menu, as described later in this chapter.)

- *Number of Columns (2 or N)*   The default setting for this option is two. To indicate more than two columns, type a number and press [Enter] .

- *Distance Between Columns (3 or D)*   The default setting is 0.5″. To specify another distance, type in a measurement and press [Enter] . (This option is useful only if you wish to set all columns at the same width. To set unevenly spaced columns, see the next option below.)

- *Margins (4 or M)*   This option is set by default based on your specifications for the Number of Columns and Distance Between Columns options (as described above), taking into account the current left/right margins across

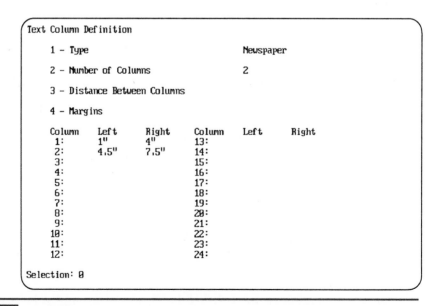

```
Text Column Definition

    1 - Type                            Newspaper

    2 - Number of Columns               2

    3 - Distance Between Columns

    4 - Margins

    Column    Left      Right     Column    Left      Right
      1:      1"        4"          13:
      2:      4.5"      7.5"        14:
      3:                            15:
      4:                            16:
      5:                            17:
      6:                            18:
      7:                            19:
      8:                            20:
      9:                            21:
     10:                            22:
     11:                            23:
     12:                            24:

Selection: 0
```

**FIGURE 11-2**   Text Column Definition menu

the full page. To change the margin settings for individual columns, enter new measurements for each column's left and right margin location.

You are not limited to the current left/right margins across the full page when setting column margins. For instance, even when the left margin of the page starts at 1″, you can still start the left margin of the first column at 0.5″.

If you set your own column margins, be sure not to overlap columns and to leave some space between columns so that the columns are easy to read. For instance, if you wish to create two columns and the first has margins of 1″ and 3.5″, you must make sure that the second column starts after position 3.6″ — somewhere around position 3.8″ or 4.1″ would be best — to ensure sufficient space between columns for easy reading.

Once all the columns are set, press the EXIT ( F7 ) key or press Enter to return to the Columns menu. A Column Definition code is inserted at the current cursor position. The Column Definition code indicates how many columns you've specified and what the margins are of each. In version 5.1, the type of column is also indicated. For instance, if you had set two columns, one with margins of 1″ and 4″ and the other with margins of 4.5″ and 7.5″, the code for 5.1 users would be **[Col Def:Newspaper;2;1″,4″; 4.5″,7.5″]**. For 5.0 users, the code reads **[Col Def:2,1″,4″, 4.5″,7.5″]**.

## Turn On the Column Feature

You're now ready for step 2 — activating the Column feature. From the Columns menu, *5.1 users:* Select On

(1 or O). *5.0 users:* Select Column On/Off (3 or C). (This selection is like a toggle switch: when the Column feature is off, this selection turns it on.) A **[Col On]** code is inserted. All text that you type following this code will be formatted into columns in whatever format you specified on the Column Definition screen. When the Column feature is activated, the status line contains a Column indicator, such as the following:

`Col 1 Doc 1 Pg 2 Ln 1" Pos 1"`

The "Col" indicator lets you know what column you are typing in.

## Type Text into Columns

The third step in creating columns is to type your text. You should type in newspaper columns as if typing a regular document. Word wrap will be hard at work to ensure that the text remains within the boundaries of the first column.

How WordPerfect starts a new column is analogous to how it starts a new page. After you type the maximum number of lines that can fit on a page, a Soft Page code **[SPg]** is automatically inserted, and the cursor jumps to the beginning of the next column. When the last column on a page is full, an **[SPg]** code is again inserted; but this time, a page bar appears on screen, and the cursor jumps to the beginning of the first column on a new page.

You can also end a column before it would normally end by pressing Ctrl + Enter to insert a Hard Page code. This forces an end to that column, just as it forces an end to a page when WordPerfect is not in Column mode. With the

Hard Page **[HPg]** code inserted in the text, the cursor moves up to the top of the next column.

The standard typing features work within columns. For instance, you can press [Tab] to indent the first line of a paragraph to the first tab setting just as you would if not in Column mode. Or, if the cursor is at the left margin of a column, you can press the CENTER ([Shift] + [F6]) key to center a short line of text over that column. Or, you can press the FLUSH RIGHT ([Alt] + [F6]) key to align a short line of text at the right margin of the column.

## Turn Off the Column Feature

The final step is to turn the Column feature off after you have completed the typing. *5.1 users:* Press COLUMNS/ TABLES ([Alt] + [F7]), select Columns (1 or C), and select Off (2 or F). *5.0 users:* Press the MATH/COLUMNS ([Alt] + [F7]) key and select Column On/Off (3 or C). A **[Col Off]** code is inserted in the text, and the cursor moves down to the left margin below the columns. You can then return to typing text as usual—across the entire line. On the Typing screen, you can tell when the Column feature is no longer active: The status line returns to its standard appearance, as you can see from the following example:

**Doc 1 Pg 3 Ln 3.5" Pos 1"**

## Practice with Newspaper Columns

Here's an opportunity to work with newspaper columns. Suppose that your job is to type the monthly R&R Wine Association company newsletter; this month's newsletter is shown in Figure 11-1. You will define two evenly spaced columns, with 0.5″ in between. Proceed as follows:

1. On the first line of a clear screen, center and type the first line of the title, **R&R WINE ASSOCIATION**.

2. On the second line, center and type the second line of the title, **EMPLOYEE NEWS**.

3. Press (Enter) four times to insert blank lines.

4. *5.1 users:* Press the COLUMNS/TABLES ((Alt) + (F7)) key, and select Columns (1 or C). [*Pulldown menu:* Layout (L), Columns (C).] The Columns menu appears:

   Columns:   1 On; 2 Off; 3 Define: 0

   *5.0 users:* Press the MATH/COLUMNS ((Alt) + (F7)) key to display the following menu:

   1 Math On; 2 Math Def; 3 Column On/Off; 4 Column Def: 0

5. *5.1 users:* Select Define (3 or D). *5.0 users:* Select Column Def (4 or D).

   The screen shown in Figure 11-2 appears. Notice that WordPerfect assumes that you want two newspaper-style columns. WordPerfect also assumes that you want 0.5″ of space between the columns, as indicated by how WordPerfect calculated the column margins for you. The left column begins at 1″, the current left margin for the page. The left column ends at position 4″ and, because WordPerfect assumes 0.5″ between columns, the right column begins at position 4.5″. The right column ends at 7.5″, the current right margin for the page. The default settings are what you desire, so no change is necessary.

6. Press EXIT ([F7]) to return to the Columns menu.

7. *5.1 users:* Select On (1 or O). *5.0 users:* Select Column On/Off (3 or C). As soon as you do, a column indicator appears on the status line to reflect that you're in Column mode. For instance, the status line may read

   **Col 1 Doc 1 Pg 1 Ln 2" Pos 1"**

   You are now ready to begin typing the first column.

8. Press the CENTER ([Shift] + [F6]) key, type the title **NEW SERVICE OFFERED**, and press [Enter] twice. Notice that the title is centered over the column rather than over the page, since you're typing within a column.

9. Type the text as shown in Figure 11-1, pressing [Tab] to indent the first line of each paragraph. Remember that word wrap will keep the text within the margins of that column—you need to press [Enter] only to end a paragraph and insert a blank line between paragraphs.

   If you type all the text as shown in the first column of Figure 11-1, you'll notice that the cursor moves automatically to the second column once the first column is full of text. (Remember from Chapter 6 that, assuming default settings, WordPerfect breaks to a new page just before line 10" so that a bottom margin of 1" is maintained on 11"-long paper. It is on the same line that WordPerfect breaks to a new column when in Column mode.)

   Or, if you are a slow typist and don't wish to type the entire text shown in Figure 11-1, then you can force a premature page break. Type part of the first column and press Ctrl + Enter to move the cursor to the top of the second column. Then type part of the second column.

10. After completing the columns, you are now ready to turn off Column mode. With the cursor positioned after the last word in the last column, press the COLUMNS/ TABLES ( Alt + F7 ) key.

11. *5.1 users:* Select Columns (1 or C) and then Off (2 or F). *5.0 users:* Select Column On/Off (3 or C).

The cursor jumps to the left margin, below the columns, and the "Col" indicator on the status line disappears. Now you can again type text across the full width of the page. (If you turn off columns after typing the last line that will fit on a page, the cursor will be positioned at the top of a new page.)

After defining columns in a document, you can turn Column mode on and off as often as you wish. For instance, after typing within columns, you could turn off the Column feature and type some text across the full width of the page. Then you could again press the COLUMNS/ TABLES ( Alt + F7 ) key and turn columns on. You could then type a second group of columns and turn the feature off. Figure 11-3 shows a document in which columns were turned on below the title "NEW SERVICE OFFERED," turned off to type a paragraph across the width of the page, and then turned on again below the title "WORLD OF WINES."

You can also insert more than one column definition in a document so that the column layout is different, as long as you enter a new column definition when Column mode is off. For instance, define columns to insert a **[Col Def:]** at the top of your document. Then turn columns on, type the columns, and turn columns off. Now, with columns off you

---

R&R WINE ASSOCIATION
EMPLOYEE NEWS

### NEW SERVICE OFFERED

All R&R Wine Association employees are now eligible for two valuable company services.

First is the new R&R Money Market Fund. Any percentage of your monthly salary can be automatically invested in the Money Market Fund, an established mutual fund with assets so far of over $1 million. The R&R Money Market Fund is just a part of a larger fund, which is over $45 million strong.

Second, and as a complimentary feature, we now offer a financial planning service, free to all employees. You'll learn how to minimize taxes, what to do about life insurance, and how to handle emergency needs. You'll also be advised on pension plan options.

**To find out more about the benefits of joining our company's Money Market Fund, call Karl Nottingsworth at (415) 666-9444. He's also the person you'll want to speak with about setting up an appointment for financial planning!**

### WORLD OF WINES

In our last newsletter, we completed a five-part series on wines produced in the United States. Next month, we begin a new series on the wines of Europe. Our first nation in Europe? By popular request, it will be France.

France is most often considered the greatest wine-producing country in the world.

The variety of wines grown here is absolutely amazing: the sparkling wines of Champagne, the red wines of Bordeaux, the red and white wines of Burgundy, the sweet wines of Barsac--just to name a few!

You'll learn about all the French wines we ship around the country in our next edition of R&R Wine News.

---

**FIGURE 11-3**  Sample of two sets of newspaper columns

can redefine columns, inserting a new **[Col Def:]** code in the document. When you next turn on columns, the columns will abide by the new column definition.

When a document with columns is printed, the text in each column is justified on both sides if full justification is on (as shown in Figures 11-1 and 11-3). If you alter the justification, then each column will be adjusted accordingly. Remember from Chapter 4 that to switch justification on or off, you would position the cursor above the text and use the Line Format menu to insert a Justification code in the text. (Also remember that full justification appears on the printed page but not on the Typing screen.) Because columns are narrower than a full page of text, uneven spacing shows up more in columns. Thus, you might find that hyphenation is especially useful in columns, especially when full justification is turned on.

To give your columns a professional look, you may wish to place graphics lines or images between columns. See Chapter 10 for a discussion of how to employ the Graphics feature. If you want the graphics between columns, make sure that the cursor is positioned after the **[Col On]** code, where Column mode is in effect, before inserting a graphics line or image.

# MOVE THE CURSOR IN NEWSPAPER COLUMNS

In controlling the cursor within columns, page-by-page cursor movement keys such as `PgUp` and `PgDn` operate the same whether or not WordPerfect is in Column mode. However, other cursor movement keys are confined to the current column. For instance, [Home], [←] moves the cursor to the left edge of the *column,* not the screen. Similarly, [Home], [→] or [End] moves the cursor to the right edge of the *column.*

When the cursor is on the first or last character in a column, use the arrow keys to position the cursor in another column. If the cursor is at the very beginning of one column—on the first character, then

- [←] moves the cursor to the bottom of the previous column.

- [↑] moves the cursor to the bottom of the same column on the previous page.

Or, if the cursor is at the very end of one column—on the last character, then

- [→] moves the cursor to the top of the next column.

- [↓] moves the cursor to the top of the same column on the next page.

To move the cursor quickly between columns when the cursor is in the middle of a column, use the key sequence [Ctrl] + [Home]. Remember from Chapter 6 that this sequence is referred to as the GOTO key combination. When you press [Ctrl] + [Home] [*Pulldown menu:* Search (S), Goto (G)], WordPerfect prompts

Go to

In Column mode, GOTO in combination with the arrow keys moves the cursor as follows:

| | |
|---|---|
| [Ctrl] + [Home], [↑] | Top line of current column |
| [Ctrl] + [Home], [↓] | Bottom line of current column |
| [Ctrl] + [Home], [←] | Preceding column |
| [Ctrl] + [Home], [→] | Next column |

*Note:* If you are using WordPerfect version 5.1, and have an enhanced keyboard, you can press [Alt] + [←] or [Alt] + [→] in addition to [Ctrl] + [Home], [←] or [Ctrl] + [Home], [→] to move the cursor from column to column. This will operate only if you use the arrow keys found on the second set of cursor movement keys and not those found on the numeric keypad.

You can also move to the very first or last column by pressing [Home] one extra time, as follows:

| | |
|---|---|
| [Ctrl] + [Home], [Home], [←] | First column (to the left) |
| [Ctrl] + [Home], [Home], [→] | Last column (to the right) |

Some of these methods for moving the cursor are illustrated as follows:

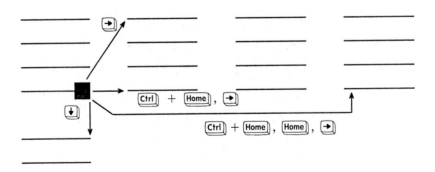

Here's some practice moving the cursor.

1. Press [Home], [Home], [↑] to move to the top of the document on the screen.

2. Press [↓] until the cursor is inside the columns and "Col 1" appears on the status line.

3. Press [Ctrl] + [Home], [↓]. The cursor moves to the bottom of column 1.

4. Press [End]. The cursor moves to the right edge of the column.

5. Press [→]. The cursor moves to the top of column 2.

6. Press [Ctrl] + [Home], [↓]. Now the cursor is located at the bottom of column 2.

7. Press [Ctrl] + [Home], [←]. The cursor moves across to column 1.

8. Press [Ctrl] + [Home], [↑]. The cursor returns to the top of column 1.

# EDIT TEXT IN NEWSPAPER COLUMNS

Certain editing features operate in columns just as in regular text. The standard deletion keys work the same way, but they are confined to a single column. For instance, [Ctrl] + [End] erases text from the current cursor position to the right edge of the column rather than to the right edge of the line. [Ctrl] + [PgDn] erases from the current cursor position to the bottom of the column rather than the entire page.

As you insert words, it may appear that the existing text laps over into the next column. When you press [↓], the text adjusts. As you add or delete text, the column readjusts. If necessary, the text in other columns shifts up or down as well, just as when you add or delete text during normal editing and the text on each page shifts.

Watch what happens when you delete a paragraph in one of the columns on screen:

1. Position the cursor somewhere within the third paragraph of the first column on the screen, which begins with "You will earn high yields. . . ."

2. Press the MOVE (Ctrl + F4) key. [*Pulldown menu:* Edit (E), Select (E).]

3. Select Paragraph (2 or P). Notice that WordPerfect highlights the paragraph, staying within that column.

4. Select Delete (3 or D). The paragraph is erased. Notice that the following paragraphs shift up to fill in the gap left by the deleted paragraph.

The Block feature key works in Column mode to highlight a chunk of a column. You can perform any of the many features possible after blocking text—copying the block, moving it, saving, printing, and so on. You can also use the Move feature to move text from one place to another in the usual way.

*Note:* Chapter 5 describes how WordPerfect allows you to move or copy not only a standard block, but a rectangle or tabular column as well. The Tabular Column option is used for a column aligned on *tab stops,* but cannot be used for columns created using the Text Column feature. Move or copy words, sentences, or paragraphs in text columns with the Block option and not the Tabular Column option, just as you'd move them in standard text.

When you reveal codes in an attempt to check or delete codes within columns, WordPerfect shows only one column at a time and always at the left side of the screen. For instance, Figure 11-4 shows the Reveal Codes screen with the cursor in the first paragraph of column 1. Notice in the bottom window, where codes are displayed, that you can see the **[Col Def:]** and **[Col On]** codes, as well as part of the first column; the second column, however, does not appear. The two columns are treated as two separate pages on the Reveal Codes screen.

Certain features are inaccessible when you're typing in columns. For instance, you cannot change margins within columns; you must alter margins above the **[Col Def:]** code and then redefine the columns to reflect the margin change. And footnotes are inoperative in columns, although endnotes work just fine.

When editing in columns, WordPerfect responds more slowly in reformatting text than when not in Column mode. Because the Column feature is quite complicated, Word-Perfect has a heavy burden in readjusting the text with

```
    NEW SERVICE OFFERED          Market Fund?  So that your
                                 investments are wise ones, so
     All R&R Wine Association    that you get long-term profit
employees are now eligible for   from your earnings at R&R.
two valuable company services.
                                     Why do we offer the FREE
     First is the new R&R Money  financial planning service?
Market Fund.  Any percentage of  For the same reasons.
your monthly salary can be
automatically invested in the        To find out more about the
Money Market Fund, an            benefits of joining our
                                     Col 1 Doc 1 Pg 1 Ln 2.33" Pos 1.5"
[  ▲   ▲   ▲   ▲   ▲   }   {   ▲   ▲   ▲   ▲   ▲   }   ▲   ▲
[HRt]
[Col Def:Newspaper;2;1",4";4.5",7.5"][Col On][Center]NEW SERVICE OFFERED[HRt]
[HRt]
[Tab]All R&R Wine Association[SRt]
employees are now eligible for[SRt]
two valuable company services.[HRt]
[HRt]
[Tab]First is the new [UND]R&R Money[SRt]
Market Fund,[und]  Any percentage of[SRt]
your monthly salary can be[SRt]

Press Reveal Codes to restore screen
```

═══════ **FIGURE 11-4**   Reveal Codes screen: cursor in the left of two newspaper columns

each revision you make. If you are planning extensive editing within columns, you can speed up WordPerfect by requesting that it stop displaying the columns side by side. Each column then appears on a separate page, with a page bar between them. Once you have revised the columns, you can again choose to display columns side by side. The Side-by-Side Columns Display feature is accessed via the Setup menu. Refer to the "Display" section in Appendix B for more details.

# ERASE AND CHANGE
# THE COLUMN FORMAT

WordPerfect's ability to reformat text into and out of newspaper columns is amazing in its flexibility. You can take text that you've already typed and format it into columns. Just position the cursor above the existing text, define the columns so that a **[Col Def:]** code is inserted, and then turn on Column mode. When you press ⬇ to adjust the text, it reformats into columns instantly. You should remember to insert a **[Col Off]** code at the end of the last line of text that you want formatted into columns.

You can also retrieve text into an already defined column layout. For instance, position the cursor below the **[Col Def:]** and **[Col On]** codes that define the columns. Then use the RETRIEVE (Shift + F10) key or the LIST (F5) key to retrieve a document. That document is inserted at the current cursor position, automatically formatted into the column layout.

You can cancel the text columns format, too, so that text again appears across the full width of the page. Simply find and erase the **[Col Def:]** code that defines the column layout. The **[Col On]** code disappears automatically, and the text readjusts to fill the full width of the page.

You can even insert a brand new **[Col Def:]** code and then turn on columns. The text would reformat into the brand new column layout that you had defined.

Suppose that you've decided that columns are inappropriate in the document on screen.

1. Reveal codes and hunt down the **[Col Def:]** code near the top of the document.

2. Position the cursor on the **[Col Def:]** code and press `Del` to erase it, or position the cursor to the right of the code and press `Backspace` to erase it.

3. Return to the Typing screen. Notice that the text is no longer in a column format.

4. Save the text currently on screen under the filename NEWCOL (standing for newspaper columns)—even though it is no longer formatted into columns. You will reformat this text into columns in the review exercise that concludes this chapter.

# CREATE PARALLEL COLUMNS

Parallel-style columns are useful whenever you wish to type columns of text in which information reads *across,* rather than down, the page. Related information is presented in adjacent (parallel) columns that are kept side by side, to get the effect shown in Figure 11-5. For example, the entry "Lonnie Chang" along with her title and telephone number is considered to be one group of parallel columns. The entries related to "Tim Fingerman" are considered a second group. WordPerfect automatically inserts a blank line between each group. Parallel style resembles standard tabular columns, except that text can wrap individually in each column.

You can employ parallel columns in two ways. Use the regular Parallel column either if entries in a group will continue for more than one page or if it doesn't matter to you that one parallel column may be split between two

---

R&R WINE ASSOCIATION: LIST OF MANAGERS

| | | |
|---|---|---|
| Lonnie Chang | Director of the Public Relations Department since 4/12/83. | (415) 333-4109 |
| Tim Fingerman | Distribution Manager, West Coast Region, since 6/1/87. Stationed in Oakland, California. | (415) 549-1101 |
| Paula Garcia | Distribution Manager, East Coast Region, since 12/2/82. Stationed in New York City. | (212) 484-1119 |
| P.J. McClintock | Assistant to the President since 5/13/86. | (415) 333-4401 |
| Sandy Peterson | President since 3/2/82. | (415) 333-4400 |
| John Samsone | Director, Office of Administration, since 3/2/82. | (415) 333-9215 |

**FIGURE 11-5**  Sample of parallel columns

pages. You may wish to use regular Parallel columns, for example, when typing a script.

Use Parallel with Block Protect columns when entries are small and you wish to protect each group of parallel columns from being split between two pages. WordPerfect inserts Block Protection codes so that each group of adjacent columns always remains together. (As described in Chapter 6, the Block Protect feature is also available when text is not in Column mode, to protect a chunk of text from being split by a page break.) Using Block Protect, an entire group is placed on the next page if one column in a group of parallel columns extends beyond a page break. This type of column is convenient to use when you wish to create mailing or inventory lists or the list shown in Figure 11-5, where each group of parallel columns is short.

Follow the same steps in creating parallel columns as when creating newspaper columns, which include defining the columns, turning on the Column feature, typing text into the columns, and turning off Column mode.

## Define Columns

To define parallel columns, proceed as when defining newspaper columns. *5.1 users:* Press the COLUMNS/TABLES ( Alt + F7 ) key and select Columns (1 or C). [*Pulldown menu:* Layout (L), Columns (C).] Then, select Define (3 or D) to display the menu shown in Figure 11-2. *5.0 users:* Press the MATH/COLUMNS ( Alt + F7 ) key and select Column Def (4 or D) to display Figure 11-2.

Indicate the layout of your parallel columns on the Text Column Definition menu as you would newspaper columns, except that you must now specify a different column type. Select Type (1 or T) and the following menu appears:

Column Type: **1** Newspaper; **2** Parallel; **3** Parallel with Block Protect

Select whether you want parallel columns, or parallel columns with block protect. Continue to define the columns and then press EXIT ( F7 ) to insert a **[Col Def:]** code in the text.

## Turn On the Column Feature

Turn on parallel columns just as you would for newspaper columns. *5.1 users:* Select On (1 or O). *5.0 users:* Select Column On/Off (3 or C) from the Columns menu. When you turn on Parallel columns, WordPerfect inserts a **[Col On]** code. If you select Parallel with Block Protect, WordPerfect also precedes that code with a **[Block Pro:On]** code, which ensures that related columns across the page are never separated.

## Type Text into Columns

As with newspaper columns, you can rely on word wrap when typing parallel columns to maintain the margins of each column. But in contrast to its use in newspaper columns, Ctrl + Enter is used constantly in parallel columns. You must press Ctrl + Enter after completing each entry in a related group of parallel columns. A Hard Page code **[HPg]** is inserted in the text, and the cursor moves up to the top of the next column, where you would type the next entry and press [Ctrl] + [Enter] again to continue. In parallel columns, you *type each parallel group across the page* before moving on to the next group.

When you complete the last column of a parallel group and press [Ctrl] + [Enter], WordPerfect accomplishes many tasks in sequence.

- If you selected Parallel with Block Protect, a **[Block Pro:Off]** code is inserted to designate the end of protection for that group.

- A **[Col Off]** code is inserted to designate the end of columns for that one group.

- The cursor moves to the left margin of a new line, and a **[HRt]** code is inserted so that a blank line is established below the group.

- The cursor moves to the left margin of a new line, and, if you selected Parallel with Block Protect, a **[Block Pro:On]** code is inserted to designate the start of a new group to be protected.

- A **[Col On]** code is inserted in preparation for your typing the next group of parallel columns.

All these tasks are accomplished in a split second, and you're ready to continue typing. Notice in Figure 11-5 that a blank line separates groups. This line is inserted automatically when you press [Ctrl] + [Enter] after completing the last of a group of parallel columns. Figure 11-6 illustrates where all the codes are inserted around the first two groups of parallel columns, assuming Block Protect. For parallel columns without Block Protect, all the same codes are inserted, except for the **[Block Pro:]** codes.

R&R WINE ASSOCIATION: LIST OF MANAGERS

[BlockPro:On][ColOn]                                              [Block Pro:Off][ColOff]

↖ Lonnie Chang [HPg]        Director of the Public              (415) 333-4109 ↙
                            Relations Department
                            since 4/12/83.[HPg]
[HRt]]
  Tim Fingerman[HPg]        [Distribution Manager,              (415) 549-1101
↗                           West Coast Region, since                           ↘
[BlockPro:On][ColOn]        6/1/87. Stationed in                [BlockPro:Off][ColOff]
                            Oakland, California.[HPg]
[HRt]

**FIGURE 11-6**  Location of hidden codes in parallel
columns with Block Protect

The standard typing features work in parallel columns just as in newspaper columns. For example, use the [Tab] key to indent the first line of a paragraph or use the CENTER ([Shift] + [F6]) key to center text within one column.

## Turn Off the Column Feature

The last step in creating parallel columns is turning off Column mode. After you've typed the very last column of the last group of parallel columns, don't press [Ctrl] + [Enter], or you'll be inserting another slew of codes to turn off columns for one group and turn them on again for the next group. Instead, follow the same procedure as when turning off newspaper columns. *5.1 users:* Press the COLUMNS/TABLES ([Alt] + [F7]) key, select Columns (1 or C), and select Off (2 or F). *5.0 users:* Press the MATH/ COLUMNS ([Alt] + [F7]) key and select Column On/Off

(3 or C). Now WordPerfect turns off the feature more permanently, inserting a **[Col Off]** code (and a **[Block Pro:Off]** code if you're using Parallel with Block Protect columns) without also inserting another **[Col On]** code.

## Practice with Parallel Columns

Here's an opportunity to practice typing the text in Figure 11-5. You'll establish Parallel with Block Protect columns, where the second column will be wider than the first and third.

1. On the first line of a clear Typing screen, center the title, "R&R WINE ASSOCIATION: LIST OF MANAGERS."

2. Press (Enter) three times to insert blank lines.

3. *5.1 users:* Press the COLUMNS/TABLES ( (Alt) + (F7) ) key, and select Columns (1 or C). [*Pulldown menu:* Layout (L), Columns (C).] The Columns menu appears:

   Columns:  1 On; 2 Off; 3 Define: 0

   *5.0 users:* Press the MATH/COLUMNS ( (Alt) + (F7) ) key to display the following menu:

   1 Math On; 2 Math Def; 3 Column On/Off; 4 Column Def: 0

4. *5.1 users:* Select Define (3 or D). *5.0 users:* Select Column Def (4 or D).

The screen shown in Figure 11-2 appears. Notice that WordPerfect assumes that you want two newspaper-style columns.

5. Select Type (1 or T). The following menu appears:

   Column Type: 1 Newpaper; 2 Parallel; 3 Parallel with Block Protect: 0

6. Select Parallel with Block Protect (3 or B). Your selection is indicated on screen.

7. Select Number of Columns (2 or N).

8. Type **3** and press ⏎. Again, your selection is indicated on screen.

9. Select Margins (4 or M) so you can set your own margins, overriding WordPerfect's suggestions.

10. Set margins for the first column: type **1"** and press ⏎, and then type **2.5"** and press ⏎.

11. Set margins for the second column: type **3"** and press ⏎, and then type **5.5"** and press ⏎.

12. Set margins for the third column: type **6"** and press ⏎, and then type **7.5"** and press ⏎.

13. Press EXIT (F7); the Columns menu reappears on screen.

14. *5.1 users:* Select On (1 or O). *5.0 users:* Select Column On/Off (3 or C); a column indicator such as the following appears on the status line to reflect that you're in Column mode:

    Col 1 Doc 1 Pg 1 Ln 1.5" Pos 1"

    You are now ready to begin typing the first group of entries.

15. Type **Lonnie Chang**, and press Ctrl + Enter. The cursor jumps to the next column.

16. Type the following:

    Director of the Public Relations Department since 4/12/83.

    and press Ctrl + Enter.

17. Type the phone number **(415) 333-4109** and press Ctrl + Enter. Notice that the cursor moves down to the left margin two lines below the text of the second column, which is the longest entry.

18. Continue until you have completed typing Figure 11-5; do not, however, press Ctrl + Enter after typing the phone number for the *last* group of entries.

19. After typing **(415) 333-9215**, which is the phone number in the last column of the last group, press the COLUMNS/TABLES ( Alt + F7 ) key.

20. *5.1 users:* Select Columns (1 or C), Off (2 or F). *5.0 users:* Select Column On/Off (3 or C). The cursor jumps to the left margin below the columns, and the "Col" indicator disappears. Now you can again type text across the whole width of the page.

# MOVE THE CURSOR IN PARALLEL COLUMNS

You can move the cursor left and right between parallel columns in the same fashion as in newspaper columns. That is, if you press Ctrl + Home, ←, the cursor relocates one column to the left, whereas [Ctrl] + [Home], [Home], [←] moves the cursor to the first column. Similarly, [Ctrl] + [Home], [→] moves the cursor one column to the right, whereas [Ctrl] + [Home], [Home], [→] moves the cursor to the last column to the right.

You can also move the cursor up or down in parallel columns as in newspaper columns—except that Word-Perfect treats each group of parallel columns separately. For example, [Ctrl] + [Home], [↑] moves the cursor to the top line of the parallel column where the cursor is located, just below the blank line separating it from the previous group of parallel columns. Also, if the cursor is at the very end of column 1 for one group, [→] moves the cursor to the beginning of column 2 in the same group, while [↓] moves the cursor to the blank line between two distinct groups of parallel columns. If you press [↓] again, the cursor moves to column 1 in the next group of parallel columns.

Here's some practice moving the cursor:

1. Press [Home], [Home], [↑] to move to the top of the document.

2. Press [↓] until the cursor is inside the columns (look for "Col 1" to appear on the status line).

3. Press [End]. The cursor moves to the right edge of the column.

4. Press [→]. The cursor moves to the top of column 2.

5. Press [Ctrl] + [Home], [↓]. Now the cursor is located at the bottom of column 2 in the first group of parallel columns.

6. Press [Ctrl] + [Home], [→]. The cursor moves across to column 3.

7. Press ⬇. The cursor moves down to the blank line between the first and second group of parallel columns.

8. Press ⬇. The cursor moves down to column 3 in the second group of parallel columns.

# EDIT TEXT IN PARALLEL COLUMNS

Because there are often many short columns created when you work with parallel columns, editing text is trickier than in newspaper columns. You must position the cursor precisely, wading through a number of codes on the Reveal Codes screen.

When you reveal codes in an attempt to check or delete codes within columns, WordPerfect shows the column text only on the left side of the screen, just as with newspaper columns. But if columns are short, you may also see part of the preceding column or the next column. This can be confusing at first.

For instance, Figure 11-7 shows the Reveal Codes screen with the cursor on the "D" in "Director" in the second column of the first group of parallel columns. Notice in the bottom window that you can see the text of all three parallel columns in the group and even part of the next group. They are all shown as if in one column in the bottom window. You must find the [HPg] codes to distinguish where one column ends and another begins within one group of parallel columns. You must find the [Block Pro:On], [Col On], [Block Pro:Off], and [Col Off] codes that surround a group of parallel columns to distinguish that group from a preceding or following group.

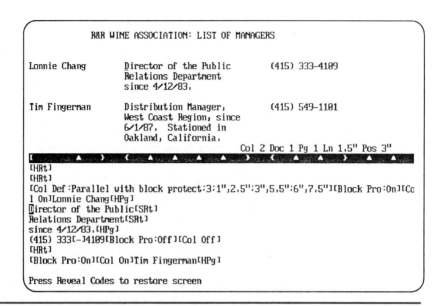

FIGURE 11-7   Reveal Codes screen: cursor in the middle of three parallel columns with Block Protect

If you wish to delete an entire group of parallel columns, make sure that you delete the codes that surround it in addition to the text itself. For instance, suppose that you wish to delete the second group of parallel columns on screen. Remember that these columns are parallel with Block Protect, so that there are Block Protection codes in addition to Column On/Off codes.

1. Position the cursor on the blank line above the "T" in "Tim Fingerman." By positioning the cursor above this group of parallel columns, you're sure to include the **[Block Pro:On]** and **[Col On]** codes in your highlighted block.

2. Press the BLOCK ( Alt + F4 ) key. [*Pulldown menu:* Edit (E), Block (B).]

3. Press ⬇ twice. Since the first column is only one line long, WordPerfect moves the cursor to the **[HRt]** code below that group, highlighting all of that group's columns, as well as the **[Block Pro:Off]** and **[Col Off]** codes that end the group.

4. Press ⬚Del⬚ and then type **Y** to confirm that you want to delete the column. You have effectively deleted the text in the parallel columns along with the accompanying codes.

5. Save this document under the name PARCOL, which stands for PARallel COLumns.

If you wish to insert an entire group of parallel columns, you must position the cursor in the last column of the preceding group on the **[Block Pro:Off]** code (or on the **[Col Off]** code if you're using regular parallel columns without Block Protect). This way WordPerfect will insert the proper codes when you press ⬚Ctrl⬚ + ⬚Enter⬚ to begin inserting the new group. For instance, if you wish to list information about another manager below the group of parallel columns pertaining to Sandy Peterson, position the cursor at the end of the column containing his phone number. Then reveal codes and position the cursor on the **[Block Pro:Off]** code, as shown in Figure 11-8. Now you can remain in the Reveal Codes screen or return to the Typing screen. Then press ⬚Ctrl⬚ + ⬚Enter⬚ and begin typing the new group of parallel columns. WordPerfect automatically inserts a set of codes for that new group of parallel columns. (You will practice adding a group of parallel columns in the review exercise.)

Parallel columns are not as flexible as newspaper columns. Because so many special codes are inserted as you type parallel columns, you don't have the ability to retrieve

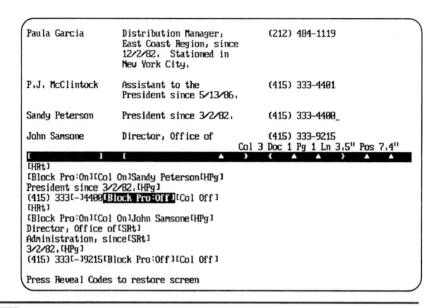

**FIGURE 11-8**  Correct cursor position for inserting a new group of parallel columns

text into the parallel column format. Nor can you type text first and then later attempt to format the text into parallel columns. So if you want columns side by side on a page, make sure to turn on the Column feature for parallel columns before typing the text.

# CREATE TABLES [5.1 USERS ONLY]

There is a new feature available in WordPerfect version 5.1, which, in many cases, will be a better alternative than parallel columns for typing text of varying lengths into columns. The Tables feature has many strengths. For instance, unlike in parallel columns, the Tables feature lets you edit the structure of the columns both before or after you enter text. You can copy, move, or delete entries easily—without concerning yourself with the position of codes. Graphics lines are automatically drawn around the table, which can be altered or removed. You can change the structure of the information from a table to tabular columns or back again. The Tables feature is so flexible that it is also useful for creating forms, where you design the structure of a table as a form and then fill out the table as a form. And, a table can be included in a style (see Chapter 14 for more on styles) or sorted (see Chapter 15 for more on the Sort feature).

With the Tables feature, you create a grid of columns and rows, such as shown in Figure 11-9, by indicating how many columns and rows will comprise your table. Each intersection of a column and a row is referred to as a "cell." Cells are labeled alphabetically (A to Z) from left to right in each row and numerically from top to bottom in each column. So, for example, the entry "Lonnie Chang" along with her title and telephone number is row 1. All the names from "Lonnie Chang" down to "John Samsone" are in column A. Thus, "Lonnie Chang" is cell A1, her phone number is cell C1, "John Samsone" is cell A6, and his phone number is cell C6.

There are two basic steps for working with tables: define the table, and type the text into the table.

## Define a Table Structure

To create a table, position the cursor where you want the table to appear, press COLUMNS/TABLES ( Alt + F7 ) and select Tables (2 or T). Then WordPerfect prompts

`Table: 1 Create; 2 Edit: 0`

Select Create (1 or C). [*Pulldown menu:* Layout (L), Tables (T), Create (C).]

WordPerfect now prompts for the number of columns and assumes that you wish to create 3. Press [Enter] to define 3 columns or type in another number and press [Enter]. Then WordPerfect prompts for the number of rows and assumes that you wish to create 1. Press [Enter] to define 1 row, or type in another number and press [Enter]. You can define up

---

**R&R WINE ASSOCIATION: LIST OF MANAGERS**

| | | |
|---|---|---|
| Lonnie Chang | Director of the Public Relations Department since 4/12/83. | (415) 333-4109 |
| Tim Fingerman | Distribution Manager, West Coast Region, since 6/1/87. Stationed in Oakland, California. | (415) 549-1101 |
| Paula Garcia | Distribution Manager, East Coast Region, since 12/2/82. Stationed in New York City. | (212) 484-1119 |
| P.J. McClintock | Assistant to the President since 5/13/86. | (415) 333-4401 |
| Sandy Peterson | President since 3/2/82. | (415) 333-4400 |
| John Samsone | Director, Office of Administration, since 3/2/82. | (415) 333-9215 |

**FIGURE 11-9** Sample of table (5.1 users only)

to 32 columns and 765 rows in a table. WordPerfect then draws a table grid on screen and displays the Table Edit menu at the bottom of the screen, as shown in Figure 11-10 (assuming that you defined 3 columns and 6 rows). The cursor widens to fill the width of the first cell in column A.

WordPerfect assumes that you want evenly sized columns based on the current margin settings and sets the width of each column accordingly. You can adjust the width of each column, however, so that they have different widths. Position the cursor in the column you wish to alter, hold down the ⟨Ctrl⟩ key, and then press the ⟨←⟩ or ⟨→⟩ key. When a column is widened, the whole table expands up until the right margin is reached; after that, for every increase in the width of a column, WordPerfect decreases the largest column to the right by a corresponding amount.

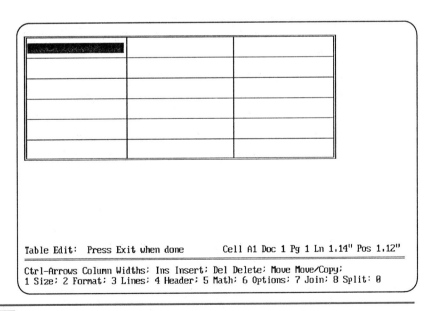

```
Table Edit:  Press Exit when done        Cell A1 Doc 1 Pg 1 Ln 1.14" Pos 1.12"

Ctrl-Arrows Column Widths; Ins Insert; Del Delete; Move Move/Copy;
1 Size; 2 Format; 3 Lines; 4 Header; 5 Math; 6 Options; 7 Join; 8 Split: 0
```

**FIGURE 11-10** Table Edit menu with 3-column, 6-row grid

When a column is narrowed, the whole table narrows. Therefore, it is best to set the width of columns starting with column A, the column at the left margin. (A second method for changing column widths is described later on in this chapter.)

Once you've established the table and adjusted the grid to your liking, press EXIT (F7) to clear the Table Edit menu. The grid remains, and the cursor sits in cell A1. You are now ready to type text into the cells. (You can return to the Table Edit menu at any time, even after you type text into tables, as described later on in this chapter.)

The grid signals where you have inserted a Table Definition code into the text. This **[Tbl Def:]** code indicates the table number, the number of columns in the table, and the width of each column. This code is then followed by additional codes that reserve space for each row and column. A **[Row]** code reserves a row, and a **[Cell]** code reserves a cell in each row. At the end of the last row, a Table Off **[Tbl Off]** code is also inserted.

For instance, suppose that you create a table containing three columns and six rows, as shown in Figure 11-10. Also suppose that the default settings are in effect when you create the table—including a paper width of 8.5″ and left/right margins of 1″. In that case, if you create a table with three evenly spaced columns, each column will be 2.17″ wide. The codes inserted to create the Table grid are as follows:

```
[Tbl Def:I;3,2.17",2.17",2.17"]
[Row][Cell][Cell][Cell]
[Row][Cell][Cell][Cell]
[Row][Cell][Cell][Cell]
[Row][Cell][Cell][Cell]
[Row][Cell][Cell][Cell]
[Row][Cell][Cell][Cell][Tbl Off]
```

Or, suppose you create a second table containing two columns and two rows. In that case, the codes inserted are

```
[Tbl Def:II;2,3.25",3.25"]
[Row][Cell][Cell]
[Row][Cell][Cell][Tbl Off]
```

Of these codes, only the first, the **[Tbl Def:]** code, can be deleted. When you do, you delete the table grid, along with the rest of the codes.

Text that you type into a table will be inserted after the corresponding **[Cell]** code. For instance, a table such as this

| Winter | Spring |
|--------|--------|
| Summer | Autumn |

corresponds to the following on the Reveal Codes screen:

```
[Tbl Def:II;2,3.25",3.25"]
[Row][Cell]Winter[Cell]Spring
[Row][Cell]Summer[Cell]Autumn[Tbl Off]
```

Of course, you can view the codes only on the Reveal Codes screen. On the Typing screen, you see just the grid and your typing.

But the Tables feature is so sophisticated that you need not be concerned with the Reveal Codes screen unless you wish to erase the table. In that case, delete the **[Tbl Def:]** code; all the additional codes that formed the structure of the table, up to and including the **[Tbl Off]** codes, are erased as well. Any text that you typed into the table remains, however, and WordPerfect formats the text based on the current tab settings and hard returns.

# Type Text into a Table

When your cursor is within a defined table, the status line contains a "Cell" indicator, such as

`Cell A1 Doc 1 Pg 1 Ln 1.64" Pos 1.12"`

The "Cell" indicator lets you know which cell your cursor is located in.

To type text into a cell, let word wrap maintain your text within the width boundaries of the cell, just as it maintains text within margins in normal typing; press (Enter) only when you wish to end a paragraph, end a short line of text, or insert a blank line of text within a cell. You can type as many lines in a cell as will fit on one page; the cell's length will automatically expand to accommodate the text. Tables can be many pages long, and WordPerfect will insert a page break between separate rows, so that rows are not split.

Tables differ from parallel columns in that with tables you can enter text into cells in any order. For instance, type all the information in all the cells in column A, and then move on to column B. Or, type all the information in all the cells in row 1, and then move on to row 2. Or, type in the information in cells at random. Once you finish typing in a cell, press (↓) to move to the next cell downward in the same column. Or, press (→) or (Tab) to move to the next cell to the right in the same row. If your cursor is in the last cell for a particular row, (→) or (Tab) moves the cursor to the first cell in the next row.

You can use features such as Indent, Center, or Flush Right to position the text in a cell. However, since pressing (Tab) moves the cursor to the next cell when in tables, to indent a line of text to the next tab stop, press the key sequence (Home), (Tab). That will produce the same effect in tables as pressing [Tab] does in normal typing. You can also use text attributes such as bold and underline in a cell. In addition, you can format particular cells or whole columns with attributes or justification specifications using the Table Edit menu, as discussed later on.

With the Tables feature, you even have the ability to construct a table based on text previously typed into tabular columns. To do so, use the Block feature to highlight the text, then press the COLUMNS/TABLES ([Alt] + [F7]) key and select Create (1 or C). The tab settings are used to determine the cell widths, and the hard returns determine the rows. The text of each tabular column is automatically inserted into the table grid.

When you print out a table, the graphics lines will print as well—providing that your printer supports graphics.

## Practice with Tables

Here's an opportunity to type text into tables. You'll create the table shown in Figure 11-9, which contains the same information as in the parallel columns you created earlier in this chapter. By typing the same information, you'll be able to compare the two features directly. Proceed as follows:

1. On a clear screen, center the title "R&R WINE ASSOCIATION: LIST OF MANAGERS".

2. Press [Enter] three times to insert blank lines.

3. Press the COLUMNS/TABLES ([Alt] + [F7]) key, and select Tables (2 or T). [*Pulldown menu:* Layout (L), Tables (T).]

4. Select Create (1 or C). WordPerfect prompts

```
Number of Columns: 3
```

5. Press (Enter), since the assumption of 3 columns is correct. WordPerfect prompts

   Number of Rows: 1

6. Type **6** and press (Enter). Now the grid and Table Edit menu appear, as shown in Figure 11-10. The cursor is highlighting cell A1.

7. To narrow cell A1, press (Ctrl) + (←) twice.

8. Press (Tab) or (→) to move to cell B1.

9. To widen cell B1, press (Ctrl) + (→) six times.

10. Press EXIT ((F7)) to exit the Table Edit menu.

11. Press (←) to move back to cell A1 and type **Lonnie Chang**.

12. Press (Tab) to move to cell B1 and type the following:

    Director of the Public Relations Department since 4/12/83.

13. Press (Tab) to move to cell C1 and type the phone number **(415) 333-4109**.

14. Press (Tab) to move to cell A2 and type **Tim Fingerman**.

15. Press (↓) to move to cell A3 and type **Paula Garcia**.

16. Continue until you have completed typing Figure 11-9. You can type each cell entry in any order: either typing row by row or column by column.

# MOVE THE CURSOR IN TABLES [5.1 Users Only]

Moving the cursor in tables is similar to moving in parallel columns in that page-by-page cursor movement keys such as (PgUp) and (PgDn) work the same as when not in tables, and other key sequences that typically work across the full width of the screen are confined to the width of a cell. For instance, ⌨Home, ⌨← and ⌨Home, ⌨→ move the cursor to the left or right edge of the current cell.

Within a cell, the arrow keys move the cursor just as on the normal Typing screen or as in parallel columns. And, like for parallel columns, there are several ways to move the cursor quickly within a cell using the GOTO ( ⌨Ctrl + ⌨Home ) key combination:

⌨Ctrl + ⌨Home, ⌨↑   Top line of cell

⌨Ctrl + ⌨Home, ⌨↓   Bottom line of cell

Between cells, the arrow keys can move the cursor if the cursor is at the beginning or end of a cell:

- ⌨← moves the cursor to the previous cell when the cursor is on the first character in a cell.

- ⌨→ moves the cursor to the next cell when the cursor is on the last character.

- ⌨↑ moves the cursor to the cell above when the cursor is on the first line in a cell.

- ⌨↓ moves the cursor to the cell below when the cursor is on the last line in a cell.

There are also other ways to move between cells when the cursor is in the middle of a cell—either by using the GOTO combination or by using the ⌨Tab key:

⌨Ctrl + ⌨Home, ⌨←                    Cell to the left

or

⌨Shift + ⌨Tab

| | |
|---|---|
| Ctrl + Home , → | Cell to the right |

or

Tab

| | |
|---|---|
| Ctrl + Home , Home , ↑ | First cell in a column |
| Ctrl + Home , Home , ↓ | Last cell in a column |
| Ctrl + Home , Home , ← | First cell in a row |
| Ctrl + Home , Home , → | Last cell in a row |
| Ctrl + Home , Home , Home , ↑ | First cell in a table |
| Ctrl + Home , Home , Home , ↓ | Last cell in a table |

*Note:* If you have an enhanced keyboard, you can move between cells by pressing Alt as a substitute for Ctrl + Home above. For instance, to move to the first cell in a column, you can press Ctrl + Home , Home , ↑ . Or, press Alt + ( Home , ↑ ), which means that you hold down the Alt key and, while holding it down, press Home and then press ↑ . Two other keystrokes offered with the Alt key are Alt + ↑ , which moves the cursor one cell up, and Alt + ↓ , which moves the cursor one cell down. But these key sequences will operate only if you use the arrow keys found on the second set of cursor movement keys and not those found on the numeric keypad.

Here's a quick exercise in moving the cursor:

1. Press Home , Home , ↑ to move to the top of the document on screen.

2. Press ↓ until the cursor moves into the table, and "Cell A1" appears on the status line.

3. Press Ctrl + Home , Home , ↓ . The cursor moves to the last cell in column A.

4. Press [Tab] or press [Ctrl] + [Home], [→]. The cursor moves to the next cell to the right, which is in column B.

5. Press [↑]. Since the cursor was at the top of the cell, it now moves to the next cell above.

6. Press [Ctrl] + [Home], [Home], [↑]. The cursor moves to the first cell in column B.

7. Press [Ctrl] + [Home], [Home], [Home], [↓]. The cursor moves to the last cell in the table, cell C6.

# DELETE/INSERT/MOVE/COPY IN TABLES [5.1 USERS ONLY]

You can delete text in tables as you would in a regular document. However, key sequences such as [Ctrl] + [End] delete only within the cell, and do not cross cell boundaries. You can also move or copy text that is part of a table in the same way as you move or copy normal text, except that the Sentence and Paragraph options on the Move menu are restricted to a single cell.

In addition, WordPerfect offers special abilities from the Table Edit menu—features to delete, insert, move, or copy that are adapted specifically to the Tables feature. You must first return to the Table Edit menu. To return to this menu, either position the cursor within the table and press COLUMNS/TABLES ([Alt] + [F7]), or position the cursor below the table, press COLUMNS/TABLES ([Alt] + [F7]), select Tables (2 or T), and select Edit (2 or E). [*Pulldown menu:* Layout (L), Tables (T), Edit (E).] Now, you can move, copy, or delete either a block of cells, a row of cells, or a column of cells.

# Deleting/Inserting from the Table Edit Screen

To delete cells from the Table Edit screen, you must first indicate the cells you wish deleted:

- For a block of cells, position the cursor on the first cell, press BLOCK ( Alt + F4 ), and position the cursor on the last cell in the block. (For a single cell, it is unnecessary to press BLOCK.)

- For a column of cells, position the cursor on any cell in that column.

- For a row of cells, position the cursor on any cell in that row.

Once the cursor is positioned correctly, press the MOVE ( Ctrl + F4 ) key. WordPerfect displays a Move menu for tables:

Move: 1 Block; 2 Row; 3 Column; 4 Retrieve: 0

Select from the first three options. Then WordPerfect responds:

1 Move; 2 Copy; 3 Delete: 0

Select Delete (3 or D).

If you deleted a block, WordPerfect clears the text from the specified cells, but the cells remain in the table. Or, if you deleted a row or column, the text and the column/row of cells is erased.

There's another option if you wish to delete either rows or columns (but not blocks). With the cursor positioned correctly and the Edit Table menu on screen, simply press Del . WordPerfect prompts

`Delete: 1 Rows; 2 Columns: 0`

Select Rows (1 or R) or Columns (2 or C) and then, when prompted, enter the number of rows/columns you wish to delete.

In case you inadvertently delete text, you can restore the last block, row, or column you deleted from the Table Edit screen. This is similar to the Undelete feature used on the normal Typing screen. Position the cursor where you want to restore the cells you deleted and press CANCEL (F1). For instance, if your most recent deletion was a block, WordPerfect prompts

`Undelete Block? No (Yes)`

Type **Y** to restore the deleted text.

You can also insert rows or columns from the Table Edit screen. Position the cursor on the row or column that, to accommodate the inserted rows or columns, you want pushed downward or to the right. Then, press Ins. Word-Perfect prompts:

`Insert: 1 Rows; 2 Columns: 0`

Select Rows (1 or R) or Columns (2 or C), and then, when prompted, enter the number of rows or columns you wish to insert.

When you're done editing the table structure, you can press EXIT (F7) to leave the Table Edit menu and return to normal typing.

*Note:* If you have an enhanced keyboard, you can quickly insert or delete a single row when in normal typing mode (that is, when the Table Edit menu is not on screen). To insert a row, position the cursor on the row that you want moved down as the new row is inserted and press (Ctrl) + (Ins). To delete a row, position the cursor on a cell in that row, press (Ctrl) + (Del), and type **Y** to confirm the deletion.

Other methods to add rows and columns are discussed in a later section entitled "Edit a Table Structure."

## Moving/Copying from the Table Edit Screen

To move or copy cells from the Table Edit screen, you must first indicate the cells you wish to be moved or copied:

- For a block of cells, position the cursor on the first cell, press BLOCK ((Alt) + (F4)), and position the cursor on the last cell in the block. (For a single cell, it is unnecessary to press BLOCK.)

- For a column of cells, position the cursor on any cell in that column.

- For a row of cells, position the cursor on any cell in that row.

Once the cursor is positioned correctly, press the MOVE ((Ctrl) + (F4)) key. WordPerfect displays the Move menu for tables:

`Move: 1 Block; 2 Row; 3 Column; 4 Retrieve: 0`

Select from the first three options. Then WordPerfect responds with the following:

`1 Move; 2 Copy; 3 Delete: 0`

If you select Move (1 or M) for a block, WordPerfect clears the text from the specified cells, but the cells remain in the table. The text is placed in WordPerfect's move/copy *buffer,* which is like a temporary holding tank; the text is preserved in the buffer so that it can be relocated. Or, if you select Move for a row or column, the text along with the column or row of cells is placed into the buffer.

If you select Copy (2 or C), the cells and text remain, but a copy is placed in the buffer.

A prompt near the bottom of the screen now reads

`Move cursor; press Enter to retrieve.`

In stage two, you "paste" the cells back into the document; that is, you indicate where you want the cells that are currently in the buffer moved or copied to. If you're ready to recall the cells from the buffer immediately, then

- If retrieving a row or column, position the cursor on the row or column that, to accommodate the row or column about to be inserted, you want pushed downward or to the right. Press Enter. WordPerfect inserts it as a new row or column.

- If retrieving a block, position the cursor in the first cell where you want the text inserted. Press Enter. WordPerfect inserts the text into existing cells, erasing any text previously typed in those cells.

On the other hand, you can wait before "pasting" the cells into a new location. Suppose, for instance, that you're retrieving a block, but need to add a row before inserting that block. In that case, instead of positioning the cursor and pressing ⟨Enter⟩, press the CANCEL (⟨F1⟩) key. The prompt "Move cursor; press **Enter** to retrieve." disappears. Now you can continue editing the cells, such as adding a row. When you're ready to reinsert the cells, position the cursor, press the MOVE (⟨Ctrl⟩ + ⟨F4⟩) key, and select Retrieve (4 or R). WordPerfect prompts with

`Retrieve: 1 Block; 2 Row ; 3 Column: 0`

Choose from this menu, and the block, row, or column that had been stored in the buffer is reinserted into the document. (In fact, a block of text remains in the buffer until you wish to move/copy another group of cells, so that you can retrieve the same cells many times: reposition the cursor, press MOVE, select Retrieve, and choose from the Retrieve menu.)

When you're done editing the table structure, you can press EXIT (⟨F7⟩) to leave the Table Edit menu.

Here's an exercise. Suppose you wish to move the row that contains information about Sandy Peterson, the president of R&R, to the top of the table. Proceed as follows:

1. Position the cursor on cell A5, which contains "Sandy Peterson."

2. Press COLUMNS/TABLES (⟨Alt⟩ + ⟨F7⟩) to return to the Table Edit screen. Cell A5 is highlighted.

3. Press MOVE (⟨Ctrl⟩ + ⟨F4⟩). WordPerfect prompts

`Move: 1 Block; 2 Row; 3 Column; 4 Retrieve: 0`

4. Select Row (2 or R). Though only the one cell is still highlighted, your choice is registered. Then WordPerfect responds

`1 Move; 2 Copy; 3 Delete: 0`

5. Select Move (1 or M). The row disappears from the text. Near the bottom of the screen, WordPerfect prompts

   `Move cursor; press Enter to retrieve.`

6. Press ⬆ until the cursor is highlighting cell A1, which contains "Lonnie Chang".

7. Press Enter. The results are shown in Figure 11-11.

8. Press EXIT (F7) to leave the Table Edit menu.

9. Save this document under the filename TABLE.

# EDIT A TABLE STRUCTURE [5.1 USERS ONLY]

When you create a table, WordPerfect makes certain assumptions about the table's design and format. These default settings include the following:

- Double lines border the outside of the table.

- Single lines border the inside of the table.

- The height of a cell is determined by the amount of text in the cell.

- Text is left-justified in each cell.

If you want to change any of these, or if you wish to redefine how you initially created a table, you can do so on

R&R WINE ASSOCIATION: LIST OF MANAGERS

| | | |
|---|---|---|
| Sandy Peterson | President since 3/2/82. | (415) 333-4400 |
| Lonnie Chang | Director of the Public Relations Department since 4/12/83. | (415) 333-4109 |
| Tim Fingerman | Distribution Manager, West Coast Region, since 6/1/87. Stationed in Oakland, California. | (415) 549-1101 |
| Paula Garcia | Distribution Manager,East Coast Region, since 12/2/82. Stationed in New York City. | (212) 484-1119 |
| P.J. McClintock | Assistant to the President since 5/13/86. | (415) 333-4401 |
| John Samsone | Director, Office of Administration, since 3/2/82. | (415) 333-9215 |

**FIGURE 11-11** Result after moving a row

the Table Edit menu. To return to this menu, either position the cursor within the table and press COLUMNS/ TABLES (Alt + F7), or position the cursor below the table, press COLUMNS/TABLES (Alt + F7), select Tables (2 or T), and select Edit (2 or E). [*Pulldown menu:* Layout (L), Tables (T), Edit (E).] Now you can choose from eight items, as described below. When the editing is complete, press EXIT (F7) to return to normal typing. By editing the table structure, you can create complex tables such as the sample invoice shown in Figure 11-12.

| SHIPPING ADDRESS | | | | INVOICE NUMBER | | |
|---|---|---|---|---|---|---|
| | | | | ACCOUNT # | | |
| | | | | DATE | | |
| BILLING ADDRESS | | | TERMS | | | |
| | | | SHIPPING/HANDLING | | | |
| ITEM # | DESCRIPTION | SHIP DATE | QTY | PRICE | TOTAL | |
| | | | | | | |
| | | | | | | |
| | | | | | | |
| | | | | | | |
| | | | | | | |
| | | | | | | |
| | | | | | | |
| | | | | | | |
| | | | | | | |
| | | | | | | |
| | | | | | | |
| METHOD OF PAYMENT | | SUBTOTAL | | | |
| | | SALES TAX | | | |
| | | AMOUNT DUE | | | |

**FIGURE 11-12** Invoice form created by editing the table structure

# Size

This item enables you to alter the number of rows or columns in the table. Select Size (1 or S), specify whether you wish to alter the size of rows or columns, and enter the total number you desire. For instance, if the table currently contains 3 columns and you wish to add 1 more column, enter 4 columns. Or, if the table contains 12 rows and you wish to delete 2 rows, enter 10 rows. WordPerfect inserts or deletes from the end of the table. (There are alternatives for inserting or deleting rows, as described previously.)

# Format

This item controls the format and text enhancements for either columns or individual cells. It also can specify how WordPerfect will determine the height of each row. You must first position the cursor properly:

- For a block of cells, position the cursor on the first cell, press BLOCK ( Alt + F4 ), and position the cursor on the last cell in the block. (For a single cell, it is unnecessary to press BLOCK.)

- For a column of cells, position the cursor on any cell in that column.

- For a row of cells, position the cursor on any cell in that row.

Next, select Format (2 or F). WordPerfect responds with the Format menu:

```
Format: 1 Cell; 2 Column; 3 Row Height: 0
```

An example is shown at the bottom of Figure 11-13. The current cell and column format settings are indicated just above the Format menu. (If you've highlighted a block, these settings reflect the last cell/column in the block.) For instance, in Figure 11-13, the settings read

```
Cell: Top;Left;Normal                    Col: 2.77";Left;Normal
```

This indicates that: (1) the cell vertical alignment is set at "Top," so that text will be aligned vertically at the top of the cell; (2) the justification in the cell and column is set to "Left;" and (3) font attributes in the cell and column are set to "Normal," meaning that all attributes are turned off.

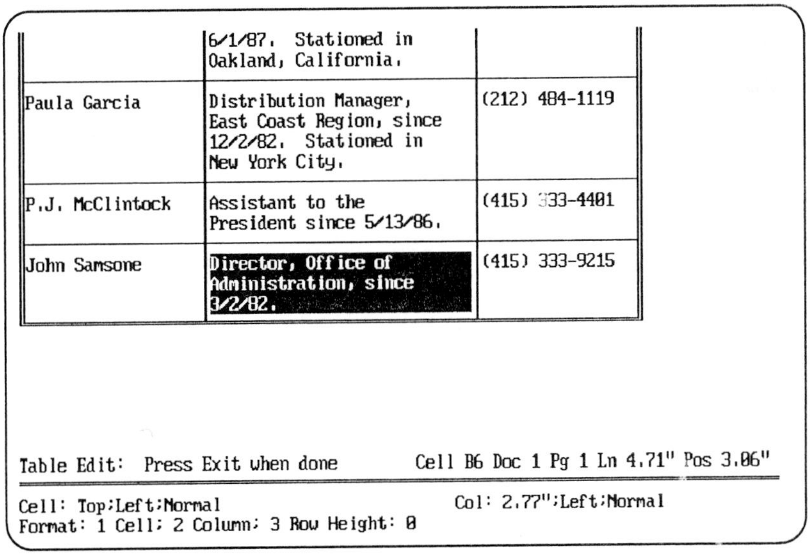

| | | 6/1/87, Stationed in Oakland, California, | |
|---|---|---|---|
| | Paula Garcia | Distribution Manager, East Coast Region, since 12/2/82. Stationed in New York City, | (212) 484-1119 |
| | P.J. McClintock | Assistant to the President since 5/13/86, | (415) 333-4401 |
| | John Samsone | Director, Office of Administration, since 3/2/82. | (415) 333-9215 |

```
Table Edit:  Press Exit when done        Cell B6 Doc 1 Pg 1 Ln 4.71" Pos 3.06"

Cell: Top;Left;Normal                     Col: 2.77";Left;Normal
Format: 1 Cell; 2 Column; 3 Row Height: 0
```

**FIGURE 11-13**   Table Format menu

When you select Cell (1 or C) from the Table Format menu, you can select from the following items:

- *Type*   Specifies either Numeric, which is the default, or Text. This item is related to the Math feature, as described in Chapter 15.

- *Attributes*   Determines font attributes for the cell, such as Bold or Underline or Italics, as discussed in Chapter 10. The default is Normal. The Reset option sets the cell attribute to whatever is the current column attribute. (Or, you can leave the cell with the normal attributes and alter an attribute as you type the text of the cell, as you would in a standard document.)

- *Justify*   Determines the justification setting, as discussed in Chapter 4, for the cell. The default is Left Justification. The Reset option sets the cell justification to whatever is the current column justification.

- *Vertical Alignment*   Determines whether text is aligned at the top, bottom, or center of the cell. The default is top. A change in vertical alignment will have an effect at the printer, but not on the Typing screen.

- *Lock*   Enables you to lock a cell so that the text in the cell cannot be edited, or to unlock a cell. When a cell is locked, the "Cell" indicator on the status line is contained in square brackets, such as **Cell [A1]**.

When you select Column (2 or L), you can choose from the following options:

- *Width*   Changes the width of a column. When a column is widened, the whole table expands up until the right margin is reached; after that, for every increase in the width of a column, WordPerfect decreases the largest column to the right by a corresponding amount. When a column is narrowed, the whole table narrows. The maximum width of a column is the width of the entire table, minus the width of the left border of the column. The minimum width is the left border of the column plus the spacing between the text and the borders (which can be altered; see "Options" later in this chapter).

(There is an alternative for changing the width of columns, as discussed in the earlier section entitled "Create Tables.")

- *Attributes* Determines font attributes for the column, such as Bold or Underline or Italics, as discussed in Chapter 10. The default is Normal. Any attributes set for a cell override the attribute settings for a column, unless you later choose the Reset option for the cell attribute.

- *Justify* Determines the justification setting, as discussed in Chapter 4, for the column. The default is Left Justification. Any justification choices set for a cell override the justification settings for a column, unless you later choose the Reset option for the cell justification.

- *# Digits* Sets the number of digits to the right of the decimal point. The default is 2. WordPerfect uses this setting to align numbers if the column is set to decimal-align justification. Also, this setting is used when math results are calculated. (Math is described in Chapter 15.)

When you select Row Height (3 or R), you can select from the following: Single-line, Fixed; Single-line, Auto; Multi-line, Fixed; or Multi-line, Auto. Single-line specifies that only one line of text can be inserted, displayed, or printed for cells in that row. (If you previously typed more than one line into a cell, the last lines are hidden.) Multi-line enables text to wrap down to the next line. Fixed sets a row height that will be maintained regardless of the size of text for cells in that row. Auto allows WordPerfect to adjust the height of each row. The default is Multi-line, Auto.

## Lines

This item allows you to dictate the type of lines in a table. First, use the BLOCK key to highlight the cells whose line settings you wish to alter. For instance, highlight the entire table if you wish to change all the lines. If you wish to change the lines for one cell only, then there's no need to use the BLOCK key.

Next select Lines (3 or L). Then select the lines you wish to redefine from the following Lines menu:

```
Lines: 1 Top; 2 Bottom; 3 Left; 4 Right; 5 Inside; 6 Outside;
7 All; 8 Shade: 0
```

Here's what these options refer to for a block comprised of four cells:

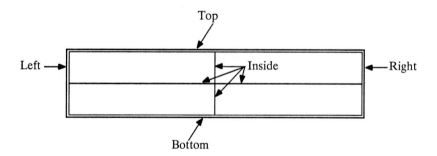

In addition, "Outside" means that you wish to set the top, bottom, left, and right borders in one command. "All" means all graphics lines that comprise the cells. "Shade"

means that you wish to shade the cells by 10%. Or, you can change the shading percentage; see "Options" later in this chapter for details. For one cell, only the Top, Bottom, Left, Right, or All options apply.

Once you select from the Lines menu, you are provided with another menu:

```
1 None; 2 Single; 3 Double; 4 Dashed; 5 Dotted; 6 Thick;
7 Extra Thick: 0
```

Select from this menu and the change appears on screen. Remember that your printer may be able to support only certain of these graphics characters.

## Header

This item is useful when your table spans many pages. It establishes one or more header rows, which are rows that are automatically repeated at the top of every page of the table. Position the cursor near the top of the table, press HEADER (4 or H), and enter the number of rows that are to become header rows. When a row is a header row, the "Cell" indicator on the status line is followed by an asterisk, such as "Cell A1*".

## Math

This item allows you to calculate results down columns or across rows. See Chapter 15 for more on the Math feature.

## Options

This item enables you to change certain settings for all cells in a table. When you select Options (6 or O), a menu as shown in Figure 11-14 appears, displaying the current default settings:

- *Spacing between text and lines*  The amount of white space between the text and cell borders

- *Display negative results*  The method in which negative numbers are displayed when WordPerfect calculates results during Math, either with minus signs, such as in −50, or with parentheses, such as in (50)

- *Position of table*  The position of the table with respect to the margins, of importance only if you decrease the width of the table from its original dimensions. Options

```
Table Options

  1 - Spacing between text and lines
        Left                        0.083"
        Right                       0.083"
        Top                         0.1"
        Bottom                      0"

  2 - Display negative results      1
        1 = with minus signs
        2 = with parentheses

  3 - Position of table             Left

  4 - Gray Shading (% of black)     10%




Selection: 0
```

**FIGURE 11-14**  Table Options menu

are to align the table against the left margin, against the right margin, centered between the margins, or at a specific distance from the left edge of the page. Or, you can select Fill, in which case WordPerfect will resize the table to fill the space between the margins

- *Gray Shading*   The percentage that a cell will be shaded if shading is turned on using the Lines item. The higher the percentage, the darker the shading; 100% is black

## Join

To combine multiple cells into one, use the BLOCK key to highlight the cells you want combined and select Join (7 or J). Text that was previously in adjoining columns will be separated by Tab codes, while text previously in adjoining rows will be separated by Hard Return codes.

## Split

To split a cell into multiple rows or columns, position the cursor on the cell and select Split (8 or S). Now you can specify the number of rows and/or columns in which to divide the cell. Or, to split a group of cells in the same operation, use the BLOCK key to highlight the cells you wish to divide before selecting Split. Each cell in the block will be split into the number of rows and columns that you specify.

# REVIEW EXERCISE

Here's some practice using the text you've been typing throughout this chapter. You'll first format already existing text into newspaper columns. Then you'll insert additional information into parallel column format. 5.1 users will also work with tables.

Suppose that you want to format text into two newspaper columns, with the right column wider than the left. Proceed as follows:

1. On a clear screen, retrieve the file named NEWCOL (the text that is no longer formatted into newspaper columns).

2. Position the cursor at the left margin on the line that reads "NEW SERVICE OFFERED," the heading for the first column.

3. Establish a new column definition for two newspaper columns; the left column will have margins of 1″ and 3.6″, while the right column will have margins of 4″ and 7.5″.

4. Turn on the Column mode.

5. Use the cursor movement keys to move the cursor downward; as you do, watch as the text reformats into the two columns you defined.

6. Save and then print this document. The result (with full justification) is shown in Figure 11-15.

Suppose that you wish to insert another person's name at the bottom of the list of managers you typed using parallel columns. Continue as follows:

1. On a clear screen, retrieve PARCOL, which contains the list of managers that you typed in parallel columns format with Block Protect.

R&R WINE ASSOCIATION
EMPLOYEE NEWS

**NEW SERVICE OFFERED**

All R&R Wine Association employees are now eligible for two valuable company services.

First is the new R&R Money Market Fund. Any percentage of your monthly salary can be automatically invested in the Money Market Fund, an established mutual fund with assets so far of over $1 million. The R&R Money Market Fund is just a part of a larger fund, which is over $45 million strong.

The R&R Money Market Fund is professionally managed by The Thomas Corporation, one of the nation's leading mutual fund companies.

Second, and as a complimentary feature, we now offer a financial planning service, free to all employees. You'll learn how to minimize taxes, what to do about life insurance, and how to handle emergency needs. You'll also be advised on pension plan options.

Why do we offer the Money Market Fund? So that your investments are wise ones, so that you get long-term profit from your earnings at R&R.

Why do we offer the FREE financial planning service? For the same reasons.

To find out more about the benefits of joining our company's Money Market Fund, call Karl Nottingsworth at (415) 666-9444. He's also the person you'll want to speak with about setting up an appointment for financial planning!

**WORLD OF WINES**

In our last newsletter, we completed a five-part series on wines produced in the United States. Next month, we begin a new series on the wines of Europe. Our first nation in Europe? By popular request, it will be France.

France is most often considered the greatest wine-producing country in the world. The variety of wines grown here is absolutely amazing: the sparkling wines of Champagne, the red wines of Bordeaux, the red and white wines of Burgundy, the sweet wines of Barsac--just to name a few!

You'll learn about all the French wines we ship around the country in our next edition of R&R Wine News.

**FIGURE 11-15** Practice exercise after formatting text into newspaper columns

2. Position the cursor just to the right of the phone number (415) 333-9215, which is John Samsone's phone number.

3. Reveal codes and position the cursor on the **[Block Pro:Off]** code.

4. Press HARD PAGE (⌈Ctrl⌉ + ⌈Enter⌉), and type **George Wilson**.

5. Press HARD PAGE (⌈Ctrl⌉ + ⌈Enter⌉), and type the following:

   ```
   Distribution Manager, Midwest Region, since 5/4/86. Stationed in
   Chicago, Illinois.
   ```

6. Press HARD PAGE (⌈Ctrl⌉ + ⌈Enter⌉), and type **(312) 731-2204**.

7. Save your practice document for creating parallel columns, again under the name PARCOL.

*5.1 users:* Suppose that you want to add a row to the bottom of the table you previously typed with the Tables feature. Proceed as follows:

1. On a clear screen, retrieve TABLE, which contains the list of managers you typed using the Tables feature.

2. Position the cursor anywhere within the table. You'll know that the cursor is in the table when the "Cell" indicator appears on the status line.

3. Press COLUMNS/TABLES (⌈Alt⌉ + ⌈F7⌉) to return to the Table Edit menu.

4. Select Size (1 or S), and then select Rows (1 or R).

5. Since the table contains 6 rows and you wish to add 1 more, type **7** and press ⌈Enter⌉.

6. Press EXIT (⌈F7⌉) to clear the Table Edit menu.

7. Now you can type entries into the new row. For instance, you can follow steps 4 through 6 in the review exercise for parallel columns to type information about George Wilson. Remember that you move from cell to cell by pressing ⊞ or ⊞Tab⊞ (and not by pressing ⊞Ctrl⊞ + ⊞Enter⊞, as is the case for parallel columns).

## Quick Review

- To define the layout of the columns, the first step in creating text columns, 5.1 users should press the COLUMNS/TABLES ([Alt] + [F7]) key, and select Columns (1 or C), Define (3 or D). Or, pulldown menu users should select Layout (L), Columns (C), Define (D). 5.0 users should press MATH/CO-LUMNS ([Alt] + [F7]) and select Column Def (4 or D). Select the type of column you desire — Newspaper, Parallel, or Parallel with Block Protect, useful if entries are shorter than a page and you wish to guard against a group of parallel columns being split by a page break. Then, select the number of columns you desire, and either set the spacing between columns or set individual column margins.

- To turn on columns, a necessary step after defining columns but before typing text, 5.1 users should press the COLUMNS/TABLES ([Alt] + [F7]) key, and select Columns (1 or C), On (1 or O). Pulldown menu users should select Layout (L), Columns (C), On (O). 5.0 users should press MATH/COL-UMNS ([Alt] + [F7]) and select Column On/Off (3 or C).

- In newspaper-style columns, text reads down the page and then continues at the top of the next column. Thus, type text down to the bottom of the page and let WordPerfect automatically break to a new column at the end of a page. Or, break a column early by pressing [Ctrl] + [Enter]. You can also format previously typed text into columns by retrieving the text into the document defined for columns.

- In parallel-style columns, related information is kept together side by side across the page. Thus, type each group of parallel columns across the page: Type the first entry, and then press [Ctrl] + [Enter]; type the second entry to its right, and then press [Ctrl] + [Enter]; and so on. After a group of parallel columns is typed, press [Ctrl] + [Enter] to start the first entry for the next group. WordPerfect inserts a blank line between each group of parallel columns.

- Turn columns off after columns are typed by positioning the cursor at the end of the text columns and following the same procedure as for turning on columns, except that 5.1 users should select Off (2 or F) as the final step.

- The variety of methods for moving the cursor quickly within and between text columns is summarized in Table 11-1.

- *5.1 users:* Create a table by pressing COLUMNS/ TABLES ([Alt] + [F7]), selecting Tables (2 or T), and Create (1 or C). Pulldown menu users should select Layout (L), Tables (T), Create (C). Next, enter the number of columns and rows to comprise the table. Adjust the column width by positioning the cursor and pressing [Ctrl] + [→] or [Ctrl] + [←]. Once the structure is set, press EXIT ([F7]).

- The variety of methods for moving the cursor quickly within and between cells in a table is summarized in Table 11-2.

- Edit the format or structure of a table by displaying the Table Edit menu. Position the cursor within the table and press COLUMNS/TABLES ( [Alt] + [F7] ). Or, position the cursor below the table, press COL-UMNS/ TABLES ( [Alt] + [F7] ), select Tables (2 or T), and select Edit (2 or E). Pulldown menu users select Layout (L), Tables (T), Edit (E). Eight options are available on the Table Edit menu for altering rows, columns, individual cells, or the table as a whole.

- A quick method for deleting a row or column when the Table Edit menu is displayed is to position the cursor on a cell in the row or column you wish to delete and press [Del]. Or, to insert a row or column place the cursor on a cell in the row or column that will be moved down or to the right and press [Ins].

- To move or copy cells within a table, display the Table Edit menu for that table. Next, position the cursor in a cell within the column or row you wish to move or copy, or use the BLOCK key to highlight the group of cells you wish to move or copy. Then, press MOVE ( [Ctrl] + [F4] ), select from the the Block, Row, or Column options, and choose Move or Copy. To "paste" the cells back into the table, reposition the cursor within the table and press [Enter].

| Cursor Movement | Keystroke Sequence |
|---|---|
| Preceding column | * [Ctrl] + [Home] , [←] |
| Next column | * [Ctrl] + [Home] , [→] |
| Top line of current column | [Ctrl] + [Home] , [↑] |
| Bottom line of current column | [Ctrl] + [Home] , [↓] |
| First column | [Ctrl] + [Home] , [Home] , [←] |
| Last column | [Ctrl] + [Home] , [Home] , [→] |

* For 5.1 users with an enhanced keyboard, a substitute for [Ctrl] + [Home] is [Alt] when using the second set of cursor movement keys, and not keys on the numeric keypad

**TABLE 11-1** Cursor Movement in Text Columns

| Cursor Movement | Keystroke Sequence |
|---|---|
| Preceding cell | * [Ctrl] + [Home] , [←] |
| | or |
| | [Shift] + [Tab] |
| Next cell | * [Ctrl] + [Home] , [→] |
| | or |
| | [Tab] |
| Cell above | [Alt] + [↑] |
| Cell below | [Alt] + [↓] |
| Top line of cell | [Ctrl] + [Home] , [↑] |
| Bottom line of cell | [Ctrl] + [Home] , [↓] |
| First cell in row | * [Ctrl] + [Home] , [Home] , [←] |
| Last cell in row | * [Ctrl] + [Home] , [Home] , [→] |
| First cell in column | * [Ctrl] + [Home] , [Home] , [↑] |
| Last cell in column | * [Ctrl] + [Home] , [Home] , [↓] |
| First cell in table | * [Ctrl] + [Home] , [Home] , [Home] , [↑] |
| Last cell in table | * [Ctrl] + [Home] , [Home] , [Home] , [↓] |

* With an enhanced keyboard, a substitute for [Ctrl] + [Home] is [Alt] when using the second set of cursor movement keys and not keys on the numeric keypad.

**TABLE 11-2** Cursor Movement in Tables
(5.1 Only)

# chapter 12

# OUTLINING, PARAGRAPH AND LINE NUMBERING, FOOTNOTING

Create an Outline
Edit an Outline
Define a Numbering Style
Number Individual Paragraphs
Number Lines at the Printer
Insert Footnotes and Endnotes
Edit Footnotes and Endnotes
Change Footnote and Endnote Options
Review Exercise
Quick Review

WordPerfect offers several special numbering features that will save you time. If you create outlines, you can have WordPerfect automatically insert outline numbers for you. Similarly, if you write documents in which you number paragraphs, WordPerfect can insert those paragraph numbers, too. Or, have WordPerfect number every line on a page.

You can also allow WordPerfect to do the work in incorporating footnotes or endnotes into the text. WordPerfect numbers the notes sequentially, and the hassle of trying to position footnotes correctly at the bottom of the page is no longer yours; WordPerfect places the footnotes on the page for you and inserts a separator line between the body of the text and the notes.

What these features have in common is that WordPerfect makes sure that the items marked by each feature are *always* numbered properly. If you delete an outline entry, the entire outline is renumbered as required. If you move a paragraph in the text, all the paragraphs are renumbered as necessary. If you insert a footnote, all subsequent footnotes are renumbered to accommodate the insertion. This chapter covers these timesaving features.

# CREATE AN OUTLINE

Before you write a lengthy report, perhaps you first create an outline to organize your thinking and guide you as you write. Or you might write agendas in outline form to make sure that you'll cover all the topics slated for a presentation. Figure 12-1 shows an example of an outline.

Of course, you can create a simple outline without using the Outline feature by simply typing in outline characters (I., II., A., 1., and so on) on your own. However, WordPerfect's Outline feature makes the job a whole lot easier. First, it inserts the outline characters automatically. Second, if you rearrange an outline — add to it, delete from it, or move entries—WordPerfect renumbers the entire outline. Since writing an outline is a fluid, evolving process, the renumbering feature is pure convenience.

WordPerfect inserts an outline character depending on what numbering style you have chosen and which tab stop the cursor is located on. WordPerfect's default for the style of characters is referred to as outline style. There are eight levels in this style; level 1 is at the left margin, and each successive level is located at the next tab stop. The style of

---

AGENDA: R&R WINE ASSOCIATION BOARD MEETING

I.   Minutes of the last meeting.

II.  Reorganization of the Finance Department.

　　A.　Who shall fill the position of department manager?  Ms. Donna Rainer's name was mentioned previously.

　　B.　To whom shall the department manager report?

　　　　1.　The department currently reports to the Vice President.

　　　　2.　The President is currently more involved in the day-to-day operations and restructuring, and works well with Ms. Rainer.

III. Authorization of a new Strategic Plan.

　　A.　The original plan, completed by the consulting firm of Burnes and Joseph on May 13th, 1984, is outdated.

　　B.　Demographics and consumer preferences have changed significantly over the past five years.

---

**FIGURE 12-1**  Sample outline using outline style for numbering

characters changes for each of these levels. Level 1, for example, is an uppercase Roman numeral followed by a period. The default styles for all eight levels are

```
Level 1    I.
Level 2      A.
Level 3        1.
Level 4          a.
Level 5            (1)
Level 6              (a)
Level 7                i)
Level 8                  a)
```

Notice that Figure 12-1 uses the first three levels.

When you're ready to create an outline, you switch on the Outline feature by pressing the DATE/OUTLINE (⟦Shift⟧ + ⟦F5⟧) key and selecting Outline (4 or O). [*Pull-down menu:* Tools (T), Outline (O).] *5.1 users:* Select On (1 or O) from the Outline menu that appears. *5.0 users:* No menu appears, and Outline is turned on automatically. For both 5.1 and 5.0 users, the message "Outline" appears in the lower left corner of the screen, reminding you that the feature is now activated; you are in Outline mode.

Four keys work together to create an outline when the feature is active.

- ⟦Enter⟧ When you press ⟦Enter⟧ to insert a Hard Return [HRt] code, the cursor moves down a line, and an outline number is automatically inserted on that new line. If you press ⟦Enter⟧ again, the outline number moves down another line. (If you press ⟦Ctrl⟧ + ⟦Enter⟧ to insert a Hard Page [HPg] code, an outline number is also inserted on the new page.)

- ⟦Tab⟧ With the cursor just to the right of an outline number (as in the case just after you press the ⟦Enter⟧ key to insert a level-1 number), the [Tab] key moves the outline number one tab to the right and increases the numbering style to that of the next level.

- *◆MARGIN RELEASE key* With the cursor just to the right of an outline number, the ◆MARGIN RELEASE ([Shift] + [Tab]) key moves the outline number one tab to the left and decreases the numbering style to that of the preceding level.

- *◆INDENT key* With the cursor just to the right of an outline number, the ◆INDENT ([F4]) key moves the cursor without moving the outline number, indenting all lines of text to the next tab stop until you again press [Enter]. (Alternatively, you can use the spacebar to insert space to the right of an outline number before typing text, but in this case, only text on the first line will be indented. Or, version 5.1 users can press [Home], [Tab] to indent the first line of text to the next tab stop.)

When you have completed an outline, you must remember to switch out of Outline mode; otherwise, an outline number will appear each time you press [Enter]. Turn off the feature the same way you turned it on: Press DATE/OUTLINE ([Shift] + [F5]) and select Outline (4 or O). *5.1 users*: Select Off (2 or F). *5.0 users*: No menu appears, and Outline is turned off automatically.

On the screen, it appears as if numbers are inserted into the text, but if you reveal codes, you will see that what is inserted are actually **[Par Num:Auto]** codes. This code means that at each location where an outline number appears, a paragraph number (Par Num) has been inserted automatically (Auto). Because of this code, the outline readjusts as you add, delete, or move an outline number so that the remaining entries are numbered in the correct sequence. (The Outline Numbering feature and the Paragraph Numbering feature—both described later in this chapter—share the same code, so don't let the term "paragraph number code" confuse you; it controls *outline* numbers as well.)

*5.1 users only:* Outline codes are also inserted at the beginning and end of the outline to mark its boundaries. An **[Outline On]** code is inserted at the top of the outline, wherever you turned on the feature, and an **[Outline Off]** code is inserted at the bottom of the outline, wherever you turned off the feature.

Let's produce the outline illustrated in Figure 12-1, to see how the feature operates.

1. On a clear screen, center the title, "AGENDA: R&R WINE ASSOCIATION BOARD MEETING," on the first line, and then press Enter to move the cursor to the next line.

2. Press the DATE/OUTLINE ( Shift + F5 ) key. [*Pulldown menu:* Tools (T).] The following menu appears:

    1 Date Text; 2 Date Code; 3 Date Format; 4 Outline;
    5 Para Num; 6 Define: 0

3. Select Outline (4 or O). (*5.1 users only:* Then select On (1 or O).) The message "Outline" appears on the status line, signifying that you're in Outline mode.

4. Press Enter . The cursor moves down a line and the Roman numeral "I." appears on that line.

5. Press the →INDENT ( F4 ) key to indent the first item.

6. Type the following:

    Minutes of the last meeting.

7. Press [Enter] twice — once to insert "II." on a new line and a second time to move the outline number down one more line, inserting a blank line.

8. Press the ➔INDENT ([F4]) key and type the following:

   `Reorganization of the Finance Department.`

9. Press [Enter] twice, inserting "III."

10. Press [Tab]. This changes the outline number from level 1 to level 2; an "A." appears.

11. Press the ➔INDENT ([F4]) key and type the following:

    `Who shall fill the position of department manager? Ms.`
    `Donna Rainer's name was mentioned previously.`

12. Press [Enter] twice, and continue until you complete the outline in Figure 12-1. Remember to use [Tab] and [Shift] + [Tab] to change the outline level, if required, before indenting and typing each outline entry.

13. When the outline is complete, press the DATE/OUT-LINE ([Shift] + [F5]) key and select Outline (4 or O). (*5.1 users only:* Then select Off (2 or F).) Now Outline mode is turned off, and the [Enter] and other keys return to their usual functions.

If you reveal codes, you'll see that codes, rather than actual numbers, have been inserted in the text. Figure 12-2 illustrates the Reveal Codes screen with the cursor on the outline number "I." near the top of the document. Notice that where outline numbers are displayed in the top window, **[Par Num:Auto]** codes rather than numbers are displayed in the bottom window.

# EDIT AN OUTLINE

An outline can be easily edited. Once you've completed an outline, you can delete an outline number just as you delete any character on screen, using the [Del] or [Backspace] key. You can move the outline number, along with the text that follows, just as you move standard text. To add an outline number, however, make sure not to type in a Roman numeral or letter followed by a period. Instead, make sure that you're in Outline mode and use the [Enter] key to insert an outline number. *5.1 users:* To return to Outline mode, simply position the cursor in the outline, between the beginning and end outline codes. *5.0 users:* To return to Outline mode, you must again press DATE/OUTLINE ([Shift] + [F5]) and select Outline (4 or O). (You can also

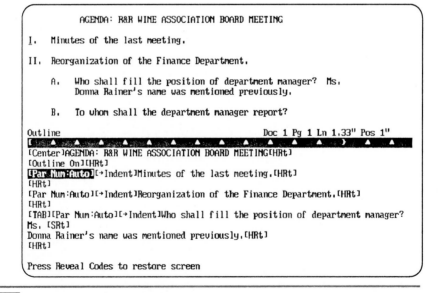

```
        AGENDA: R&R WINE ASSOCIATION BOARD MEETING
I.   Minutes of the last meeting.

II.  Reorganization of the Finance Department.

     A.   Who shall fill the position of department manager?  Ms.
          Donna Rainer's name was mentioned previously.

     B.   To whom shall the department manager report?

Outline                                   Doc 1 Pg 1 Ln 1.33" Pos 1"
[        ▲     ▲     ▲     ▲     ▲     ▲     ▲     ▲     ▲     ▲   ]  ▲     ▲
[Center]AGENDA: R&R WINE ASSOCIATION BOARD MEETING[HRt]
[Outline On][HRt]
[Par Num:Auto][→Indent]Minutes of the last meeting.[HRt]
[HRt]
[Par Num:Auto][→Indent]Reorganization of the Finance Department.[HRt]
[HRt]
[TAB][Par Num:Auto][→Indent]Who shall fill the position of department manager?
Ms. [SRt]
Donna Rainer's name was mentioned previously.[HRt]
[HRt]

Press Reveal Codes to restore screen
```

═══════ **FIGURE 12-2**  Reveal Codes screen showing numbering codes

add an outline number without switching into Outline mode by using the Paragraph Numbering feature, described farther on in this chapter.)

You can also change an outline level once you've completed the outline. Edit outline levels when you're in Outline mode by placing the cursor *just to the right* of the outline number and pressing ⟦Tab⟧ to increase or ◄MARGIN RELEASE (⟦Shift⟧ + ⟦Tab⟧) to decrease the outline level. Moreover, you can adjust the outline level when the cursor is located *on* the outline number by pressing ⟦Tab⟧ to increase or ⟦Backspace⟧ to decrease the outline level. (*5.0 users:* This latter method, where you position the cursor on the code before changing the level, also works when you're no longer in Outline mode.)

You may find that when you edit outline entries, sometimes the outline numbers on screen do not adjust until you rewrite the screen. You can do so by continuing to press ⟦↓⟧ or by pressing another cursor movement key, such as ⟦PgDn⟧, that relocates the cursor through the outline; each line is renumbered as the cursor moves past it.

You can also rewrite the entire screen without needing to move the cursor. Press the SCREEN (⟦Ctrl⟧ + ⟦F3⟧) key to display the Rewrite menu:

```
1 Window; 2 Line Draw; 3 Rewrite:   3
```

Then simply press Rewrite (3 or R) or press ⟦Enter⟧ to clear the menu and, at the same time, rewrite the screen. (*5.0 users:* This menu is numbered differently; choose 0 or R to select Rewrite.)

Let's edit the outline now on screen and observe how WordPerfect renumbers it for you.

1. Position the cursor on the "I." at the beginning of the first outline entry.

2. Press ⟦Tab⟧ to move the outline number to the next tab stop.

3. Press ⟦↓⟧ and watch as the outline number on the previous line changes from "I." to "A."

4. Continue to press ⟦↓⟧ and watch as all the level-1 outline numbers adjust, based on how you edited the first outline entry.

5. Position the cursor back near the top of the document on the "A." of the first outline entry.

6. Press ⟦Backspace⟧ to move the outline number back to the left margin.

7. *5.1 users:* The outline numbers readjust. *5.0 users:* Press SCREEN (⟦Ctrl⟧ + ⟦F3⟧) and press ⟦Enter⟧ to watch as the level-1 outline numbers readjust.

8. The cursor should now be located on the "I." at the beginning of the first outline entry. If not, reposition the cursor.

9. Press the DELETE EOL (⟦Ctrl⟧ + ⟦End⟧) key to erase the entire entry.

10. *5.1 users:* The outline numbers readjust. *5.0 users:* Press SCREEN (⟦Ctrl⟧ + ⟦F3⟧) and press ⟦Enter⟧ and watch as the level-1 outline numbers readjust yet again.

## Move the Cursor in an Outline [5.1 Users Only]

If your computer is equipped with an enhanced keyboard, and when Outline mode is on, then four key combinations help you move the cursor within an outline. Two of them move the cursor backward in an outline:

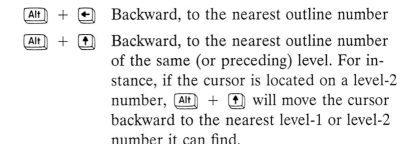 Backward, to the nearest outline number

Backward, to the nearest outline number of the same (or preceding) level. For instance, if the cursor is located on a level-2 number, ⟨Alt⟩ + ⟨↑⟩ will move the cursor backward to the nearest level-1 or level-2 number it can find.

Two key combinations move the cursor forward in the text:

⟨Alt⟩ + ⟨→⟩  Forward, to the next outline number

⟨Alt⟩ + ⟨↓⟩  Forward, to the next outline number of the same (or preceding) level

These key combinations will operate only if you use the arrow keys found on the second set of cursor movement keys, and not those found on the numeric keypad.

## Move/Copy/Delete an Outline Family [5.1 Users Only]

An outline *family* consists of the outline level on the line where the cursor is located plus any subordinate (lower) outline entries. For instance, suppose that the cursor is on the line that reads "II. Reorganization of the Finance Department." for the outline in Figure 12-1. In that case, the family includes all outline numbers and text up to the Roman numeral III. Or, suppose that the cursor is on the line that reads "B. To whom shall the department manager report?" In that case, the family includes all outline numbers and text up to the Roman numeral III.

You can move, copy, or delete entire outline families in one command. To do so, position the cursor on the first line in the family. Next, press DATE/OUTLINE (Shift + F5 ) and select Outline (4 or O). [*Pulldown menu:* Tools (T), Outline (O).] The Outline menu appears:

```
Outline: 1 On; 2 Off; 3 Move Family; 4 Copy Family; 5 Delete
Family: 0
```

Select Move Family (3 or M) and WordPerfect highlights the family. An example is shown in Figure 12-3, after the cursor was positioned on the line for outline number II. Use the ↑ and ↓ keys to reposition the family. You can

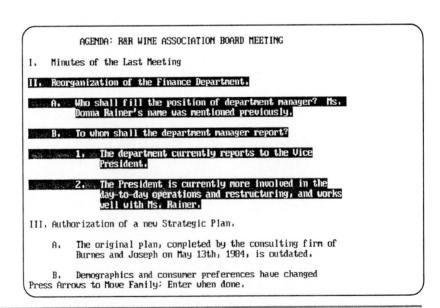

**FIGURE 12-3** Outline family highlighted for a move

also use ⬅ or ➡ to decrease or increase all the outline levels in the family at one time. Then press Enter to fix the family in place.

Or, select Copy Family (4 or C), in which case a *copy* of the family is produced and highlighted on the screen. Use the arrow keys to reposition the family. Then press Enter to fix the copy in place. The original family will not have been moved.

Or, select Delete Family (5 or D) and type **Y** to confirm, so that WordPerfect will delete the family from the outline. WordPerfect places a copy of the deleted family in a buffer, just in case you wish to restore your deletion. To restore the deleted family, position the cursor, press RETRIEVE ( Shift + F10 ), and press Enter .

# DEFINE A NUMBERING STYLE

There are several instances when it becomes necessary to define the numbering style for your outline. First, you must define a numbering style when you want to create two or more independent outlines in the same document. For instance, you may wish to create separate outlines in one document, each beginning with the first number of the first level, "I." If you don't define a new numbering style, Word-Perfect will continue numbering a second outline with the number at which the first outline left off.

Second, you must define a numbering style if you want the outline number style to be different from the default. Besides the outline style, which is the default setting, WordPerfect has three other predefined styles: the paragraph style, the legal style, and the bullets style. All four styles are illustrated in Figure 12-4. (Not all printers can print all the symbols used in the bullets style.) In addition, WordPerfect allows you to define your own numbering style, referred to as the user-defined style. For instance, you can choose uppercase letters followed by a period (A., B., C., and so on) as level 1 and lowercase letters followed by a period (a., b., c., and so on) as level 2.

*5.1 users only:* Moreover, you can use the same procedure used in defining a numbering style to customize the Outline feature—specifying how outline numbers are inserted and how the [Enter] key operates.

You can define a new style before or after you type the outline. Position the cursor above the outline or above where you're about to type the outline. (Or you can position the cursor on the Document Initial Codes screen to change the style starting at the top of the document.) Next, press the DATE/OUTLINE ([Shift] + [F5]) key, and select Define (6 or D). [*Pulldown menu:* Tools (T), Define (D).] The Paragraph Number Definition screen appears, as shown in Figure 12-5. (Items 7, 8, and 9 are absent from this screen in version 5.0.) The default is option 3, Outline, though this is difficult to decipher at first. Look at the center of Figure 12-5, next to the category "Current Definition," and you'll see that this style is identical to the style next to option 3, Outline.

Now you can do one or all of the following:

- *Restart numbering for a new outline*  Select Starting Paragraph Number (1 or S). Then type **1** (if the number 1 does not appear) and press [Enter] if you wish numbering to begin at the beginning, regardless of what numbering style you select, so that, for example, the first entry will be "I." when using the outline style or "•" when using the bullets style. Or, type the outline number and level

```
Outline Style

Level 1  I.  II.  ...
Level 2      A.  B.  ...
Level 3          1.  2.  ...
Level 4              a.  b.  ...
Level 5                  (1)  (2)  ...
Level 6                      (a)  (b)  ...
Level 7                          i)  ii)  ...
Level 8                              a)  b)  ...


Paragraph Style

Level 1  1.  2.  ...
Level 2      a.  b.  ...
Level 3          i.  ii.  ...
Level 4              (1)  (2)  ...
Level 5                  (a)  (b)  ...
Level 6                      (i)  (ii)  ...
Level 7                          1)  2)  ...
Level 8                              a)  b)  ...


Legal Style

Level 1  1  2  ...
Level 2      1.1  1.2  ...
Level 3          1.1.1  1.1.2  ...
Level 4              1.1.1.1  1.1.1.2  ...
Level 5                  1.1.1.1.1  1.1.1.1.2  ...
Level 6                      1.1.1.1.1.1  1.1.1.1.1.2  ...
Level 7                          1.1.1.1.1.1.1  1.1.1.1.1.1.2  ...
Level 8                              1.1.1.1.1.1.1.1  1.1.1.1.1.1.1.2  ...


Bullets Style

Level 1  ●                       (bullet)
Level 2      ○                   (hollow bullet)
Level 3          -               (hyphen)
Level 4              ▪           (square bullet)
Level 5                  *       (asterisk)
Level 6                      +   (plus)
Level 7                          •       (small bullet)
Level 8                              x   (lowercase x)
```

**FIGURE 12-4**  Four predefined numbering styles

you wish to start at in legal style characters. For instance, type **2** and press (Enter) to begin numbering at "II." (assuming outline style) or type **2.2** and press (Enter) to begin numbering at "II., B." or type **2.2.3** and press (Enter) to begin numbering at "II., B., 3."

- *Choose a new numbering style*    Either select Paragraph (2 or P); Outline (3 or O); Legal (4 or L); or Bullets (5 or B). That numbering style is shown next to the heading "Current Definition" in the center of the screen. (Bullets are special characters that not all printers can print. If you select the Bullets style, print the text to see the results. See Chapter 15,"WordPerfect Extras," for more on special characters.)

    Or, select User-defined (6 or U), in which case the cursor moves next to the heading "Current Definition"

```
Paragraph Number Definition

    1 - Starting Paragraph Number              1
        (in legal style)
                                         Levels
                         1    2    3    4    5    6    7    8
    2 - Paragraph        1,   a,   i,   (1)  (a)  (i)  1)   a)
    3 - Outline          I,   A,   1,   a,   (1)  (a)  i)   a)
    4 - Legal (1,1,1)    1    ,1   ,1   ,1   ,1   ,1   ,1   ,1
    5 - Bullets          •     o    —    ■    *    +    ·    x
    6 - User-defined

    Current Definition   I,   A,   1,   a,   (1)  (a)  i)   a)
    Attach Previous Level     No   No   No   No   No   No   No

    7 - Enter Inserts Paragraph Number         Yes

    8 - Automatically Adjust to Current Level  Yes

    9 - Outline Style Name


Selection: 0
```

══════ **FIGURE 12-5**  Paragraph Number Definition screen (version 5.1)

for the first level. You can then specify the outline number for each level. An outline number can be comprised of two characters (or three characters if two of them are a left and right parenthesis). The choices for the numbering style can include digits, uppercase or lowercase letters, and uppercase or lowercase Roman numerals.

| To specify an outline number with: | Enter the following character: |
| --- | --- |
| Digits | 1 |
| Uppercase Letters | A |
| Uppercase Roman | I |
| Lowercase Letters | a |
| Lowercase Roman | i |

In addition, any other keyboard character (such as a period or parentheses for punctuation) or special character (such as bullets of various sizes or typographical symbols) can also be included in a numbering style by typing in that character. (See Chapter 15 for a discussion of how to insert special characters in a WordPerfect document.) For instance, type **(A)** and press Enter to specify uppercase letters surrounded by parentheses for level 1. Type **i-** and press Enter to specify lowercase Roman numerals followed by a dash for level 2. Continue until you've defined a number style for each level.

While indicating a number style for a given level, you can also specify that the level be attached to the previous level. Here's an example of a level-2 number style that is attached to the previous level:

```
I.
     I.A.
     I.B.
 II.
     II.A.
```

*5.1 users:* Indicate this immediately after typing in the outline number; instead of pressing [Enter], press [↓] to move to the row with a heading that reads "Attach Previous Level" and then type **Y** or **N**. (If you press [Enter] and move on to another level, but then want to return to a previous level, you can't go backwards by pressing [←]; instead, press CANCEL and then reselect User-defined (6 or U) so that the cursor returns to the level-1 definition.)

*5.0 users:* Indicate that a level should be attached to a previous level by typing a period as the first character in the outline number, such as in .A or .1.

• *Determine the function of the* [Enter] *key (5.1 users only)* Select Enter Inserts Paragraph Number (7 or E). As a default, this option is set to "Yes," which means that, as you learned, pressing [Enter] inserts an outline/paragraph number when in Outline mode. You can instead type **N** to set this option to "No." In that case, you can insert outline numbers using the Paragraph Numbering feature, described further on in this chapter.

• *Determine the level chosen when a new outline number is first inserted (5.1 users only)* Select Automatically Adjust to Current Level (8 or A). As a default, this option is set to "Yes," which means that when you add a new outline number, WordPerfect inserts that number at whatever level the previous outline number was inserted. For instance, suppose you've typed the following:

```
  I.   Minutes
 II.   Reorganization
        A.   Department of Management
```

When you press [Enter], WordPerfect automatically inserts an outline number at level 2, which would be B. Then you can use [Tab] or [Shift] + [Tab] to change the level.

You can instead type **N** to set this option to "No." In that case, when you add a new outline number, WordPerfect inserts that number at level 1, regardless of the previous outline number. For instance, in the above example, when you press [Enter], WordPerfect inserts an outline number at level 1, which would be III. Then you can use [Tab] or [Shift] + [Tab] to change the level. Setting this option to "No" makes it operate like WordPerfect version 5.0.

- *Specify an outline style name (5.1 users only)* Select Outline Style Name (9 or N). Then choose an outline style from the list of styles that you previously created. These outline styles can be more complicated than the numbering styles allowed when you select User-defined; they are not limited to only two characters and can contain codes to enhance the style, such as underlining or boldfacing. See Chapter 14 for more on the powerful Styles feature and how to create outline styles.

After making selections on the Paragraph Numbering Definition menu, press EXIT ([F7] or [Enter]). The Date/Outline menu returns to the bottom of the screen. Select another option from this menu or press CANCEL ([F1]) to clear this menu. When you return the cursor to the Typing screen, a **[Par Num Def]** code is inserted at the current cursor position. (Remember that outline numbering and paragraph numbering use the same code; even though the code seems to imply a *paragraph* number definition, it also governs *outline* numbers.) The code defines a new outline style for all outline numbers farther forward in the document or until the next **[Par Num Def]** code is encountered.

As an example, suppose that you want to alter the numbering style of the text on screen to legal numbering. Here's how to do so:

1. Position the cursor on the blank line above the first outline number. (Alternatively, you can position the cursor on the Document Initial Codes screen, since you wish to alter the numbering style starting at the top of the document.)

2. Press the DATE/OUTLINE ( Shift + F5 ) key. The following menu appears:

   1 Date Text; 2 Date Code; 3 Date Format; 4 Outline;
   5 Para Num; 6 Define : 0

   [*Pulldown menu:* Tools (T).]

3. Select Define (6 or D). The screen shown in Figure 12-5 appears.

4. Select Legal (4 or L).

5. Press EXIT ( F7 ) to return to the Date/Outline menu.

6. Press CANCEL ( F1 ) to clear the Date/Outline menu and return to the Typing screen.

You have now inserted a **[Par Num Def]** code into the text, redefining the appearance of all the outline numbers. But the screen must be rewritten for this code to take effect. One way to do this is to continue pressing ↓ and watch as the outline numbers are changed. Or, press Home , Home , ↓ to move quickly through the remainder of text to

effect. One way to do this is to continue pressing ⬇️ and watch as the outline numbers are changed. Or, press Home, Home, ⬇️ to move quickly through the remainder of text to the end of the document. You could also press the SCREEN (Ctrl + F3) key and select Rewrite (3 or R) or press Enter. Now every outline number is rewritten according to the new outline style you defined, as shown in Figure 12-6.

It may be necessary sometimes to reset tabs to accommodate long legal-style paragraph numbers or Roman numerals. Position the cursor above the numbered paragraphs to reset the tabs, a procedure described in Chapter 4.

```
          AGENDA: R&R WINE ASSOCIATION BOARD MEETING

1     Reorganization of the Finance Department.

      1.1  Who shall fill the position of department manager?  Ms.
           Donna Rainer's name was mentioned previously.

      1.2  To whom shall the department manager report?

           1.2.1    The department currently reports to the Vice
                    President.

           1.2.2    The President is currently more involved in
                    the day-to-day operations and restructuring,
                    and works well with Ms. Rainer.

2     Authorization of a new Strategic Plan.

      2.1  The original plan, completed by the consulting firm of
           Burnes and Joseph on May 13th, 1984, is outdated.

      2.2  Demographics and consumer preferences have changed
           significantly over the past five years.

Outline                                      Doc 2 Pg 1 Ln 4.83" Pos 1"
```

**FIGURE 12-6**  Sample outline using legal style for numbering

*Note:* In WordPerfect you can permanently change the default numbering style from the outline style to another style by inserting a Paragraph Number Definition code on the Setup Initial Codes screen. For instance, you can request that WordPerfect assume the bullets style for every document you type unless you specify otherwise. Refer to "Initial Settings" in Appendix B for more information.

# NUMBER INDIVIDUAL PARAGRAPHS

Paragraph numbering is a close cousin to the Outline feature. The default numbering style for paragraphs is the same as for outlines and is still referred to as outline style:

```
Leve, 1    I.
Level 2      A.
Level 3        1.
Level 4          a.
Level 5            (1)
Level 6              (a)
Level 7                i)
Level 8                  a)
```

In addition, you can change that default numbering style just as you do for outlines—using the Define option on the Date/Outline menu. In fact, if your outline is composed of paragraphs, outline entries and numbered paragraphs look just the same.

Then what are the differences? There are two. Unlike outline numbers, paragraph numbers are inserted into a document one by one as you type each paragraph; you must press the DATE/OUTLINE ( (Shift) + (F5) ) key each time.

In addition, paragraph numbers can be fixed at a certain level irrespective of where on the line that number will appear. For instance, you can insert level-6 numbers, such as (a), (b), (c), and so on, at the left margin.

You can insert a paragraph number before or after typing the text of the paragraph. You first position the cursor at the tab stop where you want the paragraph number to appear. Then press the DATE/OUTLINE ( Shift  + F5 ) key and select Para Num (5 or P). [*Pulldown menu:* Tools (T), Paragraph Number (P).] WordPerfect responds

```
Paragraph Level (Press Enter for automatic):
```

Now you can proceed in one of two ways. You can press Enter , in which case you create an automatic number—WordPerfect assigns a level based on the current cursor location. For instance, if the cursor is at the left margin or before the first tab stop, WordPerfect assigns that paragraph a level-1 number and inserts a **[Par Num:Auto]** code in the text—the same code it inserts when you use the Outline feature. (In essence, this is a second way to insert the same numbering code.) If you later insert or delete tabs in front of a paragraph number, the level will change. You can adjust the level when the cursor is located *on* the paragraph number: press Tab to increase or Backspace to decrease the outline level.

Alternatively, you can type a number from 1 to 8 and then press Enter , in which case you create a fixed level; you, rather than WordPerfect, are assigning the level. For instance, if the cursor is at the left margin and you type **5** and press Enter , the number at that spot will be a level-5 number. You will have inserted the code **[Par Num:5]** into the text. That number will remain at level 5, no matter how many tabs precede it.

Just as with outlining, if you add, delete, or move paragraph numbers, the text will adjust accordingly so that the numbers are in sequential order. And if you change the paragraph numbering style, the paragraphs will be renumbered according to the new style.

As an example, suppose that you wish to number paragraphs with Arabic numerals—1., 2., 3., and so on—at the left margin. Notice from Figure 12-4 that this corresponds to the paragraph style. Let's first define the style on the Paragraph Number Definition screen. Then we'll insert some paragraph numbers and type the paragraphs shown in Figure 12-7.

1. Save the document on screen under the filename OUT-LINE and clear the screen. On the clear screen, outline

R&R WINE ASSOCIATION UPDATE

1. R&R WINE ASSOCIATION increased its market share in the United States by 2% this year as compared to the same time last year! Congratulations are in order.

2. Sales this quarter were brisk for European and Australian wines. Volumes shipped increased 12% over the same time last year. The Research Department believes that part of the increase is due to the weak dollar on international markets.

3. In the United States, there was a noticeable increase in consumer preference of Chardonnay over other white wines during the past 12 months. This is particularly true in California, where Chardonnay is produced in large quantities.

**FIGURE 12-7**   Sample document with numbered paragraphs

style for paragraph numbers is again in effect, because it's the default setting.

2. Type and center the title, **R&R WINE ASSOCIATION UPDATE**, on the first line, and press [Enter] twice to insert a blank line.

3. Press the DATE/OUTLINE ([Shift] + [F5]) key. The following menu appears:

   1 Date Text; 2 Date Code; 3 Date Format; 4 Outline;
   5 Para Num; 6 Define: 0

   [*Pulldown menu:* Tools (T).]

4. Select Define (6 or D). The screen shown in Figure 12-5 appears.

5. Select Paragraph (2 or P) to start the paragraph style.

6. Press EXIT ([F7]) to return to the Date/Outline menu.

7. Select Para Num (5 or P). WordPerfect prompts

   Paragraph Level (Press Enter for Automatic):

8. Press [Enter]. A "1.," a level-1 number, appears on screen at the left margin.

9. Press the →INDENT ([F4]) key, type the first paragraph in Figure 12-7, and press [Enter] twice to end the paragraph and insert a blank line.

10. Press the DATE/OUTLINE ([Shift] + [F5]) key [*Pulldown menu:* Tools (T)] and repeat steps 7 through 9 to type the second and third paragraphs.

11. Save this document using the filename NUMPARA (which stands for NUMbered PARAgraphs). Leave the document on screen.

What if you had wanted to number paragraphs at the left margin with lowercase letters followed by a period, such as a., b., c., and so on? Notice in Figure 12-4 that this is level 2 of the paragraph style. You could have inserted paragraph numbers fixed at level 2.

If you choose, you can align paragraph numbers with the decimal point, rather than the number, on the tab stop. Press the TAB ALIGN ([Ctrl] + [F6]) key just before you insert a paragraph number.

Make sure to refer to Chapter 14 if you will be using the Paragraph Numbering feature constantly; you'll learn about handy shortcuts for inserting Paragraph Numbering codes into your text.

# NUMBER LINES AT THE PRINTER

WordPerfect offers another feature that can automatically insert numbers on the page. Instead of numbering items in an outline or paragraphs, you can number each line on a page. With the Line Numbering feature, numbers are positioned at or near the left margin of the page. An example is shown in Figure 12-8.

Line numbering might be useful for teaching materials, where you wish to call attention to a specific section of text, as in "Please turn your attention to lines 14 through 20." Or, line numbering might prove useful when editing documents or for counting lines in case you have a line limitation in a certain document. And, line numbering is common in legal documents and can be used to create the same effect as legal pleading paper.

To insert line numbers, position the cursor at the left margin of the line where you want line numbering to begin. Then press the FORMAT ([Shift] + [F8]) key, and select

Line Format (1 or L). [*Pulldown menu:* Layout (L), Line (L).] Then, select Line Numbering (5 or N). Type **Y** to turn line numbering on or type **N** to turn it off. If you turn the feature on, then the Line Numbering menu appears, as shown in Figure 12-9. As you can see, the Line Numbering feature is preset with a variety of defaults that determine how the numbers appear:

- Blank lines are included in the line count and are numbered. To exclude blank lines from the line count, select Count Blank Lines (1 or C) and type **N**.

- A number is printed on every line. If you wish to print numbers in other increments, select Number Every n Lines (2 or N) and enter an increment. For instance, to number every other line, type **2** and press ⌷Enter⌷.

---

```
1                          R&R WINE ASSOCIATION UPDATE
2
3
4       R&R WINE ASSOCIATION increased its market share in the United
5       States by 2% this year as compared to the same time last year!
6       Congratulations are in order.
7
8       Sales this quarter were brisk for European and Australian wines.
9       Volumes shipped increased 12% over the same time last year. The
10      Research Department believes that part of the increase is due to
11      the weak dollar on international markets.
12
13      In the United States, there was a noticeable increase in consumer
14      preference of Chardonnay over other white wines during the past
15      12 months. This is particularly true in California, where
16      Chardonnay is produced in large quantities.
17
18
```

---

**FIGURE 12-8**  Printed results with Line Numbering

- The line numbers are positioned 0.6″ from the left edge of the page. You can select another position by selecting Position of Number from Left Edge (3 or P) and entering a measurement. For instance, to position the numbers 0.5″ from the left edge, type **.5** and press Enter.

- The numbering starts at 1. If you want to start numbering with another number, select Starting Number (4 or S) and enter in the new starting number.

- The numbering restarts at 1 on every page. If you want the numbering to continue—so that, for example, if page 1 ended at line 56, page 2 will begin at line 57—select Restart Numbering on Each Page (5 or R) and type **N**.

Once you've made selections on this menu, press EXIT (F7) to return to your document. A **[LnNum:On]** code is

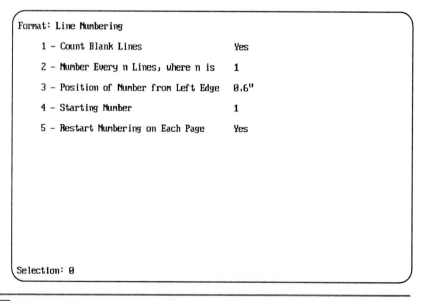

```
Format: Line Numbering

    1 - Count Blank Lines                     Yes

    2 - Number Every n Lines, where n is      1

    3 - Position of Number from Left Edge     0.6"

    4 - Starting Number                       1

    5 - Restart Numbering on Each Page        Yes




Selection: 0
```

**FIGURE 12-9**   Line Numbering menu

inserted into the text when you turn the feature on. Conversely, a **[LnNum:Off]** code is inserted if the feature had been on and you are now turning it off.

Line numbers appear on the printed page but not on the Typing screen. The feature will display on your screen, however, if you use the View Document feature. Figure 12-8 shows the printed result assuming the default line numbering settings.

If you want line numbering to appear down to the last line on a page, then either characters or hard returns must occupy each line. Thus, if text only occupies half the page, continue to press ⏎Enter to insert **[HRt]** codes down to the bottom of the page.

Be aware that line numbering is dependent on the line spacing selection. For instance, when a document is double-spaced, then line numbers are double-spaced also. If you want line numbering to be in one spacing measurement and the text in another, then use the Advance feature (see Chapter 9). That is, turn on Line Numbering at the top of the page, insert hard returns down to the bottom of the page, and, on the very last line of the page, turn off line numbering. Then use the Advance feature to advance up to the top line on the page, insert a Line Spacing code, and type the text. Or, if the Advance feature doesn't operate on your printer, you can print the same page twice; that is, turn on line numbering at the top, insert hard returns all the way down the page, print the page, and then reinsert the same page to print out the text.

If you are using the Line Numbering feature to create legal pleading paper, you should know that you can also insert vertical graphics lines down the left margin of the page next to the line numbers, as described in Chapter 10. Or, look to the discussion of the Styles feature in Chapter 14; WordPerfect Corporation has supplied a style for pleadings.

# INSERT FOOTNOTES AND ENDNOTES

Legal documents, research articles, and academic papers are commonly peppered with footnotes and endnotes. A footnote is a source citation or a supplementary discussion; a reference mark is inserted in the body of the text, and the footnote itself is placed at the bottom of the page. An endnote is like a footnote except that the endnote's text is placed at a location other than at the bottom of the page — for example, compiled with other endnotes at the end of the document.

WordPerfect offers a feature that automatically numbers footnotes and endnotes for you. Footnotes and endnotes are numbered separately so you can include both footnotes and endnotes in the same document. Each note (footnote or endnote) can be from 1 to 16,000 lines long.

For a footnote, WordPerfect automatically allows enough room on a page to accommodate the text of the footnote; gone are the days of trying to calculate the space required at the bottom of the page! (If there is insufficient room to print the text of a footnote on a page, the first 0.5″ of the footnote text is printed on that page and the rest is printed on the next page.) Endnotes are placed at the end of the document or at another location that you specify. All you need to do is type the text of the note. Should you later insert a new note or delete one, the others are renumbered for you.

WordPerfect has a predefined format for footnotes and endnotes. A sample of footnotes is shown in Figure 12-10. Notice that footnote reference marks appear as superscript text. Footnote text is separated from the main text by a 2″-long line, and the superscript footnote numbers are placed five spaces from the left margin.

R&R WINE ASSOCIATION UPDATE

1.  R&R WINE ASSOCIATION increased its market share in the United States by 2% this year as compared to the same time last year![1]  Congratulations are in order.

2.  Sales this quarter were brisk for European and Australian wines. Volumes shipped increased 12% over the same time last year. The Research Department believes that part of the increase is due to the weak dollar on international markets.

3.  In the United States, there was a noticeable increase in consumer preference of Chardonnay over other white wines during the past 12 months. This is particularly true in California, where Chardonnay is produced in large quantities.[2]

[1] The Eastern Division increased by 1.7%, while the Western Division increased by 2.2%.

[2] Marion Laramy, Wine in the United States, Parker Publishing, 1987, pages 44-45.

**FIGURE 12-10**  Footnotes within a printed document

A sample of endnotes is shown in Figure 12-11. Notice that the endnote numbers are not superscript text; they are

1. The Eastern Division increased by 1.7%, while the Western Division increased by 2.2%.

2. Marion Laramy, Wine in the United States, Parker Publishing, 1987, pages 44-45.

**FIGURE 12-11**  Endnotes in a printed document

positioned at the left margin and followed by a period. (However, endnote reference marks *are* superscript in the body of the text.) The endnotes can be printed wherever the document's regular text ends; on a separate page at the end of the document, provided that you end the document by pressing Ctrl + Enter to insert a Hard Page code; or anywhere within the document, provided that you activate the Endnote Placement option, described farther on in this chapter.

## Create Footnotes or Endnotes

Footnotes and endnotes are created in a similar way. You position the cursor in the main text where you want the note's reference mark to appear and press the FOOT-NOTE (Ctrl + F7) key. The following menu appears:

1 Footnote; 2 Endnote; 3 Endnote Placement: 0

Now select either Footnote (1 or F) or Endnote (2 or E). Another menu displays. For instance, if you selected to insert a footnote, you'll view the following menu:

Footnote: 1 Create; 2 Edit; 3 New Number; 4 Options: 0

The Endnote menu contains the same four options. Select Create (1 or C). [*Pulldown menu:* Layout (L), Footnote (F) or Endnote (E), Create (C).] A special Footnote or End-note Typing screen appears, with the reference number already inserted in the upper left corner. Press the spacebar, Tab, or ➔INDENT (F4) key and then type the text of the note, inserting any enhancements that you de-sire, such as underline, boldface, or a font attribute change.

(If you inadvertently delete the note number from the Footnote or Endnote Typing screen, position the cursor at the top of the screen and press FOOTNOTE ( Ctrl + F7 )) to reinsert the number. Do not reinsert the number by typing a numeral from the keyboard, because if you do, WordPerfect won't be able to keep all the footnotes or endnotes in your document numbered consecutively.) When you've completed typing the footnote or endnote, press the EXIT ( F7 )) key to return to the text.

On the Typing screen, a reference mark appears (though it may *not* appear as superscripted on your Typing screen). If you reveal codes, you'll find that this reference mark is actually a code. The code contains up to the first 50 characters of the footnote's text. For instance, for the first footnote as shown in Figure 12-10, the code reads **[Footnote:1;[Note Num]** The Eastern Division increased by 1.7%, while th . . .] . The **[Note Num]** within the Footnote code represents the footnote reference mark that appears in the text.

Let's create several footnotes for the document currently on screen, the document named NUMPARA. (If the document is no longer on screen, retrieve it.)

1. Position the cursor just past the exclamation point (!) that ends the first sentence of the first paragraph.

2. Press the FOOTNOTE ( Ctrl + F7 )) key. WordPerfect responds

   **1** Footnote; **2** Endnote; **3** Endnote Placement: **0**

   [*Pulldown menu:* Layout (L).]

3. Select Footnote (1 or F) to see the following menu:

   **Footnote: 1** Create; **2** Edit; **3** New Number; **4** Options: **0**

4. Select Create (1 or C). A Footnote Typing screen appears. Notice that a footnote reference number is automatically inserted for you.

5. Press the spacebar once, and type the following:

```
The Eastern Division increased by 1.7%, while the Western Division
increased by 2.2%.
```

6. Press the EXIT ( F7 ) key as suggested at the bottom of the screen.

7. Position the cursor at the end of the document, just past the period of the last sentence in the third paragraph.

8. Repeat steps 2 through 4. Now the footnote reference mark inserted is the number 2.

9. Press the spacebar once, and type the following:

```
Marion Laramy, Wine in the United States, Parker Publishing, 1987,
pages 44-45.
```

10. Press the EXIT ( F7 ) key as suggested at the bottom of the Footnote Typing screen.

If you print this document, you'll see the results as shown in Figure 12-10. To print footnotes and endnotes, WordPerfect uses whatever is the selected initial font for your document (unless you inserted a Font or Font Attribute code when typing the text of the footnote or endnote, in which case the font or font attribute you specified is used to print that particular footnote or endnote).

The text of footnotes and endnotes appears on the printed page, but is not visible on the Typing screen. To see the contents of a note before printing, you can reveal codes to view the first 50 characters of the note. Or, you can employ the Edit option, described in the next section, to see the text of the entire footnote. Or, you can view your footnotes or endnotes by previewing the document on screen using the View Document feature, as described in Chapter 9.

You can insert a new footnote or an endnote anywhere in a document, at any time—all notes will be automatically renumbered for you, although sometimes you need to move with the cursor keys down through the text in order to readjust the screen, updating the numbers. Or, you can press the SCREEN ([Ctrl] + [F3]) key and select Rewrite (3 or R in version 5.1, 0 or R in version 5.0) to rewrite the screen quickly. Let's add a footnote between notes 1 and 2 to see how the footnotes are renumbered.

1. Position the cursor after the period in the last sentence of the second paragraph.

2. Press the FOOTNOTE ([Ctrl] + [F7]) key. WordPerfect responds

   1 Footnote; 2 Endnote; 3 Endnote Placement: 0

   [*Pulldown menu:* Layout (L).]

3. Select Footnote (1 or F) to see the following menu:

   Footnote:  1 Create; 2 Edit; 3 New Number; 4 Options: 0

4. Select Create (1 or C). A Footnote Typing screen appears. Notice that a footnote reference number is automatically inserted for you.

5. Press the spacebar once, and type the following:

   Paula Fleming, "What's with the Dollar?", The New York Times, May 28, 1987.

6. Press the EXIT ([F7]) key, as suggested at the bottom of the Footnote Typing screen.

7. Press [↓] to move the cursor down through the document. Notice that the last footnote is now renumbered for you.

# Placement of Footnotes and Endnotes on the Printed Page

The vertical space occupied by footnotes is taken into account as WordPerfect readjusts soft page breaks. WordPerfect counts one blank line which contains the 2″ line separating the footnote text from the main text, one blank line preceding the text of each footnote, and all lines of the footnote text when determining where to break a page. As a result, when you create footnotes, fewer lines of your main text fit on a page.

WordPerfect reserves space at the end of the document for the endnotes, placing them either at the end of the main text or on a separate page at the end of the document if you ended the document by pressing HARD PAGE (Ctrl + Enter).

Alternatively, you can specify where you want endnotes printed by inserting an endnote placement code in the text. Position the cursor where you wish endnotes to appear when printed. The cursor must be further forward in the text from the reference marks for the endnotes. For instance, if you've created endnotes on pages 1 through 6, then the cursor must be positioned below the last endnote reference mark on page 6 in order for all those endnotes to be printed where you specify; any endnotes cited farther forward in the text will print at the end of the document or at the location of the next endnote placement code.

Once the cursor is positioned, press the FOOTNOTE (Ctrl + F7) key and select Endnote Placement (3 or P). [*Pulldown menu:* Layout (L), Endnote (E), Placement (P).] WordPerfect prompts

Restart endnote numbering? Yes (No)

WordPerfect is asking whether you wish to restart endnote numbering at 1 for all endnotes that follow the current position of the cursor. Type **Y** to begin numbering from the start, or type **N** to continue consecutive endnote numbering. WordPerfect inserts an **[Endnote Placement]** code in the text, followed by an **[HPg]** code so that additional text starts at the top of the next page. If you elected to restart endnote numbering for endnotes below the code, WordPerfect inserts a third code, **[New End Num:1]**, which dictates that the next endnote will be renumbered to start at number 1. Where the Endnote Placement code is inserted, a special comment displays on screen to remind you that endnotes will be located there when printed:

```
Endnote Placement
It is not known how much space endnotes will occupy here.
Generate to determine.
```

If you wish, you can determine how much vertical space will be occupied by the endnotes as follows: press MARK TEXT ([Alt] + [F5]), and select Generate (6 or G). [*Pull-down menu:* Mark (M), Generate (G).] Then, select Generate Table of Contents, Indexes, Automatic References, and so on (5 or G). Press **Y** to begin the generation of endnotes (as well as any tables, indexes, or automatic references—described in Chapter 15). In moments, the special comment on screen will display as follows:

```
Endnote Placement
```

The comment appears on the Typing screen as only one line long. However, position the cursor just above the comment, check the "Ln" indicator on the status line, press [→]

to position the cursor on the other side of the comment, and again check the "Ln" indicator. The status line will indicate how much space is required to print the endnotes. For instance, if the status line reads **Ln 2″** above the comment and reads **Ln 7″** below the comment, this indicates that the endnotes will occupy approximately 5″ of vertical space on the page.

You can have more than one Endnote Placement code in a document. All endnotes between the code and the previous Endnote Placement code (or the top of the document) are included at the code location when printed.

# EDIT FOOTNOTES AND ENDNOTES

To edit or review the text of a footnote or endnote, press the FOOTNOTE ( Ctrl + F7 ) key, select Footnote (1 or F) or Endnote (2 or E), and then select Edit (2 or E). [*Pulldown menu:* Layout (L), Footnote (F) or Endnote (E), Edit (E).] WordPerfect will prompt you for which note you wish to edit, suggesting the first note forward from the current cursor position. For instance, if you will be editing a footnote, WordPerfect may prompt

Footnote number? 1

Press Enter to accept the suggestion or type in the number of another note you wish to review and press Enter . That note now appears on screen. You can then use any of the standard editing keys and the Block feature to revise the text and then press the EXIT ( F7 ) key to return to the Typing screen.

For instance, suppose that you wish to edit the text of the first footnote.

1. Position the cursor at the top of the document.

2. Press the FOOTNOTE ( Ctrl + F7 ) key. WordPerfect responds

   `1 Footnote; 2 Endnote; 3 Endnote Placement: 0`

   [*Pulldown menu:* Layout (L).]

3. Select Footnote (1 or F) to see the following menu:

   `Footnote: 1 Create; 2 Edit; 3 New Number; 4 Options: 0`

4. Select Edit (2 or E). WordPerfect prompts

   `Footnote number? 1`

5. Press Enter . Footnote number 1 appears on screen, as shown in Figure 12-12.

6. Edit the percent figures in the footnote so that it reads as follows:

   `The Eastern Division increased by 1.71%, while the Western Division increased by 2.29%.`

7. Press the EXIT ( F7 ) key. When the Typing screen appears, the cursor is repositioned just to the right of footnote number 1.

You also may decide to delete a note from the text. This is quite simple. Move the cursor onto the note reference mark in the text and press Del . You can also delete by moving the cursor just to the right of the reference mark and pressing Backspace . When on the Reveal Codes screen, the footnote or endnote is erased, text and all. When on the Typing screen, WordPerfect will prompt for you to verify the deletion, such as

`Delete [Footnote:1]? No(Yes)`

Type **Y** for Yes and the note will be erased, text and all. All remaining footnotes or endnotes in the text will be renumbered accordingly.

Or, you can move a note. Delete it from the text as described above and position the cursor where you want the note inserted. Then, use the Undelete feature on the CANCEL ([F1]) key; that is, press CANCEL ([F1]) and select Restore (1 or R). [*Pulldown menu:* Edit (E), Undelete (U), Restore (R).]

When working with footnotes or endnotes, you may wish to specify a new starting number. This is useful when you want one document's numbering to begin where another's left off, as when you split a long chapter into two separate documents. To indicate a new starting number, position the cursor in the text before the footnote or endnote you wish to renumber. Press the FOOTNOTE ([Ctrl] + [F7]) key,

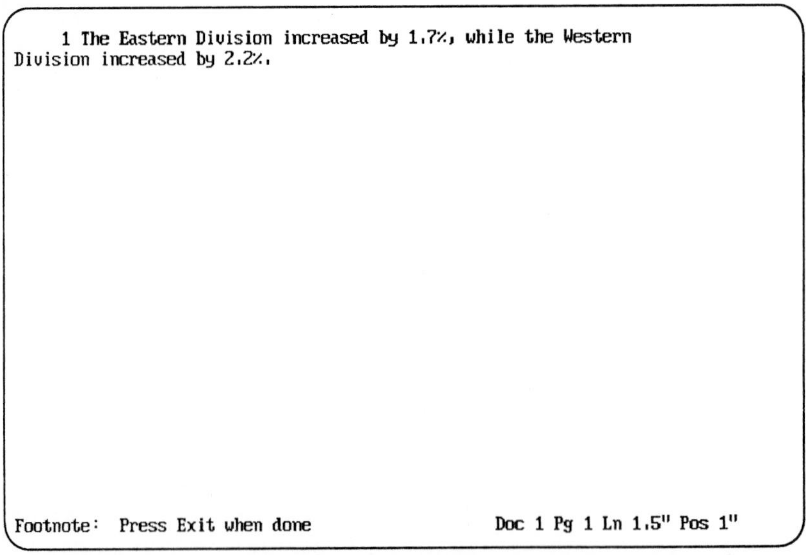

```
   1 The Eastern Division increased by 1.7%, while the Western
Division increased by 2.2%.




















Footnote: Press Exit when done            Doc 1 Pg 1 Ln 1.5" Pos 1"
```

**FIGURE 12-12** Footnote Typing screen with text to be edited

and select Footnote (1 or F) or Endnote (2 or E). [*Pull-down menu:* Layout (L), Footnote (F) or Endnote (E).] Next, select New Number (3 or N). WordPerfect prompts for a new note number. Type in the new note number and press (Enter). A code is inserted in the text. For instance, if you reset footnotes to begin at number 20, the code inserted is **[New Ftn Num:20]**. All footnotes following the code would be renumbered sequentially as 20, 21, 22, 23, and so on. Or, if you reset endnotes to begin at number 30, the code inserted is **[New End Num:30]** and all subsequent endnotes would be affected accordingly.

# CHANGE FOOTNOTE AND ENDNOTE OPTIONS

You can also alter the defaults that control how footnotes and endnotes appear on the printed page. For instance, you can change the spacing within notes to double spacing; or, instead of using Arabic numerals to reference a footnote in the main text, you can use letters or even other characters, such as the asterisk (*).

To change footnote or endnote options, position the cursor where you want the new option to take effect. For example, place the cursor on page 2 to alter an option starting on that page, or place the cursor on the Document Initial Codes screen (described in Chapter 6) to alter an option starting at the top of the document. Then press the FOOTNOTE ((Ctrl) + (F7)) key, select Footnote (1 or F) or Endnote (2 or E), and select Options (4 or O). For footnotes, the menu in Figure 12-13 appears, which indicates the default settings for how footnotes will appear when printed. For endnotes, the menu in Figure 12-14 appears, containing fewer options. The following options are available for either footnotes or endnotes:

- *Spacing Within Notes* This option is preset at 1, for single spacing within the text of the footnotes or end-notes. You can instead select 0.5 for half spacing, 2 for double spacing, and so on.

- *Spacing Between Notes* This option is preset at 0.167″ (0.17″ for 5.0 users) so that there is one blank line, 0.167″ (or 0.17″) in height, between footnotes or endnotes. You can change that setting; for instance, select 0.15″ for slightly less space between notes.

- *Amount of Note to Keep Together* This option is preset to keep 0.5″ of a long footnote or endnote on a page

```
Footnote Options

     1 - Spacing Within Footnotes          1
               Between Footnotes            0.167"

     2 - Amount of Note to Keep Together    0.5"

     3 - Style for Number in Text           [SUPRSCPT][Note Num][suprscpt]

     4 - Style for Number in Note                 [SUPRSCPT][Note Num][suprscpt]

     5 - Footnote Numbering Method          Numbers

     6 - Start Footnote Numbers each Page   No

     7 - Line Separating Text and Footnotes 2-inch Line

     8 - Print Continued Message            No

     9 - Footnotes at Bottom of Page        Yes



Selection: 0
```

**FIGURE 12-13** Footnote Options screen

before continuing the note on the next page if Word-Perfect has insufficient room to print the note on one page. You can increase or decrease this default setting.

- *Style for Number in Text*  As shown in Figures 12-13 and 12-14, this option is preset with the code string **[SUPR-SCPT][Note Num][SuprScpt]**, which means that the note reference mark—whether a number, letter, or character—will print as superscript. You can select a different style, such as removing the Superscript codes or inserting Underline or Boldface codes. (If you accidentally erase the **[Note Num]** code, use the Number Code option (version 5.1) or the Note Number option (version 5.0) on the FOOTNOTE ( Ctrl + F7 ) key to reinsert the code.)

```
Endnote Options

     1 - Spacing Within Endnotes              1
                 Between Endnotes             0.167"

     2 - Amount of Endnote to Keep Together   0.5"

     3 - Style for Numbers in Text            [SUPRSCPT][Note Num][suprscpt]

     4 - Style for Numbers in Note            [Note Num].

     5 - Endnote Numbering Method             Numbers




Selection: 0
```

**FIGURE 12-14**  Endnote Options screen

• *Style for Number in Note*    Footnote numbers are preset to be indented five spaces from the left margin and superscripted. (**[Tab]** and **[→Indent]** codes are not allowed as part of the style, so you must insert spaces instead.) Endnote numbers are preset to be followed by a period, without any indent or superscript. You can insert or delete codes to change the style. (If you accidentally erase the **[Note Num]** code, use the Number Code option (version 5.1) or the Note Number option (version 5.0) on the FOOTNOTE ( Ctrl + F7 ) key to reinsert it.)

• *Note Numbering Method*    This option is preset to numbers, which means that footnotes and endnotes will be referenced using numbers. If you select this option, WordPerfect displays the following menu:

1 Numbers; 2 Letters; 3 Characters: 0

    Select Letters (2 or L) and WordPerfect will mark footnotes or endnotes in lowercase letters (a, b, c, and so on). Select Characters (3 or C) and WordPerfect allows you to type in up to 50 characters. For instance, if you type in an asterisk (*) as the footnote character, then the first footnote will be marked with one asterisk, the second with two asterisks, and so on. If you type an asterisk and then a pound sign (*#), the first footnote will be marked with one asterisk, the second with one pound sign, the third with two asterisks, the fourth with two pound signs, and so on.

The additional options available for footnotes only are as follows:

• *Start Footnote Numbers each Page*    This option is preset to "No," so that notes are numbered sequentially throughout a document. If you wish the numbering to restart at 1 on every page, you must change this to "Yes" by typing **Y**.

- *Line Separating Text and Footnotes* This option is preset for a 2″ line separating the body of the text from the footnotes at the bottom of the page. If you select this option, WordPerfect displays the following menu:

**1** No Line; **2** 2-inch Line; **3** Margin to Margin: **0**

Your other choices are to select No Line (1 or N) or Margin to Margin (3 or M), which creates a line that extends from the left to the right margin.

- *Print Continued Message* This option is preset to "No," so that no message is printed if a footnote is split between two pages. You can instead select "Yes," so that a "(Continued). . ." message is printed at the end of the footnote on the first page and at the beginning of where it continues on the next page.

- *Footnotes at Bottom of Page* This option is preset to "Yes," meaning that even if the page is only partially full, blank lines are inserted so that the notes are printed at the bottom. If you wanted to print footnotes just below the main text on a partially full page, you would change this to "No."

Once you change one or more of the footnote options, press ⌷Enter⌷ or EXIT (⌷F7⌷) to return to the Typing screen. For footnotes, a **[Ftn Opt]** code is inserted and will affect all footnotes from the current cursor position forward. For endnotes, the code is **[End Opt]**.

Suppose you want to change the footnote reference marks to letters in the document on screen. In addition, you want a line across the entire page to separate the footnotes from the text. Since you wish to change these options for the entire document, let's do so on the Document Initial Codes screen in order to reduce the number of codes at the top of the document. (See Chapter 6 if you need a review of the advantages of placing certain codes on the Document Initial Codes screen rather than at the top of a document.)

1. With the cursor positioned anywhere in the document, press the FORMAT ([Shift] + [F8]) key. [*Pulldown menu:* Layout (L).] The Format menu appears.

2. Select Document (3 or D). The Document Format menu appears.

3. Select Initial Codes (2 or C). The Document Initial Codes screen appears.

4. Press the FOOTNOTE ([Ctrl] + [F7]) key. WordPerfect responds

   1 Footnote; 2 Endnote; 3 Endnote Placement: 0

5. Select Footnote (1 or F) to see the following menu:

   Footnote: 1 Create; 2 Edit; 3 New Number; 4 Options: 0

6. Select Options (4 or O). The Footnote Options screen appears, as shown in Figure 12-13.

7. Select Footnote Numbering Method (5 or M), and then choose Letters (2 or L).

8. Select Line Separating Text and Footnotes (7 or L) and then choose Margin to Margin (3 or M).

9. Press EXIT ([F7]) to return to the Document Initial Codes screen. You'll see a **[Ftn Opt]** code.

10. Press EXIT ([F7]) several more times until you return to your document.

11. Press the SCREEN ([Ctrl] + [F3]) key and press [Enter] to rewrite the screen.

12. Use the SAVE ([F10]) key to resave this document under the name NUMPARA.

Notice that letters now reference the footnotes. Print this page and you'll see that the page prints with letters as footnote reference marks and a separator line across the width of the page. The printed results are shown in Figure 12-15.

*Note:* In WordPerfect you can permanently change the default footnote or endnote option settings for all new documents that you create, rather than changing the defaults individually for every document, by inserting a Footnote or Endnote Option code on the Setup Initial Codes screen. For instance, you may decide that you always want a line extending from margin to margin above footnotes. Refer to the "Initial Settings" section of Appendix B for more information.

# REVIEW EXERCISE

Let's use the document on screen to practice with paragraph numbering and footnoting. As usual, WordPerfect will always renumber properly after you edit your text.

---

R&R WINE ASSOCIATION UPDATE

1. R&R WINE ASSOCIATION increased its market share in the United States by 2% this year as compared to the same time last year![a] Congratulations are in order.

2. Sales this quarter were brisk for European and Australian wines.  Volumes shipped increased 12% over the same time last year.  The Research Department believes that part of the increase is due to the weak dollar on international markets.[b]

3. In the United States, there was a noticeable increase in consumer preference of Chardonnay over other white wines during the past 12 months.  This is particularly true in California, where Chardonnay is produced in large quantities.[c]

[a] The Eastern Division increased by 1.71%, while the Western Division increased by 2.29%.

[b] Paula Fleming, "What's with the Dollar?", The New York Times, May 28, 1987.

[c] Marion Laramy, Wine in the United States, Parker Publishing, 1987, pages 44-45.

---

**FIGURE 12-15**   Printed result after altering the default footnote options

1. For the document on screen (with the filename NUM-PARA), change the paragraph numbers to the outline style (I., II., III.) rather than the paragraph style. (*Hint:* Since the default *is* the outline style, simply find the **[Par Num Def]** code previously inserted near the top of the document and erase it.) Watch the numbering style change as you rewrite the text.

2. Suppose you wish to indent the paragraph numbers to the next tab stop. Position the cursor on the Roman numeral "I." and press `Tab`. When you press `↓`, notice that the paragraph number is now "A.," because you've shifted it to level 2. Indent the other paragraph numbers to level 2 as well.

3. Position the cursor just to the right of the percent sign (%) in "increased 12%", which is located in the second paragraph. Insert the following footnote:

   Actual percent increase is 12.223.

   After you insert the footnote, notice how the two footnotes that follow it are renumbered as soon as you rewrite the screen.

4. Delete the first footnote by positioning the cursor on the footnote reference mark "a," pressing `Del`, and, if you're viewing the Typing screen, typing **Y** to confirm that you wish to delete the footnote. Notice how all the other footnotes are again renumbered after the screen is rewritten.

5. Resave this document under the name NUMPARA.

## Quick Review

- Switch into Outline mode in order to create outlines with up to eight different outline levels (I., A., 1., a., and so on) by pressing DATE/OUTLINE ([Shift] + [F5]), selecting Outline (4 or O), and, for version 5.1 users, selecting On (1 or O). Or, pulldown menu users can select Tools (T), Outline (O), On (O).

- Within Outline mode, insert outline numbers whenever you press [Enter]. With the cursor just to the right of an outline number, press [Tab] to move that number to the right and move up one outline level. Or, press ►MARGIN RELEASE ([Shift] + [Tab]) to move that number to the left and down one outline level. Once you've inserted an outline number in Outline mode, press ►INDENT ([F4]) or the spacebar to lock the outline number in place before you type the outline entry.

- Exit from Outline mode after typing an outline by using the same keystrokes as when entering it— except that version 5.1 users will, as the final step, select Off (2 or F). An outline will be renumbered if you add, delete, or move entries.

- Version 5.1 users can edit all the entries in an outline family in one command. Position the cursor on the first line in that family, press DATE/OUTLINE ([Shift] + [F5]), and select Outline (4 or O). Or, pulldown menu users can select Tools (T), Outline (O). Then choose from the Move, Copy, or Delete Family options.

- To insert individual paragraph numbers, move to the desired tab stop, press the DATE/OUTLINE (Shift + F5) key, and select Para Num (5 or P). Or, pulldown menu users can select Tools (T), Paragraph Number (P). Then, press Enter for an automatic number or enter a number for a fixed level number. You can also use this method to add an individual entry to an outline.

- To change the default numbering for outlines/paragraph numbers from *outline* style to another style, or to restart the numbering for a new outline/set of paragraphs, press DATE/OUTLINE (Shift + F5), and select Define (6 or D). Or, pulldown menu users can select Tools (T), Define (D). Make any changes on the Paragraph Number Definition menu. 5.1 users can also alter the method for entering outline numbers on this menu.

- Number lines in the left margin of your document by pressing FORMAT (Shift + F8) and selecting Line (1 or L) to display the Line Format menu. Or, pulldown menu users can select Layout (L), Line (L). Next, select Line Numbering (5 or N), and type **Y**. The default line numbering setting can be altered on the menu that displays. Line numbers appear on the printed page, but not on the Typing screen.

- Insert a note (either footnote or endnote) by positioning the cursor where the note reference mark should appear in the text. Then, press the FOOTNOTE (Ctrl + F7) key, select either the footnote or endnote option, and choose Create (1 or C). Or, pulldown menu users select Layout (L), Footnote (F) or Endnote (E), Create (C). Type the text of the note and press EXIT (F7). The text of the note itself appears not on the Typing screen but on the printed page or on the View Document screen.

- Delete a footnote or endnote by erasing the reference number in the body of the text. The remaining notes are renumbered automatically.

- Review or edit a note by pressing the FOOTNOTE (Ctrl + F7) key, selecting either the footnote or endnote option, and choosing Edit (2 or E). Pulldown menu users can choose Layout (L), Footnote (F) or Endnote (E), Edit (E). Then enter the number of the note you wish to edit. Press EXIT (F7) when the editing is complete.

- To change the appearance of your footnotes or endnotes and their accompanying reference number, press the FOOTNOTE (Ctrl + F7) key, select either the footnote or endnote option, and choose Options (4 or O). Pulldown menu users choose Layout (L), Footnote (F) or Endnote (E), Options (O). Nine options are available for footnotes, and five for endnotes.

- Specify that endnotes print at a certain location in your document, rather than at the end of a document, with the Endnote Placement feature. Position the cursor where you want endnotes to print in the text, press the FOOTNOTE ( Ctrl + F7 ) key, and select Endnote Placement (3 or P). Pulldown menu users choose Layout (L), Endnote (E), Placement (P). Type **Y** or **N** to indicate whether WordPerfect should restart endnote numbering below the cursor location. All endnotes from the beginning of the document (or from the point of the last endnote placement code to the current endnote placement code) will be printed at that location.

# chapter 13

# PRODUCING REPETITIVE DOCUMENTS AND MERGING

Work with Boilerplate Text
Learn About the Merge Feature
Merge with the Keyboard
Merge with a File
Prepare Envelopes and Mailing Labels
Enhance the Merge Process
Review Exercise
Quick Review

**W**ordPerfect offers a variety of sophisticated options for working with repetitive documents. Creating certain documents may entail simply reorganizing standard paragraphs. If so, you can create a system of "boilerplate" files, each file containing a single or several paragraphs. This lets you retrieve separate files into the document you're currently producing—effectively pasting paragraphs together to produce the document with little actual typing.

Other documents have more in common than just a few select paragraphs. These documents are identical except for bits of information that personalize each one—perhaps a name and an address. The text that changes in each copy of the document is referred to as *variable information.* WordPerfect's Merge feature can quickly create many personalized documents. The Merge feature will accept the variable information directly from the keyboard or from data provided from another file.

In this chapter, you'll learn how to produce repetitive documents quickly and easily. You'll learn first about boilerplating and then about the Merge feature—merging both with the keyboard and with a file. You'll also see how the Merge feature can produce envelopes or mailing labels in minutes. And you'll learn about some special Merge commands for added flexibility. Read on to see that given WordPerfect's power and flexibility, typing the same text over and over is a great waste of time.

# WORK WITH BOILERPLATE TEXT

Sometimes the same text appears in a variety of documents, such as a paragraph used frequently in correspondence or a chart included often in promotional materials. Rather than type that text from scratch, you can store it in its own individual file and insert it into any document you're typing. You can think of a collection of these stored paragraphs as a library of boilerplate files, any of which is ready for you to insert into your documents, as needed, without ever retyping.

# Create a Boilerplate Paragraph

There are several ways to store boilerplate text on disk. First, on a clear screen, you can type the text and then save it in its own file. Or, if the boilerplate text already exists in a document, you can retrieve that document to the screen and use the Block Save feature, discussed in Chapter 2, to save the boilerplate text in its own file. You would use the Block feature to highlight the text, press the SAVE ( F10 ) key, type a new filename, and press Enter . The document on screen would be unaffected, but now the paragraph would be stored in a separate boilerplate file.

The key to creating an effective library of boilerplate files is establishing a logical filenaming system so that it is easy to identify the contents of each file. You should give each boilerplate file a name that reminds you of its contents. For instance, you could name the paragraph most often included first in a letter as BEGIN.LET (standing for BEGINning of LETter), the paragraph that usually concludes a letter as CLOSE.LET, and the paragraph that provides background information on your company as BACK.LET. Or store a whole series of paragraphs named P1, P2, P3, and so on. You may wish to store these boilerplate paragraphs all on one floppy disk or in one directory. Be sure to keep at your desk (or in a file on disk) a list of filenames and a description of the boilerplate text contained in each file.

Here's a practical example, using a paragraph you'd include frequently in promotional material or correspondence if you worked for the R&R Wine Association:

```
R&R WINE ASSOCIATION, established in 1982, boasts a membership of
over 100 outstanding wineries from California, New York, Europe,
South America, and Australia. We disseminate information about
wine tasting, production, and enjoyment. In addition, we
distribute wine produced by our member wineries.
```

You may remember typing this paragraph as part of the document that you stored on disk under the name SAM-PLE. Let's recall the file named SAMPLE and save that one paragraph into its own file to create a boilerplate paragraph.

1. On a clear screen, retrieve the file named SAMPLE.

2. Position the cursor on the last page of the document, where you'll find the paragraph that you will save in its own file.

3. Position the cursor on the first "R" in "R&R WINE ASSOCIATION," established in . . . ".

4. Use the Block feature to highlight the paragraph.

5. Press the SAVE (F10) key. [*Pulldown menu:* File (F), Save (S).] WordPerfect responds

    ```
    Block name:
    ```

6. Type **BACK.RR** (a name that reminds you that this file will contain BACKground information on the R&R Wine Association) and press Enter. WordPerfect saves the block independently under that filename.

Nothing on the screen has changed. And yet, you've also created a new, separate file on disk that contains one paragraph. Now this paragraph can be inserted whenever you write a document in which you wish to include background information on the R&R Wine Association.

## Insert a Boilerplate Paragraph

You learned in Chapter 2 that WordPerfect retrieves a file without first clearing the screen. That's why, when you want to begin working with a completely different document from the one on screen, you must first remember to use the Exit feature to clear the screen before you retrieve another document.

If you don't clear the screen first, you can combine a boilerplate file with whatever is already on the screen. Simply position the cursor where you want the contents of the boilerplate file inserted. Then proceed in one of two ways. You can press the RETRIEVE ( Shift + F10 ) key, type the filename, and press Enter . Alternatively, you can view the List Files screen for a particular drive or directory, position the cursor on the file you wish to retrieve, and select Retrieve (1 or R). When using the List Files screen to retrieve a file onto a screen that already contains text, WordPerfect will prompt asking for verification that you wish to insert the file into the current document on screen. Type **Y** to proceed or type **N** to cancel the Retrieve command.

Once a paragraph has been retrieved, you can continue with the document at hand, typing additional text, editing text, or inserting another boilerplate file. Then you can save the document.

Be cautious if you retrieve boilerplate text onto a clear screen *first,* add additional text, and then attempt to save the document. WordPerfect will suggest that you save using the name of the boilerplate file that you first retrieved. Be sure that you type in a different filename. If you don't, you may accidentally replace the boilerplate file.

Suppose that you wish to type and store on disk the letter shown in Figure 13-1. Notice that the circled copy in Figure 13-1 is the boilerplate text you just created and stored under the name BACK.RR. You will insert this boilerplate file into the letter, thereby reducing the typing required to produce it.

---

October 15, 1990


Ms. Diane Johnston
334 Glenview Road
Boynton Beach, FL 33436


Dear Ms. Johnston:

This is a response to your letter dated September 21, 1990.  You
asked if the R&R Wine Association is a lobbying organization for
the wine industry.  We are not a lobbying organization.

R&R WINE ASSOCIATION, established in 1982, boasts a membership of
over 100 outstanding wineries from California, New York, Europe,
South America, and Australia. We disseminate information about wine
tasting, production, and enjoyment. In addition, we distribute wine
produced by our member wineries.

I believe you will instead want to contact the Winston Grape
Growers Association of America.  They are located in Baltimore,
Maryland.

Sincerely,                                    Boilerplate text

Donna Jones
Vice President

---

═══════ **FIGURE 13-1**   Sample letter to be typed with the aid of
boilerplate text

1. Press the EXIT ( F7 ) key. [*Pulldown menu:* File (F),
   Exit (X).] Then type **N** twice to clear the screen.

2. On the clear screen, type the date, the inside address,
   the salutation line, and the first paragraph of the letter
   shown in Figure 13-1.

3. Press `Enter` twice to end the letter's first paragraph and to insert a blank line, so that your screen resembles Figure 13-2.

4. Press the RETRIEVE (`Shift` + `F10`) key. [*Pulldown menu:* File (F), Retrieve (R).] WordPerfect responds

```
Document to be retrieved:
```

5. Type **BACK.RR**, and press `Enter`. WordPerfect inserts the boilerplate paragraph in the letter.

6. Move the cursor to the bottom of the document and continue typing the remainder of the letter.

7. Save this letter on disk. Because you typed text before retrieving the file named BACK.RR, WordPerfect makes no filename suggestion, but instead prompts

```
Document to be saved:
```

8. Save this document under the name **JOHNSTON.LET**.

Now you have a letter stored on disk, and you still have the boilerplate paragraph available for insertion in future documents.

Another candidate for boilerplate is a signature block. For instance, if you had stored on disk the signature block at the bottom of the letter shown in Figure 13-1 (which starts with "Sincerely" and ends with "Vice President"), you could have taken advantage of a second boilerplate file when typing such a letter.

You can also use boilerplates to store commonly used format settings. For instance, suppose that on all the reports you produce, you change the margins and establish a standard header. On a clear screen, you could make these formatting changes. Then before typing any actual text, you

```
October 15, 1990



Ms, Diane Johnston
334 Glenview Road
Boynton Beach, FL  33436


Dear Ms, Johnston:

This is a response to your letter dated September 21, 1990,  You
asked if the R&R Wine Association is a lobbying organization for
the wine industry,  We are not a lobbying organization,

-




                                     Doc 1 Pg 1 Ln 3,5" Pos 1"
```

**FIGURE 13-2**   Letter just before boilerplate text is inserted

could store this document (which contains only codes) in a file, perhaps under the name REP.FMT (which stands for REPort ForMaT). From then on, every time you are ready to create a report, you could retrieve the file named REP.FMT onto a clear screen and then type the text of the report. In this case, however, WordPerfect will suggest the filename REP.FMT the first time you save the report; make sure to save the finished report under a *different* filename so that you have the file named REP.FMT ready to use when you create a new report. (Also, see Chapter 14 for even more sophisticated methods for formatting a standard document, such as a report, with ease and swiftness.)

# LEARN ABOUT THE MERGE FEATURE

If your text has more than just a few paragraphs in common, then instead of relying on boilerplate paragraphs, utilize the Merge feature. The Merge feature automates the task of producing numerous documents that are identical except for variable information—the bits of information that change from document to document to personalize it, such as a person's name, an address, a list of products, a room number, or a date.

When using the Merge feature, you create documents with special codes, called *Merge codes,* inserted to instruct WordPerfect where to place variable information and how to carry out the merge. These codes can be placed in the main text, or, in version 5.1, in graphics boxes, headers, footers, endnotes, and footnotes. Unlike other codes in WordPerfect, Merge codes are visible on the Typing screen in addition to the Reveal Codes screen. These Merge codes are very different in version 5.1 than in version 5.0.

*5.1 users:* Merge codes are shown on the Typing screen as the Merge code name surrounded by curly brackets, such as {END RECORD}. Some of these Merge codes—those in which the user can enter information to further define the code—end with a tilde (~) to signal the finish of that code, such as in {INPUT}Name:~ or {FIELD}1~. On the Reveal Codes screen, Merge codes are surrounded by hard brackets and boldfaced, consistent with other codes, such as **[Mrg:END RECORD]** or **[Mrg:INPUT]**Name:~ or **[Mrg:FIELD]**1~. The ending tilde is not boldfaced on the Reveal Codes screen because it is a regular character. (You have the option of hiding Merge codes from view on the Typing screen so that, like other WordPerfect codes, they are viewed only on the Reveal Codes screen. See "Display" in Appendix B for more information.)

*5.0 users:* Merge codes are shown on the Typing screen as a letter preceded by a caret symbol, such as ^E. Some of these Merge codes—those in which the user can enter information to further define the code—come in pairs or, in the case of one code, end with an extra caret to signal the finish of that code, such as ^OName:^O or ^F1^. On the Reveal Codes screen, the Merge codes look the same but are boldfaced, such as **^E** or **^OName:^O** or **^F1**^. An ending caret is not boldfaced on the Reveal Codes screen because it is a regular character.

There are two basic types of merges that either 5.1 or 5.0 users can perform, depending on the Merge codes you use. First, you can merge *with the keyboard.* When you merge with the keyboard, WordPerfect displays a certain document on screen, and automatically stops at Merge code locations for you to type variable information directly from the keyboard. The second, more involved, method is a merge *with a file,* where WordPerfect automatically personalizes a document at the Merge code locations with variable information stored on disk. You store variable information on disk when you plan to use that information in many documents—perhaps one time to create personalized letters for a mass mailing, a second time to create envelopes, a third time to create mailing labels, a fourth time to create another set of personalized letters for a follow-up mass mailing. The procedure to merge with the keyboard is discussed in the section that follows, and the procedure to merge with a file is discussed afterwards.

# MERGE WITH THE KEYBOARD

Figure 13-3 is a sample of a memo that is a perfect candidate for a merge with the keyboard. It is a memo that the

MEMO FROM THE OFFICE OF PERSONNEL

To: (Marion Murphy)                         From: John Samsone

Re:  Personnel Forms

      According to our records, you have not yet completed and
returned to the Personnel office the following forms:

Withholding Tax Form
New Employee Information Form

      Please send this information as soon as possible to the
immediate attention of (Peter Strand). If you have any questions,
call (415) 333-1190.  Thank you.

**FIGURE 13-3** Memo to be produced using a merge with
the keyboard

personnel office at R&R Wine Association sends out frequently. The memo remains the same except for the circled
copy, which represents the variable information that
changes for every memo. Using a merge with the keyboard,
WordPerfect can turn the task of producing such a memo
into a quick, automated, fill-in-the-blanks job.

## Create a Primary File

To merge with the keyboard, you must first create a *primary
file,* which contains the text that does not change. In those
locations where the document is to be personalized, you
insert a special Merge code to act as a placeholder where

the variable information will later be inserted. The Merge code is used to pause for input during the merge. If you need a reminder of what variable information to input during the merge, you can also have WordPerfect display a message when it encounters a code for a merge with the keyboard.

You begin a primary file just as you begin any other document: clear the screen and type the text. You can format it—changing margins, tabs, spacing, and so forth—just as you would any standard document. Wherever you want to insert a code to pause for keyboard input, proceed as follows:

*5.1 users:* Press the MERGE CODES ([Shift] + [F9]) key, and, from the list of Merge code choices, select Input (3 or I). [*Pulldown menu:* Tools (T), Merge Codes (R), Input (I).] Now, WordPerfect prompts

Enter message:

Simply press [Enter] so that no message will display during the merge when WordPerfect pauses for input; the code {INPUT}~ is inserted at the current cursor position. Or, type a customized message and press [Enter], so that Word-Perfect will prompt you with that message when the merge is paused at that location; the code {INPUT}*message*~ appears. The primary file in version 5.1 for the R&R Wine Association's personnel office memo—with a customized message inserted only at the first and second pauses—is shown in Figure 13-4.

*5.0 users:* Press the MERGE CODES ([Shift] + [F9]) key, and, from the list of Merge code choices, type **C** to insert the ^C Merge code; no message will display during the merge when WordPerfect pauses for input. The Merge code you insert is ^C, pronounced "Control C." Or, if you wish to insert a customized message, then the process is a bit more time-consuming because you must

```
            MEMO FROM THE OFFICE OF PERSONNEL


To:  {INPUT}Type Employee Name~              From: John Samsone

Re:  Personnel Forms


     According to our records, you have not yet completed and
returned to the Personnel office the following forms:

{INPUT}List Forms On Separate Lines~

     Please send this information as soon as possible to the
immediate attention of {INPUT}~.  If you have any questions, call (415)
333-{INPUT}~.  Thank you. _




                                        Doc 1 Pg 1 Ln 3.67" Pos 2.9"
```

**FIGURE 13-4** Primary file for merge with the keyboard (version 5.1)

insert a string of three Merge codes. Press MERGE CODES, type O, and type a message. Then, press MERGE CODES, and type O to end the message. Then, press MERGE CODES and type C. The string of Merge codes you insert is ^O*message*^O^C. The primary file in version 5.0 for the R&R Wine Association's personnel office memo — with a customized message inserted only at the first and second pause — is shown in Figure 13-5.

You should know that, on some keyboards, you can also press [Ctrl] + [C] or [Ctrl] + [O] to insert the ^C and ^O Merge codes, circumventing the MERGE CODES key. Do not, however, type the caret symbol and then an uppercase "C" or "O" in an attempt to insert a Merge code. This

```
                    MEMO FROM THE OFFICE OF PERSONNEL


To:  ^OType Employee Name^O^C              From: John Samsone

Re:  Personnel Forms


     According to our records, you have not yet completed and
returned to the Personnel office the following forms:

^OList Forms On Separate Lines^O^C

     Please send this information as soon as possible to the
immediate attention of ^C,  If you have any questions, call (415)
333-^C,  Thank you, _



                                     Doc 1 Pg 1 Ln 3.67" Pos 2.9"
```

**FIGURE 13-5**   Primary file for merge with the keyboard (version 5.0)

creates a symbol which looks like a code on the Typing screen, but will not be bolded on the Reveal Codes screen, will not be treated as a code, and will therefore not work during the merge.

Once you've completed typing the primary document, be sure to check carefully for grammatical, punctuation, or spelling errors; otherwise, every mistake you make will appear every time you use the primary file to produce a new document. You can use the Spell feature, described in Chapter 7, to check the primary file for spelling mistakes.

Also, be sure to check the location and syntax of your Merge codes carefully. In version 5.1, there must be a tilde (~) following an {INPUT} code — either directly after the code if you do not enter a message, or directly after the message if you include one: {INPUT}*message*~. In version

5.0, if you do not insert a message, then insert a ^C code and no ^O codes at all, or, if you do insert a message, the ^O codes must surround that message like bookends, and be followed by a ^C code: ^O*message*^O^C. Otherwise, WordPerfect will not know where the message ends.

When the primary document is complete, save it on disk. But you will want to be able to identify this file as a primary file containing Merge codes, and not as a standard document. One good method for doing so is to choose a descriptive filename. For instance, name the file beginning with the letters PF or PRI, as in PF.MMO (which stands for Primary File MeMO) or PRIFORMS.MMO (which stands for PRImary file for the FORMS MeMO). Or, use those letters in the filename extension, as in MEMO-FORM.PF or MEMO.PRI.

For practice, let's create a primary file to use in producing personalized memos such as the one shown in Figure 13-3.

1. Beginning with a clear screen, press the CENTER (⟦Shift⟧ + ⟦F6⟧) key, press the ⟦Caps Lock⟧, and type

   ```
   MEMO FROM THE OFFICE OF PERSONNEL
   ```

2. Press ⟦Caps Lock⟧ to switch back to lowercase letters, and press ⟦Enter⟧ three times to insert blank lines.

3. Type **To:** and press ⟦Tab⟧. You're now at the location where you must insert the first Merge code.

4. Press the MERGE CODES (⟦Shift⟧ + ⟦F9⟧) key. [*Pull-down menu:* Tools (T), Merge Codes (R).] *5.1 users:* You will view the following menu:

   ```
   1 Field; 2 End Record; 3 Input; 4 Page Off; 5 Next Record;
   6 More: 0
   ```

*5.0 users:* You will view the following:

^C; ^D; ^E; ^F; ^G; ^N; ^O; ^P; ^Q; ^S; ^T; ^U; ^V:

5. *5.1 users:* Select Input (3 or I). WordPerfect prompts

Enter message:

Type the following message: **Type Employee Name.** Then, press [Enter]. WordPerfect inserts the following:

{INPUT}Type Employee Name~.

*5.0 users:* Type **O.**

Type the following message: **Type Employee Name.** Then, press MERGE CODES, and type **O** to end the message.

Next, press MERGE CODES again, and type **C.** WordPerfect inserts

^OType Employee Name^O^C.

6. Press the RIGHT FLUSH ([Alt] + [F6]) key, type **From: John Samsone,** and press [Enter] twice.

7. Type **Re:,** press [Tab], type **Personnel Forms,** and press [Enter] twice.

8. Type the first sentence of the memo, which reads

According to our records, you have not yet completed and returned to the Personnel office the following forms:

then press [Enter] twice.

9. Follow steps 4 and 5 to insert Merge codes, but change the message typing the following: **List Forms On Separate Lines**

10. Press [Enter] twice.

11. Type the next sentence of the memo, up to the next Merge code, which reads:

```
Please send this information as soon as possible to the
immediate attention of
```

12. Press the spacebar once. Now you're at the location where you must insert another Merge code, this time without any message.

13. Press MERGE CODES ( [Shift] + [F9] ). [*Pulldown menu:* Tools (T), Merge Codes (R).]

14. *5.1 users:* Select Input (3 or I). WordPerfect prompts

```
Enter message:
```

Simply press [Enter]. WordPerfect inserts the following:

```
{INPUT}~
```

*5.0 users:* Type **C**. WordPerfect inserts the following:

```
^C
```

15. Type a period to end the sentence.

16. Type the rest of the text shown in Figure 13-4 (5.1 users) or 13-5 (5.0 users). Notice in that figure that you must insert one more Merge code for a pause without a message. Follow steps 13 and 14 when the cursor is at the correct position.

17. Save this file under the name MEMO.PRI, and clear the screen.

# Merge on the Screen

Once you have stored a primary file on disk, you can initiate a merge with the keyboard at any time. You must make sure that the screen is clear. Then press the MERGE/SORT ([Ctrl] + [F9]) key and select Merge (1 or M). [*Pulldown menu:* Tools (T), Merge (M).] (Though the Merge and Sort features are accessed with the same function key, they are independent. Refer to Chapter 15 for a discussion of the Sort command.) WordPerfect prompts you for the name of a primary file; type in the appropriate filename (preceded by the drive/directory where it is stored if different from the default) and press [Enter]. Now WordPerfect prompts you for the name of a secondary file; a secondary file is used only for a merge with a file—a feature described later in this chapter; simply press [Enter] to bypass this secondary file prompt, signaling to WordPerfect that you wish to perform a merge with the keyboard.

The primary file appears on screen and WordPerfect pauses with the cursor located where you originally typed the first {INPUT} or ^C Merge code into the text. The Merge code is now erased and WordPerfect prompts at the bottom of the screen—either with the customized message you previously typed at that location, or, if you didn't type a message, with the following to remind you that you are in the midst of a merge:

```
* Merging *
```

At this pause, you can type the variable information. The information that you type can be any length. You can use the [Enter] key to insert blank lines while you are typing at the pause and also can use the arrow keys to move around in the text. Or, you can use the pause as an opportunity to retrieve a file containing boilerplate text into the document being merged.

When you are done typing or retrieving text into that first location, press the END FIELD ( F9 ) key. (*5.0 users:* The F9 key in your version is named MERGE R.) It is the END FIELD key, and not the Enter key, which tells WordPerfect to continue after a pause, so that the Enter key can be reserved to end paragraphs or insert blank lines just like in normal typing. The cursor jumps forward to the next {INPUT} or ^C code, erases that code, and pauses again. You should continue until you have completed filling in the last blank where an {INPUT} or ^C code previously resided. Then, press the END FIELD key one more time to end the merge process.

After the merge with the keyboard, a completed document is on screen. You are now ready to print the document, edit it, save it, or perform any combination of these actions. You can then clear the screen and start the merge process over again to create another personalized memorandum.

Sometimes, you may be in the middle of a merge with the keyboard and wish to quit the merge. When Word-Perfect is paused for input during the merge, press the MERGE CODES key. Then, 5.1 users see a new menu:

**1** Quit; **2** Next Record; **3** Stop: **0**

You can choose Quit (1 or Q), in which case the merge comes to an end and the primary file is displayed on screen, or you can choose Stop (3 or S), in which case the merge stops immediately, and only the file up to where you merged the text is displayed. 5.0 users see the same menu as when not in a merge; type **E** on that menu to quit the merge.

Suppose Robert Wambough, an employee at R&R Wine Association, has forgotten to complete several personnel forms. Let's send him a reminder.

1. Make sure that you clear the screen. Then, press the MERGE/SORT (⎡Ctrl⎤ + ⎡F9⎤) key. [*Pulldown menu:* Tools (T).] WordPerfect responds

   1 Merge; **2** Sort; **3** Convert Old Merge Codes: **0**

   Version 5.0 users will not see the third menu item.

2. Select Merge (1 or M). WordPerfect prompts

   Primary file:

3. Type **MEMO.PRI**, and press ⎡Enter⎤. WordPerfect prompts

   Secondary file:

4. Press ⎡Enter⎤ to bypass this prompt. The primary file appears, with the cursor positioned at the first place where you must personalize the memo, as shown in Figure 13-6. Notice that at the bottom of the screen, WordPerfect displays the message that you entered at that location, "Type Employee Name".

5. Type **Robert Wambough**.

6. Press the END FIELD (⎡F9⎤) key to continue the merge. (If you pressed ⎡Enter⎤ by mistake, press ⎡Backspace⎤ to erase the black line you inserted and then press END FIELD.) Now the cursor moves down to the next preselected place, erases the code, and pauses for your input. The message "List Forms on Separate Lines" is displayed.

7. Type **Withholding Tax Form**, and press ⎡Enter⎤ so that you can type additional information on the next line.

8. Type **Employee Emergency Form**.

9. Press the END FIELD ( [F9] ) key. The cursor moves to the next place for you to type in a name. Now, since you supplied no message, the bottom of the screen reads "* Merging *", as shown in Figure 13-7.

10. Type your own name.

11. Press the END FIELD ( [F9] ) key. The cursor is positioned for you to type the last four digits of a phone number.

12. Type **9905**.

13. Press the END FIELD ( [F9] ) key. The cursor jumps to the bottom of the document; this completes the merge process.

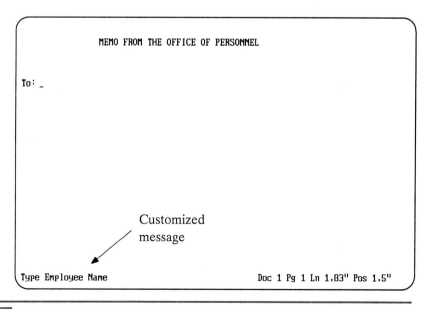

MEMO FROM THE OFFICE OF PERSONNEL

To: _

Customized message

Type Employee Name                    Doc 1 Pg 1 Ln 1.83" Pos 1.5"

═══════ **FIGURE 13-6**  Screen during a merge with the keyboard showing a customized message

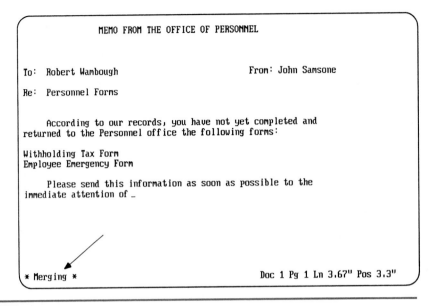

FIGURE 13-7   Screen during a merge with the keyboard showing the "Merging" message

You have completed this memo much faster than if you had to type it from scratch.

Print the document and clear the screen. You're now ready to perform other merges to prepare memos for other forgetful R&R Wine Association employees. After completing just two memos like this one, you'll see how much time and energy the Merge with the Keyboard feature saves you—not to mention the rest it provides for your typing fingers.

You can add sophistication when merging with the keyboard by inserting other Merge codes to the primary file. For instance, you can include a special Merge code that inserts the current date for you during the merge. Or, you can insert a Merge code that retrieves a certain file containing boilerplate text during the merge. Or, you can insert Merge codes to automatically print out a completely merged document, clear the screen, and then restart the merge; in this way, you can quickly produce repetitive documents without needing to manually print and initiate the merge for each merged document. See the section "Enhance the Merge Process" later in this chapter for details.

# MERGE WITH A FILE

The Merge with a File feature is most useful when you must produce and personalize the same document many times, and you wish to store the variable information for later use. Why would you ever wish to save this variable information? You may need, for example, to carry on habitual correspondence with a list of clients or members of a certain organization or committee. In that case, you will want to store the names and addresses of your clients or committee members in a file, so that whenever you merge, you won't have to type in each name and address over and over again as you would with a merge with the keyboard.

Figure 13-8 shows a letter to be sent to each person on the R&R Wine Association's wine-tasting committee. The circled copy is a sample of the variable information. The rest of the letter always stays the same.

In a merge with a file, you first store the variable information in what's called a *secondary file*. Then you're ready to create a primary file containing the text that stays the same from copy to copy, with special Merge codes inserted

Ms. Janice Smith
3559 Biltmore Street
San Francisco, CA 94123

Dear Ms. Smith

Thank you for agreeing to serve on the R&R Wine Association's
California Wine-Tasting Committee.    You are our official
representative from San Francisco!

Our first meeting will be held at the beginning of December in
Monterey, California. I'll be sure to let you know the exact date
and time as soon as it is confirmed.

I look forward to seeing you soon in Monterey, Janice.

Sincerely,

Lonnie Chang
R&R Wine Association

**FIGURE 13-8**   Letter to be produced using a merge with
a file

in those locations where the document is to be personalized using the variable information in the secondary file.

## Create a Secondary File

Figure 13-9 shows a secondary file in version 5.1, while
Figure 13-10 shows a secondary file in version 5.0. It is not
standard text; it is merely the information that personalizes
each record. A secondary file's variable information is organized into *records*. A record is one whole set of related

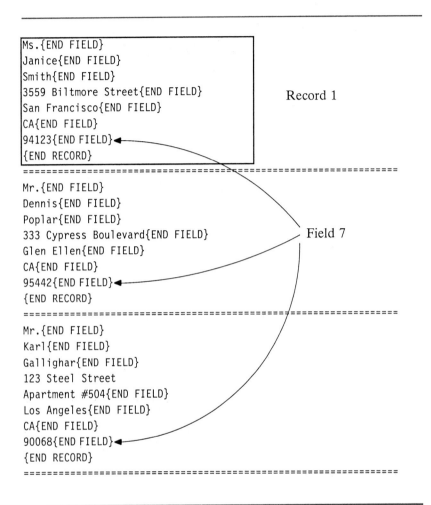

```
Ms.{END FIELD}
Janice{END FIELD}
Smith{END FIELD}
3559 Biltmore Street{END FIELD}
San Francisco{END FIELD}
CA{END FIELD}
94123{END FIELD}
{END RECORD}
===================================================================
Mr.{END FIELD}
Dennis{END FIELD}
Poplar{END FIELD}
333 Cypress Boulevard{END FIELD}
Glen Ellen{END FIELD}
CA{END FIELD}
95442{END FIELD}
{END RECORD}
===================================================================
Mr.{END FIELD}
Karl{END FIELD}
Gallighar{END FIELD}
123 Steel Street
Apartment #504{END FIELD}
Los Angeles{END FIELD}
CA{END FIELD}
90068{END FIELD}
{END RECORD}
===================================================================
```

Record 1

Field 7

**FIGURE 13-9**  Secondary file (version 5.1)

variable information, such as one committee member's name and address; each record results in the production of one personalized document. The end of a record is denoted with an {END RECORD} or ^E Merge code and is followed by a Hard Page **[HPg]** code which — as you learned

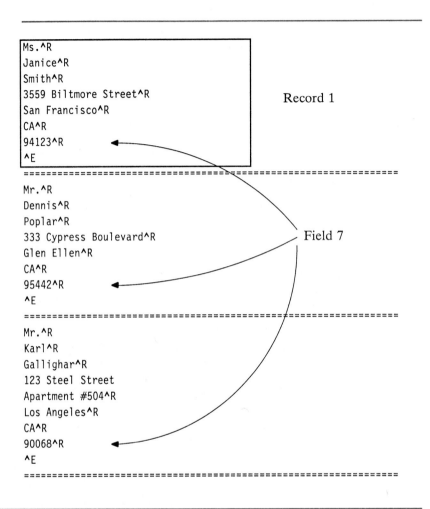

```
Ms.^R
Janice^R
Smith^R
3559 Biltmore Street^R          Record 1
San Francisco^R
CA^R
94123^R
^E
════════════════════════════════════════════════════════════
Mr.^R
Dennis^R
Poplar^R
333 Cypress Boulevard^R         Field 7
Glen Ellen^R
CA^R
95442^R
^E
════════════════════════════════════════════════════════════
Mr.^R
Karl^R
Gallighar^R
123 Steel Street
Apartment #504^R
Los Angeles^R
CA^R
90068^R
^E
════════════════════════════════════════════════════════════
```

**FIGURE 13-10** Secondary file (version 5.0)

in Chapter 6—appears on screen as a row of equal signs. Notice in Figures 13-9 and 13-10 that there are three records. Each record contains information about one person. If you use this secondary file in a merge, the resulting merged document will contain three separate letters.

Records are broken into separate units called *fields*. A field is one piece of variable information in a record, such as one committee member's first name. The field can contain letters, numbers, or both. It may be only one character long or any number of lines long. Each field is separated by an {END FIELD} or ˆR Merge code.

Each record must contain the same number of fields, and those fields must be listed in the same order. Notice in Figure 13-9 or 13-10 that each record contains seven fields. The first field (referred to as field 1) always contains a title, such as "Mr." or "Ms.", field 2 always contains a first name, field 3 always contains a last name, field 4 always contains an address, and so on.

Even if you have no information for a field in a given record, you should still insert the code {END FIELD} or ˆR to occupy a line, so that the record has the same number of fields as all the others. For instance, suppose you didn't know Ms. Smith's first name in Figure 13-9. In 5.1, for example, you would enter her record as follows:

```
Ms. {END FIELD}
{END FIELD}
Smith {END FIELD}
3559 Biltmore Street {END FIELD}
San Francisco {END FIELD}
CA {END FIELD}
94123 {END FIELD}
{END RECORD}
```

If you *forget* to insert an {END FIELD} or ˆR to occupy the blank field 2, WordPerfect will assume that field 2 is Smith, field 3 is 3559 Biltmore, and so on, and you'd get awkward results in the final merged letter addressed to Ms. Smith. For example, instead of this:

```
Ms. Smith
3559 Biltmore Street
San Francisco, CA 94123
```

you could get the following odd results as an inside address:

```
Ms. Smith 3559 Biltmore Street
San Francisco
CA, 94123
```

A field can, however, have varying numbers of lines. As an example, notice that the addresses in field 4 are one line long for the first two records. But for the last record, field 4 contains a two-line address. This is permissible in WordPerfect; it is the {END FIELD} or ^R code, not a hard return, that defines the end of a field.

To create a secondary file, consider the type of variable information you want in your documents. For instance, if only a person's name and address are required to personalize a document, then names and addresses will be the only information typed into a secondary file. But suppose that you run a dentist's office and send bills out every month to your clients. In that case, you may also want to include the amount owed as another field in each record.

Also consider how the variable information should be organized in the secondary file. For instance, if a person's address, city, state, and ZIP code are only used as part of the inside address, then they can be combined into one field, such as in this example:

```
3559 Biltmore Street
San Francisco, CA 94123 {END FIELD}
```

However, if you wish to refer to just the city, the state, or the ZIP code, in addition to using this information as part of the address, you could split the address into separate fields. The following organization would be more suitable:

```
3559 Biltmore Street {END FIELD}
San Francisco {END FIELD}
CA {END FIELD}
94123 {END FIELD}
```

This second way of organizing information is used in the secondary file in Figures 13-9 and 13-10, because the final merged result will refer to a committee member's city in both the inside address and within the body of the letter.

Once you've thought about the structure of the variable information, you're ready to type that information into a secondary file. You must start on a clear screen. Type in the first field for the first record and press the END FIELD ( F9 ) key. WordPerfect will insert an {END FIELD} code or ^R code and a hidden **[HRt]** code; the cursor moves to the beginning of the next line, ready for you to type field 2. In fact, for 5.1 users, the field number is indicated at the bottom left corner of the screen, which reads "Field: 2". Type the information for field 2 and again press END FIELD. Continue until you've typed each field for the first record.

After completing an entire record, you must insert an End Record Merge code followed by a Hard Page code. To do so, press the MERGE CODES ( Shift + F9 ) key. [*Pulldown menu:* Tools (T), Merge Codes (R).] *5.1 users:* Select End Record (2 or E); WordPerfect inserts an {END RECORD} code and an **[HPg]** code. *5.0 users:* Select E; WordPerfect inserts a ^E code and an **[HPg]** code.

After typing all the records, save the information on disk with a name that reminds you that this is not a standard document, but a secondary file of variable information. For example, name a secondary file beginning with the letters SF or SEC (both standing for Secondary File) or with the filename extension .SF or .SEC.

Suppose that the R&R Wine Association has just organized a wine-tasting committee. In the coming months,
numerous letters will be sent to the committee members.
Let's create a secondary file containing their names and
addresses, as shown in Figure 13-9 or 13-10.

1. Press the EXIT ([F7]) key, and type **N** twice to clear the
   screen.

2. Type **Ms.**

3. Press the END FIELD ([F9]) key. An {END FIELD} or
   ^R Merge code is inserted followed by a Hard Return
   code to move the cursor down to the next line.

4. Type **Janice** and press the END FIELD ([F9]) key.

5. Type **Smith,** and press the END FIELD ([F9]) key.

6. Continue to type the rest of the fields for the first record
   in Figure 13-9 or 13-10, pressing the END FIELD ([F9])
   key after each.

7. After typing all seven fields, each field followed by an
   End Field code, press the MERGE CODES ([Shift] +
   [F9]) key. [*Pulldown menu:* Tools (T), Merge Codes
   (R).]

8. *5.1 users:*Select End Record (2 or E). WordPerfect
   inserts {END RECORD} at the current cursor position
   and then inserts a Hard Page code so that a page bar of
   equal signs appears across the screen.
   *5.0 users:* Type **E.** WordPerfect inserts ^E at the current cursor position and then inserts a Hard Page code
   so that a row of equal signs appears across the screen.

9. Continue until you've completed typing the information shown in Figure 13-9 or 13-10 for records 2 and 3.

10. Save this information under the filename WTC.SEC (which stands for "Wine-Tasting Committee, Secondary File"), and then clear the screen.

## Create a Primary File

In a merge with a file, the primary file you create contains codes telling WordPerfect precisely where the information corresponding to each field of the secondary file must be inserted. The Merge code you insert in the primary file is {FIELD}$n\sim$ for 5.1 users, and ^F$n$^ for 5.0 users. The "$n$" represents a specific field number.

An example of a primary file for a letter to members of the wine-tasting committee is shown in Figure 13-11 for version 5.1 users and in Figure 13-12 for 5.0 users. The field numbers correspond to the order of fields in the secondary file. For instance, notice the following salutation line in Figure 13-11:

```
Dear {FIELD}1~ {FIELD}3~:
```

If you refer to the secondary file, you'll notice that this will result in "Dear Ms. Smith:" for the first record, "Dear Mr. Poplar:" for the second, and "Dear Mr. Gallighar:" in the third. If, instead, you wanted to address each letter by the recipient's first name, then you could have included the following salutation line:

```
Dear {FIELD}2~:
```

```
{FIELD}1~ {FIELD}2~ {FIELD}3~
{FIELD}4~
{FIELD}5~, {FIELD}6~ {FIELD}7~


Dear {FIELD}1~ {FIELD}3~:

Thank you for agreeing to serve on the R&R Wine Association's
California Wine-Tasting Committee.  You are our official
representative from {FIELD}5~!

Our first meeting will be held at the beginning of December in
Monterey, California.  I'll be sure to let you know the exact date
and time as soon as it is confirmed.

I look forward to seeing you soon in Monterey, {FIELD}2~.

Sincerely,


Lonnie Chang
R&R Wine Association
```
Doc 1 Pg 1 Ln 1" Pos 1"

**FIGURE 13-11**   Primary file for merge with a file
(version 5.1)

Typing a primary file for a merge with a file is similar to
creating one for a merge with the keyboard. You clear the
screen and begin typing the text that stays the same for
each document. You can format the document as you
would any standard document; however, if you wish to alter
a format setting, such as margins or tabs, starting at the top
of the document, it is best to include the Format codes on
the primary file's Document Initial Codes screen (as described in Chapter 6). In this way, you reduce the clutter of
codes in the text—Margin and Tab codes will appear only
once in the merged result, rather than at the top of each
repetitive document.

As you type the primary file, wherever you want to insert
a {FIELD}*n* ~ or ˆF*n*ˆ Merge code, press the MERGE
CODES ( Shift + F9 ) key. [*Pulldown menu:* Tools (T),

```
^F1^ ^F2^ ^F3^
^F4^
^F5^, ^F6^  ^F7^

Dear ^F1^ ^F3^:

Thank you for agreeing to serve on the R&R Wine Association's
California Wine-Tasting Committee.  You are our official
representative from ^F5^!

Our first meeting will be held at the beginning of December in
Monterey, California.  I'll be sure to let you know the exact date
and time as soon as it is confirmed.

I look forward to seeing you soon in Monterey, ^F2^.

Sincerely,


Lonnie Chang
R&R Wine Association

                                          Doc 1 Pg 1 Ln 1" Pos 1"
```

**FIGURE 13-12**   Primary file for merge with a file (version 5.0)

Merge Codes (R). Then, 5.1 users should select Field (1 or F), while 5.0 users should type **F**. WordPerfect then requests a field number; type the appropriate number and press (Enter). WordPerfect inserts that Field Merge code at the current cursor position. For instance, if you enter the number 5, WordPerfect inserts {FIELD}5~ or ^F5^.

Obviously, the primary file in a merge with a file is set up based on the order of fields in the secondary file. When you create a primary file, you must know which field number corresponds to which item of variable information. One way to do this would be to keep referring to the secondary file, which you can display on the Doc 2 screen, while you create the primary file on the Doc 1 screen. Or, you can keep a list of fields by your desk. For example, for the secondary file you just created, you could type up the following list and place it next to your keyboard for whenever you wished to create a new primary file.

```
Field     Information
1         Title
2         First name
3         Last name
4         Street address
5         City
6         State abbreviation
7         ZIP code
```

Once you've completed typing the primary document, remember to check carefully for grammatical, punctuation, or spelling errors, and to use the Spell feature if you so desire. Also, make sure that the Merge codes contain the correct field numbers. If you wish to edit a Field Merge code, you can use standard editing procedures to erase the field number and type a new one. And be sure to check the location and syntax of your Merge codes carefully. In version 5.1, there must be a tilde (~) following the field number, while in version 5.0, there must be a caret (^) following the field number. When the primary document is correct, save it on disk. To help you identify this file as a primary file, choose a descriptive filename. As discussed previously, you could begin the filename with the letters PF or PRI, or use those letters in the filename extension.

Let's create the primary file shown in Figure 13-11 or 13-12.

1. Make sure that the screen is clear. If not, clear the screen using the EXIT (F7) key. You're now at the location where you must insert the first Merge code, where a title will be inserted for each person.

2. Press the MERGE CODES ( Shift + F9 ) key. [*Pull-down menu:* Tools (T), Merge Codes (R).] 5.1 users will view the following menu:

```
1 Field; 2 End Record; 3 Input; 4 Page Off; 5 Next Record;
6 More:0
```

5.0 users will view the following:

```
^C; ^D; ^E; ^F; ^G; ^N; ^O; ^P; ^Q; ^S; ^T; ^U; ^V:
```

3. *5.1 users:* Select Field (1 or F). WordPerfect prompts

```
Enter Field:
```

Type **1** and press Enter . WordPerfect inserts the following:

```
{FIELD}1~
```

*5.0 users:* Type **F**. WordPerfect prompts

```
Field:
```

Type **1** and press Enter . WordPerfect inserts the following:

```
^F1^
```

4. Since you will want a space separating each person's title and first name in the letter's inside address, press the spacebar once. Now you're ready to type the Merge code where the first name will be inserted in each letter.

5. Repeat steps 2 and 3, but enter **2** as the field number.

6. Press the spacebar once. The cursor is now properly positioned for you to type the next Merge code.

7. Continue inserting codes and text as shown in Figure 13-11 or 13-12.

8. After typing this primary file, check closely for any incorrect Merge codes, spelling errors, or other typing mistakes; one mistake will show up in as many letters as records contained in your secondary file. You may also wish to perform a spell check.

9. Save the document under the name WTC1.PRI (which stands for "the first PRImary document for the Wine-Tasting Committee"), and then clear the screen.

You can use as many Field Merge codes as you like and in any order in a primary file. Notice in Figure 13-11, for example, that Merge codes referencing fields 1, 2, 3, and 5 are inserted twice. You don't even need to use all the fields contained in a secondary file. For instance, a secondary file might contain a company name in field 8 and a telephone number in field 9, but since neither of these is used in the primary file shown in Figure 13-11 or 13-12, the Merge codes referencing fields 8 or 9 would not be inserted in that primary file.

## Merge on the Screen

Once you have stored a secondary file and a matching primary file on disk, you can initiate a merge with a file. Clear the screen, press the MERGE/SORT ([Ctrl] + [F9]) key, and select Merge (1 or M). [*Pulldown menu:* Tools (T), Merge (M).] WordPerfect will prompt you for the name of a primary file. Type the appropriate filename and press [Enter]. Next, WordPerfect will prompt you for the name of a secondary file; again, type the appropriate filename and press [Enter]. Make sure to precede the primary filename or the secondary filename by the drive/directory where it is stored if different from the default. For instance, when WordPerfect prompts for a secondary file, type A:WTC.SEC if the secondary file is stored in drive A even though the default is drive C, the hard disk. (Also, 5.1 users who forget the name of a file when WordPerfect prompts to enter the primary or secondary filename can use the LIST ([F5]) key to list the files in a directory, position the cursor on the file you desire, and select Retrieve (1 or R).)

The merge happens on the screen while you wait. (To stop the merge at any time, press the CANCEL ([F1]) key.) WordPerfect automatically inserts a Hard Page **[HPg]** code after it merges the primary file with one record and before it merges the primary file with the next record. Thus, if you are merging a one-page primary file with ten records in a secondary file, WordPerfect will assemble a document containing ten pages of text—each a separate letter.

When the merge is complete, the cursor is located at the bottom of the document, displaying the letter pertaining to the last record in the secondary file. If you move up to the top of the document, you'll see the letter for the first record. Then continue to press [PgDn] to view the separate pages.

You have already stored on disk a secondary file containing variable information and a primary file that contains Field Merge codes corresponding to fields in that secondary file. You're now ready to merge these files.

1. On a clear screen, press the MERGE/SORT ([Ctrl] + [F9]) key. WordPerfect responds

   **1** Merge; **2** Sort; **3** Convert Old Merge Codes: **0**

   [*Pulldown menu:* Tools (T).]

2. Select Merge (1 or M). WordPerfect prompts

   Primary file:

3. Type **WTC1.PRI**, and press Enter. WordPerfect prompts

   `Secondary file:`

4. Type **WTC.SEC.**, and press Enter. The message * **Merging** * appears at the bottom of the screen.

5. The "Merging" message clears when the merge is completed. The cursor is at the bottom of the merged document.

6. Press Home, Home, ↑ to move to the top of the document. You're viewing the letter for the first record in the secondary file, the printed results of which are shown in Figure 13-8.

7. Press PgDn to view the second letter.

8. Press PgDn to view the third letter.

Once a merge is complete, the document on screen, which contains the personalized letters, is ready for use. You can edit any of the letters and then either print them or store them on disk. It is usually unnecessary to store the letters on disk. After all, if you want to produce an identical copy of the same letters next week, you can always merge the primary and secondary files again, since both of the files are stored on disk. By printing the merged document and not saving it, you reserve disk space for files that you cannot reproduce so easily.

You can mix and match primary and secondary files. For instance, suppose you create a separate secondary file containing a list of inactive wine-tasting-committee members. You could merge the same primary file named WTC1.PRI (Figure 13-11 or 13-12) with that other secondary file. Or suppose that next month you plan to send another letter to all active members of the wine-tasting committee. In that case, you could create a new primary file containing the text of the new letter, with Field Merge codes in each place where you want to personalize the letters. Store that file on disk, perhaps under the filename WTC2.PRI. You could then perform a merge using WTC2.PRI as the primary file along with WTC.SEC (Figure 13-9 or 13-10) as the secondary file. Or, create a new primary file for envelopes and then merge it with WTC.SEC, as discussed below.

# PREPARE ENVELOPES AND MAILING LABELS

Once you've used the Merge feature to create hundreds of personalized letters and have printed those letters, your job may not yet be complete. You may still have to produce mailing labels or envelopes so that you can send out those letters. It should not be surprising that WordPerfect can help you with this, too, by performing another merge.

You already have stored on disk a secondary file that contains names and addresses. What you must do now is create a primary file for envelopes or labels to merge with that secondary file. The primary file will contain no text; it will simply contain Merge codes in the order that the text in the fields will appear on the envelopes or labels.

The primary file will also contain Format codes so that the results will correctly print on envelopes or labels. How you format the primary file will depend on whether you wish to produce envelopes or mailing labels, the type of mailing labels you use, and whether you are a version 5.1 or 5.0 user. Instructions for creating envelopes and mailing labels are described below.

## Envelopes [5.1 and 5.0 Users]

If you wish to print addresses on envelopes (assuming that the return address is already printed in the upper left corner of the envelopes that you plan to use), then, on a clear screen, insert the Field Merge codes that correspond to the names and addresses in your secondary merge file. For instance, the codes in the primary file for envelopes — assuming a secondary file organized like WTC.SEC, which you created previously — are, for 5.1 users:

```
{FIELD}1~ {FIELD}2~ {FIELD}3~
{FIELD}4~
{FIELD}5~, {FIELD}6~  {FIELD}7~
```

Or, for 5.0 users, the primary file will contain the following:

```
^F1^ ^F2^ ^F3^
^F4^
^F5^, ^F6^  ^F7^
```

Next, you will want to format this document correctly for envelopes — changing the paper size/type, and the margin settings — starting at the top of the document. For Format codes that govern the document starting at the top, it is best to insert Format codes on the Document Initial Codes screen, and not at the top of the document, so that the Format codes are inserted only once; otherwise, if you insert Format codes at the top of the primary document, the codes will repeat at the top of each page of the merged document, which will clutter the merged document with unnecessary codes.

Display the Document Initial Codes screen for the primary file you are creating by selecting Initial Codes (2 or C) from the Document Format menu. (See Chapter 6 if you need a review of the Document Initial Codes screen.) Then, insert the following Format codes. (Depending on the size of your envelopes and your preference as to where the address should be printed, you may wish to test and then alter these settings.)

- *Top/Bottom margins* Top margin of 2.5″ and a small bottom margin, such as 0″ or .3″ (to allow room for a multiline address). Or, if you will insert the envelope into the printer manually, you can simply advance the envelope in the printer about 2.5″ yourself; in that case, you can set the top margin to 0″.

- *Left/Right margins* Left margin of 4.5″ and a small right margin, such as 0″ or .3″ (to allow room for a lengthy line in an address).

- *Paper Size/Type* Paper size/type for the envelopes on which you will print the addresses. (You must set forth a paper definition for the envelopes before you attempt to print them out, so that WordPerfect knows special instructions for printing out envelopes with your printer. Look to Chapter 9 for instructions on doing so.)

From the Document Initial Codes screen, press EXIT (F7) twice to return to the Typing screen. Save this primary file using a name that reminds you it is a primary file, such as ENV.PRI.

Now you are ready to merge the primary file, such as ENV.PRI, with the secondary file containing the addresses, such as the example of WTC.SEC used in this chapter. When you do, you'll get results such as shown in Figure 13-13. Notice that a page bar of equal signs is inserted between the addresses, indicating page breaks; this is because, as you'll remember, WordPerfect automatically

```
                    Ms, Janice Smith
                    3559 Biltmore Street
                    San Francisco, CA  94123
=====================================================================
                    Mr, Dennis Poplar
                    333 Cypress Boulevard
                    Glen Ellen, CA  95442
=====================================================================
                    Mr, Karl Gallighar
                    123 Steel Street
                    Apartment #504
                    Los Angeles, CA  90068_




                                          Doc 1 Pg 3 Ln 2,5" Pos 6,2"
```

**FIGURE 13-13**   Merged document for printing on envelopes

inserts Hard Page codes after it merges with each record from the secondary file. Each page on screen represents a separate envelope at the printer.

Your next step is to print out the envelopes. Make sure to have envelopes handy. On some printers, you will have previously set the paper definition for the "Envelope" type to feed envelopes from a sheet feeder, in which case make sure to stock the sheet feeder with envelopes. On other printers, the only way to print on envelopes is by inserting each envelope one at a time; in that case, you will have set the Envelope type to pause for you to insert each envelope, and, on some printers, will hear a beep and need to select Go (4 or G) on the Control Printer screen (as described in Chapter 2) to signal WordPerfect to print on each envelope.

# Labels [5.1 Users]

Here's how to print addresses on labels. On a clear screen, create a primary file for labels by inserting the Field Merge codes that correspond to the names and addresses in your secondary merge file. As described above, the codes in the primary file — assuming a secondary file organized like WTC.SEC, which you created previously — are

```
{FIELD}1~ {FIELD}2~ {FIELD}3~
{FIELD}4~
{FIELD}5~, {FIELD}6~ {FIELD}7 ~
```

Next, you will want to format this document correctly for the type of labels that you use — by inserting a Paper Size/ Type code on the Document Initial Codes screen. Display the Document Initial Codes screen for the primary file you are creating by selecting Initial Codes (2 or C) from the Document Format menu. (See Chapter 6 if you need a review of the Document Initial Codes screen.) Then, insert a Paper Size/Type code for the labels on which you will print the addresses. (You must set forth a paper definition for the labels before you attempt to print them out, so that WordPerfect knows special instructions for printing out labels with your printer. Look to Chapter 9 for instructions on creating a new paper definition for labels.)

From the Document Initial Codes screen, press EXIT (F7) twice to return to the Typing screen. Save this primary file using a descriptive name that reminds you it is a primary file for labels, such as LABELS.PRI.

Now you are ready to merge the primary file, such as LABELS.PRI, with the secondary file containing the addresses, such as the example of WTC.SEC used in this chapter. When you do, you'll get results that, like Figure 13-13, will show each address separated by a page bar.

But, because the paper is defined for labels, each address does not represent a separate page, but instead a section on a page. At the printer, WordPerfect will format the addresses row-by-row. If you defined one-across labels, then only one address prints across a row. For two-across labels, WordPerfect will print two addresses across. Or, as shown in Figure 13-14, a paper definition for three-across labels will print the first three addresses across the first row, the second three addresses in the second row, and so on, so that the addresses are printed on the labels. As you print, WordPerfect may pause for you to insert each sheet

```
Ms. Janice Smith       Mr. Dennis Poplar      Mr. Karl Gallighar
3559 Biltmore Street   333 Cypress Boulevard  123 Steel Street
San Francisco, CA 94123 Glen Ellen, CA  95442  Apartment #504
                                              Los Angeles, CA 90068


xx. xxxx xxxxxxxxxx     xx. xxxx xxxxxxxxxx    xx. xxxx xxxxxxxxxx
xxxxxxxxxxxxxxx         xxxxxxxxxxxxxxx        xxxxxxxxxxxxxxx
xxx xxxxxxxxxx, xxxxx   xxx xxxxxxxxxx, xxxxx  xxx xxxxxxxxxx, xxxxx


xx. xxxx xxxxxxxxxx     xx. xxxx xxxxxxxxxx    xx. xxxx xxxxxxxxxx
xxxx xxxxxxxxx          xxxxxxxxxxxxxxx        xxxxxxxxxxxxxxx
xxxxxxxxxxxxxxx         xxx xxxxxxxxxx, xxxxx  xxx xxxxxxxxxx, xxxxx
xxx xxxxxxxxxx, xxxxx


xx. xxxx xxxxxxxxxx     xx. xxxx xxxxxxxxxx    xx. xxxx xxxxxxxxxx
xxxxxxxxxxxxxxx         xxxxxx xxxxxxxx        xxxxxxxxxxxxxxx
xxx xxxxxxxxxx, xxxxx   xxxxxxxxxxxxxxx        xxx xxxxxxxxxx, xxxxx
                       xxx xxxxxxxxxx, xxxxx


xx. xxxx xxxxxxxxxx
xxxxxxxxxxxxxxx
xxx xxxxxxxxxx, xxxxx
```

**FIGURE 13-14**   Printed result of a merged document formatted for labels (version 5.1)

of labels, depending on how you defined the paper defini-tion. If so, insert the labels, and then you may need to select Go (4 or G) from the Control Printer menu, as described in Chapter 2, to begin the printing.

## Continuous Labels [5.0 Users]

Some labels are continuous; they are connected on long rolls of paper so that they can be continuously fed through the printer. Continuous sheets may be one, two, or three across. These can be used on many printers, though not on laser printers.

If you wish to print addresses on continuous labels, then start to create a primary file by formatting a document correctly for labels—changing the paper size/type and the margin settings—starting at the top of the document. It is best to insert these Format codes on the Document Initial Codes screen, and not at the top of the document, so that the Format codes are inserted only once; otherwise, if you insert Format codes at the top of the primary document, the codes will repeat at the top of each page of the merged document, which will clutter the merged document with unnecessary codes. In addition, if the labels are more than one across, you will want to define columns.

Display the Document Initial Codes screen for the pri-mary file you are creating by selecting Initial Codes (2 or C) from the Document Format menu. (See Chapter 6 if you need a review of the Document Initial Codes screen.) Then, insert the following Format codes. (Depending on the size of your labels and your printer, you may wish to test and then alter these settings.)

- *Top/Bottom margins* .25″ or less as a top margin, 0″ as a bottom margin.

- *Left/Right margins* .25″ or less as a left margin, 0″ as a right margin.

- *Paper Size/Type* "Other" size (where you indicate the width as the actual width of the paper, such as 8.5″ if your labels are three across, and a height that equals the distance from the top of one label to the top of the next) and "Labels" type. (You must define a label form definition for the Other size/Labels type before you attempt to print out labels, so that WordPerfect knows special instructions for printing out labels; see Chapter 9.)

- *Column Definition* Only if your labels are two or three across, format the document into text columns using the MATH/COLUMNS ( Alt + F7 ) key. (The Columns feature is described in Chapter 11.) Create 2 or 3 Parallel-Style columns, depending on whether the labels are two or three across. These columns should be evenly spaced, with the distance between columns set based on the distance between columns of your labels. For instance, suppose the labels are two across, each 4″ wide with 0.5″ of space between the two-across labels. If you want a 0.25″ left margin on each label, try the following settings:

| Column | Left Margin | Right Margin |
| --- | --- | --- |
| 1 | 0.25″ | 4″ |
| 2 | 4.75″ | 8.5″ |

From the Document Initial Codes screen, press EXIT ( F7 ) twice to return to the Typing screen. Then, if you have defined columns, turn on columns using the MATH/COLUMNS ( Alt + F7 ) key.

Now, you are ready to insert the Field Merge codes that correspond to the names and addresses in your secondary merge file. For one-across labels, where there are no columns, the codes (assuming a secondary file like WTC.SEC, which you created in the earlier practice exercise) are

```
^F1^ ^F2^ ^F3^
^F4^
^F5^, ^F6^  ^F7^
```

For two-across labels, your cursor will be located in column 1. In this first column, insert the ^F*n*^ Merge codes that correspond to each person's name and address in the secondary file, and also insert one extra code, a ^N Merge code (a code which is described in the next section of this chapter) on the last line. Insert the ^N code using the same method as you use to insert most other codes: Press the MERGE CODES ([Shift] + [F9]) key and type **N**. Then, press [Ctrl] + [Enter] to move the next column. Now insert the same ^F*n*^ codes again for the second column. Here's how the screen will appear:

```
^F1^ ^F2^ ^F3^          ^F1^ ^F2^ ^F3^
^F4^                    ^F4^
^F5^, ^F6^ ^F7^^N       ^F5^, ^F6^ ^F7^
```

Now, after typing the last code in the second column (^F7^), turn off columns using the MATH/COLUMNS ([Alt] + [F7]) key.

For three-across labels, the process is similar as for two-across, but you will have three columns, two which end with the ^N code, as follows:

```
^F1^ ^F2^ ^F3^          ^F1^ ^F2^ ^F3^          ^F1^ ^F2^ ^F3^
^F4^                    ^F4^                    ^F4^
^F5^, ^F6^ ^F7^^N       ^F5^, ^F6^ ^F7^^N       ^F5^, ^F6^ ^F7^
```

Then, after typing the last code in the third column (ˆF7ˆ), turn off columns using the MATH/COLUMNS (Alt + F7) key.

Save the primary file using a descriptive name, such as LABELS1.PRI (for one-across labels) or LABELS2.PRI.

Now you are ready to merge the primary file, such as LABELS1.PRI, with the secondary file containing the addresses, such as the example of WTC.SEC used in this chapter. Figure 13-15 shows the results assuming that the labels were defined for three across. Notice how each row is separated by a page bar, which represents one row of labels. (Remember that you defined the paper size such that each row of labels is considered a page.)

```
Ms, Janice Smith        Mr, Dennis Poplar       Mr, Karl Gallighar
3559 Biltmore Street    333 Cypress Boulevard   123 Steel Street
San Francisco, CA  94123  Glen Ellen, CA  95442 Apartment #504
                                                Los Angeles, CA  90068
------------------------------------------------------------------------
XX, XXXX XXXXXXXXXX     XX, XXXX XXXXXXXXXX     XX, XXXX XXXXXXXXXX
XXXXXXXXXXXXX          XXXXXXXXXXXXX           XXXXXXXXXXXXX
XXXXXXXXXXXXX          XXX XXXXXXXX, XXXXX     XXX XXXXXXXX, XXXXX
XXX XXXXXXXX, XXXXX
------------------------------------------------------------------------
XX, XXXX XXXXXXXXXX     XX, XXXX XXXXXXXXXX     XX, XXXX XXXXXXXXXX
XXXXXXXXXXXXX          XXXXXXXXXXXXX           XXXXXXXXXXXXX
XXX XXXXXXXX, XXXXX     XXXXXXXXXXXXX          XXX XXXXXXXX, XXXXX
                       XXX XXXXXXXX, XXXXX
------------------------------------------------------------------------
XX, XXXX XXXXXXXXXX     XX, XXXX XXXXXXXXXX     XX, XXXX XXXXXXXXXX
XXXXXXXXXXXXX          XXXXXXXXXXXXX           XXXXXXXXXXXXXXX
XXX XXXXXXXX, XXXXX     XXX XXXXXXXX, XXXXX     XXX XXXXXXXXX, XXXXX
------------------------------------------------------------------------


                                Col 1 Doc 1 Pg 1 Ln 0,25" Pos 0,22"
```

**FIGURE 13-15**   Merged document for printing on continuous labels (version 5.0)

To print, turn on your printer and insert the continuous labels into the printer so that the printhead is lined up with the top of the first label. Then send a print job that prints as many pages as you have rows of addresses in the merged document.

## Sheets of Labels [5.0 Users]

Some labels are purchased so that they are two or three across on a sheet of paper that is standard size (8.5″ by 11″). These sheets can be used on a variety of printers, including laser printers. The labels are printed a full page at a time.

Start to create a primary file by formatting a document correctly for labels—changing the margin settings—starting at the top of the document. It is best to insert these Format codes on the Document Initial Codes screen.

Display the Document Initial Codes screen for the primary file you are creating by selecting Initial Codes (2 or C) from the Document Format menu. (See Chapter 6 if you need a review of the Document Initial Codes screen.) Then, insert the following Format codes. (Depending on the size of your labels and your printer, you may wish to test and then alter these settings.)

- *Top/Bottom margins*   .25″ or less as a top margin, 0″ as a bottom margin.

- *Left/Right margins*   .25″ or less as a left margin, 0″ as a right margin.

- *Paper Size/Type*   If you created a paper definition for sheets of labels, insert the Paper Size/Type code corresponding to that paper definition. (This code is necessary

if you wish to indicate to WordPerfect special instructions for printing out labels—such as to pause for you to
insert each sheet of labels. But the size in the definition
will remain at standard 8.5″ by 11″, the size of the sheet
of labels.)

• *Column Definition*     Format the document into text columns using the MATH/COLUMNS (Alt + F7) key.
(The Columns feature is described in Chapter 11.) Create 3 Parallel-Style columns with Block Protect if there
are two labels across. Or, create 4 Parallel-Style columns
with Block Protect if there are three labels across. The
extra column is used to ensure that each row of labels
will contain the same number of lines when the primary
file is merged; that extra column is the first column, and
should be only .05″ wide. The remaining columns will be
evenly spaced, with the distance between columns set as
0″ to provide the maximum width across each label for an
address. For instance, try the following settings for three
labels across:

| Column | Left Margin | Right Margin |
| --- | --- | --- |
| 1 | 0.25″ | 0.3″ |
| 2 | 0.3″ | 3.05″ |
| 3 | 3.05″ | 5.8″ |
| 4 | 5.8″ | 8.5″ |

From the Document Initial Codes screen, press EXIT
(F7) twice to return to the Typing screen. Then turn on
columns using the MATH/COLUMNS (Alt + F7) key.
   Your cursor will now be located in column 1. In this first
column, press (Enter) as many times as the longest address

that can fit on a label. For instance, if the longest address that can fit on a label is six lines long, press [Enter] six times. Press HARD PAGE ( [Ctrl] + [Enter] ) to move to column 2.

In the second column insert the ˆFnˆ Merge codes that correspond to each person's name and address in the secondary file, and insert one extra Merge code, ˆN (a code which is described in the next section of this chapter). Insert the ˆN code using the same method as you use to insert most other codes: Press the MERGE CODES ( [Shift] + [F9] ) key and type **N**. For instance, based on the secondary file WTC.SEC, the codes inserted into column 2 will be

```
^F1^ ^F2^ ^F3^
^F4^
^F5^, ^F6^ ^F7^^N
```

Press HARD PAGE ( [Ctrl] + [Enter] ) to move to column 3.

In the third column for 3-across labels, insert codes identical to those inserted in the second column and press HARD PAGE ( [Ctrl] + [Enter] ) to move to column 4. (For 2-across labels, skip this step and move on to the next paragraph.)

In the last column, insert Field Merge codes identical to those inserted in the previous column. Then, instead of inserting a ˆN and Hard Page code, use the MATH/CO-LUMNS ( [Alt] + [F7] ) key to turn off the column feature.

Once columns are off and the cursor returns to the left margin on screen, type in the Merge codes ˆNˆPˆP so that the merge will start again, continuing with the next record in the same primary file. (This string of Merge codes is described in the next section of this chapter.) Insert the ˆN and ˆP codes using the same method as you use to insert most other codes: Press the MERGE CODES ( [Shift] + [F9] ) key and type **N** or **P**. Figure 13-16 shows an example of how the primary file may appear on screen. (The first column is not shown since it is invisible on the Typing

```
^F1^ ^F2^ ^F3^        ^F1^ ^F2^ ^F3^        ^F1^ ^F2^ ^F3^
^F4^                  ^F4^                  ^F4^
^F5^, ^F6^ ^F7^^N    ^F5^, ^F6^ ^F7^^N    ^F5^, ^F6^ ^F7^
^N^P^P





                                              Doc 1 Pg 1 Ln 1" Pos 1"
```

**FIGURE 13-16**  Primary file for creating mailing labels
for printing on a sheet of 3-across labels
(version 5.0)

screen, containing only Hard Return codes; also, depending
on your monitor, you may be unable to see the other three
columns at the same time.)

You have now created the primary file. Save this file
under a name that reminds you that it is a primary file for
your mailing labels, such as LABELS.PRI. You can then
clear the screen and perform a merge with LABELS.PRI
as the primary file and WTC.SEC as the secondary file.
After the merge, the addresses will be formatted into columns, with page breaks appearing after approximately nine
rows of labels, which corresponds to the number of rows of
labels on your label sheets. (Depending on your printer,
you may be unable to print on the first or last row of
labels.) Send each page of labels to the printer.

# ENHANCE THE MERGE PROCESS

You've thus far worked with several different Merge codes. You used two Merge codes in creating a secondary file: {END FIELD} and {END RECORD} for 5.1 users; ^R and ^E for 5.0 users. You also learned about the codes that are inserted into a primary file for a merge with the keyboard: {INPUT}*message*~ for 5.1 users; either ^C or ^O*message*^O^C for 5.0 users. And, you learned about the codes inserted into a primary file for a merge with a file, {FIELD}*n*~ or ^F*n*^. But WordPerfect offers additional codes as well.

In version 5.1, there are actually 70 Merge codes available; these are part of the sophisticated WordPerfect Programming Language. In version 5.0, there are 14 Merge codes available. Many of the Merge codes are quite complicated and used only by those people who have programming knowledge. But several of these additional Merge codes are easy to use, and important in order to refine the merge process for specific needs. The most useful and most frequently used Merge codes are described below for allowing added flexibility in the merge process.

## Pause During a Merge with a File

You can combine the two types of merges that you've learned about into one merge operation—so that you perform a merge with a secondary file and, at the same time, also have WordPerfect pause for keyboard input during the merge. For instance, suppose you wish to produce a letter for each record in a secondary file. In addition, you wish to type in a unique paragraph to conclude each letter. Figure 13-17 shows an example, a primary file for 5.1 users where {FIELD} codes are inserted at the top of the letter, and an {INPUT}*message* ~ code is inserted near the bottom of the letter.

During the merge, WordPerfect would take variable information from the secondary file to personalize the name and address for the first letter wherever the {FIELD} codes are located. But also during the merge, WordPerfect would pause in the first letter upon encountering the {INPUT} code, and would prompt with the message you created:

```
Type Ending Paragraph
```

```
{FIELD}1~ {FIELD}2~ {FIELD}3~
{FIELD}4~                          ◄────────Merge with file
{FIELD}5~, {FIELD}6~  {FIELD}7~


Dear {FIELD}1~ {FIELD}3~:

Thank you for agreeing to serve on the R&R Wine Association's
California Wine-Tasting Committee.  You are our official
representative from {FIELD}5~!

Our first meeting will be held at the beginning of December in
Monterey, California.  I'll be sure to let you know the exact date
and time as soon as it is confirmed.

{INPUT}Type Ending Paragraph~  ◄──────── Merge with keyboard

Sincerely,


Lonnie Chang
R&R Wine Association

                                       Doc 1 Pg 1 Ln 1" Pos 1"
```

═══ **FIGURE 13-17**   Primary file for a merge with a file *and* the keyboard (version 5.1)

You would then have the opportunity to type information into the keyboard, pressing the END FIELD (F9) key to continue the merge. Then WordPerfect would pause at the bottom of the next letter. This would continue until all records had been merged.

## Create Lists from a Secondary File

As you learned, when WordPerfect performs a merge, a page break is inserted after each record is merged with the primary file. In this way, WordPerfect creates a separate letter, envelope, or mailing label for each record.

There are times, however, when you may want to include multiple records in the same document, so you don't want WordPerfect to insert automatic page breaks. This is useful, for example, when you wish to create a list from the records in a secondary merge file. It's also used by 5.0 users when creating labels.

To stop page breaks, the primary file must contain special Merge codes at the bottom of the file. *5.1 users:* Use the {PAGE OFF} code; this code is inserted in the primary file by selecting MERGE CODES (Shift + F9) and selecting Page Off (4 or P). *5.0 users:* Use the Merge code combination ^N^P^P; each of these codes is inserted by selecting MERGE CODES and then typing the corresponding letter.

Suppose you wish to create a document that lists the members of the wine-tasting committee, along with the towns in California that they each represent. *5.1 users:* You would create a primary file as follows:

```
{FIELD}1~ {FIELD}2~ {FIELD}3~
{FIELD}5~, California

{PAGE OFF}
```

*5.0 users:* For you the primary file would look as follows:

```
^F1^ ^F2^ ^F3^
^F5^, California


^N^P^P
```

A blank line is inserted between the Field Merge codes and the {PAGE OFF} or ^N^P^P codes so that, in the merged result, a blank line is inserted between each member's name.

When such a primary file is merged with the secondary file named WTC.SEC, the on-screen display will be as follows (for the first three records):

```
Ms. Janice Smith
San Francisco, California

Mr. Dennis Poplar
Glen Ellen, California

Mr. Karl Gallighar
Los Angeles, California
```

Imagine the time savings of using the Merge feature if there were over 500 people on the wine-tasting committee, and you needed to update the list of members every month. By keeping your secondary merge file current, you could produce a list every month in just moments.

## Merge Directly to the Printer

You can direct WordPerfect to merge directly to the printer, rather than to a file on screen. Suppose your secondary file contained 500 records; if you were to merge it to the screen, you'd have a 500-page document to print.

Instead, you can direct WordPerfect to print each letter as soon as it is merged, clear the screen, and then merge the next letter.

*5.1 users:* The merge code combination to merge to the printer is {PRINT}{PAGE OFF}. (The {PRINT} Merge code alone is insufficient because WordPerfect will insert a page break after each record is merged, resulting in an extra page spewing from the printer between each letter.) These codes are placed at the bottom of the primary file; Figure 13-18 shows an example for 5.1 users.

You insert the {PAGE OFF} code as discussed previously—by selecting MERGE CODES ( [Shift] + [F9] ) and selecting Page Off (4 or P). Inserting the {PRINT} code involves an extra step because this code is not listed on the Merge Codes menu. Position the cursor where you want

```
{FIELD}1~ {FIELD}2~ {FIELD}3~
{FIELD}4~
{FIELD}5~, {FIELD}6~ {FIELD}7~

Dear {FIELD}1~ {FIELD}3~:

Thank you for agreeing to serve on the R&R Wine Association's
California Wine-Tasting Committee. You are our official
representative from {FIELD}5~!

Our first meeting will be held at the beginning of December in
Monterey, California. I'll be sure to let you know the exact date
and time as soon as it is confirmed.

I look forward to seeing you soon in Monterey, {FIELD}2~.

Sincerely,


Lonnie Chang
R&R Wine Association
{PRINT}{PAGE OFF}  ◄─────  Merge codes

                                   Doc 1 Pg 1 Ln 1" Pos 1"
```

**FIGURE 13-18**   Primary file for a merge directly to the printer (version 5.1)

the Merge code to appear, and select MERGE CODES
( Shift + F9 ). The following menu appears:

`1 Field; 2 End Record; 3 Input; 4 Page Off; 5 Next Record; 6 More: 0`

Because the Print code is not on this menu, select More (6
or M); a double-line box appears in the upper right corner
of your screen listing the first ten of the Merge codes
available in WordPerfect. Figure 13-19 shows this box on
screen. Now, use the ↓ key to move the cursor down
through the list of Merge codes until the cursor highlights
{PRINT}. (Or, you can position the cursor using the Name
Search feature; start typing the word "PRINT" until the
cursor highlights {PRINT}, and then press Enter to end
Name Search.) Press Enter , and the {PRINT} code will be
inserted on the Typing screen.

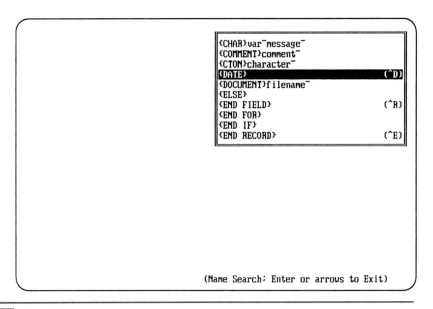

**FIGURE 13-19** Box containing WordPerfect Programming Language Merge codes (Version
5.1 only)

*5.0 users:* The merge combination for merging to the printer is ^T^N^P^P. Each of these codes is inserted by selecting MERGE CODES ([Shift] + [F9]) and then typing the corresponding letter. (The ^T Merge code, which is the code that sends the merged document to the printer, is insufficient on its own because WordPerfect will insert a page break after each record is merged, resulting in an extra page spewing from the printer between each letter.) This combination of Merge codes is placed at the bottom of the primary file.

Whether you're a 5.1 or 5.0 user, make sure that when you are about to perform a merge with a primary file that contains the {PRINT}{PAGE OFF} or ^T^N^P^P codes, that you prepare your printer; turn it on and insert the paper on which you want the merged documents to print.

## Add the Date During a Merge

You can direct WordPerfect to insert the current date during a merge (providing that the computer's clock is set with the correct date). *5.1 users:* You will insert the code {DATE} in the primary file where the date should appear in each letter of a merged document; insert this code by pressing MERGE CODES, selecting More (6 or M), using the [↓] key to move the cursor down through the list of Merge codes until the cursor highlights {DATE}, and pressing [Enter]. *5.0 users:* You will insert the code ^D by pressing the MERGE CODES key and typing **D**.

For example, you could insert {DATE} at the top of the primary file shown in Figure 13-18. After the merge, the current date would appear in each letter wherever you inserted that code.

# Accommodate for Missing Information

You may find that, for some records in a secondary merge file, you have incomplete information. As mentioned previously, even if you have no information for a certain field, you must insert the Field Merge code and leave the field empty. But that can create blank lines in the middle of a merged document.

For instance, suppose that you add an eighth field in WTC.SEC, the secondary merge file you created previously, and that field 8 contained a person's company name. Here's one example:

```
Ms.{END FIELD}
Janice{END FIELD}
Smith{END FIELD}
3559 Biltmore Street{END FIELD}
San Francisco{END FIELD}
CA{END FIELD}
94123{END FIELD}
ABC Corporation{END FIELD}  ← Field 8
{END RECORD}
```

Also suppose that for certain records, you have no company name, so you left those fields blank. Here's an example:

```
Mr.{END FIELD}
Dennis{END FIELD}
Poplar{END FIELD}
333 Cypress Boulevard{END FIELD}
Glen Ellen{END FIELD}
CA{END FIELD}
95442{END FIELD}
{END FIELD}       ← Field 8 is empty
{END RECORD}
```

If you want to merge with a primary document for addresses where the company name is placed just below the person's name, then the primary file will appear as follows:

```
{FIELD}1~ {FIELD}2~ {FIELD}3~
{FIELD}8~
{FIELD}4~
{FIELD}5~, {FIELD}6~ {FIELD}7~
```

Here are the results after the merge:

```
Ms. Janice Smith
ABC Corporation           ← Field 8 inserted
3559 Biltmore Street
San Francisco, CA 94123
===============================
Mr. Dennis Poplar
                          ← Empty line because
333 Cypress Boulevard        field 8 was empty
Glen Ellen, CA 95442
===============================
```

You can remedy this problem in WordPerfect. *5.1 users:* One method is to use the {IF NOT BLANK}*n* ~ and {END IF} Merge codes. The {IF NOT BLANK} code directs WordPerfect to check the status of the field number that you indicate, and, if the field contains information, to proceed with the commands that follow. The {END IF} code marks the end of the commands.

Here's how you would place codes in the primary file to ensure that no blank lines appear in the merged document:

```
{FIELD}1~ {FIELD}2~ {FIELD}3~
{IF NOT BLANK}8~{FIELD}8~
{END IF}{FIELD}4~
{FIELD}5~, {FIELD}6~ {FIELD}7~
```

WordPerfect checks to see if field 8 contains information; if the field contains information (and thus, is *not* blank), then WordPerfect will proceed with the commands that are between the {IF NOT BLANK} and {END IF} codes, which, in the above case, means to insert the information from field 8 and then move down a line. If the field is blank, WordPerfect simply skips over the commands between those codes.

You insert each of these codes by pressing MERGE CODES, selecting More (6 or M), using the ⬇ key to move the cursor down through the list of Merge codes until the cursor highlights the code, and pressing [Enter]. (When you highlight the {IF NOT BLANK} code and press [Enter], you must also respond to WordPerfect's prompt for a field number.)

*5.0 users:* you simply insert a question mark (?) inside the Merge code of the field that, for certain records, is blank. The question mark is inserted after the field number as follows:

```
^F1^ ^F2^ ^F3^
^F8?^
^F4^
^F5^, ^F6^ ^F7^
```

WordPerfect checks to see if field 8 contains information; if so, the information is inserted, and if not, the merge skips over that entire line.

## Reference Fields with Names Rather Than Numbers

Fields can be referenced in a primary file not only by number, as previously described, but by name as well. To do so, you must include a special record as the *first* record in the secondary merge file. This special record is different depending on whether you are a 5.1 or 5.0 user.

*5.1 users:* Create a record that assigns field names using the code {FIELD NAMES}. Position the cursor at the very top of the secondary merge file, select MERGE CODES, select More (6 or M), position the cursor on the code {FIELD NAMES}, and press [Enter]. Now, WordPerfect will prompt for you to enter field 1. Type a name and press [Enter]. Next, enter a field 2 name and press [Enter]. Continue for all fields, and press [Enter] when there are no more fields for which you wish to assign names. WordPerfect will insert the special record for you, followed by an {END RECORD} and Hard Page code. Here's an example for the secondary file shown in Figure 13-9:

```
{FIELD NAMES}Title~First name~Last name~Street address~
City~State abbreviation~ZIP code~~{END RECORD}
========================================================
```

If you wish, you can use the [Enter] key to format the special record so that it is easier to read, with each field name on a separate line as follows:

```
{FIELD NAMES}Title~
First name~
Last name~
Street address~
City~
State abbreviation~
ZIP code~~{END RECORD}
================================================
```

Once this special record is created, any primary file you create can include field codes that reference the secondary file field by name or number—such as {FIELD}2~ or {FIELD}First name~.

*5.0 users:* Create the record that assigns field names using three merge codes along with the bold feature. Position the cursor at the very top of the secondary merge file, and insert a ^N merge code and press [Enter] to move to a new line. Next, every field name must appear on a separate line, each boldfaced individually. The last field name should be followed by a ^R merge code, a hard return code, a ^E merge code, and a Hard Page code. Here's an example for the secondary file shown in Figure 13-10:

```
^N
Title
First name
Last name
Street address
City
State abbreviation
ZIP code^R
^E
==================================================
```

Here's how this same special record will appear with codes revealed, as you verify that it has been typed correctly:

```
^N[HRt]
[BOLD]Title[bold][HRt]
[BOLD]First name[bold][HRt]
[BOLD]Last name[bold][HRt]
[BOLD]Street address[bold][HRt]
[BOLD]City[bold][HRt]
[BOLD]State abbreviation[bold][HRt]
[BOLD]ZIP code[bold]^R[HRt]
^E[HPg]
```

Once this special record is created, any primary file you create can include field codes that reference the secondary file fields by name or number, such as ^F2^ or ^FFirst name^.

# Convert Old Merge Files for Use in Version 5.1 [5.1 Users Only]

When you press the MERGE/SORT (Ctrl + F9) key, the third item on the menu that display allows you to convert old merge files from version 4.2 or 5.0 into version 5.1. Retrieve the old primary or secondary file to the screen, press MERGE/SORT (Ctrl + F9), and select Convert Old Merge Files (3 or C). In moments, WordPerfect will transform all the Merge codes used in the earlier versions to version 5.1 codes, for instance, changing ^F1^ to {FIELD}1~ or ^R to {END FIELD}. Then you can resave the file and use it in a merge.

This conversion is optional if the old merge files were saved in version 5.0. (In fact, if you desire, you can still create merge files in 5.1 that look as they did in version 5.0. You can insert Merge codes that resemble version 5.0 codes by holding down the Ctrl key and pressing the corresponding letter. The merge will work properly.) However, it is imperative to convert old merge files to version 5.1 if they were saved using version 4.2.

You should also know that when merging with a secondary file, you can use not only a WordPerfect file but also a DOS text file as the secondary file. For instance, you may have an old merge file created in dBASE that contains a list of names and addresses. To use this file, convert it to a DOS text file using dBASE. Then, tell WordPerfect the delimiters in the DOS text file which separate the fields and records. (See "Initial Settings" in Appendix B for more details on the procedure.) Now you can proceed from within WordPerfect to merge, typing in the name of the DOS text file when prompted for the secondary file.

# REVIEW EXERCISE

Previously, you created a secondary file named WTC.SEC that you can now use to personalize many different documents. For practice in merging, in the following steps you'll create a primary document that you will merge with your secondary file to create a new batch of letters to the wine-tasting-committee members.

1. Clear the screen and type a primary file that will produce the document shown in Figure 13-20. The circled copy represents the variable information in each letter. Use the Date Merge code to have the current date inserted during the merge. Use Field Merge codes to have the addresses, names, and cities inserted during the merge. Save this document under the name WTC2.PRI.

2. Clear the screen and merge the primary file named WTC2.PRI with the secondary file named WTC.SEC.

3. Review the letters to make sure that the merge was successful, then print them.

4. Clear the screen and type a primary file that will produce envelopes. (*Hint:* Remember that the primary file

for envelopes is just a file of Merge codes in the same structure as the inside address and with Format codes so that the addresses will print correctly on envelopes.) Save this file under the name ENV.PRI.

5. Clear the screen and merge the primary file ENV.PRI with the secondary file WTC.SEC.

6. Assuming that your printer can print envelopes, print the addresses on envelopes.

---

〔DATE〕

〔INSIDE ADDRESS〕

Dear 〔FIRST NAME〕:

Thank you for attending R&R Wine Association's first Wine-Tasting meeting. From the response I've gotten, I believe that it was a huge success.

I look forward to seeing you at our next meeting, 〔FIRST NAME 〕. Until then, if my travels take me to 〔CITY〕, I'll see if you're available for a business lunch.

Sincerely,

Lonnie Chang

**FIGURE 13-20** Review Exercise text

# Quick Review

- Establish a collection of boilerplate files if you find yourself typing the same paragraphs in many different documents. Each paragraph can be saved into its own file. To include boilerplate text in a document you're typing, position the cursor where you want the text inserted and retrieve the boilerplate file as you would any document.

- You can create a primary file to later merge with information you type from the keyboard. In the primary file, type the text that stays the same from document to document. In addition, 5.1 users must include {INPUT}~ or {INPUT}*message*~ codes where the merge will pause for input of variable information from the keyboard. 5.0 users must include ^C or ^O*message*^O^C codes where the merge will pause for input from the keyboard. The primary file is like a fill-in-the-blanks form during the merge.

- You can create a primary file to later merge with variable information stored in a secondary file. Type the text that stays the same from document to document. In addition, 5.1 users must include {FIELD}*n*~ codes where WordPerfect will grab information from a secondary file during the merge. 5.0 users must include ^F*n*^ codes where WordPerfect will grab information from a secondary file during the merge. The primary file is like a form letter that, after the merge, results in repetitive documents which are personalized.

- Create a secondary file to store variable information that will be used over and over to personalize different types of form letters and other repetitive documents. A secondary file is segmented into records, each of which results in a personalized document after the merge. Each record contains the same number of fields, and each field contains one type of information required to personalize a document.

  In the secondary file, 5.1 users must end each field with an {END FIELD} and [**HRt**] code. Each record must end with an {END RECORD} and an [**HPg**] code.

  5.0 users must end each field with a ^R and [**HRt**] code. Each record must end with a ^E and [**HPg**] code.

- Perform a merge by pressing the MERGE/SORT ( Ctrl + F9 ) key and selecting Merge (1 or M). Or, pulldown menu users can select Tools (T), Merge (M). For a merge with the keyboard, enter the primary filename when WordPerfect prompts for a primary filename, and press Enter when WordPerfect prompts for a secondary filename. When WordPerfect pauses for keyboard input, type the text and press END FIELD ( F9 ) to continue the merge. For a merge with a file, enter a primary filename and a secondary filename. In moments, the merged result will appear on screen, with the cursor at the bottom of the document.

- Produce envelopes or mailing labels for mass mailings by creating a primary file that contains the Field Merge codes that correspond to names and addresses, and formatting the primary file for the envelopes or labels. Then perform the merge and print out the merged document on envelopes or labels.

- Produce lists from secondary files by including multiple records in the same document. To do so, 5.1 users must insert the {PAGE OFF} code at the bottom of the primary file. 5.0 users must insert the Merge code combination ^N^P^P at the bottom.

- Merge directly to the printer rather than to the screen. To do so, 5.1 users must insert the {PRINT}{PAGE OFF} Merge code combination at the bottom of the primary file. 5.0 users must insert the Merge code combination ^T^N^P^P at the bottom of the file.

*chapter* **14**

# USING MACROS AND STYLES

Y ou've learned in previous chapters how to activate sophisticated features such as font changes, text columns, paragraph numbering, and footnoting. As you've seen, it sometimes takes many keystrokes to accomplish a certain task.

You'll learn in this chapter about macros and styles, two features that are the ultimate timesavers! Macros and styles come in handy for word processing chores that you perform regularly.

Macros and styles are similar in that they are both shortcuts; by using a macro or a style, you turn a task that would typically take many keystrokes into one that takes just a few.

But each is most suitable in different types of circumstances. A macro is most appropriate for recording keystrokes that perform a series of commands. For instance, you would create a macro to resave a document on screen, print three copies, change the number of copies back to one, and clear the screen. A style is most appropriate for recording keystrokes that format parts of a document in a certain way. For example, you would create a style for chapter headings so that the headings would be preceded by paragraph numbers, centered, underlined, and printed in italics.

Macros and styles are created and executed in completely different ways. In this chapter, you'll learn first how to define and execute a macro. You'll also learn about some more advanced macro features that allow you to pause a macro for keyboard input or chain several macros together. Next, you'll work with the Styles feature. You'll create a style and use that style in a document. You'll also learn how to create a style library, so that you can store a collection of commonly used styles.

This chapter assumes that you are comfortable with fundamental features discussed in earlier chapters, such as the procedures for changing print options before you print, altering margins, and inserting automatic paragraph numbers. When a feature is mentioned that you haven't yet learned about or that you feel uncomfortable with, be sure to refer to an earlier chapter for a review before reading further.

# CREATE A MACRO

A macro is a sequence of keystrokes that WordPerfect stores for you, comparable to the speed-dialing feature on some telephones. With speed dialing, you can have the telephone store a phone number so that instead of having to press ten or more digits to dial someone long distance, you simply press the pound sign (#) and a number. Pressing # and 1 is much easier than dialing 305-734-5555.

Similarly, a macro stores a set of keystrokes, which you execute by pressing just a few keys. For instance, you could create a macro that automatically typed your company's name in a split second. You could write a macro that initiated a merge. Or, you could devise a macro that saved a document to disk, sent it to the printer, and cleared the screen—all at the touch of two keys. Create macros only for repetitive tasks, sequences of keystrokes that you press often (just as you reserve speed dialing for telephone numbers you call often), and you're ready to execute them as needed.

When you create or "define" a macro, you actually press each key one by one to record them. Thus, before you define a macro, you must prepare the screen so that you are ready to perform the task at hand. For instance, if the macro you plan to create will print a document from the screen, you must make sure that a document is on the screen and the printer is turned on.

Next, press the MACRO DEFINE ([Ctrl] + [F10]) key. [*Pulldown menu:* Tools (T), Macro (A), Define (D).] WordPerfect will respond with

```
Define macro:
```

This is WordPerfect's way of asking you for a macro name. You can name a macro in one of three ways:

- Type from one to eight characters and then press [Enter].

- Press the [Alt] key plus a letter of the alphabet. (As you will soon learn, it is easiest to execute a macro named with the [Alt] key, so reserve the [Alt] key for those macros that you use most often, but that will not be destructive to your document if you execute them accidentally. For instance, don't define a macro that will clear the screen with the [Alt] + [C] keys, or you're liable to accidentally erase the screen in the middle of typing an important document.)

- Press the [Enter] key by itself. (As you will soon learn, a macro named with the [Enter] key cannot be edited, so reserve the [Enter] key for a simple, "quick-and-dirty" macro.)

When you name a macro with one to eight characters or with the [Alt] key, WordPerfect next prompts for a macro description. Type up to 39 characters describing the macro's purpose and then press [Enter]. If you find no need for a macro description to help you later remember the tasks that each macro performs, simply press [Enter]. (If you name a macro with the [Enter] key, no such prompt appears.)

Now the message "Macro Def" starts flashing in the lower left corner of the status line. This message serves as a reminder that every key you press from now on will be recorded—just as if you had turned on a tape recorder that recorded everything you said—until you stop the recording. Type the keystrokes exactly as you want them recorded. To signal the end of the macro, again press the MACRO DEFINE ([Ctrl] + [F10]) key; the "Macro Def" message disappears, and the macro is stored on disk with the extension .WPM. For instance, a macro that you named PRINT will be stored as PRINT.WPM. A macro that you defined by pressing ⟦Alt⟧ + ⟦A⟧ will be stored as ALTA.WPM. The macro that you named with the ⟦Enter⟧ key will be stored as WP{WP}.WPM.

What if you make a typing mistake while recording a macro? Press the MACRO DEFINE (⟦Ctrl⟧ + ⟦F10⟧) key to stop recording the macro immediately. Then begin the procedure all over again; press the MACRO DEFINE (⟦Ctrl⟧ + ⟦F10⟧) key and enter the macro name again. WordPerfect will prompt, informing you that a macro by that name has already been defined and asking whether you wish to replace or edit the macro. For a macro that you defined by pressing ⟦Alt⟧ + ⟦A⟧, for instance, 5.1 users will see the following:

```
ALTA.WPM Already Exists.  1 Replace; 2 Edit; 3 Description: 0
```

5.0 users will see a slightly different menu:

```
ALTA.WPM is Already Defined. 1 Replace; 2 Edit: 0
```

Select Replace (1 or R), and then type **Y** to confirm that you wish to replace the macro. Now record all keystrokes correctly and press MACRO DEFINE (⟦Ctrl⟧ + ⟦F10⟧) when the recording is finished. (The one exception is for a macro named with the ⟦Enter⟧ key; WordPerfect will assume that you wish to replace this macro and will immediately start recording your keystrokes.)

WordPerfect typically stores a macro on disk in the default drive or directory—the same place it stores your document files. (This is the case unless another storage location has been indicated for macros in the Setup menu; see "Location of Files" in Appendix B for details.) But if you later change the default drive/directory, WordPerfect would be unable to locate the macro.

Consequently, you have various options to make sure that macros are always available. If you use a floppy disk system, you may want to store macros on the WordPerfect disk in drive A; that way you'll have access to them no matter which data disk is in drive B. To do so, precede the macro name with A:. For instance, when WordPerfect prompts "Define macro:", type **A:ALTA** or type **A:PRINT3** and press ⌷Enter⌷. If you will be creating so many macros that not all of them can fit on the WordPerfect disk, then continue to store macros on the default drive, drive B, but consider maintaining a disk that stores nothing but macros. That disk can be slipped into drive B just before you create or execute a macro.

If you use a hard disk system, you may wish to store macros in the directory where the WordPerfect program files (such as WP.EXE) are housed. Assuming that the program files are stored in \WP51, then when WordPerfect prompts "Define macro:", type **C:\WP51\ALTA** or **C:\WP51\PRINT3**. A simpler method is to use WordPerfect's Setup menu to specify that all macros be stored in their own directory. For instance, you can create a directory named \WP51\MACROS, where all your macros will be stored, easily accessible no matter what the current default. WordPerfect will always look to that directory for storing and executing macros. See "Location of Files" in Appendix B for more details on specifying a directory for storing and retrieving macros.

Here's a chance to practice creating a macro. Pretend that you work at the R&R Wine Association and you wish to create a macro that types "R&R Wine Association" on command—performing a 20-keystroke task with just 2 key-strokes. Let's define it as ⌷Alt⌷ + ⌷R⌷.

1. Position the cursor anywhere on the Typing screen.

2. Press the MACRO DEFINE ([Ctrl] + [F10]) key. [*Pull-down menu:* Tools (T), Macro (A), Define (D).] WordPerfect prompts you with

`Define macro:`

3. Press [Alt] + [R]. WordPerfect prompts

`Description:`

4. Type **Inserts "R&R Wine Association"** and press [Enter]. The following message flashes on the status line:

`Macro Def`

This message serves to remind you that every keystroke you press from now on will be recorded.

5. Type **R&R Wine Association**.

6. Press the MACRO DEFINE ([Ctrl] + [F10]) key to end the macro. The "Macro Def" message disappears from the screen, and the macro is stored under the name ALTR.WPM on the default drive/directory.

Here's another macro to practice with, one you'll name without using the [Alt] key. Suppose that for every letter you write, you print out three copies—one for the person to whom the letter will be sent, one for your boss's files, and one for your own files. Let's create a macro that changes the Number of Copies option on the Print screen to 3, prints out the letter, and then changes the Number of Copies option back to 1. We'll name this macro PRINT3 (which stands for PRINT 3 copies).

1. Position the cursor anywhere on the Typing screen. Make sure that the screen contains some text (such as

the phrase "R&R Wine Association" after recording the previous macro), so that WordPerfect will have something to print. Also, turn on the printer and make sure that paper has been inserted properly.

2. Press the MACRO DEFINE ( Ctrl + F10 ) key. [*Pulldown menu:* Tools (T), Macro (A), Define (D).] WordPerfect prompts you with

   ```
   Define macro:
   ```

3. Type **PRINT3**, and press Enter . WordPerfect prompts you with

   ```
   Description:
   ```

4. Type **Prints 3 copies of page on screen** and press Enter . The following message flashes on the status line:

   ```
   Macro Def
   ```

   This message serves to remind you that every keystroke you press from now on will be recorded.

5. Press the PRINT ( Shift + F7 ) key. [*Pulldown menu:* File (F), Print (P).]

6. Select Number of Copies (N), type **3**, and press Enter .

7. Select Page (2 or P). Three copies of the page on screen will print, and you will be returned to the Typing screen.

8. Press the PRINT ( Shift + F7 ) key. [*Pulldown menu:* File (F), Print (P)]

9. Select Number of Copies (N), type **1**, and press Enter . This returns the number to 1 for other documents.

10. Press CANCEL ( F1 ) to return to the Typing screen.

11. Press the MACRO DEFINE (Ctrl + F10) key to end the macro. The "Macro Def" message disappears from the screen, and the macro is stored under the name PRINT3.WPM in the default drive/directory.

When you view a list of files in a drive or directory where macros are stored, you can recognize all the macros by the .WPM extension. Then you can use the Look feature on the List Files menu to display the macro's description — a handy feature if you forget the tasks that a certain macro performs. However, you should never attempt to retrieve a macro; WordPerfect will display an error message.

Suppose you can't remember what the macro defined with the Alt + R key combination accomplishes:

1. Use the LIST (F5) key to display a list of files in the default drive/directory.

2. Position the cursor on the file named ALTR.WPM. (If you cannot find the file named ALTR.WPM, then someone may have redirected your macros into a different drive or directory; see "Location of Files" in Appendix B to learn the name of that drive or directory. Then you can use the LIST (F5) key to display a list of files in that different drive/directory.)

3. Select Look (6 or L) or simply press Enter to activate the Look feature. The following macro description will appear:

```
Inserts "R&R Wine Association"
```

4. Press CANCEL (F1) twice to return to the Typing screen.

# EXECUTE A MACRO

Whenever you attempt to execute a macro stored on disk, WordPerfect searches the default drive or directory as well as the drive/directory where the WordPerfect program files are stored (such as WP.EXE). If a certain drive/directory is specified for storing macro files using the Setup menu (as described in Appendix B), then when you attempt to execute a macro, WordPerfect searches that specified drive /directory as well as the one where the WordPerfect program files are stored.

When you are ready to use a macro, you must position the cursor wherever you want the macro execution to begin. What you do next depends on whether you named the macro with the [Alt] key. If you did, simply press [Alt] plus the character you named the macro with. If you didn't name the macro with [Alt], press the MACRO ([Alt] + [F10]) key. [*Pulldown menu:* Tools (T), Macro (A), Execute (X).] WordPerfect prompts with

```
Macro:
```

Now, if you named the macro with one to eight characters, type in the macro name and press [Enter]. Or, if you named the macro with only the [Enter] key, simply press [Enter]. In case you wish to stop a macro while it's executing, press the CANCEL ([F1]) key.

Let's execute the macro named ALTR.WPM:

1. Clear the screen and then position the cursor where you want the R&R Wine Association name to appear.

2. Press [Alt] + [R]. In less than a second, the company's name appears on screen.

3. Position the cursor in another location and again press [Alt] + [R]. Again, the name appears, much quicker than if you had to type it yourself.

Now let's execute the macro named PRINT3.WPM to print the short page on screen three times.

1. Make sure that your printer is on and that paper is inserted.

2. Press the MACRO ([Alt] + [F10]) key. [*Pulldown menu:* Tools (T), Macro (A), Execute (X).] WordPerfect responds with

```
Macro:
```

prompting you for a macro name.

3. Type **PRINT3**, and press [Enter]. Soon three copies of the page on screen will be printed, and the Number of Copies option will be set back to 1. How much easier than hitting the individual keys every time you want three copies of a certain page!

There's a quick way to execute a macro a specific number of times. Before you actually execute the macro, press the [Esc] key (which was discussed in Chapter 3 as a way to repeat the same keystroke a certain number of times). WordPerfect responds with

```
Repeat Value = 8
```

Type the number representing how many times you wish to repeat the macro. Then execute the macro. The following is an example:

1. Press (Esc). WordPerfect prompts

   `Repeat Value = 8`

2. Type **3**. Now the prompt reads

   `Repeat Value = 3`

3. Press (Alt) + (R). At the current cursor position, the following appears:

   `R&R Wine AssociationR&R Wine AssociationR&R Wine Association`

There's also a way to have a macro execute automatically from a merge. In Chapter 13, you learned about various Merge codes that you can insert in a primary file to control the merge process. Another command can be inserted into the primary file so that as soon as the merge is completed, the macro will begin. *5.1 users:* The command is {CHAIN MACRO}*macroname~*. *5.0 users:* The command is *^Gmacroname^G*. Place this command anywhere in the primary document. For instance, suppose that once a merge is complete, you wish to print out three copies of the last page of the merged result. You can have this macro execute as soon as the merge is completed by inserting {CHAIN MACRO}print3~ or *^Gprint3^G* in the primary document used in that merge. (In version 5.1, there is a related command, {NEXT MACRO}*macroname~*, which will cause the merge to temporarily stop whenever the command is encountered; the macro will be executed, and then the merge will continue from where it stopped.)

# LEARN ABOUT ADVANCED MACRO FEATURES

Macros can be very simple or very complex. So far, you've learned about relatively simple, straightforward macros. Often, these are the most commonly used and can save you much time and give your fingers a rest. For instance, here are some tasks that ordinarily take many keystrokes to accomplish. If you perform them repetitively, you should consider creating a simple macro for each one.

- Type your name or your company's name

- Type the closing to a letter

- Insert today's date

- Resave a file under the same name

- Display the Header screen to create a header

- Display the Footnote Typing screen to type a footnote

- Display a Graphics Box Definition screen to create a graphics box

- Display the List Files screen for a specific drive/directory

- Switch the default drive/directory

- Print several copies of a document

- Send a "Go" to the printer from the Control Printer menu

- Select a different printer from the Print screen

- Select a different initial base font from the Document Format menu

- Initiate a merge

- Capitalize the first letter of a word at the cursor

- Underline or boldface a character or word already on the Typing screen

- Display the Document Initial Codes screen to insert Format codes

You could also create macros that actually insert Format codes in the document. For instance, you might create a macro that changes left/right margins, alters line spacing, and turns on hyphenation. Or, you could create one that inserts a specific header. But keep in mind that these types of tasks can also be accomplished with the Styles feature — with the added flexibility of being able to alter a style easily; see more on styles later on in this chapter.

When creating macros for some of the tasks mentioned above, you may want to know about the more advanced macro features, features such as how to insert a pause during macro execution or how to edit an already-created macro. These advanced features are described below. But do not attempt these features until you are comfortable creating and executing basic macros.

## Display or Pause During Macro Execution

As you've seen, a macro executes at lightning speed, so fast that you don't see anything but the final result. Word-Perfect offers the ability to display the workings of the macro as it is executing. You can also request that Word-Perfect pause in the middle of macro execution, so that you can type from the keyboard and then continue the macro. A pause allows you to type different information each time you execute the macro.

Use the key combination (Ctrl) + (PgUp) to display or pause macro execution. Press this combination while defining a macro wherever you wish the display or pause to occur. For instance, press (Ctrl) + (PgUp) as the first step in recording keystrokes if you want the entire macro to be displayed during execution. WordPerfect will display the following menu:

1 Pause; 2 Display; 3 Assign; 4 Comment: 0

To display the macro from that point on, select Display (2 or D). WordPerfect prompts asking whether or not you wish to display macro execution; type **Y** to turn display on or type **N** to turn display off (the default setting). Now continue defining the macro. You'll be able to watch the progression of the keystrokes each time that you execute the macro; it will no longer be invisible.

To create a pause, a temporary stop in the macro execution, select Pause (1 or P). Type in a sample of the keystrokes to be entered during that pause (a step that can be skipped if your next keystroke in the macro doesn't depend on typing in a sample). Then press (Enter) to signal the end of the pause. Now continue defining the macro. When you execute a macro containing a pause, the macro will stop wherever you pressed (Ctrl) + (PgUp) and selected Pause during macro definition. Type your input and then press (Enter) to continue the macro execution.

For instance, suppose that you wish to create a macro that selects a different initial base font from the Document Format menu. In the macro, you want to select a different font each time the macro is executed. In that case, create a macro that pauses for user input. Proceed as follows to create a macro named IBF, which stands for Initial Base Font:

1. Position the cursor on a clear Typing screen.

2. Press the MACRO DEFINE (Ctrl + F10) key. [*Pull-down menu:* Tools (T), Macro (A), Define (D).] WordPerfect prompts you with

```
Define macro:
```

3. Type **IBF**, and press Enter. WordPerfect prompts you with

```
Description:
```

4. Type **Pause for initial base font selection** and press Enter. The following message flashes on the status line:

```
Macro Def
```

5. Press FORMAT (Shift + F8), and select Document (3 or D). [*Pulldown menu:* Layout (L), Document (D).]

6. Select Initial Font (3 or F).

7. Press Ctrl + PgUp and select Pause (1 or P). This signals a pause for you to position the cursor on the font you wish to select.

8. Press Enter to signal the end of the pause.

9. Press Select (1 or S) to select the font where the cursor is located.

10. Press EXIT (F7) to return to the Typing screen.

11. Press the MACRO DEFINE (Ctrl + F10) key to end the macro. The "Macro Def" message disappears from screen.

Now execute this macro. WordPerfect will pause on the Initial Font screen for you to position the cursor on the font you wish to select. Position the cursor and press [Enter]. The macro continues, returning you to the Typing screen. If you return to the Document Format menu, you can verify that, in fact, the initial base font that you highlighted has been chosen.

## Chain and Nest Macros

Another advanced feature allows you to chain macros together. In other words, you can write a macro that will execute a second macro — either the same macro or another one — on its own. For instance, you can create a macro that resaves a file on disk and then executes the PRINT3 macro. There are three ways to link macros together:

- A simple macro chain executes another one automatically when the current macro is completed. The last step of the current macro must include the keystrokes to execute the second macro: the MACRO ([Alt] + [F10]) key followed by the name of the second macro.

- A repeating macro chain repeats itself over and over until WordPerfect discovers through a search that a search string (a specific phrase or code) is no longer found in the text. The macro can be chained to itself only if a search is part of that macro; otherwise, the macro will repeat over and over until you press the CANCEL ([F1]) key or until the computer system locks up. The last step in the macro includes the keystrokes to execute the macro over again: the MACRO ([Alt] + [F10]) key followed by the name of the current macro.

- A nested macro executes one macro inside another. Unlike chained macros, the nested macro is executed not when the main macro is completed, but rather at the point where it is encountered in the main macro. The nested macro must have been previously created and stored on disk; also, the nested macro must have been named with the [Alt] key. Wherever in the main macro you want the nested macro to temporarily take over, insert the keystrokes to execute it: the MACRO ([Alt] + [F10]) key followed by the name of the nested macro. Then continue defining the main macro.

## Insert Comments in Macros

You can split a macro involving many keystrokes into more readable chunks for editing by inserting comments into the macro. These comments will not affect macro execution, but are helpful when you're attempting to unravel a macro's keystrokes, perhaps to figure out why the macro is not working properly.

For instance, suppose you wish to create a macro that performs a variety of tasks, including changing the default directory and appending some text to a file on disk. Begin recording the macro. Then, before recording the keystrokes that alter the default directory, insert a comment that reads "Change the default directory to \WP51\BUD." Continue with the macro recording and, later on, insert a comment before another set of keystrokes that reads "Append the text on screen to BUDGET.SSM." Continue until you have defined the entire macro.

To insert a comment, define a macro up to the point where you wish to insert the comment. You must be on either the Typing screen or the Reveal Codes screen. Then press ⟦Ctrl⟧ + ⟦PgUp⟧. WordPerfect will display the following menu:

1 Pause; 2 Display; 3 Assign; 4 Comment: 0

Select Comment (4 or C) and type in a comment. Then press ⟦Enter⟧ and continue defining the macro.

When you later edit a macro that contains comments (editing is described next), the comments will be interspersed among the macro keystrokes wherever you inserted them when creating the macro. Each comment will be preceded by the symbol (;) and followed by a tilde ($\sim$).

## Edit a Macro Stored on Disk

WordPerfect offers the ability to edit a macro that is already stored on disk. You can edit the macro description or the keystrokes that comprise the macro. Press the MACRO DEFINE (⟦Ctrl⟧ + ⟦F10⟧) key and enter the name of the macro you wish to edit, such as PRINT3. WordPerfect will prompt, informing you that a macro by that name already exists. *5.1 users:* You will see the following:

PRINT3.WPM Already Exists.  1 Replace; 2 Edit; 3 Description: 0

*5.0 users:* You will see only the first two options, Replace and Edit. The procedure to position the cursor to edit keystrokes is slightly different for 5.1 users than for 5.0 users.

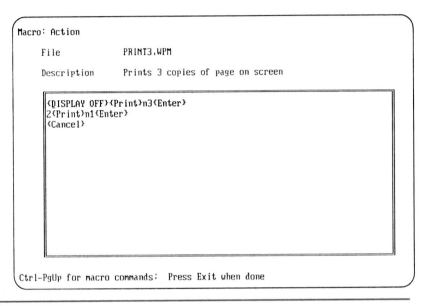

```
Macro: Action

    File            PRINT3.WPM

    Description     Prints 3 copies of page on screen

  ┌────────────────────────────────────────────────────┐
  │<DISPLAY OFF><Print>n3<Enter>                         │
  │2<Print>n1<Enter>                                     │
  │<Cancel>                                              │
  │                                                      │
  │                                                      │
  │                                                      │
  │                                                      │
  │                                                      │
  │                                                      │
  │                                                      │
  │                                                      │
  │                                                      │
  │                                                      │
  └────────────────────────────────────────────────────┘

Ctrl-PgUp for macro commands: Press Exit when done
```

**FIGURE 14-1**   Macro Edit screen for a macro named PRINT3 (version 5.1)

*5.1 users:* Select Edit (2 or E) to edit the macro keystrokes, and the Macro Edit screen as shown in Figure 14-1 appears. The cursor is located inside the double-lined box, ready to edit the actual keystrokes.

Or, you can first alter the description: select Description (3 or D). The macro description appears at the bottom of the screen for editing. After you edit the description and press Enter, the Macro Edit screen as shown in Figure 14-1 appears.

*5.0 users:* Select Edit (2 or E) to edit the macro keystrokes, and the Macro Edit screen appears as shown in Figure 14-2. Now select Description (1 or D) and then edit the description. Or, select Action (2 or A), and the cursor moves inside the double-lined box, ready to edit the actual keystrokes.

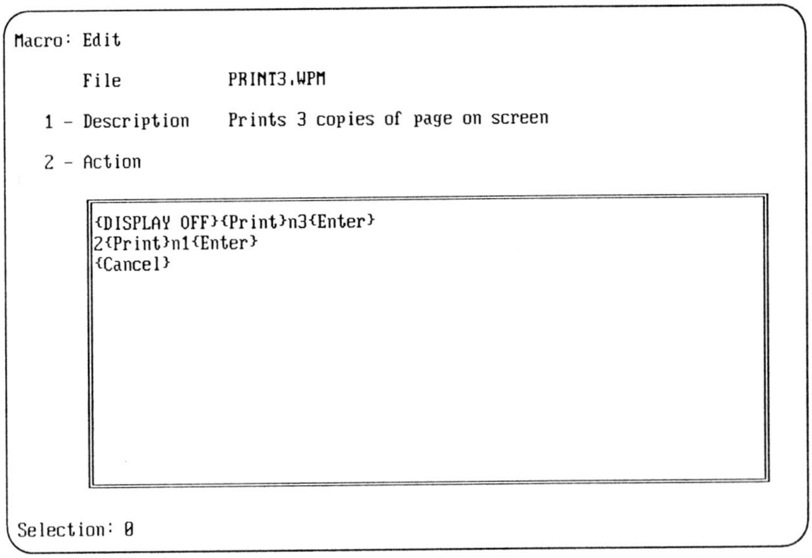

```
Macro: Edit

        File            PRINT3.WPM

    1 - Description     Prints 3 copies of page on screen

    2 - Action

        ┌─────────────────────────────────────────────────────────────┐
        │{DISPLAY OFF}{Print}n3{Enter}                                  │
        │2{Print}n1{Enter}                                              │
        │{Cancel}                                                       │
        │                                                               │
        │                                                               │
        │                                                               │
        │                                                               │
        │                                                               │
        └─────────────────────────────────────────────────────────────┘

Selection: 0
```

**FIGURE 14-2**  Macro Edit screen for a macro named
PRINT3 (version 5.0)

For both 5.1 and 5.0 users, on the Macro Edit screen, all function key names or editing key names are represented as the key name surrounded by curly braces, such as {Print}, to indicate the PRINT (Shift + F7) key. Letters and numbers represent either text typed during the macro or a menu item selection. (The keystroke {DISPLAY OFF} is automatically inserted by WordPerfect in each macro to turn off the display of the macro. See the section above if you wish to turn the display on.)

In the action box, you can use the cursor movement and editing keys to delete keystrokes and press character or function keys to insert that keystroke; for instance, press CENTER (Shift + F6) to insert {Center}. For certain editing and function keys, you must press Ctrl + V and then the key to insert the literal keystroke. For instance, press ⬅ to move the cursor to the left when editing, or press Ctrl + V, ⬅ to insert the keystroke {Left}. Press CANCEL (F1) to cancel your editing changes, or press Ctrl + V, CANCEL to insert the keystroke {Cancel}. Then press EXIT (F7) to register your editing changes and leave the action box.

Here's a simple example. Suppose that after creating the PRINT3.WPM macro, you discover that you want it to print three copies of the *full document*—whether one page or ten pages in length—and not just three copies of the *single page* where the cursor is located. You will want to alter the keystroke that sends a print job. You must change this keystroke from "2" or "P" (which selects the Page option on the Print screen) to "1" or "F" (which selects the Full Document option on the Print screen). Let's edit the macro.

1. Position the cursor anywhere on screen.

2. Press the MACRO DEFINE (Ctrl + F10) key. [*Pull-down menu:* Tools (T), Macro (A), Define (D).] WordPerfect prompts you with

   ```
   Define macro:
   ```

3. Type **Print 3** and press Enter. Because a macro by that name already exists, WordPerfect prompts you with

   ```
   PRINT3.WPM Already Exists.   1 Replace; 2 Edit; 3 Description: 0
   ```

4. *5.1 users:* Select Description (3 or D), edit the description to read "Prints 3 copies of full doc on screen," and press Enter. Figure 14-1 appears, with the cursor positioned to edit the macro keystrokes.

   *5.0 users:* Select Edit (2 or E), so that Figure 14-2 appears. Select Description (1 or D), edit the description to read "Prints 3 copies of full doc on screen," and press ⌊Enter⌉. Then, select Action (2 or A); the cursor is now positioned to edit the macro keystrokes.

5. Position the cursor on the first character in the second line. This will either be a "2," as shown in Figure 14-1, or it will be a "P," depending on how you selected the Page (2 or P) option when creating the macro.

6. Delete this character and in its place type **1** or **F**. Either will select the Full Document (1 or F) option on the Print screen once the macro is executed.

7. Press EXIT (⌊F7⌋) to exit the Macro Edit screen. (5.0 users will need to press EXIT twice.)

The altered macro is now stored on disk. The next time you execute this macro, WordPerfect will print three copies of the full document.

If you ever wish to erase a macro from the disk rather than edit it, you can do so as you would delete a document file: use the LIST (⌊F5⌋) key to list your files, move the cursor to the name of the macro you wish to delete, and select Delete (2 or D) from the menu at the bottom of the screen.

## Programming Language Commands

The ultimate in macro complexity is the Macro programming language available in WordPerfect. This programming language is for those individuals who have programming knowledge. The majority of WordPerfect users will never need to learn about and use the Macro programming language, but should know that it does exist. On the Macro

Edit screen (as shown in Figure 14-1 or 14-2), the programming language commands appear when the cursor is in the action box and you press [Ctrl] + [PgUp]. Now the cursor can be moved from command to command. If the programming language commands appear accidentally, press CANCEL ([F1]) to return the cursor to the action box without activating any of these programming commands.

For a complete discussion of the Macro programming language commands, and other features such as Assign, which is used when creating complex macros containing programming commands, you can refer to more advanced books on WordPerfect, some of which are listed in the section "Learn More About WordPerfect," following this book's introductory pages.

# CREATE A STYLE

A style is a combination of formatting codes and text. For instance, suppose that you produce newsletters once a month where you change top/bottom margins, turn justification off, type the newsletter's banner heading, and format the document into newspaper columns. You can create a style that does this work for you.

In one respect, styles are more limited than macros. A style can only be used to format text on the page. A macro, on the other hand, can be created to format a document and/or to perform a variety of *other tasks* as well, such as changing the default drive/directory, printing a document, or even executing a style.

In another respect, when you do want to format parts of text the same way, styles are more flexible. If you create a style to format chapter headings, for example, and then decide to format the chapter headings differently, you can simply alter the style; all the chapter headings will be updated immediately based on that altered style. If you use a macro to format the chapter headings and then decide to reformat the chapter headings, you must either use the Replace feature or make the changes manually, moving from chapter heading to chapter heading on your own, which is more time consuming.

As with a macro, you first must create a style for a repetitive type of format. That style becomes available for text within the document in which it was created.

To create a style, consider a document's design elements, such as the formatting you desire at the top of the document and the formatting you desire for headings, subheadings, and paragraphs. To create a style for a particular element, position the cursor anywhere in the document for which you wish to create a style. Press the STYLE ([Alt] + [F8]) key to display the Styles screen, as shown in Figure 14-3. [*Pulldown menu:* Layout (L), Styles (S).] The middle of the screen is blank as in Figure 14-3 if you have yet to define a style for that document. (On the other hand, you may see styles listed on this screen—either styles included with the WordPerfect program or styles created by someone else using your copy of WordPerfect. These are styles available to be turned on, a procedure described in the next section.)

Select Create (3 or C) from the menu at the bottom of the screen. The Edit Styles screen, as shown in Figure 14-4, appears. Define the characteristics of the style as follows:

- *Name (1 or N)* Type a name of up to 11 characters and press [Enter].
  For a paired or open style, you can skip this option and not assign a name to a style you are in the process of

```
Styles
  Name        Type      Description











1 On; 2 Off; 3 Create; 4 Edit; 5 Delete; 6 Save; 7 Retrieve; 8 Update: 1
```

═══ **FIGURE 14-3**  Styles screen

creating; WordPerfect will automatically assign a numerical name to that style. The first unnamed style you create will be called style 1, the second style 2, and so on.

For an outline style (5.1 users only), you can also skip this option, but WordPerfect will not assign a numerical name to the style. Instead, WordPerfect will prompt for a filename when you select the Type option and specify an outline type.

• *Type (2 or T)*  A menu appears from which you can select style types:

L 14-25
**Type: 1** Paired; **2** Open; **3** Outline: **0**

(5.0 users have only the first two options available, Paired and Open.) The default, as shown in Figure 14-4, is the paired type.

A paired type is for styles that must have a beginning and an end, affecting only a specific block of text. For example, use a paired type to format chapter headings,

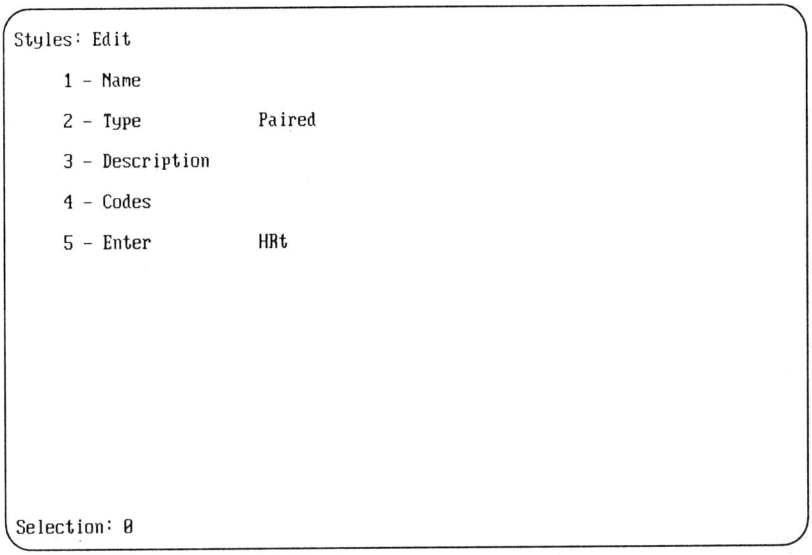

```
┌─────────────────────────────────────────────────────────────────
│ Styles: Edit
│
│      1 - Name
│
│      2 - Type              Paired
│
│      3 - Description
│
│      4 - Codes
│
│      5 - Enter             HRt
│
│
│
│
│
│
│
│
│
│ Selection: 0
└─────────────────────────────────────────────────────────────────
```

**FIGURE 14-4**  Edit Styles screen

or to format paragraphs. A Style On code is placed before the text and a Style Off code is placed after the text, in the same way that, when you underline a portion of text, an **[UND]** code is placed before the text and an **[und]** code after.

An open type has only a beginning, and affects text from where the Style code is inserted to the end of the document. For example, select Open (2 or O) to set the general format for a newsletter starting at the top of the document.

*5.1 users only:* An outline type is used in conjunction with the Outline and Paragraph Numbering features, which are discussed in Chapter 12. By creating an outline type, you can define a customized paragraph numbering style for up to eight levels of paragraph numbering. When you select Outline (3 or T), and if you have not yet provided a name for the style, WordPerfect prompts for a name; type a name and press ⌜Enter⌟. Then, WordPerfect prompts for a level number. Whatever characteristics you have already defined for the style (by having chosen the Description, Codes, or Enter options first) are assigned to that level number. Simply type **1** if you have yet to define any characteristics for the style. An Edit Outline Styles screen appears, as shown in Figure 14-5 for an outline style named REPORTS. Now you can proceed to create styles for each level of the outline style by positioning the cursor on a level number and selecting from the Type, Enter, or Codes options shown at the bottom of Figure 14-5. (The Name and Description options at the bottom of Figure 14-5 relate to the outline style as

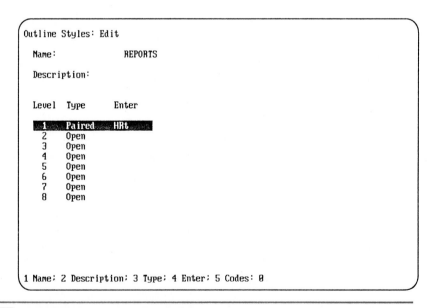

```
Outline Styles: Edit

  Name:               REPORTS

  Description:


  Level  Type       Enter

    1    Paired     HRt
    2    Open
    3    Open
    4    Open
    5    Open
    6    Open
    7    Open
    8    Open




1 Name; 2 Description; 3 Type; 4 Enter; 5 Codes: 0
```

**FIGURE 14-5**  Edit Outline Styles screen for a style named REPORTS (version 5.1 only)

a whole, and not to each level.) In essence, then, an outline style bundles together eight different "mini-styles," one numbering style for each level.

- *Description (3 or D)* Type a description of up to 54 characters to remind you what the style accomplishes and press `Enter`.

- *Codes (4 or C)* A Reveal Codes screen appears, in which you should type in the text and codes that will make up the style.

    For an open type, the Reveal Codes screen is blank; type the text and insert the codes in the order you want them to take effect in the text. As an example, insert **[L/R Mar:]** and **[Hyph On]** codes for a style that will be placed at the top of a document to alter margins and turn on hyphenation.

    For a paired type, a comment appears on the Reveal Codes screen. Look to the lower portion of the screen to locate the position of the **[Comment]** code. This code represents the text of your document that will be governed by the style you are now defining. Type the text and insert the codes that will begin the style *before* the **[Comment]** code, and then type the text and insert the codes that will end the style *after* the **[Comment]** code. For instance, position the cursor before the **[Comment]** and insert **[UND]** and **[BOLD]** codes that turn on underline and boldface. Then, position the cursor after the **[Comment]** and press `Enter` to insert an **[HRt]** code. This will turn on boldface and underlining before the text, and turn these attributes off and move to a blank line following the text. (You can insert **[und]** and **[bold]** codes after the **[Comment]** code, but this is unnecessary; WordPerfect automatically assumes that you wish to turn off attributes and Line Format codes at the end of the paired style.)

*5.1 users only:* For an outline type, what appears on the Reveal Codes screen is a **[Par Num:]** code, fixed at the level that you are defining. As an example, if you are defining level 5, a **[Par Num:5]** code is displayed and, as described in Chapter 12, this translates in outline numbering to (**1**). You can add additional codes and text to the **[Par Num:]** code, or delete this code and define a completely different style. A **[Comment]** code will also appear on the Reveal Codes screen if the level you are defining is a paired type.

- *Enter (5 or E)*    This option is applicable only if you are defining a *paired* type of style (or a paired type as part of an outline style). A menu appears from which you can select three different functions for the [Enter] key when you actually begin to use the style that is being defined:

```
Enter: 1 HRt; 2 Off; 3 Off/On: 0
```

HRt (1 or H) means that when the style is active, pressing the [Enter] key inserts a hard return, which is the [Enter] key's normal function. Off (2 or F) means that when the style is active, pressing the [Enter] key turns off the style. Off/On (3 or O) means that when the style is active, pressing the [Enter] key turns off the style and then immediately turns it on again.

Once the style is defined, press EXIT ([F7]) to return to the Styles menu. The style will now appear on that menu. Now create additional styles or press EXIT ([F7]) to return to your document.

Suppose you're about to type a report, and you want various paragraphs to be underlined and bulleted, using the asterisk as the bullet symbol. An example of the final outcome is shown in Figure 14-6. Let's create a style that can then be applied to paragraphs that you choose. It will

```
┌──────────────────────────────────────────────────────────────┐
│                                                                │
│ SALES FIGURES FOR THE WEST COAST                               │
│                                                                │
│ We predict a 15% increase in sales this year.  In the first three │
│ months of this year, the following figures are in from the West │
│ Coast of the United States:                                    │
│                                                                │
│      *    Sales of Chardonnay have skyrocketed, increasing 50% over │
│           the same time last year.                             │
│                                                                │
│      *    Pinot Noir has increased by 11%, a hefty increase, though │
│           volume is much smaller for Pinot Noir than Chardonnay. │
│                                                                │
│      *    Chenin Blanc and Cabernet Sauvignon sales have stayed │
│           about the same.                                      │
│                                                                │
│ SALES FIGURES FOR THE EAST COAST                               │
│                                                                │
│ We predict a moderate 4% increase in sales this year.  In the first │
│ three months of this year, the following figures are in from the │
│ East Coast:                                                    │
│                                                                │
│                                    Doc 1 Pg 1 Ln 1" Pos 1"     │
└──────────────────────────────────────────────────────────────┘
```

**FIGURE 14-6**  Paragraphs formatted with a paired type of style

be a paired type, since it will affect specific chunks of text and must be turned on before certain paragraphs and turned off after.

1. On a clear screen, press the STYLE ( Alt + F8 ) key. [*Pulldown menu:* Layout (L), Styles (S).] The Styles screen appears, as shown in Figure 14-3.

2. Select Create (3 or C) to display the Edit Styles screen, as shown in Figure 14-4.

3. Select Name (1 or N), type **Bullets**, and press Enter .

4. Notice that WordPerfect assumes a paired type, so there's no need to select this option.

5. Select Description (3 or D), type **Bulleted Paragraphs**, and press Enter .

6. Select Codes (4 or C) to display a Reveal Codes screen that contains a Comment code. Make sure that the cursor is on the **[Comment]** code, so that what you're about to type will be inserted before the code.

7. To define the formatting for the beginning of each paragraph, press → INDENT ( F4 ), type an asterisk (*), press → INDENT ( F4 ), and press the UNDERLINE ( F8 ) key.

8. Press →) to position the cursor to the right of the **[Comment]** code.

9. To define the formatting for the end of each paragraph, press Enter twice. (Before pressing Enter, you can also press the UNDERLINE ( F8 ) key to turn off the Underline feature; however, WordPerfect assumes you wish to turn off attributes such as underlining at the end of

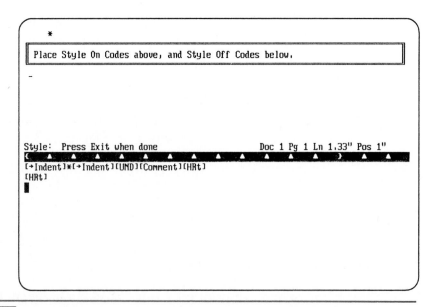

**FIGURE 14-7**  Codes inserted for the Bullets style

the style, so this step is not necessary.) Now your screen will appear like the one shown in Figure 14-7.

10. Press EXIT ( [F7] ) to return to the Edit Styles screen.

11. Select [Enter] (5 or E). WordPerfect prompts

```
Enter: 1 HRt; 2 Off; 3 Off/On: 0
```

Select Off (2 or F) so that as soon as you press [Enter], the style will turn off automatically. (If you had to type many more bulleted paragraphs in a row than shown in Figure 14-6, you could instead decide to select the Off/On option, so that you'd be ready immediately to type the next paragraph as soon as you completed a paragraph and pressed [Enter].)

12. Press the EXIT ( [F7] ) key twice to return to the Typing screen.

*5.1 users only:* the style just created is also an example of what can be defined as one level in an outline type of style. For instance, suppose you planned to type text into more of an outline format, with each paragraph bulleted with an asterisk, as shown in Figure 14-8. In that case, you could create a style specified as an outline type. Then you could define level 1 to be the style just created. Levels 2 and 3 could be defined similarly, except without underlining and with additional [→Indent] codes preceding the asterisk.

5.1 users should also know that there is a method for creating an outline style other than from the Styles screen.

```
SALES FIGURES FOR THE WEST COAST

We predict a 15% increase in sales this year.  In the first three
months of this year, the following figures are in from the West
Coast of the United States:

        *       Sales of Chardonnay have skyrocketed, increasing 50% over
                the same time last year.

                *       California sales lead the way

                        *       Northern California -- 56% increase
                        *       Southern California -- 44% increase

                *       Washington sales are growing

        *       Pinot Noir has increased by 11%, a hefty increase, though
                volume is much smaller for Pinot Noir than Chardonnay.

                *       Oregon sales show the largest increase


                                                Doc 1 Pg 1 Ln 1" Pos 1"
```

**FIGURE 14-8**   Paragraphs formatted with an outline
type of style (version 5.1)

Press the DATE/OUTLINE ( Shift + F5 ) key, and select
Define (6 or D). [*Pulldown menu:* Tools (T), Define (D).]
Then, from the Paragraph Number Definition screen that
appears, select Outline Style Name (9 or N). Now, an
*Outline* Styles screen appears, which is similar to the Styles
screen except that this screen applies only to styles that are
of the outline type. As shown in Figure 14-9, the Outline
Styles screen will display at least one style—the default
style for paragraph numbering, a style which you cannot
delete. (Your Outline Styles screen may display additional
styles that were included with the WordPerfect package.)
You then select Create (2 or C) from the menu at the
bottom of the screen, and proceed to define the characteristics of each level in the style.

# EXECUTE (TURN ON) A STYLE

When you're ready to execute an open or paired style, position the cursor where you want the style to take effect, and press the STYLE ([Alt] + [F8]) key. [*Pulldown menu: Layout (L), Styles (S).*] Then position the Style screen cursor on the name of the style you wish to execute, either by (1) using the arrow keys or (2) pressing the → SEARCH ([F2]) key to activate a name search, typing the first few letters of the style name until the cursor moves there, and pressing [Enter]. Next, select On (1 or O) from the menu at the bottom of the screen. You will be returned to the Typing screen.

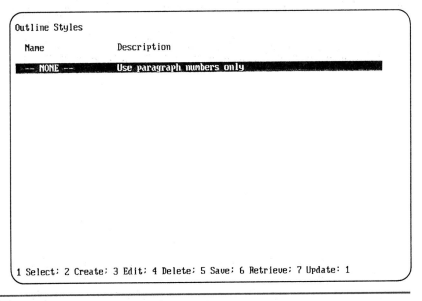

```
Outline Styles

  Name              Description

  -- NONE --        Use paragraph numbers only
```

```
1 Select; 2 Create; 3 Edit; 4 Delete; 5 Save; 6 Retrieve; 7 Update: 1
```

**FIGURE 14-9**  Outline Styles screen (version 5.1 only)

For an open style, the process is complete. An Open Style code is inserted in the text. For instance, if the style is named NEWSLET, then the code inserted is **[Open Style: NEWSLET]**. Any text you type following the code will be formatted accordingly.

For a paired style, you must also remember to turn off the style. After typing the text to be affected by the style, turn off the style either by (1) again pressing the STYLE (⟦Alt⟧ + ⟦F8⟧) key, and then selecting Off (2 or F); (2) pressing the ⟦→⟧ key, which positions the cursor outside the Style code; or (3) pressing ⟦Enter⟧, providing that the ⟦Enter⟧ key was defined to turn off a style. Style On and Off codes are inserted around the text. For instance, if the style is named BULLETS, then the pair of codes surrounding the text are **[Style On:BULLETS]** and **[Style Off:BULLETS]**.

However, in order for a paired style to execute on *already existing text,* you must first highlight that text with the Block feature. Then press the STYLE (⟦Alt⟧ + ⟦F8⟧) key, position the cursor on a style name, and select On (1 or O). WordPerfect automatically inserts the Style On and Off codes around the highlighted text.

*5.1 users only:* For an outline style, you turn on the style via the Paragraph Number Definition screen, rather than from the Styles screen. Position the cursor where you want to begin using the outline style for an outline or paragraphs. Then press the DATE/OUTLINE (⟦Shift⟧ + ⟦F5⟧) key, and select Define (6 or D). [*Pulldown menu:* Tools (T), Define (D).]

Now select Outline Style Name (9 or N) to display the menu shown in Figure 14-9. Position the cursor on the style you wish to execute and choose Select (1 or L). Now press the EXIT (⟦F7⟧) key until you return to the Typing screen.

Once you select an outline style, it becomes the style for numbering in paragraphs and outlines—whether you are in Outline mode or not. A Paragraph Number Definition code is inserted into the text. For instance, if the outline style you selected is named BOOK, then the code inserted is **[Par Num Def: BOOK]**. Any outline or paragraph numbers you insert into the text following this code will be formatted according to the Book outline style. These numbers will be inserted as Outline Style codes, either as Open Style codes or as Style On and Style Off codes. For instance, assuming an outline style named BOOK that is an open style, the following code will be inserted for a level-1 number: **[Outline Lvl 1 Open Style]**. Or, if it is a paired style, then the pair of codes surrounding the text of the paragraph will be **[Outline Lvl 1 Style On]** and **[Outline Lvl 1 Style Off]**. (Be sure to refer back to Chapter 12 if you need a review of the procedure for outlining and paragraph numbering.)

Here's a chance for you to repeatedly execute the style named BULLETS that you created previously in the document shown in Figure 14-6:

1. On the clear Typing screen where you moments ago created the style, type the heading **SALES FIGURES FOR THE WEST COAST**.

2. Press Enter twice and type the following paragraph:

   We predict a 15% increase in sales this year. In the first three months of this year, the following figures are in from the West Coast of the United States:

3. Press Enter twice. Your cursor is now positioned where you want to type a paragraph to be affected by a style.

4. Press the STYLE ( Alt + F8 ) key. [*Pulldown menu:* Layout (L), Styles (S).] The cursor is already positioned on the style named BULLETS, since it is the only style

listed. (Or, if more styles appear, then position the cursor on the BULLETS style.)

5. Select On (1 or O).

6. Type the following:

```
Sales of Chardonnay have skyrocketed, increasing 50% over the
same time last year.
```

7. Press Enter, which has been defined to turn off the style. Two hard returns are inserted because these are the codes you inserted to end the style.

8. Repeat steps 4 through 7, for the two additional bulleted paragraphs shown in Figure 14-6.

9. You may wish to continue typing this document for additional practice. Type the heading and paragraph shown at the bottom of the screen in Figure 14-6 and then use the BULLETS style to format paragraphs that you compose.

A Style code expands to show its contents when you reveal codes and position the cursor on that code. This is convenient when you've inserted a Style code into the text and can't identify the format dictated by that code from the name alone. To see how this works, proceed as follows.

1. Press the REVEAL CODES (Alt + F3) key to view the Style On and Off codes you inserted. [*Pulldown menu:* Edit (E), Reveal Codes (R).]

2. Position the cursor on the first Style On code. The code will expand to show its contents, as illustrated in Figure 14-10.

3. Position the cursor on a Style Off code to reveal its contents.

4. Press the REVEAL CODES ( Alt + F3 ) key to return to the Typing screen.

*5.1 users only:* Outline Style codes expand to reveal their contents as well.

# EDIT A STYLE

You can edit the format of a style on the Styles screen, but not on the Typing screen. For instance, suppose that you decide to remove the asterisks in Figure 14-6 and insert paragraph numbers instead. Try to position the cursor on an asterisk and you'll discover that the task is impossible. The asterisk is part of the Styles On code; the only way to edit it is to edit the style named BULLETS.

```
SALES FIGURES FOR THE WEST COAST

We predict a 15% increase in sales this year.  In the first three
months of this year, the following figures are in from the West
Coast of the United States:

    *    Sales of Chardonnay have skyrocketed, increasing 50% over
         the same time last year.

    *    Pinot Noir has increased by 11%, a hefty increase, though
         volume is much smaller for Pinot Noir than Chardonnay.
                                          Doc 1 Pg 1 Ln 2" Pos 1"
months of this year, the following figures are in from the West[SRt]
Coast of the United States:[HRt]
[HRt]
[Style On:Bullets][→Indent]*[→Indent][UND]]Sales of Chardonnay have skyrocketed,
  increasing 50% over[SRt]
the same time last year.[Style Off:Bullets][Style On:Bullets]Pinot Noir has incr
eased by 11%, a hefty increase, though[SRt]
volume is much smaller for Pinot Noir than Chardonnay.[Style Off:Bullets][Style
On:Bullets]Chenin Blanc and Cabernet Sauvignon sales have stayed[SRt]
about the same.[Style Off:Bullets][HRt]

Press Reveal Codes to restore screen
```

**FIGURE 14-10** Cursor positioned on a Style On code so that it expands

To edit a style, return to the Styles screen, position the cursor on the name of the style you wish to edit, and select Edit (4 or E). The Edit Styles screen for that style appears. Now select an item to alter the styles definition. Press EXIT ( F7 ) until you return to the Typing screen.

When you edit a style that has already been executed in a document, the results are truly amazing. The text governed by that style is revised to reflect the editing changes in seconds. As an example, suppose that you decide to alter BULLETS by indenting the bulleted paragraphs one more tab stop to the right and preceding each paragraph with a paragraph number rather than an asterisk.

1. Press the STYLE ( Alt + F8 ) key. [*Pulldown menu:* Layout (L), Styles (S).] The Styles screen appears.

2. Position the cursor on the style named BULLETS.

3. Select Edit (4 or E) to display the Edit Styles screen.

4. Select Codes (4 or C) to display the codes inserted for the BULLETS style, as shown in Figure 14-7.

5. Check the bottom window to make sure that the cursor is positioned on the first code, [→Indent], and press the → INDENT ( F4 ) to insert another [→Indent] code.

6. Position the cursor on the asterisk.

7. Press Del to delete the asterisk, press DATE/OUT-LINE ( Shift + F5 ), select Para Num (5 or P), and press Enter to insert an automatic paragraph number. Your screen should now resemble Figure 14-11.

8. Press EXIT ( F7 ) until you return to the Typing screen.

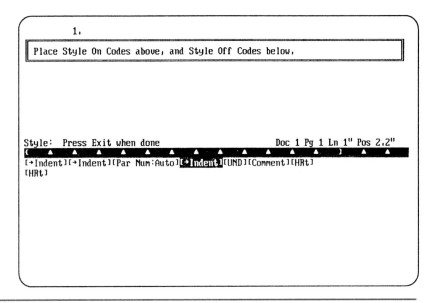

**FIGURE 14-11** Codes after editing the Bullets style

In seconds, all the paragraphs governed by the BUL-LETS style are reformatted; the results are shown in Figure 14-12.

In addition to editing an existing style, you can delete a style from the Styles screen. Position the cursor on the name of the style you wish to erase, and select Delete (5 or D). *5.1 users:* WordPerfect displays a menu of three options.

**Delete Styles: 1** Leaving Codes; **2** Including Codes; **3** Definition Only: **0**

- *Leaving Codes (1 or L)* Select this option if you wish to delete the style from the Styles screen as well as the Style codes of the same name from the text, but you want all text that had been formatted by those Style codes to continue being formatted just as the style dic-

```
SALES FIGURES FOR THE WEST COAST

We predict a 15% increase in sales this year.  In the first three
months of this year, the following figures are in from the West
Coast of the United States:

         1.   Sales of Chardonnay have skyrocketed, increasing
              50% over the same time last year.

         2.   Pinot Noir has increased by 11%, a hefty increase,
              though volume is much smaller for Pinot Noir than
              Chardonnay.

         3.   Chenin Blanc and Cabernet Sauvignon sales have
              stayed about the same.


SALES FIGURES FOR THE EAST COAST

We predict a moderate 4% increase in sales this year.  In the first
three months of this year, the following figures are in from the
East Coast:

                                      Doc 1 Pg 1 Ln 1" Pos 1"
```

**FIGURE 14-12**   Sample text after the Bullets style is edited

tated. Style codes in the text will be replace by the codes that comprised the style. For instance, if the style contained a Left/Right Margin and a Hyphenation On code, those codes will be inserted.

- *Including Codes (2 or I)*   Select this option to delete the style, the Style codes, and also the formatting that resulted from those Style codes.

- *Definition Only (3 or D)*   Select this option in order to delete the style, but keep the Style codes intact in the document. When WordPerfect encounters those codes in the document, it re-creates them on the Styles screen.

*5.0 users:* There is no choice as to how the style is deleted —when you delete a style, the Style codes remain intact in the document (comparable to the Definition Only option for 5.1 users).

# MANAGE STYLES BETWEEN DOCUMENTS

When styles are created, they are associated with a specific document. When you save the document on disk, the styles are attached to that file. The next time you retrieve that document and press the STYLE (Alt + F8) key, the Style screen appears listing those styles.

You can also save and retrieve styles separate from the document to which they are connected. In this way, you can apply styles created in one document to many other documents. For instance, a style you created for use in formatting the January newsletter can then be used when typing future newsletters.

To save a Style screen independently, select Save (6 or S) from the Style screen. Now type a filename, using the same rules for naming files as when storing a document on disk. You may wish to name this file with an extension of .STY so that you can identify it as a file containing styles by its filename. The Style screen is saved into a blank WordPerfect document, ready to be used in other documents.

To retrieve a Style screen into another document, make sure that the other document is on screen. Press STYLE (Alt + F8) to display the Style screen for that other document, select Retrieve (7 or R), and type in the name of the file containing the styles that you wish to bring into the current document. The retrieved styles are combined with any styles already on screen. If two styles have the same name, WordPerfect will prompt asking whether you wish to replace the existing style with the retrieved style. Type **Y** to replace or type **N** to stop the replacement.

You can also establish one of the Style screens that you saved independently as a *style library*. A style library is a collection of styles that will be attached to *every new* document that you create once the library is established. Reserve the style library for styles that you want to have available for all your documents. See "Location of Files" in Appendix B to learn how to specify one Style screen as a style library. Version 5.1 users should also refer to this section of Appendix B in order to specify a certain drive/directory for saving and retrieving styles. If you do not specify another drive/directory by preceding the style filename with a drive/directory path, then WordPerfect assumes you wish to save style files to and retrieve them from the default drive/directory.

WordPerfect is packaged with a list of styles under the filename LIBRARY.STY. For some of you, this file has already been defined as your style library (which is why a list of files appeared the first time that you displayed the Style screen). You may wish to examine each of the styles on this menu and decide whether any are appropriate for your needs. You can edit some of these styles and delete others. Or, if none meet your needs, you can remove this style as your style library.

If you establish a style library, you can attach this library to any document you created *before* you established the style library. Make sure that the existing document is on screen. Press STYLE ( Alt + F8 ) and select Update (8 or U). The style library will be combined with any styles already on screen. Also use the Update feature if you edit the style library and want the changes reflected on the Style screen for a document you created before the library was edited.

# REVIEW EXERCISE

Once you know about macros and styles, you'll want to take some time to think about your repetitive tasks and repetitive formatting needs. Then create your own macros and styles. The time it takes to do so will more than pay for itself in a short while. For additional practice before you start addressing your own individual needs, try the following:

1. Suppose that after typing certain reports and before printing them, you format them for double spacing and for left/right margins of 2″. Create a simple macro that

   - Moves to the top of a document (with [Home], [Home], [↑])

   - Changes the text to double spacing

   - Changes the left and right margins to 2″

   - Prints out the full document from the screen

   Name this macro DSMPRINT, which stands for Double Space, Margins, PRINT. (*Hint:* Before you begin recording the macro keystrokes, turn on the printer and type some text on screen so that WordPerfect will have something to print. Proceed slowly when recording the macro keystrokes to reduce the chance of making mistakes. Also, remember to turn off the recording after you send the document on screen to the printer.)

2. Clear the screen and retrieve a single-spaced document, such as JOHNSTON.LET, a letter you created when working with boilerplate text in Chapter 13.

3. Execute the macro named DSMPRINT to format and print this document. (*Hint:* Remember to turn on the printer before you execute this macro.)

4. For the document on screen, create a paired style that will underline and boldface a portion of text. Leave the [Enter] key defined with its usual function, inserting a hard return. Name this style UNDBOLD, which stands for UNDerline and BOLDface.

5. Execute the UNDBOLD style several places in the text. For instance, if the file named JOHNSTON.LET is on screen, then turn on the style for each occurrence of the name R&R Wine Association. (*Hint:* Since the text has already been typed, you must use the Block feature to highlight the text that you wish to be governed by the style. Then, press the STYLE ([Alt] + [F8]) key and turn on the style named UNDBOLD.)

6. Resave the document on screen. When you do, the new style that you created will be attached to that document. (If you think that UNDBOLD is a style you will use often, you can also save that style independently into its own file.)

## Quick Review

- Consider creating a macro whenever you find yourself typing a certain series of keystrokes in sequence over and over again—whether it is to type a phrase or issue a series of commands. Once you've created a macro, you can let WordPerfect do the repetitive typing for you.

- Create a macro by pressing the MACRO DEFINE (⌜Ctrl⌝ + ⌜F10⌝) key. Or, pulldown menu users can select Tools (T), Macro (A), Define (D). Type in a macro name, either by pressing ⌜Alt⌝ + a letter, or by typing one to eight characters and pressing the ⌜Enter⌝ key. Then enter a macro description. Now the macro recorder is on: Press the keystrokes that will comprise the macro. When the macro has been defined, turn off the macro recorder by again pressing MACRO DEFINE. The macro is saved on disk with the extension .WPM.

- Execute a macro named with the ⌜Alt⌝ key and a letter by pressing ⌜Alt⌝ + that letter. Execute a macro named with one to eight characters by pressing the MACRO (⌜Alt⌝ + ⌜F10⌝) key and entering the macro name. Or, pulldown menu users can select Tools (T), Macro (A), Execute (X) and then enter the macro name.

- Press the ⌜Esc⌝ key and type a number before executing a macro when you wish to repeat that macro a specific number of times in a row.

- Consider creating a style whenever you find yourself formatting certain elements in a document over and over again in the same way. Once you've created a style, let WordPerfect do the repetitive formatting for you. If you later edit that style, the text governed by that style is automatically updated to conform to the modifications.

- Create a style by pressing the STYLE ( Alt + F8 ) key to display the Style screen. Or, pulldown menu users can select Layout (L), Styles (S). Next, select Create (3 or C), and proceed to define the style, including its name, type, and the text/codes that it will contain.

  5.1 users can select from three types of styles — open styles, which are turned on but not off; paired styles, which are turned on for one section of text and turned off after that section; and outline styles, which determine the numbering format for up to eight levels when employing the Outline or Paragraph Numbering feature. 5.0 users can select from the open or paired styles.

- Turn on an open or paired style by returning to the Style screen, positioning the cursor on the name of the style you wish to select, and choosing On (1 or O).

  When you turn on an open style, the style takes effect for all text that follows the Open Style code.

When you turn on a paired style, you must also turn it off after typing the affected text by selecting Off (2 or F) from the Style menu or using the ⬗ key to position the cursor to the right of the Style Off code; the paired style takes effect for the text that is positioned between the Style On and Style Off codes.

- *5.1 users only:* Turn on an outline style by pressing the DATE/OUTLINE (Shift + F5) key, and selecting Define (6 or D). Or, pulldown menu users can select Tools (T), Define (D). Now select Outline Style Name (9 or N) to display the Outline Styles screen—a screen that shows styles only of the outline type. Position the cursor on the style you wish to execute, and choose Select (1 or L). This outline style takes effect for all paragraph numbers that follow which you insert using the Outline or Paragraph Numbering features.

- Styles listed on a Style screen are stored along with the document in which they were created. But you can save a Style screen independently on disk so that it can be employed in many different documents by selecting the Save (6 or S) option from the Style screen. You can then retrieve that Style screen into another document using the Retrieve (7 or R) option.

# chapter 15

# WORDPERFECT
# EXTRAS

Insert Special Characters
Alter the Keyboard Layout
Create Equations [5.1 Users Only]
Learn About Additional Graphics Capabilities
Work with Long Documents
Sort and Select
Perform Mathematical Calculations
Transfer Between Software Programs
Quick Review

In previous chapters, you learned about the various features most heavily relied on to manipulate words and
produce documents. In addition, WordPerfect can go far
beyond the normal bounds of word processing, offering the
capabilities to

- Insert special characters, such as mathematical or legal
  symbols, in a document

- Alter the layout of the keyboard to meet your own special needs

- Rely on an Equation Editor to create complex formats for mathematical and scientific equations (5.1 users only)

- Import graphics into documents using graphics programs not supported by WordPerfect

- Create line drawings on screen using the cursor movement keys

- Insert and update cross-references in a document

- Generate a table of contents, list, index, or table of authorities automatically

- Create a master document so that your work with long documents becomes more manageable

- Sort/select information either line by line or paragraph by paragraph in a document, or record by record in a secondary merge file document. Or, sort/select within a table (5.1 users only)

- Calculate totals and the results of formulas in columns and rows

- Perform math, convert files between different versions of WordPerfect or between other software packages and WordPerfect

These are some of WordPerfect's most advanced features, which stretch the program's limits far beyond those of a standard word processor.

Should your WordPerfect needs extend to any of the above-mentioned extras, then read on. This chapter describes the capabilities of WordPerfect's extra features. If you require greater detail on the complexities of using these extra features, Osborne/McGraw-Hill offers several excellent sources that go beyond the scope of this book, which are listed in the section "Learn More about Word-Perfect" following the book's introductory pages.

# INSERT SPECIAL CHARACTERS

With WordPerfect, you are not limited to the keys on the standard keyboard. You can produce other special symbols—for example, the degree symbol (○), the one-half symbol (½), the section sign used in legal documents (§), the paragraph symbol (¶), and Greek letters such as alpha (α) or beta (β). You can also produce digraphs and diacritical marks such as Æ, á, or ö. In fact, depending on your printer, with WordPerfect you can include a variety of multinational, mathematical, scientific, Greek, and Hebrew symbols in documents—over 1500 special characters in all.

## WordPerfect Character Set

In WordPerfect, special characters are separated into 13 *character sets*. Each character set has a name and a corresponding number, as listed in Table 15-1.

Within a character set is a group of special characters, each of which is assigned a WordPerfect character number. The WordPerfect character number is made up of the character set number, a comma, and a character number

| Name | Character Set # | Contents |
|---|---|---|
| ASCII | 0 | ASCII space through tilde — symbols commonly found on the computer keyboard |
| Multinational 1 | 1 | Common capitalizable multinational characters, diacritics, and noncapitalizable multinational characters |
| Multinational 2 | 2 | Rarely used noncapitalizable multinational characters and diacritics |
| Box Drawing | 3 | All 81 double/single box drawing characters |
| Typographic Symbols | 4 | Common typographic symbols not found in ASCII |
| Iconic Symbols | 5 | Rarely used "picture" (icon) symbols |
| Math/Scientific | 6 | Non-extensible, non-oversized math/scientific characters not found in ASCII |
| Math/Scientific Extension | 7 | Extensible and oversized math/scientific characters |
| Greek | 8 | Full Greek character set for ancient and modern applications |
| Hebrew | 9 | Full Hebrew character set for ancient and modern applications |
| Cyrillic | 10 | Full Cyrillic character set for ancient and modern applications |
| Japanese Kana | 11 | Characters for Hiragana or Katakana (the type is determined by the typeface) |
| User-Defined | 12 | 255 user-definable characters |

**TABLE 15-1**  List of WordPerfect Character Sets

from within the set. The special characters and their corresponding WordPerfect character numbers are all listed in two files, CHARACTR.DOC and CHARMAP.TST.

CHARACTR.DOC, which is over 30 pages long, lists the special characters by character set. One special character is displayed on each line, along with a description of that character and its WordPerfect character number. You'll discover, for instance, that • is referred to as the Bullet and is WordPerfect character number 4,0. Or, ÷ is the Division Sign and is WordPerfect character number 6,8. Hard disk users will find CHARACTR.DOC (if you installed it) in the directory where you installed the WordPerfect program files. Floppy disk users will find this file on the Install/Utility disk. (5.1 users) or on the Conversion disk (5.0 users).

CHARMAP.TST displays the special characters for each character set in a matrix form and without a written description of each special character, and is therefore only a few pages long. Figure 15-1 shows all the character sets, as provided in CHARMAP.TST's matrix format. To use the matrix, locate a character and take note of its Character Set (Map) number. Then, add its corresponding row value and its column value together. (The row value is counted in increments of 20 or 30, such as 0, 20, 40, 60, and so on, or 0, 30, 60, 90, and so on. The column value is any number from 0 to 29.) Now you have discovered its WordPerfect character number. For instance, the exclamation point (!) in Figure 15-1 is part of character set 0 and is at the intersection of row 30 and column 3. Thus, its WordPerfect character number is 0,33. Or, the section symbol (§) is part of character set 4, and is at the intersection of row 000 and column 6. Thus, its WordPerfect character number is 4,6. Hard disk users will find CHARMAP.TST in the directory

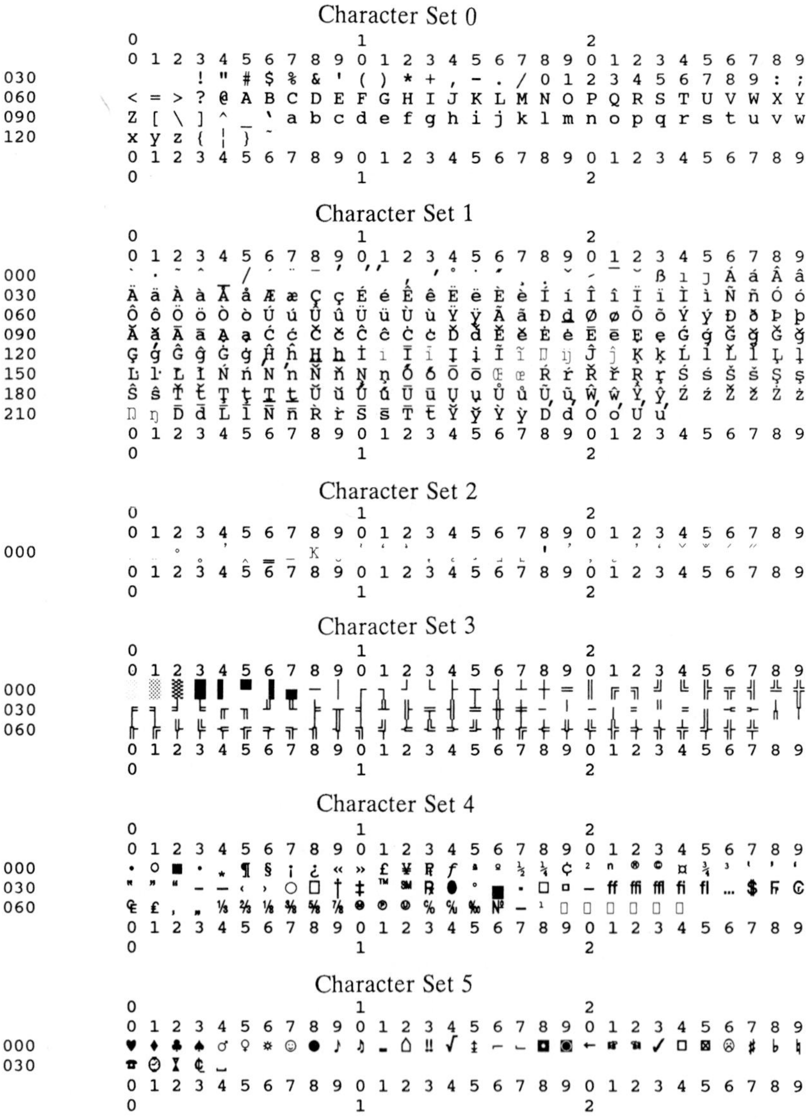

**FIGURE 15-1** WordPerfect character sets, as displayed in CHARMAP.TST

Character Set 6

| | 0 | | | | | | | | | | 1 | | | | | | | | | | 2 | | | | | | | | | |
|---|---|---|---|---|---|---|---|---|---|---|---|---|---|---|---|---|---|---|---|---|---|---|---|---|---|---|---|---|---|---|
| | 0 | 1 | 2 | 3 | 4 | 5 | 6 | 7 | 8 | 9 | 0 | 1 | 2 | 3 | 4 | 5 | 6 | 7 | 8 | 9 | 0 | 1 | 2 | 3 | 4 | 5 | 6 | 7 | 8 | 9 |

000 − ± ≤ ≥ ∝ ∕ ∕ ∖ ÷ ∣ ⟨ ⟩ ~ ≈ ≡ ∈ ∩ ∥ Σ ∞ ¬ → ← ↑ ↓ ↔ ↕ ▶ ◀

030 ▼ · · ∘ • Å ° µ ⁻ × ∫ ∏ ∓ ∇ ∂ ′ ″ ‸ ℓ ℏ ℜ ℘ ↦ ↤ → ↑ ↓

060 ↔ ↨ ↗ ↘ ↙ ↶ ∪ ⊂ ⊃ ⊆ ⊇ ∅ ⌈ ⌉ ⌊ ⌋ ◀ ▶ ∧ ⊗ ⊕ ⊖ ⊕ ∘ ∧ ∨ ∨ ⊤ ⊥

090 ⌢ ⊢ ⊣ □ ■ ◇ ◆ ⌈ ⌉ ⋆ · ⋮ ⋰ ⋱ ∮ ℒ ℭ Ʒ ℘ ○ △ ◇ ★ ‴ ∥ ~ ▪ < ≶ >

120 ≥ ∃ ∀ ◀ ▶ ⋓ ⊆ ⋒ ⊓ ⊔ ⊏ ⊑ ⊐ ⊒ ⊐ ⊒ ▲ ▽ ◀ ▶ ⋈ ⌢ ⌢ ◯ → ↦ ↤ → ⌁

150 → → ↤ ↦ ↑ ↓ ↓ ↓ ⊣ ⊢ ∪ ∩ ⊂ ⊃ ⊛ ⊛ ⊛ ⊖ ⋃ △ ◁ ◁ ▷ △ ▽ ∔ ≐ ≑ ≢ ≎ × ×

180 ⊢ ▲ ∣ ⌋ ★ ✦ ✧ ✢ ✣ ✤ ✦ ✧ ✥ ✵ ✶ ¢ ₵ ₰ ₫ ₮ ₦ ¶ ∥ ∥ ✳ ∃ €

210 ✦ ℰ ℱ C I N R ² ↳ ∃ ⋯ ⋯ ∶ ⁚ ‾ ‾ ‾ + - - ∗

| | 0 | 1 | 2 | 3 | 4 | 5 | 6 | 7 | 8 | 9 | 0 | 1 | 2 | 3 | 4 | 5 | 6 | 7 | 8 | 9 | 0 | 1 | 2 | 3 | 4 | 5 | 6 | 7 | 8 | 9 |
|---|---|---|---|---|---|---|---|---|---|---|---|---|---|---|---|---|---|---|---|---|---|---|---|---|---|---|---|---|---|---|
| | 0 | | | | | | | | | | 1 | | | | | | | | | | 2 | | | | | | | | | |

Character Set 7

| | 0 | | | | | | | | | | 1 | | | | | | | | | | 2 | | | | | | | | | |
|---|---|---|---|---|---|---|---|---|---|---|---|---|---|---|---|---|---|---|---|---|---|---|---|---|---|---|---|---|---|---|
| | 0 | 1 | 2 | 3 | 4 | 5 | 6 | 7 | 8 | 9 | 0 | 1 | 2 | 3 | 4 | 5 | 6 | 7 | 8 | 9 | 0 | 1 | 2 | 3 | 4 | 5 | 6 | 7 | 8 | 9 |

000 ⌈ ⌉ ⌋ ﹍ √ ⁻ Σ Π Ⅱ ∫ ∮ ∣ ∣ ∣ ∣ ∥ ∥ ⦃ ⦃ ⦃ ⦅ ⦅ ⦅ ⦆

030 ⦄ ⦄ ⦄ ⦆ ⦆ ∣ ∣ ∣ ∣ ∣ ∣ ∣ ∣ ∣ ⌈ ⌈ ⌈ ⌉ ⌉ ⌉

060 ∣ ∪ ∩ ✛ ⁻ ⁻ ⌐ ╲ ⟩ ∕ ∠ ﹍ ﹍ Σ Π Ⅱ ∫ ∮ √ √ √ √ ∖ ∣ ⌐ → → → ─

090 ﹍ ⇒ ⇐ = ↑ ↓ ∣ ⇑ ⇓ ∥ ⦅ ⦅ ⦅ ⦅ ⦅ ⦆ ⦆ ⦆ ⦆ ⦆ ∣ ∣ ⌈ ⌈ ⌈ ⌈ ⌈

120 ∣ ⌋ ⌋ ⌋ ⌋ ⌋ ⌋ ∣ ⟨ ⟨ ⟨ ⟨ ⟩ ⟩ ⟩ ∕ ∕ ∕ ∖ ∖ ∖ ⟍ ∪ ∩ ⊎ ⊎ ⊔ ⊔

150 ∧ ∧ ∨ ∨ ⊗ ⊗ ⊕ ⊕ ⊙ ⊙ ⊖ ─ ─ ⌢ ⋅ ─ ─ ‾ ⋅ ∧ ∧ ∧ ~ ~ ~ ⌢ ⌢ ─ ─

180 ⊖ ⊖ ⊕ ⊕ ⌈ ⌈ ⌈ ⌈ ⌈ ⌉ ⌉ ⌉ ⌉ ∥ ∥ ∥ ─ ─ ─ ─ ─ ▬ ▬ ▬ ▬ ⊣ ⊨

210 = = = = = = ∣ ∣ ∣ ∣ ∣ Π Π ⌈ ⌈

| | 0 | 1 | 2 | 3 | 4 | 5 | 6 | 7 | 8 | 9 | 0 | 1 | 2 | 3 | 4 | 5 | 6 | 7 | 8 | 9 | 0 | 1 | 2 | 3 | 4 | 5 | 6 | 7 | 8 | 9 |
|---|---|---|---|---|---|---|---|---|---|---|---|---|---|---|---|---|---|---|---|---|---|---|---|---|---|---|---|---|---|---|
| | 0 | | | | | | | | | | 1 | | | | | | | | | | 2 | | | | | | | | | |

Character Set 8

| | 0 | | | | | | | | | | 1 | | | | | | | | | | 2 | | | | | | | | | |
|---|---|---|---|---|---|---|---|---|---|---|---|---|---|---|---|---|---|---|---|---|---|---|---|---|---|---|---|---|---|---|
| | 0 | 1 | 2 | 3 | 4 | 5 | 6 | 7 | 8 | 9 | 0 | 1 | 2 | 3 | 4 | 5 | 6 | 7 | 8 | 9 | 0 | 1 | 2 | 3 | 4 | 5 | 6 | 7 | 8 | 9 |

000 Α α Β β Β ϐ Γ γ Δ δ Ε ε Ζ ζ Η η Θ θ Ι ι Κ κ Λ λ Μ µ Ν ν Ξ ξ

030 Ο ο Π π Ρ ρ Σ σ Σ ς Τ τ Υ υ Φ φ Χ χ Ψ ψ Ω ω ά ἀ ή ἠ ί ἰ ό ὀ ύ ὐ

060 ώ ὠ ἐ ὲ χ ῀ ϖ ϱ ϒ φ ϕ ; · ·

090 · ά ᾶ ᾳ ᾷ ᾷ ᾷ ᾷ ᾷ ᾷ ᾷ ᾷ ᾷ ᾷ ᾷ ᾷ ᾷ ᾷ ᾷ ᾷ ᾷ ᾷ έ ἑ ἐ ἒ ἓ ἔ

120 ἐ ἒ ἓ ή ῆ ῄ ῂ ῇ ῃ ῇ ῆ ῇ ῆ ῇ ῆ ῇ ῆ ῇ ῆ ῇ ί ῖ ῐ ῑ ῒ ΐ ῗ ί ῖ φ

150 ί ῖ ῦ ῤ ῥ ὁ ὂ ὃ ὄ ὅ ὀ ὂ ὃ ὐ ὒ ὓ ὔ ὕ ὖ ὗ ὐ ὒ ὓ ὐ ὠ ὤ φ φ φ φ

180 ὠ ὢ ὣ ὤ ὥ φ φ ὦ ὧ ὠ ὢ ὣ φ ′ ‚ Ϛ Ϝ ϟ Ϡ Ά Ε Ι Ό Υ Ω ῀

| | 0 | 1 | 2 | 3 | 4 | 5 | 6 | 7 | 8 | 9 | 0 | 1 | 2 | 3 | 4 | 5 | 6 | 7 | 8 | 9 | 0 | 1 | 2 | 3 | 4 | 5 | 6 | 7 | 8 | 9 |
|---|---|---|---|---|---|---|---|---|---|---|---|---|---|---|---|---|---|---|---|---|---|---|---|---|---|---|---|---|---|---|
| | 0 | | | | | | | | | | 1 | | | | | | | | | | 2 | | | | | | | | | |

**FIGURE 15-1**  WordPerfect character sets, as displayed in CHARMAP.TST (*continued*)

## Character Set 9

## Character Set 10

## Character Set 11

## Character Set 12

═══ **FIGURE 15-1**  WordPerfect character sets, as displayed in CHARMAP.TST (*continued*)

where you installed the WordPerfect printer files. Floppy disk users will find this file on the PTR program disk (5.1 users) or on the Conversion disk (5.0 users).

# Compose Feature

The Compose feature is used to insert a WordPerfect special character into the text of your document. The Compose feature is accessed either by pressing [Ctrl] + [V] or by pressing [Ctrl] + [2] (the number 2 using the top row of numbers on the keyboard). [Ctrl] + [V] only operates on the typing screens, such as the main screen and the Footnote Typing screen, whereas [Ctrl] + [2] operates when a menu is displayed as well. [*Pulldown menu:* Instead of using [Ctrl] + [V], select Font (O), Characters (H).]

To use the Compose feature, make sure to position the cursor where you want a special character to appear before pressing [Ctrl] + [V] or [Ctrl] + [2]. If you press [Ctrl] + [V], the following prompt appears:

Key =

If you press [Ctrl] + [2], no prompt appears on screen.

Next, you must indicate which special character you wish to insert in that location. There are four methods for doing so, depending on the type of special character you wish to insert. The first method works regardless of the special character you wish to insert, while the last three methods are shortcuts:

- Whatever the special character (whether a digraph, diacritic, or symbol), type in the WordPerfect character number and press [Enter]. For instance, type **4,6** and press [Enter] to insert the Section Sign. Or, type **6,8** and press [Enter] to insert the Division Sign. See Figure 15-1 to discover the WordPerfect character number for the special character you wish to insert.

- If the special character is a digraph, which is two vowels or consonants combined to express a single sound, type the two characters, one after the other. For instance:

| Type | Resulting Digraph |
| --- | --- |
| A E | Æ |
| a e | æ |
| o x | ¤ |
| O E | Œ |
| I J | Ĳ |

- If the special character is a diacritic, which is a vowel or consonant combined with a diacritical mark to express a single sound, type the character and then the diacritical mark. For instance:

| Type | Resulting Diacritic |
| --- | --- |
| ' i | í |
| , c | ç |
| v z | ž |
| ^ a | â |
| ` e | è |
| @ a | å |
| / o | ø |
| ~ n | ñ |
| "u | ü |
| = o | o̲ |

- If the special character is a commonly used symbol, type the combination of characters shown below:

| Type | Resulting Symbol | Type | Resulting Symbol |
|------|------------------|------|------------------|
| - L | £ | P ¦ | ¶ |
| / c | ¢ | < < | « |
| + − | ± | > > | » |
| / 2 | ½ | < = | ≤ |
| / 4 | ¼ | > = | ≥ |
| * . | · | P t | $P_t$ |
| * * | ● | Y = | ¥ |
| * o | ○ | = = | ≡ |
| * O | ◯ | ~ ~ | ≈ |
| ? ? | ¿ | = / | ≠ |
| ! ! | ¡ | t m | ™ |
| - - | — | s m | ℠ |
| r x | ℞ | r o | ® |
| c o | © | | |

Once you insert a special character into your text, it may or may not be displayed on the Typing screen. Which special characters can display depends partly on your monitor and your graphics display card. If the character cannot display, then a shaded rectangle is shown instead.

The special character is actually inserted in the text as a code. You can see this code if you switch to the Reveal Codes screen and position the cursor on that code. The code indicates the special character's WordPerfect character number. For instance, suppose you insert the section sign (§) in the text. When you switch to the Reveal Codes screen and position the cursor on the section sign, the following code is shown: **[§:4,6]**. This is because the section sign's WordPerfect character number is 4,6. As another example, you may see a shaded rectangle in your text and not know what character that shaded rectangle represents. Position the cursor on that rectangle and reveal codes to find out. Here's an example of what you may see: **[▬,4,40]**. This code indicates that the character typed into that location corresponds to WordPerfect character number 4,40.

Even if a special character cannot be displayed on screen, so that it is instead displayed as a shaded box, the special character may still print out properly as long as it is supported by your printer. What special characters can be printed depends on your printer. Some printers can print certain special symbols; with others, you must change the print wheel or font cartridge; and some printers cannot print them at all. You will have to test your printer. Either insert special characters into a document and print, or print out the document named CHARMAP.TST. If the character won't print, try inserting another available print wheel or font cartridge into the printer. If you are a 5.1 user and your printer has graphics capabilities (laser and certain dot matrix printers), then you'll find that if a certain special character is unavailable for your printer, WordPerfect prints out that character graphically; your printer is therefore capable of printing every character in the WordPerfect character sets.

There may be special characters that you insert in documents quite frequently. If so, instead of using the Compose feature to insert those characters, consider assigning them to key combinations using the Keyboard Layout feature. For example, you can assign the degree symbol to the key combination `Ctrl` + `D` or the section sign to `Ctrl` + `S`. It will thus be easier to insert these special characters than by pressing `Ctrl` + `V`, typing a WordPerfect character number, and then pressing `Enter`. See the later section entitled "Alter the Keyboard Layout" for more details.

## Overstrike Feature

You can also use the Overstrike feature to produce digraphs or diacritical marks that your printer might not otherwise produce. The Overstrike feature gives you the ability to print two or more characters in the same position. To use Overstrike, position the cursor in your document where you want the digraph or diacritical mark to appear. Press the FORMAT (`Shift` + `F8`) key and select Other (4 or O) to display the Other Format menu. [*Pulldown menu:* Layout (L), Other (O).] Then select Overstrike (5 or O). WordPerfect prompts

```
1 Create; 2 Edit: 0
```

Select Create (1 or C). WordPerfect prompts

```
[Ovrstk]
```

Now, type in the characters that you wish to print at the same location, and press `Enter`. Finally, press EXIT (`F7`) until you return to the Typing screen.

On the Typing screen, only the last character you typed will appear. For instance, if you typed **a'**, then the screen will display only the single quote ('). Reveal codes, however, and you'll find **[Ovrstk:a']**. Both characters will be printed at the same position. You can also edit the Overstrike code by placing the cursor after the code and following the same procedure as just described to view the Overstrike menu. Then, select Edit (2 or E). After editing the code, press Enter and EXIT (F7) to return to the Typing screen.

# ALTER THE KEYBOARD LAYOUT

WordPerfect offers the ability to reconfigure your keyboard to meet unique needs. You can create a keyboard definition that assigns keys to perform one of the following:

- *Activate a feature*  For instance, on WordPerfect's original keyboard, F1 serves as the CANCEL key. Other software packages, however, reserve the F1 key as the HELP key. So you may wish to set up a new keyboard definition in WordPerfect whereby, among other things, you reassign the F1 key as the HELP key.

- *Insert a special character*  For instance, suppose you frequently type legal documents and insert special characters such as the section sign (§) and paragraph sign (¶). You can set up a keyboard definition whereby all the legal special characters are assigned to certain key combinations. For instance, you'll define a keyboard such that when you press Ctrl + S, the section sign is inserted, and when you press Alt + P, the paragraph sign is inserted.

- *Execute a macro* Macros—series of keystrokes that WordPerfect stores for you—are described in Chapter 14. You can write various macros to accomplish repetitive tasks and then set up a keyboard definition whereby you press ⌷Ctrl⌷ plus a letter or a certain function key, or ⌷Alt⌷ plus a number to execute a given macro.

You can create one or many keyboard definitions. As an example, if you wish to redefine just a few keys for your personal needs, then perhaps establish just one keyboard definition. But if you sometimes type legal documents for which you want certain keys defined one way and sometimes type foreign documents for which you want certain keys defined a second way, then establish two different keyboard definitions.

When a new definition is created, it is stored on disk with the extension .WPK, which stands for WordPerfect Keyboard. You can activate a keyboard definition that you've created at any time while typing or editing a document. You can also return to the *original* keyboard—the one defined by the creators of WordPerfect—at any time.

The WordPerfect package comes with already-created keyboard definitions:

- *ALTRNAT.WPK* This file moves the Help feature to the ⌷F1⌷ key, the Cancel feature to the ⌷Esc⌷ key, and the Repeat Value feature to the ⌷F3⌷ key.

- *ENHANCED.WPK* This file reassigns more than a dozen keys for moving the cursor or enhancing text. For instance, ⌷Shift⌷ + ⌷F11⌷ will turn on italics (useful only for those of you with keyboards containing 12 function keys), and Ctrl + ↓ moves the cursor down to the start of the next sentence.

- *MACROS.WPK*   Assigns a variety of macros to the Alt and Ctrl keys.

- *EQUATION.WPK (5.1 users only)*   This file assigns a variety of mathematical and scientific characters to the Alt and Ctrl keys.

- *SHORTCUT.WPK (5.1 users only)*   This file assigns to the Alt and Ctrl keys some macros that provide quick access to some of the most common WordPerfect features.

If you wish to examine any of these keyboard definitions, floppy disk users will find these files on the Macros/Keyboards disk (5.1 users) or the Conversion disk (5.0 users). Insert that disk into drive B. Hard disk users must have previously installed these files and should specify where these keyboard definitions are found on the hard disk, as described in the "Location of Files" section of Appendix B, before WordPerfect will be able to locate these keyboard definitions.

To work with the Keyboard Layout feature, press the SETUP (Shift + F1) key and select Keyboard Layout (5 or K for 5.1 users, 6 or K for 5.0 users). [*Pulldown menu:* File (F), Setup (T), Keyboard Layout (K).] A screen such as shown in Figure 15-2 appears. Figure 15-2 shows the screen listing the five predefined keyboard definitions available in WordPerfect 5.1.

The options at the bottom of the Keyboard Layout screen allow you to select a keyboard definition, create a new one, or manage the list of keyboard definitions.

## Select a Keyboard Definition or Return to the Original

To activate an already-created definition, display the Keyboard Layout screen. Next, position the cursor on the keyboard definition name that you wish to activate in one of two ways: either use the cursor movement keys or select Name Search (N), type the first characters of the keyboard definition's name, and press Enter. Now choose Select (1 or S) and press EXIT (F7) to return to the Typing screen.

When you wish to deactivate a certain definition and revert to the original keyboard definition, again display the Keyboard Layout screen, select Original (6 or O), and press EXIT (F7) . As an alternative, you can revert to the original keyboard definition for the rest of the working session directly from the Typing screen: simply press Ctrl + 6 (the number 6 on the top row of the keyboard).

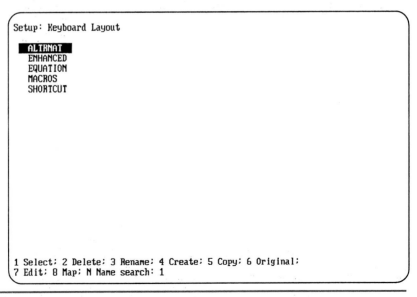

```
Setup: Keyboard Layout

   ALTRNAT
   ENHANCED
   EQUATION
   MACROS
   SHORTCUT
```

```
1 Select: 2 Delete: 3 Rename: 4 Create: 5 Copy: 6 Original:
7 Edit: 8 Map: N Name search: 1
```

**FIGURE 15-2** Keyboard Layout screen listing predefined keyboard definitions (version 5.1)

# Create or Edit a Keyboard Definition

To create a new definition, display the Keyboard Layout screen (Figure 15-2) and select Create (4 or C). Word-Perfect prompts with

`Keyboard Filename:`

Type a name of up to eight characters and press $\boxed{\text{Enter}}$. (Make sure not to also type a filename extension; the extension .WPK is automatically assigned to that file by WordPerfect.) *5.1 users only:* Select Edit (7 or E). For both 5.1 and 5.0 users, a Keyboard Edit screen displays, such as the one shown in Figure 15-3 for a keyboard definition named LEGAL.

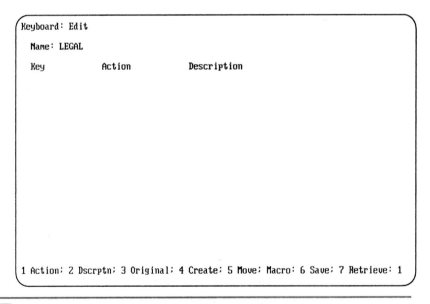

```
Keyboard: Edit

  Name: LEGAL

 Key           Action          Description












 1 Action: 2 Dscrptn: 3 Original: 4 Create: 5 Move: Macro: 6 Save: 7 Retrieve: 1
```

══ **FIGURE 15-3**  Keyboard Edit screen for keyboard definition named LEGAL (version 5.1)

The Keyboard Edit screen is also used when you wish to edit or examine key assignments for an existing keyboard definition. Display the Keyboard Layout screen, position the cursor on the name of the keyboard definition that you wish to edit, and select Edit (7 or E for 5.1 users, 5 or E for 5.0 users). The Keyboard Edit screen will display those keys that have already been defined.

Once on the Keyboard Edit screen, your task is to define or edit the action you desire for specific keys as part of a keyboard definition. You can select from the menu of options at the bottom of the screen. The first options relate to a key, while the last two options relate to a macro:

- *Action (5.1 users) or Edit (5.0 users)*  This option edits the action for a specific key. Position the cursor on a key that you wish to edit before selecting this option. The Key Edit screen reappears for the key or key combination you highlighted with the cursor. Once you edit the key-strokes, press EXIT ( F7 ).

- *Description (5.1 users only)*  This option edits the 39-character description that you can provide for the action assigned to a specific key. Position the cursor on the key before selecting this option.

- *Original (5.1 users) or Delete (5.0 users)*  This option deletes the action for a specific key, returning the key to its original definition. Position the cursor on the key you wish to delete before selecting this option. WordPerfect will prompt for confirmation; type **Y** to delete the key from the definition.

- *Move*  This option moves a key's action to a different key. Position the cursor on the key before selecting this option.

- *Create*  This option assigns an action to a specific key. WordPerfect will prompt for a key. Type the key or key combination that you wish to define, such as ⬚ or ⬚Ctrl⬚ + ⬚S⬚ or ⬚F1⬚ or ⬚Alt⬚ + ⬚P⬚.

  What happens next depends on your version of Word-Perfect.

  *5.1 users:* You are then prompted for a description; this is an explanation of up to 39 characters of the key's action, and is useful for future reference. Type in a description and press ⬚Enter⬚. A Key Action screen for that key appears, as shown in Figure 15-4 for the key combination ⬚Ctrl⬚ + ⬚Q⬚ (denoted Ctrl-Q). The cursor is inside the double-line box, ready to type in the action for that key.

  *5.0 users:* You immediately view the Key Edit screen, similar to Figure 15-4 except for (1) the header on screen which reads "Key: Edit" instead of "Key: Action", (2) the ability to type in a description on this screen by selecting Description (1 or D) and typing in up to 39 characters to describe the key's action for future reference, and (3) the need to select Action (2 or A) to position the cursor inside the double-line box.

  For both 5.1 and 5.0 users, once inside the action box, you are ready to define the key's action. The key's original function is listed in the action box, such as {^Q} in Figure 15-4, which means that when you press ⬚Ctrl⬚ + ⬚Q⬚, ^Q is currently inserted on screen. Type in the exact keystrokes that you want the key to accomplish. For instance, erase the {^Q}, press the COMPOSE (⬚Ctrl⬚ + ⬚2⬚ key), and enter the WordPerfect character number of a special character; this defines ⬚Ctrl⬚ + ⬚Q⬚ to insert a certain special character. Or erase the {^Q}, press the asterisk (*), and then press the ► INDENT ([F4]) key to define a new key that will insert an asterisk and an [► **Indent**] code.

If you wish to specify an action using an editing function, then you must press [Ctrl] + [V] before pressing the editing key. For instance, if in the action box you press [Backspace], you'll perform the editing function of erasing whatever is to the left of the cursor, but if you press [Ctrl] + [V], and then press the [Backspace] key, you'll insert the keystroke {Backspace}, which is describing the action of pressing [Ctrl] + [Q].

Once you have defined the keystroke action for the key you are defining, press EXIT ([F7]) to return to the Keyboard Edit screen. The key combination you just defined is now listed on that screen. If that key's action

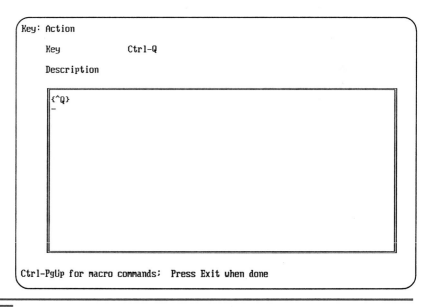

**FIGURE 15-4** Key Action screen for [Ctrl] + [Q] (called Key Edit screen in version 5.0)

was defined with more than one keystroke, it is considered a key macro, and is assigned a macro number which is displayed on the Keyboard Edit screen.

Now you can create actions for additional keys, building a keyboard definition. Any keys for which you don't create an action will maintain their original function when that keyboard definition is selected.

- *Save*   This option saves a key's action as a file macro so that the macro can be executed like other macros. Position the cursor on the key before selecting this option. At WordPerfect's prompt, type in the filename for this macro. The macro will be saved on disk with the extension .WPM, which stands for WordPerfect Macro. The macro can now either be executed as part of a keyboard definition or like any other macro. (Be sure to refer to Chapter 14 for more on macros.)

- *Retrieve*   This option retrieves a previously created macro and assigns that macro to a key. WordPerfect will prompt for a key. Type the key or key combination to which you wish to assign the macro. At WordPerfect's next prompt, type in the macro's filename. Now the macro can be executed either as part of a keyboard definition or using the standard macro executing process.

Once you create or edit a keyboard definition, assigning a variety of keys to specific functions, press EXIT ([F7]) to return to the Keyboard Layout screen; the name of the newly created or edited keyboard definition will be listed. Remember that you must still choose the Select option if you wish to start using that keyboard definition.

## Manage a Keyboard Definition

You may wish to review the keys that have been assigned in a keyboard definition—perhaps a definition created by WordPerfect, or a definition created by a co-worker on your computer. To do so, return to the Keyboard Layout screen and position the cursor on the keyboard definition name that you wish to review—either by using the cursor movement keys or by selecting Name Search (N), typing the first characters of the keyboard definition's name, and pressing [Enter]. Now, select the Edit option to display the Keyboard Edit screen for that particular keyboard definition, and then read the Action and Description for each of the assigned keys. Press EXIT ([F7]) when the review is complete.

[*5.1 users only:* You have another option for reviewing key assignments as well. You can display a map of all the keys that have been redefined—with the exception of function, cursor movement, and editing keys—by selecting Map (8 or M). A map of the keyboard definition is shown, as in Figure 15-5 for the keyboard definition named MACROS. The first pair of rows shows the assignments for all the [Alt] + typewriter keys. The row labeled "Key" shows each key, and the row labeled "Action" indicates whether the key has been defined with a special character, a one-keystroke command (C), or a macro (M). Other pairs of rows show the assignments for all the [Ctrl] + typewriter keys, and for the typewriter keys on their own, including letters in both upper- and lowercase.

5.1 users can not only check the key definitions on this screen, but also can edit all the keys except for the function, cursor movement, and editing keys, just as on the Keyboard Edit screen. Position the cursor on the key that you wish to edit—either by using the cursor movement keys or by selecting Key Name Search (N), and typing the key. Your options, similar to those on the Keyboard Edit screen, are as follows:

- *Key*  Assigns a command (one keystroke) to the current key as its action.

- *Macro*  Assigns a macro (series of keystrokes) to the current key as its action.

- *Description*  Allows you to enter a description for the current key's action.

- *Original*  Returns the key to its original function, deleting any action that was previously assigned.

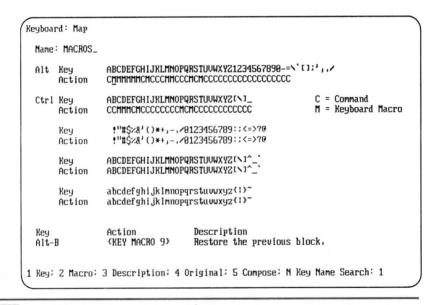

**FIGURE 15-5**  Keyboard Map screen for keyboard definition MACROS (version 5.1 only)

• *Compose* Assigns a special character to the current key as its action.

Press the EXIT (F7) key when you have finished editing the keyboard map.]

Both 5.1 and 5.0 users can also delete or rename a keyboard definition at any time. From the Keyboard Layout screen, position the cursor on the keyboard definition name that you wish to delete or rename. Then select Delete (2 or D) and type **Y** to verify the deletion, or select Rename (3 or R) and type in a new filename for the keyboard definition.

# CREATE EQUATIONS [5.1 USERS ONLY]

Inserting mathematical or scientific equations into Word-Perfect documents can be done with the Equations feature. Previously, writing an equation involved using the Advance, Overstrike, and Line Spacing features in combination with superscript and subscript. Now you can create and align complicated equations, such as the samples shown in Figure 15-6.

If your printer supports graphics, then you can print out your equations graphically. Otherwise, you can specify that the equations print out as text using the currently selected base font, such as a special font you may have purchased that can print out mathematical and scientific symbols.

To place an equation in a document, you must first insert a graphics box into your text. To do so, press the GRAPHICS (Alt + F9) key, select Equation (6 or E), and select Create (1 or C). [*Pulldown menu:* Graphics (G),

{av + ax} TIMES 2 OVER {n - ax}

$$av + ax \times \frac{2}{n - ax}$$

av ~+ ~{ax TIMES 2} OVER n ~- ~ax

$$av + \frac{ax \times 2}{n} - ax$$

x = {-a PLUSMINUS SQRT {c^3^2 - SQRT {b^3-b^2}}} OVER a^4

$$x = \frac{-a \pm \sqrt{c^{3^2} - \sqrt{b^3 - b^2}}}{a^4}$$

T = SUM P SUB i OVER {(1 + I)} SUB i

$$T = \sum \frac{P_i}{(1 + I)_i}$$

B(f) = INT SUB{-INF} SUP{INF} alpha (t) e SUP{beta}

$$B(f) = \int_{-\infty}^{\infty} \alpha(t) e^{\beta}$$

**FIGURE 15-6**   Sample of equations

```
Definition: Equation

    1 - Filename

    2 - Contents          Equation

    3 - Caption

    4 - Anchor Type        Paragraph

    5 - Vertical Position  0"

    6 - Horizontal Position  Full

    7 - Size               6.5" wide x 0.333" (high)

    8 - Wrap Text Around Box  Yes

    9 - Edit



Selection: 0
```

══════════ **FIGURE 15-7** Equation Definition screen

Equation (E), Create (C).] WordPerfect then displays a full-screen Equation Definition menu, as shown in Figure 15-7. The options on this menu, described in detail in Chapter 10, allow you to specify the location, size, contents, and caption for the graphics box. If you do not change these options, the defaults for these options mean that the equation box will (1) contain an equation, (2) be anchored to the paragraph where the cursor was positioned when you first pressed the GRAPHICS key, (3) stretch to fill the space between the left and right margins, (4) expand in height based on the size of the equation, and (5) have no caption.

With the graphics box in the text, you can now create the equation. To do so, select Edit (9 or E) from the Equation Definition menu. The Equation Editor appears, as shown in Figure 15-8. The Equation Editor has three windows:

- *Editing window*    The bottom window where the cursor is currently located in Figure 15-8. In this window, you type the text of the equation. You can type numbers, letters, and the following operators into the window:

| | | | |
|---|---|---|---|
| + | plus | = | equal to |
| − | minus | > | greater than |
| * | multiply | < | less than |
| / | divide | ! | not |

You can also insert the symbols ?. ¦ @,;: into this window. Special symbols such as '" {} ( ) have special meanings and can be entered either from the keyboard or from the Equation Palette (described next). And special characters—such as Greek symbols or arrows—can be entered either from the keyboard using the Compose feature (as described earlier in this chapter), or from the Equation Palette. When you press the spacebar, a space

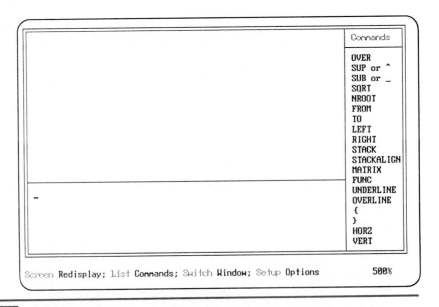

⟨⟨⟨ **FIGURE 15-8**   Equation Editor

is inserted in the Editing window to make the equation more readable, but is ignored in the equation itself.

- *Equation Palette*   The tall window at the right in Figure 15-8. In this window, you can choose commands and special symbols for insertion as part of an equation into the Editing window. When you first enter the Equation Editor, the heading "Commands" is displayed, meaning that the Commands menu is available. There are 36 commands; Table 15-2 provides a list of the most commonly used commands, and Figure 15-6 shows examples of the proper syntax for many of these commands in creating equations.

  Press LIST ( F5 ) to move into the Equation Palette. Then you can use the arrow keys to position the cursor on a command; the command's meaning and syntax are displayed at the bottom of the screen. Press Enter to insert that command into the Editing window as a word. You can instead type the command as a symbol from the keyboard. Or, press CANCEL ( F1 ) to return to the Editing window without inserting a command. From the Commands menu, another option is to press PgUp or PgDn to show the next menu of the Equation Palette. Other menus include Greek, containing the Greek symbols; Arrows, containing arrow and other special symbols such as triangles and circles; Sets, containing set, subset, and relational symbols; Functions, containing mathematical functions such as sine and cosine; Symbols, containing symbols such as primes and relational symbols; Large, containing two sizes of various symbols including sum and integral; and Other, containing miscellaneous items such as diacritical marks and ellipses.

- *Display window*   The top window in Figure 15-8. In this window, you can view how the equation will display. To do so, press SCREEN ( Ctrl + F3 ) after typing or

| Command | Application in an Equation |
|---|---|
| { and } | Signals the start and end of a group |
| ~ | Indicates that a space should be printed |
| ` | Indicates that a thin space should be printed |
| \ | Signals that the next operator or command be treated as characters rather than as an equation operator or command |
| BOLD | Signals that the next character or group be boldfaced |
| BINOM | Creates a binomial, placing the first character that follows on top, the second character on the bottom, and enclosing the binomial in parentheses |
| FROM and TO | Signals the start and end limits for operators. The FROM symbol is placed on the bottom and the TO symbol placed on the top of the operator |
| ITAL | Signals that the next character or group be italicized |
| OVER | Creates fractions, placing one character or group over another and separated by a horizontal line |
| SQRT | Creates the square root of the character or group that follows |
| SUP or ^ | Signals that the next character or group should be superscripted |
| SUB or _ | Signals that the next character or group should be subscripted |

**TABLE 15-2**  Comonly Used Commands in the Equation Palette

editing an equation in the Editing window. The equation will appear magnified; the percentage in the lower right corner on screen displays the viewing magnification. For instance, 500% means that the equation is being displayed at five times its size when printed. You must have a graphics card for the equation to display properly.

If you receive an error message after pressing the SCREEN key, then there is some type of syntax error in the equation, so that the equation cannot be displayed. The cursor relocates in the Editing window next to the syntax error. You must correct the error before displaying the equation.

You can press the SWITCH ( [Shift] + [F3] ) key to move the cursor to the display window in order to view the equation in more detail. Then, use the arrow keys to reposition the equation within the window, or use the [PgUp] and [PgDn] keys to resize the equation. To return to the Editing window, press SWITCH again, or press EXIT ( [F7] ).

While in the Equation Editor, press the SETUP ( [Shift] + [F1] ) key to change the defaults for this equation, including the font size used to print the equation, the horizontal and vertical position of the equation in the graphics box, and whether the box will print graphically or as text. (You can also change these default assumptions for every equation, rather than for the current equation, by displaying the Setup menu from the normal Typing screen. By doing so, you can also select a Keyboard Definition that will be used to help you in typing special characters in the equation; see the section entitled "Initial Settings" in Appendix B for further details.)

Once the equation is complete, and you are satisfied with its appearance in the Display window, press EXIT ( [F7] ) until you return to the Typing screen. What you see on screen will be the top of an equation box outline. The top of the box will read "EQU" followed by the equation box number.

Should you wish to alter the borders or turn on shading within the graphics box, you can change the default options for the equation box. See the section "Change Graphics Box Default Options" in Chapter 10 for more.

Keep in mind that the Equation feature is expert at formatting equations, but will do no calculations. To learn about the calculations that WordPerfect can perform, turn to the section further on in this chapter entitled "Perform Mathematical Calculations."

# LEARN ABOUT ADDITIONAL GRAPHICS CAPABILITIES

In Chapter 10, you learned about WordPerfect's ability to incorporate graphics lines or graphics boxes into a document. A graphics box can contain text or graphics images created using programs compatible with WordPerfect. If the graphics program you use to create your graphics images is not compatible with WordPerfect, you can instead use a screen capture program provided by WordPerfect called GRAB.COM. If your printer has no graphics capabilities, you can instead use the Line Draw feature to create line drawings and see if your printer will print them. Line Draw is also useful when your printer supports graphics, but you wish to create a simple line drawing on screen using the cursor movement keys.

# Screen Capture Utility

GRAB.COM is a Screen Capture program provided in the WordPerfect package. With this utility, you can copy any image displayed on screen into a file, which can then be integrated into a WordPerfect document. Given a choice, you'll want to use WordPerfect-supported graphics formats (as described in Chapter 10) rather than GRAB.COM. GRAB.COM captures images of a lesser quality, because the image you capture is only as good as the screen resolution. Nevertheless, it is a useful alternative if your graphics program cannot produce your images in a WordPerfect-supported graphics format.

To use GRAB.COM, you must load it into your computer's memory *before* you load your graphics program or WordPerfect. Therefore, exit your graphics program or WordPerfect, so that the DOS prompt appears on screen. Then, if you're a hard disk user and have installed the utility named GRAB.COM onto the hard disk, change to the hard disk directory where the GRAB.COM program is located. For instance, type **CD \WP51** and press (Enter). Then type **GRAB** and press (Enter) to load this Screen Capture utility. Or, if you're a floppy disk user, then 5.1 users should insert the Install/Utility disk that you created when you installed WordPerfect into drive A, and 5.0 users should insert the Fonts/Graphics disk into drive A. Make sure that the DOS prompt indicates that you're on drive A; if not, type **A:** and press (Enter). Then, type **GRAB** and press (Enter).

Now load your graphics program and create the graphics image. When that image is on screen, press (Alt) + (Shift) + (F9). If you hear a two-toned chime, this means you have activated GRAB.COM, the Screen Capture program. (If you hear no such chime, but instead hear a low-pitched buzz, either you are not in Graphics mode, or your monitor cannot support GRAB.COM.) A box is displayed on screen. Use the directional arrow keys to move the box, and use the key combination (Shift) + an arrow key to resize the box. Once the box is properly positioned and sized over the graphics image, press (Enter) to store the image; another two-toned chime sounds to signal that the file is being stored. You can press (Esc) to abort the screen capture.

GRAB.COM saves the image in the default drive/directory in a file named GRAB.WPG. If a file by that name exists, it is stored under GRAB1.WPG (or GRAB2.WPG, and so on). The image is now in proper WordPerfect format to be used in a document.

You can then exit the graphics program, load WordPerfect, create a graphics box, and retrieve the file named GRAB.WPG (or GRAB1.WPG, or whatever) into that graphics box—as described in Chapter 10.

## Line Draw

In addition to using the Graphics feature, you can also use WordPerfect's Line Draw feature to create illustrations. With Line Draw, you can create simple drawings that contain straight lines and sharp corners right on screen. You can use the arrow keys to produce organizational charts, design graphs, or create a work of art. The lines can be drawn around text either before or after the text is typed. Unlike the Graphics feature, with Line Draw you can see the image you've created right on the Typing screen.

To use the Line Draw feature, position the cursor on the line where you want the drawing to begin, press the SCREEN ((Ctrl) + (F3)) key, and select Line Draw (2 or L). [*Pulldown menu:* Tools (T), Line Draw (L).] The Line Draw menu appears:

1 |; 2 ||; 3 * 4 Change; 5 Erase; 6 Move: 1          Ln 1" Pos 1"

WordPerfect will assume option 1, meaning that you want to draw with a single straight line. Just start using the ⬆, ⬇, ⬅, and ➡ keys, and an image will form.

The Line Draw menu offers other choices as well. Select option 2, and you can draw with a double line. Option 3 will let you draw lines of asterisks. Select Erase (5 or E) and you retrace your steps to delete lines. Select Move (6 or M) and you can move the cursor without drawing, as if you were picking up a pencil to move it to another spot before continuing.

You can also change the third draw character from an asterisk to another character. Select Change (4 or C), and the following menu appears:

1 ‖; 2 ▓; 3 ▐; 4 ▌; 5 ▪; 6 |; 7 ¦; 8 ▀; 9 Other: 0

You can select any of these characters to draw with, or you can select Other (9 or O) and choose one of your own from the characters on the keyboard, such as the plus sign (+) or the broken line (¦). Or, specify a special character using the Compose feature (discussed earlier in this chapter). Figure 15-9 shows a graph drawn on screen by typing graph labels ("MONTHLY SALES," "JAN," "FEB," "MAR," and so on) and using three line draw characters—the single line, the asterisk, and the thick dotted line.

To draw lines more quickly, you can use the ⌂Home key in combination with the arrow keys. A line will be drawn to the next non-blank character in the direction of the arrow, up to a maximum line length of 100 characters. For instance, suppose that you've selected the asterisk as your draw character and your cursor is at the left margin of a blank line; press ⟨Home⟩, ⟨→⟩ to draw a line of asterisks to the right margin. Or, if there is a previously drawn box in the middle of the screen, then ⟨Home⟩, ⟨→⟩ will draw a line of asterisks up to the box. If you wish to move through the box, then press ⟨Home⟩, ⟨Home⟩, ⟨→⟩ instead.

Another alternative for drawing lines quickly is to use the ⟨Esc⟩ key. Press ⟨Esc⟩, type a number, and then press an arrow key to draw a line of a specific length. For instance, press ⟨Esc⟩, type **20**, and press ⟨→⟩ to draw a horizontal line 20 characters long.

As you draw using single or double lines, tiny arrows appear to indicate the direction of the line. (Two such arrows are shown in Figure 15-9). These will print out as half-lines. If you want to extend these half-lines to full

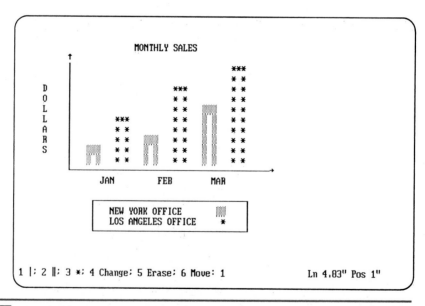

**FIGURE 15-9**   Sample graph created with three draw characters

lines, then, when the Line Draw menu is on screen, position the cursor on an arrow and press the (End) key. The arrow will be replaced by the draw character.

It is usually easier when combining text with graphics to type the text first and then activate Line Draw. Line Draw works in Typeover mode; if you draw over text, the text is replaced by the line. WordPerfect automatically inserts an **[HRt]** code at the end of each line as you draw.

Should you decide to type text *after* creating a line drawing, you should switch into Typeover mode first by pressing the (Ins) key. This will ensure that when you type on a line that contains a drawing, you won't disfigure the drawing. Don't type over the drawing or press (Enter) on a line that includes a drawing. If you do, you must find and erase the **[HRt]** code to return the drawing to its previous appearance.

When you are ready to print out your line, make sure that you are using a monospaced font, and that the justification is set to Left (5.1 users) or Off (5.0 users). Otherwise, the lines will not print correctly. In addition, you will want to retain single spacing, and may need to adjust the Line Height feature to ensure that vertical lines are not broken on the printed page.

As is the case for special characters such as § or ¶, printers that cannot print graphics may be unable to print using certain of the line draw characters. You should test your printer's capabilities. One way is to design a line drawing such as the one shown in Figure 15-9 and then print it. Should your printer be unable to print the special line draw characters, you can always draw by using some of the standard keys on your keyboard that all printers can produce, such as the broken line ( ¦ ) for vertical lines, the plus sign ( + ) for box corners, and the minus sign ( − ) or equal sign ( = ) for horizontal lines.

# WORK WITH LONG DOCUMENTS

WordPerfect offers several powerful features that enable you to manage the text in long documents. These include Cross References; Generate Tables, Lists, and Indexes; and Master Documents.

## Cross (Automatic) References

Suppose you insert the following phrase in your text: "For more on Chardonnay wines, refer to footnote 14, found on page 33." If you then edit your text so that pages are renumbered and/or edit your footnotes so that they are renumbered, you must manually update the phrase about Chardonnay wines, as well as any other phrase that cites a specific page or footnote number. That's time consuming.

Instead, employ the Cross-Reference feature (referred to as the Automatic Reference feature in version 5.0). This feature will let you refer to a specific page number, graphics box, footnote, endnote, or outline/paragraph number—called the *target*. Should you later edit your document so that the target becomes a different page or graphics box or note, all references can be updated automatically. That's a timesaver.

To create an automatic reference, position the cursor within the referring text wherever you want the reference number to appear. For instance, type **For more on the R&R Wine Association, see page.** Next, press the MARK TEXT ( Alt + F5 ) key and select Cross-Ref (1 or R). The Automatic Reference menu displays, listing three options, as shown in Figure 15-10. [*Pulldown menu:* Mark (M), Cross-Reference (R)]

Typically, the referring text and the target will already exist in the document, so that you can select Mark Both Reference and Target (3 or B). WordPerfect wants to know what you are referring to in the text. Is the target a page number? A footnote number? A paragraph number? The menu shown in Figure 15-11 appears. Type in a number that corresponds to your target, such as Page Number (1 or P) if you're referring to a page. Now WordPerfect will prompt based on your target selection. For instance, if you selected a page number, WordPerfect prompts

```
Move to page; Press Enter.
```

Position the cursor just past the target and press ⌊Enter⌋. For instance, for a target that's a page number, position the

```
Mark Text: Cross-Reference

    1 - Mark Reference

    2 - Mark Target

    3 - Mark Both Reference and Target

Selection: 0
```

═══ **FIGURE 15-10**  Cross-Reference menu (called Automatic Reference menu in version 5.0)

cursor on that page, within or just past the discussion to which you're referring, and press (Enter). For a target that's a footnote or endnote, use the FOOTNOTE ((Ctrl) + (F7)) key to view the Typing screen for that note (see Chapter 12), position the cursor just past the note number, and press (Enter). For a paragraph/outline number or graphics box, position the cursor to the immediate right of the Paragraph Number or Graphics Box code and press (Enter).

As a last step, you are asked for a target name. This target name links the referring text to the target. Type a short name. For instance, type **R&R** and press (Enter).

You are returned to your phrase in the text. That phrase now appears with the reference number, such as, "For more on the R&R Wine Association, see page 23." But the reference number 23 is really a code. Reveal codes and you will view the following: "For more on the R&R Wine Association, see page **[Ref**(R&R)**:Pg** 23**]**." This code is

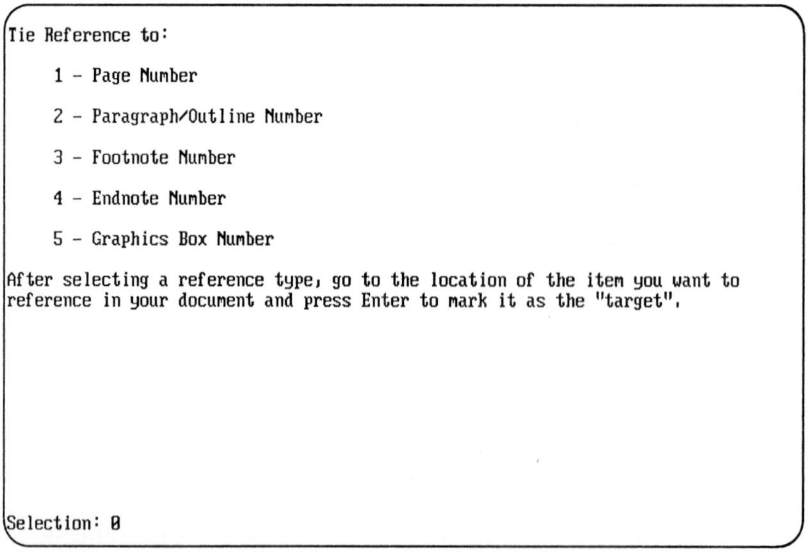

```
Tie Reference to:

    1 - Page Number

    2 - Paragraph/Outline Number

    3 - Footnote Number

    4 - Endnote Number

    5 - Graphics Box Number

After selecting a reference type, go to the location of the item you want to
reference in your document and press Enter to mark it as the "target".




Selection: 0
```

**FIGURE 15-11**  Tie Reference menu

called a Reference code, where the target name is R&R and the reference number is page 23. The target, too, contains a code. For instance, just below a discussion of the R&R Wine Association on page 23, you will find the code **[Target**(R&R)].

If you later edit the document, the location of text related to the R&R Wine Association may move from page 23 to another page, perhaps page 19. In that case, you should direct WordPerfect to generate (update) the automatic references before you save or print the document. To do so, press the MARK TEXT (Alt + F5) key and select Generate (6 or G). [*Pulldown menu:* Mark (M), Generate (G).] Then select Generate Tables, Indexes, Cross-References, etc. (5 or G). Type **Y** at WordPerfect's prompt to verify that you wish to generate (update) all automatic references (as well as tables, lists, and indexes, which are discussed farther on in this chapter). Now the phrase in the text will read: "For more on the R&R Wine Association, see page 19."

Besides marking a reference and target at the same time, you can also mark them separately. For instance, suppose that you plan to create many references to the same target. Begin your phrase in the text where you'll refer to a target, return to the Cross-Reference menu (Figure 15-10), and select Mark Reference (1 or R) to mark the referring text. Once you insert a Reference code, a question mark (?) will appear instead of a reference number. Repeat for each reference you wish to make in the text. Later, position the cursor at the target location, return to the Cross-Reference menu, and select Mark Target (2 or T) to insert a Target code. Use the same target name for all Reference codes and Target codes that are linked together. Remember to generate (update) the automatic references, as described above, to replace each question mark with the proper reference number.

# Generate Tables, Lists, and Indexes

In a dissertation, book, legal brief, or other long document, the author often prepares reference aids to help the reader easily find information in that document. WordPerfect offers assistance when you need to create reference aids, which include an index (like the one at the back of this book), a table of contents (like the one at the front of this book), up to nine separate lists (of illustrations, graphs, maps, and such), and up to 16 sections of a table of authorities (which lists various cases, regulations, and other sources cited in a legal document). Best of all, if you let WordPerfect create these reference aids for you, they can be updated by WordPerfect when you later edit your text.

The procedure for producing any of these reference aids is basically the same: (1) mark the text that will be included; (2) define the style of the reference aid; and (3) generate the reference aid.

**MARK TEXT**   You must insert codes around phrases in the text that you want incorporated in the particular reference aid. This is called marking the text. Suppose that you want to mark a heading to be included in a table of contents. Use the Block feature to highlight the heading. Then press the MARK TEXT (Alt) + F5) key. [*Pulldown menu:* Mark (M).] With Block on, the following menu appears:

Mark for: 1 ToC; 2 List; 3 Index; 4 ToA: 0

Select the option that corresponds to the reference aid for which you are marking the text; for instance, select ToC (1 or C) to mark the heading for a table of contents. Then WordPerfect will ask you how that highlighted text should be treated:

- For a table of contents, WordPerfect asks for the table of contents level number. Think of the table of contents as having a structure similar to that of an outline: level-1 text starts at the left margin and corresponds to a level-1 heading, level-2 is indented one tab stop and corresponds to a level-2 heading, and so on. You can have up to five levels in a table of contents generated by WordPerfect.

  Type a level number and press ⌨Enter. WordPerfect inserts a pair of codes around the text, such as **[Mark:ToC,1]** and **[End Mark:ToC,1]** for a level-1 entry.

- For a list, WordPerfect asks you for which list the text should be marked. For example, suppose you were creating one list of illustrations related to white wines and another list for red wines. The first could be identified as list number 1, and the second could be list number 2. WordPerfect can generate up to ten lists in a document if you are a 5.1 user and nine lists if you are a 5.0 user.

  Type a list number and press ⌨Enter. WordPerfect inserts a pair of codes around the text, such as **[Mark:List,1]** and **[End Mark:List,1]** for an entry in list number 1.

- For an index, WordPerfect asks for the index heading and then for the subheading, suggesting the highlighted text. For instance, one entry in an index might be structured as follows:

```
White Wines
       Chardonnay
       Sauvignon Blanc
       Chenin Blanc
```

"White Wines" would be the heading, and "Chardonnay" one of its three subheadings.

  Enter a heading and then a subheading. Or, leave the subheading entry blank if there is none. WordPerfect inserts one code at the beginning of the highlighted text, such as **[Index:**White Wines;Chardonnay**]**.

- For a table of authorities, WordPerfect prompts for that citation's section number. For instance, perhaps your table of authorities will have two sections: statutes and cases. Section 1 could be statutes, and section 2 could be cases. You have two possible responses when marking an authority.

  If this is the first time that you are citing this particular authority in the text, type a section number and press [Enter]. In that case, the highlighted text containing the authority is displayed on the screen. Edit the authority to determine how it will appear in the table of authorities when generated, and then press the EXIT ([F7]) key. Finally, WordPerfect will ask for the citation's short form, which will serve as a nickname for those times that the same authority is mentioned further forward in the text. Type in a short form and press [Enter]. WordPerfect inserts a code in front of the highlighted text, such as **[ToA:1;Long;Full Form]** for section 1 of the table, where Long is assigned as the short form.

  Or, if this is *not* the first time that you are citing this particular authority, but rather you have previously marked it nearer to the top of the document, then press [Enter] without typing a section number to signify that you will use the authority's short form to mark it. Then, enter the short form that you previously assigned to this authority. WordPerfect inserts a code in front of the highlighted text, such as **[ToA:;Long;]**.

When marking an index or the short form for a table of authorities, you have a shortcut available. Because WordPerfect inserts a code, rather than a pair of codes, it isn't necessary to highlight the block that you wish to mark. Instead, simply position the cursor in front of the text that you wish to block, press MARK TEXT ([Alt] + [F5]), and select the Index or Table of Authorities Short Form option.

Now respond to the prompts to mark that index or table of authorities entry.

For an index, you even have an additional shortcut available for marking text. Instead of marking each phrase individually, you can create a *concordance file,* which is a document containing common phrases that you want included in an index. On a clear screen, type the phrases, one on each line, and then save this document under a name that reminds you it's a concordance file. WordPerfect will ask for the name of this concordance file when you define the index (the procedure to define a reference aid follows); enter the filename. Then, when WordPerfect creates (generates) the index, it will search the document for those phrases contained in the concordance file and include the corresponding page numbers in the index. The phrases are assumed to be headings unless you mark those phrases in the concordance file—in the same way that you mark phrases in a document—as subheadings. Creating a concordance file does not prevent you from also marking phrases individually in the text. WordPerfect will compile both into an index when generated. But a concordance file does free you from having to mark the most frequently mentioned phrases over and over again in the text.

There's also a shortcut for creating a list of graphics boxes. Lists 6 through 10 are preassigned to assemble captions from graphics boxes. Therefore, make sure that you specify a caption for each graphics box that you want listed. That caption automatically will be included in one of the lists as follows: list 6 is for compiling captions from figure boxes, list 7 for table boxes, list 8 for text boxes, list 9 for user-defined boxes, and list 10 (5.1 users only) for equation boxes.

**DEFINE THE REFERENCE AID'S STYLE** Your next step is to define the table, list, or index that you wish to create.

Position the cursor where you want that reference aid to appear. For an index, the cursor must be positioned at the end of the document. When WordPerfect generates an index, it looks backward in the text for marked phrases, so any marked phrases that are forward from the cursor will not be included. For the other reference aids, the cursor can be located anywhere in the document. For instance, you can position the cursor on a separate page at the end of the document to ensure that the page-reference numbers are correct when you generate the aid. In this way, you can always renumber the page on which the reference aid is located after you generate it. Alternatively, you can position the cursor on a separate page at the front of the document; however, you must then remember to renumber your pages *before* you actually generate the reference aid, so that the page-reference numbers are correct. For instance, number the page containing a table of contents as page i and the next page as page 1. (See Chapter 6 for directions on renumbering pages.)

With the cursor located in the document where you want a reference aid to be generated, press the MARK TEXT ( Alt + F5 ) key. [*Pulldown menu:* Mark (M).] With Block off, a different menu appears:

`1 Cross-Ref; 2 Subdoc; 3 Index; 4 ToA Short Form; 5 Define;`
`6 Generate: 0`

Select Define (5 or D), choose the option corresponding to the reference aid you wish to define, and then follow WordPerfect's prompt to define the reference aid. In a document you can generate more than one list and multiple sections in a table of authorities, so each list and table of authorities section must be defined separately.

For a specific list, table of contents, or index, you are given the opportunity to determine how page numbers should appear once generated. Figure 15-12 shows a sample of the five numbering styles available. With a table of contents, you can also determine how many levels should be generated and whether entries in the last level should be placed together on the same line, separated by semi-colons—referred to as wrapped format. With an index, you also have the opportunity to indicate a filename for a concordance file that you may have created.

For a table of authorities, a menu screen appears where you decide whether (1) the page numbers (which will always appear at the right margin on the page) should be preceded by dot leaders, (2) the table should include underlining, and (3) a blank line should be inserted between authorities.

---

**1 - No page numbers:**
    Sales Figures for the West Coast
    Sales Figures for the East Coast

**2 - Page numbers follow entries:**
    Sales Figures for the West Coast 5
    Sales Figures for the East Coast 5

**3 - (Page numbers) follow entries:**
    Sales Figures for the West Coast (5)
    Sales Figures for the East Coast (5)

**4 - Flush right page numbers:**
    Sales Figures for the West Coast            5
    Sales Figures for the East Coast            5

**5 - Flush right page numbers with dot leaders:**
    Sales Figures for the West Coast ................................ 5
    Sales Figures for the East Coast................................... 5

---

**FIGURE 15-12**   Numbering style options for lists, indexes, tables of contents

A Definition Mark code is placed in the text. For instance, suppose you just defined list 1, where the numbering style will be flush right page numbers (option 4); the code inserted is **[Def Mark: List,1:4]**. Or suppose that you defined section 3 of a table of authorities; the code inserted is **[Def Mark:ToA,3]**.

**GENERATE THE REFERENCE AID**  The hard work is now over. You simply press a few keys and sit back while the table, list, or index is generated. With the cursor located anywhere in the document, press the MARK TEXT (⌨Alt + ⌨F5) key and select Generate (6 or G). [*Pulldown menu:* Mark (M), Generate (G).] Next, select Generate Tables, Indexes, Automatic References, etc. (5 or G). At WordPerfect's prompt, type **Y** to continue with the generation (where all reference aids as well as cross-references are updated) or type **N** to abort the command. Depending on the length of your document, the generation process could take several minutes.

After the table, index, or list is generated, you can put on the finishing touches. For example, if you put a title at the top of a table of contents that you defined as having three levels with flush right page numbers and dot leaders, you'd have a result like that shown in Figure 15-13.

# Master Documents

The Master Document feature aids you in working with a long document. You can store separate parts of a long document in individual files, referred to as *subdocuments*. Then you can create a main document that links all the subdocuments together, referred to as the *master document*. You can edit each subdocument separately, so that editing becomes more manageable. At the same time, you can work with them as a whole via the master document for tasks that require the documents to be treated as one, such as printing or generating a comprehensive table of contents, table of authorities, index, or list. And all numbering features found in the subdocuments—such as footnotes, endnotes, paragraph numbering, cross-references, and page numbering—will operate consecutively when the subdocuments are linked to the master.

The master document is basically a small file consisting of text and links to each subdocument. Suppose, for instance, you are writing a book. Each chapter can be stored on disk as a separate subdocument, using filenames such as CHAP1, CHAP2, and so on. The master document may include a title page, reference aids such as a table of contents, an introduction, and links to each chapter.

```
                          TABLE OF CONTENTS


Introduction . . . . . . . . . . . . . . . . . . . . . . . . . .  1

Wine Sales . . . . . . . . . . . . . . . . . . . . . . . . . . .  3
          Sales Figures for the West Coast. . . . . . . . . . .  5
          Sales Figures for the East Coast. . . . . . . . . . .  5

Future Projections . . . . . . . . . . . . . . . . . . . . . . .  7
          West Coast. . . . . . . . . . . . . . . . . . . . . .  8
              Short-term . . . . . . . . . . . . . . . . . . . .  9
              Long-term. . . . . . . . . . . . . . . . . . . . .  9
          East Coast. . . . . . . . . . . . . . . . . . . . . . 11
              Short-term . . . . . . . . . . . . . . . . . . . . 12
              Long-term. . . . . . . . . . . . . . . . . . . . . 12

Conclusions. . . . . . . . . . . . . . . . . . . . . . . . . . . 14




                                       Doc 1 Pg 1 Ln 1" Pos 1"
```

**FIGURE 15-13** Sample table of contents

To work with the Master Document feature, you can first type and save all the subdocuments on disk, or you can create the master document first and then create the sub-documents later. When you're ready to create the master document, start typing on a clear screen just as you would for beginning any document. In the location where you want to incorporate a subdocument, press the MARK TEXT ( Alt  +  F5 ) key and select Subdoc (2 or S). [*Pulldown menu:* Mark (M), Subdocument (S).] Word-Perfect prompts

Subdoc Filename:

Enter the name of the file to be placed at that location, including the drive and/or directory in which it can be found if different from the default, such as **C:\WP51\DATA\CHAP1** or **B:\CHAP1.** A comment box is inserted in the text, such as

```
Subdoc: C:\WP51\DATA\CHAP1
```

If you reveal codes, you'll see that the box represents a Subdocument code **[Subdoc:C:\WP51\DATA\CHAP1].** This code links the master to the subdocument named CHAP1 (which is housed on the hard disk in the directory named \WP51\DATA). It acts as a placeholder for the actual text found in that file.

Continue until all subdocuments have been linked to the master. The master document may contain very little text— just a string of Subdocument codes, one on each line. You can also separate each Subdocument code with a hard page ( Ctrl  +  Enter ) so that, when printed, each subdocument will begin on a separate page. Save the file using a filename that will remind you that it is a master document. For example, name the master document BOOK or MASTER or BOOK.MAS.

When you're ready to print the document in its entirety, including all the subdocument text, you must expand the master document. (You can also expand the master before generating a table, list, or index, but you don't have to; WordPerfect will do so automatically when you generate.)

To expand the master document, retrieve it to the screen. Press the MARK TEXT ( [Alt] + [F5] ) key, select Generate (6 or G), and select Expand Master Document (3 or E). [*Pulldown menu:* Mark (M), Master Documents (M), Expand (E).] In moments, the text of the subdocuments will be incorporated into the master, each bordered by a pair of comment boxes. For instance, the boxes around Chapter 1 will appear as follows:

```
Subdoc Start: C:\WP51\DATA\CHAP1
```

Located here would be the text of Chapter 1.

```
Subdoc End: C:\WP51\DATA\CHAP1
```

If you use Reveal Codes, you will see that the boxes represent two Subdocument codes, **[Subdoc Start:C:\ WP51\DATA\CHAP1]** and **[Subdoc End:C:\WP51\ DATA\ CHAP1]**. (Should WordPerfect be unable to locate a subdocument on disk during the expansion process, Word-Perfect will prompt asking whether you wish to continue. Type **Y** to do so, even though a certain subdocument cannot be expanded, or type **N** to stop the expansion with that subdocument.)

After printing, you can again condense the master into its short form. To do so, press the MARK TEXT ([Alt] + [F5]) key, select Generate (6 or G), and select Condense Master Document (4 or O). [*Pulldown menu:* Mark (M), Master Documents (M), Condense (C).] WordPerfect has no idea whether you edited any of the text of the subdocuments while the master was expanded, and so responds with the prompt

**Save Subdocs? Yes (No)**

Type **Y** if you made any editing changes in any of the subdocuments, in which case WordPerfect will then prompt asking whether you wish to replace the version of each separate subdocument on disk with the version on screen. Type **N** if you made no changes to the subdocuments or don't wish to save any changes made. The master will then collapse into its short form. Remember to condense a master document again before resaving it on disk, so that the master takes up the least amount of disk space possible.

# SORT AND SELECT

WordPerfect offers some of the same capabilities for use in your documents as a traditional data base manager. You can rearrange text in a specific order, either alphabetically or numerically; this is referred to as a sort. Or you can isolate information that meets certain conditions, such as those names that begin with the letter "P" or those lines that contain the name "San Francisco"—this is referred to as a select. You can even sort and select at the same time;

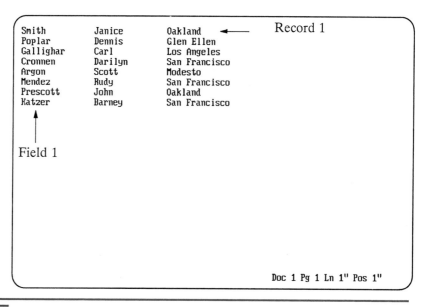

```
Smith          Janice         Oakland      ◄────    Record 1
Poplar         Dennis         Glen Ellen
Gallighar      Carl           Los Angeles
Cronnen        Darilyn        San Francisco
Argon          Scott          Modesto
Mendez         Rudy           San Francisco
Prescott       John           Oakland
Katzer         Barney         San Francisco
               ▲
               │
Field 1



                                            Doc 1 Pg 1 Ln 1" Pos 1"
```

**FIGURE 15-14**  Sample document which can be sorted by line

for instance, you could select the names of people who live in San Francisco and sort those names alphabetically.

You can sort or select text in four ways. First, you can sort or select individual lines. An example of a document appropriate for a line sort is shown in Figure 15-14. Each line is referred to as an individual record. Within records, text typed at the left margin is referred to as field 1. Text aligned on the next tab stop is referred to as field 2. (In Figure 15-14, for example, field 2 contains first names.) Text aligned on the next tab stop would be in field 3, and so on.

Besides working with lines, you can also sort or select paragraphs, such as those in Figure 15-15. Here, each record is an entire paragraph, separated by two or more Hard Return codes. Fields are again defined based on whether text is aligned on tab stops. The paragraphs in

```
        Chenin Blanc wines are white and usually range from semi-sweet
to semi-dry.

        Cabernet Sauvignon is a red grape.  The wines have a
complexity that often comes from the oak barrels in which the wine
is aged.

        Pinot Noir is light, and is often thought to lack the flavor
and elegance of other fine reds.  Winemakers have been
experimenting with this variety, and Gamay Beaujolais is one of its
clones.

        Chardonnay is a successful white wine variety.  Chardonnay
wine can be rich, full-bodied, and complex.
```

Doc 1 Pg 1 Ln 1" Pos 1"

**FIGURE 15-15**  Sample document which can be sorted by paragraph

Figure 15-15 are considered to be in field 2, since the first line of each paragraph is indented into the first tab stop. If the paragraphs had started flush against the left margin, they would have been in field 1.

You can also sort or select information in a secondary merge file. As described in Chapter 13, the end of a record in a secondary merge file is signified by an {END RECORD} or a ^E code, and fields within each record are separated by {END FIELD} or ^R codes. Figure 15-16 shows two records in a version 5.1 secondary file; each contains seven fields.

Finally, 5.1 users who created a table using the Table feature (Chapter 11) can sort rows of information in that table. Here, each record is an entire row. And, each cell in a row is considered to be a field within the record. It is best to sort a table where the cells are arranged consistently,

such as where there are the same number of cells in each
row, with approximately the same number of lines in each
cell, as in the following table:

| Friedman | Henry | $1000.50 |
| Manlikoff | Tony | $950.00 |
| Romero | Gabriela | $9040.10 |
| St. Paul | Maxwell | $245.00 |

It's a good idea to store a copy of a document on disk
before you attempt to sort or select; that way, in case you
sorted or selected in a way you disliked, or if you got

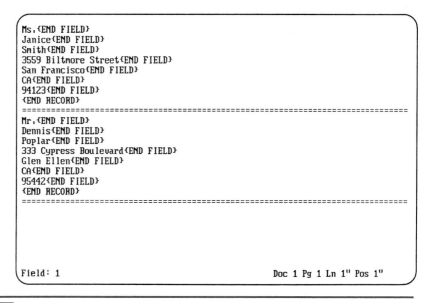

```
Ms.{END FIELD}
Janice{END FIELD}
Smith{END FIELD}
3559 Biltmore Street{END FIELD}
San Francisco{END FIELD}
CA{END FIELD}
94123{END FIELD}
{END RECORD}
=============================================================================
Mr.{END FIELD}
Dennis{END FIELD}
Poplar{END FIELD}
333 Cypress Boulevard{END FIELD}
Glen Ellen{END FIELD}
CA{END FIELD}
95442{END FIELD}
{END RECORD}
=============================================================================



Field: 1                                        Doc 1 Pg 1 Ln 1" Pos 1"
```

**FIGURE 15-16** Secondary file which can be sorted by
record

unexpected results, you would still have the original document intact on disk. Especially when you're first learning how to use the Sort command, *save a copy on disk first!*

# Sort by Line Using the Standard Defaults

If you wish to perform a sort only (without using the select function), and if you wish to sort by the first word in each line of a document, then the procedure is quick and easy. Press the MERGE/SORT ([Ctrl] + [F9]) key and select Sort (2 or S). [*Pulldown menu:* Tools (T), Sort (S).] Word-Perfect will prompt you with

```
Input file to sort: (Screen)
```

WordPerfect assumes that the file you wish to sort is the one currently on screen. Press [Enter] to verify. If the file is on disk, type the name of the file you wish to sort and then press [Enter]. Next, WordPerfect will prompt you with

```
Output file to sort: (Screen)
```

WordPerfect assumes that the results of the file should be shown on screen. Press [Enter] to accept the default, sorting to the screen. Alternatively, you can type the name of a file that the results should be sent to and then press [Enter], in which case the screen will not change after the sort; you'll have to retrieve the named file to see the results.

Next, the screen splits into two windows. The top window shows up to the first ten lines of the file you are about to sort; the bottom window shows the Sort by Line menu. Figure 15-17 shows the Sort by Line menu when Word-

Perfect is about to sort a document containing names and cities. Notice that there are seven options at the bottom of the figure.

The first option, Perform Action (1 or P), executes the sort or the select, according to the directions specified under the headings on the Sort screen. WordPerfect starts with certain assumptions about how you want the sort or the select to occur. The headings on the Sort screen indicate that if you maintained all of WordPerfect's defaults, the following will occur when you select Perform Action:

- *Key Typ Field Word*   The sort will be based on only one key (only key number 1 is defined). As you can see under this heading in Figure 15-17, the key is defined as alphanumeric ,"a," and is the first word of the first field. "Alphanumeric" means that the key will sort either

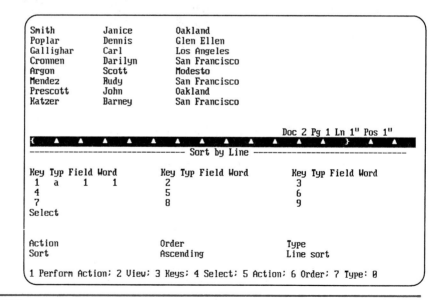

**FIGURE 15-17**   Sort by Line screen

words or numbers of equal length (such as ZIP codes).

- *Select*  No selection criteria are defined.

- *Action*  The command will sort only; no items will be selected. (Sort is the only alternative until selection criteria are defined.)

- *Order*  Text will be sorted in ascending order, which means "A" to "Z" for letters and smallest to largest for numbers.

- *Type*  The sort will occur line by line.

These settings are appropriate for sorting a document such as that shown at the top of Figure 15-17. Here's how to perform this basic sort.

1. On a clear screen, set tabs so that there are only two tab stops, at positions 2.5″ and 4.0″.

2. Type the document as shown in Figure 15-17, making sure to align first names and cities on tab stops so that they are in separate fields. For instance, type **Smith**, press Tab, type **Janice**, press Tab, type **Oakland**, and press Enter. Then continue with the other lines on this list.

3. Save this document under the name SORTTEST.

4. Press the MERGE/SORT (Ctrl + F9) key. [*Pulldown menu:* Tools (T).]

5. Select Sort (2 or S). [*Pulldown menu:* Sort (S).]

6. Press Enter twice to verify that both the input and output are to be on the screen. After a moment, the Sort menu appears, as shown in Figure 15-17.

7. Select Perform Action (1 or P). The lines in the document are rearranged by last name, from "A" to "Z."

8. If you wish, save this document again under the same filename.

Sometimes you may wish to sort or select only a portion of a document. For instance, perhaps you wish to sort a list of names on page 2 of a multipage document. In that case, first highlight the list you wish to sort, using the Block feature. Then press the MERGE/SORT (Ctrl + F9) key, and the Sort menu will appear. When you select option 1, Perform Action, WordPerfect will sort only the highlighted portion of the document.

Remember that unless you highlight a block of text before initiating a sort, WordPerfect will sort an entire document. Therefore, if you wish to sort a chart or table that contains headings, make sure to exclude the headers from the block; otherwise, the headers will become sorted as well. For instance, suppose your document contains the following:

| Last Name | First Name | City |
|-----------|------------|------|
| Smith | Janice | Oakland |
| Poplar | Dennis | Glen Ellen |
| Gallighar | Carl | Los Angeles |

If you don't block the text, excluding the line of headings, before you sort, you can get the following awkward results:

| Gallighar | Carl | Los Angeles |
|-----------|------------|------|
| **Last Name** | **First Name** | **City** |
| Poplar | Dennis | Glen Ellen |
| Smith | Janice | Oakland |

# Change the Sort Defaults for Lines, Paragraphs, and Secondary Files

What if you wish to sort the records in the document in Figure 15-14 by city name, which is field 3? Or in descending order, "Z" to "A"? What if the document you wish to sort is organized not in lines but in paragraphs, as in Figure 15-15? What if it is a secondary merge file, as in Figure 15-16? Or what if you wish to activate the Select command so that you can extract only certain information from the document? If so, you must change the defaults on the Sort menu *before* pressing option 1, Perform Action. The Sort menu's other options are described below:

- *View (2 or V)*   This option allows you to temporarily position the cursor in the top window, where the text that you wish to sort is located. You can then use the arrow keys to scroll through the document, viewing ten lines at a time, to check the document before continuing with the sort. You can view the text, but you cannot edit it. Pressing the EXIT ( F7 ) key returns the cursor to the bottom window to continue with the sort.

- *Keys (3 or K)*   This option allows you to specify what text you wish to sort or select by. You can, for example, define two keys in a sort—key 1 could be last name and key 2 could be first name. That way, if two people had the same last name, WordPerfect would perform a second-level sort for those two records by their first names. Or you can define another key to be used in a selection. For example, you could select only those people who lived in San Francisco and then sort them by last and first names. Always define the sort keys first—as key 1, key 2, and so on—and then define the select keys. You can define a maximum of nine keys.

For a line sort, you must define a key as a specific word in a specific field, and you must indicate whether that word is alphanumeric (such as a last name or a ZIP code) or numeric (such as a dollar amount). Because a record in a paragraph or a secondary merge file can contain more than one line, you must also specify that word's line for a paragraph or merge sort.

For example, suppose that for Figure 15-14 you wish to sort by first name (which is field 2) if two people have the same last name. You would define key 1 as last name, which is the default setting:

| Key | Typ | Field | Word |
|-----|-----|-------|------|
| 1 | a | 1 | 1 |

You would provide the following definition for key 2:

| Key | Typ | Field | Word |
|-----|-----|-------|------|
| 2 | a | 2 | 1 |

Or suppose that you no longer wish to sort by last name; instead, you wish to sort by city. Then you must redefine key 1:

| Key | Typ | Field | Word |
|-----|-----|-------|------|
| 1 | a | 3 | 1 |

If you were sorting paragraphs or a merge file instead of lines, WordPerfect would request not only a type, a field, and a word, but a line as well.

- *Select (4 or S)*  This option allows you to specify a selection statement. For instance, you could select only those people in the list in Figure 15-14 who resided in San Francisco. Or you could select only those paragraphs in Figure 15-15 that began with the letter "C," or only those records in a secondary merge file with a ZIP code of 94123. When you performed the action, those records that met the statement's condition would remain on screen; the other records would disappear.

A selection statement is an equation in which you include one or more keys and then indicate what criteria those keys must meet for a record to be selected. There are eight symbols you can use in the equations; they are shown in Table 15-3.

For instance, suppose you had defined key 1 as the first word of the city (as above), and wish to select only those lines in which the city is San Francisco. The selection statement you type is

```
key1=San
```

Suppose that key 2 is defined as first name. To select those lines in which the city is San Francisco and the first name is Rudy, the statement is

```
key1=San * key2=Rudy
```

| Symbol | Application |
|--------|-------------|
| = | Equal to |
| < > | Not equal to |
| > | Greater than |
| > = | Greater than or equal to |
| < | Less than |
| < = | Less than or equal to |
| + | OR (connects two key conditions together so that either condition can be true for a record to be selected) |
| * | AND (connects two key conditions together so that both must be true for a record to be selected) |

**TABLE 15-3**  Symbols Available in a Selection Statement

- *Action (5 or A)* This option specifies whether you wish to sort, select, or sort and select at the same time. If nothing is typed under the "Select" heading, then your only option is to sort. If you had entered an equation under the heading, WordPerfect assumes that you wish to sort and select. You can instead decide only to select without sorting.

- *Order (6 or O)* For a sort, this option lets you choose between ascending order (A, B, C for letters and 1, 2, 3 for numbers) or descending order (Z, Y, X for letters and 100, 99, 98 for numbers).

- *Type (7 or T)* This option specifies the type of sort you desire. WordPerfect assumes a line sort, as indicated under the heading "Type." So, for a line sort, it would be unnecessary to alter the default. But if your text were organized in paragraphs, you must change the type to a sort by paragraph; for a secondary file, you must change to a merge sort.

Once you change any of the defaults, they remain set for the entire working session or until you change them again. So each time you sort or select, make sure to check under each heading before pressing Perform Action (1 or P). And remember to save your document before you sort or select; otherwise, if you dislike the results, you'll be unable to restore the text to its previous form.

## Sort a Table [5.1 Users Only]

If you have created a table using the Table feature, then you can sort rows in the table. To sort all the rows of the table, you must display the table on screen and position the cursor on any cell inside the table. Then, press the MERGE/SORT (Ctrl + F9) key. [*Pulldown menu:* Tools (T), Sort (S).] The Sort menu appears immediately, without prompts asking for input or output files. The Sort menu automatically recognizes that the sort will be performed on a table, as is indicated by the header "Sort Table" at the top of the menu, as shown in Figure 15-18. Or, you can sort specific rows of a table by using the Block feature to highlight those rows before pressing the MERGE/SORT key.

The Sort Table menu offers the same options as the other Sort menus, except that (1) option 7, Type, cannot be altered, and (2) when specifying what key(s) you wish to sort or select by, you must define each key as a word on a certain line and in a certain cell. Lines are numbered from top to bottom, while cells and words within cells are numbered left to right.

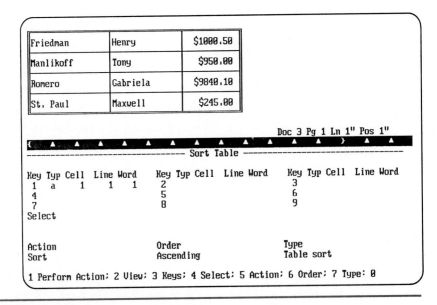

**FIGURE 15-18** Sort Table screen

# PERFORM MATHEMATICAL CALCULATIONS

With WordPerfect, you can type an invoice, calculate your yearly budget, or produce a cost estimate without running to a calculator to figure totals. WordPerfect will do the calculations for you.

There are two features that perform math calculations. First is the Math feature, where you can calculate up to 24 *math columns* on a page, where each math column is a column of numbers that are aligned on tab stops. You can calculate subtotals, totals, and grand totals in columns, and, with a bit more preparation, you can add, subtract, multiply, or divide across rows. Second is the Tables feature, available only to 5.1 users, where a variety of calculations can be performed by row or column similar to the procedure offered in spreadsheet programs such as Lotus 1-2-3 or PlanPerfect.

Both features for performing math are described below. If you are a 5.1 user, you may wish to compare the procedures involved in calculating using the Math and Tables features side by side to discover which works best for you. If you are already familiar with how spreadsheet programs operate, then you'll probably find the Tables feature easier to learn.

## Calculate Using the Math Feature's Standard Defaults

WordPerfect starts out with three basic assumptions about your use of the Math feature: that you wish to calculate only in columns, that the results of the calculations should show two digits after the decimal point, and that negative values should be displayed in parentheses. If these defaults are correct, you're almost ready to type your math columns and perform calculations.

But you must first complete two tasks. To begin, you must set tab stops for the columns you wish to create; you should be sure to set tab stops where you want the decimal points in the columns to be aligned. And, if you want the first column at the left margin to label each row, leave sufficient room for those row titles. (You cannot type your first math column at the left margin, since math columns must be aligned on tab stops.) Second, you must turn on the Math feature. Move the cursor to the line where you want the math columns to begin. *5.1 users:* Press COLUMNS/TABLES ([Alt] + [F7]), select Math (3 or M), and from the Math menu that appears, select On (1 or O). [*Pulldown menu:* Layout (L), Math (M), On (O).] *5.0 users:* Press the MATH/COLUMNS ([Alt] + [F7]) key, and select Math On (1 or M). The hidden code **[Math On]** is inserted in the document, and the message "Math" appears in the lower left corner of the screen.

Now you're ready to type your text and numbers. Each time you press [Tab] to move to the next column, WordPerfect will prompt you with

```
Align char = .Math
```

This is similar to the prompt you see when you use the TAB ALIGN ([Ctrl] + [F6]) key; it informs you that when you type a number with a decimal point, the decimal will be aligned at the tab stop. (If there is no decimal point in the number you are typing, that number will be aligned flush right on the tab stop.)

There will be some places where you will want a calculation to appear instead of a number. In those places, you type in one of the following math operators:

| Operator | Calculation | Description |
|---|---|---|
| + | Subtotal | Numbers directly above the operator in the same column are added |
| = | Total | Subtotals above the operator in the same column are added |
| * | Grand Total | Totals above the operator in the same column are added |

These math operators display on the Reveal Codes screen as [+], [=], and [*] to identify them as special codes.

When you have finished typing the math document, your screen may look like Figure 15-19, which shows columns containing a mix of text, numbers, and math operators as placeholders where the calculated numbers will appear.

After you've completed typing the math columns, you must turn off the Math feature. You should make sure that the cursor is below the last number or math operator in the columns; then repeat the process used to turn math on, this time turning it off. A **[Math Off]** code is inserted, and the message "Math" disappears from the screen.

Your last step is to perform the calculations wherever math operators are located. To do so, position the cursor anywhere within the math columns, and make sure that the "Math" prompt reappears. It will reappear whenever the cursor is between the **[Math On]** and **[Math Off]** codes.

```
┌─────────────────────────────────────────────────────────────────────╮
│ R&R WINE ASSOCIATION ── 1ST QUARTER SALES                             │
│                                                                       │
│                    Jan      Feb      Mar                              │
│ East Coast                                                            │
│                                                                       │
│    Cabernet        33.8     20.1     22.3                             │
│    Chardonnay      44.5     55.2     33.8                             │
│    Chenin Blanc    20.3     24.3     33.1                             │
│    Pinot Noir      10.5     12.8     14.2                             │
│                                                                       │
│    Subtotal         +        +        +                              │
│                                                                       │
│ West Coast                                                            │
│                                                                       │
│    Cabernet        22.9     25.4     23.3                             │
│    Chardonnay      60.5     85.2     77.9                             │
│    Chenin Blanc    22.2     18.3     36.1                             │
│    Pinot Noir       9.8      4.5      8.2                             │
│                                                                       │
│    Subtotal         +        +        +                              │
│                                                                       │
│ TOTAL               =        =        =                              │
│                                                                       │
│ Math                                   Doc 1 Pg 1 Ln 1" Pos 1"       │
╰─────────────────────────────────────────────────────────────────────╯
```

**FIGURE 15-19** Sample document containing math columns

Now return to the Math menu and select the Calculate option. In moments, you'll get results like those shown in Figure 15-20.

After you calculate, the math operators continue to display next to the calculated subtotal, total, or grand total, but they will not appear on the printed document. Leave those math operators in your document so that if you choose you can edit any number in a column and calculate again.

## Change the Default Math Feature Settings

You may wish to alter some of WordPerfect's Math feature defaults. For example, perhaps you want to have one digit after the decimal rather than two. You may want each total

```
R&R WINE ASSOCIATION -- 1ST QUARTER SALES

                    Jan       Feb       Mar
East Coast

   Cabernet        33.8      20.1      22.3
   Chardonnay      44.5      55.2      33.8
   Chenin Blanc    20.3      24.3      33.1
   Pinot Noir      10.5      12.8      14.2

   Subtotal       109.10+   112.40+   103.40+

West Coast

   Cabernet        22.9      25.4      23.3
   Chardonnay      60.5      85.2      77.9
   Chenin Blanc    22.2      10.3      36.1
   Pinot Noir       9.0       4.5       8.2

   Subtotal       114.60+   125.40+   145.50+

TOTAL             223.70=   237.80=   248.90=

Math                            Doc 1 Pg 1 Ln 1" Pos 1"
```

**FIGURE 15-20**  Math document after calculating

to appear in a column just to the right of the totaled numbers. Or you may want to calculate across rows. If that's the case, then after you reset tabs but *before* you turn on the Math feature, you must create a new math definition, which will serve to override the default math settings. *5.1 users:* Select COLUMNS/TABLES (Alt + F7), select Math (3 or M), and select Define (3 or D). [*Pulldown menu:* Layout (L), Math (M), Define (D)]. *5.0 users:* Press the MATH/COLUMNS (Alt + F7) key and select Math Def (2 or E). The Math Definition screen shown in Figure 15-21 appears.

On this screen, you can define each column separately. Your first math column is referred to as column A, the second is column B, and so on. (Remember that column A is *not* the information typed at the left margin, but the information typed at the first tab stop.) For each column, you can define the following:

- *Type* The default is 2, which, from the legend at the bottom of the screen, you can see is a numeric column. Other choices are 1, Text columns, for when you wish to fill a math column with words rather than numbers; 3, Total column, a column devoted to the calculated totals of the column to the left; and 0, Calculation columns, for when you wish to calculate across rows.

- *Negative numbers* The default is for parentheses around a calculation that results in a negative number, as in (50). Alternatively, you can select a minus sign preceding a negative number, as in −50.

- *Number of digits to the right* The default is for two digits after the decimal point; you can select from zero to four. For instance, if you wanted the results of calculations to show only one place after the decimal, you would change the setting to 1 for each column.

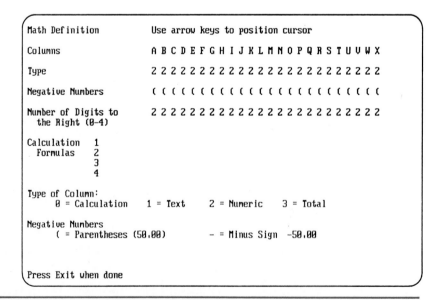

```
Math Definition          Use arrow keys to position cursor

Columns                  A B C D E F G H I J K L M N O P Q R S T U V W X

Type                     2 2 2 2 2 2 2 2 2 2 2 2 2 2 2 2 2 2 2 2 2 2 2 2

Negative Numbers         ( ( ( ( ( ( ( ( ( ( ( ( ( ( ( ( ( ( ( ( ( ( ( (

Number of Digits to      2 2 2 2 2 2 2 2 2 2 2 2 2 2 2 2 2 2 2 2 2 2 2 2
   the Right (0-4)

Calculation    1
   Formulas    2
               3
               4

Type of Column:
        0 = Calculation    1 = Text     2 = Numeric    3 = Total

Negative Numbers
        ( = Parentheses (50.00)      - = Minus Sign  -50.00


Press Exit when done
```

**FIGURE 15-21** Math Definition screen

- *Calculation formulas*  The default is for no calculations across rows. You can instead insert up to four formulas for calculations across rows, using the following symbols:

| | | | |
|---|---|---|---|
| + | addition | − | subtraction |
| * | multiplication | / | division |

In addition, there are four special formulas you can use when calculating across rows. These special formulas must be entered on their own and not as a part of a larger formula. These formulas are

| | |
|---|---|
| + | adds the numbers across all numeric columns |
| +/ | calculates the average across all numeric columns |
| = | adds the numbers across all total columns |
| =/ | calculates the average across all total columns |

To insert a formula, you must first designate a column as a Calculation column; then the cursor moves into position for you to enter a formula. For instance, suppose that you are working with four math columns and you want column D to be the average of columns A, B, and C. Assume that columns A, B, and C have all been defined as numeric columns. You must type **0** for column D at the setting "Type." The cursor will jump to the setting "Calculation Formulas," where you will type **+/** and press [Enter].

When you exit the Math Definition screen and return to the Typing screen, WordPerfect will insert a **[Math Def]** code. All math columns typed below that code will be affected by that Math Definition code. The Math/Columns menu will remain on screen; you would select Math On (1 or 0 for 5.1 users, 1 or M for 5.0 users). You would then be ready to type the math columns. You should proceed as usual; that is, press [Tab] to move from column to column. Type in a number or insert math operators (+, =, or *) where you want the calculated subtotals, totals, or grand totals to appear. If you had defined a total column, you should be sure to insert the math operators in that total column and not in the numeric columns. Whenever you press [Tab] to move to a column defined as a calculation column, an exclamation point (!) will appear. You should leave that operator wherever you desire calculations, but erase the exclamation point where you don't want a calculation to appear. Like the other math operators, the exclamation point does not appear on the printed page. (The exclamation point on the keyboard is not considered a math operator; If you attempt to enter an exclamation point from the keyboard, your formulas will not calculate correctly. You insert the math operator that resembles an exclamation point only by pressing the [Tab] key to position the cursor in a math column defined for a formula.)

As an example in defining math columns, assume that you have set tab stops for five math columns. You want column B to contain subtotals and totals of the numbers in column A. Column D will contain subtotals and totals of the numbers in column C. Column E, the last column, will contain a formula that subtracts the number in column D from the number in column B. All calculations will be displayed with one digit to the right of the decimal place, and negative calculations will also be displayed in parentheses. Here's how the first five columns would be defined on the Math Definition:

| Columns | | | A | B | C | D | E |
|---|---|---|---|---|---|---|---|
| Type | | | 2 | 3 | 2 | 3 | 0 |
| Negative Numbers | | | ( | ( | ( | ( | ( |
| Number of Digits | | | 1 | 1 | 1 | 1 | 1 |
| Calculation | 1 | E | B-D | | | | |
| Formulas | 2 | | | | | | |
| | 3 | | | | | | |
| | 4 | | | | | | |

Then, after typing the math columns, you could get results as shown in Figure 15-22. Your last step would be to position the cursor within the math columns, return to the Math menu, and select the Calculate option.

## Calculate in a Table [5.1 Users Only]

If you have created a table using the Table feature (as described in Chapter 11), then you can perform a variety of mathematical calculations within that table. While similar to the Math feature, the Table feature allows more flexibility because it allows you to reference specific cells when adding rows, or columns, or creating formulas.

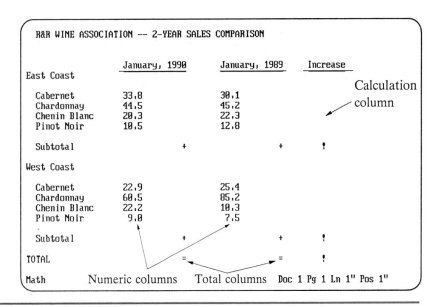

FIGURE 15-22 Math document with columns defined

To calculate, you must display the table on screen and position the cursor on any cell inside the table. Then, press the COLUMNS/TABLES ([Alt] + [F7]) key to display the Table Edit menu. [*Pulldown menu:* Select Layout (L), Tables (T), Edit (E).] Now, press Math (5 or M) to display the Math menu, as shown at the bottom of Figure 15-23. You have six options for performing calculations.

- *Calculate (1 or C)* Recalculates all subtotals, totals, grand totals, or formulas that were entered in the table. Make sure to select this option if you make changes to any cells that may affect an already-calculated result.

- *Formula (2 or F)* Enters a math formula in the cell where the cursor is located; thus, position the cursor

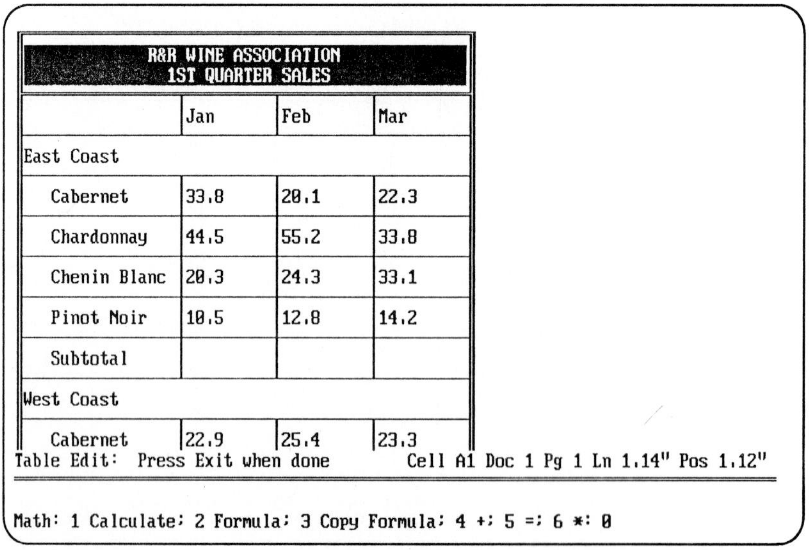

| | Jan | Feb | Mar |
|---|---|---|---|
| **R&R WINE ASSOCIATION** | | | |
| **1ST QUARTER SALES** | | | |
| East Coast | | | |
| Cabernet | 33.8 | 20.1 | 22.3 |
| Chardonnay | 44.5 | 55.2 | 33.8 |
| Chenin Blanc | 20.3 | 24.3 | 33.1 |
| Pinot Noir | 10.5 | 12.8 | 14.2 |
| Subtotal | | | |
| West Coast | | | |
| Cabernet | 22.9 | 25.4 | 23.3 |

Table Edit: Press Exit when done          Cell A1 Doc 1 Pg 1 Ln 1.14" Pos 1.12"

Math: 1 Calculate; 2 Formula; 3 Copy Formula; 4 +; 5 =; 6 *: 0

**FIGURE 15-23** Table Math menu

before selecting this option. Then select this option and type in formulas, where you use the same symbols as in the Math feature:

+   addition          −   subtraction
*   multiplication    /   division

A formula can contain numbers and/or reference specific cells, and WordPerfect will calculate the results from left to right. For instance, the formula A1*B1/2 multiplies the number in cell A1 by the number in cell B1 and then divides the result by 2. The result of the calculation will display in the cell as soon as you press ⟨Enter⟩ to enter the formula into a cell; in addition, when the cursor is highlighting that cell, the actual formula will display in the lower left corner of the screen.

- *Copy Formula (3 or P)*   Copies a formula from one cell to another cell, to a group of cells below, or to a group of cells to the right. Position the cursor in the cell containing the formula before selecting this option. After selecting this option, WordPerfect prompts you for an indication of where to copy this formula to. You can select Cell from the menu, move to the cell where you want to copy the formula, and press ⟨Enter⟩. Or, select Down or Right from this menu, and then indicate how many times this formula should be copied. The formula is copied relative to the cell where it is copied to; as an example, if you copy the formula A1+A2 one cell to the right, the formula in the new cell will be B1+B2; the calculation displays as soon as the copy is complete.

- *4 or +, 5 or =, 6 or ***   Inserts a math operator into the cell. These are the same operators as used in the Math feature:

| Operator | Calculation | Description |
|----------|-------------|-------------|
| + | Subtotal | Numbers directly above the operator in the same column are added |
| = | Total | Subtotals above the operator in the same column are added |
| * | Grand Total | Totals above the operator in the same column are added |

(However, unlike in the Math feature, do not insert a plus, equal sign, or asterisk in a table from the keyboard. WordPerfect will not treat these symbols as math operators.) The calculation displays as soon as you enter a math operator into a cell.

# TRANSFER BETWEEN SOFTWARE PROGRAMS

WordPerfect interacts easily with other software packages. First, both versions 5.1 and 5.0 are equipped with a feature so that files created in either version can be used with one another or earlier WordPerfect versions. Second, Word-Perfect comes packaged with a utility program named CONVERT.EXE, which can transform files between other popular word processing packages (such as WordStar and

MultiMate), spreadsheet packages (such as Lotus 1-2-3), or database managers (such as dBASE), and WordPerfect. Third, 5.1 users have access to the Spreadsheet Import and Link features, which can retrieve a spreadsheet created in PlanPerfect, Lotus 1-2-3, or Excel into a WordPerfect document directly. Finally, WordPerfect can work with text files written in ASCII, which is like a universal language; in that way, ASCII (DOS) text files can be used as the intermediary between WordPerfect and virtually any product not supported by the Convert utility.

## Switch Between WordPerfect Versions 5.1, 5.0, and 4.2

No special process is required if you have upgraded. For those of you who now use version 5.1, you can work with all documents created with version 5.0 or 4.2; simply load version 5.1, retrieve any document, edit the document as usual, and save it as usual. The document is saved into version 5.1 format. Similarly, version 5.0 users can work with 4.2. Be aware, however, that you may have to manually edit certain Format codes so that they operate properly in version 5.0.

Conversely, WordPerfect offers a feature when you wish to downgrade — to save a document for use with an earlier version of WordPerfect. This is useful, for example, if you use version 5.1, but the person across town who will be editing your documents uses version 5.0. In that case, you must store your documents in the earlier format for that other person. Or, perhaps some departments in your company have yet to upgrade to the newer WordPerfect version.

*5.1 users:* With your document on screen, press the TEXT IN/OUT ([Ctrl] + [F5]) key and select Save As (3 or A). [*Pulldown menu:* File (F), Text Out (O).] Then, select to save that text either in version 5.0 or version 4.2 format. A prompt will appear requesting a filename. Type a filename and press [Enter] to store the file on disk in an earlier version format. It is a good idea to type in a new filename when saving a file in an earlier format; you will thus maintain one copy of the file in version 5.1 format when you follow the normal saving procedures, and a separate copy in another format when you use the TEXT IN/OUT ([Ctrl] + [F5]) key.

*5.0 users:* With your document on screen, press the TEXT IN/OUT ([Ctrl] + [F5]) key and select Save WP 4.2 (4 or W). A prompt will appear requesting a filename. Type a filename and press [Enter] to store the file on disk in version 4.2 format. It is a good idea to type in a new filename when saving a file in version 4.2 format; you will thus maintain one copy of the file in version 5.0 format when you follow the normal saving procedures, and a separate copy in version 4.2 format when you use the TEXT IN/OUT ([Ctrl] + [F5]) key.

## Use the Convert Program

A program named CONVERT.EXE transforms files from certain other formats into WordPerfect, and vice versa. Files that contain documents (such as letters written using WordStar) can be transferred into WordPerfect's document file format, while those containing records (such as lists of names and addresses entered in dBASE) can be transferred into WordPerfect's secondary file format so that they can be used in a merge operation. In addition, Convert also changes WordPerfect files into other formats.

The following document files can be transferred to or from WordPerfect with Convert:

- WordStar

- MultiMate

- The earlier version of WordPerfect

- Files that are in Revisable-Form-Text or Final-Form-Text, such as IBM word processing packages on IBM mainframes and microcomputers (DisplayWrite, Display-Write 3, and DisplayWrite 4 enable you to transfer files into this format)

- Files that are in Navy DIF format

The following can be transferred into WordPerfect secondary merge files:

- Mail merge files (created using WordStar or dBASE, among others)

- Spreadsheet DIF files (Lotus 1-2-3 files can be transferred into this format to work with Convert)

You can also convert a WordPerfect secondary merge file into spreadsheet DIF format so that it can be used with Lotus 1-2-3. Fields become cells and records become rows. Further, version 5.1 users can convert files from Microsoft Word 4.0 into WordPerfect.

Finally, the Convert program can change a file from 8-bit to 7-bit format and vice versa to aid you in sending WordPerfect documents electronically via a modem.

If you have a document on disk in one of the formats mentioned above and you wish to convert it into Word-Perfect format, or if you want to convert a WordPerfect document to one of these formats, then start at the DOS prompt. If you have already loaded WordPerfect, you must exit WordPerfect. *Floppy disk users:* If you use version 5.1, place the Install/Utility disk that you created when you installed WordPerfect into drive A; 5.0 users should place the Conversion disk in drive A. Then, type **A:CONVERT** and press Enter. *Hard disk users:* You previously should have installed the Convert program, along with other utilities, on the hard disk. Switch to the directory where CONVERT.EXE is stored. For instance, type **CD \WP51** and press Enter. Then, type **CONVERT** and press Enter.

After the Convert program has been loaded, Word-Perfect will first ask for an input filename. This is the name of the file you wish to convert. Type the filename, including the drive or directory where it is found (for example, **B:DOC**, or **C:\WP51\DATA\DOC**) and press Enter. Next, WordPerfect will ask for the name of the output file; this is the file where the converted document should be stored— the name must be different from that of the input file. Type in a name and press Enter; now the menu shown in Figure 15-24 will appear (assuming that the input file is B:DOC and the output file is B:DOC.2). From here, select any menu option from 2 through B to convert from another format into WordPerfect. Or, select option 1 in order to convert a WordPerfect file into another format; a second menu, as shown in Figure 15-25, will appear for you to make another selection. Enter the number of the type of conversion you desire, and then respond to Word-Perfect's prompts or press the CANCEL (F1) key to abort the conversion.

```
Name of Input File? B:DOC
Name of Output File? B:DOC.2


0 EXIT
1 WordPerfect to another format
2 Revisable-Form-Text (IBM DCA Format) to WordPerfect
3 Final-Form-Text (IBM DCA Format) to WordPerfect
4 Navy DIF Standard to WordPerfect
5 WordStar 3.3 to WordPerfect
6 MultiMate Advantage II to WordPerfect
7 Seven-Bit Transfer Format to WordPerfect
8 WordPerfect 4.2 to WordPerfect 5.1
9 Mail Merge to WordPerfect Secondary Merge
A Spreadsheet DIF to WordPerfect Secondary Merge
B Word 4.0 to WordPerfect

Enter number of Conversion desired
```

**FIGURE 15-24** First menu from the Convert utility

```
Name of Input File? B:DOC
Name of Output File? B:DOC.2


0 EXIT
1 Revisable-Form-Text (IBM DCA Format)
2 Final-Form-Text (IBM DCA Format)
3 Navy DIF Standard
4 WordStar 3.3
5 MultiMate Advantage II
6 Seven-Bit Transfer Format
7 ASCII Text File
8 WordPerfect Secondary Merge to Spreadsheet DIF

Enter number of output file format desired
```

**FIGURE 15-25** Second menu from the Convert utility which converts a WordPerfect file to another format

If you converted a file into WordPerfect format, you are now ready to load WordPerfect and retrieve the output document (such as DOC.2). If you converted to another software package, you can load that other package and retrieve the output document. Be aware that certain sophisticated formatting features won't translate correctly; you will want to reformat the document. For instance, if the document you converted had been typed in columns, the conversion in columns may not work properly, and you may have to reformat the document in columns manually.

# Import and Link Spreadsheets [5.1 Users Only]

You may use a spreadsheet program such as PlanPerfect or Lotus 1-2-3, which provides sophisticated mathematical abilities, to calculate numeric information. However, when you're ready to produce a document showing your number-crunching results, those programs don't offer the sophisticated word processing capabilities of WordPerfect. With WordPerfect's Spreadsheet Import and Spreadsheet Link features, you can calculate in a spreadsheet, and then bring the completed results into WordPerfect to produce a final report.

The Spreadsheet Import and Link features are quite different. When you *import* the spreadsheet into a Word-Perfect document, you are actually retrieving it into the document—either as text (20 columns maximum) or as a table, just as if you created it using the Tables feature (32 columns maximum). The import is a one-time retrieval. Conversely, when you *link* the spreadsheet to a Word-Perfect document, you create a bond between those two files; every time that you alter the spreadsheet, you can update the data in your WordPerfect document as well.

You can use these two features with PlanPerfect version 3.0 to 5.0, Lotus 1-2-3 version 1.0 through 2.2, and Micro-soft Excel versions 2.x. In addition, the features can be used with Lotus 1-2-3 version 3.0 files that have been translated from .WK3 format to .WK1 format.

Make sure the WordPerfect document into which you wish to import or link a spreadsheet is on screen. Next, position the cursor where the spreadsheet will be retrieved, press TEXT IN/OUT (Ctrl + F5), and select Spread-sheet (5 or S). [*Pulldown menu:* File (F), Text In (I), Spreadsheet (P).] The following menu appears:

Spreadsheet: **1** Import; **2** Create Link; **3** Edit Link; **4** Link Options: **0**

Select option 1 or 2, the Import or Create Link option. WordPerfect will display a menu where you can

- Specify the name of the spreadsheet file you wish to retrieve.

- Indicate the range within the spreadsheet file you wish to retrieve. WordPerfect assumes you wish to import or link the entire spreadsheet, but you can instead specify a range. A range is entered by typing the upper-left and lower-right cells of the range, separated by a colon, such as A1:H58, or by using the LIST (F5) key to list the named ranges in the spreadsheet and then selecting a range.

- Specify the type of retrieval, either as a table or as text formatted into tabular columns.

- Perform the import or the link. When WordPerfect imports a spreadsheet file, it retrieves the spreadsheet and attempts to preserve the file's appearance; you may find, however, that you need to edit the table or text. When WordPerfect links a spreadsheet, the spreadsheet is retrieved and enclosed around two codes showing where the link begins and ends. These two codes display comments that indicate the name of the linked spreadsheet file and the range (if specified), such as the following:

```
Link:    C:\LOTUS\EXPENS98.WK1
```

Located here would be the contents of the spreadsheet.

```
Link End
```

Option 3, Edit Link, enables you to edit any of your specifications. Option 4, Link Options, is used to update your links, since the updating is not done automatically, or to hide the display of comments that surround the linked spreadsheet in the WordPerfect document.

## Transfer Files Using DOS (ASCII) Text Files

Another way that WordPerfect interacts with other software packages is by importing a DOS (ASCII) text file into WordPerfect or by exporting a WordPerfect file into a DOS (ASCII) text file. DOS text files are written using only those ASCII (American Standard Code for Information Interchange) codes that most software programs can understand. These files contain straight text, spaces, and little else—they are stripped down, containing no special formatting codes for underlining, boldface, margin changes, and the like. Thus, they are often used as the intermediary between different computer programs. This is a way to work in WordPerfect with files created by software packages not supported by the Convert program or by the Spreadsheet Import and Link feature in WordPerfect.

To import (retrieve) a DOS text file into WordPerfect, you must clear the WordPerfect Typing screen, press the TEXT IN/OUT ( Ctrl + F5 ) key, and select Dos Text (1 or T). [*Pulldown menu:* File (F), Text In (I).] The following Dos Text menu appears:

```
1 Save; 2 Retrieve (CR/LF to [HRt]; 3 Retrieve (CR/LF to [SRt]
in HZone): 0
```

Select option 2 to retrieve the text file and have each line end with a Hard Return code; this is appropriate when retrieving files that you do not want to wordwrap. Select option 3 to retrieve the text file and have each line that ends within the Hyphenation Zone end with a soft return; this is appropriate when retrieving files that you wish to then reformat within WordPerfect. Lines within paragraphs will end with **[SRt]** codes rather than with **[HRt]** codes so that paragraphs will readjust when you edit the text.

There's another option for importing, as well—this one is found on the List Files screen. When viewing a list of files after pressing the LIST ( F5 ) key, position the cursor on the DOS text file. *5.1 users:* Select Retrieve (1 or R). *5.0 users:* Select Text In (5 or T). A hard return is inserted at the end of each line—identical to selecting option 2 on the Dos Text menu.

To export a WordPerfect document into ASCII format, you must make sure that the document is on screen. Then press the TEXT IN/OUT (⌨Ctrl⌨ + ⌨F5⌨) key, select Dos Text (1 or T), and select Save (1 or S). [*Pulldown menu:* File (F), Text Out (O), Dos Text (T).] You must then type in a filename, and press ⌨Enter⌨; type in a new filename so that you can preserve the original copy of your file in WordPerfect format. WordPerfect will save that file on disk, stripping it of all special formatting so that the file could be used with another software package.

As an alternative for exporting, you can save text into Generic format. This is most appropriate when you plan to use the text in another word processing program. More of the special formatting will be preserved. For instance, text that had been centered will remain so because spaces will be inserted around the centered text. Tabs will be maintained. Also, soft returns are converted into spaces. *5.1 users:* With your document on screen, press the TEXT IN/OUT (⌨Ctrl⌨ + ⌨F5⌨) key, select Save As (3 or A), and choose Generic (1 or G). [*Pulldown menu:* File (F), Text Out (O), Generic (G).] *5.0 users:* With your document on screen, press the TEXT IN/OUT (⌨Ctrl⌨ + ⌨F5⌨) key and select Save Generic (3 or G). At the prompt, enter a filename.

WordPerfect's ability to import and export DOS text files is convenient for those of you who create DOS batch files. For instance, Appendix A describes how you can create a batch file in DOS to aid you in loading WordPerfect. You can work instead with a batch file from within WordPerfect. For example, suppose you wish to revise the batch file named AUTOEXEC.BAT. You could use the TEXT IN/OUT (⌨Ctrl⌨ + ⌨F5⌨) key to retrieve that file (selecting option 2 on the Dos Text menu so that each line ends with a hard return) and then edit it using Word-

Perfect's standard editing features. After editing, you would use the TEXT IN/OUT (Ctrl + F5) key to save the batch file again in DOS text format. Those of you who have attempted to edit batch files by rewriting them from scratch or by using EDLIN, DOS's own editor, will find the TEXT IN/OUT (Ctrl + F5) key a convenient alternative.

## Quick Review

- Depending on the capabilities of your printer, you can produce documents that contain special characters used in mathematical, legal, foreign, or technical text. The Compose feature, accessed by pressing `Ctrl` + `V` or `Ctrl` + `2`, allows you to insert special characters with just a few keystrokes. In addition, the Overstrike feature on the Other Format menu lets you type two or more characters in the same location.

- WordPerfect allows you to change the layout of the keyboard, so that you can tailor the keyboard to your special needs. Using the Keyboard Layout feature, you can, for instance, redefine the keyboard so that the key combination `Ctrl` + `S` produces the section symbol (§) and the key combination `Shift` + `F12` executes a print macro. The Keyboard Layout feature is accessed through the SETUP (`Shift` + `F1`) key.

- 5.1 users can easily create mathematical and scientific equations for inclusion in their documents. Use the GRAPHICS (`Alt` + `F9`) key to create an Equation graphics box, and then rely on WordPerfect's Equation Editor to develop an equation.

- You can take further advantage of WordPerfect's graphics abilities introduced in Chapter 10. The GRAB.COM program lets you incorporate graphics images into your documents from programs not directly compatible with WordPerfect. Moreover, the Line Draw feature, accessed via the SCREEN (⌨Ctrl + ⌨F3) key, lets you draw lines and boxes on screen with sharp corners to create organizational charts or graphs. You create horizontal and vertical lines using the arrow keys as your "paintbrush."

- WordPerfect can aid in the production of a long document, such as a book, thesis, annual report, or legal brief. The Cross-Reference feature allows you to create and update references in a document, such as "See Footnote 2, page 44." The Master Document feature helps you work more easily with lengthy documents by creating a small file consisting of subdocuments and text. The Generate Tables, Lists, and Indexes feature automatically generates reference aids, including tables of contents, tables of authorities, lists, and indexes. These features are all accessed via the MARK TEXT (⌨Alt + ⌨F5) key.

- WordPerfect has some data base management capabilities. The Sort feature can sort text in alphabetical or numerical order, whether that text is a list organized by line, a group of paragraphs, a secondary file used in a merge, or a version 5.1 table. And it can select specific text, such as all names that begin with the letter "B" or all records in a secondary file with the ZIP code 90046.

- With the Math feature, you can add or subtract numbers in a column. And you can calculate across a row based on a formula. In addition, 5.1 users can create and calculate formulas in a table.

- You can transfer files between different versions of WordPerfect or between another software package and WordPerfect. The CONVERT.EXE program allows you to take files from certain other programs, such as WordStar, and convert them to WordPerfect format so that you could use WordPerfect for all your word processing needs. Using the TEXT IN/OUT ( Ctrl + F5 ) key, you can transfer files to and from standard ASCII format, a universal set of computer symbols. And 5.1 users can import spreadsheet files directly into a WordPerfect document.

# APPENDIXES

Installing WordPerfect for Your Computer and Printer
Customizing WordPerfect with the Setup Menu
Using a Mouse in WordPerfect [5.1 Users Only]
Listing WordPerfect Files and Codes
Getting Additional Support

appendix A

# INSTALLING WORDPERFECT FOR YOUR COMPUTER AND PRINTER

Before Installation
Install WordPerfect
Create a Batch File
Startup (Slash) Options

**B**efore you can use the WordPerfect program, you must take the master disks that come inside the Word-Perfect package and prepare them to operate on your computer equipment, a process referred to as installation. WordPerfect 5.1 comes on 11 master disks: Program 1, Program 2, Spell/Thesaurus 1, Spell/Thesaurus 2, Install/Learn/Utility 1, Install/Learn/Utility 2, PTR Program//Graphics 1, PTR Program/Graphics 2, Printer 1, Printer 2, and Printer 3. The WordPerfect files on these master disks are compressed to fit on just the 11 disks.

WordPerfect 5.0 comes on 12 master disks: WordPerfect 1, WordPerfect 2, Speller, Thesaurus, Learning, PTR Program, Conversion, Fonts/Graphics, Printer 1, Printer 2, Printer 3, and Printer 4. The version 5.0 files are not compressed.

Installation is the first thing you should do after you purchase WordPerfect and remove the master disks from the package. You install WordPerfect to work with both your computer and your printer.

This appendix describes how to start the computer and then install WordPerfect for use on your computer and printer. The process is different depending on whether you are installing version 5.1 or version 5.0, and also depending on whether you are installing on a hard disk or on floppy disks. Thus, the procedure described below is, at times, discussed separately for the different versions or computer systems. You'll also learn about writing a batch file to speed the process of starting up WordPerfect for every working session—a real timesaver if you use WordPerfect every day. And, at the end of the chapter, you will also learn about special options for starting up WordPerfect.

After you've installed WordPerfect as described in this appendix, you'll be ready to turn to "Getting Started" at the beginning of this book for a basic lesson on starting up and using WordPerfect with your computer equipment. Then begin with Chapter 1, where you'll create your first WordPerfect documents.

# BEFORE INSTALLATION

Before installing WordPerfect, you must boot up your computer, which means that you turn it on and start up the

Disk Operating System (DOS) — the program that is essential to the operation of your computer. Floppy disk users must also format disks in preparation for installing Word-Perfect. These procedures are described below.

## Boot Up Your Computer

DOS is stored on your hard disk or, if you use a floppy disk system, on your DOS or boot disk. To boot up your computer, perform the following steps:

1. *Hard disk users:* Turn on the computer. *Floppy disk users:* Place your boot disk or your DOS disk into drive A and turn on your computer. Depending on your equipment, you may have to turn on your monitor separately. Now wait for a minute or so — the computer takes a bit of time to start up.

2. For some of you, the computer responds with a request for the current date; type it in. For example, if today's date is December 9, 1990, type **12-09-90**.

3. If you typed in the date, press the ⌜Enter⌝ key.

4. For some of you, the computer responds with a request for the current time; type it in. The computer works on a 24-hour clock, so if the time is 4:30 P.M., type **16:30**.

5. If you typed in the time, press the ⌜Enter⌝ key.

Hard disk users should now see on screen an uppercase "C" followed by a "greater than" symbol: C>. (Some of you may instead see a prompt such as C:\>.) Floppy disk users should see A>on screen. This is referred to as the

DOS prompt, indicating that DOS is loaded and waiting for your instructions. The "C" means that the computer believes that the instructions will involve drive C, the hard disk, while the "A" refers to drive A.

## Prepare Disks

Hard disk users are ready to run the WordPerfect Installation program as long as you have available 2.5 MB (megabytes) to 4 MB of disk space on your hard disk. (The amount of disk space required varies based on the number of WordPerfect files you choose to install.) You can then skip to the next section.

Floppy disk users have one additional step, which is to format blank disks so that you are ready to store an installed copy of the WordPerfect program. *5.1 users:* Assuming that your floppy disks each hold 720K (kilobytes) of information, you will need to format at least 11 disks—ten to copy the WordPerfect program and one disk as your first data disk, a disk that will store the first documents you create using WordPerfect. (WordPerfect 5.1 cannot run on a floppy disk system with 360K disk drives; you must have a system with disk drives with greater capacity, such as 720K or 1.2 MB, to run WordPerfect 5.1.) *5.0 users:* You will need to format one blank disk for each disk in the Word-Perfect package, in addition to two extra disks—one that will store WordPerfect's help files and one that you can use as your first data disk, to store the first documents you create using WordPerfect.

To format a disk, your DOS disk should be in drive A. If the DOS prompt does not read A>, type **a:** and press [Enter]. Next, type **format b:** and press [Enter]. WordPerfect will prompt asking you to place a blank disk in drive B;

after doing so, press ⟨Enter⟩ again to format the disk. Once the disk is formatted, you will be asked whether you wish to format another. Type **Y** and then insert a new blank disk in drive B and press ⟨Enter⟩ to repeat this procedure for another blank disk. Or, type **N** to stop formatting additional disks.

You should also format one disk specially, so that whenever you wish to start WordPerfect from a floppy disk, you can boot DOS and WordPerfect from the same disk (which is convenient unless your computer requires a special boot disk). To do so, format one disk by typing **format b:/s** and pressing ⟨Enter⟩. The "/s" that you type directs the computer to place part of DOS on the disk in drive B after the disk is formatted.

After you've formatted the disks, you should label your newly created disks. *5.1 users:* Label the disks as follows: WordPerfect 1, WordPerfect 2, Install/Utility, Learning/Images, Macros/Keyboards, Speller, Thesaurus, PTR Program, Fonts/Graphics, Printer (.ALL) files, Data disk. *5.0 users:* Label the WordPerfect program disks just like the master disks, and then label the remaining two as the Help disk and the Data disk. For both 5.1 and 5.0 users, if you formatted one disk specially with the "/s" so that DOS and WordPerfect can be loaded from the same disk, that disk must be the one that you label as the WordPerfect 1 disk.

Be extra cautious whenever you format disks. When you format a disk, any information previously stored on that disk is wiped out. Therefore, be *sure* to format only brand new, blank disks, or those that don't have anything stored on them that you wish to preserve. Also, be sure that you never type simply "format," but that, instead, you *always*, indicate a specific disk drive after typing "format" — such as typing **format b:** (or **format a:** if the disk you wish to format is in drive A). If not, you could accidentally format the disk in another disk drive, and, for example, wipe out all the

DOS program files if the DOS disk were in drive A (or erase the entire hard disk if you're a hard disk user)!

# INSTALL WORDPERFECT

To install WordPerfect on your computer, you must copy the WordPerfect program files, which are housed on the WordPerfect master disks. Hard disk users will copy the WordPerfect program files onto the hard disk. Floppy disk users will copy the WordPerfect program files onto blank, formatted disks. Then the master disks should be stored in a safe place, available in the event that a mechanical error causes your copy of the WordPerfect program to malfunction, or in case you later decide to install additional files. You need to install the program for your computer only once; you or anyone who uses your computer will then be ready to use WordPerfect thereafter. If you have any installation problems, be sure to call WordPerfect Corporation at (800) 533-9605 for more assistance.

## Install Version 5.1 on Hard or Floppy Disk Systems

5.1 users should run the WordPerfect Installation program as follows:

1. Insert the Install/Learn/Utility 1 disk that came with the WordPerfect program into drive A.

2. Type **a:** and press [Enter]. Now the DOS prompt reads A> or A:\>.

3. Type **install** and press [Enter].

4. When WordPerfect asks whether you wish to continue, type **Y**.

5. When WordPerfect asks whether you wish to install on a hard disk, type **Y** if you are using a hard disk system, or type **N** if you are using a floppy disk system.

The menu shown in Figure A-1 will appear, listing various choices for installing, updating, or copying WordPerfect files. Select one of these options to get your computer and printer ready to work with WordPerfect. Each is described below.

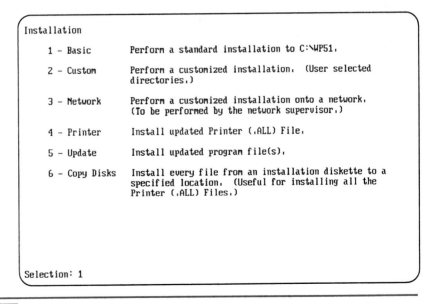

```
Installation

    1 - Basic        Perform a standard installation to C:\WP51.

    2 - Custom       Perform a customized installation.  (User selected
                     directories.)

    3 - Network      Perform a customized installation onto a network.
                     (To be performed by the network supervisor.)

    4 - Printer      Install updated Printer (.ALL) File.

    5 - Update       Install updated program file(s).

    6 - Copy Disks   Install every file from an installation diskette to a
                     specified location.  (Useful for installing all the
                     Printer (.ALL) Files.)




Selection: 1
```

**FIGURE A-1**  Installation main menu (version 5.1)

**BASIC**     This option automates the procedure of installing WordPerfect and is the appropriate choice if you are
new to computers or you wish to perform the simplest
installation. For hard disk users it assumes that you wish to
copy all the program files from the floppy disk (drive A)
into a directory that it will create with the name C:\WP51,
and also copy all the learning files (used with the Word-
Perfect tutorial, as discussed in Appendix E) into a
directory that it will create named C:\WP51\LEARN. For
floppy disk users it assumes that you wish to copy all the
program files from drive A to blank, formatted disks in
drive B. It directs you with prompts to copy the disks.
(Look to Appendix D if you wish to see a list of the
WordPerfect files that are copied from each of the master
disks and to determine whether you need to copy every
disk.)

Next the Installation program checks to make sure that
a file named CONFIG.SYS—either on your hard disk or, if
you're a floppy disk user, on your WordPerfect 1 floppy
disk—contains a FILES = 20 command. The Installation
program also checks that a file named AUTOEXEC.BAT
contains a PATH command so that, for hard disk users, the
computer will know where to find the WordPerfect program files on the hard disk. If the Installation program
needs to create or alter either of these two files, it will ask
your permission first and then will prompt you to reboot
your computer. To do so, hard disk users should remove
any disks from drive A, while floppy disk users should place
the DOS (or boot) disk into drive A. Then, press Ctrl +
Alt + Del, which means to hold down the Ctrl and the
Alt key with your left hand, and then press the Del key
once with your right hand, and follow the procedures described above to once again load the Installation
program. You will be returned to the point in the

```
 1  Acer LP-76                          Printers marked with '*' are
 2  AEG Olympia Compact RO              not included with shipping
 3  AEG Olympia ESW 2000               disks.  Select printer for
 4  AEG Olympia Laserstar 6            more information.
 5  AEG Olympia Startype
 6  Alphacom Alphapro 101
 7  Alps Allegro 24
 8 *Alps Allegro 24 (Additional)
 9  Alps ALQ200 (18 pin)
10  Alps ALQ200 (24 pin)
11  Alps ALQ224e
12 *Alps ALQ224e (Additional)
13  Alps ALQ300 (18 pin)
14  Alps ALQ300 (24 pin)
15  Alps ALQ324e
16 *Alps ALQ324e (Additional)
17  Alps P2000
18 *Alps P2000 (Additional)
19  Alps P2100
20 *Alps P2100 (Additional)
21  Alps P2400C
22  Amstrad DMP 4000

N Name Search; PgDn More Printers; PgUp Previous Screen; F3 Help; F7 Exit;
Selection: 0
```

**FIGURE A-2**  Partial list of printers displayed during installation (version 5.1)

installation procedure where you stopped to reboot the computer.

As a last task, WordPerfect prompts you to insert the Printer 1 disk into drive A to help you install one or more printers. A screen such as shown in Figure A-2 appears, listing various printers. You must now search for your printer on this list. To do so, you can press `PgUp` or `PgDn` to move up or down screen by screen. Or, use the Name Search option; type **N**, type in the first few letters of your brand of printer, and then press `Enter` when your printer appears on screen. If the printer name is preceded by an asterisk or is not on the list, then you cannot install your printer unless there is one on the list that is close enough to yours. Or order a disk with your printer on it by calling (800) 222-9409 or write to

SoftCopy, Inc.
c/o Printer Drivers
81 N. State Street
Orem, UT 84057

Once you find your printer on the list, type in the number next to your printer and press Enter. WordPerfect then copies a file with the extension .ALL, such as a file named WPHP1.ALL or WPDM6.ALL, to the hard disk or onto a floppy disk. This file contains a definition for a variety of printers, including the printer you selected. You can then select additional printers.

After you have selected one or more printers, the Installation program starts up WordPerfect, and, if this is the first time you are starting up WordPerfect, asks you to enter your license number. (This is the registration number for your copy of WordPerfect; if you enter a number, it will be accessible to you whenever you use the Help feature, which is described in the "Getting Started" chapter. Type in your license number and press Enter, or simply press Enter if you do not wish to input your license number.) Now, WordPerfect displays help screens for the printer(s) you selected, and, at the same time, creates files with the extension .PRS, one for each printer you selected. For instance, the file created for the HP LaserJet Series II printer is HPLASEII.PRS. This is the printer definition that will be used whenever you print out a document using the HP LaserJet.

Once printers are installed and you begin printing out documents in WordPerfect, you may discover that it is necessary to edit a printer definition you created; Chapter 9 discusses this procedure.

**CUSTOM**    This option allows you to customize the procedure of installing WordPerfect. The Custom Installation menu is shown in Figure A-3. It is the appropriate choice if you are interested in segregating the WordPerfect files into specific, previously created directories on your hard disk. For instance, you can copy the graphics files to C:\WP51\GRAPHS, copy the keyboard/macro files to C:\WP51\KEYMACS, and copy all the other WordPerfect program files to C:\WP51. (See Appendix D for a list of the different types of WordPerfect files that are installed.)

The Custom Installation menu breaks down the installation procedure into six separate steps that you control. You can specify the drive from and to which you wish to install the program. You can also determine whether you wish to have WordPerfect check the CONFIG.SYS and AUTOEXEC.BAT files, and whether to install printers. (See the "Basic" section above for more information on installing printers.)

```
Custom Installation                              Installation Problems?
                                                 (800) 533-9605
 └→ 1 - Install Files From              A:\

    2 - Install Files To                C:\WP51

    3 - Install Disks

    4 - Check CONFIG.SYS and AUTOEXEC.BAT

    5 - Select and Install Printer and Exit

    6 - Exit


  ┌─────────────────────────────────────────────────────────────────────┐
  │Use this option to specify the drive from which the WordPerfect Program│
  │disks will be copied.  This drive can be either a 3½" or a 5¼"         │
  │floppy disk drive.                                                     │
  └─────────────────────────────────────────────────────────────────────┘

 Selection: 1
```

**FIGURE A-3**   Custom Installation menu (version 5.1)

**NETWORK**    This option is appropriate if you are installing WordPerfect to run on a network. It is similar to the Custom option, except that it includes an option that checks to make sure that a file named WP{WP}.ENV exists on your system. If not, you are asked to specify which type of network software you are using. Then you are prompted for the location of the setup files for all users on the network; these are the files that end with the extension .SET, which are files that contain information that customizes WordPerfect for each user.

**PRINTER**    This option is appropriate if you obtain updated printer disks from WordPerfect Corporation for a printer you previously installed. The old printer files, with the filename .ALL, can be replaced by the updated .ALL files.

**UPDATE**    This option is appropriate if you obtain interim releases of WordPerfect 5.1, which contain updated files on the Program, Spell/Thesaurus, or PTR Program/Graphics disks. The old program files can be replaced by the updated files.

**COPY DISKS**    This option is appropriate if you wish to copy files from one or more of the original WordPerfect disks to a hard or floppy disk. Since the files on the original WordPerfect disks are compressed, the files are unusable unless they are expanded. With the Copy Disks option, WordPerfect files are expanded while they are copied to a specified location.

## Install Version 5.0 on Hard Disk Systems

5.0 users should run the WordPerfect Installation program as follows:

1. Insert the Learning disk that came with the WordPerfect program into drive A.

2. Type **a:** and press [Enter]. Now the DOS prompt reads A> or A:\>.

3. Type **install** and press [Enter].

The menu shown in Figure A-4 will appear, which lists the steps in the installation process. Proceed with each step consecutively.

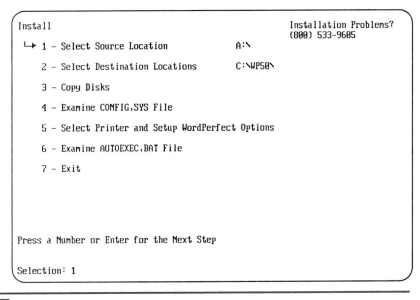

```
Install                                        Installation Problems?
                                               (800) 533-9605
 ↳ 1 - Select Source Location           A:\

   2 - Select Destination Locations     C:\WP50\

   3 - Copy Disks

   4 - Examine CONFIG.SYS File

   5 - Select Printer and Setup WordPerfect Options

   6 - Examine AUTOEXEC.BAT File

   7 - Exit




Press a Number or Enter for the Next Step

Selection: 1
```

**FIGURE A-4**   Install main menu (version 5.0)

For more background information, you can refer to the description of the Basic and Custom options in the earlier section, "Installing Version 5.1." One item that is different in WordPerfect's version 5.0 Installation program, however, is step 5, "Select Printer and Setup WordPerfect Options." Here you not only install your printers for use with Word-Perfect, but also have the opportunity to alter several of the defaults set up by WordPerfect as to how the Word-Perfect program will operate for you. Appendix B describes the Setup menu and should be consulted when you are deciding whether to alter any of the options on the Setup menu. Also look to the next section, addressed to floppy disk users, if you wish to install printers manually, rather than using step 5 of the Installation program to do so.

## Install Version 5.0 on Floppy Disk Systems

There is no WordPerfect version 5.0 Installation program for floppy disk users. As a result, you must manually copy the WordPerfect master disks onto your formatted disks, and then create a CONFIG.SYS file. In addition, you must install your printers manually.

To copy the WordPerfect program files onto your formatted disks, proceed as follows:

1. Place the master disk labeled "WordPerfect 1" into drive A and the disk that you created and labeled "WordPerfect 1" into drive B. (If you use high-density disks, then the master and your copy will be labeled "WordPerfect 1/WordPerfect 2.")

2. Type **copy wp.exe b:** and press ⌨Enter. WordPerfect's main program file is copied onto the disk in drive B.

3. Insert the disk that you created and labeled as the "Help" disk into drive B.

4. Type **copy wphelp*.fil b:** and press ⟦Enter⟧. WordPerfect's two help files are copied onto the disk in drive B.

5. Place the master disk labeled "WordPerfect 2" into drive A and the disk that you created and labeled "WordPerfect 2" into drive B.

6. Type **copy *.* b:** and press ⟦Enter⟧. One by one, all the files from the WordPerfect 2 disk are transferred onto your working copy.

7. Repeat steps 5 and 6 until the rest of the WordPerfect disks have been copied onto formatted disks, making sure to match the correct master disk with the corresponding formatted disk that you labeled.

Now you must create a special file called CONFIG.SYS so that WordPerfect operates properly. This file must contain the command FILES = 20 so that the computer knows how many files can remain open at one time, a necessity for running WordPerfect. To do so, follow these steps:

1. Insert your working copy of the WordPerfect 1 disk into drive A.

2. Type **copy config.sys + con config.sys** and press ⟦Enter⟧. WordPerfect responds with the message "CON."

3. Type **files = 20**.

4. Press ⟦Ctrl⟧ + ⟦Z⟧; that is, hold down the ⟦Ctrl⟧ key and type the letter "z." Then, press ⟦Enter⟧. In moments, the computer tells you that one file has been copied. You have just created a CONFIG.SYS file.

Finally, you must install your printer for use with Word-Perfect. To do so, you must start up WordPerfect, as described in the beginning chapter of this book, entitled "Getting Started." Once in WordPerfect, press the PRINT ( Shift + F7 ) key, choose Select Printer (S), select Additional Printers (2 or A), and select Other Disk (2 or O). WordPerfect prompts

`Directory for printer files:`

Insert a printer disk (such as the Printer 1 disk) into drive B, type the letter "b" followed by a colon, and press Enter ; that is, type **b:** and press Enter . A screen displays, listing various printers.

You must now search for your printer on this list. To do so, you can press PgUp or PgDn to move up or down screen by screen. Or, use the Name Search option; type **N**, type in the first few letters of your brand of printer, and then press Enter when your printer appears on screen. If you can't find your printer on the list, insert another printer disk—such as the Printer 2 disk—into drive B and again select Other Disk (2 or O) to view a new list of printers. If your printer is not listed on any of the printer disks, then you either must find one on the list that is close enough to yours or you must order a disk with your printer on the list by calling (800) 222-9409 or writing to

SoftCopy, Inc.
c/o Printer Drivers
81 N. State Street
Orem, UT 84057

With the cursor on the name of your printer, choose Select (1 or S). A filename with the extension .PRS displays at the bottom of the screen. For instance, the filename for the HP LaserJet Series II printer is HPLASEII.PRS. Press [Enter] to create this printer definition. This is the printer definition that will be used whenever you print out a document using the printer you just installed. Now you can read over the help screen that appears for your printer and press EXIT ([F7]) twice. Next you can define additional printers or continue to press EXIT ([F7]) until you return to the clear WordPerfect Typing screen.

# CREATE A BATCH FILE

Once you have installed WordPerfect, you may wish to create a batch file to automatically load WordPerfect for you. You can write a set of instructions using DOS so that you can start up WordPerfect quickly from now on and automatically set the proper drive/directory for storing the documents you create with WordPerfect.

The batch file is a convenience, but it is not a necessity. You can always load WordPerfect directly from the DOS prompt without using a batch file. The chapter entitled "Getting Started" at the start of this book discusses how to load WordPerfect either with or without a batch file. A batch file isn't as much of a necessity for 5.1 users since 5.1 users have the ability to set up a drive/directory for storing WordPerfect documents using the Setup menu, as described in the section "Location of Files" in Appendix B. As you read on, you can decide whether a batch file makes sense for you.

The following instructions help you create the most commonly used batch file, one that automates the following tasks: (1) sets the default directory, which is the directory for saving and retrieving files, to be C:\WP51\DATA for hard disk users or B: for floppy disk users; (2) loads Word-Perfect automatically; and (3) changes the directory back to the default directory when you exit WordPerfect. You may wish to adapt the contents of the batch file to meet your needs. Make sure that you're viewing the DOS prompt before proceeding:

1. *Hard disk users:*   Type **c:** and press Enter, and then type **cd \** and press Enter; this ensures that you are working in the main (root) directory on the hard disk.
    *Floppy disk users:* Insert the WordPerfect 1 disk that you created into drive A, type **a:** and press Enter; this ensures that you are working in drive A, which contains the WordPerfect 1 disk.

2. *Hard disk users:*   Type **md \wp51\data** and press Enter if you are a version 5.1 user, or type **md \wp50\data** and press Enter if you are a version 5.0 user. Now you will have created a directory on your hard disk that can store your WordPerfect documents.

3. *Hard disk users:*   Type the following commands, pressing Enter after typing each command so that each is on a separate line:

```
copy con: wp5.bat
cd \wp51\data  (or type cd \wp50\data if you are a 5.0 user)
wp
cd \
```

*Floppy disk users:* Type the following commands, pressing [Enter] after typing each command so that each is on a separate line:

```
copy con: autoexec.bat
b:
a:wp
a:
```

4. Press [Ctrl] + [Z]; that is, hold down the [Ctrl] key and type the letter "z." Then, press [Enter]. In moments, the computer tells you that one file has been copied. You have just created a batch file.

You can tailor a batch file to your needs. For instance, if you are a floppy disk user and your computer is equipped with a battery-operated clock, you may need to add a line in step 3 above that accesses your computer's clock program. In that case, add a new line just below the "copy con:" line that will access your computer's clock program, such as by typing **astclock** and pressing [Enter]. Or, if your computer is not equipped with a battery-operated clock, you may wish instead to add the commands so that the computer will prompt for the correct date and time when you turn on the computer. In that case, add two new lines just below the "copy con:" line: type **date** and press [Enter], and then type **time** and press [Enter].

Also, you can customize your batch file with the SET command. This command allows you to take advantage of special options each time that you start up WordPerfect. (These special startup options are described in the next section.) For instance, one of the startup options is /r. To start up WordPerfect every time using the /r startup option, include a command just above the "wp" command line (hard disk users) or the "a:wp" command line (floppy disk users) that reads **set wp = /r**. Another startup option is /nf. To start up WordPerfect every time using both of these startup options, include the command **set wp = /r/nf**. Because of this SET command, whenever WordPerfect is loaded from the batch file, these startup options will be activated.

# STARTUP (SLASH) OPTIONS

Depending on your equipment and needs, it may be advantageous to load WordPerfect in a slightly different way. Usually, the command that triggers WordPerfect to load in the computer is wp. Instead of wp, you can add the forward slash symbol (/), followed by various characters, to activate options that might make a session more productive for you. For instance, you can load WordPerfect by typing **wp/r** or **wp/d-b:**. The options take effect only until the next time you load WordPerfect. Or, you can include a SET command in your batch file (as described in the last section) so that certain options are activated automatically each time you load WordPerfect from the batch file. For instance, you can enter a command in a batch file that reads **set wp = /r**. The various startup options are described below.

## Option 1: Speed Up the Program with Expanded Memory

As you now know, WordPerfect is loaded into RAM before you begin a session. Yet the computer must still refer to the WordPerfect program on the disk drive from time to time. You can tell when the computer is referring to a disk drive: The indicator light on your disk drive is illuminated.

One reason that WordPerfect refers to the disk is that some detailed program instructions are not loaded into RAM when you load WordPerfect. The computer thus must refer to the disk periodically for further information, slowing down the processing time of the computer. Whether a hard or floppy disk user, you can avoid the slowdown if your computer's RAM is large enough. If your computer is equipped with *expanded memory* (which means more than 640K) and at least 300K of RAM is unused, you can load into RAM even the more detailed instructions. To do so, instead of typing **wp** at the DOS prompt to load WordPerfect, you can invoke what is called the /r (pronounced "slash r") option by typing (in upper- or lowercase letters) **wp/r**. Or, include the SET command in a batch file as follows: **set up = /r**.

This will load *all* the WordPerfect instructions — even the more detailed set — into RAM. As a result, WordPerfect will be able to execute commands more quickly for you.

Conversely, you can inhibit the use of expanded memory when using WordPerfect by using the /ne option. Type **wp/ne** at the DOS prompt.

## Option 2: Redirect Temporary Files

WordPerfect often creates temporary files as you make requests and stores those temporary files on whatever disk the WordPerfect program is stored. These are WordPerfect's own housekeeping duties. As a result, floppy disk users must keep the WordPerfect disk in drive A even after exercising the /r option. You can direct WordPerfect to perform housekeeping functions on another drive or directory, however, by using the /d option.

To use this option, type **wp/d** followed by a hyphen and the new drive or directory. For example, say you wanted to redirect housekeeping to the B drive. Then, to load Word-Perfect, you would type **wp/d-b:**. Or, include this option in a batch file. (If you redirect the temporary files to drive B, you must make sure that the disk in drive B has enough room to store those temporary files—64K is usually sufficient.)

A floppy disk user who employs the /d option in conjunction with the /r option can remove the WordPerfect 2 disk from drive A for most of the working session. That will cut down on the constant swapping of disks, allowing you, for example, to keep the WordPerfect 1 disk (5.1 users) or the Help disk (5.0 users) in drive A to have access to the Help facility.

# Option 3: Simultaneously Load WordPerfect and a Commonly Used File

Say that you'll be working on the same document every day for the next week. You can specify a filename so that the document and WordPerfect are loaded together. If your document is in a file called JONES and is stored on the floppy disk in drive B, type **wp b:jones** at the DOS prompt. (No slash is typed for this one startup option.) As soon as WordPerfect appears on the screen, the file named JONES is retrieved for editing.

## Option 4: Simultaneously Load WordPerfect and a Commonly Used Macro

A macro is a fast way to store phrases or execute keystrokes that you use often (as explained in Chapter 14). If you wish to start a macro as soon as you load WordPerfect, then specify that macro as you load. Type **wp/m** followed by a hyphen and the macro name. (Precede the macro name with the drive/directory where it is stored if the macro is not located where the WordPerfect program files are stored.) If your macro is named START, for example, and is stored where the WordPerfect program is stored, then type **wp/m-start** at the DOS prompt. The macro will be activated as soon as WordPerfect appears on the screen. Or, include this option in the SET command in a batch file.

## Option 5: Improve WordPerfect's Performance on Certain Types of Computers

The following options may be advantageous depending on your computer hardware and software. All of these options can be activated at the DOS prompt when you load WordPerfect or can be included in the SET command of a batch file.

*5.1 and 5.0 users:* Use the /nf ("non-flash") option if your screen goes blank periodically or windowing programs (programs that create multiple windows on screen) are resident in RAM when you use WordPerfect. At the DOS prompt, type **wp/nf**.

Use the /nc option to disable the Cursor Speed feature (as described in Appendix B). This is important when you're working with equipment or a TSR (terminate and stay resident) program that conflicts with the Cursor Speed feature. Sometimes, WordPerfect won't load without invoking this option. At the DOS prompt, type **wp/nc**.

Use the /nk option to disable enhanced keyboard commands. This is important when you're working with equipment or a TSR program and, after loading, WordPerfect locks up or the keyboard freezes. Your problems should clear up if, at the DOS prompt, you type **wp/nk**.

Use the /ss ("screen size") option to set the screen size of your monitor when WordPerfect cannot automatically discern the correct size. Type **wp/ss** followed by an equal sign and the rows and columns displayed by your monitor. For example, suppose that your monitor displays 66 rows and 80 columns (as the Genius monitor does). At the DOS prompt, type **wp/ss = 66,80**.

*5.1 users only:* Use the /cp (code page number) option to indicate to WordPerfect which code page your hardware system uses. This is important to access the proper keyboard and 256-character ASCII character set for which your system is preset. Type **wp/cp** followed by an equal sign and one of the following three-or four-digit numbers: 437 Standard, 850 PC Multilingual, 895 Czechoslovakian, 851 Greek, 8510 Greek Alternate, 860 Portuguese, 8600 Portuguese Alternate, 861 Icelandic, 863 French (Canada), 865 Norwegian and Dutch, 899 Russian. An example is **wp/cp = 895**.

Use the /f2 option if you have a computer that displays more than 25 lines and 80 columns, and are having problems displaying the text even after using the /ss option. Make sure to set the desired text mode with the software that is included with your video board (such as the Paradise Autoswitch EGA 480 or VGA Plus) before typing **wp/ss =** *rows, columns/***f2** to load WordPerfect.

Use the /nb option if you have insufficient room to resave a file on disk. Normally when WordPerfect resaves a file, it renames the original document, saves the new document, and then deletes the original; thus, at some point, it is necessary to hold two copies of your file on disk. This option instead instructs WordPerfect to overwrite the original document when you replace a file. At the DOS prompt, type **wp/nb**.

Use the /no option to disable the use of the Ctrl + 6 key. Normally, Ctrl + 6 returns the keyboard to its original mapping after you have selected an alternate keyboard using the Keyboard Layout feature. (See Chapter 15 for more on the Keyboard Layout feature.) At the DOS prompt, type **wp/no**.

Use the /ps option to indicate the location of the .SET file, which contains various setup options. Normally, WordPerfect uses the .SET file located in the directory where the main WordPerfect program file, WP.EXE, is stored. This option is especially important if you are running on a network. Type **wp/ps** followed by an equal sign and then the drive/directory, such as **wp/ps = c:\wp51\gen**.

Use the /w option to limit the space in conventional memory and expanded memory that can be used by WordPerfect. Normally, WordPerfect uses all conventional memory and 87.5% of expanded memory to run WordPerfect. Type **wp/w**, an equal sign, and then the conventional and expanded memory in kilobytes, separated by a comma, such as **wp/w = 120,512**. If you indicate no expanded memory limitation, then the default of 87.5% is used, as in the example **wp/w = 120**. You can also use an asterisk to have WordPerfect use all available memory, such as in the example **wp/w = *.***.

*5.0 users only:* Use the /i option if WordPerfect will not load, prompting with the message "Insert WordPerfect disk and press any key to continue." This indicates that WordPerfect cannot locate the program file named WP.FIL, because you installed WordPerfect either from a copy or from floppy disks before you installed the program onto your hard disk. At the DOS prompt, type **wp/i** to correct the problem.

## Option 6: Return to the Default Settings

When you purchase WordPerfect, certain settings are provided as defaults by WordPerfect Corporation. For instance, WordPerfect sets the left/right/top/bottom margins all at 1″. But, realizing that individuals have different needs, the designers of WordPerfect provided the ability to change those defaults via the Setup menu, which is described in Appendix B.

Once you change the defaults, you can load Word-Perfect and restore the original default settings for a particular working session. You do so with the /x option. At the DOS prompt, type **wp/x**. When you exit WordPerfect and later load WordPerfect *without* the /x option, the previous changes that you initiated using the Setup menu will be restored.

## Option 7: Combine More than One "Slash" Option

You can combine any or all of the options mentioned above. For example, say you used a floppy disk system with 1.5 MB RAM, which means you have enough memory to exercise the /r option. Also say you decided to redirect all temporary files to the disk in drive B so that you could place the Speller disk in drive A for the majority of your working session.

To load WordPerfect, you would type the following: **wp/r/d-b:**. Or, include this combination of options in a batch file as a SET command (such as **set wp = /r/d-b:**).

# CUSTOMIZING WORDPERFECT WITH THE SETUP MENU

Mouse [5.1 Users Only]
Display
Environment
Initial Settings
Keyboard Layout
Location of Files

The designers of WordPerfect made certain assumptions about how the program would operate once it was loaded. For example, they determined that once saved, a document's filename should appear on the left side of the status line. And they preset all margins at 1″ and established full justification. A list of WordPerfect's most important default settings is displayed in Table B-1.

Realizing that different individuals have different preferences and needs, however, the designers also provided the ability to permanently change these and other settings via

| Feature | Default Setting |
|---|---|
| Automatically Format/Rewrite | Yes |
| Backup, Original | No |
| Backup, Timed | Yes, 30 minutes (version 5.1); No (version 5.0) |
| Columns Display, Side-by-Side | Yes |
| Cursor Speed | 50 cps (version 5.1); 30 cps (version 5.0) |
| Date Format | 3 1, 4 (as in January 1, 1990) |
| Document Comments, Display | Yes |
| Fast Save | Yes (version 5.1); No (version 5.0) |
| Filename on the Status Line | Yes |
| Format Retrieved Document for Default Printer | No |
| Hard Return Display Character | None |
| Hyphenation | No |
| Hyphenation Zone, left | 10% |
| Hyphenation Zone, right | 4% |
| Justification | Full (version 5.1); On (version 5.0) |
| Line Height | Auto |
| Line Numbering | No |
| Line Spacing | Single |
| Margins, top and bottom | 1″ |
| Margins, left and right | 1″ |
| Mouse type (5.1 users only) | Mouse driver (MOUSE.COM) |
| Tabs | Every 0.5″ |
| Page Numbering | None |
| Paper Size | 8.5″ × 11″ |
| Page Type | Standard |

**TABLE B-1**   Key Default (Initial) Settings as Established by WordPerfect

| Feature | Default Setting |
|---|---|
| Paragraph Numbering | Outline Style |
| Print Options: | |
|    Binding Width | 0″ |
|    Graphics Quality | Medium |
|    Number of Copies | 1 |
|    Text Quality | High |
| Redline Method | Printer Dependent |
| Repeat Value | 8 |
| Underline Spaces | Yes |
| Underline Tabs | No |
| Units of Measure | ″ |
| Widow/Orphan Protection | No |

**TABLE B-1**   Key Default (Initial) Settings as Established by WordPerfect (*continued*)

the Setup menu — so that you can customize the program for your equipment or to meet special formatting needs.

You can access the Setup menu at any time while you are working on the Typing screen or the Reveal Codes screen. Simply press the SETUP ( Shift + F1 ) key. [*Pull-down menu:* File (F), Setup (T).] *5.1 users:* The menu shown in Figure B-1 appears, with a list of the six sets of options that can be altered. *5.0 users:* The menu shown in Figure B-2 appears.

After you alter the Setup menu and press EXIT ( F7 ) to return to the Typing screen, the changes are saved on disk in a special file, which is named WP{WP}.SET, or, if you're working on a network, a special file named WP*nnn*}.SET, where *nnn* is the user name that you entered when starting up WordPerfect. These changes take effect for each *new* document you create in the current

```
Setup

     1 - Mouse

     2 - Display

     3 - Environment

     4 - Initial Settings

     5 - Keyboard Layout

     6 - Location of Files




Selection: 0
```

**FIGURE B-1**  Setup Menu (version 5.1)

```
Setup

     1 - Backup

     2 - Cursor Speed              30 cps

     3 - Display

     4 - Fast Save (unformatted)   No

     5 - Initial Settings

     6 - Keyboard Layout

     7 - Location of Auxiliary Files

     8 - Units of Measure



Selection: 0
```

**FIGURE B-2**  Setup menu (version 5.0)

working session and each time that you start up Word-
Perfect thereafter—until you alter them again. (If you wish
to change certain default format settings for just a single
document, whether new or existing, then you can do so
using the Format menu, as explained in Chapters 4 and 6,
rather than using the Setup menu.)

This appendix will explain each of the options on the
Setup menu. It is organized based on the structure of the
Setup menu in version 5.1, since version 5.1 offers all the
items on the Setup menu in version 5.0 plus more. Word-
Perfect 5.0 users should look to Table B-2 to discover
where in this appendix to find explanations for Setup menu
items available to you, but that are housed in different
locations in the version 5.1 Setup menu.

# MOUSE [5.1 USERS ONLY]

Select Mouse (1 or M) on the Setup menu to display the
Setup Mouse menu, which shows the default settings for
how a mouse attached to your computer will be used in
WordPerfect. You may need to change some of these settings to use your mouse in WordPerfect. Other settings can
be altered based on how you prefer to work with your
mouse.

- *Type*   Indicate which brand of mouse you have attached
  to your computer from the list that is displayed. For
  many of these brands, you must also indicate whether the
  mouse is "serial," meaning that it is attached to a serial
  port at the back of your computer, or "bus," meaning
  that it is attached to a mouse card that you installed into

| 5.0 Setup Menu Item | Location in 5.1 Setup Menu |
|---|---|
| Backup | Environment |
| Cursor Speed | Environment |
| Display: | Display |
|    Colors/Fonts/Attributes | |
|    Graphics Screen Type | |
|    Menu Letter Display | |
| Display: | Display, Edit-Screen |
|    Automatically Format/Rewrite | |
|    Display Document Comments | |
|    Filename on the Status Line | |
|    Hard Return Display Character | |
|    Side-by-Side Columns Display | |
| Display: | Display, View Document |
|    View Document in Black and White | |
| Fast Save | Environment |
| Initial Settings: | Initial Settings |
|    Date Format | |
|    Initial Codes | |
|    Repeat Value | |
|    Table of Authorities | |
|    Print Options | |
| Initial Settings: | Environment |
|    Beep Options | |
|    Document Summary | |
| Keyboard Layout | Keyboard Layout |
| Location of Auxiliary Files | Location of Files |
| Units of Measure | Environment |

**TABLE B-2**   Where To Find 5.0 Setup Menu Items in the 5.1 Menu Structure

the computer. Once you specify a brand, WordPerfect can access your mouse without the MOUSE.COM file that is packaged with your mouse.

If your brand of mouse is not listed, then select MOUSE.COM (which is what WordPerfect assumes if you do not specify a type); in that case, you must make sure that you properly install the MOUSE.COM file that is packaged with your mouse.

- *Port*    If the mouse is "serial," indicate the serial port (plug number) to which your mouse is attached.

- *Double-Click Interval*    Indicate the interval in which you will double-click the mouse, measured in 100ths of a second—such as 100 for one second. If the two clicks are not pressed within the specified interval, WordPerfect considers the movement as two single clicks. (See Appendix C for a discussion of "click" versus "double-click.")

- *Submenu Delay Time*    Indicate the time that the cursor can rest on a pulldown menu item before its submenu displays, measured in 100ths of a second.

- *Acceleration Factor*    Indicate how responsive the mouse pointer on screen is to mouse movements. A greater acceleration factor means a more responsive mouse pointer.

- *Left-Handed Mouse*    If you use the mouse with your left hand, you can change this item to "Yes," so that the tasks performed by the right mouse button will be switched to the left mouse button, and vice versa.

- *Assisted Mouse Pointer Movement*    If you want Word-Perfect to move the mouse pointer automatically to a line menu when that menu is displayed, rather than retaining the pointer at its current position, change this item to "Yes."

# DISPLAY

Select Display (2 or D) on the Setup menu, and Word-Perfect displays the screen shown in Figure B-3. On this screen you can alter how text and menus are exhibited on screen as you work in WordPerfect. The options available are described below.

## Colors/Fonts/Attributes

WordPerfect supports numerous monitors and display cards, including Monochrome, CGA, PC 3270, Black and White, EGA Color or Monochrome, VGA Color or Mono-chrome, 8514/A, MCGA, Hercules Graphics Card, and

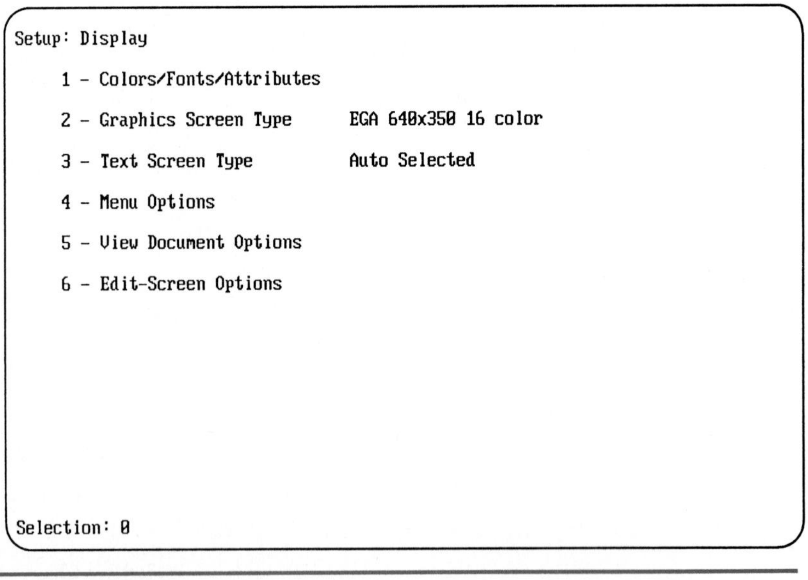

```
Setup: Display

     1 - Colors/Fonts/Attributes

     2 - Graphics Screen Type      EGA 640x350 16 color

     3 - Text Screen Type          Auto Selected

     4 - Menu Options

     5 - View Document Options

     6 - Edit-Screen Options




Selection: 0
```

**FIGURE B-3**  Setup Display Screen (version 5.1)

Hercules Graphics Card plus RamFont. You can change the characteristics, colors, and/or fonts by which normal text and text with attributes (such as boldfaced or super-scripted text) appear on screen. The text can be displayed differently on the Doc 1 screen than on the Doc 2 screen. The choices available to you for displaying on-screen text depend on your computer monitor and display card.

- *Monochrome monitors* You can select how text attributes will be displayed using the following capabilities of your monitor—Blink, Bold, Blocked, Underline, or Normal.

- *CGA/PC 3270/MCGA monitors* You can determine whether WordPerfect speeds up text display (though static may result on screen if you type *Y* for yes), and also determine the colors with which text attributes are displayed on screen.

- *EGA/VGA monitors* You first select one of five font options, so that an asterisk appears next to the selected option. Should an asterisk not appear, then there is a problem loading that font; copy all WordPerfect files ending with .FRS (5.1 users) or .FNT (5.0 users) to the same directory as where WP.EXE is located. If you select the Italic,Underline, or Small Caps Font, you can choose to see one of these fonts and/or choose from 8 colors on screen. If you choose 512 Characters, you increase the number of displayable characters in the current font from 256 to 512 (which is useful if your documents frequently contain special characters, as described in chapter15) and can choose from 8 colors on screen. And if you select Normal Font Only, than no special fonts will be shown on screen, but 16 foreground colors are available to choose from. Next, select Screen Colors (1 or S), to select your monitor's fonts and colors for specific text atributes.

- *Hercules Cards with RamFont*   You first select whether to display 6 or 12 fonts, rather than only 1 font as on an EGA monitor, so that an asterisk appears next to the selected option. Then select Screen Attributes (1 or S) and indicate which capabilities of your monitor should be activated for each of the text attributes. You can select Reverse Video, Bold, Underline, Strikeout, or, depending on whether you selected to display 6 or 12 fonts, the following fonts: 1, Normal; 2, Double Underline; 3, Italics; 4, Small Caps; 5, Outline; 6, Subscript; 7, Superscript; 8, Fine Print; 9, Small Print; A, Large Print; B, Very Large Print; C, Extra Large Print.

Whatever type of monitor you use, once you select how characters will display on the first document screen (that is, the Doc 1 or Doc 2 screen), press SWITCH ( Shift + F3 ) to assign characteristics to attributes on the other document screen. Repeat the same procedure as described above or, if you want the Doc 1 screen and Doc 2 screen to display colors, fonts, and attributes in the same way, simply press the MOVE ( Ctrl + F4 ) key; the attributes are copied from the other document screen into the current one.

Finally, press EXIT ( F7 ) to save your selections and to return to the Display menu. The changes take effect immediately.

*Note:* Remember that any changes you make affect how attributes are shown on the screen, but not how they appear on the printed page.

## Graphics/Text Screen Type

WordPerfect automatically determines what type of graphics card and monitor you have installed inside your computer. You can alter the Graphics Screen Type, which specifies the graphics driver WordPerfect uses in graphics screens, such as the View Document screen. This is useful if WordPerfect has selected the wrong graphics driver or if you have a special situation such as two monitors running on the same computer. Or, you can alter the Text Screen Type, which specifies the driver used in Text mode, such as the Typing screen.

## Menu Options

These options enable you to alter the way that menus are displayed in WordPerfect, including

- How menu letters are displayed. WordPerfect is designed with mnemonic menus, so that in addition to selecting a feature by its number or by using the cursor movement keys, you can type the mnemonic letter. WordPerfect assumes that you want the mnemonic letter displayed on screen in bold. Instead, you can choose to display the mnemonic letter with another attribute, such as underline. Your choice for how the mnemonic letter is displayed takes effect for both the Doc 1 and Doc 2 screens. You can change the menu letter display separately on menus, on the menu bar used to select pulldown menus, or on the pulldown menus themselves.

- How text (other than the menu letter) is displayed in pulldown menus.

- How to access the pulldown menus when not using a mouse—either by pressing [Alt] + [≡], which is the default, or simply by pressing the left [Alt] key.

- How text (other than the menu letter) is displayed in the menu bar.

- Whether a double separator line appears in the menu bar, and whether the menu bar appears on the Typing screen at all times or only when you press (Alt) + (≡).

## View Document Options

These options enable you to determine the following characteristics for color monitors on the View Document screen: whether bolded text will appear with color or instead as brighter characters; whether graphic images will appear in color or in different patterns of black and white; whether text will appear in color or in black and white.

## Edit-Screen Options

These options enable you to determine how the Typing screen appears and operates as you type and edit text:

- WordPerfect automatically formats text on screen immediately after an editing change. You can instead set this option to "No", so that WordPerfect only formats text when you use the cursor movement keys to scroll through the document.

- Document comments are displayed when you insert them into the text, unless you change this option to "No."

- A document's filename is displayed in the lower left corner on the status line after the first time you save that document, unless you change this option to "No."

- WordPerfect assumes that when you press (Enter) to insert a Hard Return code, the cursor moves down to the next line, but no character will display on the Typing screen. You can instead have the hard return displayed as a character, by typing a character such as ] or >or by inserting a special character using the Compose feature (as discussed in Chapter 15). Or, press the spacebar to return to the default setting of no hard return character.

- Merge codes (as discussed in Chapter 13) are displayed on the Typing screen unless you change this option to "No."

- When you press the REVEAL CODES ( Alt + F3 ) key to display the Reveal Codes screen, WordPerfect allots ten lines to the bottom portion, where codes are revealed. Instead, you can choose another value. For instance, if you allot one line, then only the line where the cursor is located is displayed with codes revealed.

- Columns you create with the Text Columns feature (as described in Chapter 11) are displayed side by side, as they appear on the printed page. You can instead decide to display each column on a separate page by changing this option to "No." This is useful for speeding up performance when editing documents containing extensive text column format. (Even when columns are displayed on separate pages on screen, they still appear side by side on the printed page.)

# ENVIRONMENT

Select Environment (3 or E) on the Setup menu, and WordPerfect displays the screen shown in Figure B-4. On this screen you can alter your working environment in WordPerfect. The options available are described in this section.

## Backup Options

WordPerfect offers two features to help protect your documents from disaster: Timed Backup and Original Backup.

*Timed Backup* instructs WordPerfect to save whatever document is currently on screen (and thus in RAM memory) to a temporary backup file on disk at specified time intervals. So, for instance, you can activate Timed Backup to save a file to disk every 15 minutes. That way, if you experience a machine or power failure—when all information in RAM disappears—you can reload WordPerfect and retrieve the temporary backup file. You will lose, at most, only 15 minutes of work. Consider activating this feature if you are forgetful about saving your documents periodically to disk using the SAVE ( F10 ) key.

Once the Timed Backup option is active, text on the Doc 1 Typing screen is stored at the time interval specified

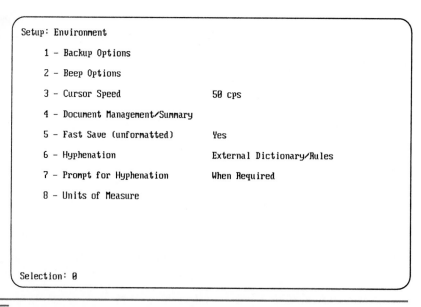

```
Setup: Environment

    1 - Backup Options

    2 - Beep Options

    3 - Cursor Speed              50 cps

    4 - Document Management/Summary

    5 - Fast Save (unformatted)   Yes

    6 - Hyphenation               External Dictionary/Rules

    7 - Prompt for Hyphenation    When Required

    8 - Units of Measure

Selection: 0
```

**FIGURE B-4**  Setup Environment screen (version 5.1)

in a temporary file named WP{WP}.BK1. Or, if you're currently working on a document in the Doc 2 Typing screen, that text is stored in a temporary file named WP{WP}.BK2. After the first backup, a document is saved again at the time interval specified only if the document is modified. For example, suppose you have indicated a time interval of every 30 minutes and are now typing a memo on the Doc 1 screen. After 30 minutes, WordPerfect backs up the document in the Doc 1 screen, creating a file named WP{WP}.BK1. The following message appears momentarily at the bottom of the WordPerfect screen:

```
* Please Wait *
```

When the message clears, the document has been backed up. Every 30 minutes thereafter, WordPerfect updates WP{WP}.BK1, provided that you have edited what is on screen during that time. You can specify a directory where timed backup files are stored using the Location of Files option on the Setup menu, described further on in this appendix. If you do not specify a directory, temporary files will be stored on the same drive/directory where Word-Perfect's main program file (WP.EXE) is found.

WordPerfect deletes the temporary backup files when you exit normally from WordPerfect using the EXIT ( F7 ) key. If instead you experience a power or machine failure, the backup files remain on disk; when you then reload WordPerfect, you can retrieve WP{WP}.BK1 or WP{WP}.BK2 and continue working. Then, assuming Timed Backup is still active, WordPerfect will prompt with the following the first time the backup is to be stored on disk after you reload:

```
Old backup file exists.   1 Rename 2 Delete
```

Select Rename (1 or R) to rename the old backup file with a different name, so that WordPerfect can save the *new* backup using the filename WP{WP}.BK1. Or, if you no longer need the text stored in the old backup file, press Delete (2 or D) to delete it.

For the WordPerfect user who experiences frequent power failures or who is a fast typist, consider indicating a more frequent time interval than every 30 minutes— perhaps every 10 or 15 minutes (or even more frequently). While this will slow down the operations of WordPerfect each time a document is backed up, a power or machine failure will cost you, at most, only 10 or 15 minutes of work.

Keep in mind that the Timed Backup feature is *not a substitute* for saving a document with a name of your choosing using the SAVE ([F10]) or EXIT ([F7]) keys. (See Chapter 2 for more on saving documents to disk.) Since WordPerfect deletes the temporary files when you exit WordPerfect normally, Timed Backup is *only* of value in case of a power or machine failure.

The second backup feature is *Original Backup.* Original Backup instructs WordPerfect to save the original file on disk each time you replace it with the document on screen. The original copy is saved with the extension .BK! (and remains on disk even when you exit normally from Word-Perfect).

As an example of how Original Backup operates once activated, suppose that you type and save a document on the disk in drive B with the filename MEMO. Next, you edit the document and save it again with the same file-name. When you save, WordPerfect prompts

```
Replace B:\MEMO? (Yes) No
```

If you type **Y**, then the old version of MEMO will be saved under the name MEMO.BK!, and the edited version will be stored under the name MEMO. The next time you edit and save the document, the contents of MEMO will be transferred to MEMO.BK! as a backup, and the edited version will again be stored under the name MEMO.

Those of you who have used WordStar, which automatically backs up an original, are familar with the advantage of the Original Backup option—it safeguards against your replacing a file inadvertently. Should you replace a file accidentally, you can simply retrieve that same file with the extension .BK! and not lose any text that you typed.

If you elect to activate the Original Backup feature, realize that files with the same name but a different extension share the same original backup file. So, for example, if you have files named MEMO.1 and MEMO.2, only one backup file will be created. Thus, if you use this feature, consider naming all your documents such that the first part of each filename—the eight characters that precede the period—is unique (such as MEMO1. and MEMO2.) so that each can be assigned its own original backup file.

## Beep Options

These options enable you to determine whether Word-Perfect sounds a beep to alert you when one of the following messages appears on the status line: (1) an error message, such as "ERROR: File not found"; (2) the message that prompts for hyphenation, which begins "Position Hyphen; Press ESC . . ."; or (3) the message indicating that the search string was not found during a Search or Replace operation, which is "* Not Found *".

## Cursor Speed

Most keys on the computer keyboard repeat when they are held down. (Keys on the keyboard that commonly do not repeat when held down include ⌈Ctrl⌉, ⌈Alt⌉, ⌈Shift⌉, ⌈Caps Lock⌉, and ⌈Num Lock⌉.) WordPerfect allows you to increase or decrease the rate at which keys repeat, measured in characters per second, or to select "Normal" if the Cursor Speed feature does not work properly on your computer or conflicts with a TSR (Terminate and Stay Resident) program that you use.

You may wish to experiment with the Cursor Speed feature to see which setting you prefer. One way to do so uses the cursor movement keys. For instance, at 30 characters per second, position the cursor at the beginning of a sentence and press and hold down the ⌈→⌉ key until the cursor moves to the end of the sentence. Then, change the cursor speed, and again move the cursor through a sentence using the ⌈→⌉ key. You'll quickly find the speed that is most comfortable for you. And, you may find that, for you, faster isn't always better—because a faster cursor speed often results in your overshooting where you want to position the cursor.

## Document Management/Summary

As described in Chapter 8, WordPerfect provides the opportunity to manage documents on disk and create a document summary, which will be attached to a specific document when it is saved as a file on disk. You can decide on four default settings regarding document management and summaries: (1) whether a document summary form should automatically be displayed when you save a new document for the first time and haven't yet created a summary for that document; (2) the subject search text, which is the preselected phrase used by WordPerfect to find the subject of a document (the default is "RE:") and to insert that subject under the Subject heading when you create a summary; (3) whether you want to name a document with a long document name (up to 68 characters or spaces) when you save the document, rather than limiting a filename to eight characters and an optional three-character extension; and (4) the default document type, which is the preselected type that WordPerfect automatically inserts under the Document Type heading when you create a summary. Be sure to refer to Chapter 8 for a fuller explanation of the Document Summary feature.

# Fast Save, Unformatted

The Fast Save option directs WordPerfect to save documents without first formatting them. By activating the Fast Save option, you reduce the time it takes to save a document.

Be aware, however, that there are trade-offs in activating the Fast Save option. As described in Chapter 2, there are two general methods for printing documents — from screen, or from a file on disk. When the Fast Save option is set to "Yes," the process for printing from disk is affected. *5.1 users*: Printing a document from disk will be slower, because WordPerfect must format the document before printing it. *5.0 users*: Printing a document from disk will be impossible unless you manually press Home, Home, ↓ before saving that document, so that it is formatted when stored on disk; if you don't format the document first and then try to print from disk, WordPerfect displays an ERROR message, and you must retrieve the document to the screen in order to print it.

If you typically print documents from screen much more than from disk, consider activating the Fast Save option; this will save you time when saving. 5.0 users must then remember to press [Home], [Home], [↓] before saving documents that you wish to print from disk. On the other hand, if you typically print documents from disk, consider setting the Fast Save option to "No."

## Hyphenation/Prompt for Hyphenation

You can indicate which of two methods WordPerfect should use when hyphenation is turned on. First, Word-Perfect can hyphenate using the hyphenation program and external dictionary contained in the files WP{WP}US.HYC and WP{WP}US.LEX (which accompany the version of WordPerfect distributed in the United States). As an alternative, WordPerfect can hyphenate using internal rules that are contained within the WordPerfect program. The external dictionary is more sophisticated and accurate than the internal rules, but occupies additional disk space.

In addition, you can indicate how you want WordPerfect to respond when the Hyphenation feature has been turned on and a word requires hyphenation. There are three alternatives. First, you can request that WordPerfect always prompt you, meaning that for every word that needs to be hyphenated, WordPerfect will prompt with the message that begins **"Position Hyphen; Press ESC . . ."**, asking your assistance in positioning the hyphen. Second, you can tell WordPerfect never to prompt you for assistance, in which case WordPerfect will wrap a word to the next line when unsure of where to locate the hyphen. Third, you can tell WordPerfect to prompt you only when required, meaning only when the hyphenation dictionary cannot determine how to hyphenate a specific word.

# Units of Measure

Numerous features in WordPerfect involve some type of measurement. As set up by WordPerfect Corporation, WordPerfect 5.1 and 5.0 assume that you want measurements displayed in inches, where the inch indicator is ". For instance, margins and tab settings on the Line Format menu are shown in inches (such as 1"), and Format codes are inserted into the text display in inches, such as [L/R Mar:2",1.5"]. Moreover, when you change measurements such as margins or tabs, WordPerfect assumes that the measurement you enter is in inches.

As an alternative, WordPerfect can display and assume that you wish to enter all measurements in different units. Your options are

| Selection | Measurement |
|---|---|
| " or i | Inches. One inch equals 1/12 of a foot. |
| c | Centimeters. One centimeter equals 1/100 of a meter or 0.39". |
| p | Points, a commonly used measurement in the publishing industry. In WordPerfect, a point equals 1/72". You should know that in publishing, a point equals 1/72.27", a 4% difference, which is small but nevertheless significant when doing precise work. |
| w | 1200ths of an inch. For instance, 600w equals 1/2". |

| **Selection** | **Measurement** |
|---|---|
| u | WordPerfect version 4.2 units, where vertical measurements correspond to lines from the top margin, and horizontal measurements correspond to column positions from the left margin. (When you select version 4.2 units, the size of a line or column varies based on the size of the font you are using in your document.) |

No matter what measurement you decide to use as your default, you do not have to enter measurements in the selected unit. You can still enter a measurement in another unit of measure as long as it is followed by a character that indicates the units—i or ″ for inches, c for centimeters, p for points, w for 1200ths of an inch, h for version 4.2 horizontal units, and v for version 4.2 vertical units. For instance, suppose that you selected that all display and entry of numbers will be in inches. You can enter a line spacing measurement of 2.5c, and WordPerfect will convert 2.5 centimeters into .984″. Enter a top margin of 90p and WordPerfect will convert 90 points into 1.25″. Or, enter a left margin of 15h, and WordPerfect will convert 15 horizontal 4.2 units into 1.5″ (assuming that the type size is 10 characters per inch). If you instead enter a number without specifying the unit of measure, then WordPerfect assumes that you are specifying inches.

WordPerfect also starts out with the assumption that you want the "Ln" and "Pos" indicators on the status line to display in inches. You can instead select one of the other units of measure, so that the status line indicates your cursor position in that other measurement:

| Selection | Example of Status Line Display |
|-----------|-------------------------------|
| " | Doc 1 Pg 4 Ln 2.5" Pos 1" |
| i | Doc 1 Pg 4 Ln 2.5i Pos 1i |
| c | Doc 1 Pg 4 Ln 6.36c Pos 2.54c |
| p | Doc 1 Pg 4 Ln 180.5p Pos 72p |
| w | Doc 1 Pg 4 Ln 3000w Pos 1200w |
| u | Doc 1 Pg 4 Ln 10 Pos 10 |

Should you decide to work with the status line in version 4.2 units, you must keep in mind that the "Ln" number indicates a distance from the top *margin,* while for the other units of measure, this number indicates a distance from the top *edge of the page.*

You may wish to change the units of measure frequently, and to suit the document you are working on. For instance, you may wish to switch into points when producing a newsletter, and to inches for standard documents. Or you may wish to stay in inches when using a proportionately spaced font and to switch to 4.2 units when using a monospaced font. Moreover, it is possible to select the status line in one unit of measure and the display and entry of numbers in a different unit of measure—although you may find this confusing rather than helpful.

# INITIAL SETTINGS

Select Initial Settings (4 or I) on the Setup menu, and WordPerfect displays the screen shown in Figure B-5. On this screen you can alter certain of the default settings established by WordPerfect as to how certain features operate and the format of your document. The options are described in this section.

## Merge

Chapter 13 describes how WordPerfect can personalize letters or other documents by merging primary and secondary files. A secondary file is the file that contains variable information, such as a list of names and addresses, and can be either a file created in WordPerfect or a file created in another program (such as dBASE III or Lotus 1-2-3) which is then converted to a DOS text file.

If you use a DOS text file as a merge, WordPerfect must know which characters are used as delimiters to separate

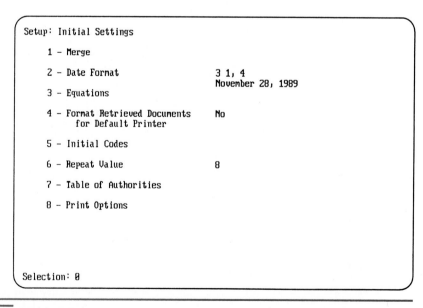

```
Setup: Initial Settings

    1 - Merge

    2 - Date Format                          3 1, 4
                                             November 28, 1989
    3 - Equations

    4 - Format Retrieved Documents           No
          for Default Printer

    5 - Initial Codes

    6 - Repeat Value                         8

    7 - Table of Authorities

    8 - Print Options



Selection: 0
```

**FIGURE B-5**  Setup Initial Settings screen (version 5.1)

each field and each record. Each field and record can have a beginning and/or ending delimiter. For instance, in the following example, the comma is used to separate each field, and a hard return (which in DOS terms is a carriage return and line feed) separates each line.

```
Ms.,Janice,Smith,3559 Biltmore Street,San Francisco,CA,94123
Mr.,Dennis,Poplar,333 Cypress Boulevard,Glen Ellen,CA,95442
```

Use the Merge option to indicate the delimiters, which will then be used when you merge with a DOS text file. To insert a carriage return, press Ctrl + M to insert **[CR]**. To insert a line feed, press Enter to insert **[LF]**.

## Date Format

Chapter 3 describes the Date feature, which can insert today's date (or time) automatically for you. Figure B-5 shows that WordPerfect assumes that you want to display the date as "3 1, 4," where the number "3" represents the month as a word, the number "1" represents the day of the month, and the number "4" represents the year with all four digits shown—for example, November 28, 1990. You can instead change the default style for the date format. Refer to Chapter 3 for more on the Date Format menu.

## Equations

This option enables you to determine default settings for working with the Equation Editor, including the font size used to print the equation, the horizontal and vertical position of the equation in the graphics box, and whether the box will print graphically or as text. (These default settings can then be overridden when you are creating a specific equation using the Equation Editor.)

In addition, you can select a Keyboard Definition that will be used to help you type special characters in the equation. WordPerfect has created a keyboard named Equation which you may wish to select; see Chapter 15 for more on the Equation and Keyboard Layout features.

# Format Retrieved Documents for Default Printer

Chapter 9 describes how you can select different printers to print out documents. Whenever you create a new document, it is formatted according to the currently selected printer. The printer name is noted by WordPerfect on the Print menu next to the Select Print option. When the new document is saved on disk, the currently selected printer is attached to the document.

This Initial Settings option determines how the document will be formatted when retrieved. If this option is set to "No," as shown in Figure B-5, then the printer selected when a document was saved will be maintained when the document is retrieved. Or, if you set this option to "Yes" and the currently selected printer is different, then when you retrieve a document, WordPerfect will format it automatically for the currently selected printer.

For instance, suppose that, with the HP LaserJet Series II selected, you type a marketing report and save it on disk. Later that day, you select the Okidata 192 and work on several other documents. Still later, you decide to edit the marketing report. If the Format Retrieved Document feature is set to "Yes," then when you retrieve the report to screen, the document will be formatted for the Okidata 192; the Okidata will be listed as the selected printer on the Print menu. If the feature is set to "No," then the retrieved document will be formatted for the LaserJet.

Keep in mind, however, that a printer must have been defined for your copy of WordPerfect in order for it to be used to format a document. For instance, suppose a document had been saved using another copy of WordPerfect on another computer with the Citizen 35 selected. If the Citizen 35 is not found on the list of printers defined on your computer, WordPerfect will format the document for the currently selected printer—regardless of whether this feature has been set to "Yes" or "No".

## Initial Codes

Every time you clear the screen, ready to begin typing a new document, WordPerfect makes certain assumptions about how the new document should be formatted. For instance, the default left, right, top, and bottom margin settings are 1″. The default line spacing is single. The default justification is set at Full (5.1 users) or On (5.0 users), meaning both the left and right margins will be justified. These initial settings can be changed *from document to document* by inserting Format codes, as explained in Chapters 4, 6, and other chapters.

But what if you find yourself changing a specific format setting in the same way *for every document?* You can change that default permanently, tailoring the initial Format codes to those you use most often. Then WordPerfect assumes the new default every time you begin typing a document.

As a general rule, don't change the Setup menu unless you find yourself altering a format setting in the same way for almost all your documents. For instance, you may wish to change the Initial Codes on the Setup menu if you consistently change the justification and margin settings for almost every document you type.

To alter the default format settings, select Initial Codes (5 or C). WordPerfect displays the Setup Initial Codes screen, which is identical to a clear Reveal Codes screen. If the bottom window on screen is completely blank, this indicates that all the default format settings as set up by WordPerfect Corporation are in effect (as listed in Table B-1). If Format codes are displayed, then you or some other user has already altered some of the initial format settings.

To change any setting, insert Format codes just as you would on the Typing screen for a specific document. For example, to change the justification setting, press the FORMAT ( Shift + F8 ) key to display the Line Format menu, and then make the change. Or, if you wish to alter WordPerfect's assumptions on footnote options (such as the spacing between each footnote), press FOOTNOTE ( Ctrl + F7 ) and select Footnote (1 or F) and then Options (4 or O), and when the Footnote Options screen appears, make any changes you desire—as you would in a document. The codes will display only on the bottom window on the screen (just as they appear only on the bottom window in the Reveal Codes screen within a document). Then press EXIT ( F7 ) to return to the Initial Settings screen.

Once you change the default format settings, those new settings will affect documents that you create from that point on. Of course, any of the newly defined default settings can still be changed in a particular document; when you're typing a document and display the Document Initial

Settings screen (as described in Chapter 6), the default initial settings can be seen, edited, or eliminated for that one document.

Be aware, however, that any change to the default format settings will have no effect on pre-existing documents. That's because an invisible document prefix (packet of information) is saved with every document that you store on disk. The invisible packet includes those codes existing on the Document Initial Codes screen; unless altered, those codes are derived from those found on the Setup Initial Codes screen at the time the document was created. For example, suppose that you created and stored on disk one document using the default left/right margin settings of 1″. If you then use the Setup menu to alter the default to 2″, that first document will remain with margins of 1″, even though the left margin assumptions for all future documents you create will be defaulted at 2″.

## Repeat Value

You can change the number of times that the ⎡Esc⎤ key repeats a keystroke. The ⎡Esc⎤ key is used to repeat a character, cursor movement, or macro. By default, when you press ⎡Esc⎤, WordPerfect prompts

```
Repeat Value = 8
```

This means that the next keystroke you press will repeat eight times. You can instead permanently change the default value for this feature. (Note, however, that you can override the default setting of the repeat value for a specific working session when viewing the Typing or Reveal Codes screen by pressing ⎡Esc⎤, typing a number, and pressing ⎡Enter⎤; see Chapter 3 for details.)

## Table of Authorities

As described in Chapter 15, WordPerfect can generate a table of authorities for you. You can decide on three default settings regarding the style for Table of Authorities entries when generated: (1) whether a dot leader should precede the page location of each authority, (2) whether to allow underlining in the generated table, and (3) whether to insert blank lines between authorities. Be sure to refer to Chapter 15 for a fuller explanation of the Table of Authorities feature.

## Print Options

As described in Chapter 9, WordPerfect makes various assumptions about several aspects of the printing process whenever you print a job. Four of these options are

- *Binding Offset*   The extra amount of space added to left/right margins to plan for binding a document like a book. The original default setting is 0″.

- *Number of Copies*   The number of copies of the job you wish to print, and whether those copies are generated by WordPerfect or your printer.

- *Graphics Quality*   The quality level at which any graphics contained in the print job will be printed — either not to print the graphics at all, or to print draft, medium, or high quality.

- *Text Quality*   The quality level at which the text will be printed—either not to print the graphics at all, or to print draft, medium, or high quality.

All of these options can be altered for a working session or until you change them again on the Print menu, accessed using the PRINT (`Shift` + `F7`) key. However, they will revert back to the default setting the next time that you load WordPerfect. For instance, suppose you change the Number of Copies option to 2 on the Print menu to print out two copies of several documents. The setting "2" stays in effect for the rest of the working session, or until you change it again. But the next time you load WordPerfect, the Number of Copies option automatically resets to the default setting, which is "1".

Instead, you can alter these print options permanently via the Print Options item on the Setup menu. For instance, suppose that you constantly change the text quality to "draft" in your documents. Instead of changing this setting on the Print menu in each WordPerfect session, alter this setting using the Print Options item, so that "draft" text quality is assumed each time you start up WordPerfect.

Moreover, you can permanently alter the method used by your printer to print out text that is redlined or modify the size attribute ratios (for instance, where Fine is 60% of normal size) for a particular font.

# KEYBOARD LAYOUT

With the Keyboard Layout feature, you can create or edit a keyboard definition to specify which key performs a certain task or feature. You can set up your own keyboard definition whereby a feature is activated, a special character is inserted on screen, or a macro is executed by pressing a key of your choosing. Chapter 15 discusses this feature.

# LOCATION OF FILES

Select Location of Files (6 or L), and WordPerfect displays the menu shown in Figure B-6. On this menu, you specify where certain auxiliary files that WordPerfect uses are located on disk, such as the speller files that are used when you spell check a document, or the macro files that are used when you invoke a macro. If you do not specify a

```
Setup: Location of Files

     1 - Backup Files

     2 - Keyboard/Macro Files           C:\WP51

     3 - Thesaurus/Spell/Hyphenation
                         Main
                         Supplementary

     4 - Printer Files                  C:\WP51

     5 - Style Files
              Library Filename

     6 - Graphic Files

     7 - Documents




Selection: 0
```

≡≡≡ **FIGURE B-6**  Setup Location of Files screen
(version 5.1)

location for certain auxiliary files, WordPerfect assumes that these files are located either in the default drive/directory or wherever the main WordPerfect program file (WP.EXE) is housed. Or, if you previously used the WordPerfect Installation program to copy files onto your hard disk, then the location that you placed these files into is recorded in the Setup menu. The menu items in Figure B-6 are as follows:

- *Backup Files*   The directory where you want the files stored that are created when the Timed Backup feature is active (described previously in this appendix).

- *Keyboard/Macro Files*   The directory where your keyboard files (with the extension .WPK), macro files (with the extension .WPM and macro resource files (with the extension .MRS) are stored. Refer to Chapter 14 for more on the Macros feature, and Chapter 15 for more on the Keyboard Layout feature.

- *Thesaurus/Spell/Hyphenation, Main*   The directory where the main speller dictionary file WP{WP}US.LEX (or another main dictionary file that you use, such as in another language), the thesaurus WP{WP}US.THS, and the hyphenation module WP{WP}US.HYC are located. (In version 5.0, the hyphenation module is purchased separately from the WordPerfect program, and is available from WordPerfect Corporation, as mentioned in Chapter 4.) See Chapter 7 for more on the Spell and Thesaurus features, and see Chapter 4 for more on hyphenation.

- *Thesaurus/Spell/Hyphenation, Supplementary*   The directory where the WP{WP}US.SUP file and other supplementary dictionary files are located. See Chapter 7 for more on the Spell feature.

- *Printer Files*  The directory where files with the extension .ALL and .PRS are located. ALL files are those that contain printer drivers for variety of printers. .PRS files are created by you when you define a specific printer to work with WordPerfect.

- *Style Files*  The directory where the style files are located — files that are employed when you use the Style or Outline Style features, as described in Chapter 14.

- *Style Library Filename*  The path and filename for the file that acts as your style library, which is your default list of styles and is retrieved whenever you display the Styles screen for a new document. Note that this is the only option on the Location of Files menu where you must indicate not only a directory, but also a specific *filename*. For instance, suppose you wish to establish as your style library the file named STYLE.LIB, which is stored on the hard disk in the directory C:\WP51. Then you would enter C:\WP51\STYLE.LIB as the style library file name. See Chapter 14 for more on the Styles feature.

- *Graphic Files*  The directory where your graphics files are kept, including the files that end with the extension .WPG.

- *Documents*  The directory where you want your documents to be stored. This directory then becomes the default directory (unless or until you change the default, as described in Chapter 8).

By specifying a location for your auxiliary files, you can arrange a hard disk's WordPerfect files into their own directories. For instance, if you specify a keyboard/macro files directory named \WP51\KEYMACS, then whenever you create a keyboard definition or macro, WordPerfect automatically stores the file in that directory. And, when you activate a keyboard definition or invoke a macro, WordPerfect looks to that directory to find the definition or macro. Therefore, you can keep all keyboard definitions and macros separate from your document files, and thus maintain a well-organized filing system.

You must create a directory before you can enter it on the Location of Files screen. Also, make sure that you copy any previously created files into that directory. For instance, suppose you create \WP51\KEYMACS after you have already stored various macros and keyboard definition files in another directory. Move those files into \WP51\KEYMACS and then enter \WP51\KEYMACS as your Keyboard/Macro files directory.

# USING A MOUSE IN WORDPERFECT [5.1 USERS ONLY]

Move the Cursor
Block Text
Select Features

**W**ordPerfect 5.1 offers the ability to use a mouse instead of the keyboard when performing the following functions: moving the cursor, blocking text, and selecting features. If you have a mouse attached to your computer, you may find that using the mouse makes it easier to perform these functions than using the keyboard. Instructions for operating a mouse in WordPerfect are summarized in Table C-1 and are described in detail in this appendix.

Before you begin using a mouse, be sure that you have installed the mouse properly according to the instructions in your mouse documentation. Also, be sure to give Word-Perfect information about your mouse—including the type

| Function | Mouse Sequence |
|---|---|
| Move cursor on screen | Move pointer and click left button |
| Move cursor by scrolling through document | Press right button and drag mouse |
| Highlight a block | Position pointer, press left button and drag mouse |
| Display the menu bar | Click right button |
| Select numbered item in a menu | Position pointer and click left button |
| Select from list in a menu | Position pointer and double-click left button |
| Cancel | Click middle button (or click left and right buttons simultaneously) |
| Exit from menu | Click right button |

Click = Press button and release

Double-Click = Press button twice in rapid succession

Drag = Move mouse while button is held down

**TABLE C-1**   Major Functions of a Mouse in WordPerfect

of mouse you are using and the port through which the mouse is connected to your computer—on the Setup menu. Refer to the section entitled "Mouse" in Appendix B for the Setup menu procedure. Then you will be ready to use your mouse in WordPerfect.

# MOVE THE CURSOR

You will know that your mouse is operating in WordPerfect when you move the mouse and a reverse-video rectangle appears on the Typing screen (▌). This rectangle is the mouse pointer.

When you use a mouse, both the mouse pointer (▌) and the WordPerfect cursor (usually a blinking dash) appear on the screen at the same time. The two should not be confused. The mouse pointer appears every time that you move the mouse and disappears as soon as you press a key on the keyboard. The cursor remains on screen at all times.

You can use the mouse to point to a specific location on screen and have the WordPerfect cursor move to that position:

1. Move the mouse pointer to a specific position.

2. Click the left button on the mouse.

When you click, that means to press a button and then release it.

You can also use the mouse to scroll through the document, point to a part of the document that is not currently displayed on screen, and then have the cursor move there:

1. Press the right mouse button and continue to hold down that button.

2. Drag the mouse in the direction that you want to scroll.

3. Release the right mouse button.

When you drag, that means to press a button, hold that button down, and then move the mouse pointer. A mouse can be used to scroll quite quickly through a document, so remember to release the right button to stop the scrolling.

Keep in mind that the mouse pointer, just like the cursor keys, cannot be used to reposition the cursor where there is no text or codes. For instance, suppose you start a new document and type only three lines of text. If you move the mouse pointer to the bottom of the Typing screen and click the left button, the cursor will move only as far as the end of the third line of text, which is the end of the document and as far down the screen as the cursor can go.

# BLOCK TEXT

As described in Chapter 1, WordPerfect offers the ability to highlight a portion of text so that you can perform a task only on that highlighted area. The Block feature can be used, for instance, to define a portion of text to be underlined or boldfaced, deleted, or printed; it is fundamental to the workings of WordPerfect. Rather than block text using the keyboard, you can use a mouse:

1. Position the mouse pointer at one end of the block.

2. Press the left mouse button and continue to hold down that button.

3. Drag the mouse until the pointer is just past the last character or code in the block; the complete block will be highlighted in reverse video.

4. Release the left mouse button.

The message "Block on" blinks in the left corner on the status line. Now you can use the function keys or the pulldown menus to select a feature that will take effect on that block of text, as discussed in Chapter 1. Or, before doing so, you can use the keyboard (such as the cursor movement keys) to change the size of the block without canceling the block. If you press the left mouse button again, you will cancel the block.

# SELECT FEATURES

The chapter entitled "Getting Started" at the front of this book describes the two different methods for accessing features in WordPerfect: the function keys or the pulldown menus. You can use the mouse in combination with keystrokes to access features, or you can use the mouse exclusively.

## Select from Pulldown Menus

Table C-2 shows how WordPerfect features are grouped into the nine pulldown menus. There are two ways to access features from the pulldown menus using a mouse. The first method takes you step by step through the menu structure, as follows:

1. Click the right mouse button. A menu bar, which lists the nine pulldown menus, appears across the top of the screen:

   File  Edit  Search  Layout  Mark  Tools  Font  Graphics  Help

**Menu Bar**

File Edit Search Layout Mark Tools Font Graphics Help

| **File Menu** | **Edit Menu** | **Search Menu** |
|---|---|---|
| Retrieve | Move (Cut) | Forward |
| Save | Copy | Backward |
| Text In | Paste | Next |
| Text Out | Append | Previous |
| Password | Delete | Reverse |
| List Files | Undelete | Extended |
| Summary | Block | Goto |
| Print | Select | |
| Setup | Comment | |
| Goto DOS | Convert Case | |
| Exit | Protect Block | |
| | Switch Document | |
| | Window | |
| | Reveal Codes | |

| **Layout Menu** | **Mark Menu** | **Tools Menu** |
|---|---|---|
| Line | Index | Speller |
| Page | Table of Contents | Thesaurus |
| Document | List | Macro |
| Other | Cross Reference | Date Text |
| Columns | Table of Authorities | Date Code |
| Tables | Define | Date Format |
| Math | Generate | Outline |
| Footnote | Master Documents | Paragraph Number |
| Endnote | Subdocument | Define |
| Justify | Document Compare | Merge Codes |
| Align | | Merge |
| Styles | | Sort |
| | | Line Draw |

**TABLE C-2**   Pulldown Menu Structure

| Font Menu | Graphics Menu | Help Menu |
|---|---|---|
| Base Font | Figure | Help |
| Normal | Table Box | Index |
| Appearance | Text Box | Template |
| Superscript | User Box | |
| Subscript | Equation | |
| Fine | Line | |
| Small | | |
| Large | | |
| Very Large | | |
| Extra Large | | |
| Print Color | | |
| Characters | | |

**TABLE C-2**   Pulldown Menu Structure (*continued*)

2. Move the mouse pointer to one of the nine options and click the left mouse button to display the corresponding pulldown menu.

3. Move the mouse pointer to one of the submenu options and click the left mouse button to select that option.

The second method for selecting pulldown menu options allows you to scan the complete menu structure and, if unfamiliar with the menu structure, search for the location of a feature that you wish to select:

1. Click the right mouse button to display the menu bar.

2. Press the left mouse button and continue to hold down that button.

3. Drag the mouse through the menu structure—either between pulldown menus or within one pulldown menu structure—until the pointer is on the submenu option you wish to select.

4. Release the left mouse button to select that option.

Be aware that whenever you use the pulldown menus, some submenu options will be displayed in square brackets, such as [Append ] or [Delete ]. Brackets signify that the submenu option cannot be selected at the present time. Certain options can be selected only after the Block feature has been turned on, so that the message "Block on" flashes on screen, while others can be selected only when the Block feature is off.

## Select from Other Menus

You are not restricted in using the mouse only within pulldown menus. You can use the mouse to select a numbered option from a full screen menu, such as the Format menu shown in Figure C-1, or from a line menu such as

1 Footnote; 2 Endnote; 3 Endnote Placement: 0

Once the menu is displayed on screen, follow these steps:

1. Move the mouse pointer to a menu item number or to any word of that option.

2. Click the left button on the mouse.

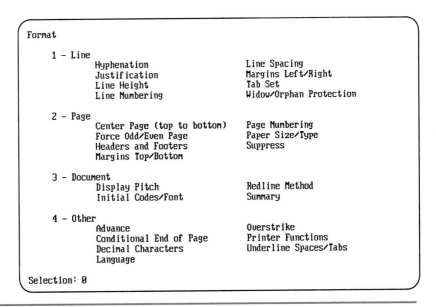

```
Format

    1 - Line
                Hyphenation                Line Spacing
                Justification             Margins Left/Right
                Line Height               Tab Set
                Line Numbering            Widow/Orphan Protection

    2 - Page
                Center Page (top to bottom)   Page Numbering
                Force Odd/Even Page           Paper Size/Type
                Headers and Footers           Suppress
                Margins Top/Bottom

    3 - Document
                Display Pitch              Redline Method
                Initial Codes/Font         Summary

    4 - Other
                Advance                    Overstrike
                Conditional End of Page    Printer Functions
                Decimal Characters         Underline Spaces/Tabs
                Language

Selection: 0
```

**FIGURE C-1**   Use a mouse to select from the Format menu

A mouse can also select an item from a list that is not in a numbered menu. For instance, from the Base Font menu shown in Figure C-2, you can select a font item as follows:

1. Move the mouse pointer to the item you wish to select.

2. Double-click the left mouse button.

When you double-click, that means to click the mouse button twice in rapid succession. Double-clicking is comparable to clicking so that the cursor moves onto an item and then pressing the Enter key. But double-clicking is more convenient when you don't wish to use the mouse in combination with the keyboard.

```
Base Font

* Courier 10cpi
  Courier 10cpi Bold
  Helv 14.4pt Bold (B)
  Letter Gothic 10cpi (Legal) (R)
  Letter Gothic 10cpi (R)
  Line Draw 10cpi (Full)
  Line Draw 10cpi 14pt (R)
  Line Printer 16.67cpi
  PC Line Draw 10cpi 14pt (Land) (R)
  PC Line Draw 10cpi 14pt (R)
  Presentation  6.5cpi Bold (Legal) (R)
  Presentation  6.5cpi Bold (R)
  Presentation  8.1cpi Bold (Legal) (R)
  Presentation  8.1cpi Bold (R)
  Presentation 10cpi Bold (Legal) (R)
  Presentation 10cpi Bold (R)
  TmsRmn  8pt (B)
  TmsRmn 10pt (B)
  TmsRmn 10pt Bold (B)
  TmsRmn 10pt Italic (B)

1 Select; N Name search: 1
```

**FIGURE C-2** Use a mouse to select from the Base Font menu

## Respond to Prompts

You can use the mouse when you select a feature and WordPerfect displays a prompt for more information. Some prompts ask a question and require a "Yes" or "No" answer, such as

```
Save document? Yes (No)
```

To respond to this prompt,

1. Move the mouse pointer on any letter in the word "Yes" or in the word "No".
2. Click the left mouse button.

Other prompts require input from the keyboard. In such instances, the mouse can be used to position the cursor within the prompt. For instance, assume that WordPerfect is displaying the following prompt:

Document to be saved: C:\WP51\DATA\SAMPLE.DOC

Move the mouse pointer to any character in the string "C:\WP51\DATA\SAMPLE.DOC" and click the left button on the mouse. Now you can edit the string using the keyboard.

There is one prompt where you will want to double-click as a response. Suppose that you've used the Move or Copy command, so that the following prompt is on screen:

Move cursor; Press **Enter** to retrieve

Text is in the Move/Copy buffer, waiting to be retrieved. Rather than use the Enter key, you can use the mouse to respond:

1. Move the mouse pointer to the location where you wish to retrieve the text.

2. Double-click the left mouse button.

# Clear WordPerfect Menus and Prompts

You learned in the "Getting Started" chapter that when you wish to clear prompts from the screen, or to back out of the menu structure one level at a time, you can use the CANCEL (F1) key. Moreover, when you wish to exit all the way out of menus or prompts in one operation, you can use the EXIT (F7) key. The same functions are available using a mouse.

The middle mouse button on a three-button mouse acts like the CANCEL key. For example, if you're viewing the Line Format menu, press the middle button to back out one level, so that you're viewing the Format menu. Should you have a two-button mouse, then cancel by pressing the two buttons simultaneously; that is, press and hold down one of the buttons and, while holding it down, click the other button.

Once you are viewing a menu or prompt, the right mouse button acts like the EXIT key. Thus, you can click the right mouse button to clear the menu immediately and return to the Typing screen. If you are currently holding down a mouse button and dragging the mouse, however, then clear the menu differently: move the pointer away from any menu selections and release the mouse button.

## Define Macros

Chapter 14 discusses how the Macro feature is a powerful method for automating tasks. By defining a macro, you record keystrokes that can then be executed at your command.

When defining a macro, you can use a mouse instead of the keyboard to select menu items; those mouse selections will be stored as the equivalent keystrokes. But you cannot use the mouse to position the cursor when defining a macro.

# WORDPERFECT FILES AND CODES

WordPerfect Version 5.1 Files
WordPerfect Version 5.0 Files
WordPerfect Codes

**T**his appendix contains lists of files that can aid you in working with WordPerfect. The first section lists files on the master disks in WordPerfect version 5.1. The second section lists files on the master disks in WordPerfect version 5.0. The last section lists WordPerfect codes that may appear on the Reveal Codes screen when you type and edit a document in WordPerfect.

## WORDPERFECT VERSION 5.1 FILES

The WordPerfect 5.1 installation program installs files from the master diskettes in groups. The following list indicates those files that are copied when you choose to install certain groups. Use this list to aid you in selecting groups of files for installation and to locate a particular file on your hard disk or floppy disks.

**WordPerfect Program Files**

| | |
|---|---|
| KEYS.MRS[2] | Keyboard macro resource file (used with the Keyboard Layout feature) |
| PRINTER.TST[1] | Printer test file |
| STANDARD.IRS[2] | Mouse driver file |
| STANDARD.PRS[2] | Text mode preview and standard printer resource file |
| STANDARD.VRS[2] | Standard graphics and text resource file |
| WP.EXE[1] | WordPerfect program |
| WP.FIL[2] | Contains a part of the WordPerfect code |
| WP.MRS[2] | Macro resource file (used with the Macro feature) |
| WP.QRS[2] | Equation resource file (used with the Equation feature) |
| WPSMALL.DRS[2] | Driver resource file (used with a floppy disk system) |

**WordPerfect Help File**

| | |
|---|---|
| WPHELP.FIL[1] | WordPerfect help file |

---

[1] Stored on the WordPerfect 1 disk if you installed to floppy disks
[2] Stored on the WordPerfect 2 disk if you installed to floppy disks

### Speller Files

WP{WP}US.LEX      Main word list (U.S. English dictionary and external hyphenation dictionary)

WP{WP}.SPW       Operates the Spell feature

WP{WP}US.HYC      Operates the external hyphenation dictionary

### Thesaurus File

WP{WP}US.THS      Thesaurus list (U.S. English thesaurus)

### Learning Files

TUTOR.COM       Tutorial

WORKBOOK.PRS     Printer resource file for WordPerfect Workbook

*.TUT           Tutorial files

*.WKB          Learning files for WordPerfect Workbook

*.WPG          Graphics images for WordPerfect Workbook

### Printer Files

*.ALL           Printer driver files (containing information for many printers)

### PTR Program Files

CHARMAP.TST      Character set printer test

EHANDLER.PS      PostScript printer file (installed only when you select a PostScript printer)

| KERN.TST | Kerned letter pair printer test |
| PTR.EXE | Printer program utility |
| PTR.HLP | Printer program help file |

**Utility Files**

| CHARACTR.DOC | WordPerfect character set documentation |
| CONVERT.EXE | Convert program |
| CURSOR.COM | Cursor program |
| INSTALL.EXE | Installation program |
| FIXBIOS.COM | Program to fix BIOS problems running WordPerfect on a non-100% IBM compatible |
| GRAB.COM | Screen capture program |
| GRAPHCNV.EXE | Graphics conversion program |
| MACROCNV.EXE | Macro conversion program |
| NWPSETUP.EXE | Network setup program |
| SPELL.EXE | Speller utility program |
| STANDARD.CRS | Conversion resource file (converts version 4.2 documents into version 5.1) |
| *.PIF | Program information files (when running WordPerfect under windows) |

| | |
|---|---|
| WPINFO.EXE | WordPerfect information program (to gather information about your computer system) |
| WP.LRS | WordPerfect language resource file |

**Fonts/Graphics Files**

| | |
|---|---|
| EGA*.FRS | Font resource files for EGA monitors |
| HRF*.FRS | Font resource files for Hercules RamFonts graphics cards |
| VGA*.FRS | Font resource files for VGA monitors |
| WP.DRS | Driver resource file (used with a hard disk system) |
| *.VRS | Graphics or text driver files for specific monitors |
| *.WPG | 30 graphics images |

**Macro/Keyboard Files**

| | |
|---|---|
| LIBRARY.STY | Style library example |
| *.WPK | WordPerfect keyboard definition examples |
| *.WPM | Macro examples |

**Files Created When Installing or Working in WordPerfect**

| | |
|---|---|
| WP51.INS | Installation file |

| WP}WP{.* | Overflow, print buffer, sort, and other temporary files (stored on the drive where WP.EXE is located or on the drive specified with the /D startup option), which are deleted when you exit WordPerfect |
|---|---|
| *.BK! | Original backup files |
| *.CRS | Document conversion files |
| *.PRS | Printer definition files (stored on the drive where WP.EXE is located) |
| *.WPK | Keyboard definition files |
| *.WPM | Macro files |
| WP{WP}.BK# | Timed backup files |
| WP{WP}US.SUP | Supplementary dictionary file |
| WP{WP}.SET | Setup file (containing all the changes to the WordPerfect default settings initiated on the Setup menu) |

# WORDPERFECT VERSION 5.0 FILES

The WordPerfect 5.0 master diskettes can be copied directly onto a hard disk or onto floppy disks during installation. The following list indicates which files are contained on which master disk. Use this list to aid you in deciding which master disks to install, and to locate a particular file on your hard disk or floppy disks.

**WordPerfect 1 Disk Files**

| | |
|---|---|
| WP.EXE | WordPerfect program |
| WPHELP.FIL | WordPerfect help file |
| WPHELP2.FIL | WordPerfect help file |

**WordPerfect 2 Disk Files**

| | |
|---|---|
| KEYS.MRS | Keyboard macro resource file (used with the Keyboard Layout feature) |
| STANDARD.PRS | Text mode preview and standard printer resource file |
| WP.FIL | Contains a part of the WordPerfect code |
| WP.MRS | Macro resource file (used with the Macro feature) |
| WPSMALL.DRS | Driver resource file (used with a floppy disk system) |

**Speller Disk Files**

| | |
|---|---|
| WP{WP}US.LEX | Main and common word lists (U.S. English dictionary) |
| SPELL.EXE | Speller utility |

**Thesaurus Disk Files**

| | |
|---|---|
| WP{WP}US.THS | Thesaurus list (U.S. English thesaurus) |

**Learning Disk Files**

| | |
|---|---|
| TUTOR.COM | Tutorial |

| LEARN.BAT | Batch file to initiate tutorial on a floppy disk system |
| INSTALL.EXE | Installation program |
| *.STY | Styles for WordPerfect Workbook |
| *.TUT | Tutorial files |
| *.WKB | Learning files for WordPerfect Workbook |
| *.WPG | Graphics images for WordPerfect Workbook |
| *.WPM | Macros for WordPerfect Workbook |

**Printer 1, 2, 3, 4 Disk Files**

| *.ALL | Printer driver files (containing information for many printers) |

**PTR Program Disk Files**

| PTR.EXE | Printer program utility |
| PTR.HLP | Printer program help file |

**Conversion Disk Files**

| CURSOR.COM | Cursor utility |
| CHARACTR.DOC | WordPerfect character set documentation |
| CHARMAP.TST | Character set printer test |
| CONVERT.EXE | Convert program |
| FC.* | Font conversion program and documentation |

| | |
|---|---|
| FIXBIOS.COM | Program to fix BIOS problems running WordPerfect on a non-100% IBM compatible |
| GRAPHCNV.EXE | Graphics conversion program |
| LIBRARY.STY | Sample style library |
| MACROCNV.EXE | Macros conversion program |
| ORDERWPG.DOC | Graphics ordering information |
| PRINTER.TST | WordPerfect features printer test |
| STANDARD.CRS | Conversion resource file |
| WPINFO.EXE | WordPerfect information program (to gather information about your computer system) |
| *.WPK | WordPerfect keyboard definition examples |

**Fonts/Graphics Disk Files**

| | |
|---|---|
| EGA*.FRS | Font resource files for EGA monitors |
| GRAB.COM | Screen capture utility |
| HRF*.FRS | Font resource file for Hercules RamFonts graphics cards |
| WP.DRS | Driver resource file (used with a hard disk system) |
| *.WPD | Graphics driver files for specific monitors |
| *.WPG | 30 graphics images |

### Files Created When Installing or Working in WordPerfect

| | |
|---|---|
| WP50.INS | Installation file |
| WP}WP{.* | Overflow, print buffer, sort, and other temporary files (stored on the drive where WP.EXE is located or on the drive specified with the /D startup option), which are deleted when you exit Word-Perfect |
| *.BK! | Original backup files |
| *.CRS | Document conversion files |
| *.PRS | Printer definition files (stored on the drive where WP.EXE is located) |
| *.WPK | Keyboard definition files |
| *.WPM | Macro files |
| WP{WP}.BK# | Timed backup files |
| WP{WP}US.SUP | Supplementary dictionary file |
| WP{WP}.SET | Setup file (containing all the changes to the WordPerfect default settings initiated on the Setup menu) |

# WORDPERFECT CODES

The following list contains WordPerfect codes that are inserted into your document when you activate features and commands. Use this list when viewing the Reveal

Codes screen to determine what feature has been activated by a certain code found in your document.

Keep in mind that there are two types of codes. *Open* codes are single codes that turn on a feature from the cursor position either to the end of the document or to the location where another code of the same type has been inserted. *Paired* codes come in twos. With paired codes, the begin code (displayed in uppercase letters) marks the location where the feature is turned on and the end code (displayed in lowercase) marks the location where the feature is turned off, such as in [BOLD] and [bold].

Those codes that appear only in version 5.1 are marked with an asterisk (*), while those that appear only in version 5.0 are marked with a plus sign (⁺).

| Code | Feature |
|------|---------|
| ^M⁺ | Merge (M = merge code letter, such as ^R or ^E) |
| - | Soft hyphen |
| [ ] | Hard space |
| [-] | Hyphen character |
| [/] | Cancel hyphenation |
| [+] | Subtotal calculation (Math) |
| [=] | Total calculation (Math) |
| [*] | Grand total calculation (Math) |
| [!] | Formula calculation (Math) |
| [N] | Calculation treated as negative (Math) |
| [t] | Known subtotal entry (Math) |

| | |
|---|---|
| [T] | Known total entry (Math) |
| [AdvDn:] | Advance down |
| [AdvLft:] | Advance left |
| [AdvRgt:] | Advance right |
| [AdvToPos:] | Advance to position |
| [AdvToLn:] | Advance to line |
| [AdvUp:] | Advance up |
| [Align][C/A/FlRt]⁺ | Decimal tab align (begin and end) |
| [Bline:]* | Baseline placement |
| [Block] | Beginning of block |
| [Block Pro:On][Block Pro:Off] | Block protection (begin and end) |
| [BOLD][bold] | Bold (begin and end) |
| [Box Num] | Caption in graphics box |
| [C/A/FlRt]⁺ | End of center, tab align, or flush right |
| [Cell]* | Cell in a table |
| [Center]* | Center |
| [Center Pg] | Center page top to bottom |
| [Cntr][C/A/FlRt]⁺ | Center (begin and end) |
| [Cndl EOP:] | Conditional end of page |
| [Cntr Tab]* | Centered tab |
| [CNTR TAB]* | Hard centered tab |
| [Col Def:] | Text columns definition |
| [Col Off] | Text columns off |
| [Col On] | Text columns on |

| [Color:] | Print color |
| [Comment] | Document comment |
| [Date:] | Date/time format |
| [DBL UND][dbl und] | Double underline (begin and end) |
| [Dec Tab]* | Decimal tab align |
| [DEC TAB]* | Hard decimal tab align |
| [Decml/Algn Char:] | Decimal align and thousands separator characters |
| [Def Mark:Index] | Index definition |
| [Def Mark:List,*n*] | List definition (*n* = list number) |
| [Def Mark:ToA,*n*] | Table of authorities definition (*n* = section number) |
| [Def Mark:ToC,*n*] | Table of contents definition (*n* = ToC level) |
| [Dorm HRt]* | Dormant hard return |
| [DSRt] | Deletable soft return |
| [EndDef] | End of index, list, or table (after generation) |
| [EndMark:List,*n*] | End marked text for list (n = list number) |
| [EndMark:ToC,*n*] | End marked text for table of contents (*n* = ToC level) |
| [End Opt] | Endnote options |
| [Endnote:*n*;[Note Num]*text*] | Endnote (*n* = note number) |
| [Endnote Placement] | Endnote placement |

| | |
|---|---|
| [Equ Box:*n*;]* | Equation box (*n* = box number) |
| [Equ Opt]* | Equation box options |
| [EXT LARGE][ext large] | Extra large print |
| [Fig Box:*n*;] | Figure box (*n* = box number) |
| [Fig Opt] | Figure box options |
| [FINE][fine] | Fine print (begin and end) |
| [Flsh Rgt]* | Flush right |
| [Flsh Rt][C/A/FlRt]+ | Flush right (begin and end) |
| [Font:] | Base font |
| [Footer *N:n;text*] | Footer (*N* = type, A or B; *n* = frequency) |
| [Footnote:*n*;[Note Num]*text*] | Footnote (*n* = note number) |
| [Force:] | Force odd or force even |
| [Ftn Opt] | Footnote options |
| [Header *N:n;text*] | Header (*N* = type, A or B; *n* = frequency) |
| [HLine:] | Horizontal line |
| [HPg] | Hard page |
| [Hrd Row]* | Hard row in a table |
| [HRt] | Hard return |
| [HRt-SPg]* | Hard return — soft page |
| [Hyph Off] | Hyphenation off |
| [Hyph On] | Hyphenation on |
| [HZone:*n,n*] | Hyphenation zone (*n* = left,right) |
| [→Indent] | Indent |

| | |
|---|---|
| [→Indent◄] | Left/right indent |
| [Index:heading;subheading] | Index entry |
| [ISRt] | Invisible soft return |
| [ITALC][Italc] | Italics print (begin and end) |
| [Just:]* | Justification |
| [Just Off]+ | Right justification off |
| [Just On]+ | Right justification on |
| [Just Lim:] | Justification limits for word/ letter spacing |
| [Kern:Off] | Kerning off |
| [Kern:On] | Kerning on |
| [L/R Mar:] | Left and right margins |
| [Lang:] | Language (for speller, the- saurus, hyphenation module) |
| [LARGE][large] | Large print (begin and end) |
| [Leading Adj:]* | Leading adjustment |
| [Link:]* | Spreadsheet link |
| [Link End]* | Spreadsheet link end |
| [Ln Height:] | Line height |
| [Ln Num:Off] | Line numbering off |
| [Ln Num:On] | Line numbering on |
| [Ln Spacing:] | Line spacing |
| [◄Mar Rel] | Left margin release |
| [Mark:List,$n$][EndMark: List,$n$] | List entry mark (begin and end, $n$ = list number) |

| | |
|---|---|
| **[Mark:ToC,*n*][End Mark:ToC,*n*]** | Table of contents entry mark (begin and end, *n* = ToC level) |
| **[Math Def]** | Math columns definition |
| **[Math Off]** | Math columns off |
| **[Math On]** | Math columns on |
| **[Mrg:*t*]**\* | Merge (*t* = type) |
| **[New End Num:]** | New endnote number |
| **[New Equ Num:]**\* | New equation number |
| **[New Fig Num:]** | New figure box number |
| **[New Ftn Num:]** | New footnote number |
| **[New Tab Num:]** | New table number |
| **[New Txt Num:]** | New text box number |
| **[New Usr Num:]** | New user-defined box number |
| **[Note Num]** | Footnote/endnote reference number |
| **[Open Style:*name*]** | Open style (*name* = style name) |
| **[Outline Lvl*n* Open Style:]**\* | Outline open style (*n* = outline level) |
| **[Outline Lvl *n* Style On] [Outline Lvl *n*Style Off]**\* | Outline paired style (begin and end, *n* = outline level) |
| **[Outline Off]**\* | Outline off |
| **[Outline On]**\* | Outline on |
| **[OUTLN][outln]** | Outline attribute (begin and end) |

| | |
|---|---|
| **[Ovrstk:]** | Overstrike |
| **[Paper Sz/Typ:*s,t*]** | Paper size and type (*s* = size, *t* = type) |
| **[Par Num:Auto]** | Paragraph number, automatic |
| **[Par Num:*n*]** | Paragraph number (*n* = paragraph level) |
| **[Par Num Def:]** | Paragraph numbering definition |
| **[Pg Num:]** | New page number |
| **[Pg Num Style:]**<sup>*</sup> | Page number style |
| **[Pg Numbering:]** | Page numbering position |
| **[Ptr Cmnd:]** | Printer command |
| **[REDLN][redln]** | Redline (begin and end) |
| **[Ref(*name*): *t*]** | Cross reference (*name* = target name, *t* = what reference is tied to) |
| **[Rgt Tab]**<sup>*</sup> | Right tab align |
| **[RGT TAB]**<sup>*</sup> | Hard right tab align |
| **[Row]**<sup>*</sup> | Row in a table |
| **[SHADW][shadw]** | Shadow (begin and end) |
| **[SM CAP][sm cap]** | Small caps (begin and end) |
| **[SMALL][small]** | Small print (begin and end) |
| **[SPg]** | Soft page |
| **[SRt]** | Soft return |
| **[STKOUT][stkout]** | Strikeout (begin and end) |
| **[Style On:*name*][Style Off:*name*]** | Paired style (begin and end, *name* = style name) |

| | |
|---|---|
| [Subdoc:] | Subdocument in a master document |
| **[Subdoc Start:] [Subdoc End:]** | Subdocument after being generated (begin and end) |
| **[SUBSCRPT] [subscrpt]** | Subscript (begin and end) |
| **[SUPRSCPT] [suprscpt]** | Superscript (begin and end) |
| [Suppress:] | Suppress page format options |
| **[T/B Mar:]** | Top and bottom margins |
| [Tab] | Left align tab |
| [TAB]* | Hard left align tab |
| [Tab Set:] | Tab set |
| **[Target(*name*)]** | Target in cross reference (*name* = target name) |
| **[Tbl Box:*n*;]** | Table box (*n* = box number) |
| **[Tbl Def:*n*;]*** | Table definition (*n* = table number) |
| **[Tbl Off]*** | Table off |
| **[Tbl Opt]** | Table box options |
| **[Text Box:*n*;]** | Text box (*n* = box number) |
| [ToA:;*text*;] | Table of authorities short form (*text* = text of short form) |
| **[ToA:*n*;*text*;Full Form]** | Table of authorities full form (*n* = section number, *text* = text of short form) |
| [Txt Opt] | Text box options |
| **[UND] [und]** | Underlining (begin and end) |

| | |
|---|---|
| [Undrln:] | Underline spaces and/or tabs |
| [Usr Box:*n*;] | User-defined box (*n* = box number) |
| [Usr Opt] | User-defined box options |
| [VLine:] | Vertical line |
| [VRY LARGE] [vry large] | Very large print (begin and end) |
| [Wrd/Ltr Spacing:] | Word and letter spacing |
| [W/O Off] | Widow/orphan off |
| [W/O On] | Widow/orphan on |

# GETTING
# ADDITIONAL
# SUPPORT

As a beginning user, you may encounter some frustration in becoming accustomed to how WordPerfect operates. Just remember that you're not alone. Many thousands of people use WordPerfect daily and have numerous questions as they learn about new WordPerfect features.

Whatever you do, don't work with WordPerfect in a vacuum. Establish a support network for yourself. If you know someone who uses WordPerfect, start sharing information; you'll both expand your comfort with and knowledge of WordPerfect.

In addition, there are many formal sources of assistance, whether you desire additional instruction on WordPerfect, or you need help answering specific questions related to a particularly complicated document or your computer equipment. Here are some suggestions:

- For quick, general answers to using features, try the Help facility. The "Getting Started" chapter describes how to use Help.

- For a more in-depth understanding of advanced Word-Perfect features, look to other books by Osborne/McGraw-Hill, available at your local bookstore. Several of these are listed at the beginning of this book.

  For a free catalog of all Osborne/McGraw-Hill offerings, fill out and return the card at the back of this book, or write to Osborne/McGraw-Hill, 2600 Tenth Street, Berkeley, California 94710.

- For help using WordPerfect with your particular equipment, your computer dealer may have the answer.

- To report software problems or to get answers to specific questions on WordPerfect, look to WordPerfect Corporation. Their telephone support is frequently hailed as the best in the business. Over 500 people staff the telephones in Customer Support, ready to answer your questions about installation, printers, or general items on all Word-Perfect Corporation products. They are extremely responsive once you get through to them, but you may be placed on hold during peak hours (11:00 A.M. to 3:00 P.M. mountain standard time). Customer Support is available from 7 A.M. to 6 P.M. mountain standard time, Monday through Friday. The phone number that you should dial differs, depending on your needs:

| Topic | Toll-Free Number | Toll-Number |
| --- | --- | --- |
| Installation | (800) 533-9605 | (801) 226-5444 |
| Printer Support | (800) 541-5097 | (801) 226-7977 |
| Graphics/Macros | (800) 321-3383 | (801) 226-4770 |

| Topic | Toll-Free Number | Toll-Number |
|---|---|---|
| Features | (800) 541-5096 | (801) 226-7900 |
| WordPerfect Networks | (800) 321-3389 | (801) 226-4777 |

Additional toll-free telephone numbers are available for information on other WordPerfect products, such as WordPerfect Library, WordPerfect Office, DataPerfect, and so on. For general questions, dial (800) 321-3349. Also, WordPerfet Corporation offers after-hours Customer Support at (801) 226-6444.

When you call WordPerfect Corporation, make sure that you're at your computer, with WordPerfect loaded. That way you can duplicate the problem you're encountering keystroke-by-keystroke for the Customer Support representative.

Alternatively, you can write to the Customer Support Department. The address is

WordPerfect Corporation
Attention: Customer Support Department
1555 North Technology Way
Orem, UT 84057

When you write, include a full explanation of the problem you're encountering, the equipment you use, and the version, release date, and license number of your Word-Perfect program. (This information will appear in the upper right corner of the computer screen when you press the HELP (F3) key while in WordPerfect.)

- For more practice with a variety of features, the Word-Perfect package contains an on-disk tutorial. The tutorial offers instruction on learning the basics in WordPerfect, such as using the keyboard, formatting a document, and moving text. The tutorial is in a file named TUTO-R.COM, and is available if you installed the learning files onto your hard disk or onto floppy disks. To access the tutorial, you must be in DOS and not in WordPerfect. Proceed as follows once you are in DOS:

*Hard disk users:* Type **tutor** and press (Enter). When the tutorial begins, follow the directions on screen to select the features you wish to learn more about.

If the tutorial program does not begin or begins but works improperly, then there is a problem with the computer's DOS PATH command. The PATH command tells the computer where to look on the hard disk in order to execute certain programs; in the case of the tutorial, this command must tell the computer where to find the learning files and the WordPerfect program files. To rectify the problem, make sure you are again viewing the DOS prompt. Now, type **path** and press (Enter). The computer will display a list of the directories contained in the command (each separated by semicolon), such as PATH=C:\DOS;C:\WP51;C:\UTIL. Now, you should enter a new PATH command that contains all the directories just listed by the computer as well as the directories where the WordPerfect program files (WP.EXE and WP.FIL) and the WordPerfect learning files are contained, if these have not already been listed. For instance, suppose that the program files are in C:\WP51 and that the learning files are in C:\WP51\LEARN. If that is the case you will need to type **path=c:\dos;c:\wp51;c:\util;c:\wp51\learn** and press (Enter). Now, type **tutor** and press (Enter) to begin the tutorial.

*Floppy disk users:* Place the WordPerfect 1 disk in drive A and the Learning disk in drive B. Type

**path = a:\;b:\** and press ⸢Enter⸣. (The PATH command tells the computer where to look on the floppy disks in order to execute certain programs; in the case of the tutorial, this command must tell the computer where the learning files and the WordPerfect program files are found.) Next, type **tutor** and press ⸢Enter⸣. In a few moments, a message on screen will direct you to take the WordPerfect 1 disk out of drive A and replace it with the WordPerfect 2 disk. Then the tutorial will begin; follow the directions on screen to select the features you wish to learn more about.

- The WordPerfect Workbook, a book included in the WordPerfect package, includes over 30 additional practice lessons. Start a lesson by loading WordPerfect as described in the chapter entitled "Getting Started," located at the front of this book. Then proceed as follows:

    *Hard disk users:* Change to the default directory on the hard disk where the learning files are stored, which most probably is \WP51\LEARN or \WP50\LEARN. One method for changing the default is to press the LIST (⸢F5⸣) key, type the equal sign (=), edit the prompt to list the directory where the learning files are stored, press ⸢Enter⸣ to register the change, and then press CANCEL (⸢F1⸣) to clear the prompt. (Chapter 8 describes in more detail how to change the default directory from within WordPerfect.) Now you are ready to begin reading the workbook and to follow along.

    *Floppy disk users:* Place the Learning disk in drive B. Now you are ready to begin reading the workbook and to follow along. Keep in mind that you will need to replace the Learning disk with other disks as you proceed with the workbook's lessons. For instance, before using the Spell feature in a given lesson, you will need to insert the Speller disk in drive B.

- For a user group devoted exclusively to WordPerfect Corporation products, there's the WordPerfect Support Group in Maryland. But you don't need to live in Maryland to get their support. They produce a newsletter called "The WordPerfectionist," which is a good source for general information and tips on WordPerfect and other WordPerfect Corporation products. In addition, the Support Group operates an electronic mail bulletin board service (for those of you with a modem), through which members can share ideas and information. You can join by writing to the following address:

  WordPerfect Support Group
  Lake Technology Park
  P.O. Box 130
  McHenry, MD 21541

  To subscribe to "The WordPerfectionist," you can also call the following toll-free number: (800) 872-4768. You can access the bulletin board service from CompuServe (an on-line service) by typing **GO WPSG**.

  Also, check local computer magazines for a WordPerfect support group in your area. For instance, Seattle, Washington, has its own WordPerfect user group.

- For a better understanding of your computer and various software packages, there are user groups devoted to your brand of computer. If you have an IBM PC, for example, there may be an IBM PC user group in your area in which you can meet other people who use WordPerfect and exchange information. User groups' names and addresses are listed in regional and national computer magazines.

# TRADEMARKS

| | |
|---|---|
| Adobe™ Illustrator | Adobe Systems, Inc. |
| AutoCAD® | Autodesk, Inc. |
| CBDS™ | International Business Machines Corporation |
| CDDM™ | International Business Machines Corporation |
| Chart-Master® | Decision Resources, Inc./Ashton-Tate |
| CompuServe® | CompuServe, Inc. |
| DataPerfect® | WordPerfect Corporation |
| dBASE® | Ashton-Tate |
| Diablo® | Xerox Corporation |
| Diagram-Master® | Decision Resources Inc./Ashton-Tate |
| DisplayWrite™ | International Business Machines Corporation |

| | |
|---|---|
| Dr. Halo™ | IMSI |
| EnerGraphics™ | Enertronics Research, Inc. |
| Epson LQ-1000™ | Epson America, Inc. |
| Microsoft® Excel | Microsoft Corporation |
| Framework II® | Ashton-Tate |
| Freelance® Plus | Lotus Development Corp. |
| GEM® | Digital Research, Inc. |
| Generic CADD™ | Generic Software, Inc. |
| Graph-in-the-Box® | New England Software |
| GRAFPLUS™ | Jewell Technologies |
| Graphwriter® | Lotus Development Corp. |
| Harvard™ Graphics | Software Publishing Corporation |
| Hercules® | Hercules Computer Technology |
| HP Graphics Gallery™ | Hewlett-Packard Company |
| HP LaserJet® Series II | Hewlett-Packard Company |
| HP Scannin Gallery™ | Hewlett-Packard Company |
| Lotus® 1-2-3® | Lotus Development Corporation |
| MacPaint® | Apple Computer, Inc. |
| Microsoft® Chart | Microsoft Corporation |
| MultiMate® | MultiMate International Corporation |
| OKIDATA® | OKIDATA, and OKI AMERICA Co. |
| Paradox® | Borland International, Inc. |
| PC Paintbrush® | Zsoft, Inc. |

| | |
|---|---|
| PC Paint Plus® | Mouse Systems Corp. |
| PFS:® First Publishing Pizazz | Software Publishing Corp. |
| Pixie™ | Sperry Univac |
| PlanPerfect™ | WordPerfect Corporation |
| PostScript® | Adobe Systems, Inc. |
| Proprinter™ | International Business Machines Corporation |
| Publisher's PicturePaks™ | Marketing Graphics, Inc. |
| Quattro® | Borland International, Inc. |
| Reflex® | Borland International, Inc. |
| SignMaster® | Ashton-Tate |
| SlideWrite Plus™ | Advanced Graphics Software |
| SuperCalc® 4 | Computer Associates International, Inc. |
| Symphony® | Lotus Development Corp. |
| VP Planner® | Paperback Software International |
| WordPerfect® | WordPerfect Corporation |
| WordPerfect Library® | WordPerfect Corporation |
| WordPerfect Office™ | WordPerfect Corporation |
| WordStar® | WordStar International, Inc. |

# INDEX

The manuscript for this book was prepared and submitted to Osborne/McGraw-Hill in electronic form. The acquisitions editor for this project was Cindy Hudson, the technical reviewer was Scott Maiden, and the project editors were Dusty Bernard and Kathy Krause.

Text design by Marcela Hancik and Mary Abbas, using Times Roman for text body and Swiss boldface for display.

Cover art by Bay Graphics Design Associates. Color separation by Phoenix Color Corporation. Screens produced with Inset from Inset Systems, Inc. Book printed and bound by R.R. Donnelley & Sons Company, Crawfordsville, Indiana.

# Command Card
## Basic WordPerfect Features

## CURSOR CONTROL

| | |
|---|---|
| Character left | ← |
| Character right | → |
| Line up | ↑ |
| Line down | ↓ |
| Word left | Ctrl + ← |
| Word right | Ctrl + → |
| Left end of screen | Home, ← |
| Right end of screen | Home, → |
| Top of screen | Home, ↑ or − |
| Bottom of screen | Home, ↓ or + |
| Top of current page | Ctrl + Home, ↑ |
| Bottom of current page | Ctrl + Home, ↓ |
| Top of page number | Ctrl + Home, *pagenumber* |
| Top of previous page | PgUp |
| Top of next page | PgDn |
| Left end of line | Home, Home, ← |
| Right end of line | Home, Home, End or → |
| Top of document | Home, Home, ↑ |
| Bottom of document | Home, Home, ↓ |

## DELETE TEXT/CODES

| | |
|---|---|
| Character left of cursor | Backspace |
| Character at cursor | Del |
| Word at cursor | Ctrl + Backspace |
| Characters right of cursor to end of line | Ctrl + End |
| Characters right of cursor to end of page | Ctrl + PgDn |
| Sentence, paragraph, or page | Ctrl + F4 |
| Block | Block text, Del, Y |
| Undelete | F1, 1 |

## SAVE DOCUMENT

### And remain in document
1. F10
2. Enter filename
3. Y/N (if resaving)

### And clear the screen
1. F7, Y
2. Enter filename
3. Y/N (if resaving), N

### And exit WordPerfect
1. F7, Y
2. Enter filename
3. Y/N (if resaving), Y

## BLOCK TEXT/CODES
1. Cursor on first character
2. Alt + F4
3. Cursor on last character

## RETRIEVE DOCUMENT

### Directly
1. Shift + F10
2. Enter filename

### From list files
1. F5, Enter drive/directory
2. Highlight file, 1

## PRINT

### Text from screen
1. Position cursor
2. Shift + F7
3. 1 (for full document), 2 (for page), or 3 (for multiple pages)*

### Block from screen
1. Block text
2. Shift + F7, Y

### Document from disk
1. Shift + F7, 3
2. Enter document name
3. Enter range of pages

### Document from list files (disk)
1. F5, Enter drive/directory
2. Highlight file, 4
3. Enter range of pages

*5.1 users only

# UNDERLINE (OR BOLD)

**While typing**
1. F8 (or F6 )
2. Type text
3. F8 (or F6 )

**Existing text**
1. Block text
2. F8 (or F6 )

# CHANGE LINE SPACING
1. Position cursor
2. Shift + F8 , **1, 6**
3. Enter spacing, F7

# RESET MARGINS

**Left/right**
1. Position cursor
2. Shift + F8 , **1, 7**
3. Enter margins, F7

**Top/bottom**
1. Position cursor
2. Shift + F8 , **2, 5**
3. Enter margins, F7

# CENTER
(OR FLUSH RIGHT)
1. Position cursor
2. Shift + F6 (or Alt + F6 )

# RESET TABS
1. Position cursor
2. Shift + F8 , **1, 8**
3. Clear Tab(s)
4. Set tab(s), F7 , F7

# SEARCH TEXT/CODES
1. Position cursor, F2
2. Type search string, F2

# REPLACE TEXT/CODES
1. Position cursor
2. Alt + F2 , **Y/N** for confirmation
3. Type search string, F2
4. Type replace string, F2

# INSERT HEADERS
(OR FOOTERS)
1. Position cursor at top of page
2. Shift + F8 , **2, 3 (or 4)**
3. Select **1** or **2** for type
4. Select frequency
5. Type the text, F7 , F7

# MOVE (OR COPY)
Sentence, paragraph, or page
1. Position cursor
2. Ctrl + F4 , **1, 2** or **3**
3. **1 (or 2)**
4. Position cursor, Enter

**Block of text**
1. Block text
2. Ctrl + F4 , **1**
3. **1 (or 2)**
4. Position cursor, Enter

# CHECK SPELLING
1. Position cursor
2. Insert Speller (floppy disk users)
3. Ctrl + F2
4. **1** (for word), **2** (for page), or **3** (for document)
5. Respond to menu options

# USE THESAURUS
1. Position cursor on word
2. Insert Thesaurus (floppy disk users)
3. Alt + F1
4. Respond to menu options

# Command Card
## Function Key Names with Pulldown Menus Comparison

| FUNCTION KEYS | | PULLDOWN MENUS† |
|---|---|---|
| **KEY NAME** | **KEY SEQUENCE** | **MENU SEQUENCE** |
| BLOCK | Alt + F4 | Edit, Block |
| BOLD | F6 | Font, Appearance, Bold |
| CANCEL | F1 | Edit, Undelete |
| CENTER | Shift + F6 | Layout, Align, Center |
| COLUMNS/TABLES* | Alt + F7 | Layout |
| DATE OUTLINE | Shift + F5 | Tools |
| END FIELD** | F9 | *(No pulldown menu alternative)* |
| EXIT | F7 | File, Exit |
| FLUSH RIGHT | Alt + F6 | Layout, Align, Flush Right |
| FONT | Ctrl + F8 | Font |
| FOOTNOTE | Ctrl + F7 | Layout |
| FORMAT | Shift + F8 | Layout |
| GRAPHICS | Alt + F9 | Graphics |
| HELP | F3 | Help |
| →INDENT | F4 | Layout, Align, →Indent |
| →INDENT← | Shift + F4 | Layout, Align, →Indent← |
| LIST*** | F5 | File, List Files |
| MACRO | Alt + F10 | Tools, Macro, Execute |
| MACRO DEFINE | Ctrl + F10 | Tools, Macro, Define |
| MARK TEXT | Alt + F5 | Mark |
| MERGE CODES | Shift + F9 | Tools, Merge Codes |
| MERGE/SORT | Ctrl + F9 | Tools, Merge |
| MOVE | Ctrl + F4 | Edit |
| PRINT | Shift + F7 | File, Print |
| REPLACE | Alt + F2 | Search, Replace |
| RETRIEVE | Shift + F10 | File, Retrieve |
| REVEAL CODES | Alt + F3 | Edit, Reveal Codes |
| SAVE | F10 | File, Save |
| SCREEN | Ctrl + F3 | Edit or Tools |
| →SEARCH | F2 | Search |
| ←SEARCH | Shift + F2 | Search |
| SETUP | Shift + F1 | File, Setup |
| SHELL | Ctrl + F1 | File, Goto DOS |
| SPELL | Ctrl + F2 | Tools, Spell |
| STYLE | Alt + F8 | Layout, Styles |
| SWITCH | Shift + F3 | Edit, Switch Document |
| TAB ALIGN | Ctrl + F6 | Layout, Align, Tab Align |
| TEXT IN/OUT | Ctrl + F5 | File |
| THESAURUS | Alt + F1 | Tools, Thesaurus |
| UNDERLINE | F8 | Font, Appearance, Underline |

\*   MATH/COLUMNS  (version 5.0)

\*\*  MERGE R  (version 5.0)

\*\*\* MERGE R  LIST FILES  (version 5.0)

†Version 5.1 Only

## Pulldown Menus Structure†

| File | Edit | Search |
|---|---|---|
| Retrieve | Move/Cut | Forward |
| Save | Copy | Backward |
| Text In | Paste | Next |
| Text Out | Append | Previous |
| Password | Delete | Reverse |
| List Files | Undelete | Extended |
| Summary | Block | Goto |
| Print | Select | |
| Setup | Comment | |
| Goto DOS | Convert Case | |
| Exit | Protect Block | |
| | Switch Document | |
| | Window | |
| | Reveal Codes | |

| Layout | Mark | Tools |
|---|---|---|
| Line | Index | Speller |
| Page | Table of | Thesaurus |
| Document | Contents | Macro |
| Other | List | Date Text |
| Columns | Cross Reference | Date Code |
| Tables | Table of | Date Format |
| Math | Authorities | Outline |
| Footnote | Define | Paragraph Number |
| Endnote | Generate | Define |
| Justify | Master Documents | Merge Codes |
| Align | Subdocument | Merge |
| Styles | Document Compare | Sort |
| | | Line Draw |

| Font | Graphics | Help |
|---|---|---|
| Base Font | Figure | Help |
| Normal | Table Box | Index |
| Appearance | Text Box | Template |
| Superscript | User Box | |
| Subscript | Equation | |
| Fine | Line | |
| Small | | |
| Large | | |
| Very Large | | |
| Extra Large | | |
| Print Color | | |
| Characters | | |

† Version 5.1 Only

## *You're important to us...*

We'd like to know what you're interested in, what kinds of books you're looking for, and what you thought about this book in particular.

Please fill out the attached card and mail it in. We'll do our best to keep you informed about Osborne's newest books and special offers.

▶ *YES, Send Me a FREE Color Catalog of all Osborne computer books*
**To Receive Catalog,** Fill in Last 4 Digits of ISBN Number from Back of Book (see below bar code) 0-07-881 _ _ _ — _

Name: _____ Title: _____

Company: _____

Address: _____

City: _____ State: _____ Zip: _____

**I'M PARTICULARLY INTERESTED IN THE FOLLOWING** (*Check all that apply*)

*I use this software*
- ☐ WordPerfect
- ☐ Microsoft Word
- ☐ WordStar
- ☐ Lotus 1-2-3
- ☐ Quattro
- ☐ Others _____

*I use this operating system*
- ☐ DOS
- ☐ Windows
- ☐ UNIX
- ☐ Macintosh
- ☐ Others _____

*I rate this book:*
- ☐ Excellent  ☐ Good  ☐ Poor

*I program in*
- ☐ C or C++
- ☐ Pascal
- ☐ BASIC
- ☐ Others _____

*I chose this book because*
- ☐ Recognized author's name
- ☐ Osborne/McGraw-Hill's reputation
- ☐ Read book review
- ☐ Read Osborne catalog
- ☐ Saw advertisement in store
- ☐ Found/recommended in library
- ☐ Required textbook
- ☐ Price
- ☐ Other _____

Comments _____

Topics I would like to see covered in future books by Osborne/McGraw-Hill include:

_____

**IMPORTANT REMINDER**
**To get your FREE catalog, write in the last 4 digits of the ISBN number printed on the back cover (see below bar code) 0-07-881 _ _ _ — _**

Osborne McGraw-Hill

*Computer*
*Books*

(800) 227-0900